PROJECT

MANAGEMENT

T0323205

Sara Miller McCune founded SAGE Publishing in 1965 to support the dissemination of usable knowledge and educate a global community. SAGE publishes more than 1000 journals and over 800 new books each year, spanning a wide range of subject areas. Our growing selection of library products includes archives, data, case studies and video. SAGE remains majority owned by our founder and after her lifetime will become owned by a charitable trust that secures the company's continued independence.

Los Angeles | London | New Delhi | Singapore | Washington DC | Melbourne

PROJECT MANAGEMENT

A Value Creation Approach

Stewart R. Clegg
Torgeir Skyttermoen
Anne Live Vaagaasar

SAGE

Los Angeles | London | New Delhi
Singapore | Washington DC | Melbourne

Los Angeles | London | New Delhi
Singapore | Washington DC | Melbourne

SAGE Publications Ltd
1 Oliver's Yard
55 City Road
London EC1Y 1SP

SAGE Publications Inc.
2455 Teller Road
Thousand Oaks, California 91320

SAGE Publications India Pvt Ltd
B 1/I 1 Mohan Cooperative Industrial Area
Mathura Road
New Delhi 110 044

SAGE Publications Asia-Pacific Pte Ltd
3 Church Street
#10-04 Samsung Hub
Singapore 049483

Editor: Matthew Waters
Assistant editor: Jasleen Kaur
Assistant editor, digital: Sunita Patel
Production editor: Sarah Cooke
Copyeditor: Christine Bitten
Proofreader: Neil Dowden
Indexer: Judith Lavender
Marketing manager: Abigail Sparks
Cover design: Shaun Mercier
Typeset by: C&M Digitals (P) Ltd, Chennai, India
Printed in the UK

Library of Congress Control Number: 2019956621

British Library Cataloguing in Publication data

A catalogue record for this book is available from the British Library

ISBN 978-1-5264-9462-7
ISBN 978-1-5264-9461-0 (pbk)

At SAGE we take sustainability seriously. Most of our products are printed in the UK using responsibly sourced papers and boards. When we print overseas we ensure sustainable papers are used as measured by the PREPS grading system. We undertake an annual audit to monitor our sustainability.

CONTENTS

LIST OF CASE STUDIES

LIST OF IN PRACTICES

ABOUT THE AUTHORS

Stewart R. Clegg is Distinguished Professor of Management and Organization Studies at the University of Technology Sydney and the University of Stavanger Business School, Norway. He has published widely in the management, organizations and politics literatures in many of the leading journals. Widely acknowledged as one of the most significant contemporary theorists of power relations, he is also one of the most influential contributors to organization studies as well as a significant contributor to project management, as acknowledged by the Project Management Institute in 2016, when they awarded him the PMI Research Achievement Award.

Torgeir Skyttermoen is Associate Professor in Project Management at Oslo Business School, Oslo Metropolitan University. He has published books on project management and has taught several disciplines for more than 20 years, including project management. A prolific researcher, he has received the Norwegian Ministry of Education's Quality Award. He is pedagogically committed to providing excellent learning processes. He is also Visiting Associate Professor at Innlandet Norway University of Applied Sciences as well as being employed as an instructor and consultant in business and public organizations.

Anne Live Vaagaasar, PhD, is Associate Professor in Management at BI Norwegian Business School. She has published widely within organizational science, in particular on temporary organizing. Her key interests are issues of organizing, relationship development, temporality, learning and innovating – always in the context of temporary organizations. She has published three books and numerous articles on these topics and won several international research awards. She is responsible for the renowned executive programmes in Project Management at BI, and teaches and lectures on a wide range of topics within the subject area.

ACKNOWLEDGEMENTS

Writing this book has been a project that, as with many projects, comes with a complicated history. Initially, a Norwegian publisher issued a much earlier version of it, in terms of both time and content, back in 2015 named *Verdiskapende Prosjektledelse*. Two of the authors, Torgeir and Anne Live, wrote this book. It turned out that they both had a friend in common with Stewart – Tor Paulson. In 2018, Tor invited Stewart to make a keynote presentation at a conference in Norway. Prior to Stewart's journey from Australia to Norway, Tor had been in touch with Stewart about perhaps collaborating with Torgeir and Anne Live in producing an English-language version of their book. The four of us met, discussed and decided to proceed with this project.

The nature of the project work has been multi-pronged. One task was to render a good English-language version of what Torgeir and Anne Live had written; another task was to turn it into a different kind of textbook. Stewart had a fair bit of experience of producing textbooks that were somewhat different from the usual run of the mill, for example *Managing and Organizations: An Introduction to Theory and Practice* and *Strategy: Theory and Practice*, both published by Sage. What marked them out was that they were written in such a way as to open up debates and perspectives rather than merely cataloguing them for easy regurgitation during the ritual examination process. Throughout this project, the three of us have followed this strategy. All three authors are very well acquainted with the project management field yet have come to it from quite different backgrounds and interests, which has made the project truly engaging. Stewart, very well versed in the organization theory and strategy literatures, was no stranger to project management, having published a number of things in the field over the years. While Torgeir has a background in organizational science, Anne Live contributes extensively to project management from a background in psychology and educational science.

All projects have their difficulties, on and off periods, which is the case for this book project as well. Nevertheless, collaborating in different time zones is a very effective way of working, in as much as it allows for a 24-hour cycle of writing and revision, and doing the work in this way proved constructive. Milestones coupled with deadlines have been helpful in terms of prioritizing and making progress. The final delivery of this project is now in your hands – literally. It will be you, the reader, who will create value from the delivery of this project, in terms of gaining new understanding, better knowledge of project management and testing this competence in real-life projects.

During this project, many people should be acknowledged. First, without Tor Paulson this would never have happened. Tor's enthusiasm for this prospect and his willingness to connect the three of us was a sparkling start for this book project. We would also like to thank the Norwegian publisher Cappelen Damm for being so positive in allowing the Norwegian textbook as a fundament to be taken further into an international textbook. Usually, the traffic is the other way – from English into another language; we find it refreshing to be engaged in a different form of trade.

For feedback we thank Kristian Kreiner, Bent Flyvbjerg, Shankar Sankaran, Graham Winch, Miguel Pina e Cunha, Marco Berti, Samuel MacAuley and Julien Pollock.

At Sage, editors Matthew Waters and Jasleen Kaur have been a great help as have the whole team at Sage; making a book is a complex project and a large team works to produce the volume you are now reading, not all of whom we meet or know but to all of whom we express our gratitude.

PREFACE
How to use this book

Project Management: A Value Creation Approach is intended as a textbook for people either learning to become project managers or who are already working in the field. The book is written in such a way as to be as useful as possible to you, the reader. There are a number of features introduced from the second chapter onwards that are designed to enhance usability. As the first chapter is an introduction to the whole book, we have not inserted the features there but we do so in subsequent chapters.

First, we have tried to be as clear as possible in the exposition of occasionally difficult ideas and while we have striven to reflect the contemporary state of knowledge we have sought to do so in an expository and descriptive way, rather than being unduly prescriptive. Above all, successful projects must combine creativity and imagination with discipline and focus. Too much of either extreme is a harbinger of unsuccessful outcomes. Often, to be frank, the excess resides on the side of discipline and focus and the deficit on the side of creativity and imagination.

Second, in engaging with you, the reader, creatively and innovatively in the text, you will find that after the first chapter of the book, there is an overview of the contents and approach that has guided us, along with a number of features designed to spark your imagination:

- **Read this!** Where you see the 'read this' text in the book, this serves as advice about where you can read material online through links on the website (https://study.sagepub.com/pm) that elaborate or exemplify a point being made in the neighbouring text.
- **Watch this!** The 'watch this' feature, when you follow it up on the website, takes you to an instructive and usually fairly short video related to the neighbouring text.
- **Extend your knowledge**. These are links to academic journal articles that we have selected from recent research that allow you to explore important points in more detail and provide you with an entry to the relevant research literature. You can find the links on the webpage.
- **In practice**. The 'in practice' feature consists of mini case studies that ask you questions that allow you to reflect on what you have read in the context of practical issues to be addressed.
- **What would you do?** These are very short vignettes that ask you to consider what you would do, given what you know, in a specific situation.
- **Marginal definitions**. Where some terms that are not in everyday use are introduced, usually either specific project management or social science terms, there are short marginal definitions to help you, the reader, with comprehension.

We have tried to standardize these features across each chapter although there will be some slight variance depending on the nature of the material being addressed.

Given what we want to achieve with this book we have made a number of assumptions about you, the reader:

- You deal with projects, in various ways, every day. These may be student projects at your college or university, they might be work-based projects, they could be IT projects, event projects, construction projects, change projects – indeed, any kind of project.
- You live and work with the outcomes of successful projects every day, as well. You attend festivals, sporting events, go to museums and galleries to see specially curated exhibitions, you organize life projects through your smart phone and other devices by making appointments, reading text, receiving emails and keeping up with your social media contacts.
- You will either soon start working in an organization in a full-time position or be doing so already, whether it is a consulting company, a multinational, a hospital, a university, an art gallery, a non-profit organization or a security or emergency service. In any of these or almost any other organization you will have to deal with projects. You will do so either as a project manager, a project owner, project team member, as an employee affected by a project or someone that has a stake-holding interest in a project.

To be able to contribute to a project, understand what a project is and how it often plays out, you need to have a thorough grounding in projects, their management and all the factors affecting them. Too often, projects and the people involved fail to recognize the main purpose of a project is to create value. Value is not just a question of profit, although in a commercial organization this will undoubtedly be important. Value can be defined in many ways, for many different categories of actors that we explore in this book. Value is sometimes hard to achieve; uncertainty, ambiguity, complexity and, most challengingly, events will often serve to distract, destabilize or destroy value. The value may be best captured in terms of use value for specific constituencies of interest, or surplus value in the form of profit for just one constituency of interest, that is, the owners and shareholders, or it may be a project with a value that is much wider, concerned with reducing pollution, inequality or social injustice.

What do all these projects have in common? We understand a project as a form of organizing that is characterized as temporary, processing through various stages, to deal with tasks and goals that could not be dealt with under the usual organizational routines. Every project starts with the intention of being a success. Many projects succeed; nevertheless, like you, we have read about many projects being over budget, over time, over and over again. We cannot guarantee that readers of this book will not be involved in such projects, as at some time it is likely to be the case that they will be so embroiled. However, we maintain that the value of this book as a project will be that it reduces the probability of 'over and over again' occurring due to a lack of good judgement about what being a project manager entails.

Now, dear reader, you are about to embark on the project that we have accomplished. Thank you for joining us.

The authors

Oslo, Lillehammer and Sydney

31 July 2020

A GUIDE TO PROJECT MANAGEMENT

The project management discipline contains a number of concepts. As you are about to dive into the complexity and ambiguity characterized by projects, it is useful to clarify some of the essential concepts. Projects appear in many shapes and formats; nevertheless, some common characteristics and processes may be found in all types of projects. Projects are increasingly used as a way of solving complex problems and tasks; their increasing proliferation across many spheres of activity has given rise to the phenomenon of **projectification**.

> **Projectification**. Projects are increasingly used to manage, organize, lead and perform actions especially those that entail change and innovation.

What is a project?

The common basis for **projects** is that they are designed to deliver *goal-oriented solutions* to relatively complex tasks in a limited time using those resources that are available. Projects are established to produce imagined and projected deliverables for which a need has been expressed by the project sponsors. That limited time horizons mean that projects are *temporary organizations* designed to **create added value** for the sponsor. Projects are designed to **deliver** results.

> **A project** is a temporary organization established by a project principal to solve a task within a specified time frame in order to enable future value creation.

Why projects?

A project is chosen as a form of organizing to deliver a specific outcome. Some organizations are entirely project-based; that is, they exist to deliver projects. Others turn to projects where there is a specific task that needs to be achieved that the existing organization design does not encompass. The reason may be that the task involves innovation or interdisciplinary work, collaboration with other organizations or dedicated skills and attention.

> **Value creation**. The processes that organizations implement as projects are designed to create value; for example, producing and marketing products, experiences and innovations; designing novel administrative procedures, legal changes or organization designs. Designs are intentions and intentions are not always met.

> **Project delivery** is a collective term describing the processes used to produce the objectives of the project. A deliverable represents the overall end product of the project.

Who are the key actors in projects?

Principal. The organization that establishes the project with the intention of achieving tangible benefits and value creation.

Project owner. The role performed by a person who takes care of the responsibilities and interests vested in the project by its principal.

The **project manager** is responsible for carrying out the project within a given framework.

The **project team** comprise the people working together to create the project's outcomes.

A **stakeholder** is any actor, whether a person, group or organization that can affect or is affected by the achievement of the project's objectives and expected effects.

Projects involve many actors representing various interests. The **principal**, *client* or *sponsor* initiates the project; often an organization that expects and strives to benefit from value creation as a result of the project's effects.

The term **project owner** has interests vested in the project by the project's principals as their responsibility. They must follow up and facilitate the success of the project by making sense of the project requirements and delivering them.

To execute a project requires organizing planning, doing and coordinating actions. The **project manager** leads the work of the group of people performing the project, the **project team**. Many **stakeholders** will be involved in any project both formally and informally, contractually and non-contractually, internally and externally.

How is the project organized?

The relationship between the project owner and the project manager is important. Different projects will have different bodies and interests involved. If the project executor is a third party this will make the relation more complex (see Figure 0.1).

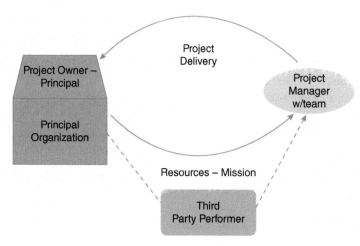

Figure 0.1   Main principles for organizing

How is the project organized internally?

In the execution of a project, the project owner, project manager and project team involved may entail collaborating with a third party assigned to execute the project. In Figure 0.2 there is a visual representation (with dotted lines for those relationships that are not always relevant) to clarify connections between the project organization, the principal organization (sometimes referred to as base organization) and any third party, when the project is executed on behalf on a principal.

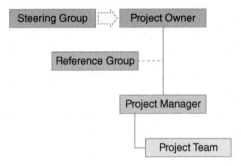

Figure 0.2   Internal organizing of a project

Project progress

Projects usually follow more or less standard phases and procedures, although there are significant variations among projects. Projects start with a need for change, after which a framework for project implementation is designed for planning and organizing the project. Implementation begins when framework planning is in place. Depending on the project, this framework will be more or less detailed in respect of specified criteria such as scope, time and resources. Follow-up and corrections of activities and courses are an important part of implementation.

> **Project execution strategy** depends on the purpose of the project, its uncertainties and complexities. Sequential execution strategies, such as a waterfall model differ from agile execution strategies such as Scrum.

The project ends when the deliverables have been delivered to the client that will be their custodian. Phases often overlap and activities can be repeated several times as the phases unfold and insight increases. Depending on the clarity of the project goals and purpose of the project, various **execution strategies** will be required.

Projects present a huge variety of delivery, size, pace, complexity, uncertainty and other contingent characteristics. Different project execution models can be utilized to capture the contingent characteristics of specific projects and the context in which they are embedded.

PRAISE FOR *PROJECT MANAGEMENT*

'Project management is traditionally framed as a discipline based in techniques and models for effective planning and execution of projects – implying a widespread neglect of emotional, behavioral, organizational and societal aspects of project-based work. In this volume, the authors provide a much needed research-based overview of these aspects, and relate them well to the practical realities of projects. It is a book not only for scholars and students of project management, but also for all those who lead projects, work in projects, hold stakes in projects or want to understand better the role of projects in industrial and societal transformation.'

Johann Packendorff, Professor of Industrial Economics and Management, School of Industrial Engineering and Management, KTH Royal Institute of Technology

'Challenges to the predominant systems paradigm in project management first espoused by Cleland and King in the 1960s have been maturing in the research literature for over 20 years. Yet our most widely used textbooks draw thinly on this new thinking and remain within the systems paradigm. These authors have created the first textbook that addresses the needs of contemporary project managers which engages deeply with this research literature. The book is, therefore, a vital contribution to our libraries and reading lists.'

Graham Winch, Professor of Project Management, Manchester Business School, University of Manchester

'This is the kind of book I wish I had when I was learning project management. It presents a very human view of projects that goes far past the simple emphasis on process common in so many texts. This book introduces the reader to a rich literature in a way that is a pleasure to read.'

Julien Pollack, Associate Professor, The University of Sydney

'The highlight of this book is that while it starts unconventionally with value as its focus in early chapters it also covers the essential knowledge on how to manage a project through its lifecycle in later chapters. Thus, both students and practitioners will also find great value from the book.'

Shankar Sankaran, Professor of Organizational Project Management, University of Technology Sydney

'There are books on project management. Then there is *Project Management: A Value Creation Approach* by Clegg, Skyttermoen and Vaagaasar! An easy-to-follow structure guides the reader through this inventive book. Beyond "simple" solutions, Clegg et al. provide any student of projects theoretically informed distillations of useful and informative practices that are useful and relevant to any setting. This book has a unique approach that is best experienced!'

Markus Hällgren, Professor of Management, Umeå School of Business and Economics, Umeå University

'Strongly rooted in a temporary organization perspective, *Project Management: A Value Creation Approach* offers a detailed and multi-layered compendium of ideas related to project management. With its contemporary emphasis on the value and valorization of projects, and through fun and creative "what would you do" exercises, this book is an indispensable guide to the modern project manager.'

Rene M. Bakker, Associate Professor of Strategy & Entrepreneurship, Rotterdam School of Management, Erasmus University

'This book is an interesting contribution to the project management debate. The dominant perception of organizing projects as technical defined matters in demarked spatial settings with a particular kind of complex tasks that have to be solved has become highly problematic. Therefore, I am very supportive to approaches that take humans as central and perceive projects as social networks of people in the process of organizing. This is exactly what the authors do in this book; exploring how projects can create value for solving contemporary social questions.'

Alfons van Marrewijk, Professor of Construction Cultures, Delft University of Technology; Associate Professor, Organization Sciences, Vrije Universiteit Amsterdam; Adjunct Professor in Project Management, BI Norwegian Business School

'This book draws a useful map of project panagement. It will help you decide where and how to travel the full gambit and terrain of workplace projects with all the tools needed to reach your desired destination. Buckle up and enjoy the journey!'

Kristian Kreiner, Professor Emeritus, Department of Organization, Copenhagen Business School

FIND US ONLINE!

Project Management is supported by a wealth of online resources for both students and lecturers to help support learning and teaching. These resources are available at: https://study.sagepub.com/pm.

For Lecturers

- **Integrate** the chapters into your weekly lectures by using the **PowerPoint slides** created by the authors.
- **Support your teaching** by making use of the **tutor's guide** specifically structured to help teach each chapter and **guide discussions** in class.

For Students

Follow along with the chapter guidance and **expand** your knowledge by clicking through to the **weblinks and further reading articles** mentioned throughout the book.

Chapter Roadmap

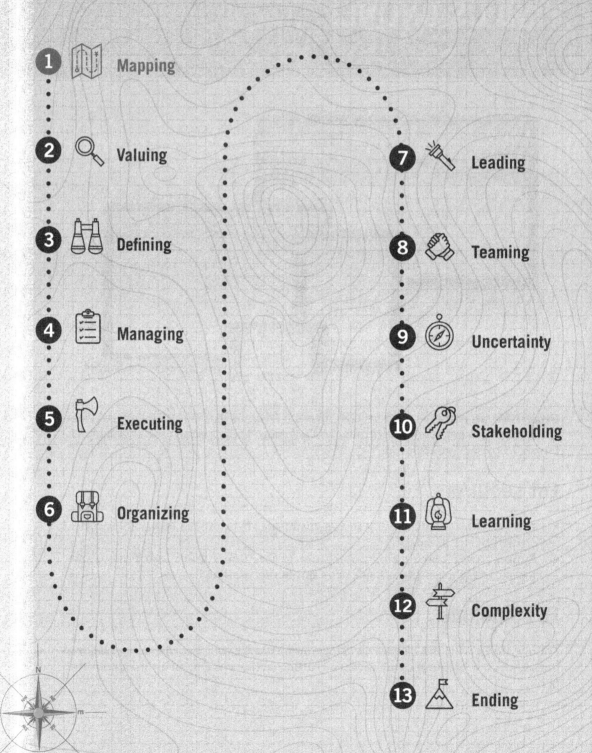

1 Mapping

2 Valuing

3 Defining

4 Managing

5 Executing

6 Organizing

7 Leading

8 Teaming

9 Uncertainty

10 Stakeholding

11 Learning

12 Complexity

13 Ending

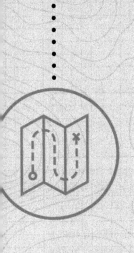

1

MAPPING PROJECTS: AN INTRODUCTION

Before you get started

The map is not the territory.

– Korzybski, 1933

Introduction

The structure of the book draws on the practical wisdom informing students of project management about basic knowledge that, in principle, is useful to them for managing projects. However, practical should not be just intended as down-to-earth or common sense; rather, what is considered to be practical is a result of the distillation of practices that relate actions to knowledge abstracted from specific contexts. Abstracted, these provide a body of knowledge useful for guiding project managers in their careers and practices. Much complexity enters into the use of knowledge in specific situations, arising from contractual and interorganizational relationships, communications, politics and local and material conditions.

There is also a considerable research-based knowledge from a broad interdisciplinary perspective, including not only organization theory but also other social science areas, that can be drawn on to inform project management. Moreover, in line with the increasing projectification of a world in which projects are used to deliver many things, in addition to engineering designs, such as innovation, change, concerts, events, festivals, weddings and wars, this book will draw examples from a wide-angle vision on projects: projects in cinemascope!

Borrowing from the philosopher, Alisdair MacIntyre (1971), who once wrote wittily about the theory of holes as a non-theoretical object of discourse,[1] we seek to reverse MacIntyre's wit, to argue for a theory of projects (which often involve holes, it should be said). We aspire to proffer theorizing of projects able to address IT projects, consulting projects, construction projects, infrastructure projects, even the project of becoming a project professional – a process whose path this book might accompany. We realize that in doing this we are making the assumption that projects are not just empirical objects, phenomena that have a material reality. Our proposition is that there is sufficient knowledge of the project phenomena, in its family resemblances from specific project to project, in order to be able to produce a general theoretical discussion of these resemblances.

To introduce a term we shall shortly define, we accept that much of the knowledge of the terrain of project management consists of a kind of practical wisdom defining the territory phronetically, rather than being a research-based science in its entirety. As a detailed discussion of the field, the book is based both upon a type of practical empiricism fostered in the *PMBOK* (*Project Management Body of Knowledge*) as well as on the kind of research-based knowledge found in various academic journals – not only those specifically of project management. There is a rapidly accruing research-based knowledge related to project management that has developed both in the emergent discipline and in cognate areas, such as management and organization studies, that we draw on to direct the reader to the book's website, where a number of these resources may be found as aids to mapping the terrain. In addition, there are many practical cases that position you, the reader, in relation to practice – what you would do in various situations, as well as inviting you to read and watch various other resources to extend your knowledge.

First, however, a word about mapping.

---

[1]'There was once a man who aspired to be the author of the general theory of holes. When asked "What kind of hole – holes dug by children in the sand for amusement, holes dug by gardeners to plant lettuce seedlings, tank traps, holes made by roadmakers?" he would reply indignantly that he wished for a general theory that would explain all of these. He rejected *ab initio* the – as he saw it – pathetically common-sense view that of the digging of different kinds of holes there are quite different kinds of explanations to be given; why then he would ask do we have the concept of a hole?' (MacIntyre, 1971, p. 260)

The map

What does it mean to say that the map is not the territory? The map of a given territory can change radically in a short time. For instance, when Captain James Cook sailed the Pacific on board the *Endeavour* in 1768 the maps that he used to chart his journey proved to be incomplete and inaccurate. As an excellent mathematician, astronomer and cartographer, as well as mariner, he charted a map of his voyage around the continent that changed understanding of the Great Southern Land. Cook revealed Australia to the rest of the world that had not shared this knowledge in the 60,000 years or so of prior human habitation. Maps are thus a testament to conventions and assumptions that his voyage's mapping changed radically.

Cook was not the first to represent the Australian landscape based on intimate knowledge. There were many maps of Australian territory in the land that he surveyed that had been transmitted through oral tradition, everyday wisdom, whose representations would have been inscrutable to European map-makers. These indigenous maps represented what was important to their makers, focusing on what was spiritually and socially significant about the landscape. Every map represents a territory using a set of conventions to do so. Just as Cook's maps aided mariners in travel so did the aboriginal maps inscribed on bark paintings and other artefacts, aiding the indigenous people in knowing their territory. A map is 'a device for organizing knowledge spatially', as Turnbull (2008: 1277) states; while its conventions are deeply embedded in the knowledge available to the map-makers this knowledge can be translated into other conventions. Maps of the Dreamtime are now recognized as legal claims to land ownership in Australian courts of law (Turnbull, 1998).

As Korzybski (1933) acknowledges, the map is not the territory. A map is an abstraction, not the thing itself and it does not exist in a literal correspondence with the thing represented. A map is a framework of symbols, conventions and rules of representation, a model of reality. A map is a reality that corresponds not to a territory so much as to the conventions of map-making, be they of mariners or hunter gathers. 'Differences are the things that get onto a map. But what is a difference?' (Bateson, 1972, p. 320). According to the purposes (and interests) of the map-makers, different elements will be either represented on or excluded from the map, in a process of social production of space, through which natural features are turned into an ordered, regimented realm (Lefebvre, 1991).

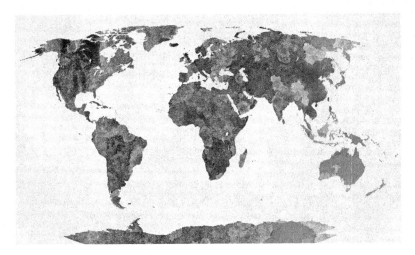

Picture 1.1   World map

Source: Image courtesy of Nicolas Raymond, via flickr.com. Shared under the Creative Commons BY 2.0 license.

Project management is a field that has largely grown out of conventions for mapping premised as much on custom and practice as on science. Conventions for mapping are a part of science but science largely derives from research-based inquiry that widens explanation and deepens understanding of phenomena. Project management has grown out of practice. Historically, there is contestation as to the specific practices that prefigured project management's development. Some, such as Peter Morris (2013), note the significant role played by defence industry contracting and provision, especially in the post-Second World War period in the United States. Others, such as Garel (2013), drawing on the work of Boutinet (1999), hark back to the construction of the great Gothic cathedrals of Europe, based on explicit design for a project, eventually creating works of profound design and construction, such as Brunelleschi's fifteenth-century Firenze Cathedral with its great dome that inspired architects and builders as far away as Oxford (the Bodleian Library) and London (St Paul's Cathedral). From this perspective, seeing the initial direction of the project residing in the hands of the architect, there is a significant shift in the late eighteenth century:

> The architect's expertise was challenged as the needs of programs changed. This marks the birth of a highly polytechnical approach with engineers who are trained in architecture and who develop an extremely authoritarian project method. In the 18th century, in the field of public buildings in France, engineers distanced themselves from architects and started to strongly influence production of space by relying on a network of new institutions and codifying their knowledge and practices. (Garel, 2013, p. 667)

The key words that Garel introduces are 'an extremely authoritarian project method'. Much later, as custom and practice were rationalized during the twentieth century from the 1930s, by the 1950s 'the management of engineering projects would lead to standardized tools, practices and roles, and the emergence of a true model' and in the 1960s, disparate corporate practices were increasingly fused into authoritative models for practice by the institutionalization of professional practice in project management bodies, such as the Project Management Institute, founded in 1969. As professional bodies these institutions have been vehicles for formulating 'principles' of project management, often codifying elements of practice in prescriptive models. The leading journal in the project management field was not published until 1990, when the *International Journal of Project Management* was first launched by one of the professional associations, the International Project Management Association (IPMA).

With its barely 70-year history, the project discipline is relatively young; nonetheless, its genealogy is contested. The Manhattan Project, which ran from 1942 to 1946, is considered as the start of project management as a discipline by many (Lenfle & Loch, 2010) although, as noted elsewhere in the book (Chapter 7), Andrew Davies regarded the construction of the Erie Canal as the first modern megaproject. The Manhattan Project hardly meets today's definition of a project. Morris (2011) states that very few of the tools or concepts used then are used in today's projects. He points out that Project management as a term was first used in a project related to the US defence industry in 1953. Nonetheless, the project discipline is characterized by its origins in major industrial projects, with an engineering bias: an emphasis on rational order, a relatively limited focus and a structural planning-oriented approach. It originated from large, complex system development. Other forms of limited 'one-off' assignments were not included during the first decades. Project management developed out of a systematization of practices emergent from large-scale engineering projects, through formalizing and routinizing knowledge of what seemed to work in context (Davies, 2017). Of course, once practices embedded in contexts are decontextualized into sets of formal routines, irrespective of context, then a degree of reification of the practices involved will occur. Formal rules will be applied because they are formalized as the principle underlying an area of knowledge; in this case they became principles codified as *A Guide to the Project Management Body of Knowledge* (Project Management Institute, 2017).

A Guide to the Project Management Body of Knowledge was first published in 1996 but was prefigured by a 1983 PMI report titled *Ethics, Standards, and Accreditation Committee Final Report*. The rationale behind this 'body of knowledge' has been the development of standards. When one contrasts this path with the embodiment of knowledge in neighbouring disciplines the contrast is quite stark. In organization theory the comparable recourse to principles characterized the early twentieth-century foundations of the field by engineers such as Fayol (1917). Although references to these early works were to be found in organization theory research conducted in the 1960s (Pugh et al., 1963), it was evident that these foundations were being superseded. Research-based knowledge that developed largely in the post-war era and beyond, multiplying rapidly with the growth of specialist journals in the field from the 1960s onwards, left the mapping of principles as a body of requisite knowledge as a relic of the past, although this approach continued to thrive in the nascent field of professionalized project management.

The early years of project management's institutionalization as a disciplinary practice – as the extraction of a discipline out of practices – lagged slightly behind the institutionalization of cognate bodies of knowledge. In terms of the politics of institution building, there was a certain logic, at least initially, in maintaining the separation between a fledgling field and others more deeply institutionalized. The time for this separation has long passed. In a world of organizations where projects are increasingly a preferred logic of action and a world of organization theory that increasingly focuses on the specificity of what is called 'temporary organizing' (*Organization Studies*, 2016, 37(12)), the time is ripe for further conciliation and synthesis. As became clear from the 2000s onwards, the field began to be engaged in increasing dialogue with other areas, such as organization theory, through the work of scholars such as Bent Flyvbjerg (2003), Alfons van Marrewijk (2008), Kristian Kreiner (1995) and Mats Engwall (2003) and their collaborators, among others. It is in this context that the present book is situated.

Any project that promotes an *entente cordiale* brings together partners with a legacy. That project management is a distinctive subject matter is widely agreed (Morris, Pinto & Söderlund, 2011). Project management thrived in many universities, often as a small part of much larger engineering or business schools and construction/architecture faculties. Nonetheless, it is fair to say that much of the orthodox knowledge constituting project management is still dominated by an engineering legacy. There are strong elements of linear rationality, of planning, that comprise project management. Traditionally, project management was approached from a *task perspective* (Andersen, 2008) focused on project management tools and methods. As with many other disciplines, there is disagreement and discussion about what the subject covers, how to define it and whether it should still be taught through the medium of principles.

Principles are a good thing, one might think. Indeed, to refer to some persons or some actions as unprincipled is not a compliment. However, principles require practice to be enacted; as codifications they may well be matters of faith or belief, much as the Koran or Bible, providing 'best practices' for action; however, action is always situated, always contextual, always a matter of practice. Sticking to a rule book makes no sense without practices that enact what these rules are, and in their enactment rules will have to be interpreted. Project management has increasingly had recourse to rugby as a metaphor in its recent iterations (for instance, the Scrum methodology in agile project management). As these words are being written their author has recently had the pleasure of watching the Rugby World Cup of 2019. The games were marked by excitement and drama, with the latter being particularly acute around controversial refereeing decisions. Refereeing rugby is a high art form; it requires a great deal of interpretive skill and fluidity because the rules of rugby are complex and, to be frank, sometimes extremely difficult to understand. They do not exist in some canonical pure form outside of the specificities of the game itself. They are enacted in game-specific contexts.

Picture 1.2   Rugby and scrum

Source: Image courtesy of PierreSelim, via Wikicommons.

The implications of the previous paragraph should be apparent for any discipline that defines itself as a body of knowledge premised on principles of best practice. These principles must be interpreted; they are always interpreted in action; action is always contextual, and there is no referee blowing the whistle enforcing interpretation of the rules. Hence, interpretations will always be a part of their enactment; thus, codification can as easily mean contestation of interpretations as compliance and consensus. What, then, is the point of these principles of best practice? At best, we might say, they reproduce a form of expert knowing formalized as knowledge that is built on precedent, rather like case law. In short, they are a form of what expertise recommends as practical wisdom. Practical wisdom is not to be spurned; it was, after all, one of Aristotle's approaches to knowledge, known as phronesis ($\varphi\rho\acute{o}\nu\eta\sigma\breve{\iota}\varsigma$), and it has been more recently recommended as the most appropriate form of practice by leading contributors to project management's body of knowledge (Clegg & Pitsis, 2012; Flyvbjerg, 2001, 2006b).

Phronesis does not constitute a form of social inquiry that seeks to construct general casual law-like covering statements. Phronesis relies on a narrative approach that can be related to Geertz's (1973, p. 6) 'thick descriptions' when he writes that those facts 'that we call our data are really our own constructions of other people's constructions and what they and their compatriots are up to', something which 'is obscured because most of what we need to comprehend a particular event, ritual, custom, idea, or whatever is insinuated as background information before the thing is directly examined … ethnography is thick descriptions' (Geertz, 1973, p. 9). Theoretical reasoning is not privileged over and above practical reasoning; we can only really grasp the nature of social reality through deep involvement in practical contexts of everyday life and engagement in the dialogues that constitute these (Clegg, 1975, represented an early attempt at doing just this). The basis for grasping social reality is not so much the construction of elegant and internally coherent models of action but an understanding that the social world has a historical and narrative structure; the one is understood through the other.

Phronesis enquires into the critical assessment of values, norms and the structuration of social reality. It is, we would argue, fair to say that the vast majority of research in the project management field does not follow a phronetic path; rather it tends to be positivist, more interested in the correlations between relatively abstracted variables from which it seeks to exploit a body of conventional knowledge that is useful for conducting various kinds of projects. Such knowledge is more than just exploitative of what is comprised as a body of objective knowledge, however. It also often seeks to bring projects in on time and on budget through fairly exploitative relations with employees, clients and stakeholders. Doing so is an important consideration in terms of the allocation and use of resources, especially capital. Even though successful projects require efficient execution in terms of time and cost, we take an approach to the field of project management premised on the simple proposition that projects should be managed for value and that value comes in more forms than being on time and on budget. Value involves employees and their relations at work in the project; stakeholder relations, whether they be internal or external stakeholders; the ecology and issues of value in terms of sustainability; and, of course, clients. The discussion of value takes in many actual projects, including one that was simultaneously both the most and the least successful project of the twentieth century – the Opera House in Stewart's home city, Sydney, a project that was completed ten years late and 1357% over budget in real terms, an accomplishment that blighted the subsequent career of its architect, Utzon (Flyvbjerg, 2005). Nonetheless, it is a magnificent, fluid construction, its sails serving to define the city along with the equally famous engineering project of the Sydney Harbour Bridge that stands nearby, spanning the two sides of the harbour. Its value to the city and country in terms of social, civic and economic value is inestimable, although in terms of the latter alone it generates over 1.2 billion Australian dollars annually. The building stands as a symbol of the necessity to approach value through plural perspectives.

The territory

VALUING

The key to delivering value in projects is to establish social and economic priorities first and only then to consider what projects are best projects suited to deliver these, as we argue in Chapter 2. Doing so requires developing independent and robust analyses on the best estimates of costs and benefits. Without such rigour and oversight, one can easily imagine the proliferation of bridges to nowhere important, an excess of power supplies and relatively empty roads, as well as innovation projects that fail to innovate. One of the things that we do in the book is to systematically chart ways in which such analysis can flourish when informed about the practices of project management. Hence, the book starts with a chapter on value whose simple premise is that projects are tools for delivering value. We look at what value is, how it can be defined and how different values are designed and created through projects. The emphasis on value creation shifts attention from assessments of whether the implementation of the project itself is successful in terms of the criteria fixed at the start of the project; instead, we determine if the project succeeded in creating value and for whom it was created. These are the most fundamental questions for delivering successful projects – such as the Opera House, despite its delay and cost blowouts.

DEFINING

In Chapter 3 we consider the main issues to clarify before starting a project. Projects meet needs defined by interests. Different stakeholders will propose different needs or, once they have been proposed, interpret these needs in different ways. To execute projects efficiently and enable future value creation, analysis is required of the ways in which these needs are being constituted in order to clarify if the project proposed is necessary. Crucial to the establishment of needs is the legitimation of project proposals, in terms of sensemaking that passes muster with project sponsors and potential owners. Sensemaking is a constant necessity in projects. The ongoing retrospective development of plausible images that rationalize what people are doing is a process that is always occurring. Sense has to be made as events unsettle plans, as value realization is challenged by unanticipated events, as considerations not known or realized at the time of planning emerge. Sometimes these considerations are unknowable, such as the location of old-established utilities in historically complex and deeply sedimented terrain in urban projects, where the records simply do not exist.

'Project' is both a verb and a noun. As a noun, it is a piece of planned work or an activity that is finished over a period of time and intended to achieve a particular purpose; as a verb it is to throw something forward. Both of these meanings enter into any discussion of projects; they are purposeful, temporal in that they will be completed and they do have a future orientation – a project produces something that, in its absence, would not have existed whether it be an opera house, a bridge, a festival, a wedding, an innovation. Hence, a project requires direction and realization. Direction means that there must be some guiding concept for the project while realization signifies that some thing or experience is the result of that direction. Connecting direction and realization are decision-making and rationalities justifying the actions pursued as approximations of how to get from the here-and-now of the projects' beginning through some stages to the there-and-then of its future coming into being.

Some projects are fairly simple. For instance, you may be reading this book in order to complete the project of gaining a professional credential that depends on you being able to demonstrate that you know what the knowledge of project management is by performing it in a piece of work for assessment or examination of some kind. Doing this is a fairly simple project. There is a deadline, the submission date for the assessment item or the date of the examination. The project delivery consists of you translating what you have learned into prose that satisfies the examiner. Memory intercedes as the storehouse of the decisions that you can recall from learning to be brought forward in the work under assessment. Put like this there is nothing too complicated about managing a (simple) project.

LEVELS

Not all projects are simple, as we begin to explore in Chapter 4. They do not just depend on you, your memory and skill in reading and retaining information from a book. Other people may be involved. Some of them will be directing you or you may well be directing some of these other people yourself. Rather than the simple goal of getting an assessment done the project may entail multiple goals, linked simultaneously in parallel as well as in a series of interlocked objectives. A pen or keyboard may deliver the content of memory in an assessment but the devices that might be involved in a project can be extremely sophisticated, expensive, dangerous, uncertain, unreliable, unavailable and unknown. Mastering a pen or keyboard is probably second nature to nearly everyone these days but mastering the vast range of project management tools can be quite bewildering: which is the right tool, what is the right way to use it, what is the right element of what kind of project on which to use it?

The most important tool may be the project management organization – people with diverse skills, experiences and identities. These people need managing. People mean skills and emotions, tasks and tensions between different trades, professions, occupations, clients and stakeholders, subordinates and superordinates. What are your people management skills? What forms of corporate governance are these exercised under? Whom are you being directed by and who directs them and who do you direct? These questions take us a long way away from the concerns of the engineering auspices of project management – we have swapped faculties and are deep in those of social sciences and business now. Things become more complicated in this territory. People have interests vested in their occupational and professional identities, the organizations they work for, the clients they serve, the stakeholders they represent, the personal projects they have in mind. Their rationalities may be more complicated as they interpolate the project than those of the project that the project designers designed.

EXECUTING

Strategy is a talismanic word for organizations of all sorts these days. You wouldn't want to be caught short without a strategy! Having a strategy is a good thing, up to a point; it is certainly better than not having one, of making it up as you go along as do many home renovators or builders if the television series *Grand Designs* provides a representative sample. Sticking to the strategy through thick and thin can be problematic though. At the time of writing a politician who sought to meet a self-imposed deadline as the chief element of his political strategy in the protracted Brexit negotiations in the UK said publicly that he would rather die in a ditch than change strategy. Not such a good idea – death by exposure is unlikely to be a persuasive strategy when it is self-inflicted. Anyway, no one that is politically sensible would believe such florid rhetoric. Strategy has to be flexible, capable of change of direction, of improvisation in the face of prescription, of changing as the facts encountered in implementing it prove resistant or different to the rationalities embedded in the strategy (Batista, Clegg, Pina e Cunha, Giustiniano, & Rego, 2016). Strategy provides focus on practice while practice puts strategy to the test of phronesis – strategy as practice (Clegg, Killen, Biesenthal, & Sankaran, 2018; Golsorkhi, Rouleau, Seidl, & Vaara, 2016; Pitsis, Sankaran, Gudergan, & Clegg, 2014), as we explore in Chapter 5.

One of the barriers to strategic flexibility apparently often seems to be the contract. The contract for a project typically tries to nail down as much detail as possible about what is to be done, how it will be done, what doing it will cost, using materials as specified, to be able to deliver the product or service contracted, according to the milestones inscribed in the project management process. Contracts, however, much as the rules of rugby, are highly contextual in their interpretation depending on which parties index their stipulations to what practices and material realities. We could say that they are highly indexical inscriptions (Clegg, 1975/2013). Moreover, contracts come in more than one form and milestones are neither immutable nor the only way to manage a project. There are other ways that take us deep into some of the more recent areas of project management where waterfalls, scrums, six sigma, sprints and agility await the enquiring project manager. Outside of the jargon that every project manager that aspires to be the very model of a modern project manager must acquire, there are other, sometimes more imaginative and creative ways, of being and doing a project, especially risky and innovative ones (Coldevin, Carlsen, Clegg, Pitsis, & Antonacopoulou, 2019).

Picture 1.3   CoffeeWorks project

Source: Torgeir Skyttermoen

ORGANIZING

Projects are often interstices. They intersect dreams and schemes; they couple professions, occupations and trades in the same harness; they create interorganizational relations, dependencies and dilemmas; they commit resources, responsibilities and roles; they mash up cultures, coordination and communication between different entities; they position, prioritize and practise power relations over, with and done to others who are doing the same reciprocally (Andersen, Soderlund, & Vaagaasar, 2010; Pinto, 2000). Projects and politics belong together, much as do salt and pepper, fish and chips, gin and tonic. Usually the one is close to the other, nearby, paired. By the time that you have got to Chapter 6 it should be evident that projects, conceived as organizing processes, have many features that are often overlooked: cultures, power relations and politics – all more or less normal effects of different identities, organizations and divisions of labour.

Power is inherent to all forms of relations in which projects are tangled: inter-personal, team, organizational, interorganizational, stakeholder. Power is ubiquitous. The very nature of all forms of organization are structures for channelling power relations of some actors over other actors, of some actors with other actors, and with some actors to achieve certain sorts of projects. These power relations are not just negative, as in the frequent zero-sum games that accompany contractual relations based on competitive tendering. A project is designed to achieve something new, something that did not exist prior to the project being attempted and successful. To achieve the project a great deal of power has to be shared with others and power sharing is always an extremely dynamic situation, easily tipping over into power struggles as autonomous actors strive to assert their autonomy, even against the will of others. Power processes need to be stabilized, however temporarily, if projects are to be accomplished. Obligatory passage points must channel the flows of process in a striving for order over fluidity, temporary stasis over permanent flows. Circuits of power need to be stabilized and many of project management's practices are oriented towards this end. The whole panoply of milestones, objectives, contracts, etc. are testament to this desire for organizing as a way of creating order (Clegg, Sankaran, Biesenthal, & Pollack, 2017). Project managers need skills of 'power steering' (Buchanan & Badham, 2020), skills that do not come easily to people from an engineering or technical background for whom the affordances of techne ($\tau\acute{\epsilon}\chi\nu\eta$) often subsumes any skill in terms of a capability for power ($\delta\acute{\upsilon}v\breve{\alpha}\mu\alpha\iota$).

It is because projects are interstices that one of the important jobs of a project manager is 'integration'. In fact, of all the knowledge areas promoted by project bodies of knowledge, integration of the various aspects of a project is usually considered the most important part of a project manager's job. While the essence of project management is to break down tasks and manage them, ultimately it is integration of everything that is broken down that adds value to projects. One central aspect of integration is achieved in projects through governance. There is often a tension between corporate and project governance that needs to be resolved between the project manager whose job is to deliver the project and the project sponsor or champion who looks after the corporate interests.

Governance is the system of rules, practices and processes by which a firm is directed and controlled. More generally, *governance* as a broad term is defined as 'the sum of the many ways individuals and institutions, public and private, manage their common affairs' (Carlsson, Ramphal, Alatas, & Dahlgren, 1995, p. 2). Relational governance aims at influencing networks to create innovation, reciprocity, trust and self-organization for organizations that require collective action, such as projects (Gil, 2017). Project governance that includes multiple firms and other agencies is more complex than the corporate governance of a single firm or organization. First, there is no necessary alignment between the many corporate governance doctrines that might be involved. Second, the project duration might require an overall code of governance separate from those of the firms involved. Third, there may well be stakeholders to govern that are not themselves directly involved as project partners in the governance of the project.

To address the latter two cases, the concept of governmentality has proven useful. Governmentality was a term first introduced by the French historian of ideas, Michel Foucault, in his collection of lectures at the Collège de France on the *Birth of Biopolitics* in 1979 (Marks, 2000, p. 128). These lectures engaged with the changing face of liberalism as a political project. For Foucault, governmentality meant combined strategies of organizational governance in a broad sense, as well as self-governance by those made subjects of organizational governance. The term *governmentality* is a fusion of *government* and *mentality* and means, actively, governing through mentalities (Müller, Pemsel, & Shao, 2014). As du Gay (2000, p. 168) suggests, governmentality 'create[s] a distance between the decisions of formal political institutions and other social actors, conceive[s] of these actors as subjects of responsibility, autonomy and choice, and seek[s] to act upon them through shaping and utilising their freedom'. What is novel about governmentality is that the personal projects and ambitions of individual actors become entangled and form alliances with those of organizational authorities and dominant organizations.

Foucault (2007, p. 108) describes three processes as the core of governmentality. The first process involves creating taken-for-granted practices, drawing both from existing institutions and procedures as well as *de novo* reflections, calculations and tactics. Foucault (1997) emphasizes that these practices are not invented by individuals but derive from the norms of cultures, societies and social groups. The second process involves deploying knowledge via a power–knowledge nexus that includes the state and learned professions. The third process involves developing technologies of the self, positioning personal identities of those governed. These technologies revolve around the question 'Who are we?' (Foucault, 1982) and represent a broader epistemological shift in seeing actors as being 'entrepreneurs of their selves' (Cooper, 2015). Together, these three processes help us understand the ways in which governmentality operates (Dean, 2010).

The practice of governmentality *aspires* to create a common sensemaking frame (Colville, Waterman, & Weick, 1999; Weick, 1995) whereby project participants will voluntarily and willingly agree to be governed in their conduct. Governmentality focuses on techniques embedded in specific rationalities that are oriented towards creating certain types of subject mentalities. Essentially, the objective is to generate compliance with governmentality premised on freedom to choose rather than subordination (Barnett, Clarke, Cloke, & Malpass, 2014). The aim of using a governmental approach in project management is for the personal ambitions of those governed to become enmeshed with those of the overall project management team. Governmentality offers an alternative to reliance on governance with its emphasis on prescribed codes, often legally framed. Governmentality relies in large part on self-surveillance (Fleming & Spicer, 2014; Sewell, 1998) and subjectification to project norms as they are situationally established.

The successful use of governmentality can have positive impacts on outcomes at both the project and organizational levels (Müller, Zhai, & Wang, 2017). Project-based organizations are temporary; thus, the key attribute of project organization governmentality is the rapid ability to develop a team of self-responsible and self-organizing people (Müller et al., 2014) blended from a larger number of organization members that constitute the project-based organization. In Clegg, Pitsis, Rura-Polley, and Marosszeky's (2002) investigations of governmentality within the project team, subtle devices aided its implementation. These devices, prominently displayed in project headquarters, included banners bearing images of the desired outcome of the project, slogans proclaiming team members to be guided by *whatever is best for the project*, as well as posters of stories of the project from media reports and notices of project-related social events. While Clegg et al. (2002) explored the practices of governmentality *internally* within the project team, where the incentives of actors are interconnected through contractual obligations, project teams can use strategies in practice to infuse governmentality *externally* to the project team, within the larger stakeholder community.

One such practice of governmentality, adopted from the sphere of consumption, is branding (Ninan, Clegg, & Mahalingam, 2019).

Forms of governmentality can be extended to less immediately involved stakeholders, in addition to those internal to a project. It is said that power can be most effective when it is least observable (Lukes, 2005), which governmentality – a key construct in the literature on covert power (Milani, 2009) – facilitates. Subtle and mundane branding strategies used in infrastructure megaprojects to manage *external* stakeholders also have an impact on internal stakeholders, especially the project team and the way their normative universe is shaped as they deploy strategies to manage external stakeholders in the project community. Not only can effective governmental strategies secure an enhanced commitment on the part of project team members and minimize conflict between them, they can also be used to advance a broader set of KPIs than is customary and to minimize fractious relationships with communities whose stakeholders have interests in the project's accomplishment.

Ninan et al.'s (2019) discussion of the use of branding in a major metro project in India provides an account of the strategic use of social media to achieve governmentality of external stakeholders. Organizations, including project-based organizations, are increasingly re-using social media to engage with audiences (Brodie, Ilic, Juric, & Hollebeek, 2013). Social media enhances the bond between the consumer and the organization by re-using user-generated content to achieve goals. In project organizations, these will likely be oriented towards specific audiences whose potential impact on the progress of the project can be significant. Social media can be used to create dominant, complementary, persuasive and legitimate discourses that seek to incorporate various communities into the sensemaking of the project team, creating a positive brand image for a project and building support and creating community advocates. Ninan et al. (2019) found that not only was the project community influenced but also the project team, in large part recruited from the broader community. Project team effects included enhanced job perceptions, an ability to attract talent, as well as the production of project team advocates. As a result of the governmentality effects on the project community, team members saw the megaproject as socially committed, safe, clean, prestigious and iconic for the city.

The use of diverse forms of branding to influence consumers has some similarity to governmentality practices as both make the exercise of power seem rational and natural (Lemke, 2002), such as consumption of specific brands as a matter of brand loyalty becoming a part of everyday rationality, as Marcuse (1964) outlined in an early critical account. Branding extends a complex set of meanings, associations and experience that create emotional, relational and strategic elements in the minds of those perceiving and enacting dispositions toward brands (Aaker, 1996). Branding increasingly penetrates everyday life, ranging from business communications to interpersonal relationships (Lect, 2012). Branding techniques include various forms of organizational self-presentation and promotion (Scott, 2010).

The use of social media is a double-edged weapon, however. Just as it is possible for project teams to use it to try and anticipate and reduce potential opposition to the depredations that a project might make on stakeholder interests by publicizing its benefits, it can also be wielded as a weapon by opponents of these projects. A good example of this is the WestConnex Action Group in Sydney, Australia, which ran a sophisticated social media and web-based campaign (see www.westconnexact iongroup.org.au/) against a major road project. On the one hand, official but limited use of social media was opposed by a contradictory use of that media that drew on social norms of community protest to create a strong sense of social purpose opposed to the development. In many ways, in terms of popular reach and mobilization, the countervailing use by the WestConnex action group appeared to have been far more effective in terms of governmental mobilization than the WestConnex project's official use. The latter's use was largely print, banner and web-based and did not use social media as successfully as the opposition, despite the opposition being powerless to stop the development.

Projects may go on in organizations, between organizations or among organizations. An example of an intra-organizational project would be the project that transformed IBM from a manufacturer of computers to a consulting company after its acquisition of PwC consulting and its sale of its computing business to the Chinese company Lenovo. An example of a collaboration project between organizations would be when Microsoft and Sony announced that they will collaborate to develop future cloud solutions for game and content-streaming services. Both companies have been rivals for more than 15 years with competing PlayStation and Xbox products, yet Sony is now working with Microsoft's vast cloud experience to enable existing and future streaming services, while Microsoft is teaming with a rival to fend off far larger gaming threats. A collaboration among organizations would be represented by the project that brought the Star Alliance into being with an alliance initially between United Airlines, SAS, Thai Airways, Air Canada and Lufthansa, which has grown into largest booking alliance for ticketing globally as a result of a major IT project that produced a common booking system.

LEADING

Projects are led. Leaders provide direction, as we discuss in Chapter 7. That direction, as we have emphasized, often came from specific forms of knowledge embedded in engineering disciplines. There are good historical reasons for this as many of the most impressive early modern projects were, in fact, engineering projects. These early engineering leaders, people such as Brunel in Britain, were extraordinarily creative and imaginative individuals, improvising both in innovation and in leading what they innovated. Today, leadership is a vast field of research and knowledge in its own right, which we draw on selectively to discuss project leadership in Chapter 7. While we might ordinarily expect to find leaders at the head of hierarchies these days, we might also find patterns of distributed leadership rather than pyramidal elegance and direction cascading down from an apex. Project managers' work becomes much more complex under these conditions as does project leadership and we consider this work and the kind of leadership qualities, personalities and styles (Müller et al., 2018) thought best able to cope with it in more detail in Chapter 7. Project leadership requires a blending of a great many skills and their embodiment in an individual for whom *planning, sociability, openness for new experiences* and *empathy* (the ability to embrace the feelings of others) are key virtues. Also, because of project management being a stressful occupation, given all the factors so far discussed, then the ability to absorb stress and manage it productively is also vital. Project managers obviously need professional skills; to be successful, however, they also need interpersonal skills to be able to manage the tensions and troubles that high pressure team-based work can generate as well as the conceptual skills to be able to concentrate on the big picture, even while detained in attending to detail.

TEAMING

Teams and their management are a topic of extensive discussion in the organizational behaviour literature, a literature that is closely related to the roots of this discipline in psychology and is a central part of the management curriculum. We discuss teams in Chapter 8 in the context of project management.

Picture 1.4   Team up

Teams are more than a collection of talented individuals; if they were the latter then there is no way in the FIFA World Cup in 2014 that Germany should have defeated a Brazilian team that was football star-studded. The best players do not necessarily make the best team. The comparison with a national football team is apt. The research on understanding and developing project teams focuses attention on interpersonal relationships and interactions in temporary organizations in which, unless project participants interact and coordinate their efforts, through being coached, mentored, trained and practised, success will not be achieved. It was the presence of these things that made Germany a winning team and their absence that made Brazil a losing team (Burnton, 2018). The project manager has to be a composite team selector, team coach, team mentor, team trainer, team disciplinarian, team strategist, all while being deeply immersed in the flow of the teaming that is ongoing (Yu, Vaagaasar, Müller, Wang, & Zhu, 2018). To be able to do all those things the project manager has to be able to engender trust with those with whom the work is being done; similarly to pulling a national team together from the talent scattered around the world in many club teams, the project manager must pool the best available talent and, where necessary, shape them into a team. In project management an artefact that is often used to try and compose teams more comparable to the 2014 German rather than Brazilian side is a team charter. A team charter is both a clarification of expectations and a concrete plan for how the team will organize their teamwork tasks, reflecting a clear expectation that everyone involved will act with a mutual commitment to teamwork. Just as in football, the motivation should be to score goals, to achieve outcomes initially predicated as the *raison d'être* for the teams' existence. Teams are liable to what is called groupthink, where everyone in the team shares a belief in the relative infallibility of the team, in a common culture, something that the project manager may need, on occasion, to combat; on other occasions boosting the team's confidence may be in order. There is no rule book that can tell you when to do which of these actions under what circumstances. Phronesis really comes into play here as the matter really is a question of practical wisdom, of wisdom honed through practice (Bygballe, Swärd, & Vaagaasar, 2016). One difference between football as a project and projects in other spheres of life is that the team players do not have to share the same pitch or be in the same arena; they can team together virtually. Virtual teamwork, based on digital communication, enables broader teams to perform than those that are co-located; however, the cues underlying communicative competence are much more difficult to interpret when being coterminous is not feasible.

COPING WITH UNCERTAINTY

All projects, as a throwing forward, a projection, a verb, have to thrive on the reality of uncertainty, the topic for Chapter 9. While tried and tested routines may be in play in the project work, they are not sufficient to keep uncertainty at bay (Loch, DeMeyer, & Pich, 2011). Each terrain built on, each innovation sought, each event organized, will always present its own sources of uncertainty for the simple reason that to project forward, to go into unknown territory, means that one may always discover something not known in advance. Venturing into the unknown is fraught with uncertainty and uncertainty always carries a risk as well as the potential for reward if the opportunities encountered can be grasped in order to add value. Order in life, as in projects, is a fragile bulwark against the perils that dealing with uncertainty can herald. While risk may be quantifiable, uncertainty is not. The project management discipline has historically focused most on the risk aspects of uncertainty. The antidote to uncertainty is widely argued to be detailed planning. Such planning reduces the likelihood that an event that is unexpected and devastating will occur. The pursuit of planning has seen the development of many useful project management tools mapping critical paths and project evaluation techniques. Nonetheless, the experience of foreseeable but unexpected uncertainty, unforeseeable uncertainty or unknown unknowns means that project planning cannot anticipate all possible factors that might shape the project's becoming into being. Uncertainty cannot be controlled just through the use of plans, rules and procedures. It must be dealt with as it arises from events that defy routines and routine categorization.

Uncertainty can be the project managers' ally when some area of work or detail that is contractually stipulated is open to interpretative ambiguity. Information is ambiguous when it can be understood in multiple and partly contradictory ways. It is indexical when different interpretations are embedded and embrained in different constituencies of interest and communities of practice that are making sense of information. In such circumstances, where there is political advantage to be gained by creating uncertainty concerning some aspect, there is a combination of power and knowledge. A project manager working in an area such as construction will be able to use their right to interpret detail to their advantage to create contractual uncertainty, which can be exploited for value, perhaps through a variation order. Since uncertainty cannot be controlled in advance, it must be managed as it arises. Uncertainty is inherent in projects throughout their life cycle. Thus, we must work with uncertainty

Picture 1.5   Thames Tideway Tunnel, London

throughout the project period as Loch et al. (2011) established. Increasingly all organizations experience rapid changes and various challenges in their efforts to develop and survive. Uncertainty is therefore immanent to all projects that strive to go, boldly, wherever crucial absences of knowledge can be experienced.

Extreme measures are sometimes required to deal with extreme uncertainties. One of the most pressing global uncertainties of present time is the future path of global warming, in part because its consequences are induced by the consequences of past, present and future actions of human agency. It is for this reason that deep inside a mountain on a remote island in the Svalbard archipelago, halfway between mainland Norway and the North Pole, lies the Global Seed Vault. The global seed vault is a store of nature's treasures held safe against the uncertainties of a changing nature and human destruction; for instance, much of the genetic material of plants from Aleppo is held in the vault as well as more than 250 types of orchid from Myanmar that are threatened by the destruction of the rainforest by logging, slashing and burning. Concerns about global warming led the Norwegian government to take additional precautions in a project designed to future-proof the seed bank against the consequences of climate changes both anticipated and those unknown in the future. It is one of more than 1700 worldwide seedbanks that serve as insurance for food crops against extinction by natural catastrophe, war or even poor husbandry. These collections, while important, are also vulnerable. Mundane accidents, such as a poorly functioning freezer, can ruin an entire collection. The Norwegian Global Seedbank serves as a back-up storage facility for the whole world. As much of the world's unique crop genetic material as possible, while also avoiding unnecessary duplication, will be stored there by the time the collection is complete.

Recently a major project, taking two years, was conducted to make the collection even safer against unknown future uncertainties. The project was carried out to provide additional security to the seed vault, based on a precautionary approach. The access tunnel leading to the seed vault has been replaced by a powerful and water-resistant concrete construction in order to make the installation resistant against a wetter and warmer climate in the future. All the technical installations have been moved to a separate service building adjacent to the vault itself in order to avoid unwanted heating. The service building also includes basic office facilities for managing the arrival and registration of seeds. Drainage ditches have been constructed on the mountainside in which the seed bank is buried deep inside to prevent melt water from accumulating around the access tunnel. A project such as this represents planning against the borders of high-level complexity, ambiguity and uncertainty. The project had to imagine possible future scenarios that might threaten the mountain redoubt of the seeds; then they had to work in Arctic conditions to construct the defences the project required. As there are only about 2000 people living there, people with specialist skills for the project had to be flown in and essential technologies either flown or shipped in.

Few project managers will encounter such harsh conditions nor, indeed, such an important project, being engaged in providing a bulwark against the consequences of the folly of human agency. The project throws into sharp relief the ways in which research and investigation (exploring/mapping out solutions) projects can face high uncertainty. In this case the project sought to ensure that uncertainty would be entirely external to the end-project by creating a wholly closed system, with access protocols, that could not be disturbed. In many ways, however, the project of producing these stable conditions under which the global seed bank would be secure mirror what project managers strive to achieve in more mundane circumstances. Every project, to manage uncertainty, must strive to create as far as is possible a stable project environment in which both internal and external sources of uncertainty that might threaten project execution are minimized. In terms of internal uncertainty, this can be due to scope ambiguity, the complexity of the contexts in which project operations occur or missing or inaccurate data or human insufficiency that fails to realize the limits of over-optimism (Flyvbjerg et al., 2003). For internal uncertainty, this can be achieved by high levels of surveillance of all areas of the project that potentially threaten uncertainty. For external uncertainty factors such as the state of the weather or the state of the markets cannot be controlled but must be monitored (Miller & Lessard, 2000). Projects, and the organizations involved in them, invest a lot of time in shaping the external environment so as to reduce uncertainties such as government policy, otherwise lobbying would not be such an extensive (and expensive) undertaking (Henisz, 2016). Internal uncertainty is almost always greatest at the beginning of the project. There are many possibilities and a great deal of uncertainty. Even though goals are established, processes are still required to turn them into sensemaking through goal hierarchies, work package structures, plans and estimates, all reducing uncertainty gradually. Through the choice of concept and design and the start-up of actual task solving, action spaces are reduced along with internal uncertainty.

Sometimes the terms soft and hard uncertainty are added to the internal/external dimension. The hard uncertainties can be quite problematic, such as securing the TBMs (tunnel boring machines) required for a major construction project, as there are only a limited number available worldwide. The soft uncertainties can be extremely problematic; these are usually either personal, interpersonal or interorganizational in origin and cannot be solved by scanning the project environment and securing some expensive technology. What is at issue are those factors that make project collaboration and teamwork problematic, often unseen or unacknowledged, often also not amenable to a quick fix, not where actions are occurring that will lead to an irretrievable breakdown of communication, trust and reciprocity. Scenario planning will rarely capture these sorts of uncertainties. In terms of planning for managing uncertainty it is worth realizing that uncertainties are not all of a piece; there is more than one kind of uncertainty that can threaten order in projects. Characterized by variety, project managers may face identifiable and unidentifiable uncertainty as well as chaotic uncertainty.

Uncertainty represents both opportunity and risk. Key elements in dealing with uncertainty will be its identification, analysis and response. As project portfolios and programmes become more and more widely used, it becomes necessary to see how uncertainty is involved and managed at the programme level as well as individually (Sanchez, Robert, Bourgault, & Pellerin, 2009). Project programmes are, of course, even more complex than individual projects, thus opening up more changes along the way to their completion, generating more conflicts and greater uncertainty than is usual in individual projects.

Collaborating and stakeholding

Individual and internal sources of uncertainty can sometimes be associated with different internal and external stakeholders, as we discuss in Chapter 10. Any project will include a number of relevant stakeholders if it is to manage the disparate knowledges tangled up in its processes (Vaagaasar, 2011). Projects often have a large number of stakeholders with whom relations can be both rewarding and challenging. The rewards flow from the positives, such as learning; the challenges arise from the interest of stakeholders in being taken into account where they have not been and may not be wanted. The project has to deal both with those stakeholders that it wishes to include as well as those that do not appear to be contributing positively to the project, those that are resisting or otherwise opposing the project, those that the project barely countenances. Stakeholders have a way of multiplying, especially on large, lengthy and costly projects. Some of these will be formally recognized, such as suppliers or contractors. Others will make claims to be stakeholders despite not being formally recognized, such as the public at large or specific sections of them who feel the impact of the project's unfolding. Other stakeholders are not able to be represented unmediated, such as the environment; sometimes it takes a young person, with extraordinary commitment, such as Greta Thunberg, to do the representing and thus mobilize millions of global citizens if not those on whose politics the health of the planet ultimately rests. The natural environment, the ecology and climate that makes life on Earth possible, is a stakeholder that cannot speak but that suffers through extinctions, global warming and a changing carrying capacity for life itself.

Some stakeholders merit inclusion because they have resources that makes project execution or delivery better while others make it problematic to implement the project. To be held at arm's length is often the fate of civil society groups mobilizing against a project – even though they may sometimes have positive ideas for improving its value by minimizing its disruption. It may be sensible to include these 'difficult' stakeholders in governance in some ways; if not, then at least adopt some governmental orientations towards them, perhaps seeking to manage them through social media (Ninan et al., 2019).

Picture 1.6   Used to be a busy airport but is now the Fridtjof Nansen Park

Source: Ivar Brodøy

Stakeholders in the project are there because they have interests that should be mapped. You need to be able to work out what their main interests are and where they impinge on the project. Are these interests likely to be positive or negative in their impact on the value of the project? Are the stakeholders manageable? What is important for these stakeholders and is it important for your project so that you can work out what resources, if any, to commit? What can these stakeholders do for or to the project? How powerful are the stakeholders, how urgent are their demands and how legitimate are their actions? In what phase of the project are their demands and interests most likely to be a factor for consideration? These are just some of the questions that you will need to consider in relation to stakeholders, working out which are marginal, which are supportive, which are antagonistic as well as those that seem to have mixed relations. Any project potentially promises a scratch orchestra of stakeholders, some accomplished instrumentalists while others are motivated to engage because of the specificities of the situation. Managing a scratch orchestra full of soloists of variable ability requires much practice.

Learning and innovating

Consult the guidebook to knowledge, follow the directions and no further learning is required, right? Wrong, as we explain in Chapter 11! Projects afford ample opportunities for learning not only because so many unknowns and uncertainties can be encountered but because their temporary duration throws many different experiences of other related and dissimilar projects into the mix. The temporary nature of the mix is both a strength and a weakness. As a strength it cross-fertilizes experiences with other experiences presenting opportunities for learning from practice. The weakness is that as the project concludes and everyone hurries off to the next project to form new teams little of the learning that has occurred is retained. Much of this learning is experiential and informal; it is learning that, by definition, is embodied and embrained in those doing the learning rather than being embedded in a text. There are signs that the times are a changing – in the UK explicit learning was encouraged in both the London Olympics project and the Crossrail metro project (see https://learninglegacy.crossrail. co.uk). Legacy is increasingly important globally in the wake of these projects.

Picture 1.7   Crossrail

Source: Image courtesy of Fred Romero, via Flickr.com. Shared under the Creative Commons BY 2.0 license.

Learning is a gerund, an active verb. While that which might have been learned can be stored in a knowledge management system or an end of project report, in all likelihood few will read these and even fewer will learn much from them because the knowledge therein is not lived, experiential knowing. Knowledge is named but not necessarily used when it is embodied in bodies of knowledge. Where these bodies of knowledge consist of rules, precepts and principles, rather similar to a catechism, faithful followers may ensue but the capability for learning further is severely truncated. Will people access it; will they read it; will they translate it from the relatively thin context of abstracted knowledge to the relatively culturally thick example of their situation and project?

Whereas knowledge may be dormant much of the time, knowing is constantly acquired through learning. Considerable learning occurs informally through communities of practice that form where people with shared interests gather to gossip, discuss issues and be social with like-minded others. Where there is opportunity for this learning to percolate an organization or a project then wider organization or project-based learning may ensue. The test of such learning is whether the organization or project becomes reflexively aware of any dynamic capabilities that learning has fostered

(Söderlund, Vaagaasar, & Andersen, 2008). Shifting awareness of these from specific situations to becoming embedded attributes is the key. These constructions, where they allow for the exploitation and recombination of knowing and expertise flexibly, enable responses to situations that require new solutions not known or embodied in guides to knowledge. Otherwise, where this enactment does not occur, learning remains implicit, tacit, unrecognized.

Shrewd project managers can strive to facilitate learning through the ways that they interact, converse, consult and liaise with others and encourage these others to do amongst themselves. A key mechanism of learning is through project and organization storytelling. Stories aid learning through thematics that memory retains. Learning becomes more intense. Individuals remember better what they learned from stories because stories are largely able to contextualise the content by placing it in relationships. Stories include and elevate emotions. Learning that activates emotions often also contributes to deeper and longer lasting learning. Stories circulate readily and rapidly because of the temporality of projects as temporary organizations. Project managers have success and disaster stories aplenty from prior projects to inform the present one. Sometimes these stories are formally recounted; other times they circulate as gossip, occasionally becoming part of the informal legends, sagas and mythologies of project life and its characters.

Workshops designed to resolve issues that the project is facing, in which external expertise can be recruited, provide for fora in which ideas can emerge, be worked over collectively, pulled apart and rebuilt. The UK Crossrail project provides an excellent example of this (DeBarro et al., 2015), which has inspired a major industry

Picture 1.8 Exhibition by Yayoi Kusama

Source: Anne Live Vaagaasar

project (www.i3p.org.uk/). Learning leads to knowing; collective knowing how to do things differently or do different things that foster innovation, creating and introducing something new. Organizations increasingly strive for innovation through project-based developments. No project lacks innovation; the projection element of projects, the throwing forward of a scheme, a collection of ideas, a design, will always create something that did not exist previously, hence something novel, an innovation of sorts. Some vanguard projects are much more innovation-focused than others, however, as they explicitly strive to generate innovation as their rationale through fostering and nurturing creativity. Practices of generating, communicating, connecting, evaluating and reshaping ideas contribute to idea work (Coldevin et al., 2019), sustaining innovative projects.

Innovation is often thought of as the production of new products, such as smart phones, Fitbits and electric cars. Usually, for these innovations to survive, there must be effective demand for them in the market. Not all innovations thrive and survive; indeed, there is a Museum of Failures in Helsingborg, Sweden that has a collection of over 100 failed products and services from some of the world's best-known companies. Innovation is not limited to companies but can also occur in processes such as the use of algorithms to transform mobility by Uber, hotel accommodation by Trivago and music consumption by Spotify. All of these innovations relied on projects attuned to processes that transformed how existing products were consumed without introducing new material products to the market. Process innovation can go further than this; it can represent transformations in internal work practices. The democratization of decision processes, changes in organizational structure, networks of relations with suppliers, vendors or other external stakeholders would all be process innovations.

Complexifying

We live in a society whose complexities are frequently delivered by projects, leading to a phenomenon known as projectification, referring to the cultural and discursive societal processes whereby projects and project-like circumstances are institutionalized in organizing through temporary organizations created to deliver value. Think of everyday things like broadband, 5G mobile networks, the television shows that you watch on Netflix or terrestrial channels, recent election campaigns that occurred – all delivered as and by projects. Sometimes these projects are running in parallel. Netflix could not provide sufficient programme content if it commissioned shows on a serial basis; instead it has many simultaneous projects, which affords them flexibility but also creates a number of challenges. Coordination of multiple projects is complex as we discuss in Chapter 12. Learning from multiple projects and ensuring that it becomes distributed into different project practices is demanding. Each project is a unique process yet all the parallel projects require managing. The complexity of an organization therefore drastically increases as the number of projects grows.

The growth in the use of projects has led to the development and spread of programme and portfolio management (PPM). In a portfolio of projects, such as Netflix's commissioning of broadcasting projects, there is often no single common goal that collects the projects together. When Saudi Aramco develops new oil fields, when Telstra expands its coverage for 5G or when Google develops a Quantum computer, the work is rarely organized as an isolated single project but is rather composed of a set of complex projects. Strategy frames and guides the projects and their interrelations. If the strategy is ambiguous and fragmented, the interrelations can slip. Project programmes may be organized sequentially, in parallel or as a network. Usually these programmes run over a long period of time, with each element being exposed to significant changes that can lead to a diminution of coherence and a lagging in progress. Hence, it is demanding to handle many projects simultaneously, which poses challenges related to resource allocation, competence development, priorities between different initiatives, organizational arrangements, use of personnel and balancing of workload: both structural and human challenges are involved. Adding to the challenges is the fact that usually there will be multiple separate organizations involved in the programme delivery, making interaction and coordination across organizational boundaries demanding. Different management systems, organizational cultures, routines and procedures that may not be compatible become entangled, making such projects risky. Drawing on the formal guides to project management, you will often encounter references to project maturity and encounter project management firms that will boast of their project maturity. By this is meant that they have mastery of most of the tools in the project management toolbox and are experienced in using them. There are more than 30 such models/frameworks on the market – and their provenance is very much that of the market. Each one claims to offer a standard for project protocols and there is competition among providers. Overall, they represent highly formalistic and standards-based approaches to management that often prove attractive to engineers and others schooled in the 'hard' disciplines.

With the emergence of projects as a major organizational form and not just a mode of delivery, not surprisingly this has become characterized as an organizational type, the P-form, used to refer to organizations that have project activities as their central core. The delivery of organizational work through multiple projects creates internal competition, tournaments between project managers engaged in innovation projects as to who can bring in projects on time, on budget and innovatively in terms of processes because project management is only a career stepping stone in such organizations. The glittering prizes are one step beyond, through promotion into the oligarchical structures of the organization that exercise strategy and surveillance over projects, where they can become project barons, quasi-feudal overlords of the projects toiling ceaselessly under their watchful gaze. The project managers in such organizations are inserted in a giant panopticon where they know that they are being watched and they know what it takes to make the break from the project to the oligarchical levels: delivering KPIs every time, on time, on budget, innovatively. Failure to do this can see the project managers permanently stranded betwixt and between the professional, scientific and technical skills that formed them originally and the managerial heights to which they aspire. All the time they are project managers they lose fluency in those professional, scientific and technical skills that formed them. Such careers can easily become dead end streets.

Many organizations are ambidextrous: they specialize some areas in creativity and others in routines. We use the Duke Ellington orchestra as a great example of this ambidexterity. Other organizations adopt polyarchic designs to manage tensions between creativity and routine by using distributed power relations between commissioning and project-based organization. Many television programmes are made this way, where showrunners look after the creativity and innovation, while the commissioning organization attend to the routines. In other industries, a project management organization might act as a subordinate part of an overall organization managing the projects.

Enough has been said already for the reader to realize that the job of being a project manager is not necessarily a carnival of pleasure; indeed, it can be very stressful. Time pressure, expectations from many stakeholders, project assignments combined with tasks employees have in their regular position in the base organization are all factors that make for stressful work. Burnout is not unusual; neither is dealing with toxic cultures at work where the stresses are widely felt as the pressures to be on time, on budget, on target with goal achievement, mount. The project manager can become the toxic handler for the pressures that flow down from above that are channelled through their office, as they simultaneously have to deal with the stresses channelled from below as resistance to the increased pressures that emanate for the project management office because of the pressures from above. Definitely not a carnival.

Ending

All things must pass, must come to an end, things good or bad. How they end is another matter. Some projects leave a joyous legacy, a favourite music album or film, a remarkable piece of engineering or construction, an innovation that changes lives. Other projects end in acrimony, in the courts, in fees that stuff barristers' wallets. Some projects just peter out, they don't really die but are absorbed into other budgets as quiet mistakes recategorized into other pieces of work, particularly prevalent in large organizations managing multiple internal cross functional projects, with diffuse accountability. Doing projects ethically may be one way of warding off the latter fault.

A project is a temporary organization, which makes it difficult to establish shared ethical platforms in the time available. The project also has a clearly defined date for termination – often leaving the issue of liability in the open. Potentially it will be easier for both the principal and other actors involved to be somewhat relaxed about ethical standards. Short deadlines can lead to ethical questions receiving only scant attention. Furthermore, many actors are involved in projects, some of whom are only involved for a relatively short duration. Many project actors represent different and partly contradictory interests, especially in interorganizational projects, where different stakeholders often have different embedded ethical cultures and values. Lack of transparency in both the structure and the collaborative relationships also contributes to making ethics problematic.

Issues can arise with implications for the project long after the project was completed. Think of the horrific fire that destroyed Grenfell Tower in London's wealthiest borough, which ended 72 lives and damaged many others. The fire raged through the cladding that a renovation project had installed on the tower block. One of the things that will be at issue in the inquiry being conducted into the disaster is the nature of the cladding used and the responsibility for it, given that an alternative cladding with better fire resistance was refused due to cost. The original contractor was dropped by the project owner because their price of £11.278 million was £1.6 million higher than the proposed budget. The contract was put out to competitive tender and won by a contractor whose bid was £2.5 million less than the original contractor's. The new contractor carried out the refurbishment for £8.7 million, with the cladding fitted by a specialist façade subcontractor, at a cost of £2.6 million.

Where the legal responsibilities reside for the decisions that led to the use of highly flammable materials will, no doubt, be decided by the inquiry when its second report is published in 2020. Phase one of the Report of the Public Inquiry into the Fire at Grenfell Tower 14 June 2017, chaired by the Rt Hon Sir Martin Moore-Bick, was published in October 2019.[2] Obviously, as well as the legal issues of responsibility,

---

[2]The full phase one report is available to access from https://study.sagepub.com/pm

which in the first report are discussed in terms of the response to the fire, there are ethical issues involved as well.

Among the ethical issues are how ethical is it to use materials that are highly flammable and proven to be highly unsafe, simply to save money? There are also ethical issues about the design of the flats – there was only one common staircase as a point of egress and exit. Ethical issues were also associated with the refurbishments to flats being conducted in part as a way of improving thermal performance as well as being a cosmetic exercise that would make the building less aesthetically unattractive to the wealthy people living in private houses in the neighbouring borough of Notting Hill. The flats were what are called in the UK council flats, social housing, with a population comprising members of many ethnic communities.

Many projects intersected on that fateful night of 14 June 2017. The projects of renovation and the project managers of the different contractors; the project management of the project owners, the Kensington and Chelsea London Borough Council; the fire safety officers' advice that if a fire broke out that they should stay put and close the doors of their flats; the lack of water pressure from the flow managed by Thames Water which was insufficient for the firemen's hoses; the absence of a high ladder from the fire service until 37 minutes after the fire service had been notified. Some endings are far worse than others; the project owners and managers, the fire personnel and safety officers, while not burnt alive, have had their conduct subject to legal and ethical scrutiny by the Moore-Bick-led inquiry. The fire service response and advice, the design of the external wall cladding and the flouting of regulations by contractors and the local authority are all subject to harsh criticism (Bulman & Shulman, 2019). We write about this event to bring home, dramatically, what the ethical implications might well be for those involved in a project that went wrong.

Picture 1.9   Grenfell Tower fire

Source: Image courtesy of Natalie Oxford, via wikicommons. Shared under the Creative Commons BY 4.0 license.

The professionalization of project management is in part a strategy intended to minimize the risks of being held to have made professional and ethical misjudgements to which legal responsibility might attach. The professional bodies have built both a common identity for and common standards within the field of project management, with strong anchoring in the task-oriented approach, based on standards and best practices. Rules for these do not easily accommodate best practices in ethical judgements, in part because ethics is not a matter of applying a rule. There is an indeterminacy about ethics that calls on human and social judgement and this requires a different type of education than the application of standards. It requires competence in deliberative democracy, in discourses in which ethical considerations have to be weighed finely in the balance. The consequences of doing otherwise may be fatal in some professional areas of project management.

The projectification of the world is seeing project management being widely used across a great many fields and practices. Although significant changes are afoot in the field of project management, represented in part by this book, many project managers and others who work with projects in film, competence development programmes or other change and development projects may find the project methodologies that these institutions promote somewhat too prescriptive, restrictive and overly oriented to material projects. Modern project management of open systems that allow multiple inputs must manage much equivocality and uncertainty and the reality of project processes being dynamic, complex and changeable. Boundaries must be drawn around the project, such as defining the project team, managing stakeholders while delivering the project on schedule, on budget, on time, innovatively, ethically and creatively. Doing this is demanding. It requires reflective practitioners (Schön, 1991) able to be engaged in the processes they are involved in, exploring and interpreting relationships, managing people and teams and being adept at sourcing and using technology, tools and procedures.

All of these people, processes, practices participating in projects will come to an end. Projects are intentionally temporary organizations (all organizations should face the probability of not being permanent, even if not intentionally so on the part of their owners and managers – nothing is for ever). When the end is nigh what are the accountabilities? Milestones, plans, decision gates and clarity of responsibilities are tools to try and control project direction (and project teams) in terms of project intention. They provide the basis for evaluating early completion of the project before the scheduled end date. Milestones are aids for assessing whether the project is on the right course in terms of project intent. If failure to achieve the milestones cannot be corrected with minor changes, the project basis might need to be reviewed again. The results of these assessments can give rise to different conclusions such as adding resources, changing delivery times, adjusting quality criteria for delivery or some combination of these, perhaps even renegotiating or exiting the project.

The project ends and what happens? A project is usually completed at the time of delivery, unless the project organization is contracted to be responsible for the project for a contracted period of time, as often happens with BOOT (Build Own Operate Transfer) contracts. In the latter case, tasks and activities will continue to be carried out in the project after it is realized. In other cases, if the project is oriented to producing a new product this product should be ready for use. If it is an event, then the event should have been staged. Depending on the type and size of the project, there will be many activities that are included in the actual completion work of the project, including contract termination; updating and disseminating activities that have not been completed; settling of project accounts and recording of project documentation. The project will be handed over, final reports prepared, the next project embraced.

Project management as a discipline must confront a rapidly changing world of projects and it is not entirely evident that its auspices in engineering best practices is the most appropriate way for it to develop the flexibility required. We conclude our book by reflecting on the contribution that can be made to project management from a concern with broader social science issues of practices, processes and sense-making; we discuss what we refer to as political phenomenology being essential for the changes required. Projects comprise much more than a matter easily captured in a task perspective. Projects relate to relationships, i.e. actors who are involved in various ways, to conditions in projects' environment, such as the way stakeholders involve themselves, to various types of uncertainty and the politics of coordinating, collaborating and communication among many different disciplines in the creation of a new reality. Projects concern people who work together in teams, who need leadership and direction in their work. Project management thus involves much more than just rational methodology. It requires an understanding of the politics of the myriad relationships that launching a project entails; it requires an understanding of the embeddedness of projects in specific forms of life and the ways that other forms of life are disrupted, intersected and transformed; it requires a degree of humility about the technical prowess and proficiency that drives projects. Projects should be seen in their broad terms as processes that make differences that matter for, to and on forms of life, differences not always anticipated or applauded at the launch of the project and its projections. Projects add value and value is not as simple as might be imagined by a fixation only on the numbers.

Picture 1.10   The research park on Svalbard

Source: Juul Frost architects/Statsbygg

Hence, our end is a new beginning, a call for new mapping that incorporates more of the territory than do abstracted standards. The territory to be incorporated resides in cognate areas such as organization studies and in the increasing research-based knowledge that the organizations, project management and related journals provide. The book does not ignore the conventions of the project management body of knowledge; after all, it is a kind of phronesis. Nonetheless, this body provides only a partial mapping largely constituted by its own conventions; we trust that this introductory textbook will unsettle some of those conventions, for improved mapping of project management in the future. As we know from Weick's (1995) recounting of a tale of two mountain ranges and one map, mapping can sometimes take us to destinations in surprising ways.

Chapter Roadmap

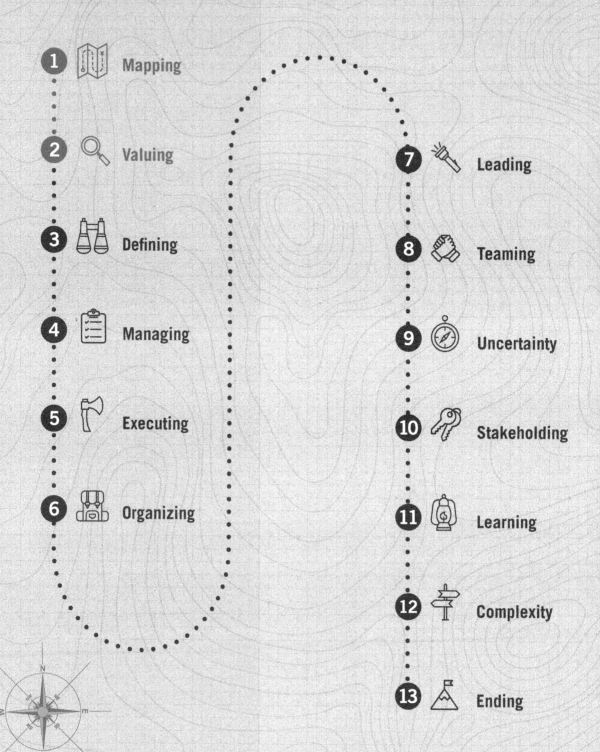

1 Mapping

2 Valuing

3 Defining

4 Managing

5 Executing

6 Organizing

7 Leading

8 Teaming

9 Uncertainty

10 Stakeholding

11 Learning

12 Complexity

13 Ending

2

Valuing Projects

Learning objectives

After reading this chapter, you should be able to:

1 Recognize the differences between project types

2 Understand that projects are tools for value creation

3 Realize that successful value creation implies project product success

4 Understand the key factors in project success and failure

5 Appreciate the multi-dimensionality of success criteria

Before you get started

He who has a 'why' to live for can bear almost any 'how'.

– Friedrich Nietzsche

Introduction

A project is a tool for creating value. This chapter highlights the phenomenon of value creation. We look at what value is, how it can be defined and how different values are created through projects. We also look into value design. The emphasis on value creation affects how we assess what constitutes the success of projects. It shifts attention from assessments of whether the implementation of the project itself is successful in terms of the criteria fixed at the start of the project; instead, we determine if the project succeeded in creating value and for whom it was created.

Value is usually conceptualized in terms of the contribution that a project makes to an accounting bottom line. Profit is an important, if a somewhat dubious social construct; dubious because figures can be manipulated in many ways to represent many things. For one thing, temporality is important. A project may come in at a substantial loss, as did the Sydney Opera House, but be a multiplier for economic value in the future as the Opera House did by becoming a tourist icon, bringing many millions of dollars into the local economy.

Value is in the eye of the beholder. It is important to note that the consideration of a project creating value or not will vary among the stakeholders. It is a subjective matter. As we increasingly organize work in projects, we must also consider, as an aspect of success, to what extent the project team members prospered through the project work. Did they learn something and utilize their potential? Did they feel motivated, safe and happy? Also, as firms increase their portfolio of projects, in order to stay competitive over time, they must manage to learn and innovate through their projects. An aspect of success is the extent to which the project facilitated organizational learning and increased the innovative capacity of the organization. What is the legacy the project leaves? Has it improved the quality of life, beauty, efficiency; has it contributed aesthetically or scientifically to humanity; did it prevent a misadventure, did it make people happier? All of these outcomes would be valuable, so we need a broad-based conception of value, tailored to specific projects and specific stakeholders and beholders.

Different project types

Projects vary widely in the types of tasks they solve, the degree of uncertainty and complexity their execution involves, as well as the contexts in which they operate. Different categories of projects can be captured in a systematic framework. A categorization of projects can increase our understanding of variations and similarities between projects and enable us to use appropriate implementation strategies. There are many ways to categorize projects. One way is to differentiate them based on the nature of the project delivery. The following categorization is a common representation (Payne & Turner, 1999):

- Technical building and construction projects
- System development projects
- Product development projects
- Event projects
- Research and development projects
- Organization development projects

Such a categorization points to substantive differences but it also represents a very instrumental understanding of projects. Additionally, it fails to recognize the way in which many contemporary projects might involve all of these elements. Think of a project such as Glastonbury, the famous rock music festival (www.glastonburyfesti vals.co.uk/). Glastonbury only lasts for five days but is a major project that crosses almost all of the categories that are listed above. It involves technical building and construction of the various stages and other facilities. There is a substantial system and organizational development project that has evolved as Glastonbury has changed since its inception in 1970, the day after the great Jimi Hendrix died. It entails product development projects: for instance, in 2015 Kanye West headlined on the Pyramid stage, despite the opposition of the old-time rockers to hip-hop (think Noel Gallagher) and the overall project is an event which is a constant site of research and development. We can think of Glastonbury as a project that crosses many fields – music festival, tribal event, logistics and planning of traffic and mobilities, ticketing and promotion, booking, agents and acts – and all before anyone comes to the fields of Worthy Farm.

The Pyramid stage at Glastonbury

Another distinction that is sometimes made is between projects delivering products and those that deliver processes, for example organizational development projects (Figure 2.1). The term 'product' refers both to a physical product such as a building, as well as services, such as an event or a seminar. A process implies several aspects, usually referring to the processes required to produce a product. It may involve an organizational division of labour or ways in which production is managed in relation to marketing or competence development.

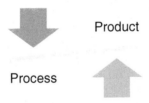

Product

Process

Figure 2.1   Project Types – two main categories as foundation for innovation

Many projects deliver both products and processes; for example, both an ICT solution and new routines for handling the refunding of travel expenses in a firm or, at Glastonbury, headliners and all the other acts as the product as well as the processes of securing regulatory permission for the detailed organization. Glastonbury each year develops a new attraction, through its headline acts. For instance, in 2017, the leader of the British opposition Labour Party, Jeremy Corbyn, spoke to popular acclaim on the Pyramid stage, a venue usually reserved for headlining musicians. Corbyn developed and delivered a product that fitted the vibe of the festival: as he said, 'Because what festivals, what this festival is about, are about coming together. This festival was envisaged as being for music yes, but also for the environment, and for peace.' Corbyn was there to promote a product – the Labour Party, its policies and his leadership. He tailored the product to fit his political project by appealing to a young festival-going crowd.

Picture 2.1   The Pyramid stage at Glastonbury

Source: Image courtesy of Paul Holloway, via wikicommons. Shared under the Creative Commons BY-SA 2.0 license.

The distinction between process and product, together with the relationship between the principal and the organization holding the ownership of the project, provides the basis for categorization by Söderlund to distinguish among development projects, change projects and delivery projects. It is a fairly useful way of classifying projects but needs expanding to include event projects, a project type increasingly used that differs somewhat from the other categories.

There are no exact differences between the types of products, and in practice, as we have established, a project could involve more than just one type. We will look into the four types (Figure 2.2).

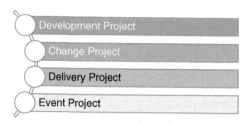

Figure 2.2   Project types

Change projects

All organizations rely on having efficient processes that provide a flow of goods and services. These processes might be organized around a division of labour, a flow of production, design for responsibilities or the integration of different activities.

Change projects aim to change the processes of the organization, aiming at process improvement, perhaps through organization re-design or revamping supply chains and networks. Examples of other targets at which organizations may launch change projects could be programmes to improve competencies, reorganize business units, achieve mergers, launch innovations, etc. Change projects are mostly concerned with introducing new methods to improve performance and new processes to try and increase efficiency – to achieve more with less effort. It is not the products of the organization per se that are the focus of attention so much as different elements related to the way the products are produced, either directly or indirectly by the organization.

Other change projects in organizations are oriented towards social relations and their improvement. For instance, in a university, a change project oriented at improving the student experience through redesigning a website to be more user friendly will not necessarily alter the grades that the students achieve – one major product of the university being the credentialing of its students – but they would be designed to make the experience of being at the university more inclusive, less fragmented and thus more enjoyable. In other instances, in recent times many organizations have been found to fall short in their promotion of a working environment that is free from sexual harassment.

READ THIS!

Read the article by Sawyer and Thoroughgood on 'How to fix a toxic culture like Uber's requires more than just a new CEO' at: https://study.sagepub.com/pm.

IN PRACTICE

THE LX PROJECT

An Australian university introduced a project portfolio of work called LX Transformation in 2019. The project was expected to run over a three-year period project to transition all the university's portfolio of subjects from Blackboard to Canvas. Blackboard was the digital platform used in the past; Canvas was to be the digital platform to be used in the future. As part of this project, consultants were brought in to map the needs of academic staff to make the transition as easy as possible. The consultants held initial workshops for academic staff. To ensure the needs of the staff were included in the planning of the transition, a broad range of staff were invited to make themselves available to attend the workshops. The workshops used human-centred design as a creative approach to problem solving that starts with the people being designed for, with the intention of producing new solutions tailor made to suit their needs. The first steps in the workshops were to find out what the academics did, when they did it, when they felt most pressured doing what at which times. A catalogue of a great many digital tools was supplied and supplemented in the meeting. The ambition was to roll all tools

(Continued)

widely used into the one platform. This was the first step towards trying to make the future demands on the academics' time that the project would require as painless and unobtrusive as possible.

QUESTION

1.   Digital skills are deeply embedded in the digital millennial generation, but for older members of the workforce they are not so deeply embedded. How might the project of digitalization of all learning in a university be best managed to ensure that there is commitment across the generations of users?

A change project is mainly internally oriented and involves the development and implementation of more efficient processes for an organization. Performance can take place on several levels and vary widely. In the case of strategic processes, it may include significant changes, such as mergers between companies. A change project can also be a competence development programme for groups of employees or other types of changes made to streamline production processes.

For the future, bearing in mind the digital revolution, project management change programmes will be increasingly digitally mediated, designed and delivered.

EXTEND YOUR KNOWLEDGE

Read the article by Whyte (2019), 'How digital information transforms project delivery models', available at https://study.sagepub.com/pm.

Delivery projects

Many organizations base their existence on products or processes which they don't develop in their own organization. They apply a third party to handle the development of the process or product. Thereby, projects are performed by others, handling all or part of the assignment. This is very common in major construction projects. Then it is a client (or a consortium of contractors) who will carry out a project, such as building a tunnel. The client usually does not build the tunnel but engages subcontractors to do so. Architectural practices are examples of organizations that rely solely on deliveries to others. Delivery projects are commonly used within the construction industry, as well as for development of ICT and telecommunications. The consulting industry is mainly based on delivery projects, by contributing to the implementation of organizational changes with a client organization, for example. Sometimes, when a client or customer asks for a delivery within a given framework, a third party is engaged to complete all or part of the project. Delivery projects imply distinctive features for the organization and distribution of responsibility (see Chapter 5), as well as for the use of contracts and negotiations (see Chapter 4).

In delivery projects, understanding client needs with as much clarity as possible is essential. Negotiations and mutual clarifications of requirements and expectations between the client and the supplier are normal. The contract is a central foundation of their relation. It specifies requirements for content and quality of delivery and specifies the financial conditions that will ensure profitability for the parties involved. Of course, these can be subject to ongoing renegotiation.

At the outset the client and the supplier should collaborate to ensure they have a common understanding of what the key needs are and how they are best understood. They should strive to develop a shared understanding of the key characteristics that the project deliverables should have, which is necessary in order to meet the aims of the project. Likewise, there should be clarity about how the collaboration required throughout the project duration is to be organized to ensure that the project deliverables meet the clients' needs. These needs may change over time. For example, it is well known how ICT projects often fail to produce their specified deliveries within the established cost and time frames (Flyvbjerg, 2008). One reason for that is that the client and the supplier have different ideas about the **scope** of the project.

> Project **scope** involves determining and documenting specific project goals, deliverables, features, functions, tasks, deadlines and costs.

Where different ideas exist it can lead to more development work which will be charged to the client (Berggren, Järkvik, & Söderlund, 2008). The technical developers at one of the major producers of mobile devices explained how this sometimes happens. First, development projects often produce potentially innovative solutions to problems that are possible to develop but will extend the scope of the project. In development projects, this might not be so unusual because the client often does not know what is required; lacking the answer, they commission a development project. Developers that present innovative solutions assume that the client will be as excited about the innovation as they are.

READ THIS!

There is a cautionary tale by Ryan Calder at Parks Canada, about a new hydro project in Muskrat Falls, Labrador that failed to consider stakeholders adequately. This is available at: https://study.sagepub.com/pm.

Event projects

Event projects differ slightly from the two types we have discussed so far. An event project deals with the planning and implementation of a specific event. Festivals, art exhibitions, sports events or other major events are examples of event projects. While many event projects are also delivery projects, we distinguish them as a separate category due to the 'event aspect'; that is, they are aimed at a particular event scheduled at a particular point in time. These projects often have multiple clients and a significant degree of volunteers doing the actual project work. Performances and exhibitions are increasingly viewed as projects, such that the cultural sector increasingly applies concepts, methods, organization and systematics from project management literature and practice.

IN PRACTICE

THE RIO 2016 GAMES: MANAGING THE 'SOFT' AND 'HARD' WARE[1]

Rio de Janeiro won the right to host the Olympic and Paralympic Games in 2009. Winning the right to host major sport events such as the Olympic and Paralympic Games, the organizing committee (Rio2016) responsible for the organization of the Games initiated negotiations with different stakeholders involved, in the planning and delivery of the event project. The Rio de Janeiro municipality was the public authority that facilitated the agreements with third parties managing the venues that would host the Games, such as GL events, who had leased Riocentro and the Aquatic Centre where some of the sport competitions were to be staged.

The agreements led to construction of venues at the Olympic Park, contributed to the development of the Barra area, the proposed construction of Pavilion 6 in Riocentro, which hosted the sport competitions of boxing and sitting volleyball competitions, and the technological development of Riocentro, the centre that hosts fairs. As part of the works undertaken to develop the clusters for hosting the Games, evictions and relocation of people living in favelas, such as Vila Autodromo, were conducted at the expense of those living there. Part of the operations included the completion of Line 4 of the metro – on which work had started decades earlier but was never completed – which connected the *zona sul* with the *zona oeste* of the city. These operations had to take place in a limited time frame, between the end of 2009 and 2016 when the event was held. During this time span many suppliers were involved in the preparation of the venues and in the delivery of the events, which took place in August and September 2016.

While the preparation comprised negotiations between different stakeholders, the delivery and staging of the event relied heavily on the work of the front-line workforce, staff and volunteers, who were recruited for the event and underwent a selection process over two years. Volunteers from all over the world applied to the volunteer programme to participate in the Games, with over 240,000 applications submitted for 70,000 slots. Volunteers with different cultures and backgrounds moved to Rio for the Games where they were expected to undertake various tasks. However, the cohort of volunteers that actually performed at the games was much less than expected, thus recruitment and selection of volunteers continued through the Games.

Problems that emerged were discontinuous communication with volunteers, who were not always available when they eventually received the invitation to volunteer. Also, volunteers paid for their travel and accommodation expenses and at short notice were sometimes unable to commit to these. Volunteers were provided with a uniform, meals and transport card to travel to the venues in which they worked. Volunteers performed in more than 60 functional areas of sport, services and job functions, spanning operations and event services to technical officials and medical services. Thus, their role was central to the staging of the event operations at both the Olympic and Paralympic Games and the diverse volunteer backgrounds were reflected in the many different languages that volunteers spoke. The contribution of volunteers was pivotal to the staging of the mega-event project as the Games had a short timespan for preparation and a shorter time for the delivery (15–20 days). Mega-events such as the Olympic and Paralympic Games are projects with a very condensed scope for the staging of the event in a limited time. For mega-events, it is a one-time project; the hosting city does not have another chance if things go wrong. Time is a crucial aspect, and all the operations have to be completed for the event project to be staged.

---

[1]Prepared by Veronica Lo Presti, UTS Business School, University of Technology Sydney

Information on RIO2016 is provided by a number of informative sites in *The Conversation*:

- 'Don't believe the doom mongers – the Olympics have changed Rio for the better' – Beatriz Garcia, 22 August 2016 at https://theconversation.com/dont-believe-the-doom-mongers-the-olympics-have-changed-rio-for-the-better-64225
- 'Vila Autódromo: The favela fighting back against Rio's Olympic development' – Adam Talbot, 12 January 2016 at https://theconversation.com/vila-autodromo-the-favela-fighting-back-against-rios-olympic-development-52393
- 'Airbnb brings Olympic tourists to Rio's poorest areas – but will locals benefit?' – Fabian Franzel, 29 July 2016 at https://theconversation.com/airbnb-brings-olympic-tourists-to-rios-poorest-areas-but-will-locals-benefit-63219

QUESTIONS

1. What value do mega-events projects such as the Games create? And for whom?

2. What are the improvements that an event project could make in the community hosting them and what are the pitfalls?

Events such as an Olympic Games and a World Cup in football are large and complex projects that include a number of project owners, multiple suppliers, and many stakes and fields of interests beyond those clearly related sports elements. Such event projects hold both the character of development projects in the form of infrastructure and construction and also have political aspects, for example in terms of community development and identity building. The London Olympics of 2012 was intended to provide the catalyst for a huge programme of urban and environmental regeneration. It was intended that a neglected part of the east end of London would be transformed into a model of sustainable urban development with benefits for residents in terms of improved sporting facilities and quality of life. It certainly improved the quality of life for West Ham United FC (https://www.whufc.com/). Their home ground is now the London Stadium, a multi-purpose outdoor stadium at Queen Elizabeth Olympic Park in the Stratford district of London. It also improved the quality of life for those working and shopping in the enormous Westfield shopping centre (https://uk.westfield.com/stratfordcity) that was a part of the legacy left by the event.

Many festivals are well planned and joyous events, well project managed. Not all are, however. In the following feature we invite you to reflect on a notorious recent case and to analyse it in terms of what you have learned from your textbook.

WHAT WOULD YOU DO?

- -

A Festival that has assumed a legendary status, for all the wrong reasons, was known as the Fyre Festival. It was 'organized' as a 'luxury music festival' by Billy McFarland, CEO of Fyre Media Inc., and rapper Ja Rule. It was created with the intent of promoting the company's Fyre app for booking music talent. The festival was scheduled to take place during 28–30 April and

(Continued)

5–7 May 2017, on the Bahamian island of Great Exuma. You can read about the festival at https://en.wikipedia.org/wiki/Fyre_Festival.

QUESTION

1. Read the case carefully and then think about what you would have done to ensure a more successful outcome to the event project by analysing the errors made in project management.

In event projects the 'timed' and efficient implementation of an event is significant. Event projects are founded on various quality criteria for the implementation of the event itself, and the defined implementation dates are almost 'absolute' (Elstad and De Paoli, 2014). A festival or Olympic site has to be fully prepared for the booked dates; it cannot be late without ruining the whole experience. Such events are best thought of as mega-events. A mega-event is defined by Li, Lu, Ma, & Kwak (2018) as an open socioeconomic system characterized by massive budget demands and multiple types of subprojects and their complex interrelationships. Such mega-events require careful project management and governance that is capable of evolving over the life cycle of the project.

Development projects

In order to survive, all organizations, especially commercial enterprises and companies, must develop continuously. Many organizations use projects as a tool for developing their products and processes. These products can encompass both goods and services in a broad sense. Today, many of the products delivered by organizations are a complex combination of both products and services, in a mix in which the service logic is dominant (Lusch & Vargo, 2014). An example might be an organization that sells machines but also offers to rent them out, repairs them and provides training in the correct use of machines. There will be significant variations regarding which projects should be classified as development projects and the degree of uncertainty which characterizes them (Söderlund, 2005). Research projects are examples of projects that often contain a high degree of uncertainty, while improvements in existing products are often characterized by uncertainty.

We have developed, based on Söderlund (2005), an overview of the differences between project types (see Table 2.1).

Table 2.1 Categorization of different project types (inspired by Söderlund, 2005, p. 64)

Type of project	Development	Change	Delivery	Event
Purpose	Develop new technology, new product or service for production to the market, to users or other recipient groups	Change the organization's organization and working methods, for better efficiency	Deliver and implement complex solutions to customers	Conduct a successful event that can lead to further ripple effects

Type of project	Development	Change	Delivery	Event
Basis of device	Product	Process	Contract	Quality criteria
Expertise problematics	Integration of knowledge between different subject areas	Change of competence structure and integration of organizational knowledge	Integration of knowledge between customer and supplier	Provide relevant competence, benefit from acquired post-graduate competence
Management focus	Specifications, technical solutions, integration of technical solutions	Change resistance, anchorage, internal marketing, decision structure	Customer dialogue, interaction, negotiations	Involvement and engagement, manage surroundings
Progress criteria	Profitability, market strategic results	Realized improvement potential, management and employee satisfaction	Profitability, customer satisfaction	Commitment. successful event

A development project involves significant interpretation of market needs and customer expectations. Whether it is a physical product or service being sold on a market or if it is a product that is part of the authorities' required tasks, this will be the case. A new prison, for instance, would be an example, as prison customers, the prisoners, are major stakeholders in the institutions that incarcerate them.

Categorizing projects draws attention to distinct differences between them. They are governed by different principles, contain different challenges and focus their attention on various aspects of planning and implementation of the projects (Söderlund, 2005). Most projects will not fall strictly within the parameters of just one type. A mix of types is far more likely. Several of these types as well what will be seen as the most prominent features will also depend on the different stakeholders' viewpoint. For example, the results to be created in delivery projects will often be either in the form of development or a change. When *Norwegian Posten* (The Royal Mail) introduced a new IT system for a part of its business, it did so by engaging external suppliers. The introduction of a new IT system will usually be categorized as a change project but it is also likely to include elements of new services and thus it has elements of both a change and development project. Event projects often feature as delivery projects, while they frequently include elements of a development project, seeking to make the event visible and expand a client's portfolio of products.

IN PRACTICE

THE RAPID BUILD PRISON PROJECT[2]

The Rapid Build Prison Project involved the primary stakeholders Corrective Services New South Wales (CSNSW), Justice Infrastructure NSW–NSW Department of Justice; Lendlease; Hansen Yuncken and the Communities of Cessnock and Wellington and, more broadly, NSW.

[2]Prepared by Daphne Freeder, UTS Business School, University of Technology Sydney

(Continued)

The deliverables sought and delivered were the rapid design and delivery of a new concept maximum-security prison for the Australian setting.

The prison design, accommodating 400 male inmates, was duplicated in two regional settings and achieved in one quarter of the time usually taken to blueprint and build a conventional prison. The concept model was a response to the NSW government's undertaking in 2016 to embark on a major expansion of infrastructure within the state prison system, to accommodate present and future increases in prisoner numbers. A bed shortage crisis existed and the need to implement urgent stopgap accommodation via the Prison Bed Capacity Program was a major driver.

A particular focus of the design was the provision of facilities that as well as ensuring security and community safety would facilitate the dispensing of programmes, to improve prospects of re-education and socialization, with the end goal of reducing recidivism. A team of researchers from the UTS Business School and the Faculties of Design Architecture and Building, and the Faculty of Engineering at UTS were invited to undertake an independent analysis of the significant variables and practices that distinguished the building of these two prisons. In particular, the task was to identify the critical lessons that could be learnt and applied to future building projects. The UTS team conducted interviews with members of the key stakeholder groups and undertook site visits to both of the rapid build prison locations: the Macquarie Correctional Centre at Wellington and the Hunter Correctional Centre at Cessnock. Strong leadership of the projects was a compelling factor in achieving success. An innovative tender process was applied, creating a high level of trust and transparency amongst the stakeholders. Speedy turnaround times by the client in response to requests for information by the builders was critical. The client's retention of risk for purposes of the build and the application of even more risk sharing between the client and building companies facilitated mutual engagement with problem solving. New benchmarks were set for the speed of delivery for government projects through collective commitment and the dedication of all involved. As a project with the highest-level risk profile in terms of the demand for speed plus quality, the Rapid Build Prisons are an exemplar for innovation in project delivery. The Rapid Build Prison projects began with a sketch drawing in May 2016 transitioning to completion in late 2017.

There were key factors enabling a speedy build. First, the holding of alignment workshops to ensure that there was universal understanding concerning the very clear mandate on the need for speed. Second, building trust with the two appointed builders by providing a clear outline of what was wanted by the client, as well as prompt client responses to requests for information and the provision of helpful information, were critical. The practice was for the builders to specify the time frame within which they required a response, which was met unconditionally. Third, there was a higher density of supervision in the field than usually applies to job sites with similar numbers of personnel.

Additional leadership components included a waterline approach. Staff were empowered to engage only with the project director in relation to issues that had the potential to 'sink the boat', issues that could create 'holes in the boat below the waterline'. Decision-making was participatory. Issues were canvassed in team meetings, with the facts of the matter and the known data pertaining to it aired in decision-making. Scenario planning and 'what if' models of different decision paths were used to explore the political and stakeholder perceptions relating to a decision: would it be harmful? The significance of issues that arose was explored for the broader project context. Whether the decision recommended was consonant with the requirements of speedy completion was a key criterion in choosing what to do. Decisions did not rely on total certainty – the decisions were not made on the basis of 'perfect rationality' but 'bounded rationality'.

QUESTION

1.   What were the chief elements in the value management of this project that made it a success, in your understanding?

Value

VALUE CREATION – THE BASIC PREMISE FOR PROJECTS

Projects are a tool for creating value for clients and other stakeholders. As with any tool that creates value, we should always ask *cui bono* – who benefits? Below we will start by explaining what value creation entails, as well as different forms of value creation. Then we look at who is affected by value creation in projects and the possible consequences of attention to value creation.

WHAT IS VALUE?

Often, we distinguish between instrumental value, moral value and intrinsic value. Money, efficiency and growth are examples of instrumental values, while care and justice are examples of moral values. That something has intrinsic value means that it also has value by virtue of itself, as when we value someone for their intrinsic worth as a person.

> The term **value** attaches to something perceived as exemplifying worth.

Projects aim to produce and deliver value through their implementation. Often when one talks about value creation one refers to returns and profits, as well as efficiency in production. The value concept includes such economic values but can also entail processes and products that are valuable, implying meaningful, engaging or useful. For example, experiences, legitimacy and sustainability can be key values that an organization strives to deliver. Organizations can have both 'hard' and 'soft' values guiding their activities. For instance, a business organization based upon the exploitation of labour power to squeeze out surplus value over and above the wages paid (and other costs) would have very different values from an organization built upon an ethos of care for the person, such as a kindergarten.

Value capture occurs when a reasonable portion of the additional economic and property value generated from new public infrastructure is used to fund these enhancements.

> **Value capture** is vital. If the project owners are unable to capture the value that flows from a project then the value is lost, a concern for many government administrations around the world.

READ THIS!

Read Lee and Liang's article on *The Conversation* about how rail works lift property prices, pointing to value capture's potential to fund city infrastructure – an interesting take on value capture at: https://study.sagepub.com/pm.

Value creation occurs through the processes that organizations implement; for example, sales of products, experiences, administrative procedures or law enforcement.

A **value proposition** is based on an innovation, service or feature intended to make an organization attractive to customers or clients.

A **service dominant logic** sees organizations applying their capabilities and competences to benefit others through the services they provide.

A **business model** can be understood as the story of how an organization creates, delivers and captures value from those opportunities it meets.

Based on the premise that organizations have been established for a specific purpose, it is crucial for them to achieve goals and also achieve **value creation**.

These value processes can be developed through projects. The field of strategy is generally keen to answer questions concerning value processes such as why are some organization units more profitable than others over time? Thus, instrumental value is the element which is measured. Significant attention is also paid to the phenomenon of *value creation* and various dimensions related to value. Within the field of marketing and parts of the field of strategy, the term **value proposition** is popular.

Organizations need to pay more attention to satisfying the needs of the recipients (customers) by creating value that their target audience desires (Levitt, 1960). Doing so is named in the literature as a **service dominant logic**.

An example of such a turning of attention to service is the Norwegian National Railway Company (NSB), stating that its mission is not to run trains but to carry passengers and goods to their destinations. The organization, in achieving success, will thus determine what its customers desire and what their product will do for the customer (Jørgensen & Pedersen, 2018). This is their **business model**.

In short, the concept of value creation denotes how an organization designs a logic for meeting its objectives, whether they be profitability or sparking wonder in young people, whether they sell or rent products, or deliver products paid for by others, such as advertisers on commercial media. For business organizations operating in a market with supply and demand, the value gap is expressed through the difference between costs and revenues. The capture of value will be the product that the customer receives, whether it is a service, product, experience or anything else. Any organization, in itself, cannot necessarily deliver value to a recipient but it can deliver a *value proposition* that the recipient will welcome. The correlation between the value proposition (creating), value deliverance (resources and activities) and value capturing (profit formula) creation can be presented as in Figure 2.3.

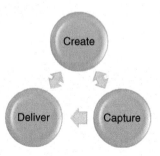

Figure 2.3   Create, deliver and capture value

For an organization, value creation will most likely be linked to achieving goals or through making contributions to reach these goals. An organization with a goal of making profits for its owners will strive to create values that yield profitable returns. However, this goal may not be the only one but is likely to be combined with other objectives, such as customer satisfaction achieved through environmentally friendly activity. These other goals may diminish the efficiency of achieving the immediate objective of economic returns but be necessary to longer-term legitimacy and sustainability. Value creation will thus differ depending on the types of values and objectives that organizations seek to achieve. When an organization tries to pursue several goals at the same time, discussing and evaluating the value it prizes can be helpful. We will look at some examples to illustrate the complexity of value creation in different contexts.

EXTEND YOUR KNOWLEDGE

Read the article by Verwej and Gerrits (2019) 'Evaluating infrastructure project planning and implementation: A study using qualitative comparative analysis', on how many evaluations of infrastructure projects rely on methods that ignore the complexity of the projects, available at: https://study.sagepub.com/pm.

An organization that assists people in a difficult situation, such as the Red Cross, acting in a famine, seeks to create values that can contribute to relief and saving lives. A fundraising campaign is an example of a value-creating element that helps the Red Cross achieve its goals. The Red Cross can organize emergency relief for a particular crisis area as a project. The value the Red Cross creates will be the emergency aid. In cases of emergency relief in a given emergency situation, the Red Cross use a project as a tool to deliver value. It is harder to consider value creation when the purpose of the organization has objectives that are not as material as saving lives or returning value to shareholders but value, however defined, is a *raison d'être* for those organizations hosting projects.

Public organizations always work to balance and safeguard different and contradictory objectives. This makes assessments of value creation demanding. Road construction projects are an example of public projects with contradictory and complex objectives. Authorities planning and implementing a road construction project to create desired values and effects in the longer term may well create considerable loss of value of amenity, access, noise, disturbance, traffic volumes and aesthetics in the short term. The idea of what is considered to be a value and what its effects are will vary among any project's various stakeholders. The development of infrastructure, such as a road, can enable business development in an area, ease the ability to move around for the residents and thus improve their quality of life in the area, and improve road safety – in the long run. At the same time, it can also increase pollution, result in loss of greenery and affect real estate values negatively.

The public sector is characterized by the fact that it has to handle a high degree of goal complexity with many objectives that may conflict with each other (Bozeman, 2007). Assessing the value creation will, therefore, be more difficult. By contrast, an organization that can reduce all calculations to the bottom line of profitability faces far less immediate challenges. It is often difficult to delimit this value creation to one clear owner or client, as the results of most projects influence a number of stakeholders.

Value creation for whom?

Many projects are managed by a client who provides clear guidelines for the types of value creation striven for as well as for whom the value should be created. For example, a sausage factory may want to develop a new type of vegan sausage to increase demand for the factory's goods, which will increase revenue and returns, thus creating higher profits for the shareowners. However, projects often do not have as clear and simple guidelines as the desire to make a sausage without meat.

Although the starting point for a project is a desire for value creation, the project involves other stakeholders who will have an opinion about the purpose of the project. The understanding of value creation then becomes diverse. Therefore, it is not sufficient to relate exclusively to the client or the permanent organization when assessing value creation. There are often many stakeholders who are, and should be, involved, both in materializing the values and judging the extent of actual value created. For example, the following stakeholders could be involved: customers, who will consume the product; employees, who will have a salary and a job that makes them feel valued; the bank, to whom the interest is due; the suppliers of raw materials; as well as the public authorities that charge taxes and fees.

Different organizations strive for different values but still have in common that their reason for establishing projects is to provide value (Shenhar and Dvir, 2007). Therefore, value creation has gained more attention in recent years in the development of project management, in theory as well as in practice. Benefits realization is a widely applied concept of value creation. When talking about extracting effects or realization of effects, it is also value creation that you are talking about.

The Oxford Handbook of Project Management (Morris et al., 2011), states that value creation and profit liberalization is one of 'the richest and most promising, yet less explored, areas within the subject' (Morris, 2011, p. 26). Some analysis of values, such as that which General Electric developed in the 1940s for looking at the relationship between the costs of implementing a project and the stakeholder benefit likely to be realized from it, is widely used. The next *extend your knowledge* feature presents a contemporary application of benefit-cost analysis. The sustainability aspects of the benefit–cost analysis for the deer are worth thinking about.

Value engineering has also attracted much attention.

Managing for value involves preparing conceptual assessments in which emphasis is placed on two questions: (1) Is the project going to be implemented? (2) If the project

> **Value engineering** means to design (in the broadest sense) a solution that unites various descriptions of perceived dividends, often by reducing costs.

is to be implemented, how can it be optimized to add substantial value? Even though value creation has gained more attention in recent years in the development of the project, in practice major projects continue to be launched – including large public investment projects – with very limited analysis of opportunities for value creation as well as limited engagement to identify and truly understand the needs of the stakeholders that will be most affected by the project. This is often due to lack of understanding of which processes should be carried out to achieve value creation, as well as who should assume responsibility for them (Cantarelli, Flybjerg, Molin, & van Wee, 2013).

To increase value creation, the concept of success and failure, and the process that determines these in different contexts requires understanding. We will, therefore, look into different criteria and factors for project success and failure.

WATCH THIS!

Videos on the value and impact of value engineering by Justin Finestone (2011) and Perry Ellis (2015) at: https://study.sagepub.com/pm.

Project success

SUCCESS FACTORS AND CRITERIA

Expectations of value creation are included when we consider what should be done for a project to be labelled a success and in assessing whether the project eventually became successful. The elements of project success have gained extensive attention over many years, especially since the 1970s. Increasingly, research has been dedicated to the elements of project success by what has been labelled 'the Success School' (Turner, Anbari, & Bredillet, 2013). Research and practice are divided into two main categories: **success factors** and **success criteria**.

> The **success factors** of the project are those elements of a project that can be influenced to increase the likelihood of success (i.e. independent variables that contribute to success).

> The **success criteria** of projects are those criteria used to measure success in the sense of the outcome of a project (i.e. the dependent variables).

It is often recommended that a project manager should, as a first priority, design success criteria for the project and then determine what would be the appropriate success factors to deliver according to these criteria (Wateridge, 1995). We will look at the design of different success criteria.

Project management and project product success

In the elaboration of success criteria, a fundamental distinction has emerged differentiating between project management success and project product success (Miller & Lessard, 2000). Project management success is often seen in terms of managing what has been seen to be the 'iron triangle' for projects. The iron triangle is a matter of trade-offs between the constraints of project budget, deadlines and scope, where changes in one constraint will usually necessitate changes in the other constraints if the quality or value of the project is not to suffer. 'Project product success' means that the purpose of the project has been achieved (Baccarini, 1996); that is, that the project deliveries contribute to the desired value creation.

Unfortunately, studies have shown, repeatedly, that projects are more successful in terms of efficient execution than in realizing the aimed-for effects. For example, it has been shown that 75% of large engineering projects have project management success, while only 45% have project product success. Research has also demonstrated a significant correlation between project efficiency and project success (Serrador & Turner, 2013). While project efficiency cannot be the only goal, since it says nothing about value creation, it cannot be omitted.

Contemporary understanding of project success implies achieving success in both project management as well as project product. However, keep in mind that while project management success can be measured at the end of the project, most of the realization of a project product success subsequently takes place after the project has ended (Andersen, 2008). The Sydney Opera House is, once again, a perfect example.

Jennings (2012) noted that political acceleration of the Sydney Opera House project led to scope creep and uncertainty. Pressure from the New South Wales government in 1959 resulted in the project starting ahead of schedule while engineering design was still incomplete. The technical problems that resulted from this have been compared with the project management problems experienced during the Concorde development, the Montreal Olympics, the Millennium Dome, the Scottish Parliament project, the Aquatics Centre for the London 2012 Olympics and the Elbphilarmonie in Hamburg.

Projects conceived within the 'iron triangle' are constrained by specified *time* frames, frames for *cost* and specifications of the *quality and functionality of project deliverables*. Success criteria, and thus success, is often defined as project execution aligned with these time–cost–quality specifications (Cooke-Davies, 2002).

The *time aspect* is central to all projects. For many projects, a defined end date shapes the expectation about when the project should be completed. This end date provides premises for the design of the project process and the deliverables that can be created. Sticking to the end date might mean that at delivery of the finished project a product or service of inferior quality to that desired is delivered because the aimed for quality was not possible to obtain within the time frame. Of course, projects cannot permanently push deadlines but if you want a good project result that delivers desired effects for the client, it may be necessary to adjust deadlines (in the form of postponement) along the way. While there may be many reasons for such adjustments, postponements often coincide with:

- New knowledge throughout the project period
- Unexpected events
- Changes in context

In some projects, however, the deadline or closing date is so crucial that it simply cannot be adjusted. An event project with a specific date, which is usually determined by external stakeholders, cannot be changed. The World Cup in Brazil 2014 and the Rio 2016 Olympics were mega-events. Although at times they were characterized by significant conflicts and extensive delays, the date of the event was immovable. There were too many stakeholders. An art exhibition project can be tiny compared to a World Cup but still you might encounter problems that tempt you to postpone the opening. Nevertheless, there are often so many external guidelines for the exhibition project that postponement is not considered as an alternative.

The *cost aspect* includes the resources available to the project, both the human resources making up the project team and the economic aspects, the amount of money that can be spent on delivering the project according to the budget. After a project budget is developed, the project manager is held accountable for executing the project accordingly. The cost aspect is limited to what affects the actual implementation until the end of the project. It does not include what may incur costs after the project has been terminated, for example related to changes or managing the delivery.

In the short term, projects are always an expense item. Projects usually develop new processes, services or products. Any gains from these rarely materialize until after the project has ended. A newly developed product does not generate revenue until it is put out for sale. A process change designed to implement more efficient production methods will not produce any gains until changes in the process have been taken into use over a period.

The third target dimension is the *quality or functionality aspect of project deliverables*. Quality is related to a specification or explanation of the functionality of the project's deliveries. It is therefore about setting the functionality criteria for the project, which indicates what the project will achieve.

WATCH THIS!

Watch this video by Jason Dodd (2014) on what a project manager does, the difference between process focus and outcome focused project managers, and the need for being outcome focused to succeed with your project at: https://study.sagepub.com/pm.

In a traditional perception of projects, great emphasis is placed on balancing the three dimensions of time–cost–quality, as they, in most cases, are interchangeably interwoven. For example, if the cost frames are being exceeded, maybe the quality can be a bit lower but still good enough in order to materialize the effects aimed for. Another option is to adjust the time frame. Even though it is crucial that managers of projects assume that their projects will be implemented within limits given by deadlines, budgets and quality criteria, this is still far from sufficient in a complex context. These criteria only provide indications of *project management success*. They do not account for the extent to which the project results provide more long-term effects and contributions to value creation, i.e. *project product success*. If considering adjustments of the time–cost–quality dimensions, consider how the considered adjustment will probably affect the value creation one seeks. Such criteria are often formulated in advance of the project, or very early in the project, and the project is, therefore, organized and managed according to them. Often these criteria of value creation are not met.

Project failure

Project failures, especially in megaprojects, are almost the norm. The difference between prediction of usage and actual traffic flows depends on the forecasts of usage. Often, as a result of optimism bias needed to gain approval for projects, these forecasts end up being costly mistakes. Hall (1980) identified that the Bay Area Rapid Transit System carried only 51% of forecast riders. Phillips (2008) noted that usage estimates of the Sydney Cross City Tunnel prior to construction were 90,000 cars per day. After completion, the financing costs could not be met by tolls from the 26,500 cars that used the tunnel daily. Prior to construction the Sydney Lane Cove Tunnel was estimated to achieve between 90,000 and 110,000 cars per day, but only achieved a daily average of 50,000 cars when the toll was introduced to the newly completed tunnel. The construction of the Sydney Airport Link provides a similar example. Ng and Loosemore (2007) identified that six months after the line was opened passenger rates were only 12,000 per day, rather than the 46,000 predicted. Jennings (2012) identified that government funding was required to support the construction of the Millennium Dome after private equity could not be secured and that the public sector was again asked to step in during the London 2012 Olympics to construct the Olympic Village after private developers withdrew. In Canada, real estate taxes were raised to pay the C\$1 billion deficit that resulted from the Montreal Olympics development. The debt was paid off only 30 years later – significantly longer than the six to seven years originally projected.

At the project outset, as Flyvbjerg (2014b) suggests, there are often good organizational reasons for bad organizational projections of costs, benefits and completion, especially in megaprojects. Megaprojects are costly, complex, involve many stakeholders, require skill level and attention in managing these projects (Capka, 2004), requiring colossal resources, budgets and management time (Sturup, 2009). The characteristics of megaprojects are bigger size, complexity, complex procurement systems, high controversy, time, scope creep, urban setting, human and environmental impacts, risks and uncertainty (Capka, 2004). These projects also have long construction schedules, huge lifespans, extreme complexity and significant social impacts (Sun & Zhang, 2011). Pitsis, Clegg, Freeder, Sankaran, and Burdon (2018) suggest the distinguishing features of megaprojects are reach, duration, risks and uncertainties, widely disparate actors, arenas of controversy and legal and regulatory issues. All these characteristics can be summarized through 6 Cs – Colossal, Captivating, Costly, Controversial, Complex and laden with Control issues (Frick, 2008). A reason for these characteristics in megaprojects is because they aim not only at practical objectives such as the delivery of the infrastructure asset and services but also involve lofty ideas, high ambitions and economic development targets (Miller, Lessard, & Sakhrani, 2017).

The benefits of megaprojects tend to be probabilistically underestimated while the benefits and completion tend to be overestimated in terms of what they deliver and how quickly they will deliver. These projections, of course, are a kind of power: they are productive in gaining commitments, harnessing resources, persuading key actors and constituencies that projects are viable. An essential element of positive power – which the cynical might call 'spin' – is often necessary to make projects happen.

Flyvbjerg (2014b) suggests four 'sublimes' of technology, politics, economics and aesthetics, to which one might add community. The technology sublime is the technical challenge that engineers and designers find in a project. Technical challenges (Frick, 2008) pose puzzles whose solution is a source of excitement and satisfaction.

Politicians find projects a source of sublimity because they are opportunities to make speeches, cut ribbons and get political mileage. What they desire is their name and picture in the media and projects enable them to achieve media coverage (Flyvbjerg, 2014b). The economic sublime is the profit motive that drive the organizations that will deliver the project and provides governments and communities with jobs and economic growth. The aesthetic sublime is the appreciation of a beautiful outcome to a project, usually a building such as the Oslo Opera or the Sydney Opera House, while the community sublime is the pride that a community takes in iconic projects, such as an Olympic Games, a World Cup or a metro.

WHAT WOULD YOU DO?

As a project management consultant, you have been asked to provide a justification for a major new piece of infrastructure, a tunnel, by the project sponsor. The project sponsor is well aware of the many problems faced by megaprojects in the past, having read some of the literature. Your task is to try and find a project that came in on time and budget and yielded the value that was projected for it.

QUESTION

1.   Using the web, conduct a search and find a case that fits the brief. Analyse what were its key characteristics.

Multi-dimensional success criteria

A project cannot be detached from the other tasks that the organizations delivering it engage in. It must be linked to their objectives, strategic orientation and formulation. Therefore, project success depends on more dimensions than those that can be linked to time, cost and quality. The development of the Balanced Scorecard (Kaplan and Norton, 1996) is based on a similar argument. Evaluating the effectiveness of an organization, they say, it seems useful to consider its strategy and vision in four dimensions. These four dimensions constitute critical success factors that results must continuously be measured against. If the results you measure differ from those you want, measures can be taken to correct the course. The four dimensions (see Figure 2.4) are:

- Financial perspective
- Customer perspective

- Internal process perspective
- Learning and growth perspective

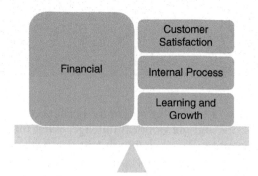

Figure 2.4 Balanced scorecard

We will not go into the ongoing discussion about the balanced scorecard's suitability for measuring performance and achieving objectives (see, e.g., Nielsen, Lund, & Thomsen, 2017). The main point is that evaluation of value cannot be limited solely to economic aspects, although financial goals are often paramount. Assessment must also include things such as customer satisfaction, work processes, learning and development. Customer satisfaction is necessary if any organization is to survive over time. Continuous improvement of production methods, related support services and organizing processes are crucial to continue delivery of value across the board. Constant adjustments to frameworks and context from project-based learning is very valuable. Organizations delivering projects have multiple opportunities to learn what has been valuable from their experience. Organizations that do not learn or innovate as a result of the projects in which they are engaged are unlikely to achieve their goals in the short term, deliver value across the board and, in the long term, even survive. The concept of balanced scorecard underlines the importance and necessity of including multiple aspects when assessing the potential of a project.

As explicated above, the key reason for an organization to establish a project is its potential for value creation to which success criteria should be closely linked. Factors to consider include the following:

1. The potential of the project as a tool for value creation for the organization in question. If there is very limited or no such potential, why should one complete the project?
2. Evaluation of success should not be solely from a short-term time perspective. The final result of the project can rarely be assessed appropriately before the project delivery has been implemented for some time. It is, therefore, necessary to adopt a long-term perspective in the assessment of projects.
3. The project involves more stakeholders than just the project principal and their considerations of and experiences with project deliverables should be reflected in the formulation of what constitutes value and success criteria.

In the development of a new office building, there will be different perspectives on the project's success. The building and preparation of the physical building will be assessed to the extent that they accord with quality requirements as well as time and cost frameworks, all of which will be significant success factors for project management success. Functionality and application will be more related to project product success.

Both during the construction of the building itself and after it is completed and delivered into use, there will be different perceptions of the project's success. The architects will have different opinions than the auditors, stressing architectural design versus financial frameworks. The top managers of the organization that use the building will have other interests than many of the employees employed in it; they will stress cost-effective use of space rather than providing ample space for personal offices. That is one reason why so many recent office buildings are premised on 'hot-desking' and 'open plan' where no one has a dedicated office or even a desk. Users and employees will be more interested in how they can work and socialize in the building, despite how mobile they have to be. Regulatory authorities will demand that the legal requirements of the building code, expectations framed by technical standards, have been met by contractors and subcontractors. Their brief will be for the achievement of environmental building standards versus improvised, albeit practical, solutions.

Nuanced perspectives on project success and a broader set of criteria have been contributed to the literature by Davis (2014), Andersen, Birchal, Jensen, and Money (2006), Morris and Hough (1987) and Pinto and Slevin (1988). Based on earlier work, Shenhar and Dvir (2007) present a model, now widespread in its adoption, with five main criteria for project success:

1. Project efficiency (implementation according to the framework set for time, cost and quality)
2. Impact on the user (end user's experience of delivery, i.e. 'customer satisfaction')
3. Impact on team members (experience and learning)
4. Profitability and direct value creation, business result, ROI, growth
5. Preparation for the future through possible long-term gains from the project

These dimensions describe the complexity in and around the project in a more inclusive way than the so-called 'iron triangle', especially because they capture both short-term and longer-term aspects of success. Below, we will discuss and elaborate these dimensions to tease out nuances and key aspects of value creation.

IN PRACTICE

NORTHERN BEACHES HOSPITAL

We will refer to a well-publicized case of a recently completed large hospital project. The construction costs of a large general hospital are roughly equivalent to the annual running costs of such a hospital. These costs can collide when a hospital is newly opened as project completion costs and operating costs have to be met out of the same budget. The New South Wales government paid a private consortium that includes Healthscope, Leighton Holdings

(Continued)

and Theiss $2.14 billion over 20 years to run a newly commissioned Northern Beaches Hospital, which cost $600 million to build.

Within days of the hospital's opening in November 2018, a senior anaesthetist resigned from Sydney's new Northern Beaches Hospital. In email exchanges that made their way into the public sphere[3] it was asserted that the facility was failing completely in its primary objective – that of patient safety. Shortages of staff, equipment and training were alleged. As the ABC reported the story:

> When the doctor at the centre of the email exchange resigned on November 23, he said there were 'fundamental systemic failings in the way the hospital has been set up and is currently running'. 'Let me be clear these are NOT "teething problems,"' he wrote. 'The hospital currently fails completely in its primary objective of patient safety,' the anaesthetist said in the email to the head of his department, adding that a recent emergency caesarean was a nightmare for clinicians.
>
> 'There was inadequate supply of equipment, insufficiently trained staff, poor protocols for simple requests such as a blood transfusion, and a complete lack of a cohesive plan for [a] worst-case scenario. This patient survived somewhat against the odds. This is clearly unacceptable.'

At issues was a caesarean section for which the blood bank despatched only two units of blood when the anaesthetist required six. Wider issues were subsequently raised with respect to a lack of training and equipment. Within three days of the opening of the hospital its chief executive resigned. It is not surprising that the word most often associated with the project is 'chaos'.[4]

The New South Wales Nurses and Midwives' Association[5] made the following statement three months after the hospital had become operational:

> Within a fortnight of receiving its first patients it was obvious the hospital was a 'shambles' with patients and staff reporting 'chronically understaffed' units, as the *Sydney Morning Herald* put it.
>
> The hospital repeatedly ran out of essentials such as insulin, adrenaline, antibiotics, drugs for heart failure and hypertension, dialysis fluids and central intravenous nutrition. Units also ran out of syringes, IV lines, medical swabs, saline bags, needles, wash cloths and alcohol rub and maternity pads.
>
> 'Nurses have filled their own car boots and back seats with basic medical equipment from the now-closed Manly Hospital as well as Mona Vale to replenish the new hospital's stockrooms,' the *Herald* reported.
>
> There was a bed shortage due to lack of staff and ED patients waited up to 17 hours for treatment.

---

[3] If you search on YouTube there are a great many videos exploring what went wrong at the Northern Beaches Hospital.

[4] See: www.smh.com.au/national/nsw/chaotic-what-northern-beaches-hospital-doctors-patients-are-saying-20181117-p50gny.html (accessed 14 March 2019).

[5] See: www.smh.com.au/national/nsw/chaotic-what-northern-beaches-hospital-doctors-patients-are-saying-20181117-p50gny.html (accessed 14 March 2019).

The hospital, as a building project, was considered a success: it was a landmark project delivered on time and on budget[6] as a public private partnership. It clearly delivered value in this respect.

QUESTIONS

Using the resources drawn on above and others that you can research using Google, answer the following questions:

1. In what ways has the Northern Beaches Hospital delivered or failed to deliver value to which stakeholders?

2. How might value have been better assured in terms of project product success?

---

[6]See: http://phnews.org.au/northern-beaches-hospital-officially-opened/ (accessed 14 March 2019).

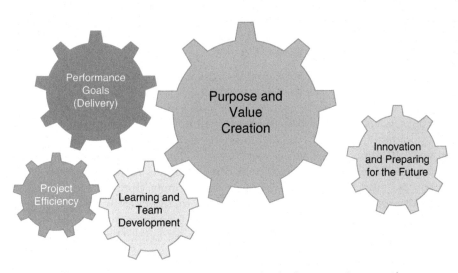

Figure 2.5   Multi-dimensional project success criteria from a value creation perspective

PROJECT EFFICIENCY

Time limits and cost frames in terms of budgets are the key elements related to the project efficiency dimension. The two elements of the project's iron triangle – time and cost – are often taken for granted as criteria for project success (Kloppenborg, Manolis, & Tesch, 2009). They are among the easiest criteria to measure and evaluate, and they are usually subject to attention if they are not fulfilled. With ever faster changes, shorter time horizons and greater demands on precision, these elements become more and more critical (Serrador & Turner, 2013). Efficiency also refers to the efficient use of project methodologies, as well as the organization and management of the project to provide adequate processes for organizing, coordinating and controlling the project.

PERFORMANCE (DELIVERY)

The performance goals describe what the project will create: the deliverables. The performance target corresponds to the quality of the project's iron triangle. When building a bridge, the goal is to complete the bridge within the quality standards set. Traditional project literature and practice has mostly emphasized project execution tools that enable goal achievement, defining traditional project management as a goal-oriented and rather introverted approach.

LEARNING AND TEAM DEVELOPMENT

As organizations increasingly carry out much of their work through projects it becomes crucial to learn from project work, both to improve solutions and to increase capabilities for flexibility under emerging conditions (Brady & Davies, 2004). For example, participants in an IT project not only learn about IT professionals but will also learn about project processes and teamwork. Knowledge and development of working methods and processes in teamwork involves learning for both the organization and the individual employee. This includes learning about project management functions (Müller & Turner, 2007). Projects are a central arena for learning at both individual and team level through the project work as well as for retention and dissemination to the team working on the next project. (We discuss this topic in detail in Chapter 10.)

PURPOSE AND VALUE CREATION

Project delivery should satisfy stakeholder expectations. These are likely to be several and variable. One might think that the construction of a beautiful Olympic stadium is a success but if the stadium is not used much after the Olympics are over the effect of the project is very limited because there will have been little value added. Thus, the project cannot be considered a success – even if the stadium has been produced in line with the time–cost–quality specifications. The value creation of the project is linked to the effects of the actual performance targets to which an assessment of project success must be particularly linked. Increasingly, the concept of social value is being discussed, particularly in infrastructure projects because of innovative social procurement legislation around the world and an increasing acceptance of the need to provide social value, rather than simply economic value (Barraket & Loosemore, 2018; Loosemore, 2016; Raidén, Loosemore, King, & Gorse, 2018). Social value has been defined by Social Enterprise UK (2012) as the collective benefit to a community when a public body chooses to award a contract. The pursuit of social value means treating external non-contractual stakeholders, such as the community, as an asset rather than a risk to be managed. A social value-driven approach sees creating and managing social value as an integral part of decision-making, organization and practice. It is very much in alignment with the United Nations' Global Sustainable Development Goals, for which the pursuit of social value provides a vehicle and a goal for organizations and projects to make long-term positive contributions, through the benefits bestowed, the procurement and employment practices deployed, often adding value to disadvantaged categories of persons.

INNOVATION AND PREPARING FOR THE FUTURE

Many projects can provide long-term gains in terms of innovation and learning, which make the organization/s involved better able to face future challenges. Some projects will be pilot projects, initiated to explore new methods, markets or technologies

(Davies & Frederiksen, 2010). The primary purpose of the project is to create learning experiences through exploration (March, 1991). Such projects can often entail significant costs during the project period but are implemented with a clear expectation that they will eventually be sustainable, meanwhile preparing organizational processes that facilitate the creation of new opportunities (Shenhar & Dvir, 2007, p. 28). Attempts of value creation can involve shaping and (re-)design of business models (Osterwalder & Pigneur, 2010).

Shenhar and Dvir (2007, p. 29) propose that creating new markets for a product, a new production line, or the development of new technology, entails asking questions such as:

- Did the project test out ideas that could result in new markets, innovations and products?
- Did the project contribute to developing new technology and new core competence?
- Are you prepared to initiate change and create a new future and rapid changes within your domain?

As Figure 2.5 illustrates, the five dimensions hang together and relate to each other to a greater or lesser extent. The size of the gears also indicates the relative significance, without being in any way intended to represent exact sizes.

The timing of success assessment

When assessing to what extent the different success criteria have been achieved, be aware of temporality. As Figure 2.6 shows, some criteria may be assessed immediately while others can only be assessed after the project deliverables have been implemented for some time, which implies special consideration when developing success criteria and assessing success.

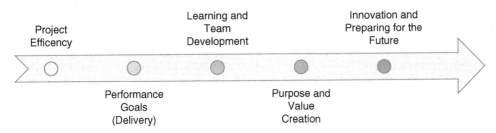

Figure 2.6   Aspect of time for the dimension related to a project's success criteria

Project effectiveness and performance goals can be measured at the end of project execution. Team learning and team development could be measured during project execution (as well as after). The same goes for learning across projects, but often this must be considered in a longer perspective – to see how the learning products from one project might impact projects in parallel and projects of the future (Schindler & Eppler, 2003). While some effects might materialize during project execution, in more agile projects with multiple deliverables, fulfilment of purpose and value creation must usually be assessed sometime after project execution. For some types of projects, it is common to practise post-evaluation, for example, two years after the project ended. Very often, the assessment of innovation and dynamic capability for handling future events have an even longer time horizon. Also, critical success factors vary across project phases (Pinto & Prescott, 1988).

Agile execution models that include more flexibility in terms of shifting the sequence of project deliveries than more classical stage gate models are a recent fashion in project management, in response to dynamic project environments. In terms of realizing benefits, they can give priority to those deliverables that have the highest potential for producing benefits or which can produce benefits most rapidly.

Sometimes, however, the dynamism of environments is one of such high velocity that events can overrun projects prepared to deal with them. At the time that asylum seekers started arriving in large volumes from Africa and the Middle East to central and northern Europe in 2016, the Norwegian government started a large digitalization project in which one of the smaller deliverables was the more efficient provision of the national security number of residents in Norway. The project made this a priority deliverable because it seemed evident that it would have rapid benefit realization due to the influx of people requiring various public services. By the time delivery was completed, most immigrants no longer reached Norway due to restrictions implemented in southern Europe. The tracking and registering system, the project deliverable, was now no longer needed to the same extent and its benefit, initially perceived as high, was now much lower.

Success depends on the characteristics of the project

The ability to meet various success criteria is obviously associated with various degrees of uncertainty. In this book we elaborate on multiple project processes: how and why can they best be understood and implemented in different types of projects? When it comes to success criteria, reflect on what success criteria and success factors needed considering in what order of significance for the different types of project and how their achievement can be enabled. For example, having a detailed plan for implementation and executing the project accordingly is perceived as a success factor in many projects. However, as Chapter 4 demonstrates, planning as a success factor is contingent on the form and amount of uncertainty inherent in a project and the need for involving users, amongst other factors.

In the past, due in large part to the heavy rationalist bias of most project management, detailed front-end planning was perceived as a true success factor for nearly all projects. As several types of assignments are solved through project work, it has been acknowledged that in some projects, for example in many development projects, it is not advisable to presume detailed front-end planning of most activities to be undertaken during project execution. The reason for this is the extensive uncertainty about what the project should deliver (establishment and choice of concept) and how it should be delivered. Flexibility is often regarded as necessary in the implementation of development projects (see, for example, Eisenhardt and Tabrizi, 1995; Takeuchi & Nonaka, 1986; Tatikonda & Rosenthal, 2000. Agile project strategies might be a way to handle the necessity of flexibility. We will investigate this further in Chapters 4 and 5.

Whether detailed front-end planning is a success factor or not depends on the nature of the project and its context and success factors should be evaluated in light of the project's characteristics. Choose factors that match the context in which the project is embedded (Engwall, 2003). At the same time, several studies of success factors across project types have pointed to some of the same factors (see, for example, Miller & Lessard 2000):

1. through work with concept assessments and user needs interpretation
2. active and skilled project owners
3. well-developed understanding of uncertainty
4. skilled project manager with considerable autonomy

Assessment and application of success criteria

The development of success criteria should be prescribed before the project is launched if they are to give desired direction to the project. In the next chapter, we will look at the process of establishing projects, including formulating project goals and outcomes in terms of explicating and operationalizing the constitutes success criteria so they can help in forming project execution that enables future value creation. Elaborating the different ways in which key stakeholders understand what constitutes success criteria will be taken into account (Jugdev & Müller, 2005). How might project managers negotiate and develop shared understandings of success criteria, the complexity inherent in striving towards their fulfilment and the contradictions encountered in the process? The elaboration process can be quite variable in its intensity and length. For internal projects, especially small ones, one may readily reach agreement on success criteria but these still require elaboration. Too often, we take for granted that all parties involved in the project share the same sensemaking (Weick, 1995). Additionally, elaboration contributes to understanding of and commitment to the project. It helps organizational actors to make *sense of the project* (Hernes, Simpson, & Söderlund, 2013). Implementation of project deliveries often involves significant changes for the organizations and other stakeholders involved, which, through reflecting and discussing success criteria, can create support and anchoring for the project.

Common sensemaking is difficult to achieve and can be deeply problematic. First, let us look at the difficulties. We should not take for granted that everyone involved understands the success criteria in the same way or even that they share success criteria. Different stakeholder interests need to be understood. Then you can establish plans and strategies for the interaction with various key stakeholders, as well as the distribution of responsibility and authority among the involved parties, which enables achieving the success criteria. Second, too much agreed upon sensemaking can be problematic because it can stifle innovation. If everyone agrees about how they are doing what they are doing, then there is likely to be little conflict or debate. Another way of saying this is to note that too much common sensemaking means too little democracy, debate and division. Democracy is not only the sign of a healthy body politic but also a key source of innovation. Debate and disagreement about approaches and ideas is the source of alternative ways of doing things; it is from the contested sensemaking characterizing debate that innovations flow.

In the next chapter, we will look at how success criteria and the idea of value creation should be the basis for what ideas for potential projects become projects and the characteristics of the process from idea to project.

READ THIS!

The Conversation is a great source of information. In a 2018 article, Darryl Carlton analyses why so many IT projects fail. The article is called 'Lack of technical knowledge in leadership is a key reason why so many IT projects fail' at: https://study.sagepub.com/pm.

Why do projects fail?

Nonetheless, despite the support that major projects can receive from their sublime sponsorship, such projects often fail dramatically. Flyvbjerg, Bruzelius, and Rothengatter (2003) studied 258 megaprojects in 20 countries to conclude that 90% of them fail to deliver on their planned objectives, time, cost or promises to stakeholders. Other indicators of failure in these projects are negative environmental effects such as noise, pollution, landscape erosion, etc. (Priemus, Flyvbjerg, & van Wee, 2008). These projects have social impacts as well, as large numbers of people are inconvenienced and sometimes displaced to achieve their accomplishment. Many projects enter into a 'debt trap' (Flyvbjerg, 2014b) where it is impossible for the income generated from a project to cover costs, thereby making the project non-viable, which can result from a combination of delays, escalating costs and increasing interest payments. The deliverables of these megaprojects are expected to provide value for the society for decades or more. Thus, even though they may have a high failure rate in the short term, in the longer term their value may be inestimable. In order to take a more holistic approach to success, we need multi-dimensional criteria to govern projects, with different conceptions of value.

Sublime sponsorship leads to optimism biases (Flyvbjerg, 2008), often leading to strategic escalation of commitment with attendant costs and time implications. Other factors on which project failure might be predicated include strategic misrepresentation of the project's potential handicaps on the part of initial sponsors (Wachs, 1989) in order to increase the chances of the project being started. One implication of this is that the riskiest projects may attract the strongest support. Failure to plan sufficiently in advance of the project (Morris, 1994) can also lead to failure by not matching the flexibility of the contract to the envisaged level of uncertainty in project variables (Stinchcombe & Heimer, 1985). Finally, the pluralism of interests vested in a project can also be a source of conflicting, contradictory and occasionally paradoxical expectations (Gil, 2015). Such pluralism not only comes from diverse stakeholders but from the project as a vehicle for occupational mobility and careers. The key project personnel that begin a project are not necessarily going to be with the project for its complete duration. Strategic changes in personnel can be made as the project politics unfold; as goals change so may personnel.

One project that suffered a significant change of personnel during its completion was the Sydney Opera House, widely regarded as a spectacular failure at the time it was being built. The Sydney Opera House was considered a failing project due to escalation of costs and completion, such that its architect, Jørn Utzon, was dismissed by the state government of New South Wales, the client organization, before its completion. The building was ten years late, and over 1357% over budget – yet it is probably the most iconic and successful building of the twentieth century.

Picture 2.2   The Sydney Opera House

WHAT WOULD YOU DO?

You are the project manager for a major IT project in an organization, working for an external consulting company, to implement a new IT project. You are having trouble maintaining top management team support from within the client organization. You suspect that some of the reasons are those alluded to by Carlton (2018) in the article from *The Conversation* referred to on page 60. However, you have recently read an article by Sayyadi (2019), 'How effective leadership of knowledge management impacts organizational performance available at: https://study.sagepub.com/pm', which you feel you also need to take into account.

QUESTION

1. Using your knowledge of the article, which you can download at online resources at https://study.sagepub.com/pm, work out a project that you can present to the top management team to ensure the success of your project.

Success and value creation can be experienced differently and judged in different ways (Crawford, Morris, Thomas, & Winter, 2006; Jugdev & Müller, 2005) by different stakeholders and at different times (Shenhar & Dvir, 1996), affecting how success criteria are established and negotiated. Designing and evaluating success criteria should be considered more broadly than just creating value for a client. Unforeseen innovations may be generated, individual project participant and organizational learning acquired, or social capital created as a result of the project.

In recent years, there has been a strong belief that projects differ widely within the project management field of study (Shenhar & Dvir, 1996) and that their success can be assessed in different ways, implying different processes, leadership styles and competencies are required to carry out these various projects (Turner & Müller, 2005). Often, success is assessed differently depending on *when* one is measuring it, *how* it is measured and *whom* one is asking.

Summary

Whatever the type of project, project managers usually want to complete them successfully. Hence, we have discussed the key and complex issue of value. After reading this chapter you should appreciate that:

- Value is concerned with usefulness, for whom value is achieved, using what methods, with what success or failure.
- Value may be expressed in monetary terms and for the majority of private sector projects profit probably will be preeminent but there are broader conceptions of value than just the surplus value gained over and above total costs and expenditures.
- Value may be expressed socially, in terms of civic benefits, as social value; ecologically, in terms of an improved natural environment; aesthetically, in terms of the appreciation of beauty in all its guises, and so on – value will ultimately reside in the appreciation of the beholder.
- Projects differ in terms of task, size, complexity and many other features. Each project must be approached in terms of its characteristics. We cannot treat projects as if they are all the same. We distinguished between four types of project: those dealing with change, delivery, events and development.
- Projects are tools for value creation and creating value entails knowing about different concepts of value, value positioning and value engineering.
- Successful value creation implies project product success and knowing about the important aspects of enabling project success.
- Determining success is equally as complex as trying to deliver value, largely because neither value nor success can be attributed to a singular variable, a calculable bottom line. The bottom line is, of course, significant but it is not the only calculus.
- In assessing the success of a project, it is important to take four perspectives: financial perspective, customer perspective, internal process perspective and the learning and growth perspective.
- There are five dimensions for evaluating success: project efficiency, project performance, learning and team development, purpose and value creation, and, lastly, innovation and preparing for the future.

Exercises

1. We have presented a commonly used categorization of projects including six categories: technical building and construction projects; system development projects; product development projects; event projects; research and development projects; organization development projects. Can you distinguish some of the similarities and differences among them?

2. Account for the difference between project product success and project management success.

3. Are project product success and project management success equally important to project work? When can each be respectively measured?

4. What is the key point about multi-dimensional success criteria – can you account for these criteria?

5. Account for the terms: value creation, social value, value proposition and service dominant logic.

6. What is value engineering?

7. What can you say about the relationship between project success and the characteristics of the project?

8. Can you mention some important reasons for project failures?

CASE STUDY

PROJECT CONCEPTUALIZATION FOR BURGER KING

More sustainable products and processes are emerging as key values for organizations competing for customers throughout the world. One such company is Umoe Restaurant Group (URG), which has the master franchise responsibility for the Burger King brand in Scandinavia.

URG is a part of Umoe and is a private-owned international company formed in 1984 in Norway. Its slogan is 'building sustainable value', and the main owner, Jens Ulltveit-Moe, is genuinely concerned about the environment on the planet. The company aims to be more sustainable and states: 'Our health and sustainability strategy is structured based on the UN Sustainable Development Goals (SDGs) and the principles of UN Global Compact'. Therefore, they aim to contribute to the UN's Sustainable Developments Goals (SDGs). This includes the subsidiary company Umoe Restaurant Group (URG) as well. URG are currently undergoing several innovation projects for redesigning their business models for a more sustainable future.

First, URG has entered into a partnership with the EAT Foundation. It is a science-based global platform for food system transformation, which recommends a diet that includes more plant-based foods and fewer animal source foods a healthy, sustainable and good for both people and planet. Second, URG executives are increasingly aware of the regulatory and reputational risks regarding single-use plastics. Society at large is also concerned about waste in general and food waste in particular, and Burger King are implementing measures to address this. On a different note, the pressure to innovate and digitalize for efficiency has led to the implementation of self-service machines in the restaurants. In addition, there is increasing uncertainty about changes in consumer preferences – food trends on display on Instagram and in other channels clearly reveal a shift in young consumers' food tastes. For this reason, Burger King has introduced new products, including vegetarian options. However, which direction the company should take – and how fast they should change – is still uncertain.

URG needs to have a long-term health and sustainability strategy that can create long-term value that is positive for people, the environment and the companies UMOE owns and operates. The executives state that this is especially the case for Burger King's business model,

(Continued)

and that they need everyone's help to integrate the UN's Sustainable Development Goals (SDGs). The most relevant SDGs are number 3, *Good health and well-being*, number 12, *Responsible consumption and production*, and number 13, *Climate action* (see Figure 2.7).

Figure 2.7   UN Sustainable Development Goals

Source: www.un.org/sustainabledevelopment/news/communications-material/

Burger King is a typical fast-food restaurant chain, where people drop in to eat a quick and cheap meal. Price, taste, effective service, etc. would be among elements for customers to choose Burger King as a place to buy food. Nevertheless, even among customers at such restaurants, environmental concerns play an increasing significance in behaviour and choice. However, before launching sustainability projects, URG wanted a more strategic consideration of such projects.

URG considered starting another project for their Burger King restaurants, related to the UN's SDG of 'Responsible consumption and production', and more specifically on the topic of food waste at the Burger King restaurants. As part of the initial start of the project on food waste at the Burger King restaurants in the Nordic countries, they wished to gain more knowledge on topics related to consumer behaviour and preferences. URG is fully aware of being a part of a larger company (Umoe) and a large international chain (Burger King), and that they have to take into account expectation, direction and guidelines from these.

Experience from previous projects on more sustainable products and processes have mostly been successful, innovation projects being an instrument often used for changing the organization's products and processes. The executive team and the board have an upcoming seminar for discussing and developing their strategy towards projects for a more sustainable development at URG. They are eager to learn more on how to obtain more value creation for their projects. To gain a more systematic insight into preparing and conceptualizing a project for creating value, they would like an 'outsider view'.

Applying insights from this description, including additional links, come up with some considerations and arguments by answering the questions below.

QUESTIONS

1. If they were deciding to start a project on food waste at Burger King restaurants, which values would be essential to include in the strategic considerations for the project? Furthermore, how might they contradict each other and how would you suggest URG should handle this in such a project?

2. What would be potential key factors for project success and how would you categorize the various project success dimensions (multi-dimensional success criteria) for such a project?

3. Essential stakeholders outside the organization would be customers in various segments – suppliers, competitors, government, Burger King international, to name a few. How does this affect the conceptualization of the project?

4. In general, what could be limitations and essential elements of uncertainty for projects like these?

Additional resources

Useful resources for a value-based approach to project management would include Raiden et al. (2018) and Loosemore and Higgon (2015). Each of these shows how the trajectory of a project, especially through its employment practices, can add value far and wide socially. The emphasis is on construction projects. More broadly, looking at how narrative techniques can create value, you could consult Green and Sergeeva (2019). Value in agile projects is addressed by Daniel and Pasquire (2019).

Chapter Roadmap

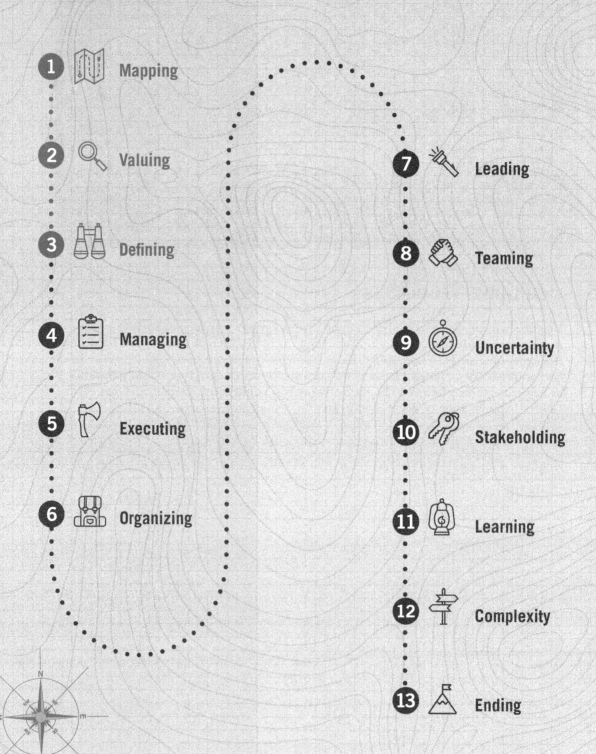

1. Mapping
2. Valuing
3. Defining
4. Managing
5. Executing
6. Organizing
7. Leading
8. Teaming
9. Uncertainty
10. Stakeholding
11. Learning
12. Complexity
13. Ending

3

Defining Projects

Learning objectives

After reading this chapter, you should understand:

1 The reasons for establishing projects

2 How to assess the suitability of projects by looking at the quality of the project idea, concept development and objectives

3 The complexity of project goals and how they affect possible project success

4 The importance of project outcomes and project goals and the relationship between them

5 The key elements of decision-making processes and potential decision-making traps

Before you get started

A good decision is based on knowledge and not on numbers.

– Plato, 1973

Introduction

A great many projects that are established should not have been started at all or, at least, not in the form in which they were planned and initiated. In this chapter, we will look at the main issues to clarify before starting a project.

That there are many different needs promulgated for projects and suggestions as to the change and renewal that such projects will help to create, increases the desire to establish projects to meet these needs. Needs, however, are always related to interests. Different stakeholders will propose different needs or, once they have been proposed, interpret these needs in different ways. To execute projects efficiently and enable future value creation entails analysis of the ways in which these needs are being constituted in order to clarify the concept of the proposed project.

> The project **concept statement** clarifies an idea or design in words, often as part of a business plan or investment proposal.

The **concept statement** may form the basis for establishing performance goals associated with implementation and impact targets, outcomes and mission critical features – the future desired effects the project will provide – that are associated with value creation. Such goal-oriented management is a vital tool for increasing success in most projects.

No matter how good you are at managing-by-objectives or goal-directed management, it can be difficult to succeed with the project and future value creation under certain circumstances. What are these circumstances likely to be? If the idea underlying the project is not well thought through; if key stakeholder commitments have not been enrolled in support of the project; if all the resources necessary to deliver the project have not been secured; or if the intra-organizational politics of the organizations associated with the project have not been processed and resolved in the form of a truce premised on agreed upon commitments. It is therefore essential to understand the decision-making processes in the project context and how a project might move in a desirable way from conception, through inception, to execution (see Figure 3.1).

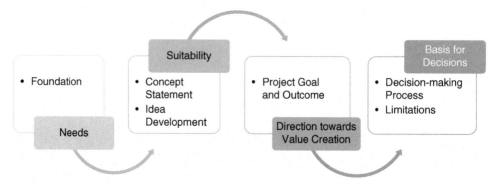

Figure 3.1   Foundation for project start-up by clarifying needs, suitability, goals and purposes, and basis for decisions

When an organization is considering starting a project it should evaluate the need for that project, the possible future relevance of potential project deliveries, as well as the project purpose. Assessments of a possible project start-up should also include details about limitations and feasibility. A list of items and questions (shown in Figure 3.2) should, therefore, be clarified.

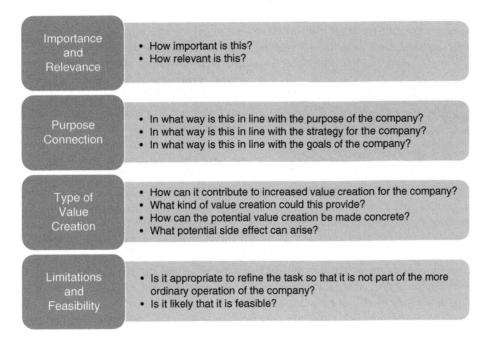

Figure 3.2   List of elements for clarifying the project's initial position

Recall the definition that preceded the previous chapter: a project means to cause to move forward or outward through collaboratively designed enterprise and organization. To move from a position or state of affairs already established to some other position deemed preferable presumes that projects arise from a necessity for change. Different needs and desires may be the basis for creating a project.

These needs and desires may have their origin in an organization's planned, long-term strategy or be more opportunistic as a result of some challenges or chances perceived in its environment. Chances and challenges can vary enormously and they may include opportunities for product development or innovation and/or change and improvement of organizing processes. In many cases, projects include a *significant aspect of innovation* (Davies, Brady, Prencipe, & Hobday, 2011). The different origins for new projects can roughly be divided into the following categories:

- The organization's strategy
- A need perceived and legitimated within the organization in question
- Idea work in the organization
- Assignments or tenders/bids

The categories may overlap and sometimes it is difficult to determine the source that triggers a project. Developing an understanding of what originated the project can indicate likely stakeholders and uncertainties associated with the project. We will look into the different scenarios.

Projects originating from an organization's strategy

Many projects stem from an organization's strategy, for the implementation of which a project is designed as a tool. When organizations design strategies, typically they elaborate purpose, values and different objectives. Although the link between projects and **strategy** is not always clear and pronounced, most projects launched are part of or based on an organizational strategy. It is particularly difficult to discover this link when the organization has multiple simultaneous goals that do not directly link to each other.

> **Strategy** concerns planning, positioning, patterning, partnering and projecting to attempt to create a desired and beneficial position for the organization in changing environments.

Organization involves *planning* as a basis for future development. In turn, future development must entail that those organizing have a view as to the desired future *positioning* of the organization. For instance, a strategy might be to gain dominance, defined as being number one or two, in all those markets for goods and services in which the organization competes. Such positioning might mean divesting aspects of the overall organization that are failing to meet these targets. Perhaps their functions will be outsourced or sold to another party. The result of this will be a different *patterning* of activity by the organization. Organizations such as IBM have transitioned in this way, by selling their computing function, based around PCs, shifting from being hardware manufacturers of computers to providers of consulting services based on offering business solutions. On other occasions, organizations may strive to achieve strategies by *partnering* with other organizations. Apple learnt about miniaturization by partnering with Sony in its early days of development. Many infrastructure projects are only deliverable because lead organizations, often in the public sector, enter into partnering with private sector providers to deliver project outcomes that the public sector organization could not deliver alone. *Projecting* is thus both a striving for future direction and the accomplishment of strategies designed to hasten the journey.

Strategies can be initiated from many factors as part of the planned strategic development of an organization. We illustrate this in Figure 3.3.

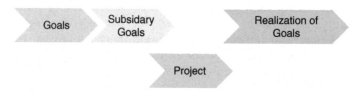

Figure 3.3 Projects as a part of a company's strategy

If organizations inhabited a world that was entirely rational and predictable this rational predictability would be the starting point for almost every project. However, organizations are only rational to a limited extent (Simon, 1965), as we intimated in the previous chapter. Given the cognitive bounds to rationality as well as those that are more material, in terms of the data which is known to be unknown as well as that which is unknown in almost every aspect, the relationship between project and strategy is often loose and random at the start of the project, while it typically becomes established more firmly during project implementation or at the end of the project, as a project rationalization. Such rationalizations are almost always post hoc and ad hoc. Major projects, such as the Iraq War, have in the past been launched with very little in the way of clear strategy or data. Consequently, as they are implemented the rationalizations for the project launched change. When weapons of mass destruction are not found the rationalizations may shift towards ridding a country of a tyrant and bringing democracy and order to a region that has lacked these attributes. As chaos reigned and civil war escalated, the rationalizations become ever more distant from the strategic objectives that were supposedly the project plan. Although the example may seem a long way from the realms of project management, it is not. Had it been managed as a political project with a clear scoping of objectives and how to achieve them it may well have been far less calamitous.

READ THIS!

There is an article by Giones, from *The Conversation*, about the most significant research strategies in the world for innovation projects: 'Horizon Europe: The EU plans to spend €100 billion on research – here's how to get the most from it at: https://study.sagepub.com/pm.

Projects based on a need perceived and legitimated within the organization in question

Organizations are dynamic with organization relationships with markets, employees, suppliers, competitors, customers, clients and other stakeholders changing continually, which means that strategic plans for further development must be constantly under review and revision. New technologies, products, processes, competitors, customers, employees and other stakeholders can affect how and what an organization does and strives to be. As organizations plan to adapt, they develop projects to manage these adaptations. Attention to the urge for change also involves attention to innovation (Clegg, Kornberger, Pitsis & Mount, 2019). Such attention can help make visible requirements that are not necessarily in line with existing strategy or business plans but that can still safeguard or change organization goals (Patanakul & Shenhar, 2012).

The extent to which organizations perceive and legitimate needs depends a great deal on their **sensemaking** capabilities.

Sensemaking, in organizational terms, involves constantly making sense, revising past rationalizations in the light of new information, knowledge and events that were not

> **Sensemaking** is defined by Weick (1995) as the ongoing retrospective development of plausible images that rationalize what people are doing, a process that is always occurring.

previously available. Project organizing is based on ongoing sensemaking; as new information arises, we redefine what we know about where we are going; moreover, retrospectively, we redefine what we thought we already knew. Often, sensemaking occurs in an overall context of uncertainty, due to bounded rationality; hence, sensemaking will always be provisional on the unfolding of events and meanings.

Events that cannot easily be accommodated in past sensemaking disrupt sense. What sensemaking does is to bracket and label the flow of events by breaking them into blocks of 'sense' that can be categorized and described. Sometimes organization leaders bring new phenomena to the attention of their members or their members do the same for their leaders, leaders who are usually more removed from the everyday occurrences in which intractable problems can arise; other times events are so disruptive it is impossible not to register the phenomena that they bring to attention. For organization projects disrupted in their sensemaking it is significant to manage the effects on the organization members and partners involved in the project.

Many cues will be used to make sense: past experience, what others say they think is happening, likely stories that you are familiar with that seem to fit the pattern that appears to be forming, previous project experiences, and so on. Different cues, different interpretations of cues and different projected courses of action can flow from sensemaking. A significant part of managing is to try and cue people in similar processes of pattern making to fit clues and cues together and make common meaning out of them. Project managers create a frame, enabling things to be connected together to make coherent sense much as a film director frames a shot, by including some detail and omitting other detail. A frame defines what is relevant. Once we have the frame then we can make sense through **framing**.

> By **framing** we decide on what is relevant from the infinite number of stimuli, behavioural cues, sense data and information that surround us.

Many good ideas do not emerge from a long and strategically founded process but emerge as rather more or less random events. Ikea's concept of flat-packed furniture was an idea that came out of a random event, for instance. Ikea did not spring into life selling flat-pack furniture. The idea for doing so sprang from an early encounter between a small car, a designer, Gillis Lundgren and a Lovet table. The table was to be delivered by Lundgren to a customer but would not fit in his car. He had the idea of designing the table so that the legs could be attached by the customer after receipt of the goods, thus making delivery much easier. Flat packing came to define Ikea. Projects may also emerge because someone in the organization had an inspiring experience, when attending a course or visiting another organization, that triggered the interest of either creating new products or processes or modifying the existing ones.

Regulatory authorities and other entities provide frameworks, such as requirements for product design, manufacturing or service delivery, which lead to organization changes. Projects can be an appropriate way to organize such change. An example of a project that arose as a result of external requirements is the GSM-R project at Norwegian National Rail Administration, which developed and implemented a 'new' communications platform for railways, which was initiated by the EU's new requirements for emergency communication by train (Vaagaasar, 2006).

Another example, which changed projects dramatically, was the Australian government's ban on branding of tobacco products. Despite fierce and costly lobbying by the tobacco industry the ban was not overturned on appeal. When this occurred in 2012 after a decision by the High Court of Australia, the big tobacco companies lost their battle against the introduction of plain tobacco packaging in Australia. All brand marks and logos on tobacco packaging were replaced with large graphic health warnings taking their place with only a small generic font exhibiting the manufacturer's brand name. The decision was an outcome with broad ramifications: at the point of sale, tobacco products could not be displayed; in terms of sales, specific brand identification lessened, as did smoking, while attempts to quit the habit increased.

The impact has been profound. No more advertising means no more lucrative projects for advertising agencies and media outlets; it means less deaths from cancer and reduced pressure on health services and reduced profits for tobacco companies. The project has been contagious, with other countries, including France and the UK following Australia's lead. In this instance, the regulatory change transformed tobacco companies' marketing projects markedly. The value delivered was in this case wide. Clearly, the quantitative value delivered in terms of lost profits to tobacco manufacturers was measurable and meaningful for their shareholders. However, it was the inestimable value delivered to health both individually and in terms of national health systems that was most significant.

Projects based on assignment or tender

Many project-based organizations compete with each other to win bids or be awarded assignments so that they might work on a *delivery project* (Chapter 2). Architectural firms, cultural companies and consulting companies are examples of organizations whose projects are assigned mainly by a third party as the basis for their business. The assignments are carried out as projects assigned to the project management delivery organization alone or in cooperation with other organizations, in a consortia or alliance.

Different routes may lead to the initiation of projects. Awareness of this influences the implementation of the project and the opportunity for project management success as well as project product success. Much of the literature within the project subject has an instrumental approach and assumes that projects start solely as well-considered initiatives in light of the strategy of the agency. On the best of occasions this may well be the case but even in these instances there is potential for many a slippage to occur between plan and project completion.

WHAT WOULD YOU DO?

John and Jim were a couple that had invested dreams in a scheme for renovating their existing inner-city terrace house in a funky part of the city. Loving the boho feel of the neighbourhood but feeling increasingly cramped in their house, which previous owners had stripped of character, they decided on a major renovation. Thinking that they knew what they wanted, they thought they knew what was needed. Jim was a theatre director while John was an antiques and curio retailer. In the course of John's career, he had filled a warehouse with old bits of houses, often sourced from demolition sites, such as fireplaces, windows and a staircase. John's plan was to use these materials in the renovation and thus keep costs down. Jim sketched out what he thought they wanted to do and then contacted Jules, an architect friend. Jules was very enthusiastic about the project and started to design a transformation for the house that would see them dig down into a basement and out into the garden, while opening up the Victorian interior by removing walls and letting light flood in from Velux windows in the roof on to the staircase that John had salvaged. Jules reckoned that the renovations would cost about $450,000.

(Continued)

John and Jim put the job out for tender and selected the quote that came in as the most reasonable, from Sandy. Jules handed the project over to Sandy at this stage.

Six months into the project a number of snags began to appear. The basement which had been dug and extended proved not to be waterproof; water was forcing its way into the basement. Research at the local library indicated that they were building on a water course that early maps had recorded but that had been left off more recent ones. The windows, which were John's dream, with their lead-lighting, were so out of true that they did not fit the apertures created in the brickwork. The staircase did not turn sufficiently tightly to fit the available space where the old staircase had been demolished.

Sandy advised them that these were not insuperable problems, only expensive ones. The budget was blowing out beyond 1 million dollars and a ceiling could not be put on the unanticipated costs. Further loans from the bank seemed increasingly difficult.

QUESTION

1. You were a project manager called in late in the project to advise John and Jim what to do. Previously Jim had been managing the project between rehearsals and performances and Jules had absolved himself of responsibility as he had only designed the renovations and his role had stopped at the design stage. Learning from this project, what advice would you offer future clients contemplating similar renovations?

Assessing the concept

If the starting point for a project is a comprehensive and dramatic statement or idea, you may not immediately proceed with the case as a project. For ideas to materialize as projects, they need to be refined (Carlsen, Clegg, & Gjersvik, 2012). They are often unclear and ambiguous, and therefore, may need work on interpreting them, clarifying what the project results should be to try and prefigure the extent to which it is possible to create these kinds of results. The idea also needs to be anchored broadly in the organization before it is decided to materialize it through a project. Many project failures are projects that should never have been started in the first place because suitability and relevance have not been sufficiently considered. Often, clients/principals are eager to get started, and therefore rush to prepare and champion the ideas (Tidd & Bessant, 2018), starting to sketch what the project will deliver and how it can be done to create the delivery, in a project description.

In the process of establishing a concept, it can be very difficult to determine what the appropriate ambition level for the project is if, for example, the project is going to create something unique and the actual project delivery is difficult to foresee. Often this is the case in research and other innovation projects – as we saw with the example of the house renovation it can also occur in more constrained projects. Where many stakeholders are involved in determining the character of the final delivery, carving out an emerging solution at the outset may well be difficult, unless considerable explicit collaboration has occurred and continues to occur though the project.

Whether it is feasible to proceed with the idea depends on the ability to clarify the concept and ambition level sufficiently, as well as to foresee the methods one can use to create the aimed for delivery. These two dimensions can be combined in a simple framework to clarify the potential journey from idea to project (Obeng, 1996). See Table 3.1.

Table 3.1   Different foundations at project start-up regarding characteristics for outcome and methods for creating desired deliverance

		What to do	
		Clear	Unclear
How to do it	Clear	Closed project	Semi-open project
		('Painting by numbers')	('Making a movie')
	Unclear	Semi-closed project	Open project
		('Going on a quest')	('Walking in the fog')

- **Closed project: 'Painting by numbers'.** In these types of projects, the task and the methods are quite clear – you know what to deliver and how to deliver the outcome. Thus, internal uncertainty is limited. Since these projects are rather predictable, they can be planned in detail and often they may also be split into a work breakdown structure in which tasks are isolated and distributed among the parties involved. The project manager's role entails directing work and sewing bits and pieces together. A simple construction project would be an example of this type of project where a new build is required on a greenfield site.

- **Semi-open project: 'Making a movie'.** In this type of project, the method is known in as much as one knows that one has to do filming, cutting and editing, record a soundtrack and add digital effects, etc., all things about which you and the team that you have become a part of are very knowledgeable. However, what the total impression will be when all these bits and pieces come together is something that you know much less about. In system development projects, for example, the methods are often given, while the characteristics of the delivery are gradually clarified and anchored in the project team, the client/base organization and other stakeholders.

- **Half-open project: 'Going on a quest'.** In this type of project, you know where to go but not how to get there. One may associate going on a quest with travellers, such as the ancient military Knights Templars who went on the road and knew they were headed to Jerusalem but knew and understood little about the events they would encounter on the way as they afforded protection to Christian pilgrims travelling through Muslim lands. The Knights' primary duty was to fight: to further this aim they built castles, garrisoned strategic towns and participated in battles until they were routed at the battle of Acre in 1291 by Sultan Saladin. Castles and garrisons were methods they understood well from their experience in Europe. As product development methods, however, they failed to be transplanted successfully into hostile territory with no network of supporting institutions. Despite their strong organizational culture, embedded in Catholicism, they embarked on a project that would never gain local support. Despite having a competent fighting team, building a good culture for task solving, supporting it with sound material garrisons and castles, their continuous learning proved fatal as they never came to terms with the culture and religion that surrounded them. Good project managers manage the cultures that their projects are embedded in (Clegg et al., 2002).

- **Open project: 'Walking in the fog'**. In this type of project both the goals and the methods are most uncertain. The project team, without the foggiest idea of where they are, can only see a short distance ahead. In such projects, it becomes crucial to exploit all team members' competencies and thus the development of team culture is crucial. The team members must elaborate visions and overall goals providing direction for the work while they navigate uncertainty with little in the way of clues as to direction and progress. In such circumstances relate to other stakeholders and involve them in the project, to capture and interpret uncertainty continuously and make the necessary decisions.

WHAT WOULD YOU DO?

A FAILING PROJECT

First, read the article by Yamuara, Muench, and Willoughby (2019) about 'Factors influencing adoption of information technologies for public transportation project inspection: A WSDOT case study', available at: https://study.sagepub.com/pm By most criteria, this looked like a relative failure as a change-management project but the paper shows that a number of factors, such as inadequate communication and training to prepare personnel for the change, were the cause of this failure as the change programme was insufficiently embedded in existing organizing processes and practices.

QUESTION

1. What would you do if you were a project manager midway in a similar change project and discovered that your project had a similar lack of embeddedness? Would you suggest putting it on hold or adopt some strategies? Explain the reasons behind what you propose.

Traditionally, it is recommended to proceed from idea to project when one anticipates the project execution to be a process of following a recipe. At the same time, where exploration and innovation are required it is necessary to organize projects that fall into the three other categories. One could argue that, due to the very high uncertainty, projects that seem foggy are the least suitable to launch but opportunities are inherent in uncertainties and many good innovations have been realized this way. It is hard to imagine that, for example, the development of the iPod or other significant innovations would have taken place without a considerable degree of search and ambiguity (Carlsen et al., 2012). In such circumstances this does not mean that working on the cultivation of ideas and concept development is not crucial; rather, that innovation projects are more integrated in the project execution process rather than their initial planning.

Sometimes projects are created solely to explore new opportunities. These can be seen as vanguard projects (Brady & Davies, 2004) such as the first moon landing. In this kind of project, it is most uncertain if the project can create deliverables nor can you be sure what kind of deliverables will ensue. Due to uncertainty about if and how deliverables will materialize, these projects are very challenging. It is difficult to relate to considerable uncertainty, which can be very stressful: the unknown unknowns make it difficult to engage key stakeholders and commit them to the project, affecting decision-making. In other chapters in the book, we will elaborate how the differences in what we know about the nature of the delivery and how it will be created, have implications for other essential processes in the project (such as management, organization and planning), choice of execution model and appropriate project team composition.

Not all ideas can be continued as projects. Idea refinement processes must be based on how the legitimate needs of the organization are defined and must work systematically to open various possibilities for alignment with these. A systematic approach to cultivating ideas is more than brainstorming and free creativity (Coldevin et al., 2019): it entails elaborating ideas, integrating information and generating material to inspire further action. It is vital to develop frameworks for designing the idea into action once the initial insight has been generated. Once the ideas have been sufficiently processed, you can go ahead with developing the project concept in a process that often leads to negotiations between people fighting for different approaches. Idea refinement is also about choosing those aspects of an idea with which to find project legitimacy.

Developing the concept

Before starting up projects, several concepts are often compared and further evaluated to determine which concept is suitable for further development and whether or not such development should be part of the operational tasks of the organization or be organized in a project.

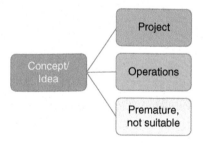

Figure 3.4 Alternatives for dealing with concepts

For concepts considered appropriate to be managed as a project, various economic and administrative consequences must be analysed. It is crucial to discuss how the concept should be anchored and clarified, as well as who would enact responsibility for developing the concept and managing it. Analysis and evaluation of multiple concepts often result in sketches of the project that gives the client and the permanent organization a better foundation for prepping the project (Figure 3.4).

In short, concept development involves clarifying what tasks should be included in the project, how these relate to the organization's strategy and plans, as well as making an overall assessment of purpose, focusing on the value creation dimension and clarification of objectives.

The relationship between the different levels is discussed here, while goal management will be explained in more detail in Chapter 4.

IN PRACTICE

REDESIGNING A UNIVERSITY WEBSITE

We have already introduced the university in Australia that is undertaking a three-year programme of work to transition all its subjects from Blackboard to Canvas and transform the digital learning and teaching experience in Chapter 2. We shall revisit the case here to ask some different questions. The programme is called LX Transformation. The initial workshops that the consultants arranged were used both to gather information about work patterns of academics, when their stress periods were likely to be and when they were unavailable, as well as when they might best be engaged. From these investigations it became clear that the antipodean year was structured around that of the northern hemisphere because the conference calendar of this hemisphere dictated the availability of researchers in the southern hemisphere as they attended and presented at the major conferences in their field. Having discovered when they were available, the consultants then sought to find out what aspects of their everyday work were significant for these academics, what they enjoyed doing most. Finally, an extremely long list of software tools known to be in use in the university was presented to the academics in the room, asking them to nominate which of these they used. The next stage in the project, after gathering all this information from a representative sample from across the university, is to make recommendations and create design assets, such as journey maps, that will inform the programme team's design and implementation decisions. Findings are also intended to inform the design of the learning interface on the website that allows users to easily access those tools that they need in order to be able to do their job.

QUESTION

1.   Bearing in mind that the university website has many different types of users, from present to intending students, academic staff and administrators, visitors from other organizations seeking to find information on people, research and courses, as well as general visitors, how do you think the further development of the project concept should be designed?

Direction of value creation

There will be many different elements influencing the direction that any organization adopts as part of its strategy for value creation, however that value is defined. All the elements are connected.

In Chapter 2, we looked at needs and values. Based on needs to be met by projects, one often formulates objectives and goals. Objectives describe the purpose, while goals are tools for directing processes towards purpose realization. These purposes can be plural. For example, an enterprise's mission may be to contribute to good user experiences for the customer, while it may also be a goal to achieve a sufficiently large profit that increasing dividends can be paid to the shareholders each year. A social welfare organization may seek to diminish homelessness by raising income to help put people in shelters more efficiently by collaborating with business partners that donate an element of income, say 5%, or an element of the time of their members, say one day a month. Thus, they have an overarching goal of reducing homelessness but beneath this goal, in order to aid its realization, they have sub-goals of partnering with business organizations inclined towards a degree of philanthropy. Looked at from the business organization's perspective, this may well produce a conflict of interest over goals: while the top executives are happy to be engaged in a socially worthwhile exercise their shareholders may not be so inclined. For them, the primary goal is profit-making rather than philanthropy that may have only a tangential relation to the overall goal.

In a perfectly rational world, each organization would have a clear and unambiguous purpose reflected at all levels, including outcomes and goals for the project portfolio. However, as we have seen before, people and organizations only have limited rationality (March and Simon, 1958). In line with the fact that values are often contradictory, as we saw in Chapter 2, there are often ambiguous and conflicting views on the organizational purpose. Is the social welfare organization really serving its mission with all those corporate events its members attend, the lunches they eat and the days in the corporate box at major sport events? For business organizations the maintenance of purposive goals is less problematic: following advice from the neo-classical economists they may well feel the business of business is business and business only and that, above all, this means making a profit. For organizations so inclined everything can be reduced to the bottom line.

By contrast, if we consider a non-business organization, such as a municipality, it will have some goals and purposes which will be in opposition to each other and organizationally it will be expected to try to handle the tensions this conflict can provoke. Part of its mandate may be to deliver efficient services to its residents. In order to do this, it initiates a change project designed to reduce council expenditures. One of the results is that it moves to outsourcing of what it considers non-core organizational operations, such as rubbish collection. The outsourced organization arranges this differently, with less frequency and larger bins, than the old council employees, many of whom have been hired – at lower wages – by the private contractor. The council can expect to receive flak on at least two fronts: disgruntled residents who see a decline in service standards and disgruntled former employees who now have to tolerate a decline in their pay and conditions. The municipality now has to manage this disgruntlement on two fronts along with all the other goals that it strives to realize, none of which can as easily be reduced to a balance sheet as in a private sector business.

Even where there is a bottom line, the creation of value can lead an organization in contradictory directions. An organization within the IT industry not only has to provide the highest possible returns to the owners. Its objectives can also include customer satisfaction, product quality and corporate social responsibility. In other words, the objectives of an organization can be multiple, ambiguous and sometimes even divergent, tensions that can drizzle down to individual IT projects' purposes and goals as well. Therefore, it is critical to work with the relationships between organization level objectives and project purposes and goals, for example using tools such as goal hierarchies and purpose hierarchies (see Chapter 4).

Visions, something that any fashionable organization should not lack, are closely linked to purposes.

> **Visions** express the desired image of the organization in terms of the ideal situation sought for the future.

Visions are overarching statements communicated through an organization's business ideas positing exploratory opportunities for the organization, based on factors such as its perceived **adaptive capabilities**.

> **Adaptive capabilities** are those characteristics of an organization that enable it to adapt an organization's resource base purposefully.

Organizations may have more or less significant dynamic capabilities (Teece, Pisano, & Shuen, 1997). These can reside in technological, knowledge or market intelligence competencies, for example. Change projects can often seek to tease these dynamic capabilities out in pursuit of new goals, such as innovative products, markets or processes (Davies & Brady, 2000). Once goals are postulated in terms of a description of the desired state to be achieved, more concrete objectives will often be operationalized. These might include raising revenue or service levels, opening new markets, or improving client satisfaction by a specific amount. Objectives enable one to see to what extent goals have been achieved. Objectives help to guide behaviour in the desired direction; they should feedback into the project development, reinforcing or rectifying its direction. It might be useful to have goals arranged on several levels in order to deduce and plan activities. We will look at the design of multi-level goals in the next chapter.

Projects can be many and varied. Next, drawing on research in Africa, we look at projects to provide shelter for the millions that have made the trek from rural poverty to urban density in search of a better life. Once arrived in the city, people from impoverished backgrounds do not find it easy to gain shelter. Many, estimated to be 1.5 billion by 2020, end up living in informal settlements that lack security of tenure, do not have durable housing and that are short of basic services. Slum dwellers are stigmatized, often subject to severe state sanctions, such as bulldozing their settlements in order to evict them forcefully. Yet, slums provide a vital refuge and shelter for millions across the planet. In Accra, in Ghana, one of Africa's most successful states, almost half of the residents of the city live in informal settlements. In the extract from the article that follows, the broader dynamics of urban housing and the rental regime that has pushed many people into the informal settlements are discussed. The authors argue that slums are more than just marginalized spaces of abject poverty and neglect.

Because of a lack of affordable, decent and secure shelter for the low-income population, there is a shortage of housing in the Ghanaian capital. This crisis was instigated by the withdrawal of the state as an active provider of housing, following IMF recommendations in the 1980s.

IN PRACTICE

SLUM DWELLERS' PROJECT

Throughout much of the world, the most basic necessities of life, such as shelter, are in short supply, as Okyere, Tasnatab, and Abunyewah write about in *The Conversation* (7 October 2018) at https://theconversation.com/accras-informal-settlements-are-easing-the-citys-urban-housing-crisis-104266.

CAN UPGRADING SLUMS HELP SOLVE THE CRISIS?

Old Fadama is the largest informal settlement in the city of Accra. In media and political circles, it is often cast as dystopian. But for many it's one of the few places they can be assured of access to cheap and alternative housing while still remaining close to core services in the city of Accra.

This informal settlement sits on public land that was initially acquired by the government of Ghana for the Korle Lagoon Ecological Restoration Project. The project was abandoned and the land remained undeveloped until the 1980s when the informal settlement began.

Since then the population has grown substantially. Between 2004 and 2007, for instance, the population doubled from 24,000 to 48,000. The most recent data suggests that nearly 80,000 people now live in the area.

This exponential growth can be attributed to the fact that Old Fadama provides cheap, centrally located housing. Moreover, not all housing is substandard. Relatively better-quality houses can be found in unplanned areas at more affordable prices than other areas in Accra. This is borne out by the fact that Old Fadama doesn't only house the informal poor. A recent study suggested that about 15% are formal sector employees.

Old Fadama is an entry point to basic housing for those in both low-paid formal and informal employment. For many in this slum, access to cheap housing in the city's economic heartland has made it possible to capitalize on their capabilities and enabled them to try and move out of poverty.

There's an urgent need for targeted interventions around slum housing in Accra. Fortunately, the 2015 National Housing Policy and the newly established Ministry for Inner City and Zongo Development are good starting points. Both emphasize support for the urban poor and low-income housing.

Additionally, civil society groups are experimenting with collective self-help housing – such as the Amui Dzor Housing and Infrastructure Project implemented by the Ghana Federation of the Urban Poor in collaboration with the government and UN Habitat – for low-income groups. In view of this, we suggest that there is a need to combine policy support with project experimentation for house improvement in urban slums.

This should be considered as part of a housing programme that involves state leadership in providing 'real' affordable housing. There is also a need to provide funds for social housing, enforce regulation of the rental market and support the informal housing sector. This would add up to a solid commitment towards every citizen's right to decent, secure and affordable housing.

QUESTIONS

1.   Search online and describe what vision, goals and policy objectives of the 2015 National Housing Policy of the Government of Ghana's Ministry of Water Resources, Works and Housing drive Ghanaian housing projects for the informal sector?

2.   What role might slum dwellers play in the urban economy for housing through self-reliance projects and what is the role of the state and civil society in these projects? (Hint: Danso-Wiredu and Midheme's (2017) article, 'Slum upgrading in developing countries: Lessons from Ghana and Kenya?, which is downloadable online, may be useful.)

Goals and objectives in projects

As can be seen from the National Housing Policy of the Government of Ghana's Ministry of Water Resources, Works and Housing, in projects one often distinguishes between objectives or impact targets, as well as performance targets. Objectives, or impact targets, describe the desired future condition of value creation a project seeks to deliver, while performance targets or goals describe the results the project will create, the project deliverables. Performance targets can be evaluated immediately at the end of a specific aspect of the project, while objectives are often not realized until the overall project is completed. Performance targets are linked to project management success, while project product success is associated with purpose (Figure 3.5). We will look at some examples.

Figure 3.5 Connection between project, project goal (performance targets) and purpose

The construction of a bridge can be organized as a project. A typical goal will be to build a bridge according to the determined quality criteria, preferably within time and cost estimates. However, the bridge itself is not a definitive goal; it is its use that matters. The use value of the bridge is its role in changing the pattern of transportation, improving access to individual sites, providing better infrastructure for residents and business activities in the area, perhaps also reducing environmental impact in the form of a changed transport pattern and improving well-being and satisfaction among nearby inhabitants and users. When an adventure park is going to develop a new product, the new product is the actual project objective, while increased visitor numbers, customer satisfaction and increased revenue may be fundamental desired purposes. If a governmental agency reorganizes, the project target may be a new organizational structure, changed division of labour or changed responsibilities. The purpose will be more efficient service production, higher quality of case processing and perhaps the integration of new tasks for the affected organization.

Sometimes it can be difficult to make the distinction between project goals and purposes, as they are often entangled. For an artist contributing to an exhibition, the project will be showing work at the exhibition and selling it to appreciative buyers. The purpose of the exhibition is increased attention and demand, as well as higher income for the gallery and the artists represented. For specific artists, however, the exhibition and the effects that might be gained from it are so interlinked that it may be difficult to separate between project goals and purposes. As these short and general examples demonstrate, there are differences in types of projects and organizations but they all have in common that project goals are not the definite goal but are rather more the tool for achieving a purpose. We have emphasized this approach several times, yet it is often forgotten both in the project literature and in project work itself.

IN PRACTICE

SAGRADA FAMILIA

There are some projects that take more than a lifetime to accomplish. One significant contemporary example is the Sagrada Familia church in Barcelona. It was begun in 1882, although it is usually credited as beginning in 1883, when Antoni Gaudí took over as chief architect. His project was only a quarter completed when he died in 1926 and the construction of the church continues to this day. During the course of its construction it was disrupted by the Spanish Civil War in 1936, when the loss of detailed project plans occurred, as well as some of the built structure, as a result of the conflict.

The project was initially wholly privately funded by donations – what today we might refer to as crowdsourcing – and today is sustained by a visitor fee levied on the 2.5 million tourists that visit it each year. At present it is about 70% complete. Hence, nearly 140 years since the project's inception, it is not yet accomplished. The style of the architecture is a highly distinctive fusion of Gothic motifs and Art Nouveau, with many organic elements represented with nary a straight line anywhere in the building.

The project is incomplete but was the purpose of the building merely to achieve completion? The building was originally inspired by a bookseller, Josep Maria Bocabella, founder of Asociación Espiritual de Devotos de San José (Spiritual Association of Devotees of St Joseph). His purpose was to build a house of worship inspired by a basilica he had seen on his travels at Loreto. Gaudi transformed this into his unique mixture of Gothic and Art Nouveau inspiration, to produce an organic, flowing building,

Picture 3.1   The Sagrada Familia

Source: Image courtesy of C messier, via wikicommons. Shared under the Creative Commons BY-SA 4.0 license.

one with many folds, as yet uncompleted. Nonetheless, its purpose has been established ahead of its completion, although its construction, with so many biblical metaphors embedded in its fabric, prefigured this purpose. With the completion of the main nave's roof and the installation of an organ in 2010, the building became available for its intended purpose of holding Catholic religious services. In November 2010 the then pope, Benedict XVI, consecrated the building at a ceremony attended by a congregation of six and a half thousand people. From mid-2017 an international mass has been celebrated in the building every Sunday.

QUESTION

1. The difference between project goals and purposes is very evident in the case of the Sagrada Familia. Separating project goals and purposes clearly can help to clarify the

(Continued)

central dimensions of objectives and to see which elements comprise dynamic objectives and which need to be more stable. The purpose of the project for most projects will be fixed, while the project objective is more dynamic, being a tool to produce the desired effects. In your estimation, what are the purposes of the Sagrada Familia as it has transpired?

During project execution, the project team and the stakeholders develop new knowledge that can facilitate better solutions in terms of the project execution itself and the deliverables. For instance, the development of Computer-Aided Design (CAD) and Building Information Modelling (BIM) technology has speeded up the Sagrada Familia project in recent years. In addition, in the absence of detailed plans for the whole structure, its design terms and conditions have had to be emergent, developing through adjusting and changing the project objectives from time to time, as obstacles were faced and overcome.

In a more commercial example than a religious and architectural icon, we could consider an organization whose project is to achieve the purpose of more efficient routines for logging and archiving information about interaction with its customers. One of the goals in the project is to develop their file concept. During the project, new technology emerges that facilitates the development of a digital archive system. This leads to a change of project goals; for example, by removing the need to develop their current (physical) file concept but retaining the purpose of more efficient archiving routines as a basis for more efficient operation, which remains the key effect aimed for that defines the purpose of the project. It should also be noted that in the process of achieving projects and project goals there can be unintended effects that are not integrated into the process of preparing project goals and impact targets. Architects can die in accidents before they have completed their design, as happened to Gaudí; civil war can destroy blueprints and plans; new technologies can speed up projects.

Figure 3.6 Project goals and possible side effects

In concept development and start-up processes, it is essential to consider and take into account potential side effects of the project (Figure 3.6). The Sagrada Familia was challenged by technological developments that were entirely unrelated to the church. In 2010 a project to construct a tunnel for a high-speed train was commenced in Barcelona. The tunnel not only runs through the centre of Barcelona but directly under the Sagrada Familia, giving rise to campaigns to change the route that were unsuccessful. The tunnel boring machines began tunnelling under the church, at a distance of four metres from the structure. Trains have been running since the beginning of 2013 on tracks that are embedded in an elastic material to reduce vibrations. There has been no damage to the building either by the boring or the trains running on the tracks. The use of an elastically embedded Dutch system for noise and vibration reduction was a desirable side effect of building under a dense and heritage-significant city. In open country or less heritage-sensitive contexts the system may well not have been required.

For product development, increased environmental emissions and cannibalization of other products in an organization's portfolio may be examples of undesirable side effects. All organizations' projects cast a shadow that you must be aware of (Jørgensen & Pedersen, 2018). A plane such as the Airbus 380 has found great favour with long-haul passengers as it is more comfortable and better pressurized than its rivals but it has not found the same acceptance amongst airlines as its large carrying capacity and four engine configuration mean that it has to fly each flight at near full capacity to make a profit in terms of the economics of the contemporary long-haul travel market. A better product as a result of the Airbus developmental project is no longer being made because the orders have dried up as it was deemed less fit for purpose than other aircraft, including smaller Airbuses.

Developing a new aircraft such as the Airbus 380 is a major long-term project. In this case the project began in 1988 with the first flight not occurring until 2005. Given a project development period of 17 years, a great deal can change in the way of the objectives and purpose of a project, the organization's strategy and that of its competitors, the specific need that triggered the project, as well as identifying the stakeholders to be involved in a holistic manner. For projects, it is a critical success factor to have both purpose and goals that stakeholders acknowledge. With the Airbus 380, different stakeholders held different divergent views on what would be the most appropriate purpose. The project was successful in bringing the aircraft to market and in initial sales, largely to Middle Eastern long-haul airlines and Qantas as the main customers. However, its purpose – to move large numbers of people long distances, cheaply and efficiently – in the long run did not form a compelling value proposition for repeat sales. On 14 February 2019, after Emirates reduced its last orders in favour of the A350 and A33neo, Airbus announced that A380 production would end by 2021.

EXTEND YOUR KNOWLEDGE

Read the article by Loch and Sommer (2019), 'The tension between flexible goals and managerial control in exploratory projects', on tensions between managerial control and flexibility in project goals, available at: https://study.sagepub.com/pm.

Be aware that the inclusion of many stakeholders in the project goal design may lead to ambiguous goals and conflicts of interest, which may require flexibility in goals. Contemporary projects often bear testament to this fact; they rarely have exclusively one-dimensional goals, yet awareness of ambiguous goals and conflicts of interest may be limited, given the optimism biases and sublimes that we discussed in Chapter 2. There needs to be deep reflection to determine the different dimensions inherent in the goals promulgated. The goal may be to produce a more efficient machine but is it also sustainable, aesthetically pleasing and appropriately priced?

Goal complexity and conflicts may be the outcome not only where there are multiple organizational stakeholders but also where multiple entities representing a permanent organization are involved. For example, the project of developing an application for hosting the Winter Olympics 2022 in Oslo, Norway, involved several clients. The Norwegian Sports Association and Oslo Municipality were the key parties on the client side but their success with the project was contingent on the support of other stakeholders involved in the project. The fact that the municipality of Oslo and the Norwegian Sports Association held different objectives probably contributed, together with the limited willingness of national authorities to fund the games, to the project being terminated.

In projects where multiple entities in an organization participate and might also be affected by the future implementation of the project deliveries, there will often be different values and agendas that may lead to complex and partly contradictory goals. For example, an organization that is going to develop a new product typically would have a technical department with more goals for the project than has the marketing department. Importantly, it will need to be clear what the overall purpose of the project is so that it will form a point of reference for the goal of all involved. One of the most talked about goals in recent years has been the development of the United Nations' 17 Sustainable Development Goals (SDGs). One of these goals is health and how it got to be there and quite what its pursuit will be turns out to be deeply political. A lot can be learnt about the nature of goals, their definition and implementation from the process of inclusion of health in the SDGs.

READ THIS!

Read the article by Hill (2015), 'More is less? Health in the Sustainable Development Goals' from *The Conversation* at: https://study.sagepub.com/pm.

EXTEND YOUR KNOWLEDGE

Read the article by Jones and Barry (2018), 'Factors influencing trust and mistrust in health promotion partnerships'. Increasingly, public sector initiatives are being delivered by projects that involve collaborations between different organizational actors, available at: https://study.sagepub.com/pm.

Decision-making

The process of developing a project concept includes many decisions. When the concept is fairly well established, it becomes the basis for deciding whether to start the project, what ambitions will be projected on to it and how it will be implemented. Decisions and decision-making processes are thus crucial in projects.

Decisions involve choices between different alternatives. Often decision-making processes are presented as a result of managers and decision-makers in organizations gathering information, assessing the information, before making a decision. Such a sequence is rare. Decision-making processes mostly entail inherent power struggles, coincidences, subjective approaches, lobbying and institutional histories (Garvin & Roberto, 2001) but it is also possible to have excellent and efficient decision-making processes. We will look into some issues that characterize many decision-making processes in projects, especially decisions about launching projects.

RATIONALITY AND DECISIONS

The belief in human beings as perfectly rational was based on a particular understanding of how people made economic and, by extension, organizational decisions (Brunsson, 2007). The term *Homo Economicus* expresses such a belief. It is assumed that the economic person, here deemed to be a man, will evaluate and decide on options based on a complete overview of the relevant data and information.

The notion of there being a perfectly rational decision-maker is now abandoned as a basis for understanding human behaviour and choices. Herbert Simon (1965), regarded as one of the foremost researchers in decision theory, claimed that even if humans wish and try to act as perfectly rational, they will never fully succeed in doing so. Rationality is only partial due to limitations in time and other resources, as well as the complexity of the decisions to be made. Instead of perfectly rational solutions, we must seek to find satisfactory solutions, suggests Simon. In practice, not being perfectly rational does not mean that we do not strive to be. Embedded rationality, rationality that is rooted in everyday sensemaking on the part of people striving to make sense with whatever tools, resources and skills are at hand, implies trying to relate analytically to an issue by evaluating different alternatives and their consequences, in order to choose the option that best fits dominant preferences and goals. The key word here is 'dominant' – some versions of sensemaking will have greater heft than others, perhaps because of the status of the person, persons, department, knowledge or political nous of those promoting them. To secure their definitions of the situation those that are dominant have to be able to fix the terms of debate so that they flow through channels that they command. These are the metaphors and forms of calculation that are made obligatory passage points in organizational decision-making (Clegg, 1989) that are normalized. No individuals are perfectly rational, politics will always be shaped by interests and interests differentiate actors. It is for this reason, if no other, that assessments and decisions in organizations cannot be fully rational.

DECISION-MAKING CONTEXTS

A decision cannot be isolated from its context. It is part of a decision-making process that includes assessments and actions that lead to a decision, as well as implementation. To choose between different options, some general elements must be clarified. One must:

- Know what one wants to achieve; that is, one should know what one's goal is
- Acquire relevant knowledge, by gathering information and assessing it as a basis for decision
- Compare and rate the options that appear feasible, given resources
- Select according to the ranking of the options

All of these elements appear to be self-evident and partly banal, yet they are fundamental to decision-making processes in organizations and in the considerations concerned in proceeding from ideas to projects. We will see how decision-making processes in organizations are complicated by the fact that there are many involved, either directly or indirectly.

READ THIS!

Vanhoucke (2018) has a downloadable PDF (link available at https://study.sagepub.com/pm) that tells the story of a young project manager, Emily Reed, in charge of implementing a new way of managing projects based on a mix of facts and figures, in combination with experience and intuition. It is an unusual presentation of a highly rationalistic approach to project management.

EVALUATING CONSEQUENCES AND DEFINING BENEFITS

One important aspect of a decision-making process is to assess the probable outcomes of different actions and choices. Doing so involves foreseeing and evaluating the potential consequences of different strategic steps, planned actions and possible measures. Typical forms of evaluation of consequences that are used when organizations consider launching projects are:

- Strategic assessments
- Conceptual assessments
- Financial assessments (profitability calculations)
- Assessment of uncertainty
- Evaluation of the implementation plan

Strategic assessments of projects should always be linked to the organization's overall strategic efforts related to value creation, depending on how value is defined. It is crucial that these assessments provide a link to and anchoring in the strategy when it comes to launching projects. Projects require legitimation to be accepted and one way of seeking to assure this is to link them explicitly to the current strategic plan and its categories. Projects that do not do this at the proposal stage are unlikely to pass further on in the process because their sponsors make it too easy for others to reject them.

Conceptual assessments imply considering the types of potential project deliveries. These projects are still at the idea stage and it is important to look into the potential quality of solutions, how they integrate with existing organizational processes, their potential for being implemented and used as well as the maintenance and operational needs that they will be likely to engender. At this stage of the process, there are very many aspects to clarify, based on available project-specific information as well as learning from similar projects.

Financial assessments. When an organization elaborates on whether to initiate a project or not and in what ways the potential project can be executed, the questions of costs and benefits will usually be close by. Often, these considerations will be expressed in terms of profitability. There are many methods for assessing profitability, as well as the need for economic resources to be committed in a project and advanced methods are commonly used to estimate both cost and profit aspects of any project proposal that passes initial scrutiny. Still, it might be difficult to calculate profitability, as projects often have extensive uncertainty inherent. Although not advanced, calculations and methodologies can reduce uncertainty and provide a basis for familiar and more qualified assessments.

Assessment of uncertainty is a key aspect of project work. Various types of uncertainty are considered, including technological, political, market, capacity-sensitive and economic. These uncertainties must be included in impact assessments. We will delve more deeply into uncertainty in the context of projects in Chapter 9.

Evaluation of the implementation plan is a stage when the feasibility of project implementation is assessed: How realistic is the project? Are the key elements related to implementation available? Some aspects central to the project, such as time, cost and resource requirements, will be considered. Questions on which to reflect include the following: Is the capacity and competence available to be responsible for implementation? What kind of cooperation with other actors is required or feasible and what kind of contractual arrangements should one opt for?

Even though an organization may find that a potential project is appropriate, it might still not be committed to launching the project. This could, for example, be due to lack of human resources with relevant expertise. Starting up a project may be harmful to other activities in the organization and therefore should be considered from a portfolio perspective. It is also relevant to consider organizational issues, such as who will manage the project, what kind of decision-making structure is most adequate for the project and relevant project context.

READ THIS!

Read about a unique experiment in blind decision-making and some of the lessons that can be learnt from it, arising from the Homeward Bound project taking 77 female scientists to Antarctica, in an article by Hamylton and Balez (2018), 'How a trip to Antarctica became a real-life experiment in decision-making', from *The Conversation* at: https://study.sagepub.com/pm.

LIMITATIONS IN DECISION-MAKING

Projects involve very many components and interfaces, factors that lead to uncertainty and complexity, not least given that decision-making is often represented as being rational when, as social scientists, we know that it is always boundedly rational (Simon, 1965).

DECISION-MAKING PROCESSES WITH AMBIGUITIES AND COINCIDENCES

The well-known 'garbage can' theory points out that when events are analysed, problems, solution options, decision-makers and decision-making flow into and out of metaphorical garbage cans. There, given random adjacencies, they sometimes connect (March & Olsen, 1976), but it is difficult to justify why and how these problems, solution options, decision-makers and decision-making connect and materialize as a decision.

Much of the explanation of why this is the case is simply because they flow into the garbage can in the same period of time, hence are adjacent. A decision about a given solution does not always fit the problem to be solved because solutions are actively looking for a problem to which to attach themselves. You often do not know what the problem you are trying to address is before the problem is solved (Cohen, March, & Olsen, 1972, p. 3). This often links problems and solutions quite randomly.

IN PRACTICE

PROJECT DELIVERY

Delivery projects are widely used in public sector management. In the past, public utilities might well have delivered projects using the in-house resources of the Public Work Department. As a result of many years of expenditure reductions and downsizing these bodies no longer have the capabilities or the capacity to deliver these infrastructure projects. Consequently, these bodies increasingly use delivery projects. Look at the link on the companion website starting with www.apcc.gov.au. Here you can read a guide to project delivery from the Australian Construction Industry Forum. The focus of this guide is the front-end of projects – project initiation, project delivery planning, delivery team procurement and project delivery. In the processes outlined, on page 10, you will find a framework for Value Management. This framework presumes a high level of rationality in the form of available knowledge for decision-making. From organization theory, we know that this rarely pertains. Instead, most decision-making is characterized by bounded rationality. Bounded rationality (Simon, 1991) means producing satisfactory rather than optimally rational decisions, a process referred to as 'satisficing', meaning accepting decisions that are both sufficient and satisfying. In later work, Simon's collaborator, J. G. March, writing with <J. P. Olsen and M. D. Cohen, said that many decision-making processes were best thought of in terms of the 'garbage can model' (Cohen et al., 1972). The garbage can model describes the chaotic reality of organizational decision-making in conditions of organized anarchy. Organized anarchies are decision situations characterized by problematic preferences, unclear technology and fluid participation.

QUESTIONS

1. Looking at the framework for value management, what are the major points at which value might not be well managed from the perspective of bounded rationality, particularly in terms of the 'known unknowns' and the 'unknown unknowns' that might have an impact on the project? (Hint: these terms pop up again in Chapter 8.)

2. Looking at the framework for value management, what are the major points at which value might not be well managed from the perspective of the garbage can model, particularly in terms of the evolution of the project over time?

The 'garbage can' theory shows us that work in projects, whether in temporary or permanent organizations, is characterized by some ambiguities that make it impossible for events to be entirely rational. We mention four types of ambiguities here:

- Ambiguity related to what the preferences are in a decision-making situation. There is a lack of consistent criteria for choosing decisions, with the consistency between the consequences of the decision not holding against criteria. Organizational preferences are neither well defined nor consistent.
- Unclear technology or system solutions characterize the project. Participants do not, or will not, understand the solutions; they interpret them differently, sometimes out of predefined power interests, other times out of a logic based on trial and error.
- Storytelling ambiguity. Participants have different understandings of the targets of the project and the relationships between these and other processes.
- Unclear boundaries for the project and its organization, as participants go in and out of it.

By being aware of these four types of ambiguity, one can elaborate on them systematically in order to reduce vagueness and contradictions involved, for example through early phase activities in projects. However, we must live with some ambiguity as part of the process. Irrational courses of events equal to those described above are also triggered by situations where it is expected that organizing will act decisively, for example in some decision forums such as the steering group of the project. Although the rationality of participants may be limited, lacking sufficient foundations to make decisions, they will still act decisively, for example by signing contracts, terminating or commencing contractual relations or distributing responsibility for uncertainty.

WATCH THIS!

Watch the Ted Talk by experimental psychologist Petter Johansson about how we can know what we know – and what we do not know at: https://study.sagepub.com/pm.

The likelihood of irrational decisions increases due to the current flow of participants entering and leaving the projects and in the surrounding areas of the projects (Vaagaasar, 2011). Skills and attention determine their capacity in the decision-making situation. In project-based organizations, many of the organizational members may be associated with several matrix projects that run in parallel. Then it is difficult to get the most competent people in a decision-making situation at the right time and with the necessary attention and understanding of the problems to be solved. Moreover, it is often the case that when a decision needs to be taken, there is often little chance of obtaining sufficient information if only because it is time-consuming to do so. Planning is essential for good decision-making.

WATCH THIS!

Watch the Ted Talk by Sara Garafalo on the psychology behind irrational decisions at: https://study.sagepub.com/pm.

RATIONAL DECISIONS AS HYPOCRISY

Some researchers, notably Brunsson (2006), claim that it is only 'false mechanisms of hope' that still leave us talking about the classical conception of rationality. It is better to acknowledge that we interact and solve tasks through three systems of actions, decisions and talks about actions and decisions in projects, suggests Brunsson (2000). Based on the idea of perfect rationality, these should match.

In practice, however, despite the intention of there being compliance on the part of actors among their actions, decisions and talk, often there is little or no correspondence. For example, in cases where some time elapses between decision, talk and action, deviations often occur among the three systems. Other times, the differences can be created intentionally for the project; for example, when it comes to a complicated stakeholder context in which one wishes to hold the coalition together (Vaagaasar, 2006). On such occasions the strategic ambiguity that slippage amongst the terms allows can be strategically useful, as Giezen, Salet, and Bertolini (2015) argue with respect to transport megaprojects in the Netherlands. Through deviations, a project can satisfy more stakeholders and thus it might be advisable to practise what Brunsson and Adler (1989) call hypocritical rationality.

We have seen that ambiguities and space for local interpretations (of preferences, knowledge of systems or contexts and of whom should take part in a decision-making situation) make decisions and behaviour in and around projects limitedly rational (Andersen et al., 2010). We have also looked at how hypocritical rationality plays its part in projects. Below we will reflect on some other phenomena that inhibit rational progress and high-quality decisions in projects.

Why do we start the worst projects?

Looking back at project failures, it's not difficult to point out projects that should not have been launched. These are projects that were initiated despite the lack of analysis indicating that the investment of money and other resources probably would lead to expected value: projects started without the users calling for the process or product being delivered; projects including highly complicated and/or uncertain solutions, which include economic risk and a further investment of funds that are difficult to defend. These are just a few of numerous reasons. Several researchers (such as Kahneman and Tversky, 2000) have asked the question, 'Why do we start the worst projects?' In extending this observation, we can ask, What are the reasons why so many projects that seem to be inappropriate seem to be implemented?'

ERRORS AND OVER-OPTIMISM

How can we explain the great number of project fallacies? The standard economic theory would say that bad results are a natural consequence of organizations taking rational risks in uncertain situations. Leaders know and are willing to run this risk because they believe that, in the long run, they will achieve some successes. This might seem like an attractive argument, especially for the leaders, because it relieves their guilt related to project fallacies. As Lovallo and Kahneman (2003) demonstrate, there are other, and perhaps better, explanations than claiming that normally, what we have, is 'rational choices gone wrong'. Rather, it is 'the result of bad decision-making – characterized by decision-making traps'. Since they can have fatal consequences for the project success, we will look at some different decision traps.

A common decision-making trap is an over-optimism that overestimates the benefits of the project and underestimates the potential for it to go wrong. Over-optimism is a human asset that we can be aware of, appreciate in some contexts but try to correct in decision-making processes related to start-up and implementation of projects. It's risky because when a project starts to go bad economically, there's almost no limit to how bad it can go.

Over-optimism allows managers to create success scenarios for projects and be led by them, which inhibits the ability to weigh the pros and cons accurately. The leaders' over-optimism can be traced both to psychological factors and forces in the organization that push in a certain direction (Lovallo & Kahneman, 2003). Research has shown that people tend to be quite optimistic most of the time when it comes to the outcome of processes that they take part in or in or for which they hold responsibility. An important reason for this is that we think we have better abilities than we in fact do (Kahneman, 2012). For example, a survey showed that when more than 1000 students were asked to evaluate their leadership skills, 70% thought they were above average. Similar results are found among athletes and workers. Most of us think we are far above average. On the question of how well one thought fellow students liked them, 25% of the students answered that they were among the top 1% (Lovallo & Kahneman, 2003). Our judgement is therefore bad. If someone cuts in while we are driving, your first thought might be 'What a jerk!' instead of considering the possibility that the driver is rushing someone to the hospital. On the other hand, when we cut someone off in traffic, we tend to convince ourselves that we had to do so. We focus on situational factors, like being late to a meeting, ignoring what our behaviour might say about our own character (Kahneman, 2012). That means that in situations where we succeed, we add this to our abilities while, when we fail, we attribute that to coincidence. Simply put, it's rare we talk about projects succeeding because we were lucky while we often talk about failing because of bad luck.

Furthermore, we tend to overestimate the degree of control in different contexts. In some experimental studies, people have been asked to press a button each time a light blinks, hitting it as often as they possibly can. The test subjects are told that the number of hits will depend on both the effort and the coincidence. Usually, the significance of your own effort for the number of hits is greatly overestimated. Your belief in your abilities and the ability to control them in given situations may be over-optimistic. For managers and entrepreneurs, this image is strengthened by two other traps, according to Lovallo and Kahneman (2003): the *anchor effect* and *competitor neglect*, which can explain much of why 80% of business ventures fail within a short period of start-up. We will look into this.

EXTEND YOUR KNOWLEDGE

Read the article by Batselier and Vanhoucke (2016) where they compare different models for predicting the future by looking at similar past situations and their outcome, available at: https://study.sagepub.com/pm.

In the assessment of project start-ups, decision-makers often submit a proposal with some estimates and a preliminary plan. Decision-makers value this and may make additional analyses as well. While the proposal makes sense, the problem is often that the starting point is incorrect. First, it is the case that those who have promoted the proclamation are probably affected by over-optimism associated with positive outcomes, abilities and control. Furthermore, they would like to have this project be accepted and try to render it beneficially. The basis being considered is therefore too optimistic.

Anchoring is the name of a psychological decision case that describes that we anchor our estimates in random estimates. When decision-makers are provided numbers (for example related to how much time and money a potential project would cost) as a foundation for their decisions, they will anchor their action in these. Even when the numbers are completely wrong, they base their decisions on the numbers. They adjust estimates based on analyses but do so insufficiently, similar to the situation we are exposed to in haggling situations, where the seller starts with a very high price.

An organization's degree of success depends on the activities of their competitors. Nevertheless, decision-makers tend to concentrate their attention on internal relationships such as capacity and capabilities, not whether competitors have better capacity, capabilities or ideas. There is often an over-optimistic trend in organizations. We have already mentioned that those who wish to win in the struggle for which projects are started will tend to make the project optimistic. Moreover, organizations and their leaders often strive for and emphasize goals that are far too ambitious (Cunha, Viera, Rego, & Clegg, 2018). It is also true that many organizations promote the people in their firm that express a belief in themselves and what they can accomplish. As a rule, there is usually no promotion and benefit associated with pessimism. All these factors mentioned contribute to over-emphasizing the benefits of the project and the possibilities for project success, undermining the possible adverse outcomes of a project. Therefore, we often start the worst projects – usually those with the worst business case (Lovallo & Kahneman, 2003), as we saw in Chapter 2.

The awareness of over-optimism and how it affects decision-making processes can strengthen the ability of decision-makers to reflect on the quality of their own decisions. Those who introduce analyses that are more systematic where they compare their focal activities with relevant activities and projects outside their own organization (labelled *outsider view*) succeed better. Research shows that it is better to assess other people's estimates than one's own and that when one sees an outsider view, optimism is reduced. For example, a group of students were asked to evaluate their performance compared to other students, with 84% answering that they were better than the average. When asked to base their views on the grades of the other students, the number of students who thought they were better than the average fell to 60%. A quick look at other people's achievements can significantly reduce over-optimism, even when it comes to project implementation. This way of overcoming classic problems with the assessment of the pros and cons of a project is what is called benchmark comparisons. In setting up projects, companies tend to focus on their own experiences, competencies and expectations in their analyses. This experience, however, is too narrow. With systematic comparisons with similar activities and projects outside of your own organization, you can achieve a more nuanced image (Lovallo & Kahneman, 2003).

One institutionally embedded area of over-optimism in regard to abilities is the field of leadership, or at least leaders' estimates of their own abilities. Politically, for instance, one might have doubts about the leadership qualities of one who claims to be a 'stable genius' yet lurches from policy mishap to mishap. The conceit of leadership is not just a quality that politicians have in excess. It is also to be found, especially, in the upper echelons of many organizations, especially when committing to major IT projects (see the study of Australian boards of directors that summarizes some of the reasons why this is the case by Carlton, 2018).

READ THIS!

- -

Read the article by Darryl Carlton from *The Conversation*, 'Lack of technical knowledge in leadership is a key reason why so many IT projects fail' at: https://study.sagepub.com/pm.

Summary
- -

We have addressed some issues that should be clarified when launching projects.

- In order to create a desired value, goals must be relatively unambiguous and the project must aim to contribute to organizationally intended goals and purpose. The connection to value creation and purpose is therefore essential for a project.
- Projects are instruments for achieving goals. Therefore, it is key to be aware of the distinction between the project's mission (the purpose of achievement) and the project's performance goals, as well as the relationship between them.
- Working on the business case, grounding the decision about materializing idea work as a project and cultivating objectives should all be part of starting up a project. These procedures must, of course, be adapted to the characteristics of a given project and its context.
- Projects, project assignments and the context of projects vary greatly and thus all mainstream project processes and practices must be adapted to fit the particular project.
- Delivery projects, for example, will follow a different logic and approach for those who will perform the assignment than would be the case in internal development projects or change projects. The size and complexity of the projects will also affect the nature and relevance of the different project processes.

Exercises
- -

1. Please account for the elements that need to be considered when an organization is considering starting a project. What can you say about limitations and feasibility?
2. What are the typical origins for new projects – do you recall the four categories?
3. What do we mean by the two terms 'sensemaking' and 'framing'? What are the function of these two processes?
4. What are the differences between: closed projects, semi-open projects, half-open projects and open projects? Why is it important to be able to distinguish between projects in this way? How would you approach a semi-open project?
5. How can we work with direction of value? What are the key tools at hand in this work?
6. What is a goal and how is a purpose different from a goal? Why are both goals and purposes important to project work?

7. What is goal complexity and how can we deal with that?
8. What are some key aspects of decision-making? What are common flaws in decision-making processes with which you are familiar? What do you know about over-optimism?

CASE STUDY

THERANOS: A VERY SECRET PROJECT
MEDHANIE GAIM, UNIVERSITY OF UMEÅ, SWEDEN

A 19-year-old Stanford drop-out founded Theranos, a consumer health technology and medical laboratory services company, in 2003 and was at once a sensation in Silicon Valley. Elizabeth Holmes was once considered the next Steve Jobs and 'fulfilled all our personal checkmarks for the mythological quirks of genius: she does not date, is a vegan, sleeps very little, quotes Jane Austen by heart, works nonstop, and dresses like Steve Jobs' (Daisey, 2015). Theranos took on the massive laboratory-diagnostic industry and envisioned 'disrupting' healthcare testing with the classic trifecta: cheaper, faster and better (Daisey, 2015). The promise was a technology 'that could provide results for nearly 200 tests with only a single, capsule-sized amount of blood drawn by a finger stick rather than a needle in the arm' (Johnson & Eunjung, 2015). On top of that, 'the company claimed that it could do the testing faster (in less than four hours) and cheaper than traditional labs'. It seemed that Theranos had solved an elusive innovation paradox: cutting costs while improving quality.

Holmes was at a point worth more than $4.5 billion and her mission was lofty: *One tiny drop changes everything* (Stewart, 2015). Ten years after its formation, Theranos began offering tests to the public by opening 42 blood-drawing wellness centres. Fast forward to September 2018, Theranos announced that it would cease operations and release its assets and remaining cash to creditors. In March of the same year, Holmes gave up her financial and voting control, returned shares of Theranos stock and was fined half a million dollars, while a California Judge ruled that trial for Holmes would start in July 2020. What happened?

Theranos was peculiar in many ways. For one it had a very impressive board of directors including a retired US Navy admiral, three former US cabinet secretaries, a US Marine Corps general and former senators, among others, rather than scientists or people with experience in the laboratory business (Pollack & Abelson, 2015). Holmes had full control of the firm and 'solidified that control in 2013 by arranging for the company to adopt a high-vote stock structure that gave her most of the votes' (Solomon, 2016). Whatever future moves the company made were up to her. Apart from the board, Theranos partnered with larger and famous companies and associated itself with politicians both for publicity, legitimacy and influence. Politicians who visited Theranos' lab included Joe Biden and John McCain (Crow & Samson, 2015). Holmes successfully lobbied for an Arizona law that allows people to get tests without a doctor's order (Carreyrou, 2015b). Moreover, Theranos had notable investors including Oracle's Larry Ellison and venture-capital firm Draper Fisher Jurvetson (Carreyrou, 2015c), and engaged in newsworthy projects such as Ebola and working with the military where there was interest in modifying its blood tests for a rugged battlefield environment. As a result, although privately held, Theranos and Holmes were in the public eye, and she amassed the accolades and riches. From media appearances to Ted Talks to tech salons, she has been a prominent presence and some believed her company could become the Google of healthcare testing (Daisey, 2015).

Regardless of the media hype and publicity, it was unclear how and whether Theranos' technology worked. Relatedly, regardless of Holmes' criticism of the diagnostics industries – which account for between 2% and 2.5% of health spending – as old-fashioned, slow, unpleasant, expensive, with huge error range, her new technology and how it worked was not exposed to the scientific community. The narrative, however, was that Theranos would change the industry by performing fast and less invasive blood tests (Harrison, 2015). With just a few drops of blood, dozens of diseases and conditions can reportedly be scanned for near instantaneously. The technology involved devices that automate and miniaturize more than 1000 laboratory tests, from routine blood work to advanced genetic analyses. 'The first, a so-called *nanotainer*, is a finger-prick vial into which a patient deposits just a few drops of blood. The second is a laboratory machine, known as an *Edison*, that can purportedly return accurate results from the nanotainers, which collect much less blood than nurses and doctors typically take from veins' (Crow, 2015). The technology promised early detection, accuracy and transparency, ultimately leading to personalized medicine.

In July 2015, the US FDA 'had approved the test for herpes simplex 1 virus and called the move a validation of the company's approach and technology' (Johnson, 2015). Although it was excellent news for Theranos, experts and scientists were sceptical of the technology as Theranos has not followed the norm of getting their new technology *peer reviewed*. One of the critics was John Ioannidis of Stanford University, who wrote a critique of Theranos' lack of transparency and what he called 'stealth research'. He said that although the FDA clearance is a 'step in the right direction' in which Theranos should be congratulated, he maintained that 'it is important also to have the full information available in the scientific community through peer-reviewed publications on methods and results, with access of other scientists to the raw data and protocols' (Johnson, 2015). The secrecy around their technology invited questions from sceptics. With scepticism from the scientific community and complaints from Theranos staff about how the technology was working, Theranos was facing external pressure to open up. Coupled with extensive coverage of Theranos in the *Wall Street Journal* and scientists questioning the technology, the impression that people had about the company was fading, which resulted in Theranos removing its 'few drops of blood' claim from its website (Goldman, 2015).

Inside Theranos, there was a struggle to turn the excitement over its technology into reality. After 12 years of development, Holmes' approach was far from proven. Unlike other technology start-ups, Theranos has always faced an extra burden because blood tests sometimes provide life-or-death answers (Carreyrou, 2015a). The disconnect between marketing and reality was important as the latter is inspected by inspectors in FDA and CMS alike, irrespective of the claims in the former (Crow & Samson, 2015). News and reports were coming out regarding the results from Theranos' lab. First, there was a problem with Edison; it worked for only 15 tests (less than 10%). There were also studies showing how Theranos' result 'differed enough from the two largest laboratory companies in the US that they could throw off doctors' medical decisions' (Carreyrou, 2016). When blood was drawn from a finger prick, Theranos reportedly needed to dilute those samples to use them in traditional lab equipment -- a controversial tactic that called into question the accuracy of Theranos' test results (Goldman, 2015). When tests are done with dilution, it means adulterating the sample and changing it in some fashion (Carreyrou, 2015a). Theranos ran tests on the Advia 1800 Clinical Chemistry System, 'by diluting small samples of blood pricked from patients' fingers to increase the samples' volume

(Continued)

to fit Advia's volume requirements, according to former employees' (Carreyrou, 2015a). Thus, regardless of the hysteria around Theranos, it was mostly relying on other firms' existing technology where needles were used to draw blood.

Confronted with these difficulties, Theranos engaged in numerous activities to cover up. In March 2014, a Theranos employee alleged to New York State's public-health lab that 'the company might have manipulated the proficiency-testing process' (Carreyrou, 2015b) and that it cherry-picked 'which data to report to regulators' (Johnson, 2015). In another case, a former employee of Theranos reported they had been instructed to deal with regulatory checks on its test results in a way that might amount to cheating (Moritz, 2015), alleged that the company underreported the rate at which the machines broke down during the study (Carreyrou, 2015d) and that some crucial parts of the devices, including polystyrene tips that drop into blood samples, were modified to improve their accuracy (Carreyrou, 2015b). Holmes defended Theranos and its technology on various occasions stating that the accusers were either stupid or the incumbent firms scared, or that those who reported discrepancies were using incorrect methods. In most cases, Holmes came out fighting against her critics, 'some of whom she casts as part of an old-fashioned medical elite, scared of the change she promises' (Crow, 2015).

Although Theranos, like Uber and Airbnb, run into regulatory hurdles, as a medical technology company, it 'bumped up against something else: the scientific method', which puts a premium on verification over the narrative. Theranos needed to present data showing that its technology worked (Solomon, 2016). Without peer-review, which is the norm, Theranos faced extraordinary scepticism about whether its technology worked, regardless of its insistent narrative that the technology might be copied, citing trade secrets for not being transparent, which experts described as highly unusual. Given the hype around the promised technology, although a private firm, Theranos was very much in the public eye. Theranos experimented and iterated, without external interference, lured talent with attractive stock options, shielded themselves from competitors and polished their product before going public. However, privacy also had a dark side as it gave a sense of false security as there are no requirements to disclose as in publicly traded firms (Moritz, 2015). In retrospect, so much about Theranos seems questionable: the secrecy, the board and the internal workings, for example. The focus on narrative and impression rather than verification, the media hype all overshadowed critical thinking. With lofty promises and association with giants in the industry and politics, people make an instant decision that everything is fine. In reality, things were far from fine.

QUESTIONS

1. What made Holmes' project goals complex?

2. If you were the project manager, what would you have done differently to ensure project success?

3. Given the resources at hand, what could Holmes have done differently to ensure project success?

Additional resources

For more thorough insight into ideas and processes, Carlsen et al.'s *Idea Work* (2012) is recommended. Decisions in organizations are an essential topic, whether the discussion is of decisions per se or decisions affecting projects more generally. Coldevin et al. (2019) is a continuation of the project that produced the *Idea Work* book. Dealing with two of the projects that contributed to that book but in more detail, there second is a contribution by Clegg and Burdon (2019) which builds on the Coldevin et al. (2019) approach to discuss a successful media project. Another useful resource is Karin and Nils Brunsson's book *Decisions* (2017), which has good insight into decision-making. For additional insight into how people think, judge and decide, Daniel Kahneman's (2012) book *Thinking Fast and Slow* is recommended.

Chapter Roadmap

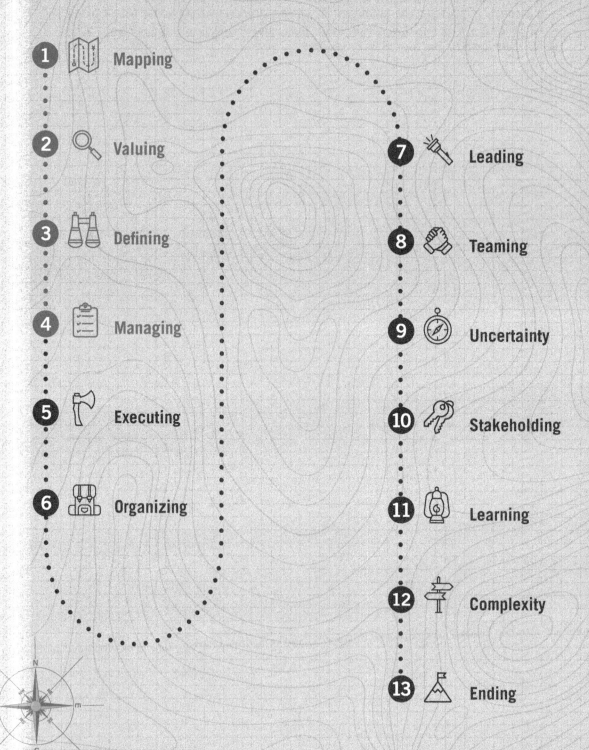

1. Mapping
2. Valuing
3. Defining
4. Managing
5. Executing
6. Organizing
7. Leading
8. Teaming
9. Uncertainty
10. Stakeholding
11. Learning
12. Complexity
13. Ending

4

Managing Projects

Learning objectives

After reading this chapter, you should be able to:

1 Understand the many levels of project management and how they relate to different execution models

2 Know the overall management framework of the project and its function

3 Understand and use devices for project planning

4 Be familiar with some widely used project management tools

5 Be familiar with key aspects of reporting and follow-up

Before you get started

Plans are only good intentions unless they immediately degenerate into hard work.

– Peter Drucker

Introduction

In this chapter, we will look at how projects are managed. We will stress project managing as an active process rather than project management as an abstract noun. Stressing the latter inclines you towards thinking that there a series of steps, stages or sequences to be followed religiously. By contrast, we think it far better to think of project planning, which takes us straight into acting, into doing – and doing so always in context. Our approach will be one that considers multi-level action. Plans are developed at different levels and decision points for the project's activities. These plans attempt to prescribe how the project's management and enactment should unfold but this management is exercised through project action, which may or may not follow management planning and follow-up procedures. Project practice and project planning do not necessarily coincide. Project management is much more a matter of processes than the unfolding of plans, which is one reason why, in complex projects, plans rarely come in on time, on budget and by design. Thinking of project processes rather than project plans and planning injects realism into prescription.

Managing projects

In order for an organization to create value and achieve its goals, it needs management. Managing refers to strategic, tactical and operational levels of performance. Strategy is the long-term vision for accomplishing the project; tactics are the improvised steps frequently taken to maintain the vision as events that threaten it arise. Different actions and behaviours at the operational level, perhaps doing things with different machines, depending on availability, or in different ways, are usually undertaken to avert threats. The strategic vision is frequently embedded in the **project charter** as the overall framework for the project.

> The **project charter** is a preliminary delineation of roles, responsibilities, scope, goals, objectives, constraints, outcomes, main stakeholders and uncertainties facing value creation and strategic execution.

> A sequential **phase-based** project locks in fixed phases in a project sequence at the outset.

> An **agile** project is completed in small *iterations*. Each iteration is reviewed and critiqued by the project team, including representatives of various stakeholders.

The project charter is a significant tool in project governance as it contributes to aligned expectations among the actors involved. It defines the authority of the project manager. It serves as a legitimate reference point for the future of the project. It is, however, an ideal document; it specifies how things will be done if everything goes to plan. In large-scale projects this cannot be guaranteed. We will discuss how processes for governance can be different depending on whether an execution strategy is chosen that is **phase-based** or more **agile**.

Whether phase-based or agile, projects will often go awry from plans such that improvisation will be necessary to get them back on track unless, alternatively, the opportunities inherent in being off-track afford innovative possibilities. As we will discuss later, projects often deviate from their planned track, due to uncertainty. Sometimes uncertainty opens up possibilities for improvement in project processes or deliverables. Improvisation occurs when the tension between learning and organizing is explored. Organizing may not go as intended in terms of the detailed project planning and that is when improvisation is valuable. Employees, learning on the job, are involved in improvisation that plays around with everyday patterns and, in context, changes them slightly. Improvisation is always based on an interplay between past, present and future, changing as events unfold or errors occur.

To enable learning and development, errors should be used as starting points for future improvisation. Improvisation is best practised as a team event, not a one-person show, where changes can be introduced under the radar. When teams improvise there is collective learning that relies on the feedback of others and their contribution to change (Carlsen et al., 2012).

There are many components included in the management of projects. In order to visualize these components, not least by positioning *managing projects* in a slightly broader context, Figure 4.1 is useful.

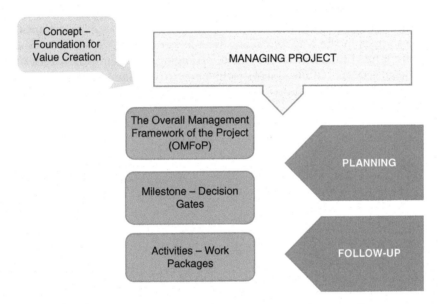

Figure 4.1   Managing of projects – central components and connections

Goals and strategies are key instruments in managing both the entire organization and the individual project. Based on goals and strategies, you can split up and integrate (coordinate) tasks, derive procedures for executing activities, allocating responsibilities and authority among those involved. The framework by which this is done is often referred to as corporate governance. **Corporate governance**, sometimes shortened to just governance, is a term that evolved from political science (Torfing, Sørensen, & Røiseland, 2019) and strategy (Clegg, Carter, Kornberger, & Schweitzer, 2019) to become a topic receiving much attention in both project management practice and research in recent years (Crawford et al., 2008; Müller & Lecoeuvre, 2014). Several forms of governance may be adopted (Pinto, 2014).

Corporate governance comprises the rules and practices governing relationships between managers and stakeholders, specifying forms of coordination, collaboration and control transparently and accountably in terms of responsibilities.

In the project literature, governance is treated as a more limited topic than in corporate governance in the strategy literature. Governance is understood as the way projects in an organization are directed and controlled, with managers being held accountable for conduct and performance (Müller, 2016, p. 14). Project governance may be aimed at the whole project from start-up to benefit realization or it may apply to a more extensive project portfolio or project programmes (see Chapter 12).

The interest in governance in and of projects has been increasing over the last decade, as the focus on benefits realization increased. The two are tightly coupled. The project owner strives to govern the project in such a manner that the project ends up with deliverables that have the potential of creating the aimed-for value. Having such an active owner, one that follows the project from beginning to end, has been seen as a key criterion for both *project management success* (i.e. execution of the project by the execution framework) and *project product success* (if the delivery is used in a desired manner).

Governance can provide strategic synergy effects as a combined effect of individual efforts, the integration of knowledge in permanent organizations and the interaction between different entities within the organization, creating a synergy that is higher than the impact of each factor uncombined. Project organizing typically uses available resources in the way that seems best as events and errors arise (Söderlund & Tell, 2009). While efficient systems enable managing, managing entails social *action* not just social *systems*. Often systems will have to be side-stepped, suspended or worked around by improvisations that are in the spirit of the project charter rather than its letter. A key issue is to design appropriate organizational project level management structures that fit the particularities of their organization's corporate governance principles without being hidebound by these.

EXTEND YOUR KNOWLEDGE

In an innovative recent paper by Müller, Drouin, and Sankaran (2019), 'Modeling organizational project management', you can learn about 22 organizational project management elements and how these can be modelled for managing in project-based organizations available at: https://study.sagepub.com/pm.

Management in any enterprise takes place in the tense relationship between control and trust (Das & Teng, 1998) in which managing plays out in practice. The two terms of control and trust are inversely related. The less trust is vested in an agent or agency the more that they are likely to be subject to formal controls of surveillance (Fox, 1974). The more an agent or agency is trusted then the less need will be perceived for formal **control**.

> **Control** involves some form of supervision or monitoring of the way employees and other agencies work on their tasks.

The opposite of control is autonomy and will be the degree of organizational trust that mediates the relationship between the two

Management will tend to use control by surveillance, based on aligning project members' expectations of how work tasks should be resolved, so goals can be achieved. Surveillance can be achieved in several ways: by direct oversight; by key performance indicators; by indirect oversight through forms of digitally mediated monitoring or through surveillance by the team members of each other.

Projects that are not subject to control by effective governance often end up failing to meet the goals for which they were established. One example of a megaproject that has failed on many fronts, but which was still continued, is Ethiopia's Kuraz sugar project, a project that failed in terms of its governance, its objectives of job generation, export earnings, sustainability and stakeholder responsibilities, despite much Chinese and government investment.

Picture 4.1   Sunset over Omo River valley in southern Ethiopia.

Source: Flickr/Rod Waddington

READ THIS!

Read the article by Kamski (2019) about the Kuraz sugar project titled 'Why Ethiopia's showcase sugar projects face huge challenges' at https://study.sagepub.com/pm.

Projects must be managed on several levels

Projects that are sub-organizational and internal to the organization are typically managed in such a way as to ensure alignment with the desired direction of the organization (Patanakul & Shenhar, 2012). Projects are tools for managing an organization in a direction desired to achieve goals but they also represent a form of *temporary decentralization* (Söderlund & Tell, 2012) when the project enjoys variable degrees of relative autonomy and decision-making authority from its organizational and superordinate components. The political realities of project managing can place project leaders in difficult situations. On the one hand, they are emissaries of the organization, seeking to secure control and compliance. On the other hand, they are involved in a project with some autonomy, especially if it is a change or innovation project, and their professional and disciplinary knowledge may well influence them to tolerate more ambiguity and uncertainty in project development than the formal controls allow. In such situations they have to chart a course between over-control that kills creativity and improvisation or under-control that threatens the project deliverables.

Managing takes place at several levels in projects (see Figure 4.2). The impact and extent of managing at the various levels may vary depending on the complexity and size of the project. It is common to stress project managing as falling into a three-level division (Müller, Turner, Andersen, Shao, & Kvalnes, 2016). The *strategic level* should clarify why the project is to be implemented, by ensuring a connection to the overall strategies, either of the project per se or the organization for which it is being conducted. Organizational project management resides at the strategic level and is the integration of all project management-related activities linking strategic decisions (where the project management-related activities are to be carried out) with business decisions (portfolio management and benefits realization) with their management (programme and project management) and their governance at both the strategic and project levels. At its most comprehensive organizational project management will include not only portfolio, programme and project management but also governance, projectification, benefits realization and organizational design. The *tactical level*, which is sometimes referred to as the intermediate or milestone level, will make clear what central contributions and expectations are associated with the project and what subsidiary goals require specifying as well as what the project controls will be. The *operational level*, which is sometimes referred to as the activity or detail level, will provide details that make it possible to specify how the various goals and plans will be achieved through planning and reorganizing of activities and resources allocated to project actions.

Figure 4.2   Managing projects at different levels

WATCH THIS!

Watch the Ted Talk by John Doerr in which he suggests that the secret of success is setting the right goals through a widely used system that focuses on objectives and key results at https://study.sagepub.com/pm.

Ownership in projects

All project management requires the use of power and authority relations in one form or another. In the context of a project, management is based on the assignment and ownership of the project. This means that there are project owners who have authority for managing the project and also power to act with prejudice against any or all of its participants if their sense of progress is unsatisfactory (Crawford et al., 2008). A project may have one or more owners. The management basis is usually simpler when there is only one client or owner and when the project is reasonably limited in scope and complexity. It becomes more complicated when there are more stakeholders involved, both in terms of multiple parties enacting the ownership role and multiple actors being involved in the project execution. Opportunities for power and authority conflicts, ambiguities and misunderstandings arise in these situations. However, to minimize these it is crucial to elucidate what the project should include and what should be omitted, by working with clarifications of concept and scope and sharing these widely.

IN PRACTICE

CANADIAN PPPS

It is often assumed that the more widely shared the concept and scope of a project, the more transparent it will be. Transparency, through clarification of the project concept and scope, is often seen as a sign of democratic accountability in terms of project stakeholders. In an article that addresses practices in PPPs (public–private partnerships), Valverde and Moore (2019) draw on socio-legal studies to analyse the documentary and other information practices that underpin and operationalize public governance in the PPP sector in Canada. Overall, they find that the information made public often presents projects out of context, as devoid of historical or comparative context, without reference to any broader regional or other plan, and when 'real' documents are made public, neither the content nor their framing enables effective openness, thus hindering accountability. The article, titled 'The performance of transparency in public–private infrastructure project governance: The politics of documentary practices', by Valverde and Moore (2019) *Urban Studies*, 56(4), 689–704), is available in the online resources at https://study.sagepub.com/pm

QUESTION

1. Based upon your reading of Valverde and Moore (2019), to what extent do you think conventional corporate governance practices minimize or amplify opportunities for power and authority conflicts, ambiguities and misunderstandings among stakeholders? Answer the question both in the context of Canadian PPPs and also as you are familiar with them from seeing PPPs reported.

The overall management framework of the project

The overall management framework of the project is presumed to be the basis for the project, which various concepts describe. The International Project Certification

System known as PRINCE2 uses the terms business plan and project proposals to refer to those premises that form the starting point or basis for project direction and execution. The use of the term 'basis' is somewhat misleading. Among other things, the foundation of the project is much broader than the business plan and concept. Different understandings and perspectives concerning the nature of project management and their differences flow from the reality that, in practice, projects are varied and are always processes that unfold in response to events as well as plans, often taking directions that either were not and indeed, sometimes could not, have been planned for.

The overall management framework of the project details the necessary clarifications for the temporary organization to be able to start planning and executing the project. The assessments made using potential success criteria, conceptualization and assessment of objectives, as described in the previous chapter, are vital elements.

Picture 4.2   Project: a bigger splash

Source: Anne Live Vaagaasar

The overall management framework of the project will both clarify and regulate the principles, stated by the client, to which the project execution strives to adhere. There are various supportive elements or project management tools useful for guiding this process. The following four project management tools are used in most projects (see Figure 4.3):

- Purpose, objectives and mission breakdown structure
- Benefit realization plan
- Stakeholder analysis
- Project charter

Mission Breakdown Structure (MBS)	Benefit Realization Plan (BRP)	Stakeholder Analysis (SA)	Project Charter
• Clarifying the project's contribution and outcome. • Systematization of potential impact targets, and clarification of goals of the project. • Contributions to delimitations.	• Description of expected gains. Identification of measures. • Organization and accountability as required. • Linked to the MBS – purpose.	• Identification of the project's stakeholders and their area of interest. • Assessment of their potential contribution. • Strategies to handle and follow up stakeholders.	• Agreement that provides the basis for management. • Regulates the distribution of responsibilities, the project framework and objectives.

Figure 4.3   Four project management tools for the overall project management framework (OPMF)

The effort expended in establishing and breaking down the structure of the mission into increments, such as the benefits realization plan, stakeholder analysis and project charter, are activities that can take place sequentially or in parallel. Often, doing these activities is an iterative process, one that always needs to be seen in context, with the realization that they can shape and influence each other (Figure 4.4). These documents are not set in stone but need to develop, aligned with process developments in the project. For example, using a mission break-down structure tool (Andersen, 2014) can clarify the significance of interfaces or overall goals that require the charter to be revised in order to work as an appropriate contract between the project and the principal.

Through work in interpreting and clarifying the project's purpose (mission) and potential value creation and gains, project goals, framework and sharing of responsibilities will also be more explicit. Mission breakdown structure is a tool for interpreting purpose while a benefit realization plan helps to prepare the client for the impact of the project.

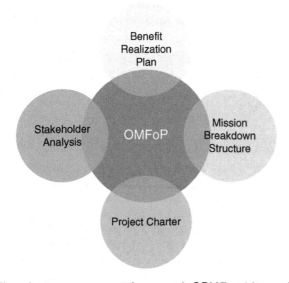

Figure 4.4   Overall project management framework OPMFand its main components

Purpose and goal as a basis for management by objectives

In Chapter 3, we elaborated on how purpose and objectives/goals in projects in the context of the processes of project concept development could be developed and evaluated. We then said that the outcome, or the *effect goal*, as it is sometimes called, describes the purpose of the project. The purpose refers to the value creation the client seeks to link to the success of the project process or product.

The goals of the project describe what the project is intended to deliver during its lifetime. Often the project framework is also defined in terms of goals. Most projects have goals related to the triple constraints of the Iron Triangle – these are goals that specify what qualities the delivery should have, what it will cost in terms of resources to produce it and how long it will take.

Purpose and goals are critical elements of the project's overall management framework because they form the basis for the widely used management by objectives approach in projects. The basic idea of management by objectives is that one must first work on developing appropriate goals. Once they are in place, one can determine the proper means for achieving these goals (Drucker, 1976). Projects often start by focusing on methods, on how to produce certain deliverables before sufficiently elaborating, clarifying and aligning expectations about what these should be. Focusing attention on discussions of goals can counteract this.

At the heart of management by objectives is that all goals for projects must be specified before activities are started. However, in many projects that are 'walking-in-the-fog projects' and 'Making-a-movie projects' (see Chapter 3) it is not possible or appropriate to specify all goals at the start of the project. Such projects are characterized by too much uncertainty. Instead, detailed goals, milestones and more general goals beyond the completion of the project can only be specified when uncertainty is reduced and available knowledge is more complete, if and when that occurs. Project managing in this way provides increased opportunity for learning along the way and capitalizing on opportunities to improvise innovations that open up in the execution of the project. In process, all projects should be learning projects, which will vary with the degree of indeterminacy and unknowns that arise during the process.

WHAT WOULD YOU DO?

BUILDING A NEW BUSINESS SCHOOL

A new dean of a business school took the opportunity of her honeymoon period to argue that the school needed a new building. She was correct; the present accommodation was dated, shabby and a rabbit warren of floors, offices and corridors that were not mutually accessible. As part of her initial period as a new dean she had held a number of strategic consultations with the faculty of the school, facilitated by a consultancy that specialized in strategic conversations. Emerging from the strategic conversation, which was influenced very much by the new dean's enthusiasm for design thinking, there came the idea of making the school a more integrated learning, teaching and research environment in which the different disciplines would work together developing solutions to business and social problems. Impressed by the open-plan offices and flexible layout of the consultant's offices, the dean started to align the case for a new building with the purpose of making learning, teaching and the research environment more integrated and collaborative, arguing that a different kind of building, with many collaborative spaces, would help facilitate this outcome. The dean was successful in persuading the vice chancellor that the new building was necessary. The goal now became the commission and completion of a new building. However, a strategic dilemma was faced. On the one hand, there was a tightly constrained site available close to the main university campus in the city. Building there would be convenient for students and staff to access as it was not far from public transport hubs. The downside was that the site was physically constrained, both by the size of the bloc of land and council regulations governing the height of the building. On the other hand, there was a secondary campus in a green-belt setting some 10 kilometres away from the site of the main campus which could be adapted to the needs of the business school at a considerably lower cost than the expense of a new build construction. The dean and the university faced a strategic dilemma. On the one hand, the purpose of a new building explicitly designed to facilitate collaborative and integrated approaches could be met on the constrained site. However, the building was only likely to be suitable for purpose in the short term because it could only just house the present staff of the school; further expansion would see it severely over crowded. The building that was available for renovation did not really meet the purpose, even if repurposed: it was designed more like a conventional high school than a building with the flexible features that the 'starchitect' who had been approached to design the new building promised. The latter served the dean's purpose far better; the former served the university's goal of most efficiently maintaining a portfolio of buildings, that is, at the lowest cost. The new build promised to be a distinctive design, was close to campus, limited in terms of further development but fit for the purpose that the new dean envisaged. The renovation of the old building was less fit for purpose. It was far from the campus; there was limited public transport available for to access it and it lacked the flexibility that the dean craved for the new approach. However, it was much more cost efficient and met the goal of the best use of the university's resources even if, in some respects, the building was less appropriate in terms of access, design for flexibility and integration.

QUESTION

1. The dean was pitching for the new build; the vice chancellor was having doubts. To resolve the situation, he calls you in as an expert consultant with experience in project management to collect evidence and weigh advice as to whether it was better to meet the goal of efficiency or the purpose of a distinctive style of business education. What would you do and how would you go about doing it?

Managing multiple goals

GOAL DIRECTED PROJECT MANAGEMENT

Goal-directed management in projects is done by starting with the overall objectives and breaking them into subsidiary goals and delimited goals (Andersen, Grude, & Haug, 2009). Before the project begins, an attempt will be made to set as many and as detailed goals as possible. Consider whether the overall goals should refer to multiple qualitatively different development paths. Should they balance in terms of people, systems and organizations (PSO)? Too much stress on any one without regard for its impact on the others can be highly dis-equilibrating for processes. While project managers are often good at focusing on systems and, to some extent, organizations, it is most often people that are overlooked. The task details get specified but they are not embedded in clear goals. Technical changes may well be achieved but cultural changes required to enact the goals are often overlooked. Goal Directed Project Management (GDPM) strives to balance technical and cultural objectives by developing people (educating, training, motivating), developing the organization (making changes to the organizational structure, improving the relationships between the staff members) and developing systems (technical solutions, routines and procedures). All need balancing in the dynamic and changing tensions of project managing.

According to its proponents, GDPM contributes to enhancing the clarity and direction of the project by providing a clear specification of what the project involves, highlighting the need for resources and constraints. Using it is supposed to build motivation and support for the project, clarifying what is in it and what is outside of its scope, establishing a basis for organization and obligations. There is emphasis on communicating results to top management, project owners and future end users as well as communicating with the project participants about tasks being undertaken.

WATCH THIS!

Watch the YouTube video from Cognology at https://study.sagepub.com/pm. on how you can establish goals, in particular SMART goals.

Who forms goals?

It is usually the top level in the client or commissioning organization hierarchy that determines who is responsible for what, establishing the goals of the project, with significant variations in practice as to how this is done. The principal is usually responsible for the overall objectives, while more detailed objectives are usually formulated in collaboration between the project organization and the permanent organization that is client or commisioner.

SMART GOALS

In SMART goals the acronym stands for:

- *Specific.* The goals should be expressed as accurately as possible so that one knows what they mean.
- *Measurable.* They should be formulated so that one can see if one has reached them or not, and then it must be possible for them to be verifiable.
- *Acceptable.* The goals must be rooted in those who are affected and those who will work to reach them.
- *Realistic.* Often some goals are something aspirational. Project goals should be credible and possible to attain. They must, therefore, be realistic.

- *Timed*. Objectives should also have a time frame so that there will be intensity in achieving the goals in time.

For SMART goals to contribute to the direction of the project and to gain support, they must be both understandable and appropriate. SMART goals are used extensively in many contexts of project management (Doran, 1981) but not without criticism and some degree of scepticism (Chamberlin, 2011). Often, strategic, long-term and more value-based goals are difficult to define and assess, being less specific and somewhat more flexible, especially if the level of commitment is high.

It may be appropriate to use SMART goals for some project management but they must be combined with commitments to longer-term goals, such as making the harbour 'less full of shit' (Pitsis, Clegg, Marosszeky, & Rura-Polley, 2003) which may not be exactly measurable but whose objective is crucial to goal formation. Measurability, as a fetish, can inhibit work to achieve excellent goals.

MOVING GOALS/TARGETS

Projects are planned and executed in a context characterized by uncertainty and unpredictable dynamics. When a project is innovative it is often unclear precisely what will be achieved. Project objectives often change along the way. TV shows such as *Grand Designs*, in their various national franchises, thrive on this happening: projects can change radically as a result of planning constraints, ground conditions, client preferences or any number of contingencies. Project work can be compared to 'shooting at moving targets' as goals change (Andersen, 2008). There may be several reasons why goals change during the project period:

- The client's views on desired delivery or what will be prioritized by the project's sub-deliveries changes.
- New insights into and knowledge about the project emerges among the project team members and actors in the permanent organization.
- The permanent organization and other stakeholders change their view of what is required.
- New demands and changes in the environment create a need for changes in the project.

Changing goals mostly relate to project level; rarely does one change the purpose unless the original goal proves impossible to achieve. The invasion of Iraq in 2003 by the US-led coalition failed to find any weapons of mass destruction, the original goal promulgated, as a necessary step to ensuring international peace and security. Consequently, the goals of the mission kept changing, from toppling the Saddam Hussein regime, to gaining access to oil reserves, to instilling democracy and installing markets in place of state monopoly. The outcome of a terrorist organization dedicated to the creation of an ISIS caliphate was never a goal although it was a major outcome. If changes in goals affect the purpose of the project, it is crucial that they be addressed at the overall level and also followed up with changes in objectives and framework. If changes occur at a milestone or at a detail level, consideration should be given to how these will lead to the need for changes and reorientations between the interim targets.

WHAT WOULD YOU DO?

- -

SMART AND STRETCHED GOALS

SMART goals, as outlined above, provide a concrete approach for formulating targets, and could be useful when dealing with short term targets in projects. However, to be able to deal with uncertainty, ambiguity, multiple stakeholders and development of new knowledge and conditions for the projects, a more flexible approach in projects often will be useful.

Stretch goals are a popular concept in many organizations and projects. The term stretch goals started to evolve as a concept in the 1990s (Kerr & Landauer, 2004) and indicates goals that you don't know how to reach. Collins and Porras (1994) in their international business best seller *Built to Last* introduced the term 'big, hairy, audacious goals'; subsequently, the idea of stretched goals became seen as equivalent to goals that are extremely novel, ambitious and difficult to reach. There is a belief that employees and managers will perform better if the goals are set so high that they are almost impossible to reach. Stretch goals might seem to be an attractive goal orientation, implying a project's freedom to govern the process as long as it focuses 'eyes on the prize'. However, Sitkin et.al. (2011) argue that positive outcomes for stretch goals only happen in the rare cases when there are sufficient slack resources combined with recent strong performance. Furthermore, stretch goals involve a contradiction between realism and imagination because they are almost impossible to achieve, implying a set of paradoxes managers and the project have to deal with (Cunha, Giustiniano, Rego, & Clegg, 2017).

Leaders applying stretch goals, on the understanding that these are big, hairy, audacious goals for projects, may trigger enthusiasm and motivation but rather more likely fear or apathy will result. In most projects when principals and project actors develop goals and work with goal setting, a combination of a flexible and concrete approach will be necessary. Companies such as Google, Apple and others have applied a combination of stretch and smart goals successfully, labelled as OKRs (Duhigg, 2016). OKRs is an abbreviation for Objectives and Key Results, where Objectives would be a qualitative statement of what you would like to achieve. Key Results would be metrics broken down for each Objective (Doerr, 2018a).

Interpreting a stretch goal as an elastic but reachable goal, applying stretch goals at the strategic level of project management, can be useful in combination with SMART goals at the tactical and operational level. Put simply, stretch goals should be applied as a foundation for developing smart goals. In projects, this normally implies stretch goals usually being defined at the strategic level, sometimes at the tactical level, while smart goals apply at both levels. For a stretch goal to be relevant in a project there has to be a certain degree of uncertainty and ambiguity about the project. The execution strategy chosen will matter: the more agile it is, the more likely will be the case that a stretch goal is relevant. The more autonomy a project has will see more inclination to use stretch goals. Those project organizations that lack experience in working with stretch goals should be aware of the need for developing competence and experience and willingness to learn, to be able to master them.

QUESTION

1.   Think of a project you know of, or are about to be involved with – could stretched and smart goals be useful here? Furthermore, in what way would you apply such goals?

PROCESS GOALS

As discussed in the previous chapter, the purpose of any project is the value creation that takes place during the actual project process. Development of higher core competence, more collaboration between different units of an organization and increased project competence are examples of such value creation. To ensure a goal-directed emphasis on these values, it is possible to establish *process goals* linked to the execution process, most often also to specific participants in the project. Many projects, change projects in particular, find process goals useful. Often it will be appropriate to establish process goals in parallel with the other objectives being formulated.

MISSION BREAKDOWN STRUCTURE

Purpose is usually placed at the top of a hierarchy of objectives while other goals are detailed as delegated operationalizations of its achievement. Often this is called a Mission Breakdown Structure (MBS) and is based on an underlying hierarchical structure where the element on top dictates what trickles down the hierarchy (Andersen, 2014). The design of an MBS starts by describing the overall effect one aims for – the purpose – and the prerequisites for reaching it by breaking the goals into increasingly limited areas and conditions (see Figure 4.5). The project objective forms the basis for interim goals, which in turn provide the basis for activities. For instance, a bricklayer may be laying a course of bricks; the architect sees these as integral to building a mosque, which the imam sees as a holy place in which to worship Allah.

Figure 4.5   Goal hierarchy as an approach

An MBS, like milestones, is an aid to visualizing what the project is about to achieve. It provides a useful representation of the relationship between goals at different levels. A Mission Breakdown Structure (MBS) will help to:

- Clarify the purpose of the project by clarifying and systematizing potential impact targets
- Achieve project objectives through clarifying expected results
- Separate goals that fall within and outside the project

On the latter point, the work on the Mission Breakdown Structure can expand opportunities both for the project itself and for the purposes that it should initially be managing. A Mission Breakdown Structure, through formulating goals, can help to provide the most accurate picture of what the project will create and contribute. Figure 4.6 shows an example of a project structure.

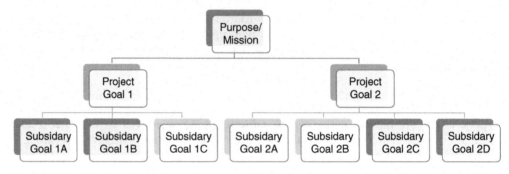

Figure 4.6 Mission Breakdown Structure, including an example on elements outside and inside the project's frame

It is usually the principal, represented by project owners, steering committee or others, that establishes the Mission Breakdown Structure (MBS). In many cases, the project manager will also contribute to this work. Work on the Mission Breakdown Structure helps to provide:

- A complete picture of the project's scope and direction
- A common understanding of the project's value-added contribution
- Clarity in project performance goals and subsidiary goals
- A common basis for the division of responsibility between project, permanent organization and possibly other stakeholders
- A picture of the whole that also provides the basis for what the project should not include but which must be solved by the permanent organization or others.

It is both demanding and complicated to work with the Mission Breakdown Structure (MBS). A future desired condition and clarity about what is required of subsidiary goals and actions is required (see Figure 4.7). Distinguishing between the different subsidiary goals and the conditions that belong together may be problematic. In concrete terms, topics should be formulated through common headings and boxes designed to create clarity in goals and communicate them to others. Often, it will be necessary to supplement these headings and boxes with explanations and clarifications while proposing solutions, distinguished by importance and responsibility.

Marketing strategy is approved
• Explanation: Implies that the marketing strategy for the new exhibition has been developed and accepted
• Requirements for solution: Must be adapted to the exhibition's purpose and target group. Concretized in terms of key measures and frameworks
• Responsibility: Project manager responsible for preparation, project owner approves
• Importance: Central to reaching target audience.

Figure 4.7   Example of a subsidiary goal (could also be a milestone) from a MBS for an art exhibition

The Mission Breakdown Structure is a particular tool that can be used in the early phase of the project. It is often perceived as useful to clarify and structure the various objectives of the project. It enables explication and elaboration of different interpretations and opinions, in order to create a shared understanding of the assignment and to determine the division of responsibility for different deliveries and processes between the permanent organization and the project.

Mission Breakdown Structure fits in many types of projects. Major projects, such as arranging an Olympics, smaller projects, such as organizing national atheletics meetings or arranging local championships, can use a Mission Breakdown Structure to clarify the purpose and thereby the value-creating element (Table 4.1).

Table 4.1   Examples of different project types and sizes, with a description of mission

Project	Development Project	Change Project	Delivery Project	Events Project
Size	*Large*	*Large*	*Large*	*Large*
	Development/building the Gardermobanen	NAV-reform, changed organization	Oslo Opera Building, construction of new building	Olympic Winter Games, Lillehammer 1994
		Mission		
	Better infrastructure in society through suitable transport source (train).	Better service that should lead to more people in work and activity, user-oriented and efficient management.	A future-oriented building that can engage a large and complex audience. A symbol building that gives national pride.	A good event that creates pride, national identity and increased sporting interest.
	Small	*Small*	*Small*	*Small*
	Development of a new ski wax type	New administrative processing routine	New booking system at hotel	Produce a short movie
		Mission		
	Better product range that contributes to increased profits.	More efficient administrative routines, which provide better services.	Implement an established system that provides more efficient booking and increased earnings.	A good artistic product that creates attention.

BENEFITS REALIZATION PLAN (BRP)

The Mission Breakdown Structure (MBS) helps highlight the value-added contribution of the project and clarifies the basis for the division of responsibility between key actors as a basis for realizing value. Value creation is the key with profit realization being the essential part of value creation. Therefore, MBS and Benefits Realization Plans are closely linked. Managing benefits realization enables clarity regarding the strategic relevance of each project, while also enabling increased effectiveness of project governance in a strategic form (Jenner, 2010; Serra & Kunc, 2015).

With value creation as a starting point for projects, attention is drawn to how the aimed for benefits can materialize. This issue is overlooked by many organizations. The process of benefits realization includes planning as organizing to harvest the **benefits**.

> **Benefits** are the positive effects that the client and other stakeholders seek.

> A **Benefit Realization Plan (BRP)** clarifies how benefits are measured, when they will be achieved, what measures must be taken and overall responsibilities and organizing.

To realize benefits, one must systematically maintain focus throughout the project's life cycle, in the form of good analyses at the forefront of the project and concrete plans for the follow-up of benefits during and after the project, through a **Benefit Realization Plan (BRP)** as in Table 4.2. The project owner has, in essence, responsibility for following up a project and realizing the expected benefits.

A Benefit Realization Plan should, at a minimum:

- Identify the expected benefits sought
- Specify the roles and responsibilities that will contribute to the realization of these benefits
- Specify measures and activities necessary to achieve these benefits
- Specify how and at what time measurement of gains should be performed
- Identify the resources required to assess the benefits

The permanent organization and other key stakeholders should engage in mission breakdown work. They are the ones who will be affected and who will be able to reap the benefits of the project. Involvement also contributes to stronger ownership of the project. The client/principal who is responsible for establishing the plan and the project owner, together with the managers of the permanent organization, will be heavily involved. In practice, it will often be a project manager who works on the plan on behalf of the client.

Table 4.2   Example on a Benefit Realisation Plan (BRP)

Benefit	Measures	Indicator	Outcome	Time Horizon	Responsible for benefit	Risk factor
Better procurement - annual savings> £ 100 000	For example: Measures to ensure that everyone is using systems.	System loyalty	Reduction in purchase prices.	100% system loyalty, within 5 years.	Finance Manager	> Reluctance to change. Close collaboration with business leader. > Not enough resources to cover roles that are needed. Leader Follow-up.

BRP is usually included in the management framework for the project and will be created before the project start-up. For many projects, it is better to wait to develop the Benefits Realization Plan until the planning phase has started. Because the assessments of potential benefits will change during the project period, it will often be adjusted as new insights are gained. With changes in the project, a changed profit potential will occur, as well as having an impact on other benefits sought. For projects characterized by a great deal of uncertainty, it is often unclear what potential gains the project can provide. It may be advisable to establish a BRP in parallel with the Mission Breakdown Structure and the project charter. The BRP is intended to be a tool contributing to the creation of value for the project; it should not be seen as a restraint.

READ THIS!

Read the article from *The Conversation* that you can access at the online resources on the dilemma between fulfilling base-load requirements for electricity generation and contributing to climate change and global warming. In such a context we should welcome megaprojects that are established to deliver energy through sustainable energy resources such as solar and wind power, shouldn't we? Well, it all depends on how the benefits are realized and shared as Zoe Cormack (2019) explains in connection with Africa's largest wind energy project and the biggest public–private investment in Kenyan history, the Lake Turkana Wind Power project at: https://study.sagepub.com/pm.

Analysing stakeholders

The project stakeholders are actors (that may include both human and other animals and habitats, as well as organizations) potentially or actually affected by project work and results (Mitchell, Agle, & Wood, 1997). Even before the project is planned and initiated, the client should identify potential stakeholders. For instance, in the Lake Turkana project the stakeholders included rival pastoralists that used the land where the project is situated for grazing and ceremonial purposes but were largely neglected by the project. It is advisable to prepare a stakeholder analysis as a systematic identification and assessment that will help the client to:

- Clarify the project stakeholders
- Identify topics or areas of interest associated with them
- Gauge the types of interest they may have
- Develop a strategy for managing them
- Assign responsibility for following up identified strategies

In an early phase, there is often considerable uncertainty associated with both the project's stakeholders and how their interests can affect the project. However, the stakeholder analysis is vital to clarify the project framework, the desired results and value creation. A stakeholder analysis prepared as a part of the overall project management framework will usually be further developed in connection with the planning and execution of the project. Read more about stakeholder analysis in Chapter 10.

IN PRACTICE

SQUATTING DIGITAL NOMADS

Stakeholders may be internal or external to the project organization. Internal stakeholders can be managed through the many processes we have already discussed. External stakeholders are more problematic, especially as they are formed by community organizations or social movement organizations with an interest in the project. The interest will not always be positive from the project point of view. New infrastructure projects, mining ventures or mega-events do not always meet with approval from the communities that experience their effects. Disaffected or anxious communities often collectively organize as stakeholders opposed to the project. Sometimes social movements will mobilize to speak up on behalf of an ecology or creature seen to be under threat from the project.

What can projects do? First, they can define key performance indicators (KPIs) that are inclusive of stakeholder concerns. For instance, they may institute ecology or community as part of their KPIs. Project champions can be nominated to ensure that these interests are represented at project leadership level. Professionals, such as communications graduates, can be employed to liaise with communities and make sure that their concerns are aired and represented to the project. Other professionals, such as ecologists, can act as consultants to monitor crucial aspects of the environment and the project's impact on them.

As well as redefining KPIs and employing people with competencies to manage these external stakeholder relations, projects can exercise initiatives through social media. Organizations can use social media to engage with audiences (Brodie et al., 2013). Social media enhances the bond between the consumer and the organization by using user-generated content to achieve goals. In project organizations, these will likely be oriented towards specific audiences whose potential impact on the progress of the project can be significant.

A recent paper (Ninan, et al., 2019) on the use of branding in a major metro project in India discusses the strategic use of social media to achieve governmentality of external stakeholders. In the project being researched – a major metro network in an Indian city – social media was used to create dominant, complementary, persuasive and legitimate discourses that sought to incorporate various communities into the sensemaking of the project team. The effect on the community of the creation of a positive brand image for the project was to build support and create community advocates. Not only was the project community influenced but also the project team, in large part recruited from the broader community. Project team effects included enhanced job perceptions, an ability to attract talent, as well as the production of project team advocates. Team members saw the megaproject as socially committed, safe, clean, prestigious and iconic for the city.

QUESTION

1. You are project managing a large urban redevelopment project in a European city. You have read about the metro project in India and want to use social media for governmentality as was the case reported there. However, there is a section of the site that is presently occupied by anarcho-syndicalist squatters who are digital nomads, with great social media skills. They have set up a contra-project website that questions everything that the project is doing; they seem to be winning the social media war as they are so media savvy. What would you do to try and reassert governmentality?

Devices for project management

THE PROJECT CHARTER

Once it is decided that a project will be implemented, as a project manager you will define the content, scope and responsibility of the project in a document that is often referred to as a project charter (other terms include project contract, project description, assignment, project plan or project directive). There is great variety in how this document is compiled and what tools are used.

There are variations as to what the document contains and there are also differences in how legally formal and binding the document will be. Somewhat simplified, we can say that the project charter is the contract between *the principal* (usually a project owner) and *the executor*. This applies to either the executor as a project team, represented through the project manager as well as where there are several parties involved.

The content of a project charter often varies according to the scale and complexity of the project but usually contains the following elements, as shown in Figure 4.8.

PROJECT CHARTER	
Name of the project	*The project name can be important, so if a suitable name is clear, use it. Apply the project mandate as the summary document that defines project frameworks and managing foundation. Benefit realization plan, mission breakdown structure and stakeholder analysis, together with the conceptual framework, will be a key basis for drawing up the mandate. Elements from these will be included in the document basis and can also be included as attachments.*
Background	*Explain the context of the project and what suggested the need for it. Preferably, describe how this fits into the organization's strategy. State whether the project will be a stand-alone activity to fulfil a particular business requirement or whether it is part of a bigger programme.*
Purpose of the project	*Why this project? The Purpose will provide a brief overview of the purpose of the project and provide enough of a description to complete the following sections.*
Project goals and main deliveries	*Explain what the project is trying to achieve by stating its objectives, which should be measurable and defined in terms of the projects major deliverables and benefits expected.*
Principal (Project Owner)	*Identify which organization(s) are the client/principal and who is the project owner, i.e. the one who safeguards the client's responsibilities and interests in connection with the project.*
Performer – Project Manager	*When clarified, identify who is the project's day-to-day manager and responsible for carrying out the project within the given framework.*
Framework	*Specify the framework conditions that apply to the project. These involve the time period, the resource boundaries and the most important quality requirements.*
Constraints	*Describe the known constraints of the project, e.g. there may be constraints on the amount of resources available to the project or the location of the project team. Include possible limitations related to what the project should not include, but which could be close or relevant for the project's purpose.*

Figure 4.8 Project charter

As part of the overall project management framework, the Mission Breakdown Structure (MBS), Benefits Realization Plan (BRP) and Stakeholder Analysis (SA) will be included as attachments or additional elements for a project charter.

A formal document such as the project charter will most often start with the *project name*. Admittedly, this is not the most significant element in the charter but at the same time a project name frames what the project entails. Names are better if they are catchy, relatively short and preferably convey some purposes associated with the project.

Project owners' responsibilities will be visible in the charter. The project charter should also specify the responsible executive unit in the project; often it will also designate the project manager; it may be useful in explaining the background for the project and gaining a clearer understanding of the project foundations (Engwall, 2003). If there are other projects (on going or completed) that may affect the focal project, include information on these. If the stakeholder analysis is adequately prepared, it may be included here. Purpose and project goals could be clarified and operationalized, for example through the use of the Mission Breakdown Structure.

Limited time and resources characterize projects, so it is vital that the project charter clarifies the framework that applies to the project regarding time, resources and quality criteria. The deadline is critical. For certain projects, the deadline is absolute – for example, an art exhibition or any other temporally specific event – while for others it may be more flexible, yet still remain necessary to set a time frame for the project that should appear in the project charter.

For many projects, the features and qualities of the delivery should be defined. For large projects, these are regulated through their agreements and contracts. Although it is often appropriate to specify such quality requirements and criteria in a separate specification, they can be outlined, at the overall level, in the charter. Projects also need resources, such as the number of working hours that should be dedicated to the project and the economic resources committed. Resources include all investments, equipment and other things that the project must be able to allocate to carry out delivery. Since the charter is set up before the project starts, it will often be uncertain what type and how much in the way of resources one might need. However, it is useful to try and clarify this in the charter. We will elaborate the issues of economy and resources later in the chapter.

The purpose of the project charter is thus to clarify and agree:

- What the project is about
- What is to be done
- Which persons and organizational units have what significant responsibilities
- The framework that applies to the project
- The objectives of the project and aimed for value creation

Working with the overall management framework for the project

Often the project owner and other key actors in the client organization establish the actual charter. In many cases, the project manager is already considered or selected, and if so will be involved. In internal projects, most key roles are involved in work on the Mission Breakdown Structure, as well as with the project charter and also the BRP. The BRP contributes both to commitment and an improved decision-making basis for the project. These tools are useful in communicating with stakeholders to gain input and to anchor the project. Doing so helps in creating project understanding, acceptance and commitment.

High uncertainty is often related to projects, as many projects are very complex. Establishing charters, including a framework that is appropriate at the outset and will retain validity over time, is a demanding exercise. Before starting a large project, it may, therefore, be beneficial to create a pre-project or pilot exercise to try and explicate needs, the probability of achievement and value creation. Doing so can reduce uncertainty while revealing what will be valid premises for the project's execution. Pre-projects are used in many different project types.

The overall management framework for the project needs preparation before planning and detailing the project. Planning contributes new perspectives on the management framework with the processes being connected and shaping each other. The framework may become perceived as inappropriate as plans start to take shape – if there is need to, change it, if feasible. The framework should evolve in dialogue between the project manager and the client. Governance may require review of the frames in use. Where new knowledge is created, changing framework conditions in the project as it is under way, the project charter will also need revising and adjusting, perhaps re-aligning the overall management framework. Projects operate in complex and changing environments and must be open to change.

Planning in projects

US President Dwight D. Eisenhower, who was responsible for the planning and execution of the Allied invasion of Europe in June 1944, drawing on his experience in conflict, became well known for the statement that 'plans are nothing, but planning is everything'. The quotation emphasizes that although plans cannot always be followed, the planning process is incredibly valuable in preparing for what is going to happen. The thoughts and reflections one can develop through a planning process, increase understanding and commitment to the assignment and help in obtaining success. However, execution seldom happens as one planned and so plans often must be revised. A piece of military wisdom by the nineteenth-century Prussian military commander Helmuth van Moltke in 1880 was that, at the first encounter with an enemy's main force, the best plan rapidly changes (Hughes, 1995). Plans can be aids only if we have realistic expectations of their validity over time and we must recognize the need to revise them as events and facts change.

Planning as a phenomenon and process

Organizations' planning is usually linked to strategy through strategic plans and action plans. There is considerable variation in the scope and detail of the plans of different organizations. For example, in the public sector over the last 30 years, significant emphasis has been placed on planning programmes of operation as a means of ensuring targeted work. The extent to which such planning has worked purposefully as well as whether due consideration has been given to the unintended consequences of such planning is open to question (Christensen & Lægreid, 2007). Planning always takes place in the face of uncertainties, deriving from socio-material conditions that are unknown in advance. Uncertainty only takes shape when we strive to act, to project, in the world (Beauregard, 2018). Scheduling helps reduce insecurity in achieving goals in uncertain conditions. There are likely to be so many unknown factors that will potentially affect an outcome on any major project so that, while it is necessary to plan, there must always be room for improvisation and change.

When operating with considerable uncertainty, planning should be seen as a process always capable of being reformulated, although there are several approaches that try to reduce the likelihood of surprises and the necessity to deviate from the plan. One that has been strongly feted is Deming's (2000) PDCA (plan, do, check, act) cycle, implying that in a planning process, a plan is being implemented, then its effects and appropriateness are examined before correcting the execution and then planning further from the experience and adaptations that are necessary. This is a somewhat mechanical formulation; it suggests that planning, doing, checking and acting are easily decomposable elements in managing a project with a linear sequentially. In practice, these stages are likely to be entangled, overlapping and unclear rather than smooth linear stages. Still, simple formulae have their attraction, even in complexity; in such circumstances attraction can sometimes prove fatal as the plan is overwhelmed by events and uncertainties.

Picture 4.3   Plans for direction

Source: Torgeir Skyttermoen

WATCH THIS!

Watch the video with the lecture by Deniz Sasal that is available at: https://study.sagepub.com/pm. After having read the previous material, watching this may be useful revision.

The purpose of planning in projects

Scheduling projects facilitates common understanding of a task, how it can be approached, as well as its most critical processes. Planning facilitates collaboration and helps project participants to become acquainted with each other and with the assignment as they meet and work together, creating a greater sense of shared sensemaking and differences in their understanding of the project. Planning can generate enthusiasm, a valuable force in a project. Planning processes also provide participants with an opportunity to collaborate and learn about different styles of work and assumptions framing project managing. Insight into what is to be undertaken and its sequencing can develop as well as more accurate forecasting of whether the project will be completed within the duration of the project. The need for key persons in the permanent organization, as well as identification of key project team members and the potential for bottlenecks to arise in terms of resource allocation (the scarcities), can be clarified.

The distribution of tasks and responsibilities between the client (the permanent organization), the project organization and other participants can be initially allocated in planning. Initial planning exercises may help build more resilient teams because they become familiar with each other at the outset and can arrive at a shared understanding of what they anticipate as the likely stress points and events that might make the project vulnerable, risk its outcomes or, more positively, provide opportunities. Such opportunities may be best for the project; however, they can just as easily be best for particular organizational interests being represented in the project. The project can as easily be a battleground as a place of harmony. As projects evolve, the project strategy and the strategies of those organizations represented in the project will very likely diverge. Tactics that are less than collegial can begin to multiply, such as project partners seeking variation orders from the contract as a result of unanticipated contingencies that they claim they have had to deal with. Conversely, at its best and most productive, long-term planning can clarify why it is crucial to initiate the project processes.

EXTEND YOUR KNOWLEDGE

Uncertainty and risk are project planning's nemesis. Read the article by Browning (2019), 'Planning, tracking, and reducing a complex project's value at risk', which presents a methodology for planning and tracking cost, schedule and technical performance (or quality) in terms of a project's key value attributes and threats to them available at: https://study.sagepub.com/pm.

The arguments for the planning of projects mentioned above assume that the overall management framework of the project has been adequately clarified as a basis for focusing attention on the milestone and activity level. Planning contributes to delivery within the framework provided for the project (Andersen, 2008). Planning in projects often facilitates execution, in particular with respect to the time and resource constraints provided. Plans make it easier to allocate and distribute resources; they legitimate decisions already made although, when resources are scarce, the tendency is to use what is available wherever it is needed.

A mechanism for coordinating resource allocation is scheduling, where activities are outlined on a time axis (Ballard & Seibold, 2003). Scheduling seeks to avoid critical resources being booked for multiple purposes at the same time. The development of plans and rules can be done both to coordinate efforts at the start of a project and later, as part of the ongoing development process in the project. The process of doing this scheduling is often interactive, where those involved develop common understanding and agreement as to how to cooperate, for example, in projects such as crisis teams and film projects (Bechky & Okhuysen, 2011). In the interaction needed to develop plans and rules, disagreements and ambiguities will often become apparent that will subsequently need to be negotiated to an accord.

IN PRACTICE

PROJECT SESAM

Project SESAM – an excellent example of a name for a project. In a project that was to establish a service management system for Norsk Data, the project name, Service System for Administration and Management, created the SESAM acronym in an analogy with 'open sesame', the magical phrase in the story 'Ali Baba and the forty thieves'. (In the story of *One Thousand and One Nights* the command 'open sesame' opens up the mouth of a cave in which the forty thieves have hidden treasure.) SESAM is described as 'an Integration Platform using a unique Datahub approach for collecting, connecting and sharing data. With SESAM, data can quickly be re-purposed, re-structured and used, without changing the systems that own the original data. In this way all the valuable data within your company will be available for the whole organization. SESAM redefines enterprise integration to be data orientated, highly agile and now. This empowers the people who need the data to act fast and derive value. SESAM is the first integration platform to care about your data' (https://sesam.io/index.html#whysesam).

QUESTION

1. Your task is to approach a major infrastructure project involving a consortium of engineering and construction companies and to try and advise them to switch to a project tool such as SESAM. Openness is its virtue, as the name describes. What do you think would be the advantages that you would stress in favour of its adoption? Are there any disadvantages that you perceive?

Opportunities and limitations in the project planning process

There are several factors to consider when planning. The amount of time, data and other information at your disposal is of great importance. Too little of these will weaken the basis of the planning process. The same applies to the extent to which you have support tools, such as planning and calculation methods as well as IT functions. Contextual relationships such as rules, laws and regulations, standards and procedures will also matter; sometimes they will be helpful, other times they limit possibilities. Competence among those involved and the norms and cultures of the organizations characterizing other key actors will also play a role in the planning process. All of these elements will, to a greater or lesser extent, provide guidance as to how the project plan will play out at different levels.

In the planning process, you need to be aware of some traps and errors that are often encountered. Not taking into account potential adversities, as mentioned above, may cause weak planning processes and unsatisfactory plans. There is always a variable level of appropriate detail and a purposeful time horizon in planning.

As uncertainty is always high, many of the tasks that must be undertaken in order to reach a goal will cause changes and adjustments to the plans in the future.

Planning should never be a fetish, involving planning for planning's sake. Doing this, one is likely to spend an inordinate amount of time and energy planning unimportant things that can be known in detail while overlooking more important things that cannot. Some studies show that detailed planning of the entire project at start-up has adverse effects on the project because it gives rise to excessive control and expectations of predictability in execution (Fitzgerald, 1996; (Serrador & Turner, 2013).

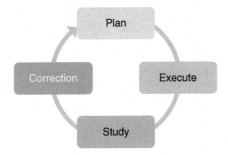

Figure 4.9   Planning as process

When planning, having an overall plan that provides a comprehensive and overall picture of the most critical conditions in the project helps provide a *gestalt* for the project (Figure 4.9). The plan should be easy to communicate. Additionally, you can have operational-level plans that provide direction for the activities to be performed, when they are to be performed as well as the sequence of activities. Detailed plans are developed based on the overall plan. As far as possible, one should plan the entire project at the overall level at the start of the project. However, detail planning should be limited to planning only the near future, as it is unrealistic to plan in detail what will happen way ahead. The higher the uncertainty within and around the project, the less appropriate it is to plan for a more extended period. Large projects usually have a hierarchy of detailed plans that follow the work package structure (see page 133). Have plans in the project that are tailored to activities, so that there are plenty of plans to provide direction for activities at the level of detail as well as plans at several levels that assume different functions.

In Chapter 3, we saw some limitations on our ability to make proper assessments of how irrationality can affect the project basis. The same restrictions also apply to the planning process. As humans, we are often optimistic when planning (Kahneman, 2012). We assume we can do more than we actually are able to achieve. We are time optimists and believe that we will finish the tasks in less time than is the case. We rarely consider *over-optimism*. The same goes for projects. We tend to make plans that are not based on learning from past experiences but from desired estimates of the future (Flyvbjerg, 2006a), which is often a future perfect (Pitsis, Clegg, Marosszeky, et al., 2003). Such forecasts, once one has decided on a date for a milestone or completion of the project, become even more optimistic in their assessments of the completion date (Andersen, 2008). This provides a meaningful explanation as to why so many projects, particularly large ones, are not completed within the time and cost frames. We need to know these conditions and try to adjust for the planning.

Planning of projects, particularly those that have an infrastructure impact, always has to take into account regulatory frameworks. These are the frameworks that government develops to guide developments that are planned. Innovation has to occur in projects that are aligned with planning frameworks but oftentimes these frameworks can inhibit innovation. One area where this is especially evident is in the provision of green infrastructure. The expertise required to create substantive and deliverable green infrastructure priorities may extend beyond the capacity of planners and needs to involve engineers, transport consultants, architects and emergency services personnel as collaborators as well as those who set design standards. One of the biggest barriers to innovative planning in this way, as you can explore online, may well be the conservatism of the planning profession in regard to new technologies and disruption to embedded practices.

READ THIS!

Read the online article from Connie Stemmie (2019) to learn about key issues of planning fallacy and advice on how to avoid the planning fallacy at: https://study.sagepub.com/pm.

Read the article from *The Conversation* by Matthews, Ambry, Baker and Byrne (2016) that discusses 'Here's how green infrastructure can easily be added to the urban planning toolkit' at: https://study.sagepub.com/pm.

Project management tools

Project management tools are many and varied. As a project manager you will be overwhelmed not only by 'solutions providers' seeking to sell software to you but also the sheer number and jargon intensity of widely used tools that are part of the project management toolbox. We shall review some of the more common tools.

MILESTONE PLANNING

When the overall objectives and framework are sufficiently clear, the next level of planning and preparation is to establish subsidiary goals or *steps* towards the main goal. Such steps or control stations are usually called milestones in the project context. Research has shown that milestones are positive organizational mechanisms. They motivate cooperation between the actors because they are often regarded as attractive. Participants want to help realize them. They help coordinate work effort and set the execution rate for the processes by dividing up processes into smaller units (Eisenhardt & Tabrizi, 1995). They can also contribute to increased strategic capability by providing an overview image for communicating and reflecting in the project (Andersen et al., 2009).

In order to ensure progression and necessary clarifications along the way towards the project goal, it is useful to divide the project into different parts. It is necessary both because projects are often large and long-lasting so that one cannot easily comprehend the whole and because the process is characterized by uncertainty in terms of available information about the future. Milestones give the work direction. Often, a project has several phases and sub-processes that differ from one another such that it may be appropriate to split it into several subsidiary goals and processes. The subsidiary goals can often be applied as significant milestones for the execution process. A **milestone** is expressed as a *condition* to be achieved, usually by a specified date, with specific prerequisites attached to it.

In agile projects, milestones are different. They are temporal milestones, structured with regularity, that specify the pace of the project but do not say anything about the results/ conditions to be achieved at each milestone.

A **milestone** is a checkpoint where concrete conditions denote whether a specific stage has been achieved in the project.

For example, in a software development project, typically one should produce a functionality (or more) each 30 days (i.e. within a sprint of 30 days).

EXTEND YOUR KNOWLEDGE

Read an article that researches the moderating influence of two project management approaches on the relationship between project complexity and project dynamism for project outcomes by Butler, Vijayasarathy, and Roberts (2019), 'Managing software development projects for success: Aligning plan- and agility-based approaches to project complexity and project dynamism' available at: https://study.sagepub.com/pm.

The milestone formulation must be understandable to the project team and other stakeholders. Conditions, achieved or not, are the benchmark for achieving the milestone (Andersen et al., 2009). A specific description of the conditions that must be fulfilled for the milestone to be met is necessary. These may be:

- Methods and measurements that make it possible to evaluate the results according to specified criteria
- Procedures or prior work that must be carried out according to specific criteria
- Decisions that must be made before proceeding

These conditions provide the basis for the establishment of various activities that must be carried out in order for the milestone to be achieved. A milestone should be solution neutral by not specifying what activities will be performed to reach it (Andersen et al., 2009). The achievement of particular tasks can form appropriate milestones.

A milestone plan is an overall and comprehensive plan for the project that will provide clarity as to the direction and scope of the project. It shows what the project must achieve during the project period in terms of a logical sequence. Figure 4.10 is a visual representation of this.

Figure 4.10   Visualization of a milestone plan

Proper milestone plans are usually set up without considering what activities must be done to reach the various milestones. A good milestone plan should be easy to understand and communicate to the permanent organization. Establishing a good milestone can be difficult. It requires both insight into the subject areas with which the project is going to work, logical sense, some creativity and also some experience with project work.

Picture 4.4 Creating a path

WATCH THIS!

Watch the video by Mike Clayton (2017) on how to define good milestones and milestone planning at: https://study.sagepub.com/pm.

The nature and complexity of the project determine what a milestone plan should consist of and the length of time between milestones. Shorter time between milestones leads to the increased pace of the project and thus increased propulsion. Motivation is considered to be a significant reason for this (Eisenhardt & Tabrizi, 1995). There is no one best way for determining how many milestones a project should have or how they should be structured.

RESULT PATH

A result path is a group or series of milestones that are related to each other, concerning the same types of deliverables (Andersen et al., 2009). Different result paths can be realized in parallel. The number of result paths that are appropriate depends on the complexity and the subject of the project but, as a rule of thumb, if there are more than five, it is often difficult to maintain an overview. By giving each path a name, themes can be communicated. It can be difficult to establish appropriate result paths that communicate the types of results the project will achieve, something especially relevant when the project has several subsidiary goals to be completed.

IN PRACTICE

BUILDING A HOUSE

Building a house is an example of a milestone plan conceived as a result path. There will be different milestones and subsidiary goals. For building a house, you will need permits, applications and other administrative procedures, which could be separated into a path. Furthermore, the building work itself will consist of various deliverables, as the basic work to be completed, raw construction of the house and so on. Getting the roof on and making the house weatherproof is often a key milestone – it enables interior work to begin. The inside work of the housebuilding project contains some elements of carpentry work, technical facilities and more, which can also be separated into a result path. Using this approach divides your milestone plan for the house-building project into separate result paths and work on this in parallel, at the same time enabling you to see the interconnections and communicate this to the actors involved. Figure 4.11 provides an illustration of how this might be done.

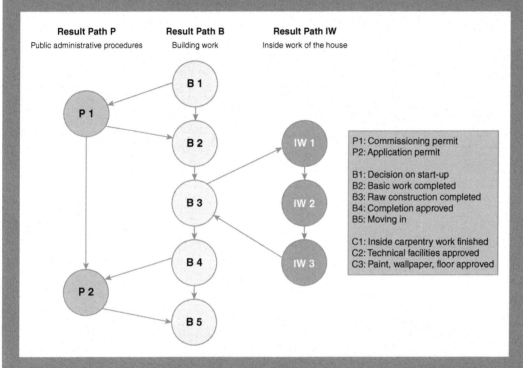

Figure 4.11   Milestone plan as a result path visualization – building a house

QUESTION

1.   You are planning to build a new house: what results path would you devise?

To obtain a comprehensive picture of the project, establish result paths. For a project to enable future benefit realization, a project culture that stresses learning and innovation is necessary (Pitsis, Clegg, Marton, & Thekla, 2003). The project culture might be outlined in terms of processes for which the project assumes responsibility, with the charter needing adjustment as the project unfolds, or it might be designed in terms of the unique processes that the project will follow (Clegg et al., 2002). The milestones' result paths and Mission Breakdown Structure should be linked and comparable, clarifying what the principal and potentially other stakeholders must do to achieve project value. Multiple result paths can be structured via subprojects, where each subproject safeguards one result path each.

EXTEND YOUR KNOWLEDGE

The article by McGivern, Dopson, Ferlie, Fischer, Fitzgerald, Ledger, and Bennett (2018), 'The silent politics of temporal work: A case study of a management consultancy project to redesign public health care', describes how unarticulated, covert and political temporal inter-dynamics produce expedient provisional temporal settlements, which resolve conflict in the short term, while perpetuating it in the longer run available at: https://study.sagepub.com/pm.

WHAT WOULD YOU DO?

Project milestones mark projection – moving forward – by achieving specific events in time and on budget in a number of different ways:

- The completion of any highly significant task, event, occurrence or decision
- Reaching a significant phase in the project life cycle
- Achieving a specific 'percentage complete' for any given amount of work
- The production of one or more planned project or process deliverables
- The usage of a specific amount of funding, the passage of a specific amount of time, or the utilization of a specific number of resource hours
- Above all, they mark any significant circumstance or event unique to a given project.

Strategically milestones define project priorities, monitor progress and script the story for the project. What you need to be able to do is ask yourself a series of questions about the importance of a task, decision or event and its impact, if it is not met on time. If a milestone is not met then there should be analysis of the failure to meet it, an analysis of its impact on the project and a plan of action for rectification. As you have been studying project management in order to become a better wedding planner you are well aware of the importance of milestones.

QUESTION

1. For one of the weddings that you are planning, with 400 guests, everything was going well until you heard that the wedding venue had burnt down in a 3.00 a.m. fire (these fires are often arson for insurance purposes) and you have two weeks to resolve the milestone in a context in which there is no other venue available with that capacity. What would you do to cover the venue contingency and what hurdles would you envisage?

ACTIVITY PLANNING

Milestones, goals and sub-goals are tools that enable detailed planning. Detailed planning of the individual activities starts by identifying all the activities that must be performed to reach a milestone. Often, some of the activities belong together in work packages. For example, work tasks associated with conducting a market analysis in a project may include more activities, which can be coordinated in a work package. The time dimension must be considered when determining the level of detail in the identification of activities for each milestone. For milestones with a long time horizon, it is often unlikely that you will be able to identify and plan all the activities, other than main ones. A rule of thumb when it comes to planning activities is not to plan and organize work on individual activities before it is needed (Eisenhardt & Tabrizi, 1995).

Key questions: What persons and entities are affected by the activity and how should they be involved? Who has the primary responsibility for the activity? How will the work effort be assessed? For most projects the hours required are planned and a plan made for who will perform the activity and when it should be executed. Separate work packages need to be managed so that their progress is aligned so as to determine whether an activity has been performed satisfactorily. Also, are the resources to do the job available? (See Table 4.3.)

Table 4.3 Detail planning. Example of a work package for a milestone

Work package for milestone MP6 when mapping tool is decided					
No.	Task	Hour	Responible	Performer	Notice
MP6. 1.A	Create requirements specification	10	Hans	Hans, Andrine	Made on the basis of previous projects
MP6. 1.B	Prepare which alternative tools are relevant	8	Hans	Andrine, Jens, Hans	Problably only Google Form and SurveyMonkey relevant
MP6. 1.C	Examine details about functionalities	6	Hans	Hans, Jens	Based on requirement specification
MP6. 1.x	Etc.	xx	xx	xx	xx

PROJECT BREAKDOWN – WORK BREAKDOWN STRUCTURE (WBS)

WBS stands for Work Breakdown Structure, sometimes known as Project Breakdown Structure (PBS), a method for hierarchically sharing project work at different levels and groupings in a 'top-down' approach where the number of levels depends on the need for detailing. The project target is the top level which is broken down into subprojects which, at a lower level, comprise work packages and activities.

WBS indicates two critical issues: what tasks are included in the project and what relationships exist between these tasks (structure). This implies that tasks and work not included in WBS are not included in the project.

Table 4.4 Different levels for WBS levels of projects, purpose and time horizon

Level	Term	Purpose	Time Horizon
1	**Programme**	Business strategy	3–10 years
2	**Project**	Measurable result	9–18 months
3	**Subproject**	Partial result	6–12 months

(Continued)

Table 4.4 (Continued)

Level	Term	Purpose	Time Horizon
4	**Work package**	Milestone	1–3 months
5	**Activity**	Measurable result	1–3 weeks
6	**Work task**	A greater effort	Days
7	**Job**	Short-term work effort	Hours

The time horizons in the Project Management Institute (PMI) table (4.4) are roughly based on technical construction projects. The table illustrates that it is common to depict a project breakdown structure as upside down. In established projects, WBS can help create a sound basis for follow-up and control through formulating an information base tailored to each organizational level. In the work of the Mission Breakdown Structure (MBS), the same logic is based, and many of the elements used in milestone planning and later detailed planning use much the same structure. WBS is widely used in project work, with PMI being one of the organizations that recommend implementing WBS logic in its models and descriptions of project management. WBS is relatively strict in its structure; many of the procedures used in project management are different variants of WBS, although they are not always as strictly defined. Bear in mind that these techniques are premised on experiential data, custom and practice.

GANTT CHARTS

The Gantt chart was developed over a hundred years ago by H. L. Gantt to provide unskilled construction team members with a visualization of what they should work with for the next planning period. The Gantt chart is thus a visualization of a project plan and progress where milestones and activities are specified on a time axis, with the status of the work symbolized (Figure 4.12).

Gantt charts are classic and widely used project planning tools, based on a WBS approach. They are easy to understand and are thus communicable to individuals not heavily involved in daily project work. They do not reveal dependency relationships between various activities clearly, however. What they do illustrate is:

- Division in part-time jobs
- Time allocation for the part-time jobs and the project in total
- Sub-job placement in time
- Necessary resources for each of the sub-jobs and the entire project

NETWORK PLANS

Network planning entails scheduling interdependent activities. The point is to determine which activities affect the duration of the project. There are mainly two networking methods or models that have been dominant, the so-called **Critical Path Method (CPM)** and **Program Evaluation and Review Technique (PERT)**. CPM is a network planning model based on deterministic time estimates.

PERT uses stochastic estimation, implying that even if one cannot predict when

> **CPM** is activity-oriented, focused on relationships between time and cost, based on a complete list of activities, timings, interdependence and endpoints for delivery.

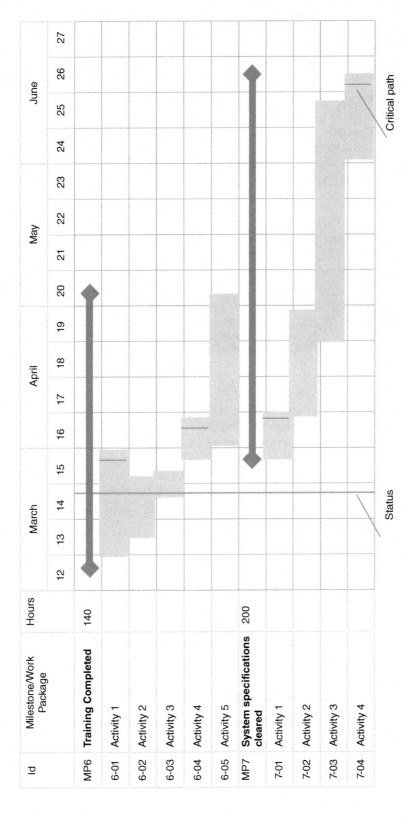

Figure 4.12 Brief presentation of a Gantt diagram

> **PERT** is a network planning model that aims to keep track of execution time by calculating uncertainty and probability.

an event will occur, one still has a known probability that it will occur. PERT is event-oriented and assumes that the duration of the different activities follows a statistical distribution with known expectations and variations (between optimistic and pessimistic duration). This calculation provides the basis for finding the critical path; that is, the one most likely to be completed within the deadline, while handling uncertainty. Quick and efficient execution is a common purpose for both CPM and PERT, with the differences being that CPM operates with predetermined projections for the duration of activity, while PERT has a more open approach and attempts to calculate the likely duration of the activity.

WATCH THIS!
- -
Watch the video tutorial about PERT from Kauser Wise (2016) to learn about how to construct the project network, find the expected duration, the variance of each activity, the critical path and expected project completion time at: https://www.youtube.com/watch?v=WrAf6zdteXI.

Both models can be visualized through two well-known activity network models – Activity on Arch (AOA) and Activity on Node (AON) models. They are used for engineering projects in buildings and installations, for example, to calculate the time of completion of partial deliveries or milestones. There is plenty of software to perform calculations with these models but all the activities to be performed and what resources are required needs to be known in advance. We do not investigate how this is done but refer to Figure 4.13, which illustrates that for AOA, the arrow is the activity, whereas, in AON, the node is an activity.

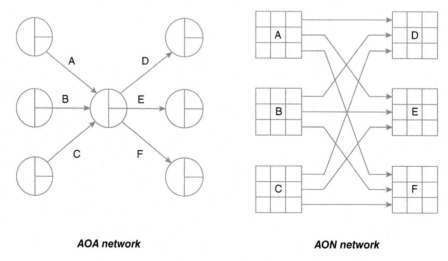

AOA network   *AON network*

Figure 4.13 Two activity networks models – AOA and AON network

The nodes contain certain conditions and descriptions such as activity number, earliest and latest start time, earliest and last calculated end time. These, with the exception of numbering, are defined in terms of duration. The arrows illustrate the order between them. See Maylor (2010, pp. 135–143), for example, for a more detailed description of how these are built and function.

WATCH THIS!

Watch the video from Engineer4Free (2014) on activity planning, how to use forward and backward passes to determine project duration and critical path at: https://study.sagepub.com/pm.

Such network models aim to help calculate activity and resource needs in order to reach the delivery or milestone within the deadline and they are a useful aid in more technical construction projects where the framework is reasonably defined. They provide the basis for systematic planning of activities linked to critical factors (milestones). The network plans created in this way are used where there is a considerable degree of unpredictability, complexity and the need for a clear framework (for example, in major construction projects). They may be useful in some complex projects as a basis for efficient management of resources and for explicating particular constraints.

Network planning can also contribute to increased control and overview when it comes to costs because it can provide better total and sub-budgeting, as well as optimization of time spent and costs. Network plans have a clear focus on time and resource assessments. In projects where such calculations form a central part of the project, relatively technical models are used to monitor and correct progress, based on network plans (Larson & Gray, 2011). Both AON and AOA are widely used in project management. AON is increasingly becoming more prevalent than AOA which, together with Gantt charts, provide better visualization of models in practice.

WATCH THIS!

Watch the video from Engieers4Free (2014) to learn about how to determine the earliest start and earliest finish of activities. Learn about slack and float in project planning. Engineer4Free (2014) 'Determine the Early Start (ES) and Early Finish (EF) of activities in a PDM network diagram', at: https://study.sagepub.com/pm.

Digital project management tools

Spreadsheets are the most widely used digital platform in projects, at least in small and medium-sized projects. For their purposes, they work well, and you should not underestimate the importance of having simple overviews that are sufficiently detailed.

Developments within IT have contributed to a variety of newer and different digital platforms. For more technical building and construction projects, customized projects are often used for project execution. For network models like CPM and PERT, as described above, there is separate software used to calculate and schedule activities and resource usage. Many large companies that extensively use projects also have developed programs for project planning and execution. Several free software tools are available for download from the web. When choosing digital devices, reflect on the ability to look forward, for example in the form of forecasts, making sure follow-up is not only of a reversible nature.

Digital project management tools aid managing of projects; they are not autonomous managing agents. Consider what does a specific digital tool require, regarding sales, training and organizational customization? Don't underestimate these aspects; many organizations do. The result often becomes frustrated employees who spend more time and energy using the tool than gaining from using the device. As a rule, if adopting such a tool, one should deploy significant resources in their implementation.

Reporting and follow-up in projects

Project management entails:

1. Establishing an appropriate framework, goals and plans for managing
2. Monitoring whether the project evolvement is aligned with framework, goals and plans
3. Putting the project back on track when it deviates from the planned course and goals and keeping track of project resources

Follow-up is a central process necessary to ensure that the project is on track. Follow-up should primarily focus on improvements and the future. Often, it is too retrospective. Mikkelsen and Riis (2017b) argue for future follow-up by:

- Taking a look at the project's final situation and the effects
- Keeping an eye on developments and events outside the project, but still relevant to the project objective
- Reporting expected final situation versus goal-determined final situation
- Applying outside-in thinking, i.e. focus on consistency, value and suitability for users

Follow-up in projects can be done in many ways: standardized reports delivered at specified times with a subsequent schedule for non-conformance management are typical. In addition, more or less systematic follow-up conversations with project members, affected users, stakeholders and others could contribute to follow-up.

REPORTING

The key idea of reporting is that decision-makers at different levels capture signals from the project that require analysis of the situation and possible correction of the development. For the reports to have some value, the deviations described must be followed up with corrective measures. Reports that are not used have no value.

Reporting must, therefore, be relevant, with routines for using the information. In short, reporting is a description of what has happened, what is the current situation, with possible reasons to explain why it is as it is, while follow-up responds to reports by assessing and implementing measures. A follow-up report may contain the following items:

- Where should we have been according to the plans?
- Where are we – what's the status?
- What is the deviation (if anything)?
- What consequences can the deviation have?
- What actions are proposed to avoid these consequences?

When projects experience deviations or when deadlines, cost estimates or other constraints are not met, the first step should not be to increase reporting requirements. As a rule, there is a need to enquire into the underlying causes of the perceived deviations. Depending on the type of deviation from the plans that have either occurred or you are aware is about to happen, you may take different measures to change this. It depends on the level at which the deviation applies, which we will focus on by following up on milestone and activity levels, respectively.

Reporting is crucial. At the same time, one must balance how extensive, detailed and time-consuming reporting is going to be with how the time and energy to be expended can best be used elsewhere in the project. In an ongoing measure used in the public sector, reporting is highlighted as one of the largest 'time thieves'. Project team members seldom regard reporting as particularly joyful and interesting, even if the report ends up taking them only a short time to do. Motivation is critical for reporting regularly and accurately. For the individual project, reporting provides increased opportunity to succeed by being up to date in knowing what's going on. For the organization, it provides the opportunity to learn across projects. Reporting can be facilitated through the use of templates that frame reporting requirements and inputting directly through digital tools, such as tablets, phones and other devices.

FOLLOW-UP AT THE MILESTONE LEVEL

Milestone plans can be communicated to the permanent organization and to other stakeholders, so that project owners and key stakeholders can understand and approve the milestone plan, making further project work more straightforward. Milestones often have financial consequences. Therefore, the better they are formulated in a clear and unambiguous manner the less likelihood that the parties will meet in a courtroom. An example of a clear wording may be '30% of the contract amount is due when the integration test is approved.'

The project manager is usually responsible for following up the milestones and reporting to project owners. Milestone reporting is aggregated from reporting at the operational level. The milestone report describes whether the milestones have been achieved, if anything is noteworthy in the accomplishment of work thus far, as well as whether the milestones need adjusting, given progress and events, either in time, quality or otherwise. The project manager's analysis of achievements vis-à-vis the current milestones may well become the basis for subsequent negotiation between project partners, even litigation.

The milestones report should be concise: if there are deviations, an account reporting the dialogue between the project manager and the overall authority (project owner) should be provided. If deviations occur at the milestone level, these can affect the achievement of the project's goals at all levels. Deviations usually lead to decisions on adjustments and changes to the milestones. Deviations do not necessarily imply negative consequences but may also involve the discovery of new opportunities for the project's objectives and potential effects.

WHAT WOULD YOU DO?

Back to the project SESAM again (see p. 126) and the infrastructure project including engineering and construction companies. They decided to implement the SESAM as their platform. This means six different companies will now start implementing SESAM within a three-month period.

QUESTION

1. Can you define three key milestones for this implementation process? How would you follow up on the progress of the work across these six companies?

FOLLOW-UP AT THE OPERATIONAL LEVEL

When checking and following up activities on a more detailed level, reporting should be easy for those doing it. Issues must be described clearly; if at all possible, responsibilities allocated. Reporting and follow-up at this detail level provides the basis for follow-up at the milestone level. Such reporting should consider the status of work achieved and any problems related to further progress. Common follow-up criteria in an activity report include resource usage, consumption and remaining needs: What are the accrued costs at a given time? How do these compare with budgeted costs for working hours and other resources? Has progress on completed activities or work done been as was planned? Any deviations from the plan as stated in the report can now be handled. First, assess any need for adjustments and changes and particular challenges or problems to be faced, detailing cause, consistency and assessments.

The report forms the basis for dialogue with the project team and other stakeholders. If there are significant deviations from the plan, possible causes and consequences need accounting. Subsequent delays in planned progress can arise when accounting is not realistic. Time optimism, overestimation of staff skills and capacity, availability of external labour and underestimation of the complexity of the work may all cause delays and adjustments. Reports require follow-up to reduce risks and correct progress and adjustment of plans at an early stage. Reports also require action: Why did the deviations occur? What is their significance? Do they need corrective measures?

Projects do not always come in as agreed on time and budget parameters. Accumulated costs over time can easily escalate beyond those predicted. Planning of costs entailed and their allocation to various elements of the work being undertaken is vital. Monitor the costs incurred (actual costs) in relation to the processes/activities performed. When calculating the earned value, the percentage of work performed of the total planned work (often set as hourly work) will be calculated for the project. Earned value can also be determined in relation to milestones achieved. By comparing the planned value with earned value, you can track categories of deviations, as shown in Table 4.5.

Table 4.5   Different types of deviation, what they show and how they are calculated

Deviation type	Shows	Calculates	Positive numbers	Negative numbers
Cost deviation	The difference between the values created and what the work done has cost	Earned value minus real costs	The performance goes better than planned	The performance goes worse than planned
Progress deviation	The difference between when work is planned and when it is really done	Earned value minus planned value	The work is performed faster than planned	The work is performed slower than planned
Budget deviation	The difference between what work done has cost and what it had budgeted would cost	Planned value minus real costs	The performance has cost less than budgeted	The performance has cost more than budgeted

To get a simple picture of the relationship between progress and costs, calculate the critical index using the following formula:

(actual work/planned work) × (budgeted costs/actual costs) = critical index

To look at the development of the project, you can also calculate the *cost performance index*. It is an index that indicates the relationship between earned value and real cost and helps to calculate what the final cost of the project is by taking the status of the ratio between earned value and real costs. Furthermore, you can calculate the *schedule performance index*, which shows whether the project deliverables are ready according to schedule, considering the relationship between the earned and planned value.

Indices can indicate how the future might be and should not be taken too seriously; they are just indicative and not a picture of what the future will be – how could they be? The more uncertainty in and around the project, the more critical it is to treat indices with caution. The above methods are good tools for monitoring project development on time and costs. As they require detailed planning, they are best suited to projects where uncertainty is relatively low.

COMPREHENSIVE FOLLOW-UP OF SUCCESS FACTORS

Follow-up must also take place on parameters other than time and cost. Doing this can be achieved by working with critical success factors directing attention to many parallel elements broader than primarily time and cost. Below is a summary of ten critical success factors (Pinto & Slevin, 1988):

1. The purpose of the project
2. Project support from management
3. Project schedule
4. The project's interaction with the users

5. Project team
6. Technical task solution
7. Acceptance of customer
8. Reporting and feedback
9. Communication
10. Troubleshooting

If the project manages all these areas, the likelihood of reaching the project goals increases.

Milestones established and met keep projects on target. Today, there is no more important target to meet than those needed for long-term planning to avoid dangerous climate change. As you will see quoted in the online feature below, if there is no plan in place for the long term, you cannot have any criteria for good decision-making in the present.

READ THIS!

Read the article by Scott Thwaites and John Ferraro (2016) in *The Conversation* titled '2050 climate targets: Nations are playing the long game in fighting global warming', in which various action plans and milestones established by different governments are evaluated in terms of their planning for low-emission targets at: https://study.sagepub.com/pm.

INPUT–PROCESS–OUTPUT MODELS FOR FOLLOW-UP

In terms of overall follow-up, *input–process–output models* (Hackman & Wageman, 2005) are sometimes mentioned. The EFQM model, developed by the European Foundation for Quality Management (EFQM) together with leading European companies and the EU, is a case in point. The relationship between input factors, processes and results in the project are stressed in such models. Input factors, processes and results may vary in different phases of the project. Each project phase can be analysed using such models as can the period between two critical milestones.

Summary

After reading this chapter, you should be able to:

- Understand the many levels of project management and realize that these differ when using a sequential phase-based execution strategy that locks in fixed phases in a project sequence at the outset from agile projects carried out through small iterations. Each iteration is reviewed and critiqued by the project team, including representatives of various stakeholders.
- Know the overall management framework of the project which will clarify and regulate the principles stated by the client to which project execution strives to adhere. There are various supportive elements or project management tools useful for guiding this process. The following four project management tools are used in most projects: Purpose, Objectives and Mission Breakdown Structure; Benefit Realization Plan; Stakeholder Analysis and the Project Charter.

- Appreciate the challenges of managing multiple goals, be able to reflect on what is a good goal, goal hierarchy and purpose. Also, understand the issue of moving goals and process goals.
- Understand the purpose of planning processes, the key aspects of planning and know about commonly used devices for project planning: milestones; Gantt charts, network plans, work breakdown structures. You should be able to reflect on what you gain from milestone planning and when it is appropriate to plan in milestones and use activity planning.
- Understand the value and key aspects of follow-up on different levels, know about the key aspects of follow-up reports, as well as the multiple dimensions of success to consider when following up a project.

Exercises

1. Account briefly for what we mean by phase-based and agile execution strategy.
2. What can you say about the many levels of managing projects? What is the Mission Breakdown Structure and how does it relate to goals? How can we work to make goals at the lowest level measurable? What do you think about stretching goals?
3. What is the function of a project charter? What are the key aspects to be clarified and agreed on through the process of establishing the project charter?
4. Can you describe key aspects of the network plan, the Gantt chart and the milestone plan?
5. What is the key difference between activity planning and milestone planning?
6. Can you account for the key aspects of the benefit realization process and why this is so important? What do you understand to be the Benefit Realization Plan?
7. What is the difference between mere reporting and follow-up? How are these two processes related? What are key issues to follow up on?
8. How many of the ten critical success factors can you remember? Which one do you consider most important and why?

CASE STUDY

NOBULIB

The student group at a business school (named NoBuLiB – 'There's No Business Like this Business') is given the responsibility for the whole arrangement of a conference on a professional topic. This includes everything from the programme content to practical elements such as food, transportation and marketing. Based on your recently gained insight on project management, you are given the role of project manager for the conference.

THE CONFERENCE TRADITION

Every second year there is an academic conference that circulates among various academic institutions. Depending on the programme and the arrangements made for the conference, it

(Continued)

normally lasts for between two and four days. Participants at the conference vary from below 100 to almost 500, depending on the event arrangement, marketing and theme for the conference. Despite it being an event shared among academic institutions, there is no knowledge base, central organization or sharing of experiences between the various organizers for the conference.

THIS CONFERENCE

This year's theme for the conference is titled 'Learning for or from better ways of organizing in a world of uncertainty'. There should be some keynote speakers, parallel sessions with various themes, a conference dinner and a welcome event. Included in the organizing of the conference is accommodation, transportation and other elements.

The university is organized in autonomous units and the business school will be the sponsor for the event. The head of the business school at the university will be the principal for the event. Nevertheless, she and the rest of the leader group are busy with other things and wants the student group to deal with the arrangement of the conference. Decisions related to the content for the conference will be taken care of by the professional staff but the project team (consisting of students) are expected to manage its staging.

The head of the business school will be the project owner. In the preliminary project assignment, the student group (NoBuLiB) receives some instructions, which you now have been handed as the potential project manager.

QUESTIONS

This is the project assignment you receive:

> At this stage of the project, you are not expected to include organizing of the project or the professional content of the programme. Neither should you consider details of the length of the conference or the number of participants. However, the ambition at this stage of the project is a conference for three days with about 300 participants.

What would be your response, if you were the project manager for this project?

Remember to focus on the essential elements in the project assignment from the head of the business school. The conference should be dealt with as a project. At this early stage, still 13 months before the date set for the conference, we want you to work out some suggestions for the following elements:

1. Based on common knowledge and your insight into the field and topic of project management, develop a draft of:

   a. A Mission Breakdown Structure, or at least a sketch consisting of essential elements

   b. A Benefits Realization Plan, again, at least some preliminary elements

   c. A list of stakeholders

2. Furthermore, founded on the above sketches of overall managerial project elements, identify some decision gates, formulate these as milestones and provide a milestone plan, primarily including a result-path structure.

3. Consider some other essential elements you regard as vital for the project to be a success.

Additional resources

Bos-de Vos, Volker, and Wamelink (2019) focus on value capture by managing risk in projects. Broadening the focus to development projects, Paul's (2019) lessons of success in managing development programmes is also very useful while, looking at environmental projects, Goggin et al. (2019) provide a useful account of how to incorporate social dimensions into planning, managing and evaluating environmental projects.

Chapter Roadmap

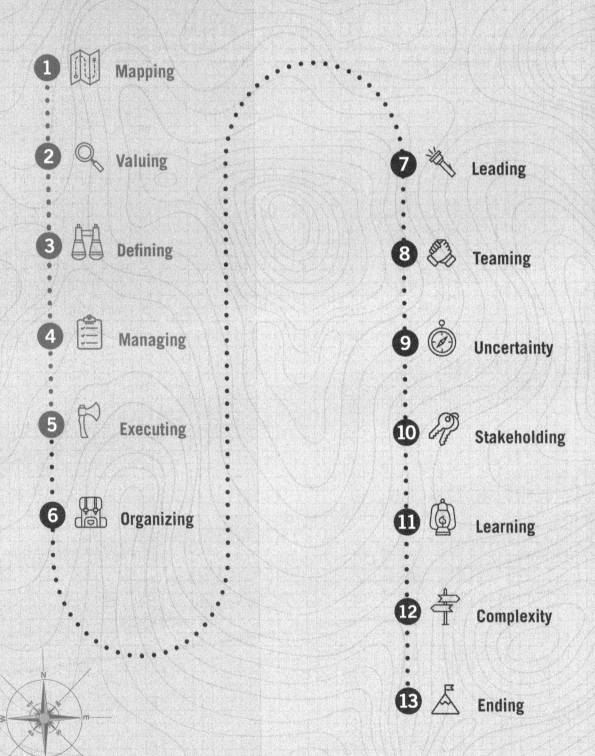

1. Mapping
2. Valuing
3. Defining
4. Managing
5. Executing
6. Organizing
7. Leading
8. Teaming
9. Uncertainty
10. Stakeholding
11. Learning
12. Complexity
13. Ending

5

Executing Projects

Learning objectives

After reading this chapter, you should understand:

1 That project execution's/design and planning has no one best strategy

2 Project type, scope and complexity, together with project competence and project objectives, provide guidelines for the development of strategy

3 Sequential phase-based execution strategies are not the only game in town, although in terms of waterfall and milestone approaches, they have been the most frequently used in the past

4 The strengths and weaknesses of more agile approaches to project management

5 The importance of appropriate contracting for the project in question

Before you get started

Make everything as simple as possible, but not simpler.

– Albert Einstein

Introduction

A common characteristic of project management is that it is a field in which execution strategies are structured and planned. Know your project! You need to understand your project and the context within which it will be executed to select the most relevant project strategy. Project type, scope and complexity, together with project competence and project objectives, provide guidelines for the development of strategy.

Many of the tools and processes of project management were intially developed to deal with technical projects (mainly concerning infrastructure) that were subsequently transferred and applied to other types of projects. As a result of being largely based in engineering expertise rather 'technical' and instrumental ways of dealing with projects were commonly used, with variable success. We encountered some of these approaches in the previous chapter in the shape of traditional project management tools. They are largely based on the assumption that there will be a sequential phase-based execution strategy. In this chapter the more contemporary approach of agile execution strategies will be the primary focus. From these more recent perspectives, rather than seek to formulate an a priori planned sequence of phases, irrespective of context and contingencies, the execution strategy is decided by whatever is best for the purpose of the project, along with competence in project methods (project maturity). Often this will involve combinations of phase-based execution with more agile approaches and methods to implement project execution.

Two specific facts to consider about value creation in general and profit are significant. First, the potential economic profit a project is intended to achieve is based on tight margins and an ideal of tight control of an open system that events can always complicate, be they political, environmental, economic or social. Second, in terms of the project's projected profit cycle almost all of the profit that accrues to the investment will occur after the project has ended. Nevertheless, during any projects' lifetime, the economy of the project will be a major consideration as a project that runs at a loss can be a career breaker for a project management team. Project budgets and management of their economy are in many ways similar to the management of non-project-based organizations in that investors expect a return on their investment. In projects in which the project is intended to be completed with a limited temporality involving subcontractors and many other participants outside the organization, contracts between the project principal and contributors, project owners and managers have to deal with far less routine than the majority of non-project-based organizations. Project execution strategies are a way of attempting to superimpose routines on uncertainties, known and unknown, that might threaten the project process.

Project execution strategies

As presented in Chapter 3, projects can be categorized in terms of the degree of clarity of goals and methods. In many projects it is neither possible nor appropriate to specify all goals at the start of the project if only because their accomplishment will be characterized by considerable uncertainty – uncertainty about events arising and uncertainty about how to deal with these unknowns, requiring different strategies for execution of a project. Having a framework of models guiding execution helps to frame communication internally within the project and also externally with relevant stakeholders.

These models contribute to structural frames supporting standardization and predictability in processes of project delivery and can simplify the execution of projects by:

- Guiding execution and incorporating a common terminology
- Providing insight into what will be done for those involved in the various steps
- Supporting planning work to ensure that there is a common understanding among the project participants of the unfolding project processes
- Contributing to project decision-making's appropriate communication, coordination and control, furthering temporal progress

The phase model, which is still widespread, has been the most widely used execution model. Over time, however, a wider range of execution strategies has emerged (see Figure 5.1) characterized by a higher degree of iterative rather than sequential logic (see, for example, a good review in Forsberg, Mooz, & Cotterman, 1996). Sequential execution is still vital for managing projects but in the past 20 years, more agile execution models that allow greater space for contingent iteration have become widespread.

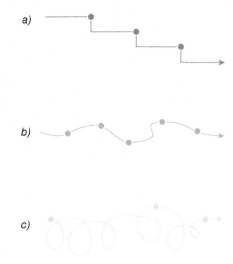

Figure 5.1   Three different execution strategies

Sequential strategy phases

It is common to split a project into different phases. How many phases are chosen varies with the conditions that are emphasized and the perspective taken in approaching the project. Roughly speaking, in terms of a broad ideal type, we can say that a project goes through the phases shown in Figure 5.2.

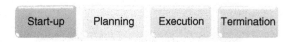

Start-up   Planning   Execution   Termination

Figure 5.2   Phases in a project

There is a common view of project realities that they can be mastered by a relentless causal logic in which one thing should prescriptively lead to the achievement of the rational next thing in a prescribed process of sequencing and temporality. There are two variants of this basic phase-based model that we will consider next: a 'waterfall' and a 'milestone' model. Both are phase-based models, with the former emphasizing streamlined sequential execution while the latter establishes a model in which projected milestones have to be achieved by specified dates.

WATCH THIS!

Watch the video by Johnny Khoury (2018) on the waterfall model and key steps in doing an ICT project using the waterfall model at: https://study.sagepub.com/pm.

WATERFALL EXECUTION STRATEGY

Water in a waterfall flows downward: it can only go one way, onward to its destination, governed by the specific topographical features relating to an area in which the water flows. Similarly, projects such as constructing a building, usually follow a fairly linear, sequential process governed by the specific materialities that have to

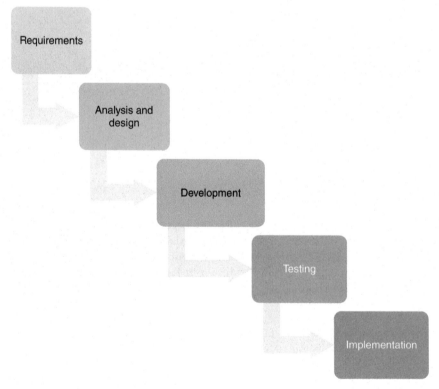

Figure 5.3   Example of a waterfall model for a project

be dealt with, such as pouring foundations before building walls. The term *waterfall strategy* refers to that sense of necessary ordering of direction. The logic here is that when the project has started, the work will flow in a sequential manner, completing one task and then moving on to the next – one at a time, moving in one direction. Not all activity for the next work package must be put on hold until the decision point for the current one is reached but the packages will follow each other in sequential execution. In order to establish a detailed plan for execution with this approach, one must be able to identify all the elements in advance and they must be able to be carried out coherently. The model can be illustrated as in Figure 5.3.

Waterfall principles for project execution are in widespread use across different kinds of project not only in construction but also in the ICT sector although, gradually, more agile execution strategies are becoming used to cope better with uncertainty in the processes of project delivery.

Whether using a more or less flexible sequential strategy it is common practice to manage by establishing control points, known as decision gates. These decision gates represent checkpoints by which time or phase specific processes should have been performed or conditions reached before the project can proceed (Cooper, 1990). Decision-making gates represent a form of formalized follow-up from the client side (see, for example, Cooper, 1990; Müller and Turner, 2005, as well as Garland, 2009, for useful insights).

IN PRACTICE

INFRASTRUCTURE DECISION-MAKING

A report by the Institute for Government in the UK written by Graham Atkins, Chris Wajzer Raphael Hogarth, Nick Davies and Emma Norris (2017) discusses 'What's wrong with infrastructure decision-making? Conclusions from six UK case studies', available online at: www.instituteforgovernment.org.uk/sites/default/files/publications/Infrastructure%20 report%20%28final%29r.pdf.

QUESTION

1. Read the report and reflect how the use of decision gates might improve the quality of infrastructure decision-making.

MILESTONE EXECUTION STRATEGY

Milestones used to dot the European countryside in earlier times. They were literally engraved stones pointing out direction and distance to the next destination. The term has become widely used in more contemporary project management, depite its somewhat archaic origins. A strategy that establishes milestones is a more flexible variant of the sequential waterfall strategy. It maintains the importance of identifying key events for the project process before the project begins and the importance of moving the project in a defined direction, yet also allows for iterations.

Projects can be conducted with a less linear approach, without the phases being strictly separated, with insights and decisions from various phases being incorporated in all phases through a series of iterations ('repetitions'). By applying milestones, the project can have an overall structure while maintaining a relatively flexible execution, transparently managing uncertainties that arise and exploiting insights gradually gained through the course of the project.

The milestone model has similarities with the waterfall approach. It is assumed that many of the key elements of the project are known when the project plan is established but it differs from the waterfall approach in emphasizing subsidiary goals as milestones that must be passed. It is less prescriptive in its approach to work packages and the activities required to reach the milestones; there can be deviation from plan if the milestones are receding into the distance rather than being accomplished and passed on time. The milestone approach also provides more opportunity for separating various milestones and work packages from each other by establishing multiple result paths.

Several extensions of milestone-based execution strategies have emerged. For example, in the 1980s the strong growth in organizing product development as projects contributed to more flexible models based on iterative thinking combined with fixed decision-making. At the decision points, the project would be subject to extensive critical review, while the project management team would have more freedom than in classic waterfall projects (see, for example, Clark & Fujimoto, 1989; Wheelwright & Clark, 1992). There is better opportunity for experimentation in order to find the best solution to arrive at decision gates (Eisenhardt & Tabrizi, 1995). Phases are more integrated than in a waterfall, so that knowledge can be transferred more efficiently between phases and form solutions across them (Lindkvist, Söderlund & Tell, 1989). Much of the thinking behind these more flexible solutions was based on Toyota's processes of continuous improvement transferred not only to product development projects but also to construction projects, as well as projects in industry and offshore oil exploration. One variant of a milestone approach, the result path, which was presented in Chapter 4, seeks to handle project execution with parallel but connected milestones and activities (see Figure 5.4).

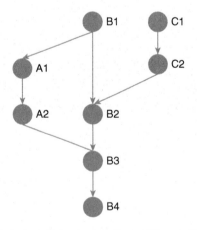

Figure 5.4   Milestone model visualizing execution with result path

Agile execution strategies

When using the waterfall approach, it is common to present activities in Gantt charts, which visualize how the project should be solved. More flexible execution strategies are often called *agile execution strategies* (Takeuchi & Nonaka, 1986). They are in many ways the opposite of waterfall strategies, seeking to identify all the elements and relationships between them at the beginning of the project and then developing scope, detailed plans and work packages based on that analysis.

In many projects in order to achieve product success it often proves necessary to engage in re-planning the process of execution, an approach that has more recently been formalized as 'design thinking' (see Clegg, Kornberger, Pitsis & Mount, 2019). Fitzgerald (1996), for instance, found that half of all design-related activities took place in other project phases than in the actual design phase. The classic dilemma faced by managers is that the need to determine specifications and plans early, with the hope of reducing uncertainty, has to be balanced against the need to maintain sufficient flexibility in execution to solve emergent problems arising in the project process. Agile execution strategies address this dilemma by relying on many recurring cycles where delivery is produced, tested and feedback received. An agile execution strategy pays great attention to continuous improvement through more or less formalized design thinking.

READ THIS!

Read the light-hearted introduction to agile execution strategies by Heslin (2019) which advises 'Three ways to achieve your New Year's resolutions by building "goal infrastructure"' at: https://study.sagepub.com/pm.

An agile approach to project execution embraces uncertainty, accepting that a project's deliverables cannot be specified in detail at the start of the project but that the specification must emerge during the project process. The essence of agile execution is to plan, using many sub-deliverables that can be tested on future users for feedback; this can then be used to rework and improve the overall delivery. Through this process, one can reduce uncertainty and develop relevant and purposeful deliveries that can contribute to value creation (Nerur & Balijepally, 2007).

The development process in flexible methods is typically product oriented in that it is not how the development is happening so much as what is taking place that is significant. Since delivery specifications will grow through the development process, it is fixed time intervals that are the structuring element in the planning. The development emerges through a series of repetitive, iterative development loops, whose time frame is set at the start of the project. This provides a structured model with a lot of flexibility to capture the learning that the members of the development team gain through their work, as well as the knowledge that comes in the form of input from the users.

Agile methods have been widespread in IT projects for a long time and have gradually been adapted for use in other types of project. Influenced by adjacent methods and strategies in production systems and innovation processes, different agile methods have emerged as ways of executing projects. Among many different agile methods, Scrum is one of the most widespread (Takeuchi & Nonaka, 1986) and frequently considered to be the first 'pure' agile project method.

THE ORIGINS AND DEVELOPMENT OF AGILE THINKING

The use of agile methods in project management has been current for a while now. There is no single source or origin of these fashionable and popular approaches, although it is widely proposed that everything started in Japan. Did it really begin in Japan? There is no doubt that the agile approach was kick-started by the ways in which the Japanese car industry developed new ways of thinking about the design of work.

These new ways were evolved very much under the tutelage and thrall of W. Edwards Deming, an American engineer involved in the US military's post-war reconstruction of Japanese industry. In 1950 Deming gave a speech expounding his ideas of how to organize work, which is largely seen as the origin of methods such as Lean, Total Quality Management (TQM) and Six Sigma, to mention some of the best-known approaches, along with agile project management. Deming was an American statistician, military engineer, later a professor and consultant. The Japanese car industry embraced his ideas. He evolved the PDCA (Plan, Do, Check, Act) cycle and this was the basis for what later became known as the Toyota way, the origin of methods like TQM, LEAN, part Balanced Scorecard, Six Sigma and Agile – especially Scrum. These methods are based on Deming's 14 principles, which he developed over the years, and presented in his book *Out of the Crisis* (2000).

1. Create constancy of purpose towards improvement of product and service, with the aim to become competitive, to stay in business and to provide jobs.
2. Adopt the new philosophy. We are in a new economic age. Management must awaken to the challenge, must learn their responsibilities and take on leadership for change.
3. Cease dependence on inspection to achieve quality. Eliminate the need for inspection on a mass basis by building quality into the product in the first place.
4. End the practice of awarding business based on the price tag. Instead, minimize total cost.
5. Improve constantly and forever the system of production and service, to improve quality and productivity, and thus constantly decrease costs.
6. Institute training on the job.
7. Institute leadership. Supervision of management is in need of an overhaul, as well as supervision of production workers.
8. Drive out fear, so that everyone may work effectively for the organization.
9. Break down barriers between departments. People must work as a team.
10. Eliminate slogans, exhortations and targets for the workforce asking for zero defects and new levels of productivity.

11. Eliminate work standards, substitute leadership and eliminate management by objective.
12. Remove barriers to pride of workmanship.
13. Institute a vigorous programme of education and self-improvement.
14. Require that management take action to achieve the transformation. Put everybody in the organization to work in accomplishing the transformation. The transformation is everybody's job.

The ideology and approach to ways of dealing with work, stated in these principles, is tangible in Lean, Scrum, TQM and other methods, and we will briefly present some of them here.

PDCA

Learning is the basis for continuous improvement in quality in products and processes. The Deming Cycle emphasizes this and is now a renowned concept applied all over the world. The Deming Cycle consists of four elements: Plan – Do – Check – Act (see more on this in Chapter 10 on learning).

THE TOYOTA WAY

Japanese car factories in general and Toyota in particular were inspired by and later based their production on the 14 principles from Deming. Even though it is almost impossible to distinguish the various approaches and methods from each other, the Toyota Way is considered to be a system designed to provide tools for people and organizations bent on continually improving their work. The Toyota way stresses the importance of becoming a bureaucratically structured learning organization through relentless reflection and empowering the teams and the individual (Adler, 1995; Adler, Goldoftas and Levine, 1999).

LEAN

Growing from the focus on continuous improvement Toyota is widely known for being the source of Lean production. Liker and Morgan (2006) defined the four principles of Lean manufacturing:

1. Defining customer-based value to separate value added from waste.
2. Front load the product development process to explore alternative solutions while there is maximum design space.
3. Creating flow.
4. Utilizing rigorous standardization to reduce variation and create flexibility and predictable outcomes.

Lean methods strive to avoid waste, whether relating to wastage of resources or time. Lean is now a widely used method for various businesses, including project management degree of clarity of goals and methods. (We will look more cosely at Lean later in this chapter.)

TOTAL QUALITY MANAGEMENT (TQM)

Based on the principle that every member of the organization must be committed to maintaining high standards of work, TQM is another management system based on quality improvement as a main area of attention. In terms of its emphasis on customer satisfaction, employee commitment, effective communication, strategic thinking and related aspects, TQM leans heavily on PDCA. TQM was an especially popular method in the United States in the 1980s–90s and is still widely applied, including in project management.

SIX SIGMA

The methodology of Six Sigma emerged as an approach inspired by Lean, PDCA and the like. Six Sigma, originally developed in 1986 by Motorola, is a data-driven review methodology to limit mistakes or defect in processes. The term 'Six Sigma' originates from the statistical normal distribution. Sigma represents the population range of standard deviation, which is a measure of the variation in a data set collected about the process. A defect is defined by specification limits separating good from bad outcomes of a process. A Six Sigma process has a process mean (average) that is six standard deviations from the nearest specification limit, providing sufficient buffer between natural variation in a process and the specification limits. Originally developed as a management method to work faster with fewer mistakes, it has become widespread in different sectors and usages, including project management.

WATCH THIS!

Watch a video (A simple explanation of Six Sigma) at https://study.sagepub.com/pm that provides a simple explanation of Six Sigma and how to use it.

COMMON CHARACTERISTICS – USER INVOLVEMENT AND VALUE CREATION

The connection to project management of Deming's ideas and principles is apparent in agile methods. The different methodologies included among the agile execution strategies have in common that they place *user involvement* and *value creation* in the centre of project work rather than timely achievement of the sequential strategies. The main characteristics of agile strategies are continuous improvement, frequent deliveries and project-based assembly of dynamic capabilities as well as an emphasis on collaboration.

SCRUM – A WIDELY USED AGILE EXECUTION STRATEGY

Among the various agile project methods, Scrum is the best known. Scrum (the name comes from the sport of rugby) is often used in product development projects, especially within IT (Meso & Jain, 2006). As a rule, Scrum is used for the more uncertain processes in the project, while the overall planning and follow-up of the project still relies on more fomal approaches.

WATCH THIS!

Watch the Atlassian Agile Coach video by Clare Drummond (2020) on 'Scrum?' and look at the text on the website as well at: https://study.sagepub.com/pm.

In the early phase of the project, you are expected to determine the framework and objectives. Based on the purpose, you will define the scope, the key qualities of the end-product and also time-based intervals. The content of each milestone is not specified, unlike the regular milestone approach; a regular temporal pattern is established so, for instance, it may be specified that there should be a project delivery every 30th day. The work period between each delivery is often called a *sprint*. The key idea is that within each sprint the team should produce outcomes that can be tested at the end of the sprint. Sprints can vary in length but the most common duration is 30 days (Meso & Jain, 2006).

At the outset, one also defines a list of project performance requirements as a set of features. The requirement list is called *Product Backlog*. Prior to each sprint, a set of features from the *Product Backlog* is picked, which will be implemented in the next sprint. The list of requirements to be implemented during a given sprint is termed the *Sprint Backlog* (Figure 5.5). The queue of actions is never completed and lasts as long as product development is in progress. The elements in the product queue are often broken down so that each of them can be estimated to take no more than 5–10 days to produce. The scope of the elements involved is estimated but these estimates are deliberately treated as speculation over time spent, as preferential rather than binding limits. The estimation of these various points is ongoing throughout the project.

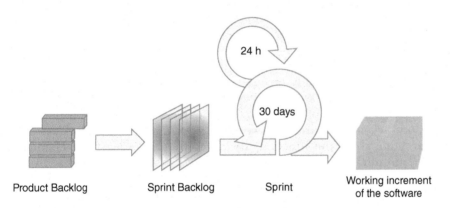

Figure 5.5   Scrum process with basic elements

In agile projects, three different roles are prescribed: *Product Owner, Scrum Master* and *Scrum Team* (Meso & Jain, 2006). The Product Owner represents the customer/user to ensure that, from an enterprise perspective, the Scrum Team works appropriately in determining the priorities of the project, using the product queue. The Scrum Team is responsible for doing the development work and delivering the product. We will return to the description of these roles in Chapter 6 on 'Organizing Projects'. The members of the Scrum Team freely choose which tasks they will perform from the sprint queue. They report progress in daily sprint meetings that focus on obstacles; they are responsible for 'achieving goals' with their tasks (Nerur, Mahapatra, & Mangalaraj, 2005).

A tool for achieving progress is the daily Scrum meetings with the Scrum Master, where all members of the team are present. The Scrum Master acts as a concierge and facilitator for the Scrum Team and ensures that the Scrum process is followed by facilitating *sprint start-up daily stand-up* meetings (short meetings where all stand) as well as capturing retrospective reflections (Meso & Jain, 2006).

This meeting typically lasts about 15 minutes. In this meeting, each team member is expected to report the remaining time to be spent on duties, while the Scrum Master reports the accumulated progress of the entire team. All group members report the following three things:

- What have you been doing since yesterday?
- What are you going to do today?
- Do you have any hindrances?

To visualize the status of the tasks within a sprint, a physical board is often used in the Project Room with Post-It notes. (Digital representations can also be used.) A note represents each task. The notes on the board give an overview of the tasks and also indicate up-to-date progress. When working on a task, the corresponding note moves from left to right on the board.

A burndown chart is also a useful management tool for the Scrum Master and team. This is a graph showing the remaining hours in a sprint as a graphical representation of work left to do versus time in which to do it. The outstanding work (or backlog) is usually on the vertical axis, with time measured along the horizontal axis. The graph can be supplemented with a capacity line, allowing the team to check if they can deliver the remaining work. If you are in danger of not being able to deliver, you will remove items from the sprint queue. If, on the other hand, you have free capacity, you will insert high-priority items from the product queue into the sprint queue (Nerur et al., 2005).

Keeping track of the amount of work done at all times entails that the reporting in Scrum projects should only include what is ready for delivery. Many teams use X and Y axes, where the X-axis shows completed sprints, while the Y-axis shows elapsed hours. A sprint is often terminated with a demonstration meeting where the functionality developed during the sprint is presented. All stakeholders are asked to provide input about this functionality and to present requests for changes. Afterwards, the product queue is revised in line with stakeholders' input. In addition, it is common for the teams to have a sprint evaluation meeting, where they reflect on their work process in the last sprint and how they want to work together in the next sprint.

In summary, we can say that a sprint typically contains the following activities:

- A sprint planning meeting
- Daily Scrum meetings
- Demonstration meeting with stakeholders
- Sprint evaluation meeting

It is often emphasized that in order to make the Scrum work, it is crucial that:

- The team is collocated
- There are mostly full-time resources involved in the project
- Each member of the Scrum team can fill more than one role
- The plan is made available, up to date and visible to the entire team
- The Scrum meeting is conducted as a short and targeted meeting
- Assignment of tasks and follow-up of status are done in daily Scrum meetings
- The length of the cycle/iteration (one sprint) is never abandoned
- The relevant executive resources should be involved in planning and execution.

Many find that agile approaches increase the possibility of value creation by producing more relevant deliveries – as teams test and gain feedback from users throughout the project. Agile approaches also involve strong customer focus and business gains, arguably reducing execution time in development projects.

EXTEND YOUR KNOWLEDGE

Explore how the iterative cycles used in agile software development create a series of deadlines for project teams. What could be the optimal iteration length under behavioural conditions for agile software projects? Read more about this in an article by van Oorschot, Sengupta, and Van Wassenhove (2018), 'Under pressure: The effects of iteration lengths on agile software development performance' available at https://study.sagepub.com/pm.

There are also some disadvantages with agile methods. They provide very limited space for defining the results of the project up front and thus can be difficult to 'sell' to project owners or secure funding. If the customer has many requests for more functionality or altered functionality, it can increase the scope of the project: it delivers too much autonomy to the customer. The fact that each member of the team has total responsibility for their activities can also lead to scope creep due to direct contact with those who specify the requirements and a continuous desire to deliver the best solutions (Nerur & Balijepally, 2007).

The main features of classic waterfall and agile execution strategies are compared in Table 5.1.

Table 5.1   Main features of waterfall versus agile execution strategies

	Waterfall	Agile
Approach	Predictable process and could be planned	Adaptable, continuing development
Organizational Structure	Bureaucratic, mechanical	Flexible, organic
Management and control	Managing, formal and top-down	Flexible, autonomous, leadership
Communication	Formal, procedures	Informal, frequent
Project model	Sequential, life cycle model	Evolutionary, iterative
Focus on customer and user	Important	Essential

As noted above, agile principles recommend a daily face-to-face meeting that takes place only within the team. It may also be done virtually. Scrum has mostly been used in rather small projects or development processes, usually with no more than nine team members. Lately it has also been scaled up to be used in multi-team projects, with the jargon being expanded to include the Scrum of Scrums. The principle for the *Scrum-of-Scrums meeting* is the same as for the Scrum meeting, only that the former is a 'between' meeting and the latter a 'within' team meeting. In multi-team agile projects, each team prepares one or more people who then meet and report on their team's status. Often there are no specifications of who should meet from each team, as that can vary according to the topics to be discussed. In these meetings the four key questions that are on the agenda for Scrum meetings are discussed. These meetings between members of individual teams can be held daily or at longer time intervals (e.g. multiple times per week) and usually are scheduled to last about fifteen minutes to one hour. The principle of Scrum can also be carried out at higher levels, taking the jargon to ever more elevated heights (Scrum of Scrum of Scrums) but doing this is not very widespread. (Which is good for those who wage war on managerial jargon! There is already more than sufficient.)

EXTEND YOUR KNOWLEDGE

BEING AGILE

Agile methods have mostly been applied to what is referred to as the 'agile sweet spot', which consists of small co-located teams working on small, non-critical, green field, in-house software projects with stable architectures and simple governance rules. These methods are increasingly being used on large projects as the article by Hobbs and Petit (2017) on 'Agile methods on large projects in large organizations' shows, available at https://study.sagepub.com/pm.

WHAT WOULD YOU DO?

THE AGILE MANIFESTO

The 12 principles defining the agile manifesto were developed during a seminar in 2001 between some practitioners and academics; all were involved primarily in software development. Since this manifesto was elaborated, these have been the guiding principles underlying much of agile development (see Figure 5.6). Building on experience and frustration with software projects, focusing mainly on plans developed ahead of the project start that ignored the importance of user-involvement and part-deliveries, among other aspects, framed the Agile Manifesto in 2001.

QUESTION

You are now handed a brief for a development project improving social care of the elderly. The top manager in the organization has heard of the agile manifesto in project management. She

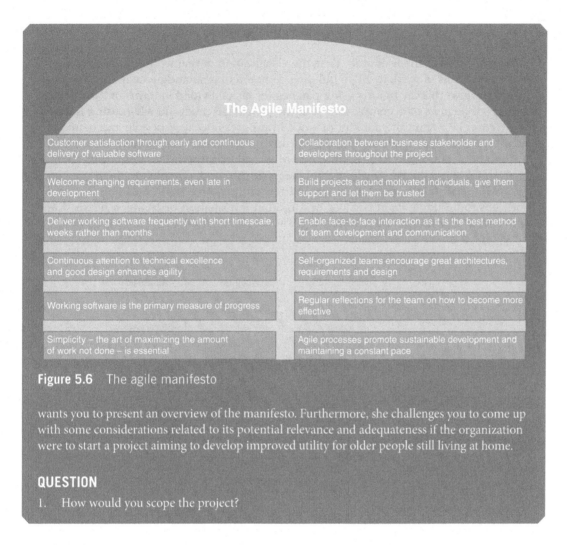

Figure 5.6   The agile manifesto

wants you to present an overview of the manifesto. Furthermore, she challenges you to come up with some considerations related to its potential relevance and adequateness if the organization were to start a project aiming to develop improved utility for older people still living at home.

QUESTION

1.   How would you scope the project?

Kanban, Lean and BIM

Other agile project execution models have emerged as ways of dealing with projects consisting of uncertainty and the need for close relationships with the customer during the project. Three models or techniques are worth highlighting here. As is the case for Scrum, these techniques are based on following certain steps and using techniques designed as a part of the method.

KANBAN

Kanban is a flexible methodology that aims to avoid waste of resources. The main idea is that you start only that work within an area that is necessary to progress further. Work initiated within an area must, therefore, be limited, balancing needs and capacity by establishing a queuing system – with blocking – which forces priority. In the same way as for a road, less traffic in the form of fewer projects or tasks at a time provides better flow and throughput. Capacity for more continuous improvement work is created through clearing time to help others (and vice versa) and to improve the system.

Kanban has a number of tools. First, the visualization of real workflow, real state and real expectations of work to aid in building common understanding enabling an immediate overview. Display boards using patches for tasks divided in terms of their status, in terms of degrees of accomplishment in the process, is a key aid when using Kanban (see Figure 5.7). Limit the amount of work in progress because people and teams are often overloaded with work. Juggling overload leads to increased overheads, poorer quality and a noticeably longer time before work is finished. The time from start to finish should be reduced. The longer it takes to finish work completely, the more extra work will occur due to time spent waiting for and juggling work, meaning that more work has to be done again because of forgotten information or changed needs. Kanban is often used as a tool when working with a Lean methodology (described below).

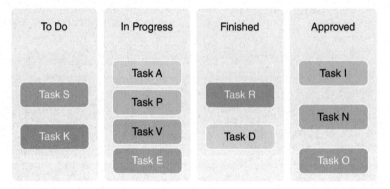

Figure 5.7   Illustration of a Kanban board

LEAN

Lean is a flexible methodology that is regarded both as an overall organizational and management philosophy and as a set of tools. The main part of this methodology is to eliminate so-called waste and increase the customer's experience of value rather than emphasizing the cost elements. The underlying goal is to improve that profitability by creating added value with less effort from resources. As waste is eliminated, quality improves while reducing production time and costs. There are several types of waste that must be considered, such as waste through overproduction, waiting for goods, people or work tasks, poor transport solutions or incorrect production. Lean is often connected to Six Sigma.

WATCH THIS!

Watch the YouTube video featuring Astrid Renata van Veen (2017) on how Lean was applied in the design and construction of the Bergen Art and Design School at: https://study.sagepub.com/pm.

Lean has many principles and tools. Among the tools in the Lean methodology, is *the customer commitment* plan that seeks to ensure that the customer makes decisions at the right level at the right time in the project. Doing this increases the possibility of successful implementation by keeping decision speed up and successful value creation occurring through allowing the customer to decide which solutions are best suited.

IN PRACTICE

LEAN AND HEALTH

Lean management is increasingly being adopted in health care. Rotter, Plishka, Lawal, Harrison, Sari, Goodridge, and Kinsman (2019) ask in their article, 'What is lean management in health care?', available at https://study.sagepub.com/pm.

QUESTION

1. How applicable is Lean to health care? What innovations in Lean are necessary to make it applicable in health care?

LEAN AND BIM

Lean has been widely used in various production systems and for improvement processes in various businesses, ranging from assembly line production to municipal home help services. Lean is also becoming widespread in construction projects. In this connection, Lean is often linked to tools such as BIM (Building Information Modelling) and 'last planner', which is decentralization of planning to the lowest possible level and a reduction of the planning horizon, so that the uncertainty surrounding execution is reduced. The principle is that more is known about the near future than something that is far ahead, thus detail planning should be done as close in time to the actual processes of implementation as possible.

BIM is a process for creating and managing information on a construction project across the project life cycle. The Building Information Model, a digital description of every aspect of the asset to be built, is the key output in this process. Such a digital model draws on information assembled collaboratively and updated at key stages of a project. Creating a digital model enables those who interact with the building to optimize their actions, resulting in a greater whole life value for the asset.

BIM makes it possible for anyone to access that information for any purpose, e.g. to integrate different aspects of the design more effectively. In principle, the risk of mistakes or discrepancies is reduced and abortive costs minimized. It allows for updated information flow so that all team members should be working to the same standards as each other. Difficulties can arise, however, when different professional relevancies focus attention on different levels of the elements in the design; decisions made at one level may have unanticipated consequences for decisions made at another level. What the heating engineer sees in the plans and what the electrical contractor sees reflects their ways of seeing, not the reality of the representation. In practice they may end up in each other's space, literally, because they were not paying attention to the overall model.

Picture 5.1   What is really real?

BIM data can be used to illustrate the entire building life cycle, including spaces, systems, products and sequences. By signalling conflict detection, it can also reduce errors at various stages of development/construction. The BIM model is a combination of many things:

- Information content that defines a product
- Product properties, such as thermal performance
- Geometry representing the product's physical characteristics
- Visualization data giving the object a recognizable appearance
- Functional data, such as detection zones, that enables the object to be positioned and behave in the same manner as the product itself

BIM has caused a digital revolution within the global construction industry. Indeed, today 'digital twins' are becoming increasingly used in projects, where an exact digital replica of a product, process or service is created as a model representing the physical in the digital world.

Replicating objects digitally, using the internet of things, enables simulations, testing, modelling and monitoring based on the data collected by sensors. Data is the primary driver and output of digital twins. This data can help companies in making decisions.

Digital devices are not only increasingly being used in the design phase but also in construction.

IN PRACTICE

ROBOTS

Can a construction project be built by robots? It might seem a prospect for the future or something out of a science-fiction script, but it is not. The majority of houses built today and constructed out of brick use a brick veneer approach. Laying bricks is a laborious and skilled trade, when done properly. In future, it may be done by robots. An Australian robot is set to take on bricklayers the world over, after building a three-bed, two-bathroom, 180-square-metre home in less than three days. Built by ASX-listed Perth company Fastbrick Robotics (FBR), the Hadrian X machine recently successfully completed a series of tests, proving it was capable of complying with various building requirements.[1] Once these tests were completed, the robot was free to build its first full-home structure, which it completed within the allocated three-day time period. In 2017 the company behind the development of Hadrian X signed a non-binding memorandum with Saudi Arabia potentially to use the Hadrian X's to build 50,000 houses in the Kingdom by 2022. About 100 robots are reported to be needed to do this.

A number of recent high-profile studies of robotics and artificial intelligence (or AI) in economics and sociology have predicted that many jobs will soon disappear due to automation, with few new ones replacing them. While techno-optimists and techno-pessimists contest whether a jobless future is a positive development or not, a 2019 paper by Peter Fleming that you can access in the online resources at https://study.sagepub.com/pm, addresses the employment effects of digitalization. Despite successive waves of computerization (including advanced machine learning), he suggests that jobs have not disappeared and probably will not in the near future. He proposes that the concept of 'bounded automation' demonstrates how organizational forces mould the application of technology in the employment sector. If work does not vanish in the age of artificial intelligence, he argues that poorly paid jobs will most certainly proliferate.

---

[1] You can watch a video about the technology at www.fbr.com.au/view/hadrian-x.

Design thinking

Project management that is hidebound by predetermined phases, stages and milestones is much less likely to be creative in resolving issues as they arise. Design Thinking, an approach widely used as a methodology in innovation projects, is being linked to the project management literature and methodology (Elsbach & Stigliani, 2018). It is a process designed to try and maximize creative innovation through a conjoined process of *inspiration*, *ideation* and *implementation*:

- *Inspiration* derives from making a problem material through mock-ups, sketches, scenarios and so on.
- *Ideation* is the process of generating, developing and testing ideas through building prototypes, piloting and 'testing the waters' – idea work (Coldevin, Carlsen, Clegg, Pitsis, & Antonacopoulou, 2019).
- *Implementation* is the clear development and specification of the idea, its effective communication, the enrolment of others in its support and the translation of the idea into action or practice.

Design Thinking comprises an approach to problem-solving using tools and methods in a process to innovate new products or processes, utilizing cross-disciplinary collaboration in a creative way. Design Thinking has been applied to a great extent, especially in innovation projects. Its origins are in the 1960s when scholars evolved Design Thinking as a method for creating new forms of artefact and new knowledge (Elsbach & Stigliani, 2018). The consulting firm IDEO has developed and advocated the use of Design Thinking for solving abstract and multifaceted problems in a business context as well as for social innovators. Design Thinking has now become a widespread methodology for innovation processes in a great many project-based sectors.

WATCH THIS!

Tim Brown (2009), guru among design thinkers, can be seen talking about design thinking in a Ted Talk at: https://study.sagepub.com/pm.

Schön (1992) suggests that for, designers the production of artefacts is essential to their business. Therefore, practitioners in the field of design sciences, including, among others, professional designers, architects and engineers should be focused on prototyping action and being solution centred (Michlewski, 2008). The idea of prototyping includes the objectives of creating a physical prototype to enable organizational thinking and learning to occur more rapidly by making prototypes small and thus, by testing them, being able to minimize the impact of failures. Prototypes also encourage employees to explore new behaviour (Coughlan, Suri, & Canales, 2007, p. 127).

An example of Design Thinking using prototypes occurred in the construction of a project designed by the famous architect Frank Gehry. The project, the construction of a new business school, involved windows and bricks being mounted on a sub-structure of non-linear but 'folded' metal (see Picture 5.2). How to do this was challenging, as there were no precedents for using bricks and windows in this way. The project team resolved the innovation challenges posed by constructing a mock-up full-scale model of the detail in question, incorporating the sub-structure, bricks and window frame, to arrive at a practical solution involving innovative brick ties as a means of fastening the bricks (see Naar and Clegg, 2015, 2018).

WATCH THIS!

Watch a video from the University of Technology Sydney (2015) exploring the finished design of the Gehry building in Sydney at: https://study.sagepub.com/pm.

Design Thinking addresses the challenges facing organizations, business and societies for dealing with uncertainty, ambiguity and the urge to change and innovate. As for other agile methods, Design Thinking is a non-linear process. Moreover, it is relevant especially for resolving 'wicked problems' or ill-defined problems (Buchanan,

Picture 5.2   Window detail of the Frank Gehry designed UTS Business School

Source: Image courtesy of Ignatzschatz, via Wikicommons. Shared under the Creative Commons BY-SA 4.0 license.

1992). Visualizing, prototype-driven and experimental behaviour are essential elements for Design Thinking projects. Design Thinking in projects operates between intersections of:

- **Desirability** – what is desirable from a human point of view
- **Viability** – what is economically viable from the organization owning the project
- **Feasibility** – what is technologically and practically feasible to develop and implement

Design Thinking tools in innovation processes consist of visualizations such as drawings, models, figures, narratives and prototypes. Making use of visual and physical elements makes it easier to imagine the product or processes the project is supposed to deliver. Furthermore, it provides communication and enables involvement with participants and stakeholders that is more concrete. Design Thinking provides a method to apply in innovative projects, related to which there are a range of adjoining approaches and methods (Figure 5.8).

Design approaches practise interventions that are improvement- and solution-centred (Trullen & Bartunek, 2007), based upon a set of fundamental values that include collaboration; a focus on solutions rather than on analysis; belief that experiment is necessary for successful intervention processes, and that each situation is unique in its context and solutions should be goal oriented – even if these goals change in the process (Trullen & Bartunek, 2007, p. 27).

Visualization and Narratives

- Making use of elements such as charts and graphs, as well as storytelling, metaphors and analogies

Deep Understanding of the Users

- Making use of participants' observation, interviewing, journey mapping and the like

Structured Collaborative Sensemaking

- Creating a 'common mind' by making use of mind mapping, brainstorming and concept development techniques

Identifying Assumptions

- Focusing on identifying assumptions around value creation, execution and other elements that underlie the attractiveness of the a new idea

Prototyping

- Techniques which facilitate making abstract ideas tangible, by applying storyboarding, user scenarios and the like, providing more vivid manifestos for the future

Co-creation

- Incorporates techniques for engaging users in generating, developing and testing new ideas

Field Experiments

- Testing the key underlying and value-generating assumptions of a hypothesis in the field with stakeholders

Figure 5.8 Design Thinking tools and the tasks they aim to achieve

EXTEND YOUR KNOWLEDGE

DESIGN THINKING

Read the article 'Contribution of Design Thinking to project management in an innovation context', by Mahmoud-Jouni, Midler, and Silberzhan (2016), arguing for the relevance of integrating Design Thinking into project management approaches in practice available at https://study.sagepub.com/pm.

WHEN COULD DESIGN THINKING BE USEFUL IN PROJECTS?

Design Thinking is differentiated from Lean, Scrum and Kanban in its human-centred and creativity-focused approach. For Design Thinking to be an adequate methodology in project management, it depends on the type of project to which it is supposed to apply. In innovation projects, where uncertainty and ambiguity are prevalent, elements from Design Thinking can be useful in creating value for a project. Furthermore, Design Thinking tends to be more useful in projects where there is a degree of open-endedness in designing solutions. Under these conditions the process can generate and nourish ideas, testing and improving solutions before implementing them.

Design Thinking provides just one of multiple approaches for dealing with creative processes in projects. Carlsen, Clegg, and Gjersvik (2012) emphasize certain elements that often appear in projects and works involving creativity and innovation. Prepping, craving wonder and generative resistance are among ten sets of practices they categorize into interwoven, affective, material and controversial qualities for idea work.

Choosing execution strategy

In general, we can say that the development of execution strategies has become more flexible because of the increasing realization that uncertainty occurs. Recognition of the likelihood of uncertainty requires different types of plans as well as plans at different levels. In short, it requires execution strategies and planning processes that take into account the nature of the delivery and the environment surrounding the delivery. Hence, the waterfall approach, in the strict sense, is now rarely used in modern project management.

A principal question in project planning is how detailed plans should be when starting project work. The literature suggests three possible starting points:

1. You can create a complete network plan where all the activities and relationships between them are described. The assumption is that at the start of the project all the activities to be performed and how long will be spent on each is determined.
2. A less demanding approach is the informational use of milestone planning and determining the milestones of the project and the relationships between them. The time allocated to reach each milestone is not calculated but the key activities one knows are demanding should be elaborated. Detailed planning for each milestone is done when required – as close as possible to starting actual work on the milestone.
3. The agile strategy requires the least information in the early stage, as it only determines the overall principles and features and then just focuses on the results that can be reached during the next fixed time frame, normally 30 days. When the 30 days have passed, the team considers the next task to be targeted.

When project managers and their teams start a project (or enter new project phases), they should reflect on what approach is best suited to the information available, as well as the importance of including the users/customer in the process and how much need there will be for learning.

COMBINING STRATEGIES

One way to combine a traditional milestone-based execution strategy with a flexible strategy can be to establish some key decision points in the form of certain milestones and then set up an agile execution with frequent iterations, repeating a process several times, with partial delivery of the project elements. Flexible execution techniques can be used to work with concept preparation and with parts of the project other than actual execution. The key is that the strategy is sufficiently flexible to capture necessary changes and add new knowledge and solutions that increase the effectiveness of the project, at the same time as the project lands within reasonable time and cost limits.

Picture 5.3   Virtual idea work?

With increased attention to value creation and the need for faster adaptations and changes, many projects can be placed upwards to the right in the mode represented in Figure 5.9. Doing this reduces the timeliness of locked, sequential execution models. Any execution model should support the project instead of placing it in a project management approach that is a straitjacket. Choosing this strategy is a matter of the competencies involved in the project connected with execution, as well as the competence and experience that you have as a project manager.

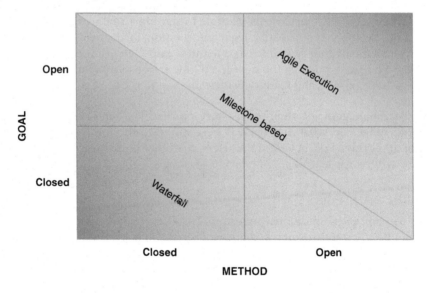

Figure 5.9   Choosing execution strategy depending on goal and method

CONSIDERATIONS WHEN CHOOSING AN EXECUTION STRATEGY

It is usually the project owner who has the decisive word in terms of the choice of execution strategy. How project managers handle this in practice is discussed in more detail in later chapters. Typically, some reviews of proposed strategy will be made before the project starts. Noteworthy variables to consider will be issues such as the degree of uncertainty, the possibility of adjusting the course along the way, the importance of user involvement, the possibilities for detailed activity planning, the importance of interaction, whether the project is an alliance delivery mode and what are the demands for pace of execution. See Figure 5.10.

Before proceeding with the project, understandings of the project assigned before commencing will be clarified. The project owner should be a party to shared conversations in which an understanding of the project is negotiated so that this can be the starting point for later design of the project charter and the framework for the project. Clarifying communication and expectations at the outset spreads understanding and common sensemaking between key stakeholders.

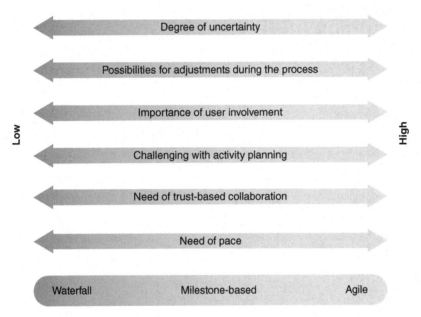

Figure 5.10   Decisive elements for choosing execution strategy

To sum up:

1. If you have little information about what is actually going to be delivered along the way and assume that there is high uncertainty, a high need for customer/ user involvement and a great need for learning, an agile execution model is more appropriate.
2. A milestone-based execution will be appropriate if there is ample room at the outset for reflection and interpretation of what the mission really is and how it should be resolved in processes between the milestones.
3. We know that flexible approaches are used most in IT projects while network planning is used primarily in technical projects. In recent years many projects are

being implemented in a more agile way than previously, due to the recognition that projects are almost aways characterized by uncertainty and that participation is crucial for delivery to users that is as relevant as possible, maximizing the potential to gain value.

A multinational survey of over 1000 projects showed that flexible methods were perceived as very appropriate and efficient in many contexts (Serrador & Pinto, 2015). On the other hand, the transition from traditional execution strategies to flexible approaches has been perceived as demanding because of a loss of a 'controlled' delivery process, with established procedures for development, governance and interaction (Boehm & Turner, 2005). Introducing flexible models requires time for conversion, change and training, often forgotten in practice when enthusiastically converting to agile approaches. Used well, flexible methods can be an efficient tool to increase both project success and project product success (Serrador & Pinto, 2015).

WHAT WOULD YOU DO?

Waste and the execution of projects to deal with it is a major contemporary problem. You are engaged as a project manager by a municipality to scope a project for recycling waste as a result of China and other countries no longer accepting waste. Various solutions present themselves:

- Increased landfill in the municipality
- A solid-waste-processing unit to pick out and recycle metal, paper and plastic from the waste generated by the municipality. The plant would be intended to convert food waste into biogas for injection into the local gas grid, mix paper into recyclable pulp for egg cartons and transform plastic film into fuel briquettes for energy generation. In the process, the plant would reduce greenhouse gases such as carbon dioxide compared with landfills and incineration.
- A food-waste digester to make biogas to provide heat and power. Applying such methods to inconsistent waste materials such as garbage and wood is not as simple as turning coal into gas or natural gas into hydrogen. Moreover, gasification has yet to prove itself profitable. Even if technically successful, it will still fail if an adequate return is not generated.

QUESTION

1. How would you develop an execution model to scope what to do with the waste? What would be the key factors for consideration? (Hint: the web page for Chemical and Engineering News is a useful resource.)

Project economics and resources

How a project is executed depends in part on the abundance or scarcity of resources available. The scarcity problem in the allocation of competing resources is a classical economic problem. For project execution to happen, the project must have resources of different kinds. When starting up, projects are empty entities. They must be resourced so that they can unfold and be implemented as planned. However, there are a number of factors that make project economics different from those of organizations more generally. Any project is not itself profitable during its existence. It is the effects of the project that will create value and contribute to profitability. Therefore, there are usually a few specific expectations and conditions that apply to finances in projects than for the organization in general.

When assessing whether a project is to be started or not, as described in Chapter 2, one must consider its potential for value creation in light of a number of factors, not least the resources one needs to expend to complete the project. Cost estimates, profitability calculations, investment analyses and other more or less qualified assessments can be used. These are done before a possible start-up and will not be further elucidated here. They are therefore expected to be completed before the project starts. On the other hand, for the vast majority of projects, it is appropriate to plan the economic aspects of the project process through a project budget that is updated by an evolving project statement. Before looking at the use of internal resources, we will briefly explicate these aspects.

Project budget and following up

A budget is a planning document intended to provide an overview of expected expenses and revenues. Thus, a project budget will be an overview of the projected expenses and revenue for the period the project is scheduled to last. To manage overall project resources, a project budget is essential, backed up by the use of accounting and other follow-up routines to monitor resource utilization. A project budget will be followed up at both the overall management level, at the milestone level and the activity level.

There is a considerable difference between the financial constraints for the construction of a major highway project and a project where the key delivery is a competence development plan for a small organization. The difference between the two projects can be counted in billions of dollars. Nonetheless, external stakeholders will be involved in both and economic and resource assessments will be required despite the different financial constraints, details and needs.

The variance in types of projects, from megaprojects, such as building a national broadband network or a major opera house, to simple projects, such as a garage or home extension, means that it is difficult to convey a joint presentation of the resource aspects of a project in an abstract and overall statement. In both, however, despite the difference in scope, scale and sensemaking, profitability assessments have to be made before the start of a project. A common feature of the vast majority of projects will be that they contain both income and expense items. However, there will be significant variation in the proportion of the project budget as a time resource spread between the various projects. Time consumption in this context adds labour costs on the expenditure side (see Figure 5.11).

There are differences between what are called *external and internal costs*, depending on the type of project and the extent to which *external resources* outside the permanent organization are used. If it is a robust delivery project, costs will basically be almost exclusively external costs in terms of working hours (salary) and any investments that are included as part of the contract for the project execution. These external costs are direct costs that are included in the budget. The project is budgeted in balance so that the revenue (transfers from the client) is equal to the expenses (cost of the project itself).

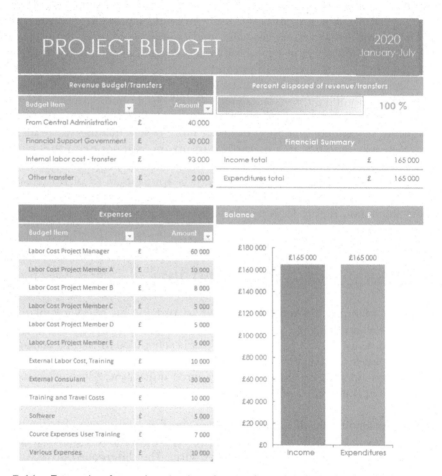

Figure 5.11 Example of a project budget for the introduction of new administrative processing procedures in a municipality

There will always be *indirect costs*. Such indirect costs may include time resources and travel expenses incurred by the permanent organization or client when working on the project. Project-management functions, such as planning, decision-making and follow-up, as well as participation in the design of the project's content also need to be costed. These are usually not included in the budget, although it would often be appropriate to do so. There could also be indirect costs borne by externalities such as ecology and the community.

In internal projects, the work effort, investments and other costs are covered by the permanent organization itself, such that costs are therefore internal. The budgets established for such projects vary greatly in detail. However, it is fruitful in such projects to apply budget and accounting controls as the basis for project execution and to assess potential profitability and value creation for the project. Resource usage in the project should be planned and followed up by budget and accounting on all three levels of project management: OPMF, the overall project management framework, milestone and detail level.

EXTEND YOUR KNOWLEDGE

PROJECT BUDGETS

Read the article by Kwon and Kang (2019) to learn about how project uncertainty is a critical factor in estimating project budget, which is available at https://study.sagepub.com/pm. Project managers still face the challenge of completing projects within given budgets but often without the relevant tools to deal with unidentified risks. A three-point estimation technique which can improve budget accuracy and precision is suggested.

Project planning often adheres to a top-down approach: it starts with overall planning and then focuses on more detailed levels to establish project budgets. It is usually not the activity undertaken in the project that is the basis for the budget. It may seem strange that one does not start with summarizing all the activities to be undertaken, including the investments, to use as the basis for budgeting. For a purely technical project, such a model could work (Andersen et al., 2009) but not for projects that deliver change or which involve a significant degree of innovation. In such projects, a great deal of uncertainty and many unpredictable processes may be expected. Top-down budgeting fits these contexts better since it is the overall objectives of the project that will set its premises. In such projects, project managers need to be prepared to adjust direction and budget along the way.

The project charter and the overall project management framework define the main elements for the budget. The project charter is particularly crucial for delivery projects. When the project is in progress, reporting and follow-up from the subordinate levels will be the basis for how any changes regarding budget overruns will be followed up, which also applies to the project budget. The overall budget is initially distributed and attributed to the different work packages or is associated with the milestone level. It is based on an assessment of what is required to reach the individual milestone. Detailed planning of the achievement of the milestones will further provide a basis for budgeting activities at the retail level. Once the level of detail is planned, it will reveal the need for budget-level adjustments. In some cases, it will eventually necessitate changes to the overall project management framework.

As we can see, top-down budgeting often means that when elaborations are made on a subordinate level, whether at the milestone level or one of more detail, they can result in adjustments. The project of building the opera house in Bjørvika in Oslo was significantly more expensive than the original estimate made on the basis of a three-dimensional model, taking into account previous experiences with similar construction projects. The first concrete estimates of about 1.8 billion Norwegian kroner were subsequently converted to 3.3 billion at construction start in 2002, and eventually ended at around 4.4 billion when the building was completed in 2010. The example emphasizes that early cost estimates are not definitive calculations and thus are highly uncertain. Communication to stakeholders about calculations and uncertainties in early phases of a project avoids or mitigates reactions that often arise when the detail estimation is made, showing substantial deviations from the original estimates. Of course, optimistic cost forecasts might propel a project into action whereas more realistic projections of cost would not succeed in launching the project.

Knowledge acquired in project execution often results in the need for adjustments in resource use. As we have included in the description of the Iron Triangle of the project, transgression in resource use in one area often means that one has to compensate by reducing resource utilization in another area. The option is to change the deadline or quality of work if one does not want to change the overall goals.

Using internal resources from the permanent organization

We have stated that internal projects primarily have internal costs that are covered by the permanent organization. Whether it is a development project that renews or creates a new product or a change project such as improving the workflow of a manufacturing process or reorganizing process, these will often be primarily performed by the permanent organization. Only some technical investments together with course and training costs, and any external consultancy contributions that make up external expenses, will be required.

There are several good reasons for including internal resource use when the project budget is prepared and followed up; it provides the basis for assessing profitability and the value-added contribution the project will provide to the organization. Visualizing the project's resource needs in the execution of the project aids budgetary control. Both resources and attention regarding work effort and other contributions from the staff members and managers of the permanent organization, as well as the inclusion of internal resource use in the planning of the project work and the allocation of employees contributing to project execution, require budgeting. By explicating these costs in the project budget, it also becomes clearer which obligations accompany employee resources from the affected departments and line managers. If the allocation of the crew is not included in the resource assessments, both the project organization and the employees themselves may find that the relevant line managers will not allocate resources to the project because this limits their availability for other more routine tasks.

Contracts in projects

Most projects include the use of goods or services purchased and delivered from external suppliers in the market. In projects where there are many external suppliers, follow-up of these is a crucial part of project execution. Agreements need to be managed to ensure that purchases are of the agreed quality, price and delivery time.

The type and extent of deliveries or procurement can differ greatly among projects. In projects delivering large facilities, such as roads and offshore installations, compared with projects that involve internal conversions or conference events, the procurement range will be highly variable. Because purchases are so different and involve varying degrees of uncertainty, they must be regulated in different ways, usually through contracts. A contract is in the legal sense a written or oral agreement between two or more parties on matters of a legal nature. Different forms of contract have been established to reflect differences in scope and uncertainty.

Procurement agreements are entered into when the project accepts an offer made by the other party (often as a result of the project requesting it). If the agreement concerns simple purchases such as PCs for project staff, the goods can be delivered from the permanent organization or purchased in local retail outlets or online. If the delivery involves many PCs, it makes sense to negotiate a framework agreement on scope and content. If custom PCs loaded with specialist software are required, a separate competition for development, establishing and delivering them, requiring rigorous follow-up from the project organization will probably be inititated. Clarification of external deliveries the project requires and procures is a necessary part of the project's permanent management. This is often called the project's *contract strategy*.

In many projects, procurement is crucial and comprehensive work that will often be attended to by contract specialists (usually lawyers). In projects with large acquisitions, it is common for the project team to have members whose role it is to take care of the contract strategy (contract managers). Anyone working on projects needs a clear understanding of the main principles related to contract work, while at the same time recognizing that it is a separate field bounded by legal conventions that cannot be covered within the constraints of this book. Therefore, we will only look at the key principles.

A well-balanced agreement between the parties is a prerequisite for good delivery. The project must describe what is to be delivered in an appropriate manner. Doing this can be accomplished through using detailed technical specifications where appropriate or with a more general description of the function of the delivery. When the project is to procure goods and services, the following key factors should be addressed:

- When is it advisable to involve the supplier?
- What are reasonable criteria for choosing a supplier?
- How to negotiate? (Should you negotiate with one or many?)
- What kind of relationship do you want and how is it best to regulate this?
- How should the delivery be paid for?
- What incentives should you include in the contract? (For example, bonus if delivery takes place quickly and negative incentives such as daily fines if delivered late or inadequate.) A target price contract is a contract of incentives for both parties, for example, through the fact that savings are shared between them.
- How is risk to be distributed? In any kind of agreement, the risk should be distributed appropriately, with the key principle being that the party that is best suited to managing the risk owns it. The total contract is the form of contract which entails the least risk to the principal.
- How is the contract to be followed up?

In order to ensure delivery, it is vital that the project, in advance, considers the quality features of the delivery carefully and how quality should be verified before the project accepts delivery. How extensive such verification processes should be varies from a simple check when receiving delivery, to extensive testing plans during the production phase, to a long-term operational and warranty phase before delivery is finally taken over. For many situations, standardized contracts and industry-based agreements will be widely used. Larger companies will have standardized procurement and contract templates. Using these will usually offer advantages for the project since familiarity makes them easier to use, involving less risk to the suppliers than contractual forms specially developed for the individual project.

All of the contractual forms mentioned above are common in the project context but neo-classical contracts, based purely on competitive tender, are the most widely used instrument for regulating the relationship between projects and their suppliers. In these, suppliers will be chosen based on offering the lowest price. Using this approach may be beneficial but it often means that any changes will be separately accounted for as variation orders. It is not recommended to choose a supplier solely on the basis of price, especially if there are complex deliveries to purchase. The supplier who offers the lowest price may not necessarily be the most competent. Both professional competence and delivery capacity should be considered. One should also consider the entire life stage of the delivery project: what responsibility should the supplier receive for project product success and what incentives should follow this responsibility?

Payment for delivery is, of course, a salient element in the project's contract strategy. Fixed price, unit price and cost plus price are the most common options for compensation (Zaghloul & Hartman, 2002).

- *A fixed price* (a certain price is agreed for the entire assignment) for delivery results is a small risk for the project because the supplier must then cover any costs that the delivery may incur.
- *Unit price.* If the project chooses the unit price, the supplier should be compensated for all units included in the delivery, such as working hours and materials. This form of agreement includes a great deal of risk for the project if it is not identified which units are part of the acquisition beforehand but at the same time it provides the opportunity to add and subtract units during the process. For example, if you have a construction project to be financed through the sale of existing housing, you often choose to do so because you are uncertain about what the sale will bring about. The cost of the new building will then be the sum of the price of all units included in the acquisition.
- *Cost plus price* (settlement after bill + one surcharge). In this payment model, the contractor receives all his expenses and has a profit margin (cover contribution) agreed in advance. If the scope of the assignment is difficult to define or there is a need for many changes along the way, often cost plus settlement is used.

There are four main types of contract used in the project context: classical, neoclassical, relationship and alliance contracts. The main distinction between them has to do with the degree of integration between the parties. Classical and neoclassical contracts are integrated primarily by the written agreement around matters such as delivery, price and quality; we can think of this as system integration. Relational and alliance contracts are integrated much more by mechanisms of social integration involving trust and shared purpose.

Figure 5.12 Contract types with different degree of integration between the parties

Very simplified, these types can be described as:

- **The classical contract** is primarily used for purchases justified in conventional market logic. The transaction has low uncertainty because what is procured is a 'finished' product. Laws and regulations usually govern disagreements.
- **Neoclassical contracts** are used for longer-term transactions and are more difficult to define exactly. The contract defines the delivery and compensation (payment). It is crucial to determine delivery as well as acknowledge that there may be changes in it. Changes can create conflicts between the parties. Therefore, these types of contracts contain procedures for conflict resolution and working towards establishing trust between parties.
- **Relationship contracts** are used in relationships where the parties plan transactions that cannot be fully described at the time the parties enter into the agreement. Therefore, descriptions of the interaction process are emphasized more stringently than the deliveries.
- **Alliance contracts** (also known as partnership contracts) are used to integrate the parties into a close and mutually beneficial partnership. Benefits that can be achieved in the collaboration can be sharing knowledge and other resources and reduced transaction control costs. In partnering it is crucial to work for unforeseen goals, distribution of incentives, mutual commitment and trust. Being able to achieve this requires good communication.

Relationship and alliance projects are more likely to be used in contexts where there is considerable uncertainty; where the factors that might produce these are better accounted for and known, then the variants of the classical contract will be more likely used. Sometimes, where there is mutual agreement, an open book contract will be used. In these the buyer and seller of work/services agree which costs will be remunerable and the margin that the supplier can add to these costs. Many domestic construction projects, for instance, proceed on a 10% cost-plus basis. The project invoices the customer based on receipts for materials and time incurred plus the agreed margin. Sometimes these are known as cost-plus contracts. Suppliers sometimes work on a risk/reward basis where the supplier gets a bonus or penalty calculated as a percentage of the difference between the real cost of the project and initial estimations.

EXTEND YOUR KNOWLEDGE

Read the paper by Wang, Chen, Zhang, & Wang (2018) on contractual complexity in construction projects, available at https://study.sagepub.com/pm.

We have looked at some main forms of contract settlements. For larger deliverables, hybrid forms are often combined. It is crucial that the contract form best suited, given the desired flexibility and degree of uncertainty, is chosen. In some megaprojects, especially, more realistic estimation at the contract stage might negate the project ever being attempted.

For public projects in the EU, there are detailed rules governed by EU regulations and regulations for public sector employees. Deficient contracts or the choice of the incorrect contractual form are a significant reason for cooperation problems among contractors, creating time and cost overruns (Zaghloul & Hartman, 2002).

One principle is that risk must be allocated where it is to be handled. Contract management involves using the contract as a tool throughout the project's life cycle, from establishing an appropriate contract strategy to following up contractual obligations in the contract.

Research in the field of projects has shown great interest in the field of cooperation across organizational boundaries in projects and how to formalize this cooperation. For example, there is research work on issues such as partnering (Bresnen & Marshall, 2002), alliances (Clegg et al., 2002; Miller & Lessard, 2000; Pitsis, Clegg, Marton, et al., 2003), project networks (Cova, Ghauri, & Salle, 2002), private/public relations (Kwak & Anbari, 2009) and interorganizational projects (Jones & Lichtenstein, 2008; Bygballe, Dewulf, & Levitt, 2015).

Within project management, there is a separate contract school interested in the relationship between contract management and project management. Much attention has been focused on how legal entities should be handled in project execution.

Managing risk and contracts

Andi (2006) claims it is crucial to identify risks and allocate them to the contractual parties for efficient risk management. Peckiene, Komarovska, and Ustinovicius (2013) highlight that the sole purpose of construction contracts is to allocate risks between the parties along with rights, duties and responsibilities. Contracts legally bind risks such that the party to whom risk is allotted is assumed to act responsibly in managing that risk. Risks are thus transferred to another party or shared on the basis of relevant contractual conditions. Bing, Akintoye, Edwards, and Hardcastle (2005) argue that when the burden of risk is transferred to the contractor, they will levy higher implementation prices.

Risks that are mismanaged can cause project inefficiencies and result in adversarial contractual relationships (Andi, 2006). Equitable risk allocation subsequent to risk analysis is important and random shifting of risks to other parties is inequitable and unreasonable (Peckiene et al., 2013). Arndt (1998) calls for risk allocation to be symmetrical and balanced so as to create maximum incentive for managing the risks efficiently. He advises that if the partner is exposed to a downside risk, they should also have the advantage of a corresponding upside potential. Risks and rewards should be balanced for both public and private sectors (Grimsey & Lewis, 2002). Fisk (1997) notes that before risk is allotted to a party, it needs to be ascertained whether the party has the required competence to assess the risks fairly and the required expertise to manage the risk. The European Commission's (2003) guidelines stipulate that risks should be allocated to the party best able to manage the risk at the least cost.

Irwin, Klein, Perry, and Thobani (1998) include the end user as a party to whom risks should be allotted. Bing et al. (2005) advise, on the basis of their study of UK infrastructure projects, that the preferred risk allocation should involve risks allotted to the public sector project owner, the private sector contractor, with some shared and some strongly dependent on the project. They suggest that the public sector is best able to handle political risks, such as nationalization, expropriation, political opposition and unstable government. The public sector should also be accountable for poor public decision-making processes and the risks relating to site availability. Sastoque, Arboleda, and Ponz (2016) advise that above the political and project selection risks, the public sector should also be accountable for social risk. Bing et al. (2005) suggest that the private sector is best able to handle financial risks such as high financing cost, interest rate volatility, availability of finance, poor financial market, etc. The private sector should also be accountable for construction and project management risks such as coordination risk, poor quality, cost overrun, time overrun, frequency of maintenance, availability of labour or material, insolvency of subcontractors, design deficiency, etc. Economic risks arising from operational revenue being below expectation should also be borne by the private sector. Bing et al. (2005) advise that the risks that can be shared between the public and the private sectors are *force majeure* risks, lack of commitment from partners and legislation change. Supporting this, Arndt (1998) also suggests the *force majeure* risks be shared so as to provide incentive for the private player to design the infrastructure in such a way as to minimize any damage due to these events.

Arndt (1998) note that a fair and transparent system for risk allocation should be followed when no party is able to manage the risk. He calls for such a mechanism to be flexible over the life cycle of the project and that it be able to deal with risks not envisioned. Mok, Shen, and Yang (2015), in their study of external stakeholders in megaprojects, note that the project teams with their limited cognition are unable to identify all the external stakeholders, let alone the risks arising because of them. Supporting this, Chang, Hatcher, and Kim (2013) note that the size and complexity of large projects causes difficulty in discerning which actors or elements can influence the project. Clegg and Kornberger (2015) note that stakeholders can materialize from unlikely places, such as the natural environment.

Albalate and Bel (2009) propose the use of a variable model, i.e. Least Present Value of Revenue (LPVR) and Least Present Value of Net Revenue (LPVNR), to mitigate risks and thereby improve social welfare. Through these, they suggest flexible-term rather than fixed-term contracts so that the risk is internalized in the contractual framework and what actually occurs in practice dictates the length of the concession period.

The conventional way of allocating risks encourages a blame game rather than problem solving. Alternatively, a risk/reward regime can be set up as a cost or benefit for each participant according to project outcomes, rather than individual contributions by the relevant participant. This sharing of risks, by which all participants benefit or suffer together, incentivizes all of them to prevent and solve problems, rather than seek to allocate blame. Pitsis et al. (2003) provide an example of just such an approach in the construction of the Northside Storage Tunnel in Sydney.

Describing the entirety of a complex product and process makes writing a detailed contract nearly impossible (Brown, Potoski, & Van Slyke, 2018). The up-front costs of reducing uncertainty through finely detailed prescriptive definitions can be steep and sometimes prohibitive. There needs to be a focus on flexibility while delivering complex products such as infrastructure projects.

Risks can be categorized into risks in the pre-development phase, risks in the development phase and risks in the operation phase (Jin, 2009). The risks in the pre-development phase include planning fallacy risk, renegotiation risk and financial closure risk. The risks in the development phase include planning and design risks, delivery risks and commissioning risks. The risks in the operating phase include operating risks, market risks and asset ownership risks.

EXTEND YOUR KNOWLEDGE

A systematic analysis of risk in project management is provided by Williams (2017), available at https://study.sagepub.com/pm.

WHAT WOULD YOU DO?

You are the project manager for a large urban light rail project that is planned to run down the main street of your capital city. The street is quite old and has been settled for hundreds of years. Building a rail line along the street was always going to be difficult, not just because of city traffic, but because of what lurked below: two and a half centuries of pipes, conduits and cables, some of which were documented and some of which were not. These risks were exacerbated by planning and governance arrangements that skipped important assurance steps. The project was accepted by the contractor, for whom you work as project manager, on the understanding that the electricity company had agreed with the government that there was a plan in place to deal with its utilities under the route. This proved not to be the case. After work had commenced the electricity provider submitted requirements that the contractor had to meet, such as additional spare conduits and enlarging pits for cables as well as many more relocations of services. Weeks of extra work at key intersections followed, sending the project way off schedule and budget with ongoing legal disputation occurring as to who should carry the risk.

QUESTION

Who, in your opinion, should carry the risk and its costs? (Hint: this case is based on an actual set of events surrounding the construction of a light rail line down Sydney's main thoroughfare, George St., which opened in 2019. A Google search will uncover considerable news coverage of the case and its litigation.)

How to manage – practical examples and tools

In this chapter, we have presented various aspects and characteristics of project management. We have stressed both planning and follow-up and that project management takes place on several levels. It is challenging to make an overall description of how all types of projects can be managed, given the vast range of difference and complexity that projects can present. However, we will present as an abstraction a concrete, step-by-step representation of how project management can be planned and implemented. The presentation provides a summary of this chapter and an instruction manual for the most central project management tools.

Chapter 3 concluded with a proposal on how to prepare the project by clarifying importance and relevance, identifying expected value creation and assessing feasibility, i.e. the overall project management framework. These elements form the basis for developing the next step: *project management*. Defining the key principles for the project is the first step in project management, as presented in the previous chapter, by establishing a mission breakdown structure, benefit realization plan, stakeholder analysis and project charter (see Figure 5.13).

It is desirable and often necessary that actors such as project managers, senior management and line managers in the permanent organization, as well as others that might be profoundly affected, should participate in the preparation of the overall project management framework.

As the project progresses, there will also be greater clarity and emerging needs as a result of changes and new knowledge. This will often necessitate changes and

Mission Breakdown Structure	• Clarify the purpose. What will the final result of the project lead to? What value creation should it contribute to? • Systematize potential impact targets. • Obtain the project goals by clarifying expected results. • Separate goals and sub-goals that fall within and outside the project. • Practical. Break the purpose, performance goals and sub-goals down on different levels and detailing. Design a hierarchical presentation, with descriptions, explanations and clarifying what's inside and outside the project framework. Attract key actors into developing the project work.
Benefit Realization Plan	• Identify expected gains from the project. • Identify what specific steps are needed to achieve the benefits. • Prepare and assign responsibilities and roles about who will contribute to the realization of the benefits. • Explain how and what time measurement of gains should be possible. • Consider what resources are required to evaluate the benefits.
Stakeholder Analysis	• Identify who may be the project's stakeholders. • Identify which area or topic stakeholders may have their interests in. • Identify what kind of interest they may have, how they can affect the project and its results. • Develop a strategy for managing stakeholders. • Assign responsibility for following up the strategies.
Project Charter	• Clarify the objectives of the project and contributions to value creation, regarding project goals and impact targets. • Obtain clity what the project is about, what is to be done. • Clarify which individuals and agencies have important responsibilities, where PL and PO are the most important. • Enter the framework conditions that apply to the project. It implies a period, the resource framework and the most important quality requirements. • Use the mandate as the summary document that defines the project framework and management basis. Any other documents may be attached or included in the documentary basis. • Include the background for projects and give the project a suitable name.

Figure 5.13 Strategic level. Overview for overall project management framework (OPMF) and other essential elements

adaptations. The organizational project management elements give the strategic framework that provides the basis for establishing framework and management tools at the tactical level (Figure 5.14).

Responsibilities and roles are often included in the charter, although many projects also draw up their own documents for these. The use of principle responsibility cards (Andersen et al., 2009) is an example of that. In Chapter 9, we will focus on stakeholders and how to involve them in the project. We will present stakeholder analysis more thoroughly there and discuss why and how it can be used. As a rule, it would be useful to include stakeholder analysis as part of organizational project management.

Once organizational project management is established, you have an excellent foundation with which to start work on milestones and milestone follow-up (Figure 5.15).

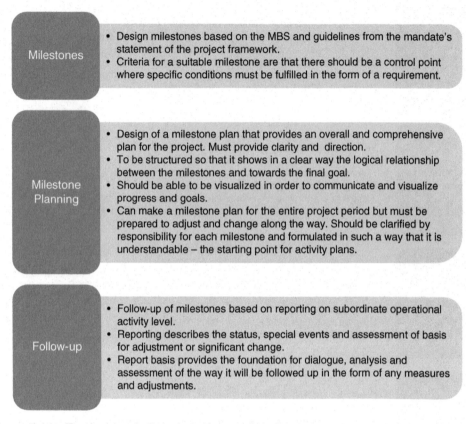

Figure 5.14 Tactical level. Overview of essential elements

The milestones are established to define what activities and actions must be taken to achieve them. They provide a basis for detailed planning and follow-up.

Risk has to be managed and we have introduced some of the literature relating to risk management. Finally, we would like to emphasize that it is not possible or desirable to offer universal recipes and procedures for project management, since projects are so different. Project management needs to base execution on the project's specificity and needs, using or discovering the tools best suited to reach the project's objectives.

Summary

In this chapter we have emphasized that all project managers must know their project and the contextual contingencies and select the most appropriate execution strategy accordingly. To do so we suggested that the project manager should know about:

- Execution strategies and how they guide execution through providing shared terminology, expectations about what will be done, when, a common platform for planning and contributing to project decision-making's appropriate communication, coordination and control, furthering temporal progress.

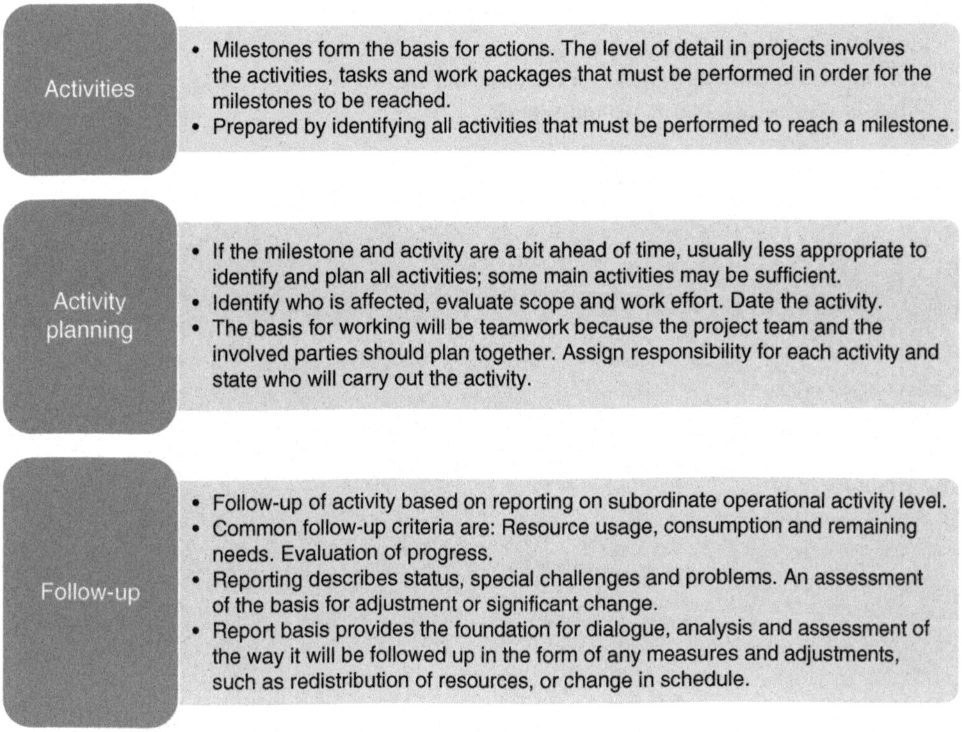

Activities
- Milestones form the basis for actions. The level of detail in projects involves the activities, tasks and work packages that must be performed in order for the milestones to be reached.
- Prepared by identifying all activities that must be performed to reach a milestone.

Activity planning
- If the milestone and activity are a bit ahead of time, usually less appropriate to identify and plan all activities; some main activities may be sufficient.
- Identify who is affected, evaluate scope and work effort. Date the activity.
- The basis for working will be teamwork because the project team and the involved parties should plan together. Assign responsibility for each activity and state who will carry out the activity.

Follow-up
- Follow-up of activity based on reporting on subordinate operational activity level.
- Common follow-up criteria are: Resource usage, consumption and remaining needs. Evaluation of progress.
- Reporting describes status, special challenges and problems. An assessment of the basis for adjustment or significant change.
- Report basis provides the foundation for dialogue, analysis and assessment of the way it will be followed up in the form of any measures and adjustments, such as redistribution of resources, or change in schedule.

Figure 5.15   Operational level. Overview of central elements

- Key principles and underlying logics of the main project execution strategies; namely waterfall, milestone and agile strategy and be able to judge the appropriateness of each of these strategies in light of various contingencies.
- Strengths and weaknesses of the different execution logics.
- Where risks should be allocated. The aspects of project type, scope and complexity to consider when choosing the execution strategy for your project. These, together with project competence and project objectives, provide guidelines for the development of strategy.
- A variety of ways to do contracting in projects and what considerations frame the appropriate contracting for the project in question.

Exercises

1. Explicate the key principles of the waterfall execution strategy, the key principles of the milestone execution strategy and the key principles of agile execution strategy.
2. What are the key features to consider in selecting the most appropriate execution strategy for the project in question?
3. Explain the relationship between uncertainty and choice of execution strategy.
4. What are the three things group members must report on in the daily stand-up meetings when using Scrum?
5. What are the key principles of Design Thinking and when is it relevant to apply Design Thinking in projects?

6. What is most important to consider when following up on budgets and at what level should one follow up?
7. Explain three different ways to do contracting.
8. What is risk? How can it be managed?

CASE STUDY

- -

EXECUTION STRATEGY FOR A REORGANIZING PROJECT AT A GOVERNMENTAL CULTURE AGENCY

BACKGROUND

Political authorities have decided governmental organizations need to be more efficient and that the taxpayers' money should be audited as being well spent. The Agency for Cultural Promotion is no exception. More specifically, they are told by the Ministry of Culture to find a better way of organizing their work.

The Agency for Cultural Promotion (ACP) is a governmental operator implementing governmental cultural policy, coordinating strategies for subunits in cultural sectors, financed by the state. The National Art Exhibition and the National Museum of Art and Design are examples of the dozen or so subunits. ACP consists of about 100 employees and four departments and is located in the capital.

REORGANIZING AS A PROJECT

Reorganizing of the agency will start soon. The new director for the agency, Steve Cook, has decided that this implies a reorganization of three out of the four departments in the organization. There is a mutual understanding in the agency about the necessity of this, as well as among the subordinate organizations, one of which will be directly affected by the reorganizing.

The reorganizing process will be organized as a project. Cook is aware of the importance of involvement from those affected and the importance of having focus on the effects of the reorganization, not merely the project itself. In addition, due to necessary process requirements, the project must deal with some significant decision gates or milestones.

Director Cook is excited to get started and recently he has become aware of Scrum as a way of executing projects. He has read some articles on the issue. However, during a discussion in the previous management meeting, there was quite strong disagreement about the relevance of Scrum as the most appropriate way to execute this project.

Cook understands that for a project like this to be successful, it will be important to apply a suitable execution strategy. He would appreciate some enlightenment and advice on some issues, before starting the project.

QUESTIONS

1. What characterizes Scrum as a methodology? Given the *limited information* on the project you have available, what would be the potential advantages and disadvantages of applying Scrum as an execution strategy?

2. If a pure Scrum methodology is not going to be used in this project, how can a reorganization project like this apply agile methods and elements, while at the same time including the decision gates (milestones) for the project?

3. What would be potential critical elements for succeeding with an agile execution strategy for this type of project?

Additional resources

In the book by Larson and Gray (2017) you can go deeper into a variety of tools and processes and how these are framed by what is conceptualized as the prevailing culture of the organization and interpersonal dynamics of the people involved (we would argue that there are *cultures*). In Pries and Quigley's 2010 book you can gain an overview of Scrum project management. Turner (2017) gives valuable insights into issues of contracting for project management. Smyth (2014) provides insights on how to manage relationships in projects.

Chapter Roadmap

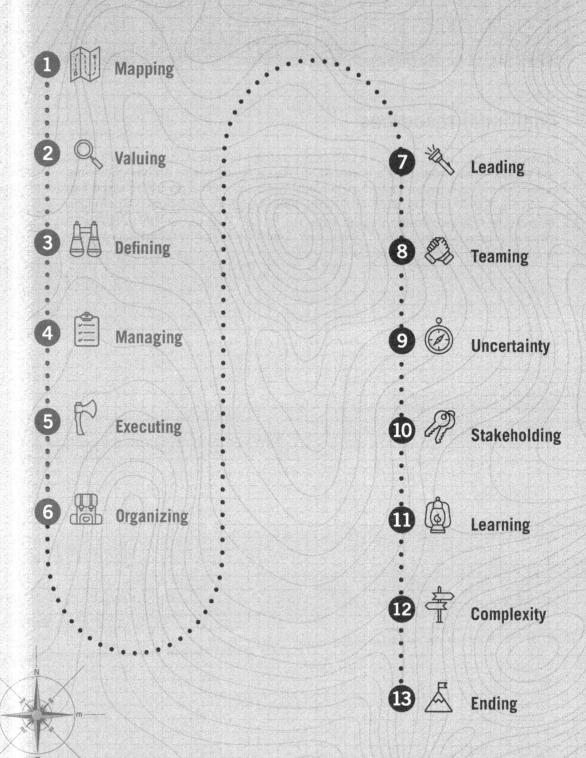

1. Mapping
2. Valuing
3. Defining
4. Managing
5. Executing
6. Organizing
7. Leading
8. Teaming
9. Uncertainty
10. Stakeholding
11. Learning
12. Complexity
13. Ending

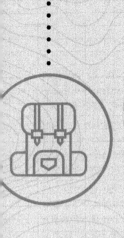

6

Organizing Projects

Learning objectives

After reading this chapter, you should:

1 Understand that external project organizing is about the relationship between the permanent organization and the project, and the project manager's decision-making authority over the project team members (the hours they are allocated to the project)

2 Know that internal project organizing refers to the sharing of responsibility and authority among the various roles involved in project execution and knowing the most important roles

3 Understand the importance of organizing and coordinating and how this is contingent on the context

4 Be aware of the different elements of organizational culture that feature in the project context

5 Know about the dimensions and distribution of power in the project context

Before you get started

Management combines art, craft and science in variable measures of creativity, phronesis and techne.

– Stewart Clegg.

Introduction

Thus far we have concentrated quite a lot on *techne*, or technical aspects, of project management. The many acronyms of project management as a discipline that we have already encountered are testament to this technical aspect. Nonetheless, as we have stressed, projects are temporary organizations whose goal is to create a delivery that involves value *creation* for another actor. Often, the actor aiming for increased value creation is the project's principal. In order for the project to succeed in project execution and for value to be created when deliveries are implemented, a close positive connection between the client and the project is crucial. This is where *craft* enters the picture. What is at issue is how responsibility and authority should be shared between the two parties and how they should interact in order that the organization design for project execution and deliveries is efficient and effective. Another critical issue is the design of the internal organization, i.e. the distribution of responsibility and authority between actors/roles in project execution and how they interact.

In this chapter we will put the most emphasis on the formal structures that indicate the allocation of responsibility and authority, as they are the main premises for project organizing. They do not determine the actual organizing, as organizing emerges as an entangled process including formal and informal structures, people, organizational culture, power and influence. Neither the prescription of roles nor the power relations associated with the roles will be definitively defined. Project organizing is an ongoing development process influenced by the interaction between individual participants. The pattern of interaction reflects the actual organizing of the project and forms the identity of the project. Project organizing is thus not primarily boxes and arrows on an organization chart (formalized structures) – that is, the organization's design. It is practice and understanding this is where both *art* and *science* enter the picture.

Organizing and success

Project organizing is one of the topics that has gained increasing attention in recent years and is often ascribed as a key cause of project failures (Flyvbjerg et al., 2003). One reason is that sometimes the permanent or client organization does not make available to the project those human or financial resources promised, seeing a greater need for them in more pressing routine matters (Engwall & Jerbrant, 2003). Other times, the client organization does not provide the project with clarifications that are necessary for it to keep on track as envisioned; the project becomes relatively autonomous and somewhat semi-detached. Under these circumstances the most critical issue for the client organization is to ensure timely clarifications (Berggren et al., 2008). If the client doesn't follow up in a way that contributes to efficient work processes and good governance in the project (there may be too much as well as too little follow-up), the probability of project management success will also be reduced (Jugdev & Müller, 2005).

The likelihood of project management success is reduced if the permanent organization is not adequately prepared for taking over and implementing project outcomes (Andersen, 2008). Many a project has delivered excellent policy and strategy frameworks to organizations that they find difficult to accept, integrate or implement. Avoiding such an outcome is particularly important from a value creation perspective. In addition, the relationships between the project and the permanent organization in terms of scope, scale and time is not always clear. If a project's outcomes are not used by those organizationally responsible, the potential for project success is obviously reduced. The responsibilitities of the project, as well as those of the client organization, relate both to implementing the project and using its outcomes. Organizing to manage these predictable issues is closely linked to project success.

External project organizing: The interface between project and permanent organization

Typical permanent organizations are often relatively hierarchically structured, with many different organizational units and specified functional roles. Their organizing reflects the overall purpose of the organization. Organizational structures in permanent organizations are designed for the stability of the tasks and the way they are distributed; therefore, they are not very flexible. Projects serve as organizational mechanisms, enabling flexible operation when called for, often where there are demands for renewal. Through projects, a company can, for a period, break up organizational structures to solve specific assignments that are not accomplished within the existing functional hierarchy of the organization. The temporary organization of the project can draw on resources from many parts of the organization, forming interdisciplinary teams. For any project assignment to be resolved appropriately for the permanent organization the connection between the project and permanent organization needs to be defined.

We will now look at three forms of project organizations, referring to the interface between projects and their permanent organization: *autonomous projects*, *departmental projects* and *matrix projects*. These types of organization are used in many project-based companies in the field of construction, oil, industry, ICT and product development. However, they are not applicable to projects where several organizations collaborate on the ownership side, either in delivery projects or most event projects.

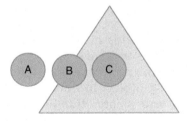

Figure 6.1   Three organizational forms for projects' connection to the base organization

The triangle in Figure 6.1 represents the permanent organization while the circles represent the three different connection types the project may have. The main difference between the three types of organizing is the extent to which the project manager has decision-making authority over project team members during the time they are allocated to the project (Andersen, 2008). Put another way, does the creation of the project mean a change in the permanent organization's imperative authority over the employees?

In Figure 6.1 – a widely used representation of three different types of organization – A refers to autonomous projects, B to matrix projects and C to departmental projects.

Picture 6.1 Autonomous Project

Source: Statsbygg/Trond Isaksen

Autonomous projects

An autonomous project is entirely separate from the permanent organization. Large construction projects as well as major change projects are often organized as autonomous. If projects are autonomous in their organizational form, project team members work 100 per cent in the project for as long as they are part of it (Cicmil & Marshall, 2005). The project manager has approximately 100 per cent decision-making authority over resources regarding professional tasks. Many project managers prefer this organizational form as do project team members. The attraction is in being employed 100 per cent in the same project, providing a greater sense of belonging than switching among projects.

A potential disadvantage of working in autonomous projects, especially if they have a long-term horizon, is that sometimes you lose touch with what is happening in your department during the project period. Tension related to what project team members will do after the project has ended is not uncommon as projects can be intensely purposeful and identity-fulfilling, such that switching back to routines, especially if the team members have been part of a project for a long time, maybe for years, will not be attractive. Can they return to line assignments or can they transfer to other projects? Employees can also miss the opportunity to be engaged in other exciting tasks and projects during the period they work in an autonomous project.

The members of autonomous projects are often physically collocated, something that enables knowledge translation and interaction between project participants (see Chapter 10), hastening project progress (Vaagaasar, 2015a). Autonomous projects often make it easier to build good teams. The employees are in the project throughout their working hours, working closely together and intending to work on this project for a long time. Hence, it is easier for them to invest in relationships so that trust is created (Swärd, 2013). They also learn more about each other and thus it is likelier that they will develop better shared understanding and goals (Cicmil & Marshall, 2005). All of this common sensemaking is positive for project execution.

One difficulty with an autonomous project organization is that its members become too well socialized together as a team. If this occurs, it may be that the project and the permanent organization become too detached from each party. They are unable to entrain their actions, to provide adequate information to each party, make the necessary decisions to ensure the project's progress and deliverables, to achieve the quality and relevance desired on both sides to create the required value (Andersen, 2008). Since autonomous projects, by definition, are independent, it can be demanding to achieve synergies between seperately autonomous projects. Sharing knowledge between projects and employees across projects where team members are committed to a specific project does not make it easy for them to switch between several projects or to remain active in their line jobs. We will later look at what steps can be taken to address these challenges.

Departmental projects

C refers to the departmental project where the structure of the permanent organization is not altered. It is the permanent organization, in each department, which has decision-making authority over employees. The project is part of a department and the project manager has limited authority. In departmental projects, all members of the project work in the same department. Departmental projects are often relatively small projects, requiring only specific and limited knowledge and skills. They may also arise from a department wishing to change its day-to-day operation or as change projects that treat highly sensitive information, not intended for widespread distribution. In practice, project managers of such projects often have relatively small decision-making authority. Such projects are often conducted in a relatively informal and ad hoc manner. An advantage of this form of organization is that knowledge and learning developed in the project can easily be incorporated into the department's work. There are no problems associated with being detached from one's department and community of practice. Nevertheless, these types of projects tend to be relatively unstructured and not tightly managed relative to the outcomes they produce; indeed, there is a high risk that they will not produce much in the way of increased value creation.

Matrix projects

Many contemporary organization projects are organized as *matrix projects* (Larson & Gobeli, 1987). In matrix-organized projects, as in A, employees perform some of their departmental responsibilities while participating in the project, hence their identity is both that of being a part of the project while they remain partially overseeing line tasks. We will see that the project manager's decision-making authority can be quite variable in various forms of matrix-organized projects. Project team members work in a given project while working on other projects or with line assignments. The project manager has to make agreements with various line managers about the commitments of team members to the project. The project manager's degree of decision-making authority relative to the line managers must be clearly specified. Failure to do so can generate intra-organizational conflicts about the use of human and other resources.

The apparent advantage of the matrix organization, from the perspective of the permanent organization, is that it provides flexible utilization of organizational expertise. It allows for the temporary establishment of a project organization in which those persons most fitted for the task at hand can collaborate in goal achievement. There are different forms of matrix organization: *a weak, balanced* or *strong* matrix (Larson & Gobeli, 1987).

- In a *weak matrix*, the project manager has a small degree of decision-making authority over project staff and works more as a coordinator across the functional areas than as a leader. Line managers retain responsibility and authority for their respective parts of the project. They make decisions for the project's work within what they define as their area of responsibility in the permanent organization.
- In a *strong matrix*, the project manager is more of a real leader, a chief executive of the project, with employees taking greater responsibility and holding more decision-making authority within their segments of the project.
- In a *balanced matrix*, project manager and line managers are notionally equal in terms of responsibility and authority for the decisions that must be made in the project. Research has shown that project matrixes located between balanced and strong often provide the most efficient project execution in which the project has relatively large control over project resources.

PROS AND CONS OF MATRIX PROJECT ORGANIZATION

Individual employees working in a matrix organization can participate in projects that take them out from routines while keeping them in touch with these routines and other colleagues. The opportunity to participate in project assignments can be potentially exciting while providing departmental continuity in routine staffing and operations. Matrix organization also facilitates knowledge transfer between the project and the permanent organization (Swan, Scarbrough, & Newell, 2010). When a project ends, employees have a base to which they can return, although the transition from being in the project to working in the department is more difficult when a staff member has been wholly committed to the project for a long time. Project leaders, especially, can find themselves in the awkward situation of having lost touch with departmental knowledge and colleagues while gaining project experience and autonomy that fits ill with the expectations of returning to the routines in the department that they are expected to slot back into.

An obvious and significant disadvantage of a matrix organization is that the employee has two or more managers simultaneously, potentially leading to higher pressure and stress. When both managers request delivery, time and commitments require balancing and priorities ordered that may well have political consequences. If the project member tries to manage the potential conflict by communicating different and possibly contradictory messages then they may end up in more serious longer-term conflicts, as the contradictions mount. Where they are subject to these contradictory commands their position becomes increasingly ambiguous: who should they follow, where and when? Working in matrix projects often involves interaction with many people and opportunities that can be enriching but also challenging for interpersonal and interorganizational communication, coordination and control, from which conflicts and stress may result.

Matrix organization is demanding but potentially rewarding as an organizational form. It requires high levels of awareness of possible contradictions, clarification of interfaces as well as willingness on the part of the host organization to train members in the execution of projects and the challenges they bring. Despite the risks, there are many benefits associated with matrix organization that include the following (Larson & Gobeli, 1987):

- Flexible and efficient use of human resources in the firm (in principle, it also means that all projects can have access to relevant competencies)
- Good coordination across projects because many employees are coupled both to the permanent organization and one or more projects
- Attention to customer needs and good customer understanding in the project if there is an internal customer for the project's delivery
- Well-established actor networks of employees across the organization will be generated through experiences shared across projects and over time

The disadvantages of matrix organization can be summed up as the corollaries of those aspects of its design that make participation in the matrix demanding. The permanent organization can find it quite challenging to cope with a project portfolio based on the matrix principle because:

- Conflicting needs are nurtured in the permanent organization and the project
- Additionally, there may be clashes between commitments to different projects; for example, such conflict can arise in allocating resources to individual entities
- Attention and resource allocation must be balanced so that line assignments are well taken care of while projects are also executed as planned
- The matrix involves prioritization between the various projects, which can cause 'noise' and inhibit the planned progression of some projects

For employees, having two or more managers (and potentially multiple signals) may be confusing and politically problematic and their relations with multiple other employees, interfaces, tasks and deadlines belonging to different entities can be challenging.

WHAT WOULD YOU DO?

You are to be the project manager for a project starting up soon. The project aims to implement a new IT system software in a medium-sized business. The software development side of the project is rather straightforward. However, when the system is implemented, it will affect three of the departments and their routines and procedures, and quite a few of the employees in several departments. You work as an IT specialist in the IT department. The principal, as well as the CEO and the leader group of the company, have argued for a departmental organization

(Continued)

of the project. Nevertheless, some arguments against this form of organizing for the project were raised in subsequent discussions. You accepted the challenge of considering the most appropriate form of organizing for this type of project.

QUESTION

In general terms, think about what proposal you would make to your boss, the IT director, about how to organize the project. What, why and how would you argue?

PROJECT AND LINE MANAGER RELATIONS IN MATRIX ORGANIZATION

Matrix organizing requires a high degree of shared responsibility between different actors. Divisions of labour and responsibilities must be combined with collaborative work oriented to building close dialogues and establishing informal relationships characterized by trust and mutual respect. Given these affordances, knowledge will be shared and managed to clarify decisions efficiently, helping enable project success. To minimize the negative effects of matrix organization it is crucial to elaborate the interfaces between the project team members' charters and outline expectations related to task solution, terms of type and scope.

Matrix organization requires that the type and amount of human resources assigned to the project from their department be released as a part of line managers' responsibilities for project execution. In accomplishing the project, project managers will deploy resources gleaned from elsewhere in the organization. When these are people whose skills are dedicated to the project, it is best that the line manager is responsible for designating the employee. The manager assesses how the expertise in his department can contribute to the project and the extent to which the department can live up to the resource-related commitments it is taking on – does doing so conflict with more local and immediate needs or political interests?

Conflicts in matrix projects are neither inevitable nor unlikely. Line managers will have to shield employees who have a heavy burden of project tasks from other tasks, while redirecting responsibilities in the department and assessing the general deployment of resources. The line manager must manage the department's obligations to the project and the organization, which can often create sub-optimal goal displacement: for instance, do I send the best person for the job to the project? Or, shall I send that person I have been trying to get rid of for some time? The temptation to do the latter can sometimes be too great.

The distribution of decision-making authority over organization members while working in a project is an essential issue for any external organization. We have discussed three external organizational forms – autonomous, departmental and matrix – pointing out that a matrix organization is the most common. In practice, it is rare to see such organizations in as pure a form as we have described them. They appear, more usually, as hybrid forms. For example, many of the team members in autonomous projects work 100 per cent, while the project team also has members that only take part for a short period or are just engaged in resolving minor issues. Similarly, in matrix projects, some employees may have a minor or part-time job involvement while project managers and a few other key employees, whose skills are vital for project success, spend their entire working hours in the project. Moreover, many projects involve external stakeholders, such as consultants whose assignments are defined through a separate contract with the project.

EXTEND YOUR KNOWLEDGE

Putting a project team together involves many risks. Projects are under constant pressure to improve performance. Read the article 'Organizational justice, project performance, and the mediating effects of key success factors', by Unterhitzenberger and Bryde (2019) to learn about their framework for success, available at https://study.sagepub.com/pm.

Internal project organizing: Governance

We will now look at internal project organizing, specifically at how different functions, roles and relationships are arranged to run a project. A role is the sum of the norms and expectations that relate to a particular responsibility, position or group in the project. The range of critical roles in classical project execution include the following:

- Project managers
- Project team members
- Project owner
- Steering groups
- Reference groups
- Project councils

By establishing roles with varied tasks and responsibilities, a structured division of labour is designed which aligns with structured design of flows of communication and coordination in governance, as an overall control mechanism (Müller & Lecoeuvre, 2014). Ambiguity and conflict can easily occur where there are contradictory expectations of what a project role should be. Different expectations may well be embedded in subordinates (those reporting), superordinates (those to whom reports are made) and peers (those with whom the role incumbent collaborates on an equal footing). Excessive strain can be caused by overloading work expectations for the role.

Any organizational role is a continuous and fluid process, emerging through the interaction of more or less established guidelines about the role, as well as other actors' attitudes and expectations towards it (Bechky, 2006), none more so than when that role is project-based, outside of normal organizational routines. Hence, people assigned to roles must be able to adapt these to the evolving project's purpose and have the competencies and commitment to be able to perform the duties expected. Projects are always in process, emergent, fluid.

Formal roles and structures are designed to enable communication and coordination to produce effective collaboration in the project. In practice, however, formal design rarely suffices: communication and coordination processes will be characterized by some degree of improvisation (Kamoche & Cunha, 2001). Improvisation in almost all forms of endeavour requires preparation and capabilities that frame emergent action as reflective practice (Schön, 1983) – think of great jazz or football. Improvisation entails intensely well-trained and accomplished practitioners being able to work intuitively with similar others in their craft.

These powers of improvisation also matter for projects (Bechky & Okhuysen, 2011).

Ownership – main responsibility for the project

The project owner has a critical role in the project (Miller & Lessard, 2000)). The owner holds the primary responsibility for the project in the permanent organization. Ownership entails responsibility for communicating, coordinating and controlling flows of information between project and organization processes (Turner & Keegan, 2001). Interests are at stake in these flows: the project manager's interest in being seen to be delivering an exemplary project; the project teams' interest in being part of a success story; the clients' interest in obtaining exemplary project outcomes; the project owners' interest in safeguarding the client's interests.

Delivering on the complex of interests, which is a major responsibility of the project owner (usually and optionally in cooperation with the steering group), requires governance (Müller & Lecoeuvre, 2014) that includes some or all of the following:

- Ensuring that the project receives the necessary attention in the permanent organization and that critical decisions for the project are taken
- Providing overall management and control throughout the life of the project
- Ensuring good transitions between project phases, including determining decision gates
- Establishing the project's charter
- Recruiting a project manager
- Approving an execution model, including plans, organization and resource allocation at the overall level
- Monitoring and controlling progress, results and financial conditions in the project
- Ensuring that the project receives necessary human and financial resources
- Nurturing a strong 'for project' culture and liaising with other key actors in realizing the project
- Anchoring the project in the organization, its strategies and cultures, throughout the entire lifespan of the project
- Terminating the project, if necessary

Governance responsibilities might be vested in a project owner or a steering group. Sometimes, the project owner will lead the steering group as a decision-making body that supports the project owners' efforts to facilitate and control the project. Either way, governance is ordinarily a concommitant for projects having operational and skilled project owners (Turner & Müller, 2005) and/or steering groups (Lechler & Cohen, 2009).

Governance is often linked to the establishment of phase models with decision gates. The idea is to achieve improved project execution and increased likelihood of success by stopping along the way (at the gates) and systematically evaluating what has been completed and considering the future direction. The decision-making gates ensure that decision-makers in the organization regularly evaluate the project's direction and progress, which also contributes to organizational learning (Morris, Pinto, & Söderlund, 2011).

There has been a significant increase in attention and emphasis on the project ownership role in the last decade as a part of the increasing attention being paid to issues of corporate governance (Clegg et al., 2020). Paradoxically, projects are often led by competent project managers with experience and formal competence in project management, while middle managers often assume project direction as owners, even when lacking project experience or competence. Professionalizing this element of governance involves staffing the ownership function with people who have knowledge of project execution, making governance part of the project's management system, using mechanisms that enable competent project owner practice by making sure that people assigned to this role have time and other resources to be committed.

The project owner may be a departmental director/line manager who has relevant professional responsibility. Sometimes the line manager responsible for the area in which project delivery will be implemented holds the project owner role. In projects of highly strategic importance, it may be that the top management (CEO) assumes the role of project owner (or steers the steering group).

Project owners and project champions

Project owners should be appointed in the project's early phases, often in the conceptual phase, to be a champion for the project. A decision framework will already be in place in the sponsoring organization and the champion's role is to ensure that project delivery creates the required value. Often, the project owner is relatively uninvolved in project execution after establishing the project charter, except for mobilizing against project-threatening events. The project owner role is often assigned to relatively experienced individuals with high authority in the organization (Helm & Remington, 2005). Being busy and with many other obligations, the champion's attention may be diluted. High degrees of professionalism and education are usually a sine qua non, including, in many contexts, appropriate certification. An already burdened top executive team member may not be the best project owner, unless their role as such is clearly articulated in the organization. A project owner may, in turn, nominate project champions to represent various aspects of project delivery. These roles can often be developmental with engineers becoming champions for ecological management and ecologists championing engineering solutions, for instance.

The project owner thus has a role both in relation to the project, by facilitating it, as well as towards the owner organization, by ensuring that the project is conducted in a manner that is in line with the interests of this organization and with relevant deliverables. Nominating and delegating project champions can be a useful device for achieving these outcomes.

Project owners or their representatives seek to ensure that the project achieves what is designated (Turner & Müller, 2005). In principle, we can say that project owners follow up on the project's alignment with the agreed framework and constraints defined in terms of key performance indicators. These may not just prescribe expected schedule/cost parameters but can be broader; they could, for example, include obligations to manage ecology, community and health and safety (Pitsis, Clegg, Marton, et al., 2003).

When the steering group or the owner make decisions, it is usually because they have the requisite decision-making expertise and authority although the decision-making authority of the project owner (and the steering group) is not linked just to these areas. A rule of thumb is that the senior leader with the most appropriate expertise will make the decision. From the discussion thus far, you can see that the project owner's key task is both controlling and facilitating the project. Often emphasis is placed on control as the central aspect. With regard to execution and also the implementation of project delivery, the facilitation role is often overlooked. The probability of project success is increased by the project owner being involved and responsible for facilitation rather than being an 'absentee landlord' (Helm & Remington, 2005; Muller, 2009).

THE ROLE OF THE PROJECT OWNER AND DECISION-MAKING

The term project owner is familiar nomenclature. Other terms are used, however, such as *project responsible* or *project director*. 'Project responsible' is mostly used for a permanent organization representative that oversees the daily follow-up of the project on behalf of the project owner. The owner is sometimes referred to as a *project sponsor*, implying that the organization implementing the project also financed it. We will use the project ownership nomenclature generically.

The project owner needs to ensure that the project receives timely decisions providing direction. Often, the execution rate of projects is hampered by the fact that decisions are slow in coming; perhaps the decisions that the project needs are taken by decision-makers, such as a steering group, that does not meet often (Berggren et al., 2008), perhaps because it is difficult to convene (Lechler & Cohen, 2009). The frequency of steering group meetings, as far as possible, needs to be adapted to the project's requirements for timely decisions (not from a calendar logic, for example, once a quarter). *Agile* approaches, especially, in line with other execution models in which not all of the premises are established at the start of the project, require many decisions being made throughout the project duration. Some decisions *must* be made in the steering group while others can be delegated.

The project owner is responsible for deciding who should participate in decision-making (Berggren et al., 2008). End users may well be significant for these processes even if not formally part of the decision-making apparatus in the project process. User involvement in the project may mean less project team control over the quality of the completed delivery. Overall project expectations from multiple stakeholders must be balanced against client wishes related to the quality of delivery and constraints related to future economy and time. Managing these processes may be demanding.

The project owner is the project's chief decision-maker and the project model should prefigure the most likely decision points in the project as well as overall procedures for decision-making processes and involvement. In longer-term projects, sponsoring organizations' needs and context may change with implications for the relevance of deliverables (Kreiner, 1995). The project owner bridges between the project and changing requirements from the permanent organization whilst being mindful of increases in project scope and mandate greater than those initially assigned (Vaagaasar, 2006).

WHAT WOULD YOU DO?

You are to be the project owner for the IT project implementing the new IT system software (see p. 196). The system will affect the routines and procedures of three departments. An IT specialist in the IT department is the project manager and most of the members of the project team are coming from the IT department but there are also several people coming from the accounting and finance department as well as the HR department. As you are feeling busy and a bit scared of not truly understanding the core of the project, you have started wondering about establishing a steering group. Who would you invite to the steering group and why? Would you include the CEO in this group? Would you still be the leader of this group or do you suggest only having a steering group – not the project owner role at all?

PROJECT OWNER–PROJECT MANAGER

While the owner exercises overall control and prepares the ground for the project, the day-to-day management of the project is carried out by the project manager. Project owners and project managers have to enjoy relatively close interaction, which may range from having regular (e.g. monthly) meetings or reports, usually related to the project's iron triangle; at the other extreme, they may have intensive contacts, maybe even several times daily, that are a mixture of formal and informal discussions.

Project owners may primarily follow up on what has been done or they may be a more active partner. In general, the more uncertainty that characterizes the project, the less it can be clarified and formulated in advance. Hence, close and frequent interaction throughout the project, both to interpret what is happening and the extent to which it is in line with the principal's definition of the project's interests, is more critical under these circumstances. Communication on the part of project owners and managers that is open and reflective will always pay attention to unfolding uncertainties in the project (Müller & Turner, 2005).

Project managers and project owners have relatively different expectations of each other's roles (Helm & Remington, 2005). Project owners tend to emphasize that project managers explicitly report on time and cost while project managers tend to want owners close to the project that take greater responsibility for it and the project teams' motivation. Project managers also want owners to be sparring partners, reflecting on and interpreting ambiguous information, proposing solutions. Project owners' need for control can conflict with project managers' desires for a learning partner in sensemaking. Organizations perceived as highly successful in executing complex projects become classified as having a high degree of project maturity because they often have an ownership function that is active and close to the project.

What do project managers want from project owners?

1. Experience, authority and power within the organization providing political knowledge, contacts with other relevant actors in the organization and a willingness to fight on their behalf for decisions and resources.
2. Someone to help them situate the project in a broader context, providing necessary clarifications and resources, especially legitimacy for the project.
3. Connection with stakeholders that are vital for the project by acting as brokers between sources of knowledge and users (Hargadon, 2002); creating action nets; leveraging social relationships (Hydle, Kvålshaugen, & Breunig, 2014); linking knowledge and experience among projects in a project portfolio (Koskinen, 2008); connecting with users, researchers, developers or people making regulations and designing procedures.

4. Learning: project owners often run several projects simultaneously. The lessons learned in one project can be useful for another, if collected, collated and communicated. By contributing to a knowledge network, the project owner increases the overall competence available for the project, so that innovation and problem-solving ability is increased.
5. Challenging and motivating the project team and manager as a partner (Helm & Remington, 2005).

WATCH THIS!

In some projects a function as a project coordinator is included in the organization design. Watch a video from Henrik Kniberg (2012) to learn more about this role at: https://study.sagepub.com/pm.

Steering group

The ownership role may be distributed to a *steering group* or *committee* (Lechler & Cohen, 2009). Where there is also a project owner, they usually lead the steering group as overseers of project quality assurance and follow-up. Steering groups may monitor and follow the overall project while the project manager is responsible for closer detail relating to execution. Participation in the steering group and its scope will be determined by the organizational context and those roles that are critical. In extensive projects, owners, managers and management team may all follow the project closely. Often, line managers for whom the deliverables or the project process are strategic will lead the steering group.

There are arguments for and against having a steering group for the project. The main argument against a steering group is that bringing in more actors reduces decision-making speed; in the worst-case scenario, the steering group hampers the project by providing it with additional work. Against this, having a steering group enables anchoring the project and its deliverables in more oversight. Involving line managers can help ensure relevant resources for the project. A steering group provides more actors to share the burden, useful if there is great uncertainty or complexity in the project, or where the project owner has a heavy workload. Where several companies join forces to establish a project, a steering group representing all companies can ensure managed information flow, involvement and anchoring. In situations where project owners are unable to follow up the project appropriately, due to low capacity or expertise, a steering group can also contribute positively.

Steering groups are responsible for the project charter and the other areas of responsibility assumed by project owners and can help to define and control projects to execute them in accordance with an organization's procedures for project execution (Lechler & Cohen, 2009). Steering group work can vary depending on the project being managed. For instance, decisions, or the basis for them, can be established in more informal arenas than board meetings, such as in a steering group that makes frequent site visits to innovation labs, shop floors or construction sites, as the case may be, in which some board members may be involved. Steering groups, especially where they gain first-hand knowledge of the arenas requiring oversight, can contribute to value creation in light of the overall goals of the company (Table 6.1).

Table 6.1 Steering group's possible work areas

Contribution	Influence surroundings and find resources	Advice, knowledge and resources	New thinking and innovation	Independent reviews
Tasks that lead to value creation	Networking, anchoring and legitimization	Consultations	Strategic input	Control and decisions
Necessary resources among board members	Social competence, reputation and relations	Experiences and professional competence Dynamic competence	Diversity, different experiences, time, creativity. Absorbent capability	Independent members, analysts and decision-makers, steering group experience. Understanding of the business
Use of resources requires	Engagement	Openness and generosity. Availability	Acceptance of different perceptions and understandings	Preparation, follow-up and critical assessments
Chairman of the Board as	Front figure	Adviser	Creative challenger	Strategic thinking

Reference group

A reference group is an organizational body designed to contribute to project delivery. It is a sparring partner for the project, often related to the qualities of the project deliverables. Often user representatives will be members of the reference group. There may also be professionals not directly involved in the project but with significant, relevant competence for project delivery. The reference group assists with managing stakeholders and quality assurance of project delivery. Typical responsibilities for a reference group are:

- Giving professional advice that emphasizes the interests of users, project owner and project team
- Specification of quality requirements and quality control of the products, both from a user and a professional perspective
- 'Sparking', talking very positively about the project, anchoring it in the line (primarily users and managers of the delivery) by communicating the value and effects of the project outcomes
- Overseeing and improving line management's abilty to receive and use project outcomes

Reference groups require user representatives able to ask wise questions, act as devil's advocates and be active listeners. Reference groups will be skilled both in capturing users' experiences and needs, as well as interpreting and communicating these. Reference groups do not have decision-making authority. They are advisory bodies for the design of the project's deliverables. If a project has many different types of deliverables several reference groups may be required.

Project councils

Reference groups focus most of their attention on the qualities of delivery, while project councils often have a broader focus. Project councils are advisory bodies for projects. They advise both on execution in relation to the project's charter and technical matters. A project council can be broadly composed of stakeholders, representing an excellent opportunity for the project to conduct stakeholder management. Project councils do not make decisions but recommendations. The minimum design for project organizing consists of the project manager and team, and a project owner. A more elaborate design can also include a steering group, project manager, project council and reference group(s). It is relatively common to have project councils on public projects in many countries, especially in Scandinavian social democracies, as inclusive representatives.

WHAT WOULD YOU DO?

The IT system implementation project presented briefly earlier in this chapter is moving on. Again, the principal asks you for some advice and arguments for organizing the project. The principal now favours a matrix-based organizing of the project. However, he still is not sure whether to include a reference group, a project council or none of these in the project.

What would be your arguments for ranking these three options?

Roles in agile projects

In agile projects, and more specifically in Scrum, there are three key roles: *Product Owner, Scrum Master* and *Scrum Team*. The terminology for describing responsibilities is characterized by the fact that we often talk about them in connection with product development (especially in IT technology).

AGILE PRODUCT OWNER

An agile product owner represents the customer or user to ensure that the Scrum Team is working appropriately from the clients' perspective. This is done by controlling the scope of the project, as well as ensuring that the project's delivery accords with the interests of value creation objectives. Agile product owners control the scope of project delivery according to a list of priority areas described as a user history (product queue) and update it continuously. The product owner is responsible for regularly prioritizing the product queue so that functionality is prioritized (Meso & Jain, 2006). Also, they are responsible for analysing and processing proposals for changes affecting the scope of project delivery. In addition, they provide funding and support for the project, formulating overall requirements, return on investment (ROI) and overall launch plans. In summary, we can say that the product owner must:

- Defend the specifications of delivery features
- Set the date of launch and the content of the launch
- Be responsible for product yield (ROI)

- Prioritize functionality in line with market needs/market value related to functionality
- Customize and prioritize functionality regularly, for example, every 30 days

Typically, the product owner has one person fully responsible for the scope and the direction of development (Nerur & Balijepally, 2007; Takeuchi & Nonaka, 1986). Fulfilling this role can be very demanding in complex systems built of many subsystems. A hierarchy of product owners can be established relative to each subsystem. The owners of the subsystems will have a charter attached to their part but be subordinate to the overall system.

In large, complex projects with multiple Scrum teams working in parallel, the product owner will probably lack the necessary expertise in all aspects of delivery; therefore, they will need to rely on a product owner team. The product owner coordinates, oversees, prioritizes and communicates decisions in a way that is adapted to the specific situation. The level of innovation and complexity, whether the product is aimed at a customer or a more open market, as well as the size of the project (number of stakeholders and Scrum teams), determine the amount of adjustments likely to occur.

WATCH THIS!

Watch this YouTube video by Heinrik Kniberg on the key tasks and issues you have to know for practising the product owner role, at: https://study.sagepub.com/pm.

In a project where delivery is characterized by a high degree of innovation, a visionary product owner might be able to create enthusiasm around a fairly unfinished idea, which communicates well with the outside world. Product owners in innovation-oriented projects must be able to live with a high degree of uncertainty, sometimes even with the realization that the project is failing. If little innovation occurs in a project developing an established product, attention may shift to process improvement, and customer satisfaction and communication with users as a key focus.

Strategies for customer involvement, such as meetings where the development team and customer team meet and develop user stories, will need to be designed. Market analysis of user needs, technological possibilities as well as business opportunities and competitor analysis may be required. The product owner is responsible for representing all the stakeholders in the project, understanding their perspectives and how they experience success. As discussed in Chapter 2, success is a multi-faceted term (Serrador & Pinto, 2015; Shenhar & Dvir, 2007).

AGILE SCRUM LEADER

The main task of the Scrum leader is to facilitate scrum teamwork for delivery according to the approved sprint plan. Sprint start-up, daily stand-up meetings and retrospective reflections need organizing, with the daily stand-up meetings and sprint check-ups (see Chapter 4) being the most important processes. Scrum managers are more facilitators than leaders (since the delivery teams are autonomous) but are responsible for the team working for agile execution and minimizing disturbances (Meso & Jain, 2006). In smaller projects, both the project manager and the Scrum leader role can be taken care of by a single person. In larger projects, it is often a project manager who manages the project and a Scrum leader that facilitates delivery production in line with the Scrum principles.

WATCH THIS!

In pure Scrum projects there is no project manager, with the Scrum master being similar to a traditional project manager. In the video by Joshua Partogi (2020) 'What Are the Differences Between Project Manager and Scrum Master' the differences and similarities between these functions are explained at: https://study.sagepub.com/pm.

SCRUM TEAM

The team is central to agile execution. It is responsible for doing development work and delivering product. It organizes itself and is an autonomous group. A Scrum team often consists of 3–9 people with different skills, such as designers and developers. Since it is a self-directed group, which requires a high level of interaction, the number of participants is limited. The members of the team choose through joint decision-making those tasks from the sprint queue they will do in the next sprint. Progress in daily sprint meetings focuses on overcoming obstacles to goal achievement (Meso & Jain, 2006).

Autonomy. Management facilitate autonomy by providing some overall principles but does not interfere with the team's development and direction.

Change mastery. Professionals and developers seeking to create something new often succeed by working on initially contradictory goals for which new solutions are generated.

Cross-fertilization. A conscious combination of complementary skills and different personalities.

If the members can be collocated, the flow of information and knowledge between them will be maximized. Takeuchi and Nonaka's (1986) research points to three key features of well-functioning, autonomous groups in flexible projects: **autonomy** and **change mastery** as well as **cross-fertilization**.

Different types of projects – different roles

We have presented the most common roles for project execution. Many other roles can be part of the project execution, varying from project to project in their relevance. Some projects have a *project coordinator* overseeing the coordination of activities and resources and project planners who take care of the planning work. Other projects may have a project controller who has the primary responsibility to control information registered by the project manager and general follow-up of the project. In large projects, you can find roles such as a contract manager and communication manager. In addition, there are roles related to different subject matters that are often relatively industry specific. IT projects typically have system administrator and system integrator roles, respectively responsible for system deployment and for testing and documentation.

In addition to the roles mentioned above, many project-based companies operate with roles such as programmme coordinator/director/manager (we will use manager here). They have overall responsibility for all projects that are part of a project programme. The programme manager coordinates across the projects that are part of the programme and ensures that the projects are connected with organization strategy. The programme manager is responsible for providing the internal link between the projects so that they complement each other and may also be responsible for allocating resources between the projects and maintaining contracts with suppliers. We will elaborate these roles further in Chapter 12.

WHAT WOULD YOU DO?

The IT software implementation project presented two times previously in this chapter, is still at the planning stage. Your boss, who is also the IT manager and project principal, as we know, has been away on a course and has returned excited about agile project execution, though restricted to Scrum methods. He considered recommending Scrum as an execution strategy and method for this matrix-organized project, having been informed about the possible benefits of applying Scrum. However, in the cross-divisional project team, there will be members without Scrum methodology experience and most of them will only be part-time engaged in the projects, dealing with their original job task as well.

QUESTION

1. Based on this limited information, what would be your arguments for and against Scrum as an execution strategy for this project?

EXTEND YOUR KNOWLEDGE

In their article 'Toward an improved understanding of agile project governance: A systematic literature review', Lappi, Karvonen, Lwakatare, Aaltonen, and Kuvaja (2018) provide a literature review and identify new practices emerging in agile projects, available at https://study.sagepub.com/pm.

Tools and processes for organizing

The charter is a document that defines the relationship between the project and the permanent organization, the scope of the project and the projects' action space in an 'Overall Management Framework'. We emphasized that a coherent understanding of goals and purposes contributes to increased awareness of areas and role responsibilities both within the project team and in the relationship between the project and the permanent organization. The same applies to the Mission Breakdown Structure. An additional tool for increased understanding of responsibilities and interfaces in projects is the *responsibility chart*. Responsibility charts, first linked to system development (King & Cleland, 1975), have been used for a long time in project contexts at various levels:

- **Overall level**. The chart explicates the main principles of accountability between different units in the permanent organization and the project, outlining who takes what responsibility to realize the purpose.
- **Milestone level**. The chart shows the different actors' responsibilities for achieving milestones. These may be actors in the permanent organization and in the project.
- **Operational level**. The chart shows the various project employees' responsibilities for various activities in the project.

Responsibility charts for the three levels all have the structure, as shown in Figure 6.2 (Andersen et al., 2009).

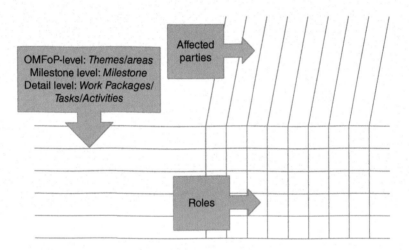

Figure 6.2 Responsibility chart principles applied to the three levels.

The charts may also include stakeholders that are not part of the internal structure but that execute the project and create value. Responsibility charts acknowledge both who is in charge and participates in the execution of activities, who is responsible for decisions and who can or may be consulted in different situations.

Below you will find a common set of abbreviations for the kind of responsibility and involvement different stakeholders will have in different activities and processes (in line with Andersen et al., 2009). An organization will use a system of abbreviations that are well known and accepted among all those involved in project execution. Responsibility charts are prepared in all shapes, with colour codes, symbols, letter codes and more.

Instead of responsibility charts, some projects use the RACI matrix to clarify many of the same themes. RACI is an acronym for *responsible, accountable, consulted* and *informed*. responsibility charts and RACI matrices are key tools used

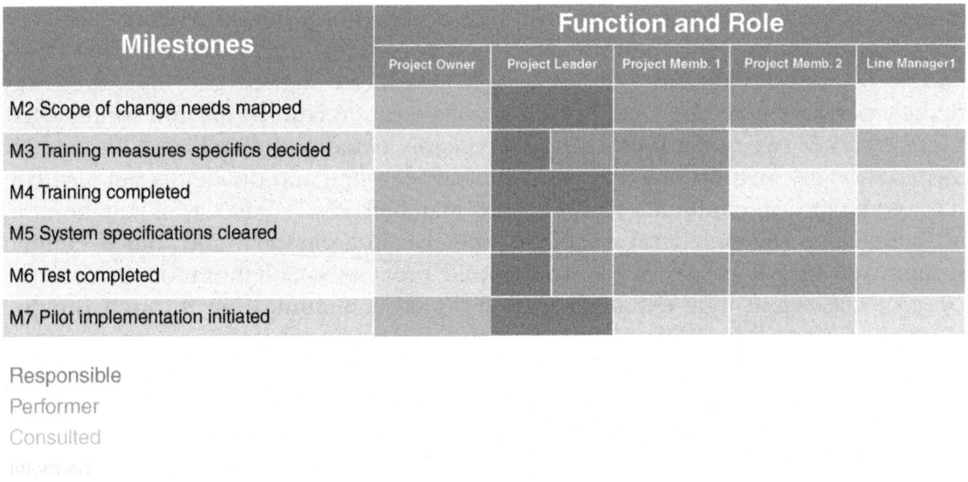

Milestones	Function and Role				
	Project Owner	Project Leader	Project Memb. 1	Project Memb. 2	Line Manager1
M2 Scope of change needs mapped					
M3 Training measures specifics decided					
M4 Training completed					
M5 System specifications cleared					
M6 Test completed					
M7 Pilot implementation initiated					

Responsible
Performer
Consulted
Informed

Figure 6.3 Example of a milestone responsibility chart, with shaded function selection for the various roles in projects

to clarify the responsibility and authority of parties involved and affected in the project work (Figure 6.3). Other tools or processes used to clarify responsibility and authority in projects are the purpose structure (Chapter 4) and the kick-off meeting (Chapter 8). The kick-off meeting is an arena for clarifying the interface between the permanent organization and the project, in which the project team can develop a more unified understanding of what it will deliver and how it will do it (Halman & Burger, 2002).

ORGANIZING IS CONTINGENT ON CONTEXT

Templates will vary with the size, complexity and uncertainty of the project (Shenhar, 2001). Two issues commonly arise. First, participants can become too concerned with the technical aspects of the project and forget to elaborate sufficiently the distribution, responsibility, authority and explanation of expectations. Second, the project becomes over-bureaucratized. *Over-bureaucratization* tends to occur when techniques such as network planning, net-present-value calculations or different forms of follow-up activities are used without sufficiently reflecting on whether they fit the specific project. Also, given the plethora of jargon and different roles and responsibilities in use it is easy to see how over-bureaucratization might happen. Not all projects require extensive formal organization appropriate for large and complex projects. At different stages the same project may also need different designs, for instance, during the idea phase, the start-up phase and the planning phase. Having the same project team throughout or with the same organization design in all phases may not be necessary. Since projects are characterized by uncertainty and learning, design should adjust according to the project tasks.

COLLABORATING

It is easy to think that building common understanding and sharing action patterns in temporary projects is unnecessary, since relations will end once the task is resolved.

However, flexible divisions of responsibility and authority are at the heart of organizing project tasks. Interaction and cooperation, referring to the coordination of multiple actors carrying out a series of activities in an aligned and integrated way, are the essence of collaboration. Collaborations create relationships and some degree of reciprocity between the parties (not necessarily equality or similarity). In practice, collaboration can involve not only mutual understanding and dividends but also conflicts and reciprocal exploitation (Bresnen & Marshall, 2002). Successful collaboration and interaction will be characterized by effective interpersonal and digital communication, resulting in cooperation and shared processes. Collaboration in construction projects increasingly entails entrained digital communication through Building Information Modelling (BIM). However, both social and work processes must support the use of BIM. Reciprocity requires a mutual flow of knowledge and information supported by social, structural and cultural factors in which the availability and dissemination of information and knowledge to all relevant actors needs to be managed. Collaboration is increasingly used in infrastructure projects (Bygballe et al., 2016), often based on an interaction contract (see Chapter 4). The results, at best, will be shared sensemaking and, at least, exchange of experiences and knowledge, in pursuit of conjoined or similar goals.

WATCH THIS!

BIM can be used for collaborative creativity. Watch this Canadian video by Julie Trottier and Marie Andrée Forrest (2018) on the contributions of BIM to innovative practices, from the planning to the commissioning phase, at https://study.sagepub.com/pm.

IN PRACTICE

INTEGRATING VR IN A BIM

Project visualization can be important in projects, especially where collaboration across various disciplines and organizations is necessary. A project based on building information modelling (BIM) is useful in overcoming potential misunderstanding and providing necessary support in discussing a project. In a project in Barcelona, virtual reality (VR) was included as an additional tool in a project (Zaker & Coloma, 2018).

Normally BIM models provide scaled models of the constructions or computer-generated visualizations where you can zoom in and out. With VR this literally provides a new dimension of visualization of the construction. Often a BIM project requires a physical presence in a room, but '… Virtual Reality as the most immersive medium for visualizing a model, has the promise to become a regular part of construction industry. The virtual presence of collaborators in a VR environment eliminates the need of their physical presence' (Zaker & Coloma, 2018, p. 1). Furthermore, research from the case of the building project in Barcelona shows that the participants on the project found benefits from the technology and VR could be an effective tool for collaboration in projects.

READ THIS!

There is a fascinating open access case study of a VR BIM project in Barcelona by Rezza Zaker and Eloi Coloma (2018) that discusses advanced collaborative approaches based on digital technologies at: https://study.sagepub.com/pm.

Coordinating

In organizations, a basic principle is the division of labour so that a task may be accomplished *more quickly* by dedicating more hours in parallel or that it can be solved *better* because it involves multiple specialized expertise. The division of labour entails a need for coordination, entrainment and integration of different efforts. The greater the interdependence between the task elements, the more coordination mechanisms are required.

A wide range of coordination mechanisms have been identified and sorted into different categorization systems. In a review article of these, Okhuysen and Bechky (2009) class them into five main categories:

- Plans and rules
- Objects and representations
- Roles
- Routines
- Proximity

The use of the mechanisms creates conditions for coordinated efforts by providing accountability, predictability and a common understanding of the task to be solved. We look at the mechanisms below.

PLANS AND RULES

Plans and rules, principles and procedures are mechanisms for coordinating effort in projects. Strategic and operational plans at different levels are widely used to coordinate projects. Rules guide project participants and other organizational members in their decision-making, especially when it includes conflicting alternatives. Rules and plans contribute to coordinated efforts by providing a direction for task solution. They help define what actions must be taken to complete a task. Responsibilities can be defined according to the plans and rules to establish roles that take care of the various areas. Enhanced predictability and control over the work of the project team occurs when activities do not fall into structural gaps in the project (Pinto, Pinto, & Prescott, 1993).

OBJECTS AND REPRESENTATIONS

Visualizations, such as drawings and models, are also useful in coordinating efforts, as they carry considerable knowledge (both technical and social). Sharing this knowledge mobilizes effort (Latour, 1988). Such drawings, models and figures function as representations, termed boundary objects (Star & Griesemer, 1989), that aid transla-tion of efforts and sensemaking across organization boundaries, internal and external through their visual and material qualities. Many organizations use representations, such as spreadsheets, to coordinate processes across subprojects. Drawings can help project participants address task solution and aid in identifying what they do not understand and what they need from others.

ROLES

Assignments can be distributed among different roles in a team or by setting up sub-project managers for different types of deliverables included in the project task. There may be one subproject leader for technical delivery and another for competence development when implementing the delivery and/or being responsible for various processes in execution (for example, one responsible for communication work, one for project planning, one for documentation, etc.).

Different roles can be identified in the project that report to the project manager coordinating efforts. The project manager reports on the progression and quality of project delivery to the steering group and/or owner, which coordinates across projects and oversees activities as consistent with strategy. Many organizations sys-tematically rotate the role of members of the project team for them to learn about different areas, contributing to a common understanding among members. Individual members gain more comprehensive understanding that simplifies coordination and provides opportunity to replace each other as needed.

ROUTINES

Routines represent embedded knowledge and are vital for coordination (Nelson & Winter, 1982) and in providing clear expectations about how to act (Gersick & Hackman, 1990). They serve as a template for how tasks have been solved in the past, contributing a common perspective on 'how to do things' across groups and actors. Routines estab-lish the order in which sequenced activities should be addressed (Feldman & Pentland, 2003; Feldman & Rafaeli, 2002); the non-routine, representing unembedded knowledge, is more threatening of project order.

PROXIMITY

Physical proximity is another mechanism for coordination. Distance inhibits interac-tion and communication between project members (Allen, 1977). Therefore, collo-cation of project teams is often used. Through collocation, project participants can more easily gain an overview of how what others do aligns with their own activities. Collocation makes it easier to shape behaviour and see the needs of the current situ-ation. Proximity affords transparency of processes that facilitate the coordination and alignment of task-solving activities. In projects where physical proximity is not possi-ble, participants attempt to create this transparency through frequent communication of project status, sharing information through e-spaces, such as Dropbox or by e-mail or social media.

Collocation of team members is common in autonomous projects but in matrix projects it is more difficult to obtain because the members often work in parallel with several projects or tasks. One solution is to have one or more 'project day(s)' where team members gather physically. A rule of thumb suggests that the earlier the project life cycle, the more the members should be encouraged to gather together regularly.

Different organization designs are differently structured to match different contexts, such as uncertainty related to production technology (Woodward, 1958), task complexity (Perrow, 1967), workflow integration (Hickson, Pugh, & Pheysey, 1969) or task dependency (Thompson, 1967a). The more uncertainty is inherent in organization, the less appropriate it is to impose highly formal and impersonal structures with little flexibility. High uncertainty makes mechanisms such as hierarchical decisions, rules and programmes for coordinating more difficult. In conditions of high uncertainty organization becomes more dependent on frequent adjustments and clarifications; thus, informal communication and information flow through personal relationships can be more efficient than highly formalized structures (Ven, Delbecq, & Koenig, 1976).

Formal coordination mechanisms provide accountability, predictability and a common understanding of the task to be solved (Okhuysen & Bechky, 2009). Project managers strive to achieve common sensemaking using both planned coordination tools from the start of the project as well as emerging processes. Coordination is a continuous and dynamic process throughout the project. Even where prior coordination has established accountability, predictability and common understanding, these conditions must still be re-created anew in novel projects. Events occurring throughout a project, such as the replacement of members and changes in the needs of the stakeholders, can destroy or erode accountability, predictability and common understanding.

We have said a lot about mechanisms for coordination in projects. Organization in general and coordination, in particular, are especially demanding in projects that span several organizations because members of the various organizations come from different organizational cultures with their respective procedures, routines and management systems. In such circumstances, working with unambiguous goals systematically to establish common understanding by eliminating ambiguities and establishing clear roles and interfaces facilitates the use of more informal coordination mechanisms.

As it is difficult to define and measure informal communication and unplanned interaction, little emphasis has been placed on facilitating them, although there is great potential for better project execution by taking these into consideration. Project participants must coordinate their efforts when something unexpected happens, no matter what organization design is the basis for their actions. Unplanned events will happen. It is how you respond to them, their impact and what you learn that becomes important for success, especially in projects characterized by high uncertainty.

Coordination and organization become most challenging when a project is run virtually because team members' opportunity for informal contact is reduced, processes become less transparent and members are more distant, socially, from each other. When there is a high degree of uncertainty, running projects on a solely virtual basis is not advisable.

IN PRACTICE

ACHIEVING PROJECT SUCCESS

There are many ways of achieving project success. One of them is to develop a specific and strong identity for the project as an autonomous entity through committing to a project

(Continued)

culture at the heart of which is to do 'whatever is best for the project', especially where the project relies on coordination, collaboration and communication across a number of different member organizations of the project. Clegg, Pitsis, Rura-Polley, and Marosszeky (2002) discuss a case where this occurred; however, there are risks in doing this when the project is intra-organizational because the best for project may not be the best for the organization overall. It is for this reason that the project needs to keep close touch with the organization and its relevant management to ensure that the twin goals of project and organization are aligned.

QUESTION

1. Think of a project that you are familiar with. In what ways do you think cooperation could be, or could have been, better facilitated? Please describe what you are familiar with and what you would recommend and why.

Allocating resources

Basically, there are no a priori resources in a project as all resources, whether human or other resources, must come from the permanent organization or elsewhere. Human resources can either be seconded or rented. The overall allocation of resources will be based on the project framework conditions (time, cost and quality), assumptions about the nature of the tasks and estimates of costs and hours projected as necessary to create the desired outcomes. After the project has been established and a work plan is developed, the project manager can allocate human resources to the project's activities on the basis of the work plan. Here, resource allocation is made by specifying the amount of time considered necessary for each resource to contribute. The project manager can then try to reserve different resources needed for different parts of the project, especially where resources are known to be scarce or completely critical for the project. Such scarcity might be related to either human resources or material resources, such as machinery and locations. Formalized resource allocation keeps track of availability of project participants and more general resources (such as equipment and machines).

Projects often experience scarcity of resources. Executives can be overoptimistic in terms of what they can achieve (discussed in Chapter 3), thus underestimating the need for resources. Projects sometimes start up with fewer resources than scoped in the initiation phase of the project. Often, project proposals compete against each other, leading to negotiations about which project to start. To achieve start-up, project managers often accept a cut in resources (Flyvbjerg et al., 2003). Starting with less than planned resources might well appear a better option than not starting at all; in the future, negotiations may ensure that the appropriate level of resources ensues.

Plans define when various resources are required in the project, creating commitment for the project and the person managing the resource. Relevant resources must, therefore, contribute to the project at the right time and in an appropriate manner (Eskerod, 1998). Sometimes this is almost impossible because insufficient resources are available to carry out all the activities to which the organization is committed. Although various techniques for multi-project planning (Wiley, Deckro, & Jackson Jr,

1998) and strategies have been developed, including allocation of resources in project portfolios, projects can still suffer from being under-resourced.

Resource shortage has traditionally been seen solely as a planning problem but there may be other causes. Resource scarcity may be a result of commitment to an increasing number of projects without looking at their effect on existing projects (Wheelwright & Clark, 1992). When management is overwhelmed by efforts to prioritize and allocate resources between activities to be solved, a resource allocation syndrome applies. The resource allocation syndrome (Engwall & Jerbrant, 2003) emphasizes that resource allocation can best be understood as a negotiation rather than a planning process (Eskerod, 1998).

In the midst of resource crises, short-term thinking may see redistribution of resources between projects, making the situation unpredictable, which can create negative feelings, forcing the management to further short-term solutions (Engwall & Jerbrant, 2003). Short-term solutions for a scarcity of resources trigger short-term responses, such as constant negotiation and bargaining over resources that can become part of an internal policy supported by other, deeper structures in the organization such as incentive systems, measurement systems and career paths.

Negotiation of resources takes place at various process stages in projects:

- As part of the project launch procedures
- When triggered by a crisis or a problem
- As a consequence of the available capacity the permanent organization makes available to the project
- When new opportunities arise that the project can work with using increased resources (often this happens when the volume of activity increases)
- As interpretations (often value-driven) making things look new in ways that redefine definitions of the situation
- Where proposed solutions are highly subjective and cannot be supported with more rational arguments; often, power probes stronger than rationality (Flyvbjerg, 2002)

One must be aware of these processes where resource allocation occurs, with each project considered in light of them. At the same time, as we will see in Chapter 12, one must take a look at how these processes affect entire portfolios of projects.

Culture

Clear goals and strategies, defined tasks and responsibilities, all help to provide direction and clarity about how people behave and interact in organizations. These clarifications form key parts of the formal organization, facilitated through organizational design that defines structures for the organization's work. However, organizing, as practised, is not identical to the organization's design. One reason is that people are autonomous and do not act entirely in line with organizational design. Another reason is that work tasks are complex and require interaction that often cannot be resolved or determined solely through descriptions and instructions. Through such interaction, employees develop an experience of 'this is the way we do it here'; that is, they create an organizational culture as a

pattern of common basic assumptions taught by the group as it addresses its external adaptation and internal integration problems, which have worked well enough to be considered valid and are therefore taught to new members as the right way to perceive, think and feel in relation to these problems. (Schein, 2010: 18)

The definition of organizational culture emphasizes it as something shared by many of the members of the organization. When members interact with each other, there is a more or less common shared opinion on how to behave, what is right and proper (Trice & Beyer, 1993). Project cultural norms emerge and become embedded.

While previously most attention was devoted to *one* organizational culture (usually leader-led), it is now acknowledged that organizations will be constituted by multiple, slightly different cultures in different departments, projects and other groups (Martin, 1992). Moreover, cultural alliances will spring up over issues in a fragmented way as different issues arise in the project. In any project organization a culture is constituted in process; culture is something that is existentially shared and made by the members rather than being something objective that the project organization may be said to possess. Culture develops under the following conditions (Schein, 2010):

- Shared time and shared significant problems
- Opportunities to solve problems and observe the effects of the solutions
- Socialization of new members to (potentially different) established ways of framing problems

When members share many contacts and feel close, with common personal characteristics, the likelihood of a common culture emerging increases, such as when there is some aspect of identity binding people together, such as ethnicity, gender or shared experience. Many projects are well suited for the development of a distinct subculture, especially in the case of innovation projects where there is a counterculture to that of a more conservative host organization.

In organizational culture, the *content* of the culture and its expression are often distinguished (Hofstede, 2001; Schein, 2010). The cultural content is represented by the norms and values that members share while action patterns and structuration of practices are the visible manifestations of cultural content. Objects and rituals are typical cultural expressions, such as topping out, planting a tree on the roof when the last beam (or its equivalent) is placed atop a structure during its construction. The ceremony often becomes a media event for public relations purposes. The practice of 'topping out' a new building is traceable to ancient Scandinavian religious rites that consisted of placing a tree on top of a new building. Ritually, this was supposed to appease the tree-dwelling spirits displaced in its construction – bear in mind that most buildings were made of timber because hardwood forests were plentiful, so appeasing the tree spirits made sense. The ritual has been retained long after the spirits require placating in most contexts.

> **Values** are 'broad tendencies to prefer certain states of affair over the others' (Hofstede, 2001, p. 5).

Values may in practice vary from those that are represented formally (Argyris & Schön, 1996). Such values embedded in practice manifest themselves in what is given status, what is rewarded, what is included in rituals in the organization (Schein, 2010). For example, a project manager may emphasize that 'in this project, everyone should participate on equal terms and we shall be flexible' (expressed value) while at the same time scolding project participants who have not followed correct progress in project work (practised value).

Norms emerge when employees work together over time as common considerations about what are acceptable and unacceptable ways to behave become shared (Hackman, 2002). Over time, they can become informal but deeply held rules defining the appropriate behaviour for the group. The normalization of a project group is associated with how the project manager, in particular, is regarded as handling critical events (Schein, 2010). There are frequent opportunities for such normalization to occur when project participants have many experiences of other project situations to draw on, comparatively. Norms accepted by individuals in the group may differ from person to person; quite likely so, when the members have been plucked from different divisions, areas and disciplines. However, when a crisis occurs, people talk and cultural sensemaking often emerges, sometimes in a fragmented and differentiated way, from the common experience. Differences contribute both to positive refractions but also to conflicts and frustration in the project group. The amount of talk time you contribute in weekly project meetings as a norm may vary greatly if you are a young and inexperienced employee compared with that of an old timer with experience from many complex projects.

Participants in a project group can develop common beliefs about what is true and how different phenomena are linked (Schein, 2010). Sometimes this is positive because it makes it easier for them to interact and because self-definition as the 'world champions in technology projects' or as 'the A team' can increase motivation and belief in achievements which, in turn, may be positive for project progress. Just as readily, however, project members can come to the realization that the project is a lemon; not keeping scheduling, riddled with errors and host to many misgivings.

The project manager may try to underline the experience of group identity by talking about 'we' and 'our mission' and using symbols that signal identities, such as coffee cups bearing the project's name and logo. While such common assumptions can be positive they also reduce the ability to see phenomena differently as, to the extent that the members come to believe they share a common culture, it may stifle innovation and learning from relevant experiences because of a belief that 'we are unique'. We will look at this phenomenon, called groupthink, in more depth later (Janis, 1972; see Chapter 8). Under these circumstances a project may be associated with great uncertainty clearly visible to project participants; however, the project participants do not address it, discuss it or take action, even 'when all the warning lights flashed red', perhaps because of the commitments to belief in the project and its culture being so strong. When participants develop concerns about a project, shared and strong common assumptions may inhibit their ability and willingness to send negative signals. Common assumptions, both encouraging and inhibitory to the project, can become taken for granted such that we do not see them anymore. As long as project participants relate to common perceptions of reality as if they are true, these are self-reinforcing and will categorize those in the project that raise doubts as deviant.

We have looked at cultural content, values, norms and common assumptions. As mentioned earlier, the cultural content is not directly visible but is expressed in different ways. The relationship between cultural expressions and cultural content is mutual: cultural content is reflected in cultural expressions, while cultural expressions help create, maintain and change the content of the culture (Schein, 2010).

Cultural expressions can be divided into four categories: behavioural expressions, verbal expressions, material expressions and structural expressions.

- *Behavioural expressions* can be divided into subcategories: meaningful social actions, repeated organizational behaviours and expressed emotions (Trice & Beyer, 1993). Social actions that display meaning and behaviours that repeat routines indicate what an organization appreciates (its values) and what is considered the appropriate way of behaving (norms). Expressed emotions revolve around those projections of value that employees show in different situations. Examples may be collective celebrations in the project when milestones are achieved, collective disappointment when a key stakeholder in coalition with other stakeholders opposes the project's wishes and collective rage (or relief) when the project manager decides to go to the competitor – rage or relief depending very much on how the project manager is viewed.

- *Discursive expression.* Values, norms and reality contexts are communicated through the stories, myths and legends reported in the organization (Martin, Feldman, Hatch, & Sitkin, 1983). In a railway organization's development of an emergency communication systems (GSM-R), the project started as a development project but eventually became a story of a large, complex and adventurous project. It became the story of the 'world championship in GMS-R development', expressed through stories of musk oxen in a national park, big helicopters, extreme weather and elements of technological innovation. From being a statutory project to ensure good emergency communication in the future, it led to a presentation of 'The Railway company of tomorrow – the high-tech railroad commission' (Vaagaasar, 2006). Such stories matter because they contribute to commitment and dedication and become lodged in collective memory; indeed, they become memorialized.
- *Material expression* of culture can be embedded in both objects and things as well as physical structure and architecture. Physical objects can signal that in this project we are 'productive' because common areas are characterized by plans and information boards that continuously indicate progress. Everyone having a hard hat on their desks signals that we are always prepared and all equal. Colourful furniture, bricks and other toys can signal that 'we are creative and innovative' in our projects. A project manager who chooses to sit in an open-plan office or has an open-door policy makes this a material expression of availability to project participants. Numerous expressions can be used to signal cultural content.
- *Structural expressions*, such as rituals, procedures and ceremonies (Deal & Kennedy, 1982; Trice & Beyer, 1993) also maintain project culture. The turning of the first sod by a silver-plated spade performed when a construction project is commenced or the ringing of a bell when a new functionality has been tested and works in an IT project as well as the kick-off meeting in a municipal project signal a collectively recognized meaningful event as a ritual of the project.

READ THIS!

There is an interesting story about how objects assume a cultural significance when associated with nationally significant infrastructure, the objects in question being a silver spade, a wooden mallet and a glossy programme, in a short article by Louise Maher (2018) at: https://study.sagepub.com/pm.

The cultural content and cultural expression of projects can work positively because it simplifies collaboration and contributes to motivation and team spirit in the project. At the same time, it can cultivate negative effects that the project manager will seek to minimize or avoid.

In this context, we are solely interested in organizational culture and how it manifests itself in the project context. Many projects are global and include participants representing multiple cultures embedded in different national and hybrid ways of being. In some highly multicultural cities, such as London or Sydney, many people will be hybrid in their ethnicities, origins and cultural attachments. For project managers that regard national culture as a key contingency it probably makes sense to try and staff overseas project with home nationals that can communicate in the host language. For instance, Mandarin-speaking Chinese Australians will probably do better in China than monolingually English-speaking ones or people with multiple linguistic capabilities other than Mandarin.

Most projects are interdisciplinary, and so many of them involve different professions. Many of the points associated with clarity about roles and interfaces, the importance of communication, learning environment and project culture are of even greater significance in projects that include different languages, national cultures or strong professional cultures. If one handles cultural differences well, they can be a significant source of enrichment in terms of learning and innovation. Handled badly, they can create turmoil and conflict, leading to processes that threaten project success. In multicultural teams there can be a number of challenges and the conflict level, particularly in multicultural project teams, is known to be high. If not dealt with properly by management and other actors in the project this may have severe negative impact on project performance. Conflict management can, however, contribute to team effectiveness through the mediation of team coordination. Sometimes conflicts need to be explicated and actively addressed but at other times avoidance is better in terms of enabling project performance.

EXTEND YOUR KNOWLEDGE

Read the article by Tabassi, Aldrin, and Bryde (2019) discussing 'Conflict management, team coordination, and performance within multicultural temporary projects: Evidence from the construction industry'.

In the article by van Marrewijk, Ybema, Smits, Clegg, and Pitsis (2016) 'Clash of the Titans: Temporal organizing and collaborative dynamics in the Panama Canal megaproject', you can learn about how national culture affects interorganizational project relations. Both articles are available at https://study.sagepub.com/pm.

Power relations

Above we looked at different roles in the internal organizing and emphasized key roles from the client side: the project owner and the steering group. These roles have legitimate power by virtue of their formal role being defined by the governance structure. They have positions that the governance structure affords authority (Clegg, Hardy, Lawrence, & Nord, 2006). Even though you may formally have authority, you do not necessarily 'have' power in practice. Power is not a given entity that someone 'has' but a social relation. Power, as it is defined through formalized positions, roles and charters may be significant but informal aspects can be equally influential in determining outcomes. There are a number of reasons why this might be so, such as personal qualities of charisma (Weber, 1978), positions in a network's obligatory passage points in circuits of power (Clegg, 1989), or control of key resource dependencies (Pfeffer & Salancik, 2003) or strategic contingencies (Hickson, Hinings, Lee, Schneck, & Pennings, 1971).

> **Power** is often defined as A being able to make some agency B do something they would not otherwise have done.

> **Authority** is the attribution of legitimacy to an office or a person holding that office and the imperative commands they produce, often seen as the source of power to get things done.

> **Legitimacy** is the 'generalized perception or assumption that the actions of an entity are desirable, proper, or appropriate within a social system' (Suchman, 1995, p. 574).

The terms **power** and **authority** are often used interchangeably. The power a supplier is able to exercise facing a project manager depends on how strongly the project and the project manager want the product or delivery that the supplier has but it also depends on the alternatives that exist for the project.

Authority is primarily expressed in terms of positioning, such as a project manager having authority to make decisions by virtue of his position as leader. However, authority can also be expressed in more informal ways, such as through personality or competence. **Legitimacy** attaches to authority and is always dependent on the degree of affirmation of those over or for whom the authority is being exercised; legitimacy implies that something is justified and perceived as correct. If a project manager loses authority, perhaps because they are not meeting their milestones, they may still exercise power but lack a degree of legitimacy in doing so.

Legitimacy is the perception of someone being entitled to something – often defined through formal decisions, procedures, standards or regulations – but it can also have an informal basis in norms and values, i.e. 'the right way to do things'. The concepts of legitimate power and formal authority are often used interchangeably, with both including notions of responsibility. Power can be exercised through orders, hidden threats, established expectations or the structuring of a field of action, embedded in routines, imperative commands and normalized expectations. A does not need to say anything to get B to do what A wants if B knows already in anticipation what A wants and the consequences of B not acting accordingly. Power is not just a matter of achieving a favourable self-interested or project-interested decision at a meeting between project owners and project managers. It also concerns who has the power to put things on the agenda (Lukes, 2005), thus deciding what issues and matters for decision are being discussed and decided. Impact through norms and perceptions of what is right and proper is also a form of power exercise. For example, external consultants in a project can provide solutions, methods and deliveries that appear to be fashionable and legitimate, as well as being expensive, adding to their legitimacy, thus materially affecting the outcomes of the project.

To be able to exercise power and make decisions, you must be able to convey the message that the decision is legitimate. We all participate in the 'power game', whether we want to take part or not, with some succeeding better than others and some having much better odds, due to their positioning in the field of power, enabling them to dominate the game. Project owners and project managers need to know how to play power games, how to exercise power steering (Buchanan & Badham, 2020) to build power and influence at work. The ability to communicate effectively and define the obligatory passage points through which communications must flow is a very substantial skill (Clegg, 1989).

It is often suggested in the literature that power is based on access to resources and their utilization, afforded by being in key positions in power relations. Often it is assumed in organization design that individuals can draw on different resources, called power bases (Bourne & Walker, 2005) to achieve desired outcomes. Power bases, it has been suggested in the past, may derive from *formal position* (position power); using *rewards* (reward power); through the use of *force and punishment* (sanction power); from being an *expert* in an area (expert power); becoming a *role model* (reference power); through possessing *information* that is useful to others (information power) or through *powers of reasoning* in arguments (argumentation power). In reality, whatever is a power base will be contextually defined so these bases may well be inoperative or be supplemented by other local features of the situation. There is little point, analytically, in nominating specific bases of power as these will always vary with context. In the case of the 9/11 tragedy the possession of craft knives and rudimentary flying skills, aligned with a commitment to altruistic suicide in the service of an ideology, proved to be resources powerful enough to end over 3000 lives, transform United States homeland security and lead to the United States' longest war – the Afghanistan campaign.

IN PRACTICE

STRAWS AND POWER

On a previous project the Project Council, known as the Leadership Team, did not function as well as it should have, largely because some members dominated the meetings and did not provide spaces for others to participate. You had recently been reading Clegg (1989) on power relations and non-decision-making for your uni subject and you reckoned that you recognized what was happening as involving non-decision-making in practice if only because the opportunity to discuss some issues did not arise. For the present project you decided to implement a slight procedural change to negate the possibilities of domination and consequent non-decision-making. The small innovation consisted of a mug in front of each place around the project table with half a dozen straws in each mug. You explained the procedural rule innovation for the meetings to the members of the Project Council at their first meeting. To make the Council a more participative event, one in which everyone had an opportunity to air their issues and deliberate democratically, you told them that you were implementing a rule that each time someone wanted to speak they forfeited a straw and that once the straws were exhausted, their opportunities to speak had ceased. You explained that this innovation was designed to implement a level playing field for participation.

QUESTION

1. How do you think the innovation would play out in practice? What are likely to be its results?

PROJECT MANAGER: POWER AND POLITICS

By virtue of position, a project manager has legitimate authority to make decisions. Real power depends, however, on whether the assembled team members have the competencies and equipment to accomplish the project as well as on the project manager's competence related to the project's deliverables and management processes. Informal aspects of power in projects can be expressed through networking between stakeholders, controlling resources, information and managing agendas. The project manager must, therefore, try to understand and relate to power struggles taking place to advance personal or project interests (Clegg, 1975). Project managers tend to be located outside the structure of a permanent organization and therefore are particularly reliant on network power and mobilization of support and influence among other actors in the permanent organization through both persuasion and negotiations to secure project management interests in the organization's power struggle.

Projects are often associated with prestige because they are 'something different' from the day-to-day operations of an organization. They are outside of routine. Prestige can lead to political processes where different stakeholders connected with the organization seek to exert influence through the fluidity of power and its relationships (Kreiner, 1995). All projects entail power relations (Clegg & Kreiner, 2013). Power is exercised within or in breach of a set of norms (Clegg, 1989, p. 132). Within joint commitments, stakeholders in and around the project (such as project participants, the management team, users and other stakeholders) use different strategies to try and create legitimacy for themselves and reduce the legitimacy of others. Indeterminacy about the norms in action becomes a useful device, which is why contracts strive to establish a normative framework that is legally binding. Chapter 10 looks into how different stakeholders can greatly influence the opportunities and limitations of projects for success.

Those who master power's tools and concepts can use standards and competence in project management to help maintain their position of power, through the knowledge project managers possess (Hodgson & Cicmil, 2007). Different outcomes in the project context can be achieved by creating a 'governmental' culture (Clegg, 2019; Clegg et al., 2002; Ninan, Mahalingam, & Clegg, 2019) (see the section on culture above) that extends to external stakeholders, often through social media strategies. In the context of a project, great professional expertise often bestows power by being able to identify shortcuts, access networks, navigate through or around obligatory passage points, and so on. Such experts are good at managing symbols for efficient project execution (such as Gantt charts).

It must be remembered that organizing the project is a process. It is created in the interaction between people, organizational structures and tasks and through the impacts of phenomena and events that generate uncertainty. It is necessary to have a large toolbox of power/knowledge devices available with which to improvise and orchestrate to achieve concerted performances (Vaagaasar, 2006). Work on roles, coordination processes and other organizing processes matters considerably but collaboration cannot be taken for granted (Chapter 6) any more than can project teams (Chapter 8).

Summary

- -

As we have seen in this chapter, at the heart of organizing is the division of responsibility and authority.

- The relationship between the project and the permanent organization needs to be clear. We have looked at how various forms of these relationships are associated and how and why the matrix is often preferred.
- From a value creation perspective, a matrix organization increases an organization's ability to utilize competence flexibly while facilitating good knowledge transfer between the project and the foundation organization or other projects. In addition, it can increase the probability of product success because it enables good contact with potential users, which can increase the likelihood that delivery will be worthwhile for future users.
- We have presented significant roles in project work and, in particular, emphasized that an operational owner, whether it is a steering group or a project owner (or combination of them), is important for both project product success and project management. It is the project owner who controls and facilitates the project.
- In addition, we have considered a number of other roles in the project execution. How these roles are designed will be characterized by the project and the current situation of the project. The individual's role in the central project processes can be made visible through, among other things, the use of responsibility charts.
- In projects, activities and processes are distributed to many actors, so they need to be integrated into a whole, a delivery, as desired. There are a number of coordination mechanisms, such as planning routines and collocation, which can be used to coordinate efforts throughout the project. We have also discussed the importance of culture in the project organization and how power is also always part of all projects.

Exercises

1. What is the most commonly used form of organizing projects – autonomous, departmental or matrix organizing? Can you account for the key similarities and differences of these organizational forms?
2. What is most challenging for project managers when their project is a matrix project? Why do firms often prefer matrix organizing over autonomous or departmental projects?
3. What are the key responsibilities of project owners? What factors are often considered in appointing a project owner?
4. When is it often advisable to have a steering group in addition to a project owner role? Do the project owner and the steering committee hold the same areas of responsibilities?
5. What distinguishes the project council and the reference group?
6. We have presented five ways in which coordination can be enabled in projects. What are they and what can you say about them?
7. Resource allocation is challenging, in particular for firms with expanding project portfolios. What are the key issues in allocating resources? When, during project execution, are resources often negotiated?
8. Power dynamics are always present in organizational life. What are the key contents of the concepts of 'power', 'legitimacy' and 'authority'?

CASE STUDY

ASTRAPTIVE HOSPITAL – NEW IT SOFTWARE FOR DETECTING LUNG DISEASE

Project 'Into the body' aims to develop and implement new IT technology software for identifying a rare disease affecting some people's lung functions. The software development involves an upgrade, integrating three existing software apps with some brand-new developments.

Astraptive Hospital, consisting of 2000 employees and seven departments, is well-regarded for its professionalism and reputation. IT systems applied at the hospital are delivered from a national hospital IT centre but Astraptive Hospital have their own IT department, considered to be professional with good skills.

Even if the project appears to be a small and simple project to develop, it could be a crucial innovation for treating the disease and implies significant changes in the logistics of the hospital procedures and routines. The doctors and the other professions involved are excited about the prospect of implementing the project and are eager to participate. However, in terms of the projects' resources, only a limited number of people from outside the IT department are included. It has been decided to apply Scrum as project execution methodology, with some adaptations.

The project is just about to start. The project owner, Annie Geturgun, is the head of the IT and Support department at the hospital. She is quite new in the job, coming from a large international consultancy office. She intends to organize the project mainly using members from the IT department, supported by some hospital professionals. A project council is about to be established, consisting of various representatives for the professions involved and other stakeholders, such as people from the national IT centre and elsewhere.

Before the project is about to commence, she receives an email from one of the senior clinicians from the department which is going to be most affected by this project and its outcome. The clinician tells her, in quite frank terms, that this project will fail if doctors and other key actors among those who will apply the new software and thereby treat the patients, are left outside the development of the software. 'If you think you can develop a system like this, affecting our procedures and routines in a big way, and not at how to treat the patients, the project is doomed to fail!'

This make Annie think: 'For the project to be able to produce functional deliverables and maintain progress, we must be agile and the IT experts are the only ones who can develop the technical aspects here.' Annie sees the importance of including the doctors, as well as other key actors, but it would be difficult to include them in a Scrum team. She thinks of alternative ways of organizing this but cannot come up with any satisfying solution. She needs some advice.

QUESTIONS

1. Given the restricted information available, how should she organize the project without turning around and starting all over again?

2. How should the key actors be involved?

3. Should the project have a project manager as well as a Scrum master?

4. How would you design the RACI matrix for this project, and what would your argument for doing so be?

5. Is there any other advice you would give related to the organizing of the project?

Additional resources

The chapter has concentrated on aspects of project organizing. For management and organizing more generally Clegg et al. (2019) is a very good source. Flyvbjerg et al. (2003) provide a good presentation of megaprojects if you want to immerse yourself in these. Power and influence matter in connection with projects, as well as in the workplace as a whole. Linda Lai gives an interesting presentation of this in the book *Power and Impact* (2014) with the best overall source being Clegg and Haugaard's (2009) *Handbook of Power*.

Chapter Roadmap

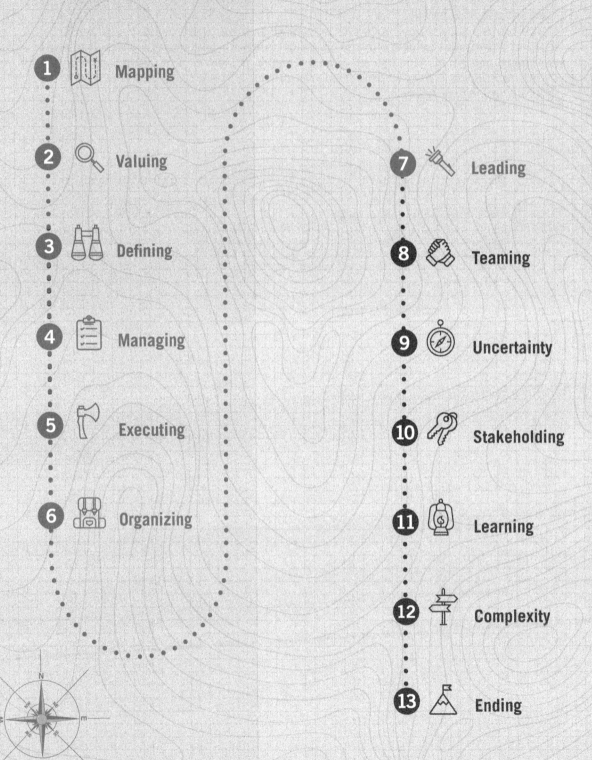

1. Mapping
2. Valuing
3. Defining
4. Managing
5. Executing
6. Organizing
7. Leading
8. Teaming
9. Uncertainty
10. Stakeholding
11. Learning
12. Complexity
13. Ending

7

Leading Projects

Learning objectives

After reading this chapter, you should know:

1 What leadership is and how it relates to specific aspects of leadership in projects

2 The essential aspects of the project leader's role and how it can be understood in terms of information, relations and action plans

3 The most critical tasks a project manager is responsible for, using the project manager's compass

4 The attributes of the project manager and what they mean for the ability to lead different project teams and project processes

5 How the project manager can use different leadership styles and what these mean for the management of the project team

Before you get started

A leader ... is like a shepherd. He stays behind the flock, letting the most nimble go out ahead, whereupon the others follow, not realizing that all along they are being directed from behind.

– Nelson Mandela, former president of South Africa

Introduction

Managing, organizing, leading and working methods are interlinked (Table 7.1). The leadership role will primarily provide added value for the projects by enabling collaboration among the team members, inducing the collaboration with a direction and purposefulness (Bass & Riggio, 2006; Yukl, 2013). Contemporary project management involves creating high-performance project teams through a supportive leadership style and a relatively high degree of autonomy in the team.

Management typically relates to certain tasks that have to be accomplished. Management includes the professional, rational reasons for decisions, while leadership involves 'creating support for collaboration by making sense' (Arnulf, 2014, p. 13). Decisions about which tasks are to be prioritized, and how and by whom they should be performed, are all embedded in relationships of imperative command that those who are affected by the commands that follow decisions should identify as legitimate (Bass & Riggio, 2006).

One or more team members should be able to enact leadership of project processes or assume leadership roles, formally and informally, as required. As seen in Chapter 5, the project owner and the steering group may also enact leadership of the project but in this chapter attention will focus on leadership within the project, in particular, the project leader role.[1]

We will elaborate on the actual and recommended attributes of project managers, their leadership actions and leadership appearance. We look into the issues and processes for which project managers are often assumed to take responsibility and the key contributions expected. Based on a comprehensive model, we highlight the characteristics of this role and the functions that are assumed to be included in the role. Finally, we discuss the key aspects to consider when assigning a project manager.

Projects and leadership

It has become quite common to distinguish between leading and managing, although it is impossible to distinguish them completely from one another. Together, these two dimensions make up *leadership*.

Table 7.1   Different aspects of project leadership

Leading	
Managing	**Leadership**
Technical validation	**Social validation**
Professional, rational reasons for decisions. Plans and professionally based insights as the basis for decisions.	Decisions are valid because they are perceived as correct. Social confirmation of the decision that is in accordance with existing reality understanding.
Make decisions about organization, a division of labour, resource allocation.	Create support through making it meaningful
Assumes power – formal authority, from above.	Building on informal authority – from below, trust.

[1]Again, we apply the terms project manager and project leader. They both are related to the same role but, as we discuss in this chapter, the role implies both managing and leading, and therefore both terms could be useful. However, the role is the same.

Leading	
Experience decisions as sensible.	Experience decisions as meaningful.
'Make people do things right'.	'Make people do the right things'.
Characteristics	
Clarify frameworks, professional reasons, plans, control, power and obedience.	Communicate vision and direction, give autonomy, motivate, create engagement.

Leadership is a much-discussed phenomenon. It is a phenomenon that has concerned philosophers, planners of military campaigns as well as captains of industry. There had been much discussion of leadership in realms of statecraft by writers such as Machiavelli (1961), and warfare by military historians such as Thucydides (1963), both of whose books are classic discussions. Indeed, any project manager taking on a complex project today would benefit from the advice contained in both of these major contributions to discussions of leaders and their strategies.

An explicitly business organizational approach to management emerged in connection with the establishment of 'the company' as a business form after the spread of limited liability legislation in the mid-nineteenth century. Limited liability legislation saw a gradual end to the debtors' prison in which entrepreneurs whose businesses failed might be interred if their personal effects and property, once seized on behalf of those to whom they were indebted, did not cover their losses. The legislative changes limited liability merely to the money invested in the business which, together with the institution of the joint stock company, provided a vehicle for investors to invest their capital. Investment could be made by a range of investors that need not fear the risks of failure as entailing prison. These institutional innovations enabled businesses to become much larger consolidations of capital. Many significant early projects involving the construction of railway and earlier, canal infrastructure, were established as companies with the goal of creating a specific infrastructure.

READ THIS!

Read this article by David Tuffly (2017) to learn about how to motivate the emerging type of worker who usually knows more about their job than anyone else in the organization and is not likely to suffer fools gladly. This type of worker is difficult to manage as they don't consider themselves to be subordinates in the traditional sense. Available at: https://study.sagepub.com/pm.

IN THE DAYS BEFORE PROJECT MANAGEMENT …

Projects were often risky ventures. The early means of communication that linked markets in the Industrial Revolution, canals and then railways were spectacularly unprofitable in many instances. The absence of institutional supports did not deter many risky and often unprofitable projects being developed in the early stages of the Industrial Revolution. Without investment of capital by many capitalists in the networks of canals that were to be superseded by railways, the Industrial Revolution could not have happened. As Davies (2017, p. 12) notes, neither the British nor the American industrial revolutions could have occurred without 'large scale projects delivering canals, railways, telegraph and telephone networks carrying large volumes of raw materials, people, information and goods; the factories, plants, and machinery of mass production; the energy, lighting, water, sewer, and other utility systems; and the built environment of rapidly industrializing cities'. Building these canals and railways were projects, often of great accomplishment. Any resident or visitor to the great cities of the world is, whether they realize it or not, in debt to the legacy of these past projects.

How were these massive inputs to industry delivered? 'Almost everything was contracted out to multiple independent parties working jointly on a shared activity in a temporary organization that disappeared on completion of the task' (Davies, 2017, pp. 12–13). These early projects were, perhaps surprisingly, given the vastness of their accomplishment, rarely an inspiration for early management theorists. In many ways Fredrick Taylor's *Scientific Management* (1911) formed the foundation for the field of management. The influence of this engineering-based approach to the management of detail work through efficiently designed exploitation of combined human and machine labour can be seen in earlier chapters of this book, where complex specifications of roles, rules and responsibilities that are common in project management have been laid out. Some of this engineering approach to managing and leading in organizations entered into practice through the training of military officers at the West Point Military Academy in the United States, north of New York, marking a fundamental shift in both US business and military strategy in the mid-nineteenth century.

As recorded by Clegg, Pitelis, Schweitzer, and Whittle (2020), during the American Civil War (1861–1865), the role of a general staff, who were separate from direct surveillance of the battlefield but schooled in logistics and planning, was decisive in the industrialized North's victory over the agrarian South. Military strategy learnt from this victory that control of resources was decisive. A modern agenda for military strategy was being formed that broadened the vision from the field of battle to the whole campaign. Much of this knowledge, based in engineering, was then applied to civilian campaigns such as building the continental railroad infrastructure. At the core was professionalism, based on success in 'written, graded examinations' qualifying personnel as 'successful, disciplinary experts' capable of careful examination of specialist problems' (Hoskin, Macve, & Stone, 1997). A formalized structure of stable power relations and a body of codified expert knowledge emerged as the norm. In short, those at the top of the chain of command should 'think', 'plan' and 'instruct' and those beneath were expected to 'do' as instructed. In the twentieth century this professional engineering approach joined forces with Taylor's scientific management, designing work on the shopfloor, to form the rudiments of modern management theory (Clegg, Kornberger, Pitsis, & Mount, 2019; Clegg et al., 2020).

Taylor's timing was lucky. He came on the scene after the explosion of interest in popular mechanics of the latter half of the nineteenth century (Shenhav, 2003), after the emergence of electric machine power and lighting and after the institutional innovations of the joint stock company and limited liability. What was significant about these innovations was that they enabled industry to consolidate and grow on a scale hitherto rarely seen. The institutional innovation in finance initially ran ahead of the capabilities to manage it. Interestingly, it was the methods used in the major project of the early nineteenth century in the United States that formed the basis for the early management of the emerging industrial behemoths in industries based on steel and the railways, prior to the adoption of scientific management and those clones spawned by its success.

Prior to the professionalization of an engineering approach to management there were major engineering projects mounted in various countries. In the United States the largest and most significant of these early projects was the project to build the

Erie Canal. The canal was both a political and commercial project, inspired by New York elites that wanted to maintain its ascendancy as a port and commercial centre, against the growing influence of centres such as Baltimore, Philadelphia and New Orleans, all of which had better communication networks with the increasingly settled interior of the vast continent. Money was invested, feasibility studies conducted, politics mobilized around the idea of a canal linking the Hudson River to Lake Erie between 1807 and 1817 (Davies, 2017).

Construction of the project began in 1817 and it was opened in 1825. This was not some grand, integrated megaproject planned from conception to execution in formal design prior to commencement, with plans guiding the whole process. Instead, the overall project was broken down into three smaller sections defined by topographical features of the landscapes to be navigated. In turn, each of these was built in small parcels, using contracts let to contractors to build short sections of the canal between about a quarter of a mile and three miles, under the overall supervision of the two chief engineers employed by the State of New York.

There was a project management body of knowledge about how to build canals available to the small contractors that accepted the contracts. They initially used customary and rudimentary methods, with much human labour, which they supervised and exploited as ruthlessly as they were able to in order to ensure that they made a profit from the competitively tendered contract. Rapidly, however, innovations were realized in practice around processes, tool and materials, such as the innovation of waterproof cement. Some contractors developed an expertise that others lacked and became more successful in winning contracts and building canal sections. Against the tendered price they were advanced finance to pay for wages, materials and tools – manly horse powered. Failure to provide satisfactory work on time led to the advance having to be repaid with interest. To minimize incorrect works an open book design process was adopted in which specification changes were recorded, encouraging more transparency in the project. By developing this instrument of control early project entrepreneurs transitioned into becoming project leaders, successful in gaining further project commissions and being observed as models for other project leaders to emulate in a process of mimetic isomorphism (Clegg et al., 2019) or, more simply, imitation.

INTERNAL CONTRACTING

The essence of major projects such as the construction of the Erie Canal, a megaproject of its day, was internal contracting. The contract was let on a competitive tender then it was up to the contractor to organize, innovate and make a profit. Not all succeeded. The internal contract became the nineteenth-century standard for best practice. As the factories and steel mills of the industrial northeast of the United States grew enormously in the latter quarter of the nineteenth century, internal contracts provided the basic methods of managing but their early elaboration occurred in the field of what we would now term project management.

Early industrial enterprises such as the Erie Canal provide an exemplary if not explicit model for the industrial enterprise of later in the century, as internal contracting became the enterprise norm. In internal contracting a contractor used materials, plant and equipment, sometimes supplied by owners, and managed the labour contracted to deliver a certain quantity of product. Standards, machinery and innovations were highly variable. The system of internal contracting flourished from the late nineteenth through to the early twentieth century, with variable lags in different countries, being developed earliest and superseded fastest in the USA. Given that the internal contract was a fixed sum agreed between the internal contractor and the employers of capital, then the middleman, the internal contractor, stood to gain the most by paying the least for the quantity contracted, so there was plenty of opportunity for downward pressure on wages to occur and for variance in the quality of the product.

ENGINEERING RULES

Clegg et al. (2019) expound that if limited liability legislation solved the problem of how to raise capital and increase scale, it did not resolve the problem of how to manage the vastly expanded enterprise. It was the 'master' rather than the impersonal authority of the 'company' that held sway in 'the enterprise, and even the company was identified with a man rather than a board of directors' (Hobsbawn, 1975, p. 214). But how could a single master exercise mastery over so many? How was the master to achieve effective governance over a vastly increased scale of operations? While the internal contracting system solved some problems, it created others, largely due to a lack of standardization in contracts and working practices.

Scientific management, born of engineering, introduced standardization and systematization into management and project management is very much its heir, maintaining many family resemblances with the parent. Project management's prescriptivism and lack of flexibility (especially the PMBOK) is directly attributable to this lineage. Let us explore the foundations of this lineage in a little detail next.

It was in steel factories in Pittsburgh in the north east of the United States that F.W. Taylor first developed the field's systematic statements from his experience as a practical engineer. Engineering was a discipline with great reach and authority, legitimated by major projects such as the railways and earlier, the Erie Canal, as well as its professionalization at West Point. Popular engineering journals and magazines in the nineteenth century constructed the discipline as *the* locus of professional managerial expertise (Shenhav, 1999). According to the new engineering approaches to management, corporations and organizations could be managed on the basis of facts and techniques. Engineers trained in the management of things and the governance of working people sought to establish principles that aligned functions and responsibilities in a scientifically proven manner.

Armed with a checklist and a stopwatch, F.W. Taylor (1967 [1911]) developed and popularized scientific management around a set of principles for making people's work more visible. He observed and timed work, and then redesigned it, so that tasks could be done more efficiently. The assumption was that there is one best way to organize work and organization based upon principles of standardization of time and routinization of motion. Taylor was the founding father of work study – fitting the person to the job – and work design, and the pioneer of productivity-related pay systems. Taylor produced a set of principles for a political economy of the body (see Clegg, Courpasson & Phillips, 2006) that became adopted by many others (see Watts, 1991). From Taylor's point of view, the working body should be maximally productive and minimally fatigued to become more efficient.

Management and leadership

Management as Taylor envisaged it left little room for leadership other than by slavishly following the one best way that he and his scientific managers dictated. In the time that has elapsed since Taylor initially developed scientific management a great multiplicity of understandings of the term 'management' have developed both within organizations and within the field of organization science (Clegg et al., 2019). However, unlike Taylor, who tried to remove decision-making from management by promulgating one best way of doing things, more contemporary conceptions of management hold that management is mainly concerned with making decisions to create results that contribute to achieving goals (Yukl, 2013). The normative and empirical stipulation of how these decisions should best be made is something that we have covered in prior chapters, in some aspects of which, as we have stated, the ghost of Taylor's influence is still visible.

WHAT WOULD YOU DO?

You are leading a consulting practice project for a client that owns three restaurants. These are mid-market restaurants, neither fast food nor fine dining, being squeezed in the middle by cost pressures that do not enable them to compete with the fast-food joints and cost pressures from above that do not enable them to compete with fine-dining restaurants with their seasonal produce, specialist providores and skilled wait staff. The owner of the restaurants has heard about 'best practice' and has suggested that you follow this line. You have recently read a book by Ritzer (2008) on McDonaldization and to your way of thinking this sounds like Taylorism applied to fast-food sales which, without the branding (and advertising) to support it may well be a race to ruin. On the other hand, the only other categories that the restaurants might be adapted to are either specific ethnic cuisines (which they presently are not) or some other niche, such as vegan or some other theme.

QUESTION

1. What are the pros and cons of adopting a best-practice model premised on the fast-food project models pioneered by McDonald's? What advice might emerge from your consulting project?

Picture 7.1 The Silverback leading his flock in the mountains of Rwanda

Source: Anne Live Vaagaasar

Leadership

It is because of the focus on designing the one best way and rigidly sticking to it, forbidding innovation, that Taylor (who claimed a trained gorilla could do one of the jobs he designed) has had little influence on contemporary approaches to *management*, *leadership* and *leading*. While these concepts are often used interchangeably some authorities assume that leadership as a term includes both management and leadership components. Others draw a distinction between management and leadership (Bass & Bass, 2008) and we will draw on this distinction to address project leadership in more detail (see Table 7.2).

Leadership comes into its own not when dealing with routines, with predictability and order but when dealing with events, with uncertainties that disorder routines. The routines of everyday reality are fundamentally challenged by uncertainty and change but it is necessary to deal with the uncertainty and meaningfulness that unanticipated events can produce (Bass & Riggio, 2006). If everything made sense for everyone, management would be unnecessary. Projects would never go askew, lose time, cost much more than budgeted or have unfortunate unanticipated consequences.

Leaders must handle a multitude of requirements and principles for dealing with the project processes and the context of projects (Birkinshaw, 2013). Projects are always in a constant process of becoming, of smaller or larger changes. The individuals involved in projects as well as the context in which projects are embedded are also always changing. Contingencies, such as the different skills of employees, the tasks to be solved, the company's terms of action, have an impact on the way leadership is exercised. Within the literature on leadership and management there is some disagreement about the importance of such contingencies and to what extent the performances of leading and managing should depend on them. At the same time, it is obvious that the characteristics of those unanticipated events that occur will frame how effectively specific instances of project management can be exercised (Frame, 2003; Turner, 1999; Turner & Müller, 2005).

High uncertainty and ambiguity are inherent in many projects. Such uncertainty and ambiguity cannot be removed through rules, routine descriptions and procedures and it is precisely in managing these features that leadership will be required. Projects often present considerable uncertainty, increasing opportunity for leadership.

WHAT DO LEADERS DO?

There are many themes and directions within management and leadership research; we mention some main themes here that address aspects of what leaders do and how they do it:

- Leadership traits
- Role of the leader
- Leadership style
- Sensemaking/creation of meaning

LEADERSHIP TRAITS

Traits such as personality, intellect and temperament are often used to describe leaders. The importance of such traits to the performance of leadership has been stressed in the past. There has been considerable research in this field and although there are a number of recipes, recommendations and assumptions about what is required or desirable for leadership skills, there is no commonly shared idea about what the ideal qualities of a leader are (Northouse, 2017).

ROLE OF THE LEADER

What a leader actually does and what features the leader should possess have been compared by Mintzberg. He looked at the roles of leaders in 1973 and 2009 and found that leaders at different levels, in different types of organizations, basically fulfilled the same roles. A relatively huge variety of different tasks and functions that had to be handled in parallel were part of these roles, which were subject to frequent interruptions as issues emerged and flared up that had to be dealt with. Project managers will be extremely familiar with such scenarios.

LEADERSHIP STYLE

Leadership style is often classified as task-oriented or relationship-oriented (Hersey and Blanchard, 2007). While the task-oriented leadership style focuses on the work to be done, the relationship-oriented style emphasizes the development of trust, involvement and job satisfaction in doing the work. Later, the binary distinction was extended to include a change-oriented leadership style, where the project manager is particularly concerned with understanding the environment and stakeholders' needs and adapting strategies, products and processes to them (Yukl, 2013, p. 65). The choice of leadership style depends on the context in which the manager and business operate. In situational management, leadership is adapted to the employee's competence and motivation, characteristics of the task to be carried out, as well as the context in which it occurs.

SENSEMAKING

The leadership function should create added value for an organization by the leader's provision of vision, direction for the project and motivation of work with a sense of meaningfulness. Sensemaking is a key value-creating element that leadership provides, especially in interpreting unanticipated and unplanned for events that may have considerable consequences for the project. The term transformational leadership is often used to label the form of leadership that provides inspiration that engages employees. When the project manager enables employees to perform at a high level by adjusting tasks and processes to trigger motivation, provides intellectual stimulation and frames collective sensemaking, it not only enables high performance from the employee but also contributes to employee satisfaction (Bass & Riggio, 2006).

We can use these concepts of traits, role, style and sensemaking as a basis for understanding the leadership of projects.

Picture 7.2   Courageous leadership encourages

Source: Torgeir Skyttermoen

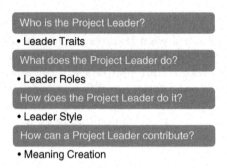

Figure 7.1   Project leader – different aspects

Much of the literature on leadership originates from the United States and West-ern Europe but much of the phenomenon of leadership can be considered universal while, at the same time, being subject to cultural context, irrespective of the frame-work conditions for the management function. For instance, there have been charac-terizations of the Nordic approach to leadership, typified by collaboration and shorter power distance between leaders and their subordinates (Czarniawska & Sevón, 2003).

We will approach the project manager function in terms of understanding derived from a Nordic context (Kreiner, 1995) because, normatively, as authors we are all committed to a social democratic approach to organization and project relations that seeks to empower personnel rather than disempower them. Hence we focus on approaches that start from the assumptions of power relations in projects being framed by 'power with' and 'power to' (Clegg et al., 2006) rather than the exercise of 'power over' through highly disciplinary management, hierarchical power relations and highly autocratic styles.

Project leadership

The role and function of the project manager are both complex and varied accord-ing to the project type and the relevant terms of action. The terms of action include both the client's guidelines and constraints related to project execution, the relation-ship between the permanent organization and the project as well as the impact of stakeholders (Figure 7.1). The size and complexity of the project, available resources and policy guidelines also affect the project managers' role and functioning. Clearly, executing project management in the development of something such as a new oil platform compared with the introduction of a project that delivers a management development programme in a county municipality or a music festival will be different.

A project manager usually has solid professional competence within the area in which the project operates. Such prior experience and competence is not always the case, however. The Glastonbury Festival, for instance, was first organized on Worthy Farm by Michael Eavis who had no project management experience. He learnt as he went along and now, in his 80s, he has handed the leadership role over to his young-est daughter, Emily, who likewise has no professional background as a project man-ager. Nonetheless, they project manage the world's most successful music festival. Her key task is to make sure that the project is carried out efficiently and properly, aligned with the requirements of the festival goers, the musicians, the regulatory authorities, while managing all the supply chain and logistical complexities.

Project Glastonbury is concerned with delivering fun in all the guises that the festival goers enjoy while providing an authoritative framing within which the fun can unfold. It is not easily characterized as a task-focused project dominated by Iron Triangle thinking and rigorous project methodology. Glastonbury teaches all project managers that still need to learn that relational aspects and inspirational leadership matter greatly for project execution.

Leading a project-based temporary organization entails managing a vast number of relationships, including clients, stakeholders, subcontractors, regulatory authorities, security, sanitation, food and beverages as well as employees. Contemporary project managers must manage both efficiently and lead inspirationally (Figure 7.2).

The project manager – and what is special about leadership in projects	Limited time period, resources and task
	Project workers have more managers – one line manager and one project manager
	To lead interdisciplinary teams with people who previously have not worked together
	Relationship to project owners, base organization and stakeholders
	Dealing with uncertainty

Figure 7.2   Project manager – and what is special about leadership in projects

LIMITED TIME, RESOURCES AND TASK

The predefined limited duration of projects frames the work of the people involved, both employees and managers, as well as interaction and organizational processes. The pressures timely completion entails are exacerbated when the project is highly time specific, such as organizing a major sports tournament or a music festival, that have to take place at a specified date. Often these pressures of schedule may lead to stress (Zika-Wiktorsson, Sundström, & Engwall, 2006) and negative emotional feelings of anxiety and chaos (Lindgren, Packendorff and Sergi, 2014), and reduce the possibility of trust development (Meyerson, Weick, & Kramer, 1996) and knowledge sharing (Prencipe & Tell, 2001).

Building better project management on more democratic footings is not helped by the fact that many project employees know that they are only going to relate to the project leader for a limited period of time, which may restrict the project leader's influence and ability to develop and empower the employees in developing their own role. At the same time, the limited period provides potential for learning and development *if* learning from the project is something that can be transferred to other projects. That Glastonbury is an annual event means that a great deal of learning has been acquired in running it over 40 years. The fact that it is highly time-specific, in that it has a scheduled calendar date when everything must have come together, also increases the need for action and the ability to make decisions within shorter periods of time.

PROJECT TEAM MEMBERS HAVE MULTIPLE LEADERS

A project manager is often responsible for a project team made up of members coming from different parts of the organization, or a mix of internal and external members. The project team can also be composed by members outside the client organization, such that the project manager leads people who also have one or more other managers: functional middle managers. In addition, they may have one or more other project managers managing them.

Project managers often have limited means to reward or follow up employees' needs and wishes. In organizing something similar to Glastonbury, project team members' loyalty and effort may be dedicated mostly to their line manager in a professional event organization, doing the sound, the lights, the staging and more. These employers possess the skills and know the routines that produce a successful event. The project manager's role is to frame how these evolving tasks relate to each other in terms of schedule and related matters; rewarding and supporting these employees is often undertaken by their line managers (Andersen, 2008), who will usually be sub-contractors.

LEADING NEWLY FORMED INTERDISCIPLINARY TEAMS

Project managers often find that they are working with, coordinating or managing team members and teams that do not know each other. It is harder to create good relationships and efficient interaction when employees and teams are not acquainted or have had the time to develop trust. Their routines might not easily mesh; they may have different perspectives and different competencies, with different views about problem-solving and interaction.

EXTEND YOUR KNOWLEDGE

Read the article by Koeslag-Kreunen, van den Bossche, Hoven, van der Klink, & Gijselaers (2018) on how and when leadership powers team learning, available at https://study.sagepub.com/pm.

RELATIONSHIPS WITH THE PROJECT OWNER, PERMANENT ORGANIZATION AND STAKEHOLDERS

Project managers need to pay attention and be more proactive towards the project owner and the permanent organization than middle managers often need to be. Doing this can increase the complexity of the project managers' role and make it more demanding. Change and innovation are inherent in the nature of projects and the potential for resistance, scepticism and moderate enthusiasm can be greater than for more ordinary operating tasks (Davies & Hobday, 2005). For instance, booking Stormzy, a UK grime star with only one CD to his credit, for the headlining Pyramid Stage at the 2019 Glastonbury Festival was 'intriguing … On the one hand, an artist who's only released one album being elevated to such a rarefied status – up there with Jay-Z, Paul McCartney, U2 and the Rolling Stones – seems unprecedented. On the other, a persistent rumour around the site suggests that Stormzy's show cost more to stage than any other in the festival's history' (Petridis, 2019). Booking a relatively new rap-based artist to a stage graced typically by guitar heroes was not entirely innovative, as Kanye West had previously headlined in 2015, when he received a mixed reception. Hence, it was a risky decision. The project manager must lead key stakeholders (project owners, users and managers of the delivery) to ensure that value can materialize, which can oftentimes be a risky business.

Leading stakeholders and aiming at a maximal value creation is increasingly central to the project leader function. Value is not purely monetary; as well as the bottom line of Worthy Farm the value that Glastonbury delivers is captured by the experience of participation by the hundreds of performers and many hundreds of thousands of festival goers. The project manager, much as Michael Eavis was and Emily Eavis has become, acts as a project champion, a 'project master' (Pinto & Slevin, 1989), defending the project's unfolding against competing priorities and stakeholders as well as 'selling' and anchoring the project.

DEALING WITH UNCERTAINTY

Projects involve uncertainty, which means that the project manager must be able to change the agenda quickly. The project leader must be able to solve problems, handle deviations, work with knowledge development, find solutions and make decisions within the mandate she has been given (De Meyer, Loch, & Pich, 2002). She must be able to interpret uncertainty and communicate about uncertainty with decision-makers and other key stakeholders. Emily Eavis spent years trying before finally booking Beyoncé in 2011. Failure to book an act means that, sometimes at relatively short notice, another headline booking has to be made.

Many of these features are also present in other leadership roles but they are particularly apparent in the management of temporary organizations. In addition, many of the team members in projects are often not collocated. This means that many project managers lead people who are not physically working together or whom the manager does not meet face-to-face. In global projects, where the people involved are located in several countries, sometimes in many parts of the world, the project leader must also relate to different work practices and cultures.

WHAT WOULD YOU DO?

You are the project manager for a leading North American project-management organization, project managing a major dam building project in equatorial Brazil. There is considerable unrest about the project both from local indigenous people and from pastoralists. In addition, you are having major problems with the local contracting organization who resent what they see as *cultura imperialista* being inherent in the professional dealings of the project management team who speak only English. The response of the local contractors is to break out in Portuguese, thus shutting the Yankees out of the conversation in meetings. You seek advice from a prominent cultural anthropologist familiar with the issues that major projects have to manage in similar locations to that in which you are working. His advice consists of setting out in executive summary the findings of two quite separate research projects. Both involved major infrastructure projects dealing with culture and water. One was the study by Selznick (1949) on TVA and the grass roots; the other was a study of the third lock project on the Panama Canal, by van Marrewijk, Ybema, Smits, Clegg, and Pitsis (2016). The first consultant recommended a strategy of co-optation; from the second, the advice was to reflect on the context and situatedness of temporary work to try and align mutual expectations and to stimulate learning between principal and agent.

(Continued)

PROJECT MANAGERS EMPOWERING OTHERS

The key to efficient project management lies in processes that enable the proficiency of team members. Project work is complex and usually requires project teams that perform very well (Hoegl & Gemuenden, 2001). The project manager must contribute to the high performance of the individual and the team as a whole by exercising supportive leadership. Attention must be focused on the individual employee, the job done, as well as individuals can be helped to succeed (Dysvik, Buch, & Kuvaas, 2015). An essential task for the project manager is to enable the experience of meaningfulness in the team and for the individual member (Yu & Zellmer-Bruhn, 2018). Doing this involves engaging with the employee to stimulate and motivate them, which must be done continuously throughout the project, with efforts adapted as a result of changes in the project, its context, economy and temporality.

Empowered team members can assume flexible responsibilities for activities and processes in the project and at times might also enact leadership of the project as well. This means that the leadership of projects may, for smaller or larger parts, be distributed between several of the team members and shift between project team members and the project manager – depending on the expertise required at any given point in time (Müller, Drouin, & Shankar, 2018). Such a non-traditional view of the managerial function, not as a purely hierarchical structure but as one with distributed powers and responsibilities, enables much more flexibility in practice (Drouin, Müller, & Sankaran 2018). Leadership becomes regarded as a collective act rather than something done by one person with formal responsibility. Everyone must help define the direction and structure of the team's work and make sense (Hackman, 2002, p. 211).

Distributed leadership in projects is clearly an emerging trend. We anticipate this trend will be strengthened in the future (see, for example, Lindgren and Packendorff's (2009) literature study on leadership perspectives). Through distributed leadership, increased team efficiency can be achieved through what is called heterarchy. In heterarchies, the leadership of various processes shifts among team members depending on who is best suited, in terms of having the most relevant skills and/or information. For the project manager, it implies that decision-making authority is given to the team or some team members on behalf of the project. Trust between team members and the leader is a necessary condition for this, as well as ensuring that team members have the necessary competencies and autonomy.

Project manager roles are shifting; increasingly they are:

- Primarily concentrating on task-solving to an emphasis on relationships – not just management but management and leadership
- Task-oriented to acting as a leader imbuing project work with purposefulness and direction
- Imbued with generic leadership skills that take care of specific management processes to becoming someone with a capacity for situational leadership
- Focused on a strong leadership role to emphasizing the development of high-performance project teams through distributed leadership and management support.

To succeed in such a project leader role, project managers must continuously aspire to be reflective practitioners who do leading by reflecting on their own management and leadership practices (Crawford et al., 2006), inspired by Schön's (1991) ideals of reflective practitioners.

PROJECT MANAGER: ROLES AND FOCAL AREAS

The project manager must relate to a number of stakeholders (actors), matters and relationships. The *project manager's compass* (Briner, Geddes, & Hastings, 1993) is a widely used visualization of what a project manager should focus on (see Figure 7.3).

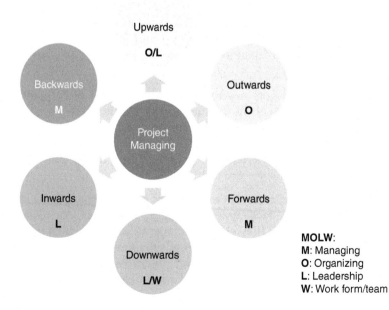

Figure 7.3 A project manager's compass

The compass shows that the project leader role entails both leadership and management.

Forward. The project manager takes care of the project's progress and plans, involving planning at the milestone level as well as detailed planning. Project leaders must be aware of possible hindrances in realizing the plan, as well as maintain goal-oriented management. Changes in plans and objectives should be done in collaboration with the project owner.

Backwards. The status quo needs to be compared with plans and schedules; therefore, reporting and monitoring are key issues to which a project manager must attend. While doing an evaluation of the status quo, project managers need to keep looking forward – since it is easier to influence the future than the past. The past can be reconstructed, however, and often is. Think of the way that the Sydney Opera House was deemed a failure because of a 1400% cost overrun and being delivered ten years beyond schedule, leading to the dismissal and shaming of its architect Jørn Utzon. Today it is widely recognized as one of the significant, if not *the* most significant, examples of twentieth-century architecture. The point is that reality is always being socially constructed and today's failed project may well become tomorrow's landmark.

Upwards. The project manager's relationship with project owners and the permanent organization involves both liabilities and duties. It is vital these parties are aligned and have shared understanding of the key deliverables of the project and how they, overall, can be created. Since any project entails uncertainty and change, project managers often have to have continuous dialogue to interpret and clarify various issues emerging as the project moves along. Utzon failed in this respect, quite spectacularly, deliberately not communicating with key others on the Opera House project.

Outwards. A project has many stakeholders, and the project manager must involve the stakeholders in a purposeful way. The amount of stakeholder collaboration will be dependent on the project type. Stakeholder collaboration means having interaction evenly with them to anchor the project and gain necessary clarifications; again, something that Utzon failed to do, contributing to his dismissal by the New South Wales government.

Downwards. Project managers need to develop close and high-quality relationships with the project team to move the project in the right direction through maintaining a well-functioning team. The project manager must follow up and ensure necessary progress and task allocation, provide clarifications and decisions. Doing this is part of supportive leadership and enables interpretation of the task and information needed to solve the task.

Inwards. Project managers must also evaluate the role that they play and how they are handling it, while also facilitating learning and development related to their efforts as a project manager. They should be able to identify which behaviour and leadership style seems appropriate, in different situations, in the current project and reflect on the actions to be undertaken to affect the project processes and the people involved. In other words, the project manager must carry out tasks on three levels – in the face of all activities and actors involved in the project. They must be a buffer and occasion for sorting and disseminating information coming from different teams, managing *communication and information dissemination*; they must build trust, creating meaning and direction for the team and establishing knowledge relationships with other key actors, *by establishing and developing relationships* as well as being able to work on scientific problem-solving and managerial tasks in the project, by being oriented to *task solution*.

PROJECT LEADER ROLES AT DIFFERENT LEVELS

Project leaders have to fulfil many roles, shifting from stage to stage as they perform, here and now in front of the labourers on site and then later in the day before the project sponsors. Figure 7.4 is based on a combination of the 'project leader's compass' and Mintzberg's (2009) categorization of the leadership role. It is, of course, a simplification but, nonetheless, does identify four central groupings to which the project manager must relate.

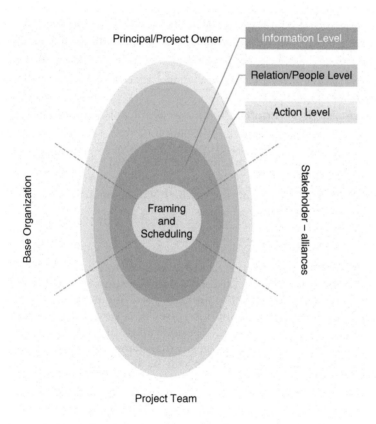

Figure 7.4 Project leader – different levels

The most central and dominant grouping is the one being led, namely the *project team*. *The principal* is also essential, often in the form of a project owner, to whom the project manager reports overall and for whom the project should contribute to value creation. *The permanent organization* will be the beneficiary of the project delivery. *Collaborators and other stakeholders* will be central for the project manager to some degree.

The different plans or levels indicate the functions and roles that the project manager must take care of for these different bodies. The size and position of the three levels illustrate the relative importance of the different groups. As we can see, both the project team and project owner are key actors (see Figure 7.4).

In order to ensure proper information flow and good relations, the project manager should create a framework for guiding the project that involves:

• Prioritizing individual tasks for more thorough review and decision-making than other matters
• Giving some relationships more care than other relationships
• Defining individual activities and processes as more strategic than others, such as stakeholder management.

The project manager designs and works to an agenda. The agenda concretizes the work tasks and enables the project manager to utilize their space in the project optimally (Mintzberg, 2009). The framework thus defines what will actually be done and prioritizes how the project manager will act to safeguard the project team and project interests.

INFORMATION PLAN

The project manager is, most often, the most significant actor when it comes to collecting, disseminating and designing information. Not all information can be communicated directly. Much needs to be processed before it is conveyed and the project manager must also be able to cache the information and monitor parts of the project for flows of information. Much of the project manager's time and attention must, therefore, be devoted to communication, which will mean acting as a generalist with information across a wide range of topics.

COMMUNICATION – SOME BASIC ELEMENTS

Communication affects almost all relationships linked to projects – it is the lifeblood of organizations by fostering interaction. Communication involves information and although these are related terms, they are not synonymous. While information is the content of communication, communication itself is a process that relates people to and associates them with each other. Communication, at best, transmits content that creates a common understanding but given that communication is always receiver-based, there are no guarantees that this will be the case. What is said or written and what is heard or read may well differ. Communication is a process that involves sender(s), content, medium or media and recipient(s). Management communication concerns how a manager develops and communicates knowledge.

Projects apply many different tools generating a great deal of information that becomes the subject matter for communication. As the project manager's compass illustrates, a project manager usually relates to many actors, stakeholders and tasks. It involves *communicating and passing on information downwards*. For their project team staff and workgroups, the project manager will handle and communicate considerable information as *the information and communication centre* in the project (Mintzberg, 2009, p. 56). Both through the various project plans, reporting routines and information flows contributed by project management, much of the time will be spent in relation to this information. The Internet and e--mail are the usual dissemination devices, sometimes contributing to so-called *information overload*.

In addition to monitoring and absorbing a wealth of information, the project manager must also ensure the dissemination of relevant information to recipients. A further task is to be the project team spokesperson when *external stakeholders* from outside of those contractually involved with the project make demands or requests for information; the project manager is usually also the recipient of information from stakeholders. Appropriate information and communication plans help to make these tasks clearer.

IN PRACTICE

COMMUNICATION PLANS

A communication plan will be a useful tool in a project in general and for a project leader in particular. The purpose of a communication plan is to clarify the importance and responsibility for communication in the project, so that the stakeholders are informed about the project's development. The communication plan can be designed on the basis of the stakeholder analysis. In addition, a communication plan can help to clarify both responsibility and central principles for information flow internally within the project organization.

For a project manager, it would be easier to prioritize communication when you have many other urgent tasks. In order to achieve the project's effects, it is important that users and other stakeholders are informed and included in the process, and a communication plan can help achieve this outcome. Regular information about the project, about achieved results and repetitions of the project's purpose and value-adding aspects, is important for raising awareness and for ensuring key stakeholders' involvement in the process at the right time.

WATCH THIS!

Developing a communication plan can be difficult. Watch a YouTube video by Ken Wright (2013) to see some recommendation as to how a culture of engagement can be communicated at: https://study.sagepub.com/pm.

RELATIONAL PLAN

A project manager must engage employees on a relational level, creating motivation and energy, as Wright (2013) suggests. To ensure that the project performs what it is assigned to achieve and has progressed in accordance with the client's requirements, the project manager works to develop a mutual understanding with the client of the project processes and outcomes. Doing so involves building mutual trust and affords the opportunity to discuss and negotiate solutions and use of resources. Most often, the task is relational, relating to project members as well as other actors in the permanent organization, suppliers, partners and other stakeholders. Here, networking, negotiation and attempts to convince others of the project's eligibility, direction and objectives are key processes. It is often crucial to build *networks and coalitions* with key stakeholders. These must be maintained throughout the project period. A project manager represents the project to the outside world which, for many projects, often means convincing others of the soundness of the project and overcoming any resistance. Again, the relational aspect is central. The project manager should also be a *buffer* that, in many contexts, shields the project team from pressure from stakeholders.

ACTION PLAN

The project leader often contributes to specific task solutions, whether this involves implementing a computer system, conducting an art exhibition or operationalizing a competency development project. Other key actions are to handle external disturbances on behalf of the project and the team, as well as conflicts in the team. Many of the governance processes discussed in Chapter 4, such as the preparation of plans, reports and daily management of the project, are key tasks for the project manager.

WATCH THIS

Being a project leader, how can you engage your people? Watch this video by Ken Wright (2013) on how to engage colleagues. 'How to engage project team members?' Available at: https://study.sagepub.com/pm.

Power and authority – project manager's action space

The project manager has authority not only by virtue of their position in the project but can achieve enhanced authority because the project's prestige, if successful, is represented by the project management office. That a project manager or project management office are engaged in a project, and will create something successful and often innovative, enhances their authority (Clegg & Courpasson, 2004, p. 528); successful project managers, particularly of innovation projects, provide a springboard with their success for promotion to higher corporate levels. Success in these circumstances usually means on time, on budget, to specifications, achieved innovatively.

At the same time, the position of project manager is subject to expectations and demands from many sides. Should a project manager succeed in an environment characterized by political tensions in the base organization, between stakeholders or in the project team, they will have to be able to communicate closely with the key actors in the project. In many contexts, they appear as a personal guarantor for the success of the project. Uncertainty associated with projects can contribute to ambiguity about how to accomplish them (De Meyer et al., 2002). Project owners and key representatives from the permanent organization can come up with new requirements and expectations that narrow the room for action and diminish the authority of the project manager (Clegg & Courpasson, 2004). For example, a project to introduce a new IT system into a business will provide the project manager with a basis to enhance their authority. Doing this will mean responding to the expectations of those who will use the system; it will also mean leading project team members to use their skills to develop a better IT system. In this way the client's expectations of a more efficient organization, created by using a better system can be delivered. When unexpected problems arise that cause delays or require the project to stall, authority will be impaired if they fail to convince key stakeholders and team members that the issues will be resolved.

It is difficult to distinguish managing and leading clearly from each other, underlining the close connection between them. A project manager must both focus attention on the tasks to be done (managing) but also keep a close eye on the relational aspects (leading) of the team, with the principal and the others involved. The project manager must gain the trust of others to implement their decisions and procedures, which we previously described as having social and technical validation. Validation, or actions, conduct and decisions that appear to be valid, are therefore also conditional upon how the project manager's characteristics and behaviours affect the project, employees and other actors.

Project manager – leadership attributes

A number of conditions affect how project managers and other managers appear and act to significant project others. Among other things, there has been much discussion about whether the manager's characteristics in terms of personality traits are primarily innate or developed through training and management experience (Yukl, 2013). Today, it is generally agreed that leadership skills can be changed and affected, while we know that people have relatively stable personality traits that affect the ability to be a good project manager.

PERSONALITY TRAITS OF THE LEADER

Personality traits are relatively stable characteristics of individuals. They are thus largely innate. Although they can be changed and developed, they are more or less manifest in the individual. Many studies have worked to identify similarities and differences between people to try to explain that some people are more suited to specific functions and tasks (including leadership) than others. There are a number of assessments, models and tests used to try to measure personality. There is also a lot of disagreement among professionals about what can be measured and how it can be done. However, there is widespread consensus that the 'Big Five' or five-factor model is well suited as a basis for assessing the personality of people in work situations, including leaders (Barrick & Mount, 1991; Judge, Heller, & Mount, 2002).

FIVE-FACTOR MODEL: 'THE BIG FIVE'

The model and its link to management indicates a correlation between personality and the leader's impact on an organization. It is based on the fact that five overall factors together can give a good description of the personality. A brief presentation of these displays the main points:

Conscientiousness (efficient/organized vs easy-going/careless). People who score high on this trait are motivated, dutiful and thorough. Good leaders show the ability to set goals, be thorough in their work and follow up on what is planned. Efficient managers thus show a significant degree of ability at planning.

Sociability (friendly/compassionate vs challenging/detached). People who score high on this trait are humble, attentive and warm. Efficient executives show high levels of sociability and the ability to support, accommodate and include employees.

Openness to experiences (inventive/curious vs consistent/cautious). People who score high on this trait are liberal, have imagination and a sense of aesthetics. Good leadership often requires some degree of creativity and being open to new experiences through imagination and a liberal approach to issues.

Neuroticism (sensitive/nervous vs secure/confident). Describes a tendency to be worried, anxious and emotionally unstable. Good leaders score low on this trait and show a low degree of depressive mood. Project managers need to have the ability to withstand pressure and stress at work. Project leaders have a significant degree of emotional stability.

Extroversion (outgoing/energetic vs solitary/reserved). People who score high on this trait tend to be social, self-confident and outgoing. These elements are linked to being a leader, although the relationship is not always linear.

IN PRACTICE

PERSONALITY TESTS

Personality tests are often used when hiring leaders, also project leaders. In a transcript from a TED 'Worklife' podcast, Professor Adam Grant (2018) says,

> A personality test doesn't explain why you are the way you are. It just describes what your traits are. You want to know your traits so you can work better with others, but there are times when your success and your happiness depends on stretching beyond your traits.

Whether a personality test is adequate when hiring a project leader is debated. Often it depends on how the persons using the test integrate the test and its results.

WATCH THIS!

A video by William Obenauer (2015) on YouTube explains the Big Five and personality at: https://study.sagepub.com/pm.

READ THIS!

Read an article by Oscar Williams-Grut (2016) in *The Independent* on how some companies use machine learning and predictive analysis, where a personality test is a part of it, to find the right candidates for hiring at: https://study.sagepub.com/pm.

QUESTION

If you were to take a personality test when applying for a position as a project leader, what would you think of that, and how would you respond to this?

A project manager's approach to leadership depends in part on personality, while the ability to lead can be developed. Furthermore, the context in which the project is situated determines which of the personality characteristics will be most significant. Personality traits, as presented in the Big Five, may help us identify key features of the project manager but it is more appropriate to concentrate on certain characteristics relevant for project managers in most projects. Research shows that the situation and context in which a leader is going to work frames the personality traits that will be perceived as significant for a leader. For a project manager, *planning, sociability, openness for new experiences* and *empathy* (the ability to embrace the feelings of others) are key features.

Conscientiousness

Managing projects means considerable coping with high time pressure in the face of which the project manager must be realistic in planning and in monitoring possible progression of plans. Conscientiousness implies more than the ability to plan. As a personality trait, it also includes a tendency to work thoroughly, attending to detail purposefully. It is associated with the general need for mastering the tasks one is assigned. For a project manager, who is responsible for both the development and follow-up of plans, reports, relationships, professional development and more, it is, of course, essential to have significant elements of conscientiousness in one's personality (Müller & Turner, 2010). Project managers who have this personality trait are usually performance-oriented, concerned with getting things done with a high activity level.

Sociability

Sociability is a personality trait that project managers require in order to be able to handle a multidisciplinary team, the relationship with the project owners, the permanent organization and a number of other stakeholders. To do that one must be inclined to support and help others. In order to empower and support them, the project manager should not have a dominant and competitive instinct or be self-centred. It is the project, its purpose and the project owner's needs, that are primary.

Open to new experiences

A project manager is open-minded, capable of using one's imagination and hold a preference for new experiences. A project is usually innovation-driven and is supposed to create something new that is not part of the regular operation of the client firm, and thus it is appropriate to have a project manager eager for innovation and thinking outside the box. Creativity is not a typical characteristic of project managers in all types of projects but while being open to new experiences and being able to embrace new opportunities is not a requirement, it is an advantage (Müller & Turner, 2010).

WATCH THIS

Watch this video by Simon Sinek (2014) on the power of caring, helping others releasing their strengths, values and capacity. Available at: https://study.sagepub.com/pm.

Extroversion and neuroticism

Project managers that are extroverts probably fare better with the interpersonal dynamics demanded of project leaders than those that are introverted; likewise, while being neurotic might be advantageous in a project with highly critical parameters such as a major science or innovation project, where infallibility in the deliverable is a critical parameter, for many other projects a high degree of neuroticism, with its unusually sensitive, obsessive, or tense and anxious behaviour would simply be likely to slow the project down too much.

Introverted people tend to find their energy in solitude, as opposed to extroverts who get energy in social settings discussing and speaking – often out loud. One might think that introverts do not enjoy teamwork and contribute only to a limited extent. If the extrovert sets the premises for the way the team works, that might be the case. There is a likelihood that some members will tend to be introvert in a team. To handle this so they can contribute to the project, Susan Cain (2013) suggests:

- Allocate time for all members to speak and be heard
- Ask for a written discussion to be distributed as contributions in the team prior to a meeting
- Instead of open brainstorming processes, ask for written ideas on new and innovative ways to improve
- Rotate the role of leader of team meetings
- Give members time to think things over and reflect before conclusions are made
- Encourage everyone to try to improve their public speaking skills
- Consider dividing a team into sub-teams when working on specifics issues. Keep in mind that introverts perform better in small groups.

There is an additional factor that is extremely important. Project managers will often need to be empathetic in leadership and relations with other people over a period of time (Keegan & Den Hartog, 2004). Projects are often composed of people who do not necessarily know each other, yet the team members often have to work closely together, very intensively. The leader should, therefore, have the ability to be attentive to signals, listen to team members and give them attention when appropriate. Self-control and sensitivity make for better project managers, especially when things go wrong. Self-control is an ability to channel emotions into behaviour that is appropriate for the situation. This means that strong impulsive reactions are held down when they are not appropriate; for example, to manage anger when a vendor has not delivered at the agreed time or a project employee has reported incorrectly. Sensitivity makes it possible to adapt and react appropriately in different situations. A project manager relates to changing and complex issues and surroundings and therefore needs to have a significant degree of sensitivity (Müller & Turner, 2010).

READ THIS!

To previously specified tips Lina Davey(2013) adds some more. Read her article 'The introvert's guide surviving teamwork' at: https://study.sagepub.com/pm.

When working in project teams (or in student groups for that matter) you should be aware of differences between the members and their personalities. As indicated in this chapter, discussion and clarifications on preferences in ways of working and collaborating, along with developing guidelines for teamwork, can increase the possibility for effective and enriching team processes. One method of ensuring that one or two more extrovert people do not dominate team meetings is, as suggested previously on page 221, to place a container with, say, half a dozen straws, in front of the place each team member sits. If they wish to contribute by speaking in the meeting, they have to lose a straw. After all straws are gone, they have no right to speak. Doing this helps to concentrate discussion of what is worth saying and to minimize those who talk simply to be heard to do so. It creates space for those who feel more inhibited to contribute.

IN PRACTICE

PERSONALITY AND TEAMWORK

The importance of diversity in project teams indicates that a team should consist of different personalities. If you aim to design a team with the ambition of achieving a perfect composition of various and balanced personality traits, you will probably fail. To do so requires a personality test and identification of all possible candidates for the team, balanced with required competencies and other elements, doing which is seldom realistic. In a project, team members have to accept who they work with and make the best of it. Hackman (2011) suggests that previous experiences in teamwork that prior teams can provide references for will be more reliable than personality tests.

QUESTION

1. Think about project teams that you have worked with as a student doing your degree or diploma. What criteria, in retrospect, would have been most useful to you in choosing team members with whom to work? Would it have been prior knowledge of their work or their personality or both? Provide reasons for your argument.

Little research has been done on exactly what personality traits are most significant for project managers to possess; in part this is because these are very dependent on the different situations as well as the types of projects involved. We have highlighted four features of a project manager's personality, which we believe to be particularly relevant, based on research. Different projects and circumstances will naturally lead to different requirements. Change projects will require more social and emotional intelligence than a road construction project (Müller & Turner, 2010).

Personality traits are difficult to change in the short term; however, they can be adjusted over time as people encounter experiences and reflect on them. Nevertheless, based on research findings one can claim that those that are efficient in the leadership role tend to have a higher tolerance for stress and are likely to be outgoing, creative, thoughtful and conscientious. Extroversion and openness also correlate with being efficient in the management function.

WATCH THIS!

Amy Cuddy (2012) suggests in a Ted Talk that body language can boost feelings of confidence and shape how you are perceived at: https://study.sagepub.com/pm.

PROJECT MANAGER COMPETENCIES

It is common to divide general managerial skills into three main categories (Northouse, 2017) that can also be used for project manager competence:

- *Professional skills*. Knowledge of relevant methods, processes and procedures. Ability to use relevant tools and utilities. Administrative skills.
- *Interpersonal skills*. Knowledge of behaviour and relational processes. Ability to understand feelings, reactions, attitudes and motives of others based on what they say and do. Ability to communicate clearly and efficiently, establish good relationships and cooperate.
- *Conceptual skills*. General analytical skills, ability to do logical thinking and to see complex and ambiguous connections in a conceptual context. Knowledge of idea development and creative activities based on various issues. Ability to reveal opportunities and potential problems through analysis and put them into context. Strategic skills.

In addition to these three leadership skill categories, one can include a competence category specific to project managers:

- *Project-related skills*. Knowledge of project management-related relationships. Ability to lead temporary organizational units with many stakeholders and a significant degree of uncertainty.

Different practices will stress different competence areas and skills when a project manager is to be engaged but the specialist competence often weighs heavily, especially when the project is considered highly advanced and complex. A subject-matter expert is not necessarily a skilled project manager. On the other hand, it is often claimed that a competent and experienced project manager can lead all types of projects. The suitability of the project manager will usually be subject to both professional and project competence (Bredillet, Tywoniak, & Dwivedula, 2015). In practice, personality traits, skills and leadership styles are entangled.

EXTEND YOUR KNOWLEDGE

Read an article by Gruden and Stare (2018), 'The influence of behavioural competencies on project performance'. The article provides some insight on the value of the behavioural competencies of project managers on efficient project performance. You can access the article in the online resources for the book at: https://study.sagepub.com/pm.

Transformational leadership and sensemaking

In projects, attention is often directed to routines and standards for project management (Tyssen, Wald, & Spieth, 2014). Usually, it is argued that projects are so time-consuming that a project manager should focus attention almost exclusively on the task-oriented elements of the project (Müller & Turner, 2007), at the cost of elaborating vision and sensemaking. Such a strategy will only succeed in smaller projects that are clearly defined for purpose, organization, frameworks and content. In other projects, the project manager must contribute to general sensemaking and be able to perform transformational leadership that changes the sense project members are making with respect of key issues that prove difficult.

Many employees think it is rewarding and inspiring to work on projects. It can provide a 'kick' to be deeply involved in an exciting project with much in the way of dynamics, development and hectic activity. At the same time, it may be difficult for a team member to oversee the totality of the project and see where their contribution fits into the bigger picture. Although team members may be captivated by the processes of programming a delivery they will still need to be inspired as well as recognized by the manager and to understand their work in the bigger picture. Project employees usually appreciate individual attention and follow-up that shows this interaction is in play.

EXTEND YOUR KNOWLEDGE

An article by Tabassi, Roufechaei, Bakar, and Yusof (2017) reports on how team condition and team performance is interlinked – a transformational leadership approach, available at https://study.sagepub.com/pm.

Much of the theory of leadership, not least leadership style, is premised on the relationship between managers and employee, based on transactions where the employee receives a reward for work performed (and punishment if the work is not performed). The transaction is the basis for the relationship, thus determining the manager's ability to influence the employee. Such management theories are labelled transactional leadership (Bass & Bass, 2008).

Over the past 40 years, research has focused more attention on the leader's contribution to sensemaking through transformational leadership (Burns, 1978). Transformational leadership attaches particular importance to four elements, the 'four Is', which will give the employees meaning in work:

- *Idealised influence.* The leader is a role model whose influence increases when the manager appears to be self-reliant and willing to share benefits and also take part of the blame when things do not turn out as expected.
- *Inspiring motivation.* The leader creates and conveys a vision for the work and formulates this clearly and comprehensively through appealing statements, optimistically communicates emotions and creates the belief that the organization will succeed.
- *Intellectual stimulation.* The leader stimulates the employee through constantly providing challenges that contribute to the development of independent thinking.
- *Individualized consideration.* The manager accommodates different needs on the part of members. A relationship between leader and employee emerges and the individual experiences recognition.

Transformational leadership does not replace so much as supplement transactional leadership, contributing with meaning and added value to the employee and enlarges their action space (Bass & Riggio, 2006).

We have previously mentioned the project manager's challenge in leading employees who have at least one other leader, the line manager. Employees relate to their regular line manager in terms of rewards and career development, which leaves the project manager with limited authority over the employees, accentuating the need for stimulating work through elaborating visions, inspiring and giving value to work in itself. If the project manager is unable to do these things convincingly, team members will dedicate effort elsewhere, at the cost of project work, especially if they maintain their regular position in the permanent organization (Tyssen, Wald, & Spieth, 2014).

Clarification of visions and objectives for the project is crucial to get the project workers to engage themselves in the project and understand its purpose. Projects often have to manoeuvre in terrain with considerable uncertainty and in a direction that is not always given. Therefore, for the employees' involvement and perception of meaningful work it is of considerable importance that the project manager has good communication skills and manages to convey messages regarding goals and objectives clearly and with enthusiasm. Transformational leadership can, therefore, have a major impact on the project team's commitment and thereby the potential for project success. Transformational leadership and intellectual stimulation can have a more significant impact on development projects where knowledge workers will contribute to innovation and exploration, and for whom facilitation of creativity and novelty is crucial (Keller, 2006).

Empowerment. Giving employees freedom in how to do their work and set goals for themselves often has sound effects on commitment and performance (Amundsen & Martinsen, 2014). This means that the project manager should try to create an inspiring and challenging work environment for their team members, giving them considerable independence and decision-making authority over tasks they are competent to handle (Dwivedula & Bredillet, 2010).

In this part of the chapter, we have emphasized meaning creation and transformational leadership. Both transactional and transformational leadership need to create the necessary involvement among project team employees. Different contextual and situation-related elements will influence the design of management in the individual project.

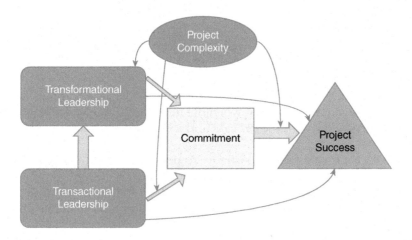

Figure 7.5 Transactional and transformational leadership and influence on project success (based on Tyssen et al., 2014a, p. 384)

The model by Tyssen, Wald, and Heidenreich (2014a, p. 384) illustrates some important dimensions (see Figure 7.5). It illustrates that both transaction and transformational leadership are of significance for project participants' engagement and commitment and contribute to the project's performance. Transformational leadership has a greater impact on project participants' engagement than transactional leadership but the interaction between the two types of management affects commitment and goal achievement significantly. There is a great deal of knowledge concerning different tools managers can use that affect employees' job performance, derived from what is called evidence-based management (Pfeffer & Sutton, 2006). Research on the impact of managers on employee performance shows that management support in the form of attention to the individual employee and the way the job is done is, in most cases, far more significant than the size of wages alone (Dysvik & Kuvaas, 2013).

Leader support has a positive impact on project success, as it helps team members feel appreciated and empowered and also enables the development of a community feeling (Laub, 1999, p. 81). The project manager striving to be successful will create an environment in which the team can perform (Thompson, 2010, pp. 111–112), for example, by engaging in *authentic leadership* (Lloyd-Walker & Walker, 2011). Authentic leaders demonstrate a passion for the goals and purpose of the project, aligning their ways of working with their values and using both passion and reason in their leadership conduct. They establish meaningful relationships and present themselves with integrity – not pretending to be something and someone they are not (George, 2003, p. 130). Project teams consisting of competent employees who want to do a good job in some situations require a leader able to provide direction, support and inspiration, a key task for a project manager, in addition to the management aspects of the role (Crevani, Lindgren, & Packendorff, 2010).

Why become project manager?

... IT JUST SEEMS TO BE STRESS!

The project, as a form of work, is often perceived as engaging, both at the organizational and individual level, because it has a clear purpose and is usually time limited so that one can see results related to efforts. Perceived as an appropriate and purposeful way of organizing and performing work it delivers results. Not surprisingly, many are attracted to the project manager role. There are many motives and reasons for this. Some factors that explain motivation are:

- *Time limitation.* It can be inspiring to manage under a condition of clear time limitation. Many experience that when the beginning and end are clearly defined, they have an overview of the process and a deadline to direct their work, which is appealing.
- *Experience.* It provides the opportunity to develop leadership skills. Projects are crucibles for initiative.
- *Impact.* Whoever seeks to make an impact can do so by being a project leader.
- *Dedicated employees.* It is inspiring to be the leader of an interdisciplinary team of dedicated specialists.
- *Depth.* It provides the opportunity to apply and develop one's own professional competencies but also use these to influence the development of others.
- *Doing innovation.* It is perceived as meaningful to be responsible and contributing to creating something concrete and new – and often based on a need.

These moments overlap and are not exhaustive. Of course, there are variations regarding both the project type and the industry and sector in which the project is included. For a project in a public sector, where the structure sometimes can be rigid and the career opportunities somewhat limited, it allows for a break from ordinary, operational tasks. It is an opportunity to try something new and to obtain managerial experience. In a business that is based on the delivery of projects, the project will be a key part of the job, for example for an employee of a consulting firm that carries out assignments on behalf of clients. For a staff member in business, there may be an opportunity to immerse themselves in a field of expertise and help create something new, such as moving from being an HR employee to becoming a project manager for a competence development project.

There are multiple potentially negative aspects associated with being a project manager. A project manager usually is subject to considerable pressure and high expectations regarding the function, often associated with deadlines and meeting requirements' specifications. Conflicts between stakeholders and the permanent organization's requirements and expectations are a source of pressure (Zika-Wiktorsson et al., 2006). It is therefore not uncommon for a project manager to experience adversity and moments of anxiety, stress and despair. Being a project manager, especially in innovation projects, can mean gradually losing touch with the disciplinary knowledge that formed one's professional identity and if the new role of project manager does not translate into alternative career opportunities, one can become stranded with an identity that is satisfactory in neither camp of being a project manager nor a discipline expert. In the media, we constantly read about project managers who choose to leave their role or who are exposed to considerable pressure and criticism. In such cases, a good relationship with and support from project owners is vital.

What to look for when recruiting project managers

How the project manager can best perform the job varies between different projects and from different contextual circumstances in the individual project. Moreover, it also varies with personal qualities and specification of those qualifications that are necessary and desirable, making it impossible to identify one ideal type for the project manager function (Turner & Müller, 2005). The humorous job description shown in Figure 7.6 illustrates how difficult it is to find the perfect project manager:

Required	Young (in her twenties)
	PhD in current special field
	PhD in Project Management
	PhD in Psychology
	Minimum 10 years of relevant professional experience
	Minimum 10 years of project experience
	Long time experience as project manager
	Broad network
	Flexible
	Co-operative and independent
	Other personal features…

Figure 7.6 Humorous description of job requirement for an ideal project manager

Looking at the expectations of employees, principals and other stakeholders and what the management literature conveys as ideals for managers in general, the requirements of the project manager might seem totally unreasonable (Mintzberg, 2004). Requirements stated in job announcements for project managers also tend to be a bit unrealistic (Bredillet et al., 2015).

This chapter has shown that a wide range of qualities, competencies and behaviours are important for becoming a good project manager. Based on the elements that have been highlighted above, Table 7.2 would help organizations wanting to engage a project manager. The table will also be relevant to those aspiring to become a project manager and can be used for self-assessment of suitability as a project manager.

In choosing a project manager, it is essential to be clear about what kind of project is being addressed. Müller and Turner (2010, p. 86) present a model in which the project type and key areas of competence are categorized. By adapting this overview to our categorization of projects, we get the ranking of competency areas related to project type (see Table 7.2).

The competency areas that are presented in the table are quite general and a project manager cannot be chosen solely based on this. However, it illustrates some key areas of expertise for different project types that it is useful to know about when deciding who to engage as a project manager. Developing the ideas in Table 7.2 further, we can refer to Table 7.3 in which these roles are elaborated processually through the unfolding of a typical project.

Table 7.2 Managing and leadership characteristics

Competence	Project type			
	Development Project	*Change Project*	*Delivery Project*	*Event Project*
Main competence	Conscientiousness Sensitivity (Vision)	Communication (vision)	Communication Self-awareness Developing others	Communication Developing others Inspiration
Situational competence	Managing resources, Empowerment, Critical analysis and judgement, Strategical perspective, Emotional resilience, Influence, Structured			
Supporting competence	Achieving, Intuitiveness			

Table 7.3 Key process elements of the project manager function

Element	Subject	Areas for attention
Choosing Project Leader	Who decides	Type of project, and who is the principal and who will be the project owner (PO) are key elements
	When to decide	Should the project manager be involved in designing the framework, or should the framework set premises for who is best suited as project manager (PL). What candidates are available?
Characteristics of the Project Leader	Personal characteristics	The importance of conscientiousness, sociability and involving others.
	In-depth or managerial skills	What is important?
		In-depth expertise in the subject area of the project. Professional managerial skills
	Contextual knowledge	The importance of knowledge for the project's professional action conditions, the base organization, stakeholders and networks.
	Motivation	The candidates' motivation for entering the project and becoming a project manager. Incentives and career opportunities.
Start-up		**Framing**
	Framing and Scheduling	Consciousness of own function. Clarify framework condition, such as deadlines, main task, quality criteria and content aspects.
	Project administration methods	Evaluate and clarify project management tools. Clarify your own and the team's competence needs.
	Selection of team members	Clarify the degree of freedom and importance of the project manager to be able to assemble the project team themselves.
		Information Plan – Communicate
	Team Team function	Preparation of frames and tasks the team should do. Communicate task, framework and project content.
	Relationship with project owner, base organization, other stakeholders	Prepare communication channel, establish and use communication plan.

Element	Subject	Areas for attention
		People Plan – Building Relationship
	Team Establishing the team	Attention to important areas for establishing good teams. Awareness of team establishment and development. Carry out the start-up meeting for the team.
	Working method	Find and develop a work method for the project, based on a clarification of expectations, norms and values (team contract).
	Relationship to Project Owner	Establishment and clarification of relationship with project owner client. The degree of autonomy is assessed and clarified.
	Relation to the base organization	Establishment and clarification of relationship with line managers and key users and stakeholders.
	Relationship with other stakeholders	Establishing and clarifying relationships with suppliers, authorities and others
		Action Plan
	Decide and contribute	Facilitate team start-up with preparations; do project administration (preparation) tasks. Decide on the choice of project tool, team composition.
		Clarify the requirements specification and understanding of the concept.
Execution		**Framing**
	Self-assessment	Awareness and work with their own role and function. Reflections and learning processes.
		Information Plan – Communicate
	The Team	Be nerve centre and buffer that sorts, screens and processes information to the team. Ensure that agreed forms of communication and channels are used. Ensure that reporting is done along the way, using reporting as a basis for follow-up internally.
	Relationship to Project Owner	Inform, report on the progress of the project. Collect information and interpret.
	Relationship with Base Organization	Gather information and interpret, be the nerve centre for the project.
	Other stakeholders	Be the project team spokesperson.
		People Plan – Relationship Development
	Being the Team Leader	Leadership support. Vitalize and develop the individual. Assign tasks and responsibilities that are appropriate. Further develop the team as a unit, strengthen the culture.
		Distribute work tasks and functions through project plans and project management tools. Expertise and capacity as a basis.
	Relation to the base organization	Clarify expectations and further develop relationship. Convince about the project's direction and importance, make adjustments.
	Relationship with client and other stakeholders	Build and develop networks, enter into agreements. Suppress and clarify project expectations. Convince and adapt.

(Continued)

Table 7.3   (Continued)

Element	Subject	Areas for attention
		Action Plan
	Handle changes and uncertainties	Be problem solver, fire extinguisher and able to handle chaos. Look ahead and consider uncertainty.
	Solving tasks	Contribute content-related tasks in the project.
	Learning and development	Learn along the way by establishing and developing learning and reflection arenas.
Termination		**Framing**
	Self-reflection and learning	Evaluate your own efforts, learning. Prepare for termination of function, consider what becomes new function after project completion.
		Information Plan – Communicate
	The Team	Design final report, evaluate team process.
	Project Owner	Submit the final report. Communicate learning and central information.
	Base Organization and other stakeholders	Prepare the users for the function and content of the delivery. Inform about the project's final results.
		People Plan – Relationship Development
	The Team	Dissolve the team. End the relationships in the team and prepare team members for new tasks.
	Base Organization and other stakeholders	Clarify further relationship. If PL is internal, prepare for re-entry into function in the basic organization.
		Action Plan
		Complete tasks. Design and submit evaluation report. Prepare for a new function.

Selection of project managers

It is usually considered ideal that the project owner decides who will be managing a given project, based on a specification of qualifications and characteristics. However, quite often, the project leader question is settled before the project is clearly defined and adopted. It is also common, where there are strong guidelines from the permanent organization, that someone is already perceived as suitable and political direction will frame selection. In the competition between subject matter expertise, managerial competence and project management skills, the subject matter expertise is often given heavy weight. As we have seen above, this is often not necessarily a very good solution. Being a disciplinary expert does not translate into the generic skills for managing projects. The managerial function must be filled with relational competence and suitability, as should be the case for project management skills.

If you choose a project manager before the project has been adequately clarified, it may turn out that the project manager does not have the necessary skills when the project specification is completed. On the other hand, the early appointment of a project manager can help shape the role and contribute with input to the project.

Other factors that also arise in the selection of project managers are the availability of good candidates, decision-makers' experience in selecting a project manager and guidance from the permanent organization.

The project manager can be linked to the project in several ways. The type, scope and competence of the project will, together with the organizational structure, often be decisive for a project manager's terms and condition of employment. In delivery projects, the project manager is usually employed in the providing organization. In other projects, temporary employment conditions are used. The person who is engaged may come from the permanent organization or from outside. The employment relationship is limited to the management function of the project itself and ends after the project is completed. In internal projects, the employment relationship often leads to exemption from certain tasks that are part of the regular position. Employees who are responsible for tasks related to their regular position and being part-time project managers often feel the strain of a lot of work pressure, an organizational challenge that has become acute in some organizations as their project portfolio has increased. It illustrates the need for competence and the importance of resource allocation across projects, as well as considering the ordinary operations that need to run as normal. However, one must always remember that the availability of a resource is not the most important thing when selecting a project manager. Competence is.

WHAT WOULD YOU DO?

In a newly developing project at an advertising agency, the principal of the project has some hesitation as to which person to choose as a project manager. Right now, the choice is between an internal employee or hiring in an external person, who previously has worked for the company. They have about the same experience and competence. The principal turns to you and asks advice before choosing. He knows you do not know anything about the project, nor the specific qualifications required. Therefore, he approaches you for some general arguments about choosing an internal or external person to be project manager.

QUESTION

1. What would your arguments be?

Project management and process – final reflections

Project management is a multi-faceted and complex process. Having arrived at this point we have moved, seemingly, a long way from the Erie Canal, internal contracts and Taylor's scientific management. However, not quite as far as might be thought. The competitive tender is still dominant in most projects; most major infrastructure projects are still 'chunked' and highly formal and prescribed sets of relations still systematize most major projects. While the latter echoes some elements of scientific management in its emphasis on clear prescription of roles, a major impetus comes from another stream of project management: the management of complex innovation systems.

The precursor of contemporary systems management of complexity occurred in the context of the Second World War. In Europe, in 1944, under the control of General Eisenhower (who was later to become US president in the 1950s), the Normandy landings, which assured the defeat of Germany in the Second World War, were planned and strategized with enormous attention to detail. In America, a parallel campaign in long-range planning was under way, designed to end the war in the Pacific. The campaign was known as the Manhattan Project: its mission was to build the atom bombs that landed at Hiroshima and Nagasaki and ensured the surrender of Japan.

No one had built such innovative and deadly devices before. As Davies (2017, p. 39) writes, there were few precedents and little structure to guide the scientists and engineers overseeing the project. Consequently, they had to create a system coordinating, communicating between and controlling a vast network of people, resources and organizations. Not only did the Manhattan Project design a new and indiscriminate form of death and destruction on a mass scale, it also designed a new approach to managing projects to deliver it. The design was that of a complex systems approach.

War marked the origins of the systems approach to major projects and it also framed the subsequent development of complex systems theory and its impact on project management through the Cold War of Soviet–United States rivalry that lasted from the end of the Second World War to the demise of the Soviet Union in 1991. Major projects during this period, including the development of intercontinental ballistic missiles, the various National Aeronautical and Space Administration (NASA) projects associated with space exploration, as well as the Vietnam War, were all administered using systems approaches. (A full account of these auspices of systems theory can be found in the excellent book on *Projects* by Davies, 2017.)

At the outset, in the Normandy Landings and the Manhattan Project, there was little in the way of formalized wisdom to guide what were major projects facing considerable uncertainty. By the 1950s however, the systems approach became much more explicit and achieved explication in a number of influential texts, notably von Bertalanffy (1968), which laid out the principles of systems-based approaches to scientific enquiry. These principles soon became widely adopted and formalized in the emergent discipline of project management, signified by the growing professional institutionalization of the field. For instance, the Project Management Institute (PMI) was founded in 1969, two years after the International Project Management Association (IPMA) and three years before the Association for Project Management (APM) in 1972.

These events, signalling the institutional formation of claims to professional practice, are of considerable significance. Much of what we have taught in this book thus far would hardly have been possible if these bodies had not spurred the formalization of the field. These bodies, creating a body of knowledge, led to a formalization and standardization of prescriptive practice worthy of the most committed scientific managers. Indeed, there were many similarities between the two projects in the focus on the one best way of doing things. It is to these bodies that much of the nomenclature, process and prescription that constitutes project management is due. The PMI, in particular, has been in the forefront of these pressures for standardization and formalization, with much of what we have written about thus far and subsequently will also address, owing a debt to the practices that they have facilitated and encouraged.

Nonetheless, there is a considerable limit to systems approaches that are translated from the relatively closed systems of space travel and missile trajectories to the messy business of social realities open to an uncertain range of issues, interests and stakeholders vested in these. Highly prescriptive planning presuming high degrees of rationality embedded in systems which are self-contained has far more difficulty in managing the complexities of projects that are open to uncertainties of finance, available resources, interest and their resistances marking a seeming rejection of planning rationalities.

These early systems megaprojects, such as the Manhattan Project, initially had access to bountiful state funding from a Keynesian Warfare State. After the disasters of the Vietnam War, run by Robert McNamara on systems principles (the system outputs were 'kill-rates'), widespread opposition and agitation against open social systems liable to become permanently failing became evident (Meyer & Zucker, 1989). With the failures of the NASA shuttle programme, in which two crews of astronauts were 'lost', even closed systems began to look problematic despite the resources invested in them (Vaughan, 1996). Increasingly, the project management body of knowledge, highly systematic and rational, with its milestones, work breakdown structures, packages of work (chunks), planned budgets and schedules that were rarely met (Flyvbjerg et al., 2003), its prescriptions of roles, its hierarchy and order, began to give way to increasingly 'agile' approaches to project management. Increasingly agile they might have intended to be; this did not stop them becoming trapped in a thicket of jargon of their own adaptation centred on sports metaphors from rugby, as we explored in the previous chapter.

It should be clear by now that there will always be variation in the factors and processes that are valid in different projects and not least in how they unfold. The term 'project' and its management cover a vast panoply of practices. An event project, such as mounting an art exhibition, will have to emphasize different matters from the construction of an oil platform, a task that pales into insignificance against the tasks from which the systems approach emerged – and failed. The overview is nevertheless suitable for summing up many of the topics we have addressed thus far in the book, highlighting the diversity of moments that apply to the project manager. It can also be useful in many contexts as a checklist and a starting point for defining and using the project manager function, at least as a baseline for more creative and agile approaches as events and uncertainties occur – and they usually do.

In this chapter, we have concentrated most on the project-management role in projects. There are also other management functions, such as the project owner and line manager to be taken care of in projects – many of the moments that concern the project manager's skills and attributes can also apply to these features. A project manager is primarily the leader of a project team. In the next chapter, we will look into the working methods and functions of the project team and how they relate to the management of the project.

Summary

In this chapter, we have:

- Elaborated what leadership entails and explicated the specific aspects of leadership in projects: limited time period, resources and task; project team members having multiple leaders; leading interdisciplinary teams with people who previously have not worked together; relationships with project owners, permanent organization and stakeholders, as well as dealing with uncertainty.

- Demonstrated how projects have evolved from being merely engineering-based techniques, to focusing on the increasing role of management and the increased emphasis on leadership, elaborating some of the key aspects of leadership and management.
- Looked at the attributes of the project manager and what they mean for the ability to lead different project teams and project processes. We have looked into the personality traits of the leader, for example the Big Five model, and the importance of conscientiousness, sociability, openness to new experiences as well as empathy.
- Elaborated on the role of the leader and the style of leading and sensemaking while also pointing out the most critical tasks a project manager is responsible for, using the project manager's compass.

Exercises

1. Can you explain the different lenses for understanding the project leadership and what they help us understand/emphasize?

    - Leadership traits
    - Role of the leader
    - Leading style
    - Sensemaking

2. How can we enable distributed leadership and empowerment in project teams?
3. What are the major shifts in focus in the contemporary project management role from earlier times?
4. What do you understand being a project leader entails? What are the key aspects you would focus on? What are the challenges related to project team members having more than one leader?
5. What are important leadership attributes for project managers? Can you describe what each element means?
6. What is the project manager's compass? What can you say about the different directions of the compass? Do you find some of these directions more important than others?
7. What can you say about the 'Big Five' and project leadership?
8. What is the difference between transformational and transactional leadership and what are posited as the positive effects of transformational leaderships on projects?

CASE STUDY

LEADING BREXIT

One of the most simultaneously successful and unsuccessful projects in recent years has been Project Brexit. Brexit, getting Britain to leave the European Union (EU), began as the sole policy of a small political party, UKIP (United Kingdom Independence Party), which in the 2010s grew into an effective right-wing social movement that had links with the right wing. The Conservative Party had long had an anti-EU rump. Harried by the growth of UKIP and fearful of his right wing, the prime minister, David Cameron, pledged during the 2015 election campaign that he would hold a referendum on Britain leaving the EU, which was duly held on 23 July 2016, resulting in a narrow decision to leave by a 4% majority. Cameron resigned immediately after the referendum and Theresa May was elected leader to carry out the withdrawal. Seeking additional legitimacy, she called a general election held less than a year after the 2015 election and lost her majority, obliging her to form the government in a coalition with a right-wing Protestant party from Northern Ireland.

What followed was two years of tortuous negotiation with the EU that demonstrated, convincingly, that with a logically impossible project charter, leaving the EU was never going to be easy. The problem was one of too many stakeholders with conflicting goals, all of which May sought to vest in the negotiations. These conflicting goals were leaving the single market and having no customs union but insisting that the land border in Ireland must remain invisible and unchanged. By virtue of the fact that the EU, as an institution, abolishes borders, it cannot be left by a country with a land border with another EU country, without creating borders. The Project Charter, May's 'red lines', were from the outset incompatible, in large part because little thought had been given in Westminster to the peculiar position of Northern Ireland as Britain's first and one of its last remaining colonies in another country, albeit one formally integrated into the sovereign state of the United Kingdom. May resigned as prime minister to be replaced by Prime Minister Boris Johnson, elected by just over 100,000 Conservative Party members. He promised to leave the EU by 31 October 2019, 'do or die, deal or no deal'. However, Parliament, the sovereign body of governance, passed an act forbidding the government to leave with 'no deal' and demanding that if , by 19 October 2019, no deal had been organized, an extension be sought for a period in which either or both of a general election and a second referendum on leave or remain should be the options. Brexit did not occur by 31 October and the whole project, which has now consumed three and a half years' political energy, is scheduled to be completed by the end of 2020 (while the UK left the EU on 31 January 2020, the transitional period lasts until 31 December 2020). By the time that you read this the implications of the outcome may be more apparent.

The moral of this story is that the Project Charter lacked analysis of many essential ingredients from the outset:

Project title and description	Yes
Project purpose or justification	Yes
Measurable project objectives	No
Description of the output of the project	No
Assigning the project manager and setting her authority level	Yes
High-level assumptions and constraints	Unclear
Pre-assigned resources	Yes – but inadequate
Name of main stakeholders	Yes – but incomplete with respect to the 48% of Remainers
Expectations	Unclear
High-level project and product requirements	Unclear
Acceptance criteria	Unclear

(Continued)

Summary of important milestones	Unclear
Estimated budget	Unclear
High-level risks	Yes

QUESTIONS

1. In retrospect, how could the decision to launch Project Brexit have been better led as a project, especially with regard to the inclusivity of stakeholders?

2. How would you judge the value achieved by Project Brexit?

Additional resources

One would think that when there are so many textbooks in project management the topic of project leadership would be well covered in these books. It is not the case. One of the exceptions is Müller and Turner's book *Project-oriented Leadership* (2010). There is a great deal of literature that deals with leadership on a general basis. We recommend the following three books: *Managing* (2009) by Henry Mintzberg; *Become a Better Boss: Why Good Management is so Difficult* (2013) by Julian Birkinshaw; *A Brief Introduction to Leadership* (2014) by Jan Ketil Arnulf. In addition, Armenio Rego, Miguel Pina e Cunha and Stewart Clegg's (2012) *The Virtues of Leadership: Contemporary Challenge for Global Managers* (Oxford: Oxford University Press) might also be interesting. The literature references in the chapter as a whole indicate the sources we consulted.

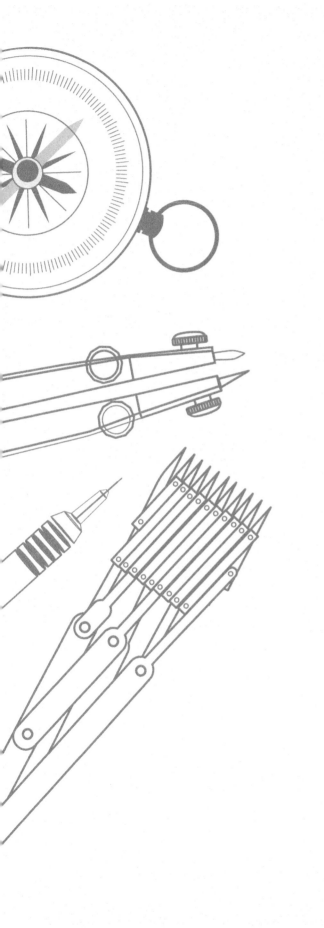
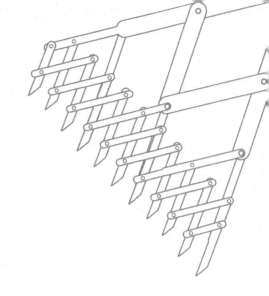

Chapter Roadmap

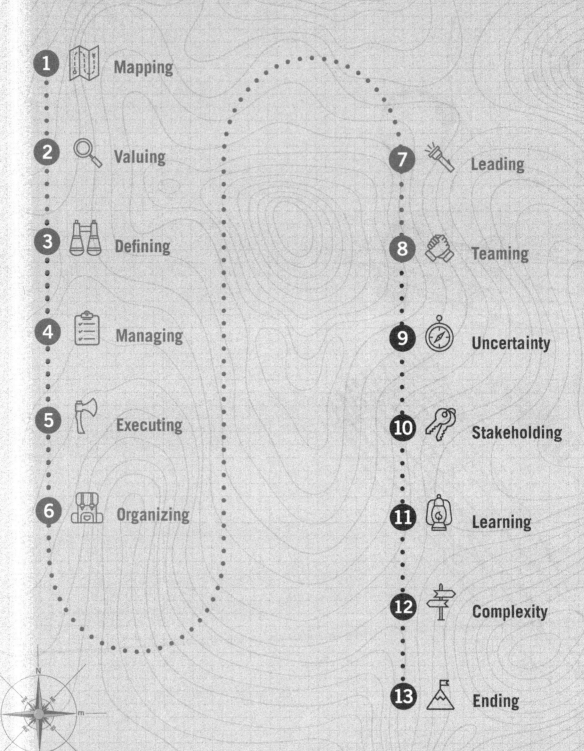

1. Mapping
2. Valuing
3. Defining
4. Managing
5. Executing
6. Organizing
7. Leading
8. Teaming
9. Uncertainty
10. Stakeholding
11. Learning
12. Complexity
13. Ending

8

Teaming in Projects

Learning objectives

After reading this chapter, you should know:

1 The key characteristics of project teams and their development processes

2 The importance of trust in the project team and processes for trust to emerge

3 What processes provide high-performance project teams, what motivates team members and what facilitates team capabilities

4 How to organize project teams in different ways

5 How to manage virtual teams' virtual working

Before you get started

I have no question that when you have a team, the possibility exists that it will generate magic. But don't count on it.

– Richard Hackman

Introduction

Project work can often be exciting and motivating. Participants in interdisciplinary project teams often work to solve difficult tasks and have to deal with considerable uncertainty and many unanticipated events. These present challenges and for the prepared person challenges can be a source of creativity, excitement and even fun. At the same time, especially when they seem insuperable, they can be a major source of stress.

Both stresses and excitements shared are better appreciated. This is where teams come in. A project provides an opportunity of building a project team to meet and come to know new people, enter into new collaborations and explore new tasks. The team is a construct: lifespan is limited and defined at the start of the project and its members often will not have forged a prior organic unity but it is likely that some, at least, will have worked on many projects previously, some of which may be similar to that anticipated. The interactions among the team members will be situated in an awareness of the temporary nature of the relationships that will unfold. All of these conditions will affect the individuals involved in the team and the relationships between them. Teamwork can be hard work and extremely difficult because it depends on interdependency and thereby involves interpersonal psychological issues. As highlighted in the previous chapter personalities matter in collaboration.

In this chapter we discuss how to establish and develop project teams, how to establish meetings as efficient collaboration mechanisms, as well as the pitfalls in project collaboration. We will describe a number of conditions and development processes that apply in many projects.

Project teams

In rare cases, one-person projects are established, such as an artist creating the score for a symphony, fabricating a mural or sculpting a monumental piece of statuary.

> **Team dynamics** are concerned with the formation, development and structuring of the processes guiding how the team functions and evolves.

More likely, however, is that a project will consist of a number of individuals working together. To be able to work effectively in a project we must be able to understand the dynamics of collaboration between individuals working together – the **team dynamics**.

We have previously seen that an organizational approach to understanding and executing projects has grown over the last 30 years. At the same time, there has been an increasing interest in considering what are often seen as the 'softer' aspects of projects, such as leadership and project team development, conflict management and work processes in the project team (see, for example, Allen et al., 1988; Hoegl & Gemeunden , 2001; Turner, Anbari & Bredillet, 2013). Research on understanding and developing project teams focuses attention on interpersonal relationships and interactions. Temporary organizations, including projects, cannot deliver unless project participants interact and coordinate their efforts (Bechky & Okhuysen, 2011).

Sometimes the term project group is used for those who work in the project, other times the term used is a project team. It is common to distinguish between teams and groups by indicating that members of a team have a more unified understanding of goals, performance requirements, work distribution and interaction than members of groups. Members of teams usually express higher commitment than group members. Teams are social systems consisting of at least three members who consider themselves as members of the team, a view shared by others, working together towards a mutual goal (Hackman, 1987).

Assigning a number of people to solve a shared task is not sufficient for them to become a project team; a group may be formed but more has to happen to turn a group into a team. First, the members must work with an understanding of goals, the assignment and expectations of performance (Hoegl & Gemuenden, 2001). The processes of establishing project goals and hierarchies of objectives, plans and roles can facilitate shared understanding of the assignment and the expectations related to it. A team has to have some common sensemaking about what it is doing even if there is dissensus about how it should be done. The dissensus is usually based on disagreement about how best to manage the issues at hand, which are commonly understood. Extensive discussions about what is expected help achieve an understanding grounded in common sensemaking early in the project to facilitate interaction, and project resolution and resilience.

To become a **project team** there are certain conditions that must be fulfilled:

> A **project team** develops a shared purpose with a limited duration and a clear relationship, sharing perceptions of performance requirements.

- A mutual understanding of the project's goals and when the different goals are to be met, founding common sensemaking for a common purpose
- A mutual understanding of the tasks, how to solve them and how they should be distributed. The project team will often be interdisciplinary and diverse expert knowledge will require integrating
- Clear norms of conduct guiding demands that can be made on the team as a whole
- Interdependent trust in a team built through collaboration, even when faced with uncertainty.

The unique feature of project teams, compared with other types of teams, is the distinctive element of finite temporality focused on a specific set of tasks to accomplish, often in conditions characterized by uncertainty, high intensity and integration of diverse knowledge and practices (Ancona & Caldwell, 1992; Meyerson et al., 1996).

Members constantly interact and communicate to find solutions to issues arising (Pinto & Pinto, 1990) by exploiting and integrating team members' diverse knowledge and skills. Team-building success is characterized by an ability to integrate skills, coordinate activities and adapt interactions, including improvising (Bechky & Okhuysen, 2011; Cunha, Neves, Clegg, & Rego, 2015). Uncertainty related to projects as well as demands for creative processes makes it increasingly probable that teams can improvise and adjust to events in their collaboration (see, for example, Bakker, Boroş, Kenis & Oerlemans, 2013; Cunha, Clegg, Rego, & Neves, 2014; Nordquist, Hovmark, & Zika-Viktorsson, 2004). Improvisation and creativity in a project require open communication founded on no barriers to entry into discussion as issues are addressed and mutual learning and testing of ideas occurs (Hoegl & Gemuenden, 2001; Pinto & Pinto, 1990; Weick, 1993) between the project team and the client, between the project and subcontractors and between the project and other key stakeholders (Eskerod & Jepsen, 2013).

COMPOSING PROJECT TEAMS

There are certain elements to be taken into account when composing a project team as they can be assembled in many ways, sometimes quite randomly. Less randomly, some members will be involved because they have specific competencies, while others will be assigned simply because they are available. Often, the project manager or other team members have experience with some people they want to involve because they believe they will make a fruitful contribution to the project. From an organization perspective, involve people with relevant knowledge and skills by efficiently exploiting the availability of resources across the host organization, making sure everyone required can be as fully engaged in the work all the time, as necessary for the project.

In many projects, there are strong guidelines from the permanent organization for types and sizes of resources that will enter the project. Some teams are assembled only by members of the permanent organization, while others consist entirely or partly of resource or persons drawn from outside of the permanent organization. Particularly in large, often unique, projects it is the principal who will engage external members to source the competencies required. In other projects, it is the project manager that chooses resources and determines the composition of the project team.

In an ideal situation, to be able to achieve the goal for the project, one should recruit the most competent personnel that are available for the task at hand in order to develop a good project team (Nicolini, 2002). The following questions can guide the assignment of project team members:

- What characterizes the project assignment (project delivery)?
- What work processes and activities must be carried out to accomplish the project?
- What competencies are needed to carry out the work processes and activities?
- Where can we find the most relevant and available expertise to participate fully in the project?

Three factors to consider in establishing well-functioning project teams are the composition of interdisciplinarity, special competencies and legitimacy.

- *Interdisciplinarity.* Efficient project teams often work with complex tasks and within complex environments, requiring multidisciplinary teams. The most competent people are required, independent of where they might be in the organization and what they presently do. The team will probably have to transcend organizational and professional boundaries and have expertise in several areas (Holland, Gaston, & Gomes, 2000).
- *Special competencies.* When a task is to be solved in a way that differs from traditional operations, a certain degree of innovation is needed. Innovation often requires special skills, providing unusual competencies.
- *Legitimacy.* The composition of the project team also influences its legitimacy. A multitude of members from several units and agencies can contribute to anchoring the project positively for stakeholders. From the viewpoint of different entities in the permanent organization, it may be important that the team represent their interests and perspectives in order to influence project processes and outcomes.

In addition, one can also build the team by emphasizing diversity in gender, age, culture, geographical representation or representation from many arenas in the organization. The *available capacity and motivation* of the individual employee must also be considered. Staff that are really committed to and engaged in a project can positively affect the rest of the team members; thus, it is best not to form a team through imperative command of someone that does not wish to take part.

Project tasks contain many known knowns; these are usually resolvable through well-rehearsed routines. There will also be known unknowns – those matters it is predictable will arise even if one is not sure where, when or how. Most problematic are the unknown unknowns – those events that are unanticipated and irregular for which there has been no prior routine or rehearsal. Thus, it is uncertain how to solve them and what expertise is the most relevant for solving them. In such projects, we can increase the likelihood of obtaining relevant expertise through a stepwise assignment of the team (Hoegl & Gemuenden, 2001). First, we can assign a *core team* to start working on the task, find out what the project entails and what processes and skills are likely to be able to solve the tasks, then recruit other relevant employees (Nicolini, 2002). Doing these things cannot afford guarantees against events and unknowns but they constitute a form of insurance.

One should think of a project team as a form of provisional organization in which the number of members who participate varies over time in line with the project's need for a specific type of expertise and resources. In some projects, because the need for competencies alters during the project, one must replace project team members to bring in requisite and new competencies. Nevertheless, it is often the case that the project teams staying stable over time and across several projects have greater success than teams with frequent change of members. The value of the members understanding each other and trusting one another seems more valuable than whatever is to be gained by adding new skills. When the composition of the team is changed by replacing members there should be a certain overlap between 'old' and 'new' staff, especially for the most significant roles. Overlap represents a form of socialization and training in the workplace. It is also necessary to document critical events and decisions so that new team members have the opportunity to understand the course of events and contribute to the team as soon as possible.

TEAM SIZE

Research on efficient teams suggests that they usually operate with 4–12 members as the most appropriate number of members (Levi, 2015). Increasing team size reduces the potential closeness of relationships, making it more difficult to establish trust, common understanding of goals, procedures and performance requirements – common sensemaking (Weick, 1995).

The development of cohesion (the experience of being in the same group) (Sydow, Lindkvist, & DeFillippi, 2004), has a clear effect on performance which is easier to achieve in small teams (see, for example, Mullen and Copper's 1994 meta-analysis). The project's characteristics and context determine the best size for a project team, although a project team should always be flexible in terms of size, depending on the tasks to be solved. Hackman (2011) argues that a typical team working together on a task will have the size of 4–6 members; if the team becomes larger, he argues that relational bindings tend to be weaker. Furthermore, the chances of the phenomena of social loafing, or free riding, will increase, where members of a team put less effort into the work than do their peers. These considerations are really rather psychology-based however and one cannot imagine them being of much use for really large and very complex projects such as those that NASA runs.

WHAT WOULD YOU DO?

THE 'TWO PIZZA' RULE

The number of a team should not be larger than that they can share two pizzas, is a statement from the founder of Amazon, Jeff Bezos. This implies a size between 4–7 team members. The pizza statement is easy to remember and even though it is not founded on scientific evidence, rather on experience, it sums up in a loose way most of the research on the field. So, even if you as a project manager lead complex and large projects, requiring multiple competences and consisting of many tasks, a large team will not necessarily be better for solving the task. The *number of links* between the members will go up, almost at an accelerating rate and managing the links between the members is the complicated thing in a team.

READ THIS!

Read this interesting article by Jacob Morgan (2015) explaining why and when smaller teams are better than bigger ones at: https://study.sagepub.com/pm.

WHAT WOULD YOU DO?

Imagine you are a project manager leading a project team of ten people. One of the members has just read the article about small teams and the two-pizza rule. She asks you to come up with some arguments for why the two-pizza rule has relevance and to explain what the arguments are as to why and when a team can be larger than the two-pizza rules indicates.

QUESTION

1. What would be the main points of the argument that you would compose?

Team roles in project teams

Roles are central to project work: both functional roles (Chapter 6) and team roles. Research shows that many of the face-to-face relationships in projects are guided by the understandings and design of roles that are common to most projects (Bechky, 2006). In order for the team to be high performing, there should be multiple team roles included. Often the roles will not be prescribed so much as emerge to ensure progress in the project team. One commonly used approach is presented by Belbin (2011). Belbin (2011) defines five success criteria for team and team roles to function appropriately:

- Each member contributes to the achievement of goals by performing a professional role
- Optimal balance between functional roles and team roles
- Each member registers and adapts to the strength of the team
- Personal traits and intellect determine the role allocation
- An adequate balance between the various team roles

Through a series of team studies, different team-role preferences were identified, as shown in Table 8.1.

Table 8.1 Belbin's team roles

Role	Description	Weaknesses
Plant	Creative, imaginative, unorthodox, and a problem solver	May be too preoccupied to communicate effectively with other people
Resource Investigator	Extroverted, enthusiastic, communicative, explores opportunities and networks	Over-optimistic, loses interest easily once enthusiasm offload their work to others
Coordinator	Mature, confident, and able to delegate well, clarifies goals, and promotes decision-making	Can be seen as manipulative, and can sometimes offload their work to others
Shaper	Challenging, dynamic, and thrives on high-pressure situations. Has drive and resilience to overcome obstacles	Prone to aggression, and can offend people, can lack emotional intelligence (ability to read people's emotions and to empathize with others)
Monitor Evaluator	Strategic and discerning and makes rational decisions based on carefully weighed-up information. Tends to be an accurate judge	Can lack drive and passion, has problems in inspiring others
Teamworker	Cooperative in nature and is democratic, perceptive, and diplomatic. They are good listetners, good at developing people, and have the ability to disarm conflict and aggressive situations	May be prone to indecision at critical times
Implementer	Well disciplined, reliable, and dependable, usually quite conservative and efficient. Good at turning ideas into practical actions	Quite inflexible and resistant to change. Slow to respond to change
Completer/Finisher	Conscientious and detail oriented. Searches out errors and omissions, and deliverson time	Anxious, inclined to worry too much, and uncomfortable in delegating responsibility
Specialist	Sinle-minded, self-motivated, and dedicated, provides knowledge and skills that are in rare supply	Contribution is specific and narrow, overly concerned with the technicalities

Source: Belbin, 1993, 2000, 2011. This figure was published in R. M. Belbin, *Team Roles at Work: Beyond the Team*. Oxford: Butterworth-Heinemann. Copyright Elsevier (1993, 2000).

Role preferences can be mapped through a team-role test for preferences for different roles in different situations. A project team member will not assume the same role in all the project teams they are involved in but, in general, will prefer certain role(s). A role preference is not the same as a personality trait, which denotes much more stable characteristics of the individual. The team-role preferences that emerge from such a test do not provide a basis for interlocking action patterns in a team but they can be a tool for exploring the expectations and needs of the team, as well as a basis for clarifying how the various roles can be filled within the team.

Different team roles facilitate different aspects of the teamwork process. For example, in an early phase of a task-solving process, it will be necessary for the ideas feature and its creative sides to appear, while in the final stage of the task the finisher role will be assumed by one or more team members. Working in teams it is not individuals alone that exercise creativity and imagination but the team as a whole, interrogating data, tossing around ideas, drawing on implicit and explicit theories, doing idea work. Such idea work is often neither as linear nor as stage based as much of the creativity literature.

Project team members often experience a conflict of interest when there is an inconsistency between what is best for the project and the interests of the organization to which the team member is attached. To reveal the multiplicity of implicit roles and potential conflicts of interest, openness and discussion of roles is required as members enter a team. All team members can be encouraged to assume multiple team roles, in a spirit of creative ambiguity, rather than strictly defining who fits specific team roles. Trust and psychological safety are the essence of performing in project teams.

Trusting

A well-functioning team is characterized by a high degree of trust. Trust implies that one party is willing to be vulnerable to another party, by assuming a benign intent, rather than one that cannot be trusted, on the part of the other party. Trust promotes achievement by facilitating open communication, learning and sharing of knowledge between members. It enables the emergence of innovative solutions and value creation. Trust is also closely linked to psychological safety, a phenomenon we will discuss in greater detail below. Trust is something that must be developed through interaction over time through shared experiences. It can be challenging to develop, as well as maintain, trust in a team.

According to Luhmann (1979) and Ring and van de Ven (1994) developing trust implies an attitude towards the future that makes one party willing to interact with another party – despite not being able to predict what will happen in the future. These expectations of each other and what will happen are based on track record. To be able to act under conditions of uncertainty, which are prevalent in projects, we must have trust (Smyth, Gustafsson, & Ganskau, 2010). As project members interact over time, they build up organizational stories about the project that can increase or decrease trust among them. When there is consistency between past expectations and what actually happened with respect to critical incidents in the life of the project, a positive spiral of trust develops.

It takes time to build trust. That is why researchers are fascinated by the fact that in many projects, including those with a relatively short time frame, the interactions display apparent high trust among team members (Meyerson et al., 1996, p. 167). The phenomenon is called *swift trust*. Understanding this phenomenon can provide mechanisms for accelerating trust in projects. The emergence of swift trust in projects is partly explained by team members' previous experience of success being dependent on the team's success ('everyone is in the same boat' principle). It might also be affected by the team members' future thinking; knowing that they might meet again in future projects, present behaviours and dispositions shadow the future. They strive to construct future perfect representations of their selves that present their best reflected self (Roberts, Dutton, Spreitzer, Heaphy, & Quinn, 2005). There is also the old adage that you meet the same people on the way up as you do on the way down. Prudence would suggest striving to maintain reputation and acting cooperatively. We should never rule out that actors may act opportunistically or recklessly in ways that are negative for the development of trust (Simmel, 1990, p. 179).

When clear roles and expectations are apparent, all project team members know what is anticipated of them and what they can expect from each other, which has a positive effect on the development of trust in the team but which does not necessarily lead to the development of swift trust. Team members have degrees of freedom in relation to design of their role (Seligman, 1997). Research shows that *swift trust* gradually evolves through displays of commitment by team members over time. In projects, this can happen quite quickly when there is a high intensity in interactions from the start-up. Team members' experiences of the team and its members and protocols rapidly build in a short period of time, which can lay the foundation for the development of trust and predictability.

In order for trust to occur, one or more of the members must actively choose to trust another. Theories point to how trust in relationships increases as one actor, B, shows another actor, A, that he or she wants to cooperate. The gestures that others make that one wishes to reward with positive action are called 'leaps of faith' (see, for example, Giddens, 1991; Seligman, 1997). If team members experience a leap of faith during their collaboration it can ease stress related to the uncertainty inherent in project work. Members learn a way of collaborating that is implicit in the emergence of these leaps of faith, making actions rather predictable, for example, by sharing an implicit code of conduct on how to collaborate.

THICK AND THIN TRUST IN THE PROJECT TEAM

Trust can be classified into different types (Figure 8.1), exhibiting different degrees of 'thickness'. Thick trust is premised on multiple and longer, in terms of temporality, experiences of being trusted and being trustworthy. One often distinguishes between trust based on deterrence, knowledge, roles and identification (Table 8.2).

Table 8.2 Thick and thin trust in projects

Type	Characteristics
Deterrence-based trust	The thinnest form of trust, where it relies on A trusting B because A knows B fears the sanctions that may occur if B does not act in line with A's expectations. This form of trust only works when there are sanctions involved; it is clear what one expects of the other and the consequences related to deviating from expectations. Since the deterrence-based trust is a fragile form of trust that is not so good for collaborative relationships when looking at them in a broader perspective, it is more fruitful to work with other forms of trust in projects, such as role-based and knowledge-based trust.

(Continued)

Table 8.2   (Continued)

Type	Characteristics
A knowledge-based trust	A thick form of trust that develops over time as team members interact and learn to know each other. This means that they, to a large extent, can anticipate how the others will act. Mutual trust can then be built through a spiral of self-fulfilling prophecies, where A has experienced that B collaborates; thus A believes that B will continue to cooperate. When A thinks B will cooperate, it increases the likelihood of B actually cooperating. The knowledge-based trust is thick and perceived as personal, so it is also difficult to re-establish if it is broken in a project team.
Role-based trust	Assumes that A will trust B due to the fact that B is included in the project based on his/her competencies. Since B has joined the project and demonstrated the ability to contribute positively, A trusts that B has the ability and willingness to provide for the project team's best. The trust in B is based on expectations that B will fulfil his/her role. In a project team where there is not enough time to develop a knowledge-based trust, working with role-based trust can be a very good option. This form of trust is thicker and more positively loaded than the deterrence-based trust. It also provides a good foundation for further development of knowledge-based trust.
Identification-based trust	In some projects, one makes an effort to develop the thickest form of trust between team members, where the parties identify with each other in a manner that makes it possible for them to act as an agent for the other. This trust is only developed when the parties have developed some sort of personal relationship and a strong sense of shared identity. Since this is often time-consuming, it is only relevant in a project team where the relationships between team members last for a long period of time.

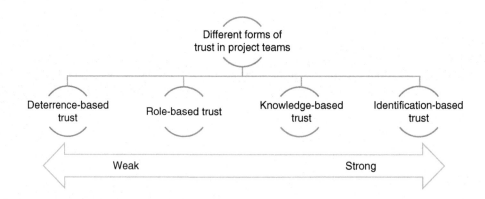

Figure 8.1   Different forms of trust in project teams

The time it takes to build trust in projects diminishes the more that team members clearly appear to be orderly and predictable in their standards for role and task execution as well as how their interactions support integrity and predictability in action pattern (Tuomela & Tuomela, 2005). One must show the other trust and actively choose to trust the other to create a positive trust spiral. The presence of trust also helps to reduce unwanted behaviour in relationships between members and thus the need for control. Mistrust of others' intentions, perhaps assuming that they may have a hidden agenda will, in turn, be a very efficient way of destroying relationships and making interactions difficult.

Psychological safety

For teams to be real teams, the importance of **psychological safety** should not be underestimated. Amy Edmondson (1999, p. 354) states that psychological safety concerns 'a shared belief that the team is safe for interpersonal risk taking'. Uncertainty

> **Psychological safety** is a belief that one will not be punished or humiliated for speaking up with ideas, questions or making mistakes.

and interdependence are underlying conditions for the requirements of psychological safety in project teamwork.

Trust and psychological safety are not equal terms. Trust refers to interactions between individuals, actors or parties. Psychological safety, on the other hand, is experienced at a group level and pertains to expectations about immediate interpersonal consequences (Edmondson, 2018). To establish psychological safety in your project there are three things you can do:

- *Frame the work as a learning problem, not as an execution problem.* Recognize and make explicit that there is enormous uncertainty at different levels in the projects and that the interdependence between team members and participants is crucial. 'We never been here before, and we have got to have everybody's voice and imagination involved.'
- *Acknowledge your own fallibility.* Be open, say you are not sure, you may have missed something, what do you reckon? This encourage speaking up.
- *Model curiosity.* Ask a lot of questions, which also is a necessity for making people open up to contribute with their thoughts.

The individual's positive involvement in the team needs to be supported, basic psychological safety created, as well as a shared story developed. Then kick-off meetings, team development seminars and celebrating milestones can facilitate clarity, engagement and the feeling of a shared history.

WATCH THIS!

Watch Professor Amy Edmondson (2014) speak on the topic of psychological safety in this Ted Talk video on psychological safety. Listen to what she underlines as significant. A. Edmondson (2014), 'Building a psychologically safe workplace', available at https://study.sagepub.com/pm.

WHAT WOULD YOU DO?

QUESTION

1. What would Professor Edmondson underline as significant work for a project team that has just started?

Picture 8.1 Team work

Source: Image courtesy of Thómas Tan and @Begoon. Provided under the Creative Commons Attribution 3.0 license via wikicommons

Start me up – establishing a project team

The project team will often start its work when the kick-off meeting is held. We have previously presented how the premises for the team's work are explicated in the project charter, through the use of responsibility maps and discussions on the mission breakdown structure. Activity responsibility charts, milestone plans and activity plans are useful tools for distributing tasks between team members in an initial meeting. The organizational culture also provides guidance for the interaction between team members. Therefore, both the members and the project manager should reflect on what kind of culture they want and how they will act to promote this.

For a team to function in a desired manner, attention should be paid to the start of a project team's life cycle. Putting effort into getting to know each other should be a focus for the project leader. How to do this will vary, depending on the project type, whether the members know each other beforehand, the composition of the team itself, as well as many other elements. Starting the teamwork with a gathering where there is an open dialogue is a useful way to start, which can begin with each member talking about their self, past projects, what they have learned from and what they hope to learn from the present project.

TEAM CHARTER – FACILITATING TEAMWORK

Projects usually have clear time frames and goals, and project teams composed on the basis of the respective competencies of the members and expectations of their contribution. Often members neither have a clear opinion about the project's purposes

IN PRACTICE

TEAM BUILDING

Robert Cialdini, an American psychologist, suggests that one way of building relations at an early stage is to do a simple exercise where all the team sits together and explores the following:

- First, find five things you have in common
- Second, find three things which you do not have in common
- And, then again, find another two things you share

The things you raise could be related to the project in one way or the other but do not have to. The central aspect is to build a relation to each other and create points of contact in the team, perhaps through liking the same music, artists or sports teams. According to Cialdini (2016) this simple exercise can have great impact on the team and its collaboration.

QUESTION

1. In your work team for assignments as a student, conduct this exercise. Write up the process and results and then share them with the other members of the team.

and objectives nor knowledge of the project manager or the others in the project team. Such uncertainty often hinders the team members in getting the collaboration started, in collaborating efficiently and purposefully. By establishing a team charter, the project team can outline shared principles as to how they will collaborate (Courtright, McCormick, Mistry, Wang, & Chen, 2017). Working together in a project team will also bind members together in an implicit **psychological contract**.

> A **psychological contract** can be defined as the assumptions, beliefs, expectations held between persons within a group set to work together, about the nature and function of the relationship between them.

A team charter is both a clarification of expectations and a concrete plan for how the team will organize their teamwork tasks (Mathieu & Rapp, 2009). The term *team charter* reflects a clear expectation from everyone involved in acting with a *mutual commitment* to teamwork. The team charter is based on four key elements that should be clarified: goals, roles, inter-relational behaviour and processes. Together these provide the GRIP framework:

- **G** – Goal of the project team
  - The goal is an expression of the future condition aimed for. Often, many of the project goals are established before the project team members are assembled and start their work together. The team members work to interpret them and develop a shared understanding of what the goals are and how they should be understood. In addition, the project team can design objectives related to their own work and learning (process goals).

- **R** – Roles in the project team
  - The roles in the team should be clarified as early as possible, through discussions of functional roles and team roles. In addition, members should discuss what each member's expectations are of themselves for the project's tasks and for the other team members. If there are opportunities for conflict of interest these should be raised and appropriate ways to deal with them determined.

- **I** – Inter-relational behaviour
  - Team members should discuss how social interaction will take place, what social norms they want and what to do to promote the desired culture.

- **P** – Processes (decision-making and procedures in the project team)
  - Discuss and agree how teamwork will take place. For example, members should clarify the routines for preparing, implementing and following up activities and decisions. It may also be necessary to clarify what to do in case of disagreement about how information should be shared.

In order to get a good foundation for efficient teamwork, it makes sense that it is prepared in the listed order (see Figure 8.2).

Figure 8.2 GRIP – the key elements for a team charter

Working on the team charter, one can facilitate a quick start-up of the actual collaboration among the team members and aim for more efficient teamwork. The content and scope of the team charter should be tailored to the project team's situation. It does not, of course, have to be formal in style or be very extensive but all parties involved in the team engage in developing the team charter to create a shared understanding of and a commitment to this way of working. Nor does it have to be formally designed; the point is that it must be drafted jointly and recognized by all implicated. Courtright et al. (2017) propose that a team charter can serve as a control mechanism that builds task cohesion through a structured exercise (Figure 8.3). They juxtapose the team charter with a control mechanism that they see as influencing the emergence of task cohesion more organically: team conscientiousness. A team charter primarily has an impact on team performance for teams that are low (vs high) on conscientiousness.

Evolving project teams

Project teams go through different stages and processes during their lifetime, which a project manager, as well as the project principal, and the team itself, need to be aware of. In Chapter 10, we investigate learning and development in project teams but raise some further elements here concerning the development of teams.

GRIP	Description
	– Name of the team
	– Members: names, device attachment
	– Date of conclusion of the charter
G – Goals	**Goal for the project team**
	– What are the goals of the team (related to the project and possibly the process)?
	– How do we concretize the goals so we can reach them?
R – Roles	**Roles in the team**
	– What expectations do we have for each other?
	– Based on the Belbin test, how should we handle the role distribution that emerges and compensate for any deficiencies?
I – Interrelational	**Interrelational behaviour**
	– How should we behave towards each other?
	– How should we communicate?
P – Processes	**Processes – procedures and decision-making**
	– How are decisions taken?
	– How are the tasks to be distributed?
	– How should information be shared?
	– How will the meetings be conducted?
	– How will the team cope with any conflicts?

Figure 8.3   Example of a template for a team charter – GRIP

PROJECT TEAM STAGES AND MIDPOINTS

A widely popular approach and model for understanding team stages is Tuckman and Jensen's (1977) stages of group development, an approach that has been criticized for being outdated and irrelevant in describing teamwork as a linear process. The more contemporary view, after Gersick (1988), is to see teams develop through processes of punctuated equilibrium at the mid-point of the team process. The strength of the linear model is that it provides a simple framework. Depending on the type of team, the goals it will reach and the context within which the team operates, teams will have a varying time span in the different phases, but roughly the project team is seen as going through five phases. The five phases are labelled Forming, Storming, Norming, Performing and Adjourning (Table 8.3). Each phase has its own distinctive features. The starting point for this approach is the work of Tuckman and Jensen (1977) and this work can be used as a prompt, to help teams become focused on what they are doing, rather than being regarded as a literal description of the processes that the teams must follow. Using Gersick's (1988) approach, if the team hasn't worked out how it will do what it will do by the halfway stage – be very worried!

Table 8.3   Stages of team development

Stage	Description
Forming	During this phase, the team is put together, and the members get to know each other and the project's goals. The team starts work on preparing the foundation for the project and the team's basic rules.

(Continued)

Table 8.3   (Continued)

Stage	Description
Storming	The basic and most necessary are set, and the phase of testing, resistance, disagreement and any hidden agendas and prejudices will appear on the surface.
Norming	Team members develop clearer procedures for work and agree on basic norms and advances. They seek cooperation with each other, develop closer relationships between themselves and commit to the project's progress and processes.
Performing	Team members work together to complete the tasks and reach the goals of the team. They develop and adjust procedures as needed. The members challenge each other but have constructive attention aimed at carrying out the tasks.
Adjourning	The project ends when the tasks are completed and the goal is reached, or possibly for other reasons, and the team dissolves. The members switch to other tasks and cooperation with employees.

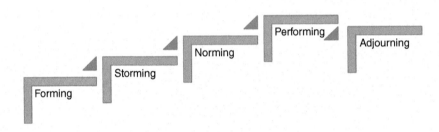

Figure 8.4   Tuckman & Jensen's team development model

Project managers might try to accelerate the forming, storming and norming phases so that the team gets the quickest possible start (Figure 8.4). Team charters (see below) can help by clarifying goals, work methods and norms for teamwork.

PUNCTUATED EQUILIBRIUM

Returning to Gersick (1988), her research suggests that project teams often dramatically change their way of working about halfway through the period of time set aside for project execution. Often, project teams quite quickly establish the method they will use to solve the task, working accordingly until half of the project's scheduled time has passed. By this time a period of intense and concentrated search to find new ways of solving the task arises, followed by re-planning of the project work, with new methods being put into use that advance the work towards the final project deadline. The recognition that one is midway in the scheduled execution time 'wakes' the team members up and makes them begin to evaluate their own methods and progression (Engwall & Westling, 2004). Such development is reminiscent of processes seen in evolutionary biology, for which the term *punctuated equilibrium* was coined. Hackman and Wageman (2005) argue it is useful for a team leader to evaluate and/or reorganize the team at this point, as this affords a learning opportunity for the team and the project. If there is not a natural midterm, a crucial milestone could be applied instead.

TEAMING

Much has been written about how project teams can plan their work ahead, often based on the assumption that the project will operate for a relatively long period of time.

Although that is often appropriate and desirable, hastiness, unforeseen events and short time horizons are often the case. In many projects, teams have to be assembled quickly and be able to perform well within a short period of time before they are dissolved in projects of very short duration. There may also be various internal, temporary sub-teams that will perform specific tasks in the project, such as workgroups. In such cases, *teaming* is important (Edmondson, 2012).

Teaming is the dynamic activity that occurs at the establishment of a team but also takes place in the whole project execution. It involves active coordination, the establishment of rapid cooperation and flexibility in interaction and staffing. Examples of project situations where teaming is applicable would be a military operational unit in the field or a crisis team put together by experts to solve an acute problem in business. In the project context, it is often a subproject work team that is part of the main project that drives teaming. Teaming can be facilitated through three steps:

1. *Framing how* the task is designed, needs elaborating, determining the direction of the work. In projects, this is usually done in connection with the development of the project charter during the planning of the project or as part of setting milestones.
2. *Structuring* the way of working, involves determining the equipment and virtual platforms supporting the work processes.
3. *Prioritizing* activities and processes, contingent on the mutual dependence between participants, activities and other resources. The key issue is how to make communication and interaction effective among those involved. Project management designs and clarifies the basis for coordination, priorities and decisions.

Contemporary organizational forms and rapid demands for changes mean that projects must increasingly be prepared for *teaming*, especially where there are high levels of uncertainty. A project manager should be aware of the characteristics and behaviours that can promote teaming. Table 8.4 shows some forms of attitudes and behaviours that, according to Edmondson (2012), support teaming.

Table 8.4   Behaviours driving teaming success

Speaking-up	Direct conversation between individuals, including asking questions, seeking feedback, and discussing errors.
Colloboration	A collaborative mind-set and behaviours – both within and outside a given unit of teaming – to drive the process.
Experimentation	A tentative, iterative approach to action that recognizes the novelty and uncertainty inherent in every interaction between individuals.
Reflection	Teaming relies on the use of explicit observations, questions, and discussions of processes and outcomes. This must happen on a consistent basis that reflects the rhythm of the work, whether that calls for daily, weekly, or other project-specific timing.

Source: Edmondson, 2012, Figure 2.1. Reproduced with permission of Wiley.

Teaming is not a new method of teamwork or a concept specifically designed for teamwork in certain contexts. Rather, there is an extra dynamic and intense activity where proactive coordination and the establishment of rapid cooperation and flexibility in interaction and staffing are central elements.

WATCH THIS! IN PRACTICE

Watch Professor Amy Edmondson (2017) explain teaming, using the mining collapse in Chile in 2010 as an example at: https://study.sagepub.com/pm.

QUESTION

1. What were the teaming factors that saved the lives of the Chilean miners?

Project team member: Motivation and progress effects

MOTIVATION

In contemporary working life, motivation is considered a significant determinant of individuals dedicating time and energy. Motivation is seen as triggering behaviour, maintaining it and determining its intensity (Locke & Latham, 1990). Elaborating and establishing adequate goals, working on how to interpret them and, of course, focused activities to achieve them, are significant for almost all projects. When the principal specifies the direction of the project team's work, as well as creating a shared perception of the direction among the team members, motivation can be triggered. Objectives can motivate and are therefore an essential force for successful projects.

> **Motivation** is defined as the psychological process that drive behaviours towards the attainment or avoidance of some object.

The psychological concept of **motivation** has been applied within organizational and management contexts since the Hawthorne studies (Roethlisberger & Dickson, 1939) in the 1930s.

Motivation affects action in three ways. It:

- Initiates action
- Provides direction for action
- Determines the duration of action

If the project team is highly motivated, it will start task solving activities faster and dedicate more effort to these activities over time. Team members will also choose a more challenging course than if they were less motivated. Extensive attention has been paid to how one can achieve consistency between the organization's requirements and the needs of individuals so that the latter are motivated for action (Argyris, 1957). Jobs must be designed so that they are enriching in order to increase employee satisfaction (Herzberg, Mausner, & Snyderman, 1959). Aspects of work trigger psychological conditions that contribute to increased performance (both quantity and quality) (Hackman & Oldham, 1980). One must perceive work as meaningful, hold responsibility for the outcomes, and perceive the emerging results to be as expected. Work that creates these conditions has five characteristics. It:

- Requires a multiplicity of skills and has an ambition level that enables the further development of skills and talents
- Implies completing tasks with observable results (a visible part of a larger whole)
- Has a positive impact on other people – appears attractive
- Implies large relative freedom in the planning and solving of the task
- Follows up with concrete and positive feedback so team members know what is expected from them and what they can do to improve their work

Common to the theories we have mentioned is that the individual becomes motivated when experiencing cognitive (i.e. mental) development.

WHAT WOULD YOU DO?

You are assigned to a project as a team member that you have not asked to join. The project requires much attention for a relatively short period of time and implies prioritizing the project in favour of other tasks you are involved in. However, this is a project where you can apply your skills and expertise and the project seems to be highly interesting and considered significant for your organization. You have just read the characteristics of motivation (in the text above) and, as you reflect upon this, you are informed about the new project in which you are supposed to participate. Before you will be formally included in the project team, everybody has to write a motivation letter to the project manager, describing how and why they are motivated to join the project.

QUESTION

1. What emphasis would you stress, based on what you know about motivation?

GOALS AND MOTIVATION IN THE PROJECT TEAM

Goals are known to have an impact on motivation. Goals have the greatest impact on motivation when they are perceived as specific and relatively difficult to reach; when the team members commit to the goals and when team members are given concrete feedback on how their performance relates to possible and actual goal achievement. Thus, ambitious goals contribute to increased team efficiency (Durham, Knight, & Locke, 1997). Teams involved in solving complex tasks should be encouraged to establish their own goals since individuals and teams tend to commit more strongly and be more affected by the goals that they establish for themselves. Doing so fits well with the value of a team charter where the project team elaborates the project goals. Where the client is also working out goals, these represent information the project team requires. They will advise the team of the level of ambition the client has for the teamwork and the project deliverables. Establishing their own goals often helps motivate teams. In addition, of course, the principal's objectives are to provide direction for the project work. Therefore, it is recommended that the project's client should work out goals in conjunction with the team working on goals. The combination can have a considerable impact on motivation, thus on project team performance, ultimately also on project success (Hoegl & Gemuenden, 2001).

EXTEND YOUR KNOWLEDGE

Read the article by Zhu, Gardner, and Chen (2018) at https://study.sagepub.com/pm to learn about how motivation predicts tacit knowledge sharing in project teams and how project managers need to promote knowledge sharing through facilitating a team culture that satisfies members' needs for autonomy, competence, and relatedness. For project performance it is important that all members use their tacit and explicit knowledge.

SELF-EFFICACY IN THE PROJECT TEAM AND MOTIVATION

Another mechanism included in motivation is self-efficacy (Bandura, 1986). Self-efficacy is the team's belief that the team *can* succeed in their tasks (Durham et al., 1997, p. 208), a belief significant for project team performance (Bandura, 1986). Self-efficacy affects the goal, as well as short- and long-term efforts, and cooperation and communication. It does so by:

- **Goal setting**. What tasks do team members choose to solve and what goals do they set? Low self-efficacy can lead to simple tasks and low goals because one assumes that one cannot complete a task in a successful manner.
- **Effort**. How quickly do team members get started with their actual task solving and how much effort do they dedicate? Low self-efficacy can reduce the effort made due to triggering the assumption that 'my effort does not matter'.
- **Endurance**. How long will team members maintain high effort? A team member with high self-efficacy, a belief in one's own ability to solve tasks and derive good solutions efficiently, will work harder to find solutions when they encounter problems in the task solving by recognizing their strategy is wrong and trying to change it. A person with low self-efficacy is likely to interpret problems from the perspective that they cannot solve them and will thus be less motivated to try harder to find a solution. They interpret problem resolution resistance as signifying their lack of ability to succeed. Thus, the project team with high self-efficacy will select more difficult tasks and set higher goals than members with a lower ability to master efficacy. Furthermore, they will start their tasks faster and maintain higher performance over time. Project teams often need to perform under unsafe conditions.
- **Cooperation and communication**. Often, if the project team believes that it will succeed, it will choose more appropriate strategies and methods to solve its tasks (Wood and Bandura, 1989). The use of more appropriate methods contributes to the experience of mastery and increased confidence in what can be achieved (Locke & Latham, 1990). The belief that one can succeed, the belief in mastering something, is thus a positive spiral that seems to have a very high impact on the motivation of teams (Bandura, 1997).

Many, including Gully, Incalcaterra, Joshi, and Beaubien (2002), who conducted a meta-analysis of 67 studies in the field, argue that a team's self-efficacy is a very good indicator of team efficiency. Team efficiency is vital for project success.

EXTEND YOUR KNOWLEDGE

Read the article by Terhorst, Lusher, Bolton, Elsum, and Wang (2018), 'Tacit knowledge sharing in open innovation projects'. It can help you understand the importance of a collaborative team climate for fostering creativity and motivation in project teams, available at https://study.sagepub.com/pm.

EXTRINSIC AND INTRINSIC MOTIVATED PROJECT MEMBERS

For more than 30 years, efforts have been made to distinguish between inner and outer motivation and to understand how these mechanisms can be used to enable work processes. Both **intrinsic** and **extrinsic motivation** are significant explanatory models for behaviour.

> **Extrinsic motivation** is the motivation that is conditioned by external rewards (such as praise, money, promotion), i.e. sources outside the activity itself.

> **Intrinsic motivation** is the motivation that is conditioned by inner rewards such as the feeling of pleasure, interest and satisfaction in performing the tasks.

If project workers are driven solely by extrinsic motivation, it is mainly the results that follow from their activities that drive them. Repeated observations of project staff emphasize that they enjoy project work due to the exciting and challenging tasks they work on in projects, the intrinsic challenges, from which they learn as they find social stimulation.

Rewards still matter as project team members that make an effort to perform very well also like to be rewarded for doing so, as long as the reward is perceived as fair among the project team members. In order to maintain intrinsic motivation, it is best to reduce the emphasis on the relationship between performance and external reward and rather work to support the employees in their work.

Principals tend to overestimate the value of extrinsic motivation for others and intrinsic motivation for themselves (Heath, 1999). In addition, it is common for clients to assume that the project team members' interest diverges from the interest of the client; thus team members are thought best managed and monitored through the uses of incentives. In order to enable high performance, clients should instead assume that employees want to perform well and concentrate on the kind of support they need to perform their best, which the client can support. As we mentioned in the chapter on the project manager's role, research shows that management support is a major factor in the employees' job effort and performance, and that payments and other rewards do not have an enduring impact on employee performance. However, the sole element that tends to drive behaviour towards better performance over time is progress, which seems to be a rather overlooked factor, according to Amabile and Kramer (2011). When they examined people's daily reports from projects, they found one factor, progress, was the key indicator. The findings are relevant to understand how and what you need to be aware of as a principal or project manager, if you intend to get the best out of your team and make them thrive and perform well.

CREATING CONDITIONS FOR GREAT PERFORMANCE IN PROJECT TEAMS – THE PROGRESS PRINCIPLE

In a permanent organization, finding ways for a manager to make co-workers perform and enjoy work is a major challenge. Of course, there is no quick fix for such a complicated matter. However, recent studies have revealed some elements as being vital ingredients for good performances at work: the keyword is progress. Much the same mechanisms and factors affect temporary as well as permanent organization. After presenting some of the core elements of what Teresa Amabile and Steven Kramer label 'The Progress Principle', we will look more closely into how this could affect a project manager and team.

Progress principle: positive forward-facing achievements that act as catalysts and nourishment for further achievement.

Inner Work Life (IWL) can be defined in terms of conditions fostering positive emotions, internal motivation and positive perceptions of colleagues and work.

Despite much of the conventional wisdom in the field of management and leadership, it is not just extrinsic incentives that drive people to be successful and happy at work. Self-determination, feedback and managerial support are some of many elements enabling people to thrive when at work. When Amabile and Kramer examined over 200 people, consisting of 12,000 daily reports, they found one factor as the key indicator: the **progress principle**, which they related to what is described as **Inner Work Life (IWL)**.

Positive IWL makes co-workers perform better, with higher productivity and creativity, as well as feel happy and engaged in their work. Seeing progress is essential, whether it is a substantial breakthrough, goal completion, forward movements, or 'small wins' (Weick, 1984). Two groups of factors influence the sense of forward momentum, of achievement. These are events that act as catalysts in supporting work that encourages one to continue striving positively, and nourishment – the realization of events that support the person. Elements in these factors are outlined in Figure 8.5:

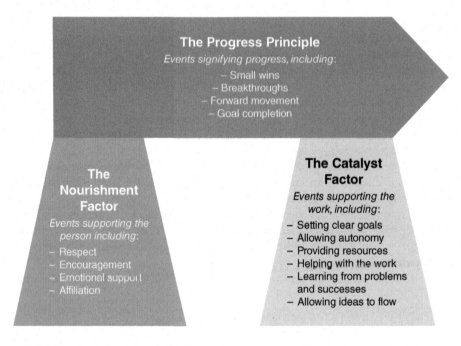

Figure 8.5 Elements and factors influencing progress – the progress principle (inspired by Amabile & Kramer, 2011)

Some guiding principles for implementing the progress principle include:

- **Celebrate progress every day**. Progress in meaningful work is an event so celebrate the 'small wins' and the progress you and your team make.
- **Deal with setbacks constructively**. When setbacks occur, deal with them constructively and use them as learning opportunities.
- **Supply catalysts and nourishers to support progress**. Provide clear goals and sufficient resources among other elements. As a project leader, focus on encouragements and recognition.
- **Build on progress**. When progress has been made, introduce new realistic challenges.
- **Minimize the negatives**. Do not ignore them but be aware that setbacks have a greater impact on emotions than progress. Deal with negatives quickly and effectively when they occur.
- **Once in a while, take your foot of the accelerator**. Remember that high time pressure requires time for breaks as well as concentration on urgent tasks when required.
- **Keep a daily journal**. Doing so helps you remember small wins and progress, as well as recording opportunities for learning.

So how could and should this affect the project manager and team? It would require more space than we have to outline this in a proper way. However, we outline some elements that can be used as guidelines for a project manager in some instances. If you want to delve deeper into this topic, you will find more on this in *The Progress Principle* (Amabile & Kramer, 2011), even though it is not tailor-made for project managers. Nonetheless, the contribution is one from which project managers can learn.

WATCH THIS!

Watch the YouTube video of Teresa Amabile (2011) explaining 'The progress principle', its importance and how leaders can enable such progress at: https://study.sagepub.com/pm.

Dysfunctional project teams

Project teams that perform well can produce great results and contribute to value creation in a highly efficient manner. Above we have looked into the conditions for successful teams, detailing the characteristics of such teams. However, many project teams are not so successful. It is seldom that teams are established with very strong enabling conditions, where all team members align with requirements for filling team roles and functional roles, with the optimal interdisciplinary combination, and so on. These enabling conditions include phenomena such as the team composition, the start-up processes and establishing the key principles for project execution, which are all dimensions that affect goal achievement. When there is a failure to achieve fit between these enabling conditions and the reality of available resources of personnel, time and budget, project teams must adapt to this mismatch between the ideal and the real, which may reduce the potential gains from teamwork.

If one risk is insufficient teamwork another risk, paradoxically, is too much teamwork. Too much teamwork can produce the phenomenon of **groupthink**.

Just as dissensus between team members on team composition, the start-up processes, establishing the key principles for project execution and so on may spell danger for a project so can the exact opposite, where everyone is of the same mind about the processes, risks and practices of the project. When everyone is sharing the same script there is always the possibility that the script, which provides its own satisfactions in promoting agreement as everyone has learnt it, may obfuscate pitfalls that lurk outside the shared comprehension of the team – the danger of groupthink.

> **Groupthink** refers to the tendency of members of a group to seek and maintain harmony in a group, at the cost of ignoring or avoiding major decisions that may disrupt harmony.

The origins of the term groupthink go back to 1961 – 17 April, to be precise. On that day a counter-revolutionary project against the Castro regime in Cuba was launched by 1500 exiled Cubans from the United States. These Cubans were supporters of the regime of Batista, the dictator who, supported by the Mafia, had made Cuba a corrupt and decadent state dependent on Mafia investments in casinos and in which ordinary Cubans, not part of the corrupt elite, had hard and miserable lives. These Batista supporters invaded Cuba on this day using ships from the US Navy and United Fruit Company. They planned to land in the Bay of Pigs (*Bahia de Cochinos*), an area that has many mangroves and is therefore relatively inaccessible. On the eastern side of the Bay of Pigs, the landscape consists of ordinary beaches and savannah vegetation.

The idea of the invasion of the Bay of Pigs was developed by the CIA and Eisenhower but the action was conducted in John F. Kennedy's subsequent presidential term. It has become world-famous as an example of bad judgement as the counter-revolutionaries were defeated by Castro's troops. 'How could we have been so stupid?' Kennedy said later, when reflecting on the debacle that became the Bay of Pigs' incident, which far from toppling Castro proved to be a propaganda coup as Yankee imperialism was represented in Cuba as being defeated by the solidarity of the socialist regime. Arthur M. Schlesinger, a member of the Kennedy administration who worked out the proposal and plans for invasion but who opposed enacting them, said, four years later, that he regretted that he had not strongly opposed the project. He explained that the urge to protest was hampered by the circumstances surrounding the discussions that took place (Schlesinger, 1965, p. 255). The idea of the invasion was an idea – however foolish later events proved it to be – that had embedded itself in the reasoning of those planning it.

The point is that in retrospect members of a group can know that the group's reasoning was too limited in its decision-making yet, still, they become swept along by and with the prevailing sentiments. Research has, over time, shown many examples of this phenomenon of *groupthinking* (Janis, 1972) when highly skilled people working in teams with difficult projects become blinded by their own processes. Often, they make decisions quickly without making sufficient or necessary impact assessment of several alternatives. History has shown that doing this can produce bad decisions and fatal project deliveries. Groupthinking is characterized by the following symptoms:

- **An illusion of invulnerability**. The group members feel that they are invincible together, hold a high degree of optimism related to what they can achieve, perceive a shared understanding and identification with one another, hold high standards for themselves, believe in their own excellence and the quality of their own decisions.
- **Ignoring critical thinking**. The group discusses few alternatives, ignores other alternatives and chooses not to consider critical objections that do not match their preferences, allowing stereotypes and heuristics to play important roles in decision-making.
- **Negative perceptions of deviants**. The group has a black and white stereotype where they perceive those who may have somewhat different perceptions as incompetent deviants who counteract the team.
- **Direct pressure**. When a group member questions the direction of the group, this pushes it towards conformity. The pressure for uniformity means not all information is presented, self-censorship occurs, furthered by pointing out that tempo is important and that there is no room for delay.

Taken together, these symptoms indicate that groupthinking is characterized by conformist pressure. When project team members work intensively together over a period of time, experiencing their work as successful and progressing, it is likely that the groupthink syndrome may emerge.

WATCH THIS!

Watch the video on Groupthink and the Challenger Disaster which explores the phenomenon of groupthink through the *Challenger* case at https://study.sagepub.com/pm.

HOW DO WE AVOID GROUPTHINKING?

The idea of groupthinking has gained massive attention since it was launched and has been followed up with case studies and laboratory experiments, generally indicating that the core of groupthinking is conformity that reduces decision-making quality. Project groups characterized by high conformity often perform what Sunstein and Hastie (2015) call **Happy Talk**. The term expresses something that usually happens when team members convey that everything is going well, it is just getting better, and there is no need to worry. It is a form of self-deception that can explain why teamwork often goes wrong.

> **Happy talk** is an indicator of groupthink where team members say that all is going well and likely to go better, and there is nothing to worry about.

Sunstein and Hastie (2015) argue that executives need to surround themselves with employees that collectively represent a multitude of skills and personalities. It is useful to have some Cassandras and deviants in the team that are not afraid to be different and to oppose the majority viewpoint. Of course, the deviance should be positive, premised on alternative analysis and courses of action other than those being pursued as conventional wisdom (Courpasson, Dany, & Clegg, 2012). Productive resistance in the workplace is better listened to and acted on rather than suppressed, either by project leadership or by the resisters, anticipating that their resistance premise on positive critique of the direction being given and taken, will not be welcome. Sometimes, having the courage of your convictions is worth holding on to.

Conformity under pressure is a common psychological condition. The relationship between conformity and decision-making quality was examined in a piece of classic research. Solomon Asch conducted a well-known experimental series in the 1950s (see Figure 8.6), where subjects were asked which line in exhibit 2 is of the same length as the line in exhibit 1 (Asch, 1956). The answer is obviously A. The subjects were included in a group comprising seven, eight or nine people, who were instructed to respond incorrectly.

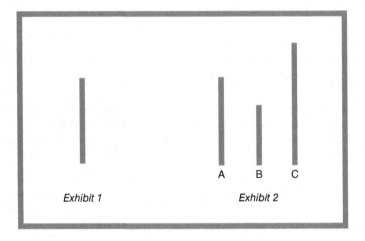

Figure 8.6 Illustration of lines and differences

The test subject was asked to answer the question second to last, after almost everyone had responded. In the experiments, it was found that when the first person answers incorrectly, the subject clearly expresses that this is incorrect (smile, eyesight, surprise) but this gradually decreases as one after the other answered wrong. If all others answered incorrectly, 37% of the test subjects also responded incorrectly, even if they demonstrated clear signals that doing so was stressful. If only one of the actors answers incorrectly, only 6% of the subjects are consistent. (The background to this experiment in social psychology is most interesting. In common with a number of other studies that investigated conformity with authority in various forms it was conducted by a Jewish scholar, Solomon Asch. In a BBC podcast called *The Science of Evil*, the background to this experiment, and others related to it, is elaborated in terms of the Holocaust.)

There have been many studies of the conditions in which this type of conformity is taking place. Overall, the following findings have been made: if there is only one non-conforming group member, the effect is drastically reduced; furthermore, conformity appears to be low when there are fewer than four members in the group. When the project group has more than nine members, the pressure also decreases towards conformity. At group sizes of between four and nine members, the pressure on the individual to be consistent is, therefore, the strongest. Measures that reduce groupthinking also reduce conformity, since the core of groupthinking is conformity. Conformity reduces when:

- The individual has another person to support them who does not respond as do the others

- There is opportunity to discuss the situation openly with others
- Divergent information/opinions are available

It is worth noting that conformity lasts beyond the situations where the project participants are gathered because the individual internalizes (private conformity) others' messages or opinions. It can happen when there is persuasive communication (which plays both mental and emotional aspects) and identifies it as a competent source of information (reference group).

WATCH THIS!

Watch the video by Phillip Zimbardo (2012) where he talks about the very famous experiment by Salmon Asch demonstrating conformity at: https://study.sagepub.com/pm.

READ THIS!

Read an article by Saul McLeod (2016) on the nature of conformity and its effects at: https://study.sagepub.com/pm.

What can project leaders do to obviate these tendencies to groupthink and conformity? Sunstein and Hastie (2015) suggest those leaders that seem to be *anxious* or worry-driven are more capable of identifying resistance related to the project process or outcomes, disadvantages and the challenges. Leaders can prevent the emergence of groupthinking by asking: 'What's wrong, what do you think about this, why have we not planned for this?' Successful project managers will facilitate critical feedback and show appreciation of such feedback and take it into account. Disagreements and conflict can be fruitful for developing valuable solutions, yet when a decision is made after various options have been canvassed, members must strive for implementation. In order to reduce the likelihood of groupthinking, the team should make space for reflection and debate as well as reduce the effect of having a strong leader in decision-making processes. Democratic decision-making and discussion is the best defence against groupthink. For projects, the advice in Table 8.5 can be useful in order to avoid groupthinking.

Table 8.5 Efforts to avoid groupthinking

Be curious and moderate leadership role	Both the project manager and the individual team member should attach importance to being critical and seek knowledge to always arrive at the best solution. At the same time, the leader should moderate his leadership role in order not to dominate the process. It is important that anyone with relevant inputs is encouraged to come up with suggestions and opinions.
Priming critical thinking	Within social psychology, the term 'priming' means that using certain terms can activate action in a particular direction. So, use 'critical thinking and critical input' rather than 'supportive suggestions and compliance'. It can in itself contribute to critical thinking.

(Continued)

Table 8.5 (Continued)

Reward team success	The team's work, decisions and rewards should be collective. This means that the team member is not primarily concerned with his own rewards and consequences, but with the team as a whole.
Ensure clear role assignment	Awareness and design of teamwork based on the team is responsible for different functions and different skills.
Change perspectives	In the teamwork, it may be important to change the perspective of one thing. By trying to assess the problem from another point of view, for example by imagining how a new project manager would look at the matter, new approaches can be obtained.
Be the devil's advocate	The project team should try critically to review a case or a possible decision by asking unpleasant and highly contentious questions.
Appoint a critical opponent – a 'red team'	In connection with a decision, two groups can be formed where one should defend and argue for the proposal to the team while the other will try to find weaknesses and counter-arguments. This is a further development of the devil's advocate. You can also include external groups or people who take the critic role.

WATCH THIS!

You would want to avoid the development of groupthink in your project. To understand this phenomenon better and how it develops please watch what Cass Sunstein (2015) has to say about how to go beyond groupthink at: https://study.sagepub.com/pm.

We have shown an example of a social psychological phenomena that can cause project groups to make bad decisions and also lead individuals to underutilize their skills. Within the scope of this book, there is insufficient room to discuss the breadth of research underlying these insights. We have elaborated only on the most common pitfalls and mechanisms that you need to be aware of in order for you to try and reduce their impact on project deliveries. While all experiments have limitations in the sense that they show general tendencies related to human behaviour, not everyone will be affected by the bystander effect or groupthinking to the same extent. Both our personality and the situations we participate in affect our behaviour. Nevertheless, groupthink is a common phenomenon so many of us can expect to experience its negative effects. Sometimes the groupthink phenomenon can extend into a 'We-Feeling', where the team sees those who stand outside as either opposing them or being unable to understand what they are doing. Sometimes this tendency is called 'projectitis' or 'project sickness' (Larson & Gray, 2011).

CONFLICTS IN THE PROJECT TEAM

All relationships contain the potential for conflict, i.e. an inconsistency between different parties with different views and/or interests. Research shows that the project teams are likely to experience less collaboration, more relative conflicts and develop fewer conflict management strategies (Druskat & Kayes, 2000) than non-project based teams. We have seen that cohesion is a major factor in the performance of project teams (Sydow et al., 2004) and conflicts have a negative effect on cohesion. The erosion of cohesion is most damaging for relatively long-lasting projects (Saunders & Ahuja, 2006), while teams involved in short-term projects can, at least sometimes, strive to minimize the conflict in order to 'just get the job done' (Knoll & Jarvenpaa, 1998). Where the conflict is fundamental, clearly creating two opposing camps, this can lead to abortive projects as one side strives to undermine the other. Often this can occur where external stakeholders are deeply opposed. Such a situation sometimes occurs in major projects that are highly political such as the UK's HS2 rail project, bitterly opposed by many powerful stakeholders in wealthy 'Home Counties' locales near London whose amenity would be potentially threatened by its construction, while strongly supported by interests in the Midlands and North of that country.

DIFFERENT TYPES OF CONFLICT

It is necessary to disagree in order for a conflict to occur but not every case of disagreement ends up in conflict. Conflicts may be of different types. We can divide them into two main types:

- *Task/content conflict.* Disagreement about the task, the goal or the details of the contents, linked to people having different preferences and interests, which is the most common form of conflict.
- *Process conflict.* A variant of task conflict where it is not necessarily the task, the objective or the case content that leads to disagreement but rather how the work process is being designed and the nature of the work required to reach the target.

Interpersonal conflict occurs in relationships between the actors. In such conflicts, strong feelings come to the surface that can be difficult for organizations and projects to handle. Conflicts can be both functional and dysfunctional, with personal conflicts being less functional than task conflicts. A *functional conflict* can help the project approach the goal, by bringing forward matters that revitalize the process. A *dysfunctional conflict* is the opposite because it inhibits communication and information exchange, and thus impedes project work. However, there is often no clear distinction between what is a functional and a dysfunctional conflict. Clarifying roles and responsibilities and setting up project work to share visions, advance direction of the project and perceptions of how the work should be done helps build accord. The team charter can also be a concrete aid if dysfunctional conflicts arise.

In projects, clear frameworks, plans and objectives seem to reduce the number and level of conflicts. Projects usually use methods to clarify both direction and procedure. Project management tools will provide clear guidelines for how things are to be done, when to do them, who will attend to them, as well as prioritizing tasks. Using these tools, well known and widely accepted, can reduce uncertainty and the potential for conflicts both internally in the project teams, between project managers and project owners as well as between the project organization and a base organization. Of course, good project management tools are not a form of magic that remove conflict but they can decrease the potential for conflicts through discussion and planning ahead, which can surface tensions about expectations, task matters and direction.

IN PRACTICE

HAVE A GOOD FIGHT AND THEN UNITE

Conflict in team meetings can imply different things. Morten Hansen (2018), in his article 'Great at work: How to fight and unite', advocates having open discussions before decisions are made. You should allow the discussion to be heated, as long as it is related to task not person. Be prepared, craft an opinion but stay open to other's ideas. After the fight, unite. Implying you need to let the argument win, when the decision is made, everybody stays behind it. He labels this as 'Fight & Unite' at: https://doi.org/10.1002/ltl.20369.

WATCH THIS!

Watch the YouTube video by Morten Hansen (2018) explaining 'What is fight and unite', in which he discusses strategic proposals for uniting and fighting at: https://study.sagepub.com/pm. Reflecting on your own experiences, consider the following questions.

QUESTIONS

1. What strategies would you use as a project manager to unite?

2. Reflect on past fights in teams that you have experienced: What might you have done to move from fight to unite?

Efficient project teams

Awareness of the importance of trust and establishing an environment conducive to psychological safety, as well as the importance of team composition, are all central aspects that we have highlighted for performing as a project team in an adequate manner. Many studies identify factors that contribute to efficient project teams. Recurrent factors identified are that teams have a clear task; there is adequate composition of the group in terms of personnel and the resources available to them; a supporting organizational context; excellent team processes (including functional coordination and communication) as well as a supportive culture at the team level through which members support each other (see 'What would you do?', below). Mathieu, Gallagher, Domingo, and Klock (2019) review the team effectiveness research literature, exploring the contextual factors that have an impact on team outcomes.

It is often the sum of a number of small signs that signal the level of performance a leader can induce in the project team. A pivotal factor for the efficiency of a project team is high involvement of all team members being equipped with adequate resources. Some leaders have a consulting style, meaning that they strongly encourage the team members to participate in decision-making and enact more of a coordinative role themselves; others will be more inclined to command and control. In a project team where the project manager has a consulting style, teams often develop better procedures for solving tasks, which has a positive effect on the project team's performance (Durham et al., 1997).

Project managers need to be aware of how they can enable team members' engagement and release 'the good forces in the team'. A virtual cycle in which good forces, once released, further energize is the ideal. If the manager, together with the other team members, is able to establish positive values, a positive spiral can be initiated. Research has shown that positive forces, such as being generative and creative in idea work, acting supportively and interacting with each other, creating a 'caravan of resources' (Hobfoll, 2011). If one manages to trigger a positive resource, it will trigger more.

Richard Hackman studied teams for several decades. In his book *Collaborative Intelligence* (2011), he summarized central findings on how to use teams to solve difficult problems. Even though the context for the book was military and civil intelligence (FBI, CIA, and the like), the findings are highly relevant for other contexts, including project teams. Hackman identified six enabling conditions for team effectiveness, much of these being in alignment with elements that we have mentioned above (see Figure 8.7). These six enabling conditions are:

- *Create a real team.* Have members working together to achieve a common purpose, with a shared understanding of contributions and the way they should work and collaborate, providing at least moderate stability, giving members time to learn.
- *Compelling purpose.* Energizing the team, orienting them towards their common objective and engaging their talents.
- *Right people.* Well-composed teams consist of the right number and mix of members, often with task expertise as well as collaborative skills. Teams should be as small as possible and diversity contributes to the range of views.
- *Clear norms of conduct.* Norms specifying acceptable behaviour reduces the amount of time spent on managing member behaviour. Norms should promote development and learning to perform better.
- *Supportive organizational context.* Organizational support is required for project teams to be able to perform well and reach desired outcomes. Besides necessary

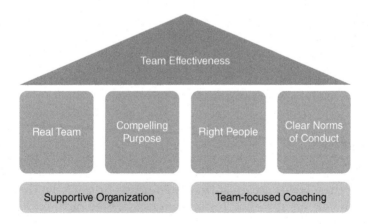

Figure 8.7 Six enabling conditions for team effectiveness, according to Hackman (2011)

resources, adequate reward systems providing recognition and positive consequences for excellent team performance are needed.

- *Team-focused coaching*. Well-timed and competent team coaching increases the chances of operating in ways that generate synergistic process gains, fostering competent teamwork by facilitating learning, feedback and reflection.

EXTEND YOUR KNOWLEDGE

Read the article by Wu, Rivas, and Liao (2017), 'Influential factors for team reflexivity and new product development' to learn about the importance of existing knowledge, task familiarity and procedural justice to facilitate project success by encouraging team reflexivity. You can access the article in the online resources for the book at https://study.sagepub.com/pm.

Hackman (2011) suggests if you want to succeed in leading a team you should put your energy into the '60–30–10 rule'. This implies that if you are a project leader you should put 60% of your energy where it will have the most impact, with 30% for the next most and 10% for the third most.

- *Prework – 60%* should be put into the design of the team. The leadership task concerns how well you can get the first five of the six enabling conditions in place.
- *Launch – 30%* involves launching the team. When the team meets and starts working together, the team charter should be emphasized.
- *Coach – 10%* should be hands-on coaching. If the first five conditions are present the team will be robust and the last – 'team-focused coaching' – will be used to aid the team in responding well to challenges, adding value to the team process.

Organizing project teams

Projects will vary in their nature, type and context and for the same reasons project teams will be different. In the open source software (OSS) community of practice, a large number of people contribute to the project of developing new or upgraded versions of software. They might have the same goal but there are weak ties related to interdependency, so it is more a group than a team. OSS software development is based on an underlying open and non-proprietary code, where anyone across the globe can contribute in a development process. The web browser Mozilla Firefox and the blog hosting platform WordPress are both examples of OSS products.

CLASSIFICATION OF ORGANIZATIONAL FORMS FOR PROJECT TEAMS

To understand project teams better, it is useful to categorize them in the way they are organized. Project teams can be organized in several ways and how the team is organized can vary across the different phases of a project. Also, large-scale projects can contain multiple teams that are organized indifferently or similarly. The project manager needs to reflect on how the project team can best be organized in light of the nature of the assignment and other relevant characteristics of the project. Commonly used classifications of organizational forms for project teams have been identified by Frame (2003) (see Table 8.6).

Table 8.6   Different types of project team organizing

Type	Characteristics
Isomorphic team structure	The organizing structure reflects the task structure of the project. The task is broken down into parts (for example using a work break down structure), and the team is organized with responsibility for the different parts of the deliveries. The project manager must arrange to coordinate between the various sub-deliveries.
Specialist team structure	All assignments are distributed, based on who has the most relevant skills to solve them. In practice, it is a matrix organizing of the team, where tasks are matched with competence, with each team member contributing to several task-solving processes simultaneously with their distinctive competence. The project manager coordinates the entirety of the deliveries, monitors the different task-solving processes and integrates them. The manager must ensure that all tasks are solved and that the right resources are linked to the various tasks.
Egoless team structure	The community, rather than the project manager, determine the solutions in this autonomous model. Management is distributed, as is often the case when using an agile execution model. In principle, one can imagine this organizing form used in more waterfall-oriented project executions but it is quite unusual to do so because the project manager role is so central, being considered the natural and formal leader in classical project implementation.
Surgical team structure	The strong project manager (surgeon) is responsible for all deliveries and results, and he/she has the authority to order the rest of the participants to deliver the person in need to create the overall delivery. The individual employee has little freedom in choosing tasks or solutions.

It may be appropriate to vary the organizing of the project team during the life cycle of the project. Often the structure can be quite flat early in the project before the task is clearly interpreted. Once the assignment becomes clearer, try to use everybody's skills to get the best assignment solution possible and to do this a matrix structure may be useful. Often most uncertainty is associated with delivery in the early phase of the project. Consult the best expertise in discussing how the task can best be interpreted and solved. In general, the greater the degree of uncertainty, the flatter the team (rather than hierarchical).

HETERARCHY

In recent years, the concept of 'heterarchy' has gained more attention (Aime, Humphrey, Derue, & Paul, 2014), referring to organizations in which leadership is distributed amongst different expertise in the project team rather than arranged hierarchically in a singular chain of command. These experts, on their own initiative, can shift leadership among the team members as situations, events or processes demand. Leadership at any given time will depend on the kind of expertise required for critical matters at that juncture. This form of distributed leadership works where the team members have confidence in each other's competencies, affording the different leaders' legitimacy. A structure in which leadership shifts among the team members increases the probable creativity of the team (Aime et al., 2014). Therefore, projects whose assignments specifically involve the need for creative solutions can benefit from the promotion of heterarchy. Closely allied to heterarchy is the idea of a project leadership team in which roles are related, such as being chair and project champion for different areas that are arranged under key performance indicators (KPIs), a design that can enrich mutual sensemaking, facilitate learning and encourage innovation.

SYNCHRONICITY AND TEAMWORK

Project teams needs to collaborate in different ways, depending on their tasks, the stage of the project process and geographical location, amongst other factors. Often project teams, disaggregated in their work packages, need real-time interaction and work together on the task as a whole team. Other times individual members can work asynchronously on their tasks. One way in which to categorize types of project team, depending on the variation in levels of synchronicity and responsibility, is represented in Figure 8.8:

		Responsibility for task, output	
		Individual work on tasks	Team as a whole
Level of synchronicity	**Real time synchronicity**	Surgical Teams	Face-to-Face Teams
	Asynchronous interaction	Coacting Teams	Distributed Teams

Figure 8.8 Four types of teams depending on responsibility and synchronicity (based on Hackman & Wageman, 2004)

For a project leader, awareness of different aspects of responsibility and synchronicity is vital for the ways in which teams are coached, powers and responsibilities distributed as well as deciding on when collocation aids project processes. As we shall see next, with virtual teams, collocation is not a constant factor.

Virtual project teams

Changes in technology and the extensive use of the Internet, video conferencing, social media and other communication platforms have changed the way we work and collaborate, including in project teams. If you go to airports, sit in cafes or in other public spaces, you might have wondered how many people using PCs, tablets or mobiles are working virtually with others. The possibility of collaboration regardless of geographical distance and time zones makes physical collocation less necessary for working together in teams. When employees do not collaborate synchronically and are not physically collocated, collaboration is virtual, with the project team becoming a **virtual team**.

> A **virtual team** primarily communicates virtually, using a combination of telecommunications, social media, the Internet and video conferences.

It has become common to collaborate virtually in projects. For a project team, virtual work also involves network-based project management tools. Virtual project teams do not have to work synchronously at all times. The nature of the project and the tasks will help to provide guidance. It is the proportion of team members who communicate virtually, along with the proportion that work outside the project office, which determine the degree of virtuality for a team. The higher this degree is, the more management should offer physical meeting points when needed. The necessity is significant when milestones are coming up for review, when critical incidents have to be dealt with, or events occur that are project critical.

POTENTIAL BENEFITS AND PITFALLS OF VIRTUAL TEAMWORKING

In modern organizations and projects where collaboration, development and innovation are key, projects often rely on teamwork workers with special skills, and often the employees with the most suitable competence are not collocated. Teamwork will then take place across geographical distances, offering great benefits, if used appropriately. When competent resources can contribute to the project deliverables, albeit working from a remote location to the project office, it makes sense to include them virtually.

Virtual teams present challenges in managing and in integrating their workflow. The challenges that apply to management and work in teams, in general, are enhanced by the use of virtual teams (De Paoli, 2014). In particular, it is difficult to obtain adequate sharing of information and coordination in virtual teams (Hoegl & Proserpio, 2004). The informational content of face-to-face interaction is far greater than that of a virtual conference where attention is focused in the room, on the others, their words, deeds and body language, the ways they use material props, such as documents, drawings and other informational aids. For leaders in virtual teams it is even more essential to engage in reflective leadership than it is in teams where participants meet physically (Carte, Chidambaram, & Becker, 2006). Managing virtual project teams, managers can face difficulties related to both emotional distance, lack of physical proximity and control as well as in building trust-making activities.

Distributed leadership may be a particularly relevant management model in virtual teams (Hoegl & Muethel, 2016). In order to achieve the best results, however, the project manager must employ coaching, monitoring and giving feedback in a regular way. Being at a distance can mean being distantiated.

WORKING IN A VIRTUAL PROJECT TEAM

Virtual team culture requires norms, values and working methods to be clarified, understood and shared (Furst, Reeves Rosen, & Blackburn, 2004) as in regular teams. For projects involving actors and team members in several countries, this will be an especially challenging task. Cultural differences expressed in values and norms can create difficulties when establishing an appropriate and shared team culture (van Marrewijk, Ybema, Smits Clegg, & Pitsis, 2016; Zander, Mockaitis, & Butler, 2012). As van Marrewijk and colleagues identified, different languages can cloak, constitute and challenge project politics in many ways that can prove subversive of project goals. If there is not a close relationship between team members, one should expect to spend more time building trust and establishing good working methods. In practice, being in different time zones can also create problems for synchronous work and the implementation of joint team meetings. If possible, use physical meeting places in the start-up phase to develop a relationship that goes beyond the formal and task oriented.

There is a wide range of possible communication tools for virtual teams, such as e-mail, electronic bulletin boards, web pages, filing, video conferencing tools, text messages and other social media. Develop a code of conduct for how and when to use different digital tools. Otherwise, the situation may become chaotic, with unnecessary delays and misunderstandings. For example, it may be convenient to use video conferencing when making joint resolutions or surveys where everyone should be prepared for specific conditions, or use e-mail for specific cases and specific patterns, a common project management platform according to specific instructions. What guidelines and communication patterns are appropriate will vary from project to project with different contextual relationships. The key is to have a well-thought-out communication strategy to prevent delays and misunderstandings.

Summary

In this chapter, we have:

- Presented the key characteristics of project teams and their development processes, focusing on the mid-point transition of project teamwork, as well as the importance attributed to more linear models.
- Looked into the nature of trust in the project team and the importance it has for engaging in collaborative project work, the quality of the teams' work in tasks, such as knowledge sharing. We have looked at different degrees of trust, i.e. thick and thin, and the nature and development of swift trust which is so necessary in projects.
- Elaborated on the processes that provide high-performance project teams, the value of external and internal motivation of team members, as well as activities that can start up project teams and bring them up to speed quickly.
- Considered how to organize project teams in different ways, for example in isomorphism with the work breakdown structure, specialist structure, egoless or surgical structure and how the most appropriate way of organizing a focal project team can vary across the project life cycle.
- Discussed how to enable efficient collaboration in virtual teams, the potential benefits that can be realized and how to reduce the emergence of potential pitfalls.

Exercises

1. What conditions must be fulfilled to be a project team?
2. Why are project teams often interdisciplinary and what is important in facilitating efficient collaboration in such teams? What would you consider significant when putting together a project team?
3. What is the difference between thick and thin trust? How can trust and psychological safety be enabled in project teams?
4. What is a team charter? What are the key aspects of a team charter?
5. What would you do to facilitate motivation in a project team?
6. What would you do to decrease the possibility of groupthink in a project team?
7. What are the potential types of conflicts that might occur in the project team and how would you handle these conflicts?
8. What are the key pitfalls and strengths of virtual project teams?

CASE STUDY

PROJECT ARISTOTLE AT GOOGLE – FINDING THE BEST WAY TO WORK IN TEAMS

Google's People Operation wanted to conduct a project identifying what makes a successful team and started Project Aristotle in 2012. The working hypothesis was that employees could perform better by working together than alone. Abeer Dubay, Director of People Analytics, was set to lead the project. Julia Rozovsky joined him and together they composed a project team consisting of experts with different professional skills. These were the best statisticians, researchers in organizational psychology, engineering and sociology, gathered to find out what characterizes the perfect team.

Two years into the project, they had studied over 180 teams, made over 200 interviews and analysed over 250 different team attributes. Still, after analysing the data, they were not able to find any clear patterns of characteristics, helping them to create a perfect dream-team algorithm. It should be mentioned that the project team also had reviewed nearly 50 years of academic studies on how teams work, which they found quite inconsistent. However, being confused with the lack of clear patterns in their own data, they looked into academic studies focusing on group norms.

Usually, you would expect to find a correlation between team membership, meaning the skills, personalities and so on, and team success. However, they did not find any such correlation. Then they moved from focusing on 'who', and more into 'how' they interact. After some closer examination, they found something. What they gathered was that the specific people who are on a team almost did not matter but the main factor was *how* those people interact. The way they treated each other, as long as there was a certain culture, meant they would gel. More specifically, they found the most significant elements were:

- *Equality in conversational turn taking.* Meaning when they met and had meetings everybody spoke roughly the same amount.
- *Ostentatious (active) listening.* Meaning that the people who listen to the person who is talking have to show attention. By active body language, having eye contact, mirroring, repeating what the person said or the like, you both encourage people to speak up, and also make sure that what is being said is understood.

This creates what Professor Amy Edmondson and other experts refer to as *psychological safety* (see pp. 279 for more on this). On these findings, the people in Project Aristotle concluded that psychological safety was the single greatest correlate with a team's success (see Figure 8.9).

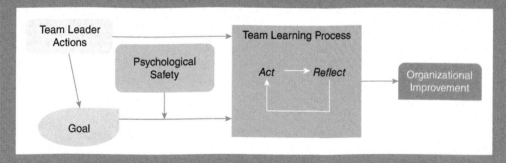

Figure 8.9 Psychological safety and team learning processes

Source: West, Smith, & Tjosvold, 2003

Building on these findings, they further studied the data and added direction from academic studies on collective intelligence and collaboration, identifying five characteristics

(Continued)

of an enhanced team and developed some guidelines for teamwork (see Figure 8.10). The five characteristics, briefly presented, are:

- Psychological safety
  - Solicit input and opinions from the group.
  - Share information about personal and work style preferences and encourage others to do the same.

- Dependability
  - Clarify roles and responsibilities of team members.
  - Develop concrete project plans to provide transparency into every individual's work.
  - Talk about some of the conscientiousness research.

- Structure and clarity
  - Regularly communicate team goals and ensure team members understand the plan for achieving them.
  - Ensure your team meetings have a clear agenda and designated leader.
  - Consider adopting Objectives and Key Results (OKRs) to organize the team's work.

- Meaning
  - Give team members positive feedback on something outstanding they are doing and offer to help them with something they struggle with.
  - Publicly express your gratitude for someone who helped you out.

- Impact
  - Co-create a clear vision that reinforces how each team member's work directly contributes to the team's and broader organization's goals.
  - Reflect on the work you are doing and how it affects users or clients and the organization.
  - Adopt a user-centred evaluation method and focus on the user.

Of all these elements, psychological safety was the single most significant element. Meaning what matters for team performance is the feeling of being safe. You could and should be open to others in the team and be an active listener. Everybody should talk, have equal time to talk, and not feel stunted, cut off or criticized about what you say when you choose to speak up in front of the team.

OUTCOME AND FOLLOW-UP OF THE PROJECT

When Project Aristotle concluded its findings, Dubay, Rozovsky and their fellow team members began sharing their results with the executives and the employees of Google (Duhigg, 2016). The company is now more attentive to factors used in creating a great team, resulting in guidelines and a change in the culture for teamwork. See https://rework.withgoogle.com/subjects/teams/ for more on this.

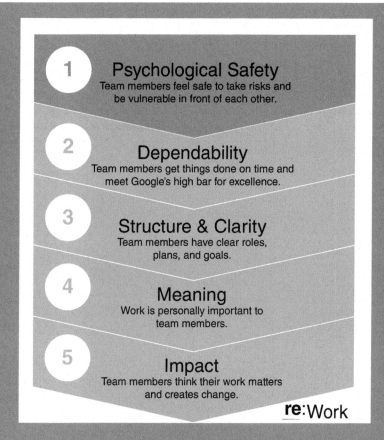

Figure 8.10 Five characteristics of enhanced team development

QUESTIONS

1. Building on findings from Project Aristotle, how would you argue for the importance of the composition of a team and what would you emphasize if you, as a project manager, were to present these recommendations to the principal of the project?

2. Compare and discuss the five elements found by Google, with activities of team start-up and applying a team charter.

3. What would you characterize as the main driving forces for the way that you wish to run the project and what are your arguments for doing so?

4. To what extent would you say this is a closed project?

5. What is the main anticipated project outcome and what kind of value creation will you argue the project has contributed?

Additional resources

Read more about team, multi-team and team effectiveness in the book by DeChurch and Mathieu (2009), or in Katzenbach (1998). In Edmondson (2012) you can read more about teaming, and in Edmondson (2018) more on the role of psychological safety in teams and at workplaces. Hackman and Oldham's *Work Redesign* book (1980) is also still worth reading. A book by Daniel Coyle (2018), *The Cultural Code*, provides an easy approach to how to establish a culture for teams to succeed.

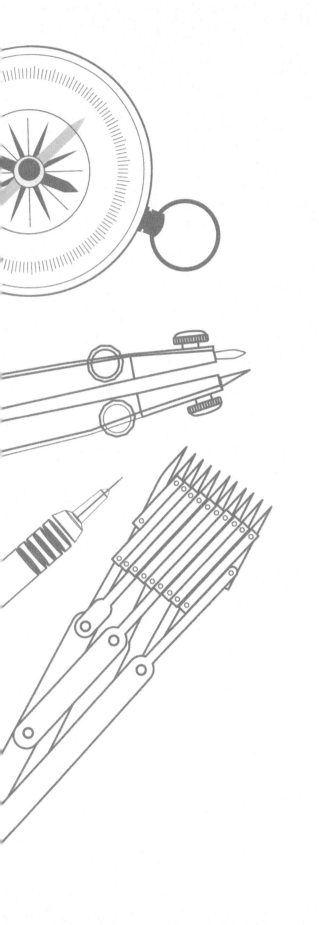
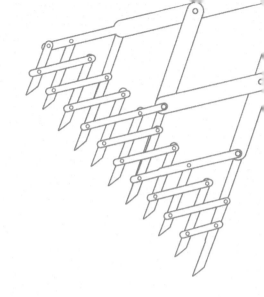

Chapter Roadmap

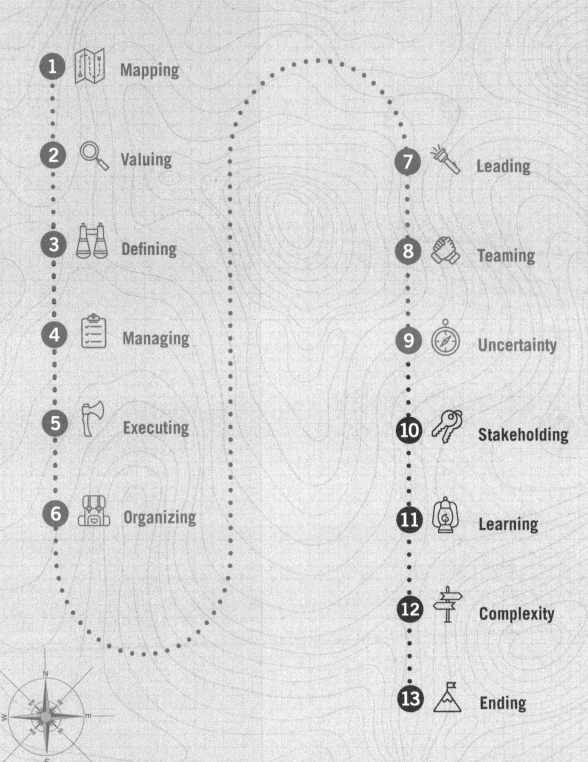

1. Mapping
2. Valuing
3. Defining
4. Managing
5. Executing
6. Organizing
7. Leading
8. Teaming
9. Uncertainty
10. Stakeholding
11. Learning
12. Complexity
13. Ending

9

Managing Uncertainty in Projects

Learning objectives

After reading this chapter, you should:

1. Understand how uncertainty is the outcome of the unknown and represents both opportunities and risks for any project

2. Be able to distinguish various forms of uncertainty

3. Know the basic principles of uncertainty management, where the most important element of practice is to identify, analyse and manage uncertainty by developing appropriate strategies

4. Understand that project managers must adapt their behaviour to the different forms and degrees of uncertainty

5. Know the important aspects of a culture of uncertainty management and what is important for creating such a culture

Before you get started

The future's uncertain and the end is always near.

– Jim Morrison, 1970, 'Roadhouse Blues'

Introduction

All projects entail uncertainty that potentially involves both negative (risks) and positive (opportunities) consequences. Projects must be prepared for uncertainties and able to manage uncertainties that they are not prepared for in order to succeed. Uncertainty can entail radical disjuncture for the project, opening up possibilities for more efficient project execution and/or creating deliveries that, to a greater extent than anticipated at the project's outset, enable benefit realization. Uncertainty can also entail events that lead to major project failures in terms of cost and time overruns, as well as the impossibility of creating the results aimed for. Therefore, this chapter is about how we can understand and work systematically with uncertainty in contemporary projects. Discussion includes processes for identifying and analysing uncertainty as well as how to act on these analyses. Uncertainty is always ambiguous and potentially disruptive. We will look at how we can best approach uncertainty by constantly trying to make sense of the relationships and contexts in which we are embedded and through developing capabilities for acting flexibly. Uncertainty management in projects aims at reducing risk as much as possible through perception and decision-making while looking for opportunities. Uncertainty is potentially inherent in all projects and their contexts. Plans may minimize uncertainty but can never eliminate it. Events happen and events are the source of uncertainty.

Uncertainty: Risks and opportunities

All projects are characterized by **uncertainty**; that is, they encounter unexpected **events** framing situations, incidents and interpretations (De Meyer, Loch, & Pich, 2002; Deroy & Clegg, 2011; Geraldi, Lee-Kelley, & Kutsch, 2010). The term 'uncertainty' is often used to denote 'what we do not know' in a project.

> **Uncertainty** is the difference between what we know and what we don't know that we need to know to resolve equivocality.

> **Events** constitute the element of unpredictability and uncertainty that threaten order.

Uncertainty can lead to both opportunities and risks (Ward & Chapman, 2008). Uncertainty will occur when working on projects (Hällgren & Wilson, 2008; Söderholm, 2008). It is not a question of whether it will occur, but *when* it occurs (Perrow, 1994). Theorists inspired by Knight's (1921) seminal distinction between 'risk' and 'uncertainty' and by Keynes' (1937) conception of uncertainty refer to uncertainty characterizing situations in which 'decision makers cannot collect the information needed to anticipate either the possible outcomes associated with a decision nor the probability of those outcomes' (Alvarez & Barney, 2007, p. 14).

Management researchers have long recognized the importance of uncertainty (Cyert & March, 1963; March & Simon, 1958). For instance, innovation projects involve processes of discovery, evaluation and exploitation of novelties (Crossan & Apaydin, 2010) that takes place, by definition, under conditions of uncertainty because at the outset it is often unclear what will be the outcome (Austin, Devin, & Sullivan, 2012; Colarelli, O'Connor, & Rice, 2013; Tidd, 2001) and how it is to be achieved.

Risk and uncertainty

The project management discipline has historically focused most on the risk aspects of uncertainty. Risk is often considered as something negative that may occur and destroy the planned project. Risk minimization through detailed planning reduces the likelihood that an event that is unexpected and devastating will occur. Traditionally, uncertainty management and calculation of uncertainty (the likelihood of it occurring and the consequences of it doing so) has been based on the belief that uncertainty can be controlled through planning and estimation. By working earnestly and systematically to reduce uncertainty, especially risk, the prognosis is that uncertainty can be reduced if not eliminated; it will at least make one better prepared for handling it. Most of the attention has been directed to uncertainty associated with the project's delivery and how uncertainty here will affect project execution (i.e. alignment with the triple constraint), thinking that developed at a time when the term project was largely equivalent to infrastructure projects. However, as variation of project types and the contexts they are embedded in increases, conceptions of uncertainty are also likely to change.

Uncertainty has always been an important element in planning within the project discipline. As the attention to network planning of activities (CPM and PERT) increased towards the end of the 1950s, project managers sought to identify the critical path for all projects, even those

Picture 9.1   Representing risk

Source: Harald Nikolaisen

that included thousands of activities. The critical path indicates when delays or changes will affect the project's ability to reach planned goals on a timely basis (see page 134). Thus, the activities that were included in the project were considered as given. Decision-making processes that create incidents that affect project execution may also occur and the important thing was argued to be understanding what incidents might occur. Possible future incidents would be envisaged, with the likelihood that they will occur and the consequences they can have, calculated.

WATCH THIS!

Watch a YouTube video by Mike Clayton (2017) on 'What is project risk management?' at https://study.sagepub.com/pm.

Theorizing uncertainty

In the academic literature 'there are almost as many definitions of uncertainty as there are treatments of the subject' (Argote, 1982, p. 420), and scholars across disciplines continue to propose alternative taxonomies (Bradley & Drechsler, 2014;

De Meyer et al., 2002; Dequech, 2011; Packard, Clark, & Klein, 2017; Townsend, Hunt, McMullen, & Sarasvathy, 2018).

Inspired by Knight's (1921) distinction between quantifiable 'risk' and unquantifiable 'uncertainty' and Keynes' (1921; 1936) conception of evidential weight and uncertainty (Bewley, 2002; Ellsberg, 1961; Feduzi, 2007), contributors to the literature on uncertainty have argued that decision-makers' beliefs about uncertain contingencies are commonly 'loosely held and ill defined' (Einhorn & Hogarth, 1986, p. 227), especially when the available information is 'incomplete', 'scanty', 'noisy', 'unreliable' or 'conflicting' (Keynes, 1921; Knight, 1921; Ellsberg, 1961). In extreme cases, decision-makers might not be able to attach numerical probabilities to some events at all. These considerations led to the introduction of the concept of *ambiguity* or *Knightian uncertainty* (Bewley, 2002; Ellsberg, 1961) to characterize choice situations where, in addition to the uncertainty about which of the set of states of the world is the true one, decision-makers are also uncertain about the probabilities to attach to the states of the world (Camerer & Weber, 1992, p. 330).

Management science scholars have used terms such as *unforeseeable uncertainty* or *unknown unknowns* to characterize situations in which, at the outset of highly novel projects, agents do not have a complete representation of all possible states of the world at their disposal typically because they cannot anticipate all possible influence factors (Loch, Solt, & Bailey, 2008; Sommer & Loch, 2004; Sommer, Loch, & Dong, 2009). Post-Keynesian economists (e.g. Dequech, 2000) have used the term *fundamental uncertainty* to refer to choice situations in which the list of states of the world available to the decision-maker at the decision point is incomplete because the future 'is yet to be created' and where the information necessary to anticipate some states therefore does not exist. In a similar vein, innovation economists (e.g. Dosi & Egidi, 1991) have used the term (strong) *substantive uncertainty* to identify all situations in which decision-makers have to face future 'unknown events' – partly because there is an information gap they cannot fill – and where '"events" are not in any proper sense "states of nature" but are partly endogenous to the decision process of the agents, so that events are not independent from actions' (1991, p. 148). Here creative individuals can generate new knowledge and, through discoveries and innovations, endogenously generate uncertainty in the environment, 'since each innovation is in act the appearance of a new, unexpected event' (Dosi & Egidi, 1991, p. 165; see also Arrow & Hahn, 1999 and Dequech, 2011).

WATCH THIS!

Watch the video by Donald Rumsfeld (2009) talking about the 'Unknown unknowns' at: https://study.sagepub.com/pm.

For most decision problems '[a]lternative actions are typically not well specified and often need to be discovered' (Levinthal, 2011, p. 1517). Decision-makers are often called to adopt previously unidentified courses of action during the implementation of a project or strategic initiative (Adner & Levinthal, 2004; Loch et al., 2008; Mintzberg & Waters, 1985). However, they might be unable to identify possible courses of action, even in situations where the list of possible future states of the world and outcomes is fully determined. To see this, consider a decision-maker who has 'a given or desired outcome in mind but no known solution' (Packard et al., 2017, p. 6), leaving the set of means for achieving the desired outcome open. While the outcome set is closed – the desired outcome can either be achieved or not – the decision-maker has to populate the set of options by imagining possible courses of action and has to choose at least one of the possible solutions. The set of possible courses of action considered by the decision-maker is constrained by the availability of resources as well as their creative ability 'to imagine possible solutions to the preferred outcome' (Packard et al., 2017, p. 8) and the key uncertainty stems from 'the fungibility of the set of options and the ignorance of possibly superior alternatives' (Packard et al., 2017, p. 6). Even if the set of outcomes is closed, different 'creative solutions generated by innovation will typically vary in effectiveness in achieving a given outcome' (Packard et al., 2017, p. 6). Packard et al. (2017) refer to a situation of this type as one of *creative uncertainty*, the situation commonly faced by innovation projects.

Risk and opportunities

In the last 10 to 15 years, attention has been drawn to uncertainty in three ways:

1. It has evolved from the fact that uncertainty is exclusively negative (in terms of risk) so that uncertainty can also be seen as potentially positive as it opens up new opportunities.
2. At the same time, more attention is being given to the fact that uncertainty is not a phenomenon that primarily belongs only to the early stage of a project. Uncertainty is a constitutive part of the project throughout all its phases, which the project team must relate to.
3. Uncertainty cannot be controlled just through the use of plans, rules and procedures. It must be dealt with as it arises from events that defy routines and routine categorization.

It is becoming widely recognized in organizations that work a great deal through projects that the unexpected events that the project encounters can be both positive and negative, either a source of new opportunities or a threat to the project. Uncertainty affords not only risks but also opportunities. **Opportunities** afford great potential for value creation.

Wide involvement of users and other key stakeholders can help to discover opportunities in events, especially when these actors see things differently from project members. These stakeholders may have useful knowledge lacking in the project with which to make sense about possible solutions. Reflecting on interpretations, understandings and possible solutions can also help in sensing opportunities.

Risk is always present in projects. Project management often strives to minimize the inconvenience of unforeseen events and incidents that occur, while increasing the ability to manage predictable risks (Chapman & Ward, 2012). Actors vary in their risk propensity, their tendency towards taking or avoiding risks, which is also called risk-taking tendency.

> **Opportunities** occur when events are interpreted that make it possible to do something that otherwise would not have been attempted.

> **Risk** means the possibility that adverse consequences will flow from something unexpected that has occurred.

Uncertainty and ambiguity

Uncertainty is often defined as a lack of information while it may more often be that the available information is ambiguous (Thiry, 2002) or more likely indexical: different interests will interpret it differently (Clegg, 1975). Participants 'index' the meaning of the project plans deliberately differently, in order to exploit those elements that are 'indexical'; that is, those elements susceptible to more than one interpretation and that offer an advantage for the interested party doing the interpreting (Clegg, 1975).

Information is ambiguous when it can be understood in multiple and partly contradictory ways. It is indexical when, from a power/knowledge perspective, the different interpretations are embedded and embrained in different constituencies of interest, communities of practice and disciplinary normalization of the ways in which sense is made of information. When uncertainty is associated with the absence of information, decision-making and work can be improved by *obtaining* more information. In the case of ambiguous information, the project team can proceed through arriving at an *interpretation* of what they have available. In the case of indexical information, the likelihood is that conflicting interpretations emerge that rapidly become locally institutionalized.

WATCH THIS!

Watch a video on indexicality of contractual language by Jeff Connor-Linton & Mike Petit (2010), 'Indexicality', https://study.sagepub.com/pm.

As project processes unfold and events occur, these create opportunities for change, so that the potential for ambiguity and indexicality to enter into interpretation of initial information and planning is high. Changes often result in different interpretations of initial plans (Thiry, 2002), making it important for project managers either to work on creating common sensemaking or, when differentially specific sensemaking favours their interests, strive to open up different forms of indexical accounting for action. Uncertainty and ambiguity are most likely to be greatest at an early project stage. Often, it is the case that the space in which changes can be made, whether indexically or sensemaking inspired, is largest at the early stages of the project; also, this time is usually the most propitious in cost effectiveness to make changes. Thus, it is smart to work to uncover possible changes as early as possible. Particularly where the project is operating on tight margins, these initial plans may afford opportunities for contrary interpretations on the part of differently interested project participants.

EXTEND YOUR KNOWLEDEGE

Read Browning's (2019) article on how to plan, track and reduce the value at risk in complex projects and learn about the challenging task of meeting goals and delivering anticipated value in complex projects due to uncertainty. The article outlines multiple types of value and two general types of risks, and how to systematically plan and track costs, schedule and technical performance (or quality) in terms of key value attributes and threats to them. You can access the article in the online resources for the book at https://study.sagepub.com/pm.

A project manager would be mistaken to think that uncertainty can be controlled; events will happen and the important thing is to try to manage them. Since uncertainty cannot be controlled in advance, it must be managed as it arises. Uncertainty is inherent in projects throughout their life cycle. Thus we must work with uncertainty throughout the project period.

Project teams often consider uncertainty management to be a burden. Work spent on managing uncertainty can contribute to better project execution, however. Neither projects nor their surroundings are perfectly rational, functional or easy to understand. They are often characterized by complex relationships, irrational processes, ambiguous information and unexpected events. Uncertainties can be both easy and difficult to grasp, open to reflection and to acting proactively.

The potential for value creation increases when work is done deliberately to reduce risk associated with execution. The potential for value creation increases by focusing on project learning and development that can lead to improvement of project processes and delivery as well as the discovery of new areas for value creation for further development in future projects.

Increasingly all organizations experience requirement for rapid changes and various challenges in their efforts to develop and survive. Uncertainty is therefore imminent. The term VUCA world has become a way of describing this in the business world (Millar, Groth, & Mahon, 2018). VUCA as a term could be traced back to Warren Bennis and his book *Leaders: Strategies for Taking Charge* (1985) written together with Burt Nanus, where they described conditions leaders must be ready to face. The acronym VUCA means: Volatility, Uncertainty, Complexity and Ambiguity.

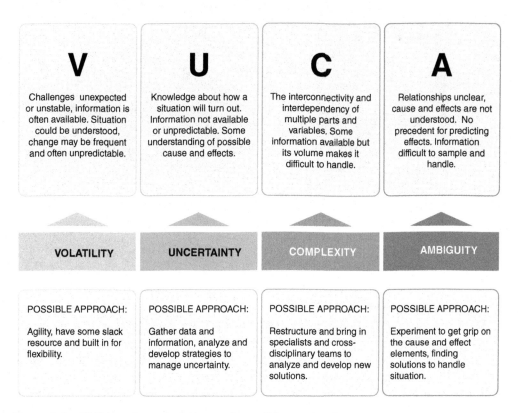

Figure 9.1   VUCA – characteristics and possible approach

VUCA represents different dimensions of how much the organization knows about the situation and the possibility of predicting the result of planned actions. Analysing situations applying a VUCA approach may provide a more nuanced approach to uncertainty for organizations as to how to handle challenges related to change and innovation (Figure 9.1).

Projects in organizations for innovations and changes in a VUCA world require an adaptive and flexible approach in various stages for the process. This implies an agile execution strategy in single projects, but also in project programmes and in portfolios (see Chapter 5 for agile projects and Chapter 12 for more on project programmes and portfolios). Willingness to adapt and change during the process of implementation is crucial. To sum up, VUCA represents a term for addressing various forms of uncertainties in the organizations' attempts to implement strategies and adapt to challenges. Applying agile project principles could be an adequate way of dealing with challenges. An article by Bennett and Lemoine (2014) on understanding threats to performance in a VUCA world and Millar et al.'s (2018) overview article on managing innovation in a world characterized by VUCA provides further insight into the phenomenon.

IN PRACTICE

A VUCA WORLD IS A TERM APPLIED IN BUSINESS: HOW DOES THIS RELATE TO PROJECTS AND UNCERTAINTY?

In October 2019 the host nation for the Rugby World Cup, Japan, on the eve of critical elimination matches, suffered the worst typhoon in 65 years which meant that several matches had to be cancelled. The typhoon also disrupted the Rugby World Cup. Two matches in Yokohama just outside Tokyo were cancelled and a third between Canada and Namibia was cancelled in Kamaishi in north-eastern Japan, in the direction the storm had travelled.

QUESTION

The typhoon was a tragedy for Japan in terms of loss of life and damage to infrastructure. Look into this through the link starting with www.smh.com.au.

It was also a major problem for the project organizers of the Rugby World Cup. Revenues from three matches were forfeited and nations whose progress hinged on key matches had to accept a compromise score artificially awarded.

1. What contingency planning might have minimized the uncertainty?

Understanding and classifying uncertainty

The kinds and degrees of uncertainty inherent in a given project are variable. Research and investigation (exploring/mapping out solutions) projects are often encumbered with heavy uncertainty. Complex IT as well as innovative product development projects pose conditions of high uncertainty. The sources of this uncertainty can be either internal to the project or a result of external factors.

INTERNAL AND EXTERNAL UNCERTAINTY

Uncertainties directly related to a project are labelled as *internal uncertainty*, some-times related to all aspects of the project, such as the choice of the concept, design, goals and plans (Turner & Cochrane, 1993). Internal uncertainty factors can also include collaboration in the project, its communication, management, competence and well-being. These are aspects of uncertainty that the project manager and the others associated with the project can exercise surveillance over and manage. Relationships in the environment of the project constitute *external uncertainty*. Common external uncertainty factors include stakeholders, regulations, the economic and political situa-tion, and weather conditions (De Meyer et al., 2002). More abstract but no less import-ant external factors would include competitors, as well as the condition of the local financial and foreign exchange markets. Such uncertainty is largely beyond the scope of the project but can have an impact on the work and/or delivery of the project. These uncertainties may not affect the project much while extreme uncertainty can make many assumptions underlying planning invalid. Such uncertainty is often called *force majeure* (from the French for 'greater power') and is a widely used clause in contracts. One or more parties will be absolved from liability for default when extraordinary incidents beyond the control of the parties (flood, war, rebellion, natural disasters) prevents them from fulfilling the obligations specified in the contract.

The project manager needs to understand both internal and external uncertainties as much as is possible. We will start by looking at internal uncertainty. The main dif-ference in the analysis of internal uncertainty is between uncertainty associated with project delivery (what is the project actually to deliver?) and uncertainty associated with methods (how will the project actually proceed to delivery?) (Obeng, 1996; Turner & Cochrane, 1993).

If uncertainty is low (a closed project) it requires relatively little attention but when uncertainty is related to delivery (in a semi-open project) there will be more interaction with users and the client. Where delivery is quite well defined but there is uncertainty about the method of creating it (semi-closed project), it is important to have competent teams well oriented to solving tasks and learning through trial and error. In these projects, one cannot plan activities in detail early, as it is uncertain which activities are best suited. Since planning cannot be done at the level of detail, it is all the more important to work with milestone planning to give direction to the work and motivation for the task. In projects where uncertainty is related to both goals and methods (open project), it is important to utilize all the team members' competencies to provide direction for the work (De Meyer et al., 2002).

Members of project teams must be able to cope well with great uncertainty in most of the processes in which they are involved. High-quality relationships in the project team integrate the knowledge and skills of each team member. Embedding the project in multiple relationships among these actors aids continuous capture and interpretation of uncertainty. Uncertainty accentuates the importance of having fora for interpretation of uncertainty and ambiguity as well as for decisions (Berggren et al., 2008). Uncertainty creates situations for which decisions need to be made. Starting up projects with high uncertainty it is important to ensure that relevant deci-sion-makers regularly gather so that the project is not hampered by lack of decisions.

As mentioned in the discussion of agile projects (Chapter 4), agile execution is often selected in situations of great uncertainty, especially where this is related to the nature of the delivery or where there is uncertainty about both goals and meth-ods. Through repeated cycles, sub-deliveries are reproduced, tested and feedback provided, leading to a gradual decrease in uncertainty as the delivery takes shape.

Uncertainty in estimates

We have previously stated that projects are often commenced on weak foundations, such as estimates that prove wrong as the project develops. We have discussed decision traps (Chapter 2) and dysfunctional team processes (Chapter 8) that can lead to estimates with considerable inherent uncertainty. It is very difficult to estimate the kinds of activities required to complete project delivery and what kind of resources are required. Sources of uncertainty in estimates may be several:

- Missing or unpredictable specifications of what is needed.
- The activity is unique (*novel*) and therefore you do not know what is needed.
- Complexity, where it is difficult to overview all the factors that are part of the project, how they are linked and how they interact. It creates uncertainty about addictions between factors.
- Possible incidents and conditions may occur.
- Biases, such as over-optimism among those who estimate (Atkinson, Crawford, & Ward, 2006, p. 688).

Many projects start with uncertainty in estimates due to ambiguity, complex contexts, missing or inaccurate data or human insufficiency that fails to realize the limits of over-optimism (Flyvbjerg et al., 2003). Many times, project teams also lack an understanding of the efforts needed to reduce uncertainties in estimates, so the work required fails to be done (Chapman & Ward, 2008).

Hard and soft uncertainty

Uncertainty associated with technical solution estimates or execution models is often called *hard uncertainty*. In addition, one must consider what is often called *soft uncertainty,* which is uncertainty associated with the actors involved in or who participate in the project. More specifically, it relates to the participants' competence and their ability to utilize these competencies effectively (Atkinson et al., 2006). Conflicts or other obstacles, such as having different organizational loyalties, coming from different cultural backgrounds or different disciplines, can all make it difficult for team members to solve their tasks collaboratively. Even projects that are extremely well planned cannot succeed if the participants have neither the motivation nor competence to perform the work. Soft uncertainty can also include the risk that the time allocated for their contribution will not be spent by project participants in an appropriate manner; other obligations may overwhelm their time and energy. For matrix projects including multiple resources that work in numerous projects in parallel the risk of being commited to other obligations represents a significant level of uncertainty. Plans often assume optimal commitments that may not occur, such as people becoming ill, having accidents and being unable to perform at their best or they may become disillusioned with the project and lose motivation. Many project team members lack judgement about how long it will take to perform certain tasks and the appropriateness of their skills for undertaking these tasks.

Uncertainty – in the eye of the beholder

Both hard and soft uncertainty can be found in all projects. Their incidence will vary through the life cycle of the project and uncertainty is a relatively subjective phenomenon, with different actors experiencing and interpreting uncertainty differently (Atkinson et al., 2006). Project managers and staff must understand these dynamics when they are present in their teams and among relevant actors outside the team. Having several or all of the team members included in the effort to identify and interpret uncertainty facilitates recognition. Doing so can help in identifying aspects of the different understandings of participants as a good source of a more comprehensive and nuanced understanding of uncertainty (De Meyer et al., 2002). If there are huge differences among perceptions, one should discuss which perceived uncertainties seem more real and prevalent and which are more stereotypical in nature. One could also discuss which types of uncertainty should be focused on and how these uncertainties can be elaborated so that team members can be proactive. Responsibility for work on various types of uncertainties can be distributed among project employees. Responsibility charts (Chapter 6) can be useful tools for this activity. Uncertainty management is more than methodology. One has to build a culture that includes uncertainty management as a reflective practice throughout the project, involving all project participants (Hillson & Murray-Webster, 2007). Developing a positive attitude towards understanding and working with uncertainty and building a suitable vocabulary with which to discuss its characteristics is important. Knowledge of typical uncertainties and their consequences in different contexts can be built up in the project. Structural measures, in terms of reporting and discussion can be built into routines so that they are regularly, systematically and operationally addressed. One way is to have as an item, 'concerns, issues and feelings', located early on the agenda of project meetings. Anyone can raise an issue for this agenda and the issue should stay on the agenda until the person that raised the issues is certain the equivocality associated with the issue has been resolved. In order for such a culture to develop well, participants must have commitment and respect for each other and their work, and resources must be devoted to resolving the uncertainty.

A culture of uncertainty management is in many ways similar to a culture of learning (see Chapter 10). What is at issue is elaborating how things are developing, reflecting on why things are not developing as expected and sharing this knowledge. Continuous elaborations mean that you learn about how to deal with uncertainty throughout the project. It is important to create a psychologically safe space in which people can feel free to talk about the uncertainties they perceive. People who are insecure about the willingness to discuss uncertainties that they experience will spend a lot of time processing risks so they do not have time to think about opportunities; a positive psychological space can overcome these tendencies.

Project leaders can work to create *a culture of uncertainty management* by stimulating the ability to engage in wondering and reflecting, so as to be actively detecting and interpreting uncertainty. Often, there are mechanisms in the overall organization that can constitute the biggest barriers to succeeding in managing uncertainty. For example, there might be a very narrow view of what constitutes uncertainty. Pressure to complete the project's early phase quickly often leads to overlooking uncertainties in estimates or how goals and purposes are to be achieved, given the pressure for results.

A framework for measuring where you are at in terms of the following four stages of uncertainty may be helpful (Hillson, 1997):

- *Naivety.* Project team members or others in the organization are not aware of the need to deal with uncertainty.
- *Novitiate.* A few of those who work in and around projects pay some attention to identifying and understanding uncertainty. Such work is not part of the organization's ongoing dialogue or a structured part of business.
- *Normalization.* Uncertainty is included in the company's processes in and around projects. Uncertainty is part of the dialogue, with structured tools and processes deployed to deal with its sources and consequences, such as workshops.
- *Naturalization.* Uncertainty is considered a part of all processes. In addition to structured processes for dealing with uncertainty, there is a culture of uncertainty management rather than its neglect. There is a great deal of acceptance for talking about uncertainty, demanding that it be worked on and resources be committed to coping with it. An opportunity perspective is pervasive – seeing not obstacles but opportunities.

WHAT WOULD YOU DO?

You are a project manager at the start of a project. It is a delivery project that entails developing a new product for another company, i.e. the sponsor. The project principal resides in the sponsoring company. You and your project team consist of members from the sponsor organization, as well as your own organization, which is a consulting company. The team members hold different areas of expertise and their familiarity and experience with project work is also variable.

Most of the members have experience in rather simple and straightforward projects, such as the 'painting-by-numbers' projects presented in Chapter 3.

The project charter and its purpose and project goals are rather open, since the development entails innovation in conditions of uncertainty. Both you and the principal are well aware of this situation. The principal challenges you to identify some important elements for establishing a project culture dealing with this type of uncertainty. Furthermore, the principal expects you to develop contingency plans and measures to deal with uncertainty.

QUESTION

1. What would you do to establish a project culture for dealing with uncertainty in the project and what emphases for action would you establish in the project?

When do most uncertainties occur in projects? Different execution models and uncertainty

If we consider internal uncertainty and how it develops during project execution, it is almost always greatest at the beginning of the project. In many projects, the goal and method are relatively open, the project members do not yet know each other, nor do they know what solutions they can create. There are many possibilities and a great deal of uncertainty. Even though goals are established, processes are still required to turn them into sensemaking through goal hierarchies, work package structures, plans and estimates, all reducing uncertainty gradually. Through the choice of concept and design and the start-up of actual task solving, action spaces are reduced along with internal uncertainty. It usually becomes simpler and easier for the project team to see what they really are about and how it should be done. At the same time, the room for opportunity is reduced – the *dilemma of project planning* (Figure 9.2).

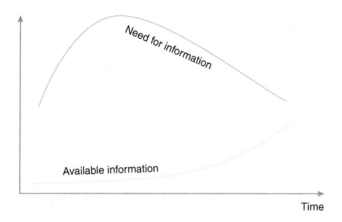

Figure 9.2   The dilemma of project planning

Internal uncertainty in the execution phase, in which delivery is to be produced and completed, is primarily related to the quality of delivery and the description of scope and processes. In a traditional execution model based on waterfalls and decision gates, internal uncertainty is significantly reduced through the transition from early stages to the completion phase. Unfortunately, this recognition often results in uncertainty gaining attention early in the project and at the start of the execution phase, while the later project work becomes more oriented to 'getting the job done'. Less attention is paid to uncertainty, since it is now perceived as relatively limited. Uncertainty management is thus often characterized by initial 'all-out efforts' rather than being part of continuous work, a dangerous attitude because external uncertainty can pursue the project throughout its life cycle. Therefore, uncertainty management must be an active and continuous process throughout the project. To achieve these objectives it is important to have in place structures, processes and cultures for uncertainty management.

With an agile execution model, it is key that decisions are made throughout the project's lifespan. This happens in a dialogue where the project tests solutions and receives input from relevant decision-makers. As mentioned earlier, such a model is often chosen in development projects where there is assumed to be relatively high uncertainty, especially related to the nature of the delivery. With such an evolutionary delivery model, internal uncertainty will be more prevalent throughout the project lifespan. Nevertheless, uncertainty is gradually reduced as deliveries take shape, although uncertainty reduction is not so clearly linked to *phase transitions*.

Some project team members find it quite natural that you have to figure things out along the way. Others experience it as extremely exciting and motivating that solutions can gradually emerge. Still others experience it as stressful if many possibilities are kept open for a long time. It can thus be very demanding for the project participants deliberately to keep multiple opportunities open through the project.

Project product success often requires that the project manager lives with internal uncertainty through much of the project process.

When working actively to reduce uncertainty in projects, one must be careful about when and how to do so. Practices are often influenced by project managers who are quick to make choices and decisions, believing that this shows momentum. Good project managers might instead ask, 'How late can we make this decision?' They know that uncertainty is reduced by access to information (planning dilemma) and wait to make more informed decisions.

In practice, project teams often try to reduce uncertainty by designing goals and plans in detail. As we have already seen, this is good to the extent that it provides project direction and opportunity for follow-up. However, it is also a problematic practice because it imposes decisions at premature times. Often, important premises for the project lay in its early stages. There is plenty of need to lay down some premises early in order to proceed with the work but it is also during this period of execution that we have the least knowledge both of the nature of the work, the delivery, the context and how the project team actually works together. We can conclude that you need to establish a number of assumptions to get started with project work but they should not be more than is absolutely necessary and you must be open to some of them being reviewed later in the project process when the actors have gained relevant knowledge. The more uncertainty that characterizes the project, the more valid is this claim.

READ THIS!

In an open access journal, *Heliyon*, you can find an article that outlines the adoption of agile methods for the management of projects in collaborative research initiatives. The article, by Hidalgo (2019), is titled 'Adapting the scrum framework for agile project management in science: Case study of a distributed research initiative' at https://study.sagepub.com/pm.

IN PRACTICE

AGILE PROJECT MANAGEMENT

Based on Hidalgo's case study, what do you take to be the key conditions for successful agile project management? What are the main features of being agile and what are the main drawbacks and benefits?

Managing uncertainty

The relevant actors in and around the project must acknowledge that uncertainty can always be present. The three key questions actors must relate to are the following:

1. What kind of uncertainty will occur and when will it occur?

2. If an uncertainty occurs, what will the likely effect be?
3. How will our response to uncertainty affect the outcome?

There are different frameworks for uncertainty management that all have the following steps in common:

1. Identification of uncertainty.
2. Analysis of uncertainty.
3. Choice and execution of measures to deal with uncertainty.
4. Follow-up and evaluation of how efficient the management of uncertainty had been.

Some frameworks split one or more of these four steps into substeps but the main point is the same. For example, in a start-up phase, it might be useful to ensure necessary clarifications related to questions such as: What should be the goal of the uncertainty analysis? How is it going to be implemented? What information should it be based on? Who should be included and who will take responsibility for what in this process? These need clarifying in order to deal with uncertainty efficiently. Projects often have routines for finding the answer to these questions.

Picture 9.2   One way of reducing uncertainty

WATCH THIS!

Watch the video on understanding risks and risk management in projects at: https://study.sagepub.com/pm.

Assigning responsibility for uncertainty management

Responsibility for uncertainty management varies in different organizations. Many times, the project manager takes the main responsibility for this work, a responsibility that experienced project managers know to take seriously. In other situations, there may be experts who lead uncertainty management. These may be individuals who are always used across projects or who work with uncertainty in different parts of the project; for example, in the early phase and phase transitions. If the company has a project management office, this often has experts who can contribute to the individual projects' uncertainty management. Companies that have a project management office often have long experience with the project form and have thus developed procedures that help clarify areas of specialization, responsibility and basis for the work of uncertainty. The specialists, the project management office and support staff, can assist with methods, techniques and professional knowledge but the project owner and project manager cannot be exempt from the responsibility for the uncertainty management. Often the project owner should become involved more strongly because much of the uncertainty will be outside the project manager's responsibility.

If the organization has limited expertise with uncertainty management or it is going to carry out a project that differs significantly from those it usually executes, it may be advisable to include external experts who are familiar with uncertainty management from similar projects. Below we will look at how we can understand and work with uncertainty management.

READ THIS!

Read Rick Clare's (2011) overview of the top ten mistakes made in managing project risks at: https://study.sagepub.com/pm.

Identifying uncertainty

The first thing we should do is be able to identify the sources of uncertainty. Often this is done as a group process. Here it is important to be aware of which groups are represented by the individual members participating in this process and what types of uncertainties they may identify and encounter. Are they able, together, to establish an uncertainty landscape that is complete/complex enough in terms of representing the project? The committee should not be too unilateral in composition and should comprise relevant expertise in terms of the uncertainties seemingly appropriate to the project in question; seemingly, because events that are wholly unexpected can always occur.

As we have seen above, individuals often have different *perspectives* on uncertainty, so it is important to envision all the perspectives of all participants. A complicating factor in the identification of uncertainty is the lack of a common defined position when making uncertainty analysis. In order to identify the most relevant uncertainty, it may be advisable to involve experts familiar with uncertainty in the particular project type, delivery type or context. These can be employees of the same company or people from outside who have experience from similar projects. The project's history or previous projects directly related to the project can also provide valuable information about potential risks and opportunities.

Obviously, it is useful to have a good knowledge of various types of uncertainty so that they can be systematically assessed. An example would include uncertainty related to technical or economic conditions, the contract and the people involved in the project or the organization of them. Furthermore, uncertainty can be analysed based on the project phases it is associated with.

Below is an overview of typical uncertainties encountered in the various phases of the project's life course, exemplified by a product development project (Atkinson et al., 2006; Ward & Chapman, 2003). There is considerable internal uncertainty but also some external uncertainty, in relation to stakeholders, for instance. The fact that there is less emphasis on external uncertainty in the table does not mean that this type of uncertainty is less important, only that it is less connected with the phases of the project life cycle. The overview is intended as an aid to identifying uncertainty in projects in a broad way by addressing it phase by phase, based on an execution model of qualitatively different phases. The discussion of execution models in projects (in Chapter 4) showed that the project often moves through overlapping phases (milestone-based execution model) or repeated cycles (agile). Many of the activities and processes presented in Table 9.1 are relevant irrespective of the execution model.

Table 9.1　Overview of typical uncertainties in phases

Stages in the project life cycle	Uncertainty theme
Create the product/idea/concept	Appropriate degree of definition
	Defining execution criteria and goals
	Stakeholders' expectations
	Business case
Strategic product design	Novelty in design and technology
	Determine points for design freeze
	Control of changes
Strategic planning of implementation	Identify and adjust according to changes in regulations and look for opportunities
	Identify degree of parallel activities
	Identify dependencies
Tactical allocation of resources	Resource estimation
	Responsibility
	Contract preparation
	Selection of partners/recruitment of employees

(Continued)

Table 9.1 (Continued)

Stages in the project life cycle	Uncertainty theme
Execution	Coordination and control – in practice
	Suitable levels and systems for control and follow-up
	Effective communication to capture risk and opportunities
	Effective leadership
	Ensure continuity in personnel and division of responsibilities – who safeguards, for example, profit realization
	Ensure continuity in non-human resources
Delivery of the product/process	Adequate testing
	Adequate training
	Expectation management for stakeholders
Evaluation/closing process	Evaluation
	Capture, store and possibly disseminate knowledge related to uncertainty and other learning experiences
	Finish in a way that is perceived as safe for participants in the project and recipients of the delivery

Other aids to identify relevant uncertainties are checklists, reports and summaries of critical uncertainties in similar projects. Often the identification of uncertainty proceeds through brainstorming processes that creatively conjure the widest possible sources of uncertainty. Being involved in uncertainty management helps many project employees gain a more comprehensive understanding and ability to perceive and deal with uncertainties. Such involvement can also contribute to an increased sense of ownership of problems arising and to clarification of expectations useful in further project work.

Analysing uncertainty

Two well-known analytical methods for analysing uncertainty are incident analysis and estimation analysis.

Incident analysis. This is a qualitative analysis of incidents. The uncertainty is not related to whether an incident does occur; it is the likelihood that it may occur and an assessment of the likely consequences for project execution that is important. The answers to these questions may be quantified such that uncertainty is calculated as the probability that an incident occurs multiplied by the consequences of it so doing. In an incident analysis, each incident is placed in a criticality matrix where the vertical axis indicates the probability of the incident occurring and the horizontal axis showing the effects, if it occurs.

The location of an incident in the criticality matrix in Figure 9.3 is shaded as follows: medium green indicates a low criticality, pale medium, and dark green very critical.

Estimate analysis. In this method, it is the effects of the consequences that are calculated. The most used example of estimation of uncertainty is a dice. Rolling a dice, the outcome must be between 1 and 6, but what the number will be is uncertain. It is the number between 1 and 6 that can be estimated. There are many ways to systematize and quantify uncertainty. A common way to quantify uncertainty is in intervals: up to 33% probability (low), 34–69% probability (medium), over 70% (high). The figures indicate the estimated probability of carrying out the project within its limits for time, cost and quality. This allows us to calculate the uncertainty associated with a given incident and how it will affect the iron triangle of the project.

Figure 9.3   Matrix for criticality

Picture 9.3   A considerable source of uncertainty

Source: Image courtesy of Visuals3D via Pixabay

When working with estimation we often try to determine confidence levels which represent the proportion, or the frequency, of possible confidence intervals that contain the true value of the unknown population parameter. Then confidence intervals that consist of a range of potential values of the unknown population parameter can be constructed. The interval computed from a particular sample does not necessarily include the true value of the parameter. Also, one should note that larger samples tend to produce better estimates of the population parameter, when all other factors are equal.

To analyse the risk landscape, exercises such as the Monte Carlo simulation can be used. The technique helps visualize most or all of the potential outcomes to provide a better idea regarding the risks associated with a decision; however, this will only work with the known uncertainties, those that are statistically probable and might occur. The probability of different outcomes can be based on repeated sampling of similar projects. The basic idea is to use randomness in problem solving based on experientially derived knowledge pooled from many projects. One issue is that this approach hardly includes very low probability regions in the samples. If we want to broaden the range, we could also use scenario planning (Clegg, Pitelis, Schweitzer, & Whittle, 2020) as this gives equal weight to all scenarios.

Table 9.2　Probability and impact scale

Probability scale	Impact scale
1 = Not expected to happen	1 = Insignificant
2 = May happen but probably will not happen	2 = Small
3 = 50% probability that it happens	3 = Damaging
4 = Expected	4 = Serious
5 = Will very likely happen	5 = Accident threatening the existence of the project

Assessing uncertainty: Probability and consequence

Above we have considered uncertainty in terms of probability intervals. Another widely used method is grading on a five-point scale capturing the risk aspects for the project (Table 9.2). Such scales might extend from risk to opportunity, although in practice the risk of uncertainty tends to be the focus.

Once the risk is analysed, it is common to insert it into a chart, as in Table 9.3, in order to gain a better overview of the contexts to be managed.

Table 9.3 Managing uncertainty

Uncertainty element	Probability	Presumably caused by	Action

The advantage of such as a chart is that it captures both possibilities (light green) and risk (dark) in the same representation, as well as the continuous development from catastrophic risk on the one hand to very large opportunity on the other side.

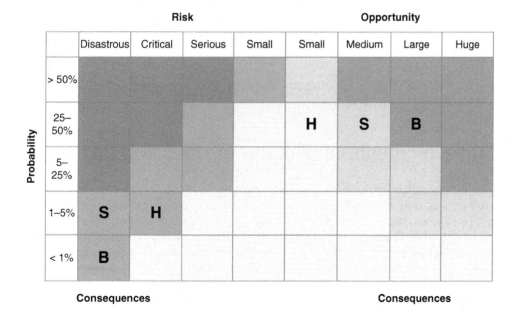

Figure 9.4 Example of risks and opportunities

Figure 9.4 represents an uncertainty analysis of the work of a project team collaborating in writing a master's thesis. The analysis has three zones of uncertainty, each marked with a letter. S stands for collaboration in the group, H stands for health and physical form in the group, while B stands for the organization they have chosen. We see that the uncertainty elements have both an upside (opportunities) and a downside (risk). There is a high likelihood that participants will be able to cooperate well, providing them with medium opportunities. There is a small (estimated at only 1–5%) probability of a breakdown of cooperation, but should it happen the consequences will be disastrous for the project. It is a high probability that the participants will stay healthy but this provides little in the way of opportunities. There is a low probability of illness, mental imbalance or the like in the group; however, should a member become ill it can have critical consequences. The organization that the participants have chosen is exciting and presents a high probability of winning with great opportunities. There is little likelihood of risk, but if something happens to cooperation with the organization the consequences will be disastrous.

To communicate an image of uncertainty where both risk and opportunity arise, a so-called tornado diagram can also be used (see Figure 9.5).

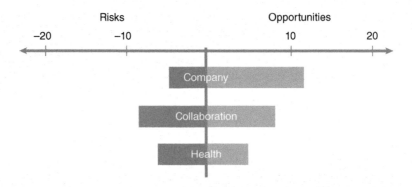

Figure 9.5 Example of a tornado diagram, including risks and opportunities for multiple dimensions simultaneously

Multiple incidents may occur at the same time

It is absolutely crucial to understand that incident analysis looks at uncertainties in terms of single incidents. Incident analyses fail to capture the cumulative effect of a project's uncertainty if multiple incidents occur at the same time. The question you can ask is this: Does the individual incident have more or fewer consequences when more incidents occur at the same time? In other words: Will the sum of 1 + 1 be smaller or larger than 2 in such cases? It does not matter that multiple incidents occur simultaneously; that is, that the effect of the individual incident is 'constant', whether it occurs alone or in conjunction with other incidents. The answers will be situation-dependent; nonetheless, it is important to reflect on how different incidents that are likely to occur may be assumed to have an impact on the project overall.

The uncertainty scenario in a project is extremely *dynamic*. The scenario will change throughout the project, both in terms of the amount and types of uncertainty that apply. As the team is working on the project, their understanding of the project and the task to be solved and its related uncertainty will change. That means, for example, incident analyses can have different outcomes over time, depending on the level of knowledge. Thus, it may be useful to analyse the uncertainties you experience as most likely and most critical several times throughout the project process. It may also be useful to test these analyses on experts or by seeking information on similar cases.

Following up and evaluating uncertainty management

We have emphasized that follow-up is important for good project execution and learning across projects (Chapter 4). The previous discussion of follow-up more generally also applies to follow-up of uncertainty more specifically. When you conclude that things have required more resources (economic and labour resources) than planned, it is usually because unexpected uncertainty has occurred. In dealing with uncertainty a systematic approach and a high level of reflection is required. Documentation should be updated and as accurate as possible in order to provide a good basis for follow-up.

Checklists and traffic lights provide easy tools with which to follow up risk in execution. Applying a traffic light is an easy way to discuss and visualize present status versus the plan for a project (see Figure 9.6 for an example in which the traffic lights would be red, yellow and green respectively):

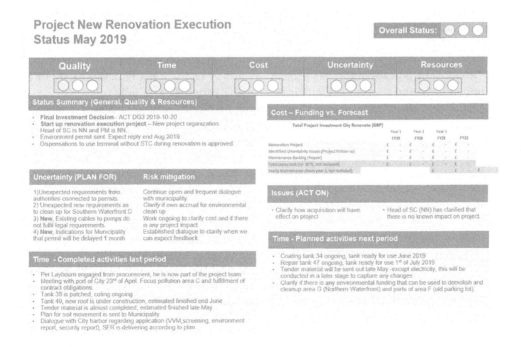

Figure 9.6 Example of a status report

In order that uncertainty is followed up throughout the project the methods and processes presented above are important as simple indicators. They need to be accompanied by more forensic investigation into uncertainties. Questions to consider are the following: Does the accompanying plan have space for regular discussions of uncertainty and changes in this landscape? Are such discussions summarized in an updated list of uncertainties? The plans should include the uncertainties related to the project as well as the likelihood that they will occur and their consequences.

Formalized or planned follow-up of uncertainty does not diminish the importance of informal and daily dialogue and reflection on observations in the management of uncertainty. It is important to be attuned, listening and learning about uncertainty, throughout the project. Realism is required as well. The degree of control one may have over uncertainty may be slight. Systematic preparing for uncertainty causes many to believe that they control uncertainty. If an active and exploratory attitude is inculcated, risks will be better handled and opportunities more easily seized, yet this does not guarantee that uncertainties will not have a major impact on a project. Therefore, it is important to establish reserves and buffers so as to be available when required.

Measures for dealing with uncertainty

Measures can be taken to deal with uncertainties, reduce risks and seize opportunities by assessing whether or not the opportunity can and should be realized, how to determine who will take responsibility and who will take part in further work. Key stakeholders must often be included to assess the value of the opportunity, what it will demand in the way of resources and the uncertainty associated with these developments. In other words, there has to be consideration of benefits realization (see Chapter 4). It is important when handling uncertainty to put the following measures into action:

1. Provide a clear action strategy for various uncertainty scenarios
2. The most important actors, as project owners or users, must become aware of the uncertainty and the importance it has for the progress and deliveries
3. Check that the project has a clear charter mandate to take necessary measures when uncertainty occurs
4. Identify the other actors who need to be involved.

As we saw in Chapter 4, uncertainty is also one of the most important aspects to consider when signing contracts in collaborative projects. Different types of contracts provide a different distribution of risk and opportunities among the parties involved.

Project teams are often better at identifying and analysing uncertainty than at taking measures beforehand to reduce risk or exploit opportunities. It is good risk prevention to work with estimates, conditions and constraints in the early phase as well as with the business case, and the foundation and the anchoring of ideas to ensure relevant project deliveries. Other risk mitigation measures may be to choose proven technology and reputable suppliers and putting together a team of employees you know are competent and motivated.

The core of achieving risk reduction is to make good and well-informed choices in as many areas as possible, realizing that it is difficult to make good choices when little information is available that will hold true over time when there is a high rate of change in and around the project. Both hard and soft uncertainty are part of the execution of the vast majority of projects. Acknowledging uncertainty, talking about it and looking for its sources will help mastery better than just hoping to avoid unexpected incidents, a recognition that must be reflected in the choice of execution model, plan level and goal level.

The more uncertainty is associated with a project, the less appropriate it is to use a waterfall model, with associated detailed plans and targets. The direction of the project must instead emerge over time, along with relevant decision-makers learning through practice. If uncertainty is quite limited (either at start-up or by virtue of its gradual reduction), try to schedule the sequence of activities and set the time for them to be achieved. Often, projects contain some processes that are associated with considerable uncertainty while some other processes are associated with little uncertainty. The latter can then be planned in detail, while planning more loosely overall in the longer term. Goal-directed project management will focus on the most central areas of the project, while keeping open a number of choices and discussion of methods.

WHAT WOULD YOU DO?

You are one of seven team members in a project developing a new communication platform for student groups at your university, in which you are made responsible for dealing with uncertainty. About halfway in the project you find that there is more uncertainty than expected associated with the posited technical solutions. In particular, there are ambiguous results related to information security for cloud solutions. There are also some bugs related to merging documents, including visualizations. In addition, at this point in time, the project duration estimated at the beginning of the project seems overly optimistic.

QUESTIONS

1. What kind of analysis would you use to get to know more about the uncertainty you are sensing here?

2. Whom would you include in these analyses?

3. What might be appropriate actions to take when you have analysed the uncertainty?

Uncertainty and sensemaking

We have so far talked about uncertainties that can be identified and analysed, towards which one can assume a proactive attitude and behaviour; however, there will be elements of uncertainty that cannot be identified at the start of the project.

Early project phase work on uncertainty will primarily be concerned with identifying and analysing uncertainties that can be classified either as a variation or identifiable uncertainty. Variations stem from uncertainty, for example, about how long the basic work of a construction project will take. Planning might have suggested 34 weeks in good weather but 36 weeks if the weather is adverse. The uncertainty will then be two weeks. Another typical source of variation may be sickness among project staff or currency fluctuations. These are factors we know may be present to varying degrees so we can try to calculate to what extent they will occur by looking at how they have been historically spread over time. The project team can thus plan with some variations built into their assumptions and set time or economic buffers (reserves/slack in time and cost) to buffer against these uncertainties when they occur. One can, in order to prevent slack becoming a self-fulfilling prophesy, make the team collectively responsible for maintaining the buffer. Another way of dealing with this form of uncertainty is to create slack or flexibility into the product by designing a performance level into the product to be delivered that is thought to be higher than necessary.

Identifiable uncertainty is uncertainty you know and understand but are uncertain about whether or when it will occur. Such incident uncertainty is what we primarily think of when talking about uncertainty management. Here uncertainty can be identified and analysed, and action plans developed. An example might be a pharmaceutical project developing a new drug for which unanticipated side effects would be typical uncertainties. Given experience in developing similar drugs previously, the project team can anticipate some possible side effects and make plans for action if they arise. The plan of action may not be used but if the side effects occur you are ready and prepared.

Unidentifiable uncertainty is a form of uncertainty that is much more difficult to relate to than those mentioned above. It occurs especially in the project's early phase or planning phase. Such uncertainty is referred to as the 'unknown unknowns', using the phrase credited to Donald Rumsfeldt, who used it in a speech about how the United States had planned and carried out its invasion of Iraq in the Second Gulf War. It is a form of uncertainty that cannot be identified, especially its risk elements. Being beyond control, because of its essential unknowability, means that no illusion of control is possible; hence, it is particularly difficult to manage. Nevertheless, unidentifiable uncertainty also implies opportunities. The more the project is innovative, unidentifiable uncertainty probably increases. One well-known example of the possibilities of unidentifiable uncertainty occurred in a project developing cardiac medicine, which during the trial found that this medicine caused blood to rush to the penis, causing an erection, enhancing male readiness for sexual activity. The drug company that ran the project chose to invest in this opportunity and capitalized on the drug Viagra. Many development projects are characterized by this type of uncertainty.

Chaotic uncertainty is the most demanding uncertainty for any project and relates to conditions of chaos. Chaos occurs when projects have fundamental uncertainty related both to the delivery and the project structure itself in a context of considerable external uncertainty, such as COVID-19. Under these conditions it is difficult to decide how and what to deliver. Research projects and highly innovative development projects are examples of projects often characterized by such fundamental uncertainty. We will focus on these last two categories of uncertainty in our discussion of innovation (Chapter 11).

EXTEND YOUR KNOWLEDGE

Read the article by Mengis, Nicolini, and Swan (2018) on how to cope with uncertainty through knowledge integration. It is based on a study of collaboration among scientists involved in developing a highly novel bioreactor and demonstrates how knowledge integration is not a homogeneous process but requires switching between different knowledge integration practices over time, available at https://study.sagepub.com/pm.

How to cope with extremely uncertain projects

The project manager and the client are jointly responsible for uncertainty management and the distribution of this responsibility should be clarified early in the project, especially in relation to external or contextual uncertainty. Internal uncertainty will typically be a project management responsibility. Who is in charge of external uncertainty and early-stage uncertainty is often unclear and important uncertainties can fall between the two responsibilities rather than being allocated. In construction, such uncertainty can often arise as a result of unknown unknowns, such as the precise extent and position of the beneath ground location of utilities in dense urban regeneration projects.

We have looked at four types of uncertainty based on the ability to identify them, characterized by variety, identifiable and unidentifiable uncertainty, as well as chaotic uncertainty. Whether and how the project manager and team relate or not to these different types of uncertainty can be crucial. It is important to note that one and the same project can be characterized by all these uncertainties to a greater or lesser extent, with their combination and strength varying over time throughout the project process.

Many projects are not successful because conventional project planning is not adapted to dynamic environments. Planning, execution and management of projects must be adapted to the environment and the nature of the project. Key questions for analysis include: What characterizes the nature of your project and the environment that it enacts? What skills will be required to manage this enacted environment and what is the gap between these skills and the skills available to the project?

Table 9.4   Project management and risk management

Type of uncertainty	Project manager role	Managing tasks	Managing relationship
Variation	**Troubleshooter and expeditor** Managers must plan with buffers and use disciplined execution	**Planning** Simulate scenarios Insert buffers at strategic points in critical path Set control limits at which to take corrective action **Execution** Monitor deviation from intermediate targets	**Planning** Identify and communicate expected performance criteria **Execution** Monitor performance against criteria Establish some flexibility with key stakeholders
Foreseen uncertainty	**Consolidator of project achievements** Managers must identify risks, prevent threats and develop contingency plans	**Planning** Anticipate alternative paths to project goal by using decision-tree techniques Use risk lists, contingency planning and decision analysis **Execution** Identify occurrences of foreseen risks and trigger contingencies	**Planning** Increase awareness for changes in environment relative to known criteria or dimensions Share risk lists with stakeholders **Execution** Inform and motivate stakeholders to cope with switches in project execution

(Continued)

Table 9.4   (Continued)

Type of uncertainty	Project manager role	Managing tasks	Managing relationship
Unforeseen uncertainty	**Flexible orchestrator and networker as well as ambassador** Managers must solve new problems and modify both targets and execution method	**Planning** Build in the ability to add a set of new tasks to the decision tree Plan iteratively **Execution** Scan the horizon for early signs of unanticipated influences	**Planning** Mobilize new partners in the network who can help solve new challenges **Execution** Maintain flexible relationships and strong communication channels with all stakeholders Develop mutually beneficial dependencies
Chaos	**Entrepreneur and knowledge manager** Managers must repeatedly and completely redefine the project	**Planning** Iterate continually and gradually select final approach Use parallel development. **Execution** Repeatedly verify goals on the basis of learning; detail plan only to next verification Prototype rapidly Make go/no-go decisions ruthlessly	**Planning** Build long-term relationships with aligned interests Replace codified contracts with partnerships **Execution** Link closely with users and leaders in the field Solicit direct and constant feedback from markets and technology providers

Table 9.4 represents that the project manager should think and act differently depending on the task to be solved, the relationships that are part of the project and how uncertainty characterizes the project. The table shows that the role of the project manager and team changes as uncertainty becomes more unknown and chaotic, as analysis moves from using calculations and traditional analysis of uncertainties to more interpretative integration of knowledge available in diverse networks from relevant stakeholders. 'Painting by numbers' projects can utilize traditional project management tools for a detailed breakdown, planning and organization but 'Walking in the fog' projects must live at ease with uncertainty.

The more a project is characterized by unidentifiable uncertainty and chaos, the more iterative execution models will be required. A few assumptions have to be made at the start and then the structure and processes can emerge gradually, through trial and error. It is important to work with prototypes and visual aids, practising design thinking (Brown, 2009) and have good resources on standby (Berggren et al., 2008; Shenhar & Dvir, 2007). As we have previously mentioned, such projects require a manager and team members with open minds, good skills to reflect on and interpret the actions and consequences of the project and, not least, a good ability to live with uncertainty.

While project management in projects with low uncertainty often resembles the discharge of routine administrative functions, the project leader role in projects with high uncertainty requires highly demanding professional and managerial skills. The project manager must bring out the best in the team and ensure that everyone is able to apply the best of their skills. At the same time a good understanding of the technical aspects of delivery is required in order to keep track of project progress. Often the organizing of the project must reflect its uncertainty, in terms of the number of stakeholders that must be involved in the interpretation of what to do and how it should be done. Since many of the premises are not set in stone at the start of the project, it means that many decisions must be taken along the way. It also means that decision-makers must be available and ready to make decisions at the right time to avoid delays.

Sometimes the uncertainty is associated with high complexity due to many organizational interfaces. In such projects, the project team needs more time for preparation than when complexity is low. The uncertainty here relates to the understanding of roles and their interfaces (Shenhar & Dvir, 2007). Complexity is reduced when everyone involved in the project is taught, to some degree, to think about procedures, execution models and important tools related to execution. Attention will be especially directed at coordination, control and communication (Table 9.5).

If much of the uncertainty is related to progress, it is important to have relatively autonomous employees with high skills that can respond appropriately and promptly to issues that arise (Shenhar & Dvir, 2007). There is often not the time to discuss all decisions in the project management team and/or in the steering committee. When there is a high degree of uncertainty, it is not possible to try or plan a large number of responses to every uncertainty that might occur. One must build structures and norms for behaviour, as well as work to empower employees, support them and facilitate interaction patterns that are positive in decision-making and performance. The key elements of leadership and project team development (Chapters 6 and 7) are vital to success in the management of uncertainty.

Table 9.5   Features of projects and areas of attention

Features of project	Areas of attention
High degree of novelty	Important to find out if there is a market for the delivery and how to prepare the ground for this
High degree of technological uncertainty	Great likelihood of failure of the quality of the delivery (important to the customer) – requires many iterations and often work with prototypes
High degree of complexity	Requires formalized processes
High degree of pace	Quick response is important. The project must be able to act adequately on different situations immediately; it should therefore prepare contingency plans where possible

Black Swans

Sometimes there are events labelled **Black Swans.** The idea of Black Swan events originally began as a philosophical point made by the Austrian philosopher Karl Popper, who during the Second World War was sent by the British authorities as an enemy alien from his academic position at the London School of Economics to the University of Otago at the foot of the South Island of New Zealand. In the Antipodes swans are black not white. Popper's point was that one only has to see one black swan to disprove the hypothesis that all swans are white.

> **Black Swan** events are negative results that are very unlikely to happen but that can have a huge impact when they do occur.

Picture 9.4   Black Swans

Source: Image taken by Alexas, from Pixabay.

More recently Taleb (2007) wrote a book called *The Black Swan: The Impact of the Highly Improbable* in which he defined Black Swan events as having three attributes in common:

1. The event is unpredictable (to the observer)
2. The event has widespread ramifications
3. After the event has occurred it will be asserted that it was indeed explainable and predictable – the bias of hindsight

Black Swan events often hit major IT projects. In fact, Flyvbjerg and Budzier (2011) found that one in six projects has a cost overrun of 200% and go over schedule by 70%. One example that they point out is when top managers at Levi Strauss sought to revamp the information technology system. As their IT network was old-fashioned and included a 'balkanized mix' of incompatible systems, it was decided to migrate to a single SAP system. A team of Deloitte consultants led the project with a budget of no less than $5 million and the risks seemed small. The $5 million project led to an almost $200 million loss in a case of a classic black swan event and the chief information officer, David Bergen, was forced to resign. Flyvbjerg and Budzier (2011) point to how mismanaged IT projects routinely cost the jobs of top managers and have sunk whole corporations in what has been the largest global study ever of IT change initiatives, including 1471 projects, comparing their budgets and estimated performance benefits with the actual costs and results. They concluded that CEOs of companies undertaking significant IT projects should be acutely aware of the risks of becoming a black swan. Based on their study Flyvbjerg and Budzier (2011) offer the following advice for avoiding the black swans:

1. Stick to the schedule
2. Resist changes to the project's scope
3. Break the project into discrete modules
4. Assemble the right team, including IT experts from both companies, outside experts, and vendors
5. Prevent turnover among team members

6. Frame the initiative as a business endeavour, not a technical one
7. Focus on a single target – 'readiness to go live' – measuring every activity against it

Communicating

We have looked at the relationship between uncertainty and plans, goals and execution model. Uncertainty also relates to the exchange of information and other communication. Projects with a low degree of uncertainty can be based on formal and solid information and often have relatively low frequency communication between project members. However, projects with a high degree of uncertainty must be based on considerable communication and interaction to achieve feedback on solutions, anchoring solutions for users and decision-makers and making the necessary decisions. With a high degree of uncertainty, there will often be considerable formal and informal communication.

It is important to think in nuanced ways about uncertainty when analysing projects. Denver Airport, in the United States, provides an example of a project failing (partly) due to uncertainty management being insufficiently nuanced (Shenhar & Dvir, 2007). Although this was a large and complex project, it was considered that it shared the basic characteristics of most other construction projects. Among other things, the technological uncertainty was considered to be rather limited. Construction (construction, runways, access roads, etc.) was considered as technologically risky; however, it was the luggage handling system that should have been characterized by a high degree of uncertainty and risk. Due to the difficulties involved in establishing the luggage handling system, the airport project was much more expensive than expected and extremely delayed, although construction work was completed in accordance with the plans. If the luggage system had been separated from the construction work as a distinct complex high-tech system, the outcome of the project might have been different.

IN PRACTICE

RISK AND ESCALATION OF COMMITMENT

The tendency of an individual or group facing increasingly negative outcomes in terms of risk from a decision, action or investment, is often to continue doing what they are doing,

(Continued)

investing more into it, instead of altering course. This phenomenon is known as escalation of commitment, a term that became associated with the United States' escalation of commitment to the Vietnam War during the time that it was fought (Herring, 1986). With each setback the military sought more troops and resources which did not ensure victory – far from it.

Escalation of commitment occurs when investment in a course of action that is failing is maintained because of not wanting to appear wrong or inconsistent with the initial decision-making. Escalation of commitment often relates to three risk-related variables: risk propensity, risk perception and outcome expectancy. In short, research shows that risk propensity and outcome expectancy are often positively related to escalation of commitment, whereas risk perception was negatively related to escalation of commitment. Also, the perception of risk partially mediates the effects of risk propensity, while risk perception is mediated by outcome expectancy. There is an illuminative article by Drummond (2018) on escalation of commitment in megaprojects.

QUESTION

1. Identify a well-known project in which escalation of commitment occurred (it could be any kind of project for which you can find web-based resources). What went wrong, why and how did the commitment escalate?

Those who are successful are responsive

Research shows that those who are successful in dealing with uncertainty have the ability to respond quickly. Quick responses are often associated with flexible behaviour, such as the ability to change within the established framework of a project with agility and the ability to use available skills in new contexts (Geraldi et al., 2010). The ability to operate flexibly and quickly is strengthened by top management support for project managers but it should also provide them the freedom to decide what uncertainty they will respond to and how they will do it. It is important that project owners are active, taking responsibility for and managing uncertainty where appropriate, so that implicit opportunities can also be seized. Sometimes you should aim at the opportunities and let the project be measured on how it realizes them.

The key aspect is that to succeed, one must try to understand as much as possible at the outset and then keep close surveillance on proceedings throughout the project to gain knowledge about uncertainty and be willing to take action. At the outset the project team can start by mapping out understanding of the uncertainty landscape by clarifying what is known about the states of the world, action effects and the adequacy of this knowledge. The adequacy of this knowledge can be refined: What are any shortcomings due to – are they there because of ambiguity or lack of understanding (complexity) (De Meyer et al., 2002)?

Learning and adapting and selecting relevant cues from the project environment can enable coping with ambiguity and complexity. For example, if you are developing a product and there are three possible solutions to providing a key feature of this product, with high uncertainty about which one would best meet user needs, then one can launch three simple prototypes and see which pays off the best. Taking a 'continuous learning' and adapting approach in terms of dealing with uncertainty has consequences for planning. Instead of detailed planning of critical paths and scheduling of the project activities at the outset of the project, one can use visions to move the team toward the 'future perfect', in combination with plans for the next tasks, while also having plans in place for learning actions. Taking such an approach the team will need to re-plan, so time, tools and capacity for re-planning should be included in the project execution.

Stakeholders often resist change, so in taking a 'continuous learning' approach an extensive part of the project leader's work will be to soften resistance, by keeping stakeholders well informed and maintaining flexible contracts. The steering committee can be a valuable unit, not only as competent discussion partners in making sense of uncertainty and in deciding on how to act on it, but also as a way of involving and incorporating stakeholders. Project managers not only decide on the adequacy of the situation at hand but also create an infrastructure around the project to deal with the uncertainty landscape.

Final reflections

The most important thing about managing uncertainty is the recognition that uncertainty is present in all projects and any project team must relate to it throughout the project. Uncertainty represents both opportunity and risk. Some uncertainty is known. From experience, we can say something about the probable uncertainty that may occur in projects. In addition, we know that there may be some uncertainty that is completely unknown at start-up. We have considered key elements in dealing with uncertainty: identification, analysis and response.

We have pointed out that some uncertainties cannot be identified in the early phase of the project, so it becomes important that the project manager and other team members try to detect and understand uncertainty by taking a proactive attitude towards it.

Since uncertainty is present in all projects, it is key to document some of the work done to resolve different types of uncertainty. Such documentation can provide important learning experiences for other projects. Unfortunately, however, we are not always so good at learning from projects nor at distilling experience with uncertainty. The succession of unsuccessful campaigns waged by the US military in the wake of their failure in Vietnam are cases in point of the difficulty of learning from failed projects of intervention. If they had, then the invasion of Afghanistan, now the longest war the United States has been involved in, as well as the invasion of Iraq, would not have occurred.

One last important point to note about uncertainty that also applies to many processes and tools related to project management is that theories generally talk about individual projects and have the project as their perspective. As project portfolios and programmes become more and more widely used, it becomes more important to see how uncertainty is involved and managed at the programme level as well (Sanchez et al., 2009). Project programmes are, of course, even more complex than individual projects, thus opening up for changes along the way, having more conflicts and greater uncertainty than usual in the individual projects.

Summary

After reading this chapter, you should:

- Know the definition of uncertainty, understand that uncertainty is the outcome of the unknown and represents both the opportunities and risks to the project, and how various types and ranges of uncertainty should be considered when selecting project execution strategy.
- Be able to distinguish various forms of uncertainty, such as uncertainty ranging from variation, to chaos, including known knowns and the unknown unknowns. Also distinguishing between soft and hard uncertainty and internal–external uncertainty.
- Know the basic principles of uncertainty management, where the most important element of practice is to identify, analyse and manage uncertainty by developing appropriate strategies.
- Understand that project managers must adapt their behaviour to the different forms and degrees of uncertainty and also that the uncertainty often shifts in form and degree through the project.
- Know the important aspects of a culture of uncertainty management and what is important for creating such a culture, requiring not only time and resources to work with uncertainty but also management attention to creating psychological safety.

Exercises

1. Account for the two aspects of uncertainty.
2. How would you define uncertainty and how does uncertainty relate to ambiguity?
3. Explain the key aspect of uncertainty management. What are the main steps in managing uncertainty?
4. Can you explain soft uncertainty? What would you do to cope with soft uncertainty?
5. Why do we have uncertainties in estimates? How can you make sense of this uncertainty?
6. What are three sources of uncertainty?
7. What are the key measures for dealing with uncertainty?
8. What do you think is important in order to create an uncertainty culture?

CASE STUDY

INDEXICALITY AND CONTRACTS

Two sections follow. The first represents conclusions drawn from research in a construction site. The second section represents contractual principles that the members of an alliance building a major piece of infrastructure designed as their commitments.

CONTRACTS

Contractual documents are never unproblematic, never unambiguous, because they can never be unindexical. Indexicality is a technical term. It refers to a situation where the meaning of something is always contingent upon someone interpreting it. Such an interpretation always 'indexes' the particulars of the occasion of its interpretation. It is dependent on who is making the interpretation, from what interests, from what knowledge, at what time in the unfolding drama of the project. The contract is something which is never, nor never can be, apparently matter-of-factual, that is without need for interpretation. By the notion of an 'interested interpretation' one means to suggest that no interpretation is ever innocent of interest. Different knowledges, different positions in a hierarchy, different personnel in a network of interorganizational relations, different times in the temporal flow of events or spaces in their spatial location, can always produce differentially interested interpretations of the matter-at-hand. Hence, indexicality is irremediable. It is, if you like, a part of the human condition. Thus, conflict is ever potential wherever there is indexicality. And, where there are attempts to frame matters unindexically, in complex organizational contexts extending across space, time and knowledge, through contractual documents, there will always be indexicality, thus the possibility of conflict. It is endemic.

Uncertainty is not a naturally occurring state or an act of God. It is something made, produced, by the project organization members out of their grasp of the indexical nature of the documentation contained in the contractual materials. These formal organizational contractual documents provide the constitutional and constitutive grounds and framework within which the meaning of the contract is negotiated, contested and sometimes contained. (Adapted from Clegg, 1992)

ALLIANCE PROJECT CULTURE

The text below is the principles of organizational project management that the interorganizational collaborators on a major piece of infrastructure came up with to govern their project.

1. Build and maintain a champion team, with champion leadership, which is integrated across all disciplines and organizations

2. Commit corporately and individually to openness, integrity, trust, cooperation, mutual support and respect, flexibility, honesty and loyalty to the project

3. Honour our commitments to one another

4. Commit to a no-blame culture

5. Use breakthroughs and the free flow of ideas to achieve exceptional results in all project objectives

6. Outstanding results provide outstanding rewards

7. Deal with and resolve all issues from within the alliance

8. Act in a way that is 'best for project'

(Continued)

9. Encourage challenging *BAU* (business as usual) behaviours

10. Spread the alliance culture to all stakeholders

QUESTION

1. What do you think the implications for indexicality would be in a project that followed the ten principles outlined in the second statement? How would you expect implications to differ from those of a competitively tendered contract?

SOURCES THAT MIGHT BE HELPFUL

1. Clegg, S.R. (1975) *Power, Rule and Domination: A Critical and Empirical Understanding of Power in Sociological Theory and Organizational Life*. London: Routledge & Kegan Paul, International Library of Sociology. Reprinted 2013 as Clegg, S.R. (2013 reprint) *Power, Rule and Domination: A Critical and Empirical Understanding of Power in Sociological Theory and Organizational Life*. London: Routledge Library Editions, Organization: Theory & Behaviour, Volume 6.

2. Clegg, S.R. (1992) Contracts cause conflicts. In P. Fenn and R. Gameson (eds), *Construction Conflict Management and Resolution* (pp. 128–144). London: E. & F. N. Spon.

3. Clegg, S.R., Pitsis, T., Rura-Polley, T., and Marosszeky, M. (2002) Governmentality matters: Designing an alliance culture of inter-organizational collaboration for managing projects. *Organization Studies*, 23(3), 317–337.

4. Pitsis, T., Clegg, S.R., Marosszeky, M., and Rura-Polley, T. (2003) Constructing the Olympic Dream: Managing innovation through the future perfect. *Organization Science*, 14(5), 574–590.

Additional resources

Many books in project management pay significant attention to risk and risk assessments. More insights into calculations and techniques for attempting to handle risk can be found in Chris Chapman and Stephen Ward's (1996) *Project Risk Management: Processes, Techniques and Insights*. Bent Flyvbjerg (2014) increased insight into uncertainty in megaprojects in his book *Megaproject Planning and Management: Essential Readings* and he also has a very interesting article on the risks of megaprojects in 'What you should know about megaprojects and why: An overview' (Flyvbjerg, 2014b). The following articles are classics within the field of project uncertainty management – and worth looking at: Stephen Ward and Chris Chapman's (2003) 'Transforming project risk management into project uncertainty management'; Tzvi Raz and colleagues' article on 'Risk management, project success, and technological uncertainty'; and De Meyer and colleagues' (2002) discussion of 'Managing project uncertainty: From variation to chaos'.

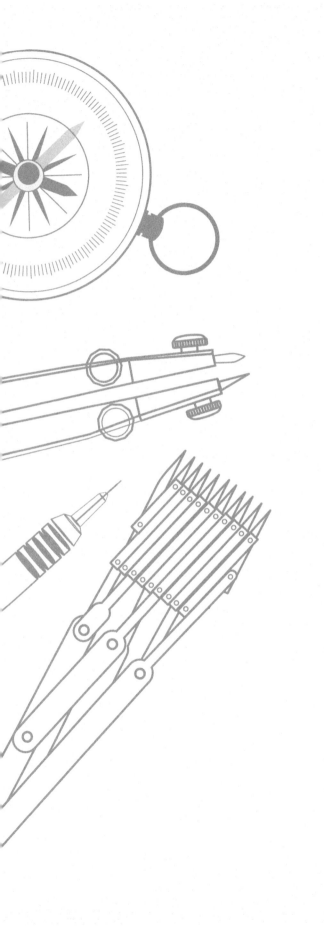
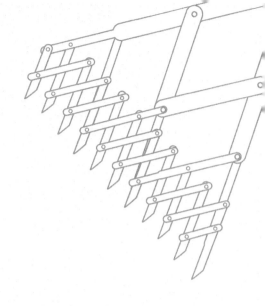

Chapter Roadmap

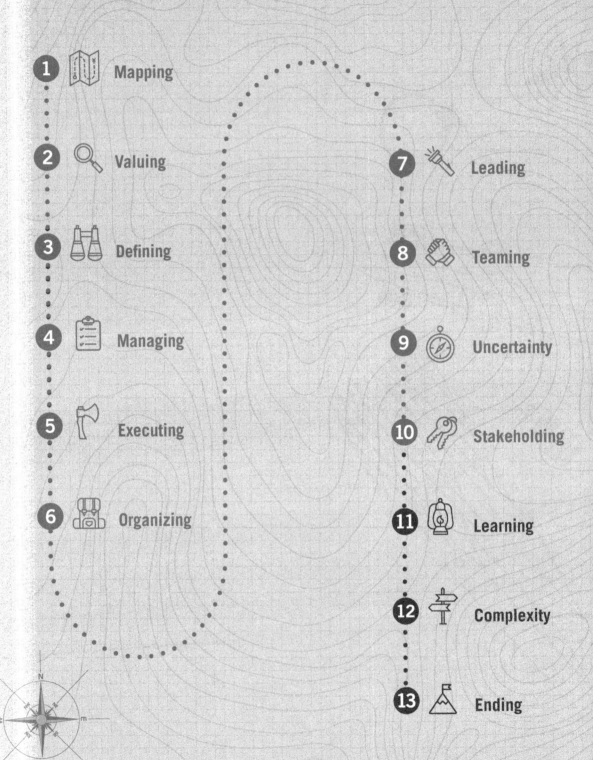

1. Mapping
2. Valuing
3. Defining
4. Managing
5. Executing
6. Organizing
7. Leading
8. Teaming
9. Uncertainty
10. Stakeholding
11. Learning
12. Complexity
13. Ending

10

Collaborating with Stakeholders in Projects

Learning objectives

After reading this chapter, you should:

1 Know what constitutes internal and external stakeholders

2 Know how stakeholders can be identified, analysed and interpreted

3 Understand how and on what basis appropriate interaction strategies can be developed with different types of stakeholders

4 Appreciate the dynamic and continuous processes involved in managing stakeholders throughout the project

5 Understand why it is expedient to work with stakeholders from a value creation perspective

Before you get started

It is the long history of humankind (and animal kind, too) that those who learned to collaborate and improvise most effectively have prevailed.

– Charles Darwin

Introduction

This chapter is about identifying the project's stakeholders, how we can understand them and the strategies we can use in relations with them. Recurring questions related to stakeholder management include which stakeholders should be included in the project work as well as the extent to which they should be included and how their inclusion is to be managed.

Project delivery, ideally, leads to value creation for the client. The likelihood that value will be added increases when more relevant stakeholders are included in the project, such as the users. They can contribute valuable input to the design of the delivery. Incorporating different stakeholders provides them with the opportunity to develop knowledge and attitudes that, subsequently, make it easier to deliver a better outcome, be it a product, process or service.

Projects often have a large number of stakeholders. For those who work in a project, sharing tasks, activities and processes with others can be both *rewarding* and *challenging*. Rewarding, because social relationships are entailed, with more sharing of different forms of knowing and increased opportunities to learn. Challenging, because stakeholders contribute choices, schemes and dreams to projects and expect to be taken into account. Any project thus faces difficult choices. What inputs can or should be taken into account and how is it best to do so? Making changes as a result of input from stakeholders may make it more difficult to complete a project according to the design framework developed at the outset (Kreiner, 1995). Collaborators have a habit of wanting to make contributions and these contributions can disturb existing project routines. This chapter addresses significant ways of dealing with that network of relationships that stakeholders constitute as well as activities and processes related to managing collaboration.

Stakeholders and stakes

Paying attention to stakeholders means embedding the project in relationships with other actors, organizations as well as individuals. Engwall (2003) points out that 'no project is an island'. For the project to be successful and create something valuable, it must be anchored in history, include stakeholders and otherwise be embedded in a larger context. Interacting with stakeholders can accelerate learning and the probabilities of success (Crawford, 2005). Interacting with collaborators can also introduce disorder into project organization as different systems, both soft human relations and hard technological protocols, fail to gel.

Placing the project in multiple relationships in this way can provide new perspectives on many aspects of the project, particularly goals and purposes, as well as how the project should be implemented (Smyth, 2014). At the same time, from Chapter 2, we know that transaction costs associated with coordination and communication escalate with an increasing number of actors (Shenhar, 2001) and that the potential for conflict increases. Nevertheless, any project should include a number of relevant stakeholders if it is to manage the disparate knowledges tangled up in its processes. The project has to deal both with the stakeholders that it wishes to include and those that do not appear to be contributing positively to the project, those that are resisting or otherwise opposing the project. However, resistance can be a source of project learning and should not be automatically opposed or discounted (Courpasson et al., 2012).

Stakeholders

- -

Approaches to understanding **stakeholders** in project contexts are usually based on more general understandings of stakeholders drawn from the strategy literature. Freeman (1984, p. 46) offers a well-known definition of a stakeholder, stating 'a stakeholder is any group or individual who can affect or is affected by the achievement of the organization's objectives', which we have adapted in our definition to a project context.

Stakeholder collaboration is an integral part of project execution as those affected or affecting a project have to be managed. Their impact may be on actual project execution and/or project deliverables (Miles, 2012). Sometimes, stakeholders have interests in both the execution and the delivery

> A **stakeholder** is any actor, whether a person, group or organization that can affect or is affected by the achievement of the project's objectives and expected effects.

(and these interests may be contradictory); sometimes they only have interests related to one or the other. The development of major infrastructure projects in crowded metropolitan areas often engage angry stakeholders, property owners fearful of noise, subsidence, pollution and loss of property values in consequence. The same property owners may subsequently appreciate that the new road or railways makes their commuting much easier. Stakeholders, however, tend to be engaged in the here-and-now effects rather than the promise of a more perfect future. The former they live with every day; the latter is difficult to imagine if you are not the engineers, designers, project managers moving all that dirt, making all that noise, polluting the air 24/7 as the infrastructure is built.

READ THIS!

- -

Stakeholders have recently sprung into focus in US business as Mark Roe (2019) writes when he asks – and answers – why America's CEOs are talking about stakeholder capitalism. He points to changes in the political economy leading to changes in thinking if not yet in practice. M. Roe (2019), ' Why America's CEOs are talking about stakeholder capitalism', Project Syndicate, 4 November 2019, available at: https://study.sagepub.com/pm.

POSITIVE AND NEGATIVE STAKEHOLDERS

Roughly speaking, we can say that stakeholders have *positive* or *negative* interests (or both) in the project and that one can choose to include or exclude their voice in the project. Some stakeholders merit inclusion because they have resources that make project execution or delivery better while others are being held at arm's length because they make it problematic to implement the project, according to its adopted framework (Savage et al., 2010). To be held at arm's length is often the fate of civil society groups mobilizing against a project – even though they may sometimes have positive ideas for improving its value by minimizing its disruption. It may be sensible to include these 'difficult' stakeholders. Doing so may introduce problems for project management by inviting in stakeholders that cannot be managed in the traditional way, through contract; nonetheless, the probability of project success may well be significantly enhanced. Therefore, inviting the resisters to have a role can be worth the challenges it creates. Other times, it may be perceived as inappropriate or impossible; the stakeholders are just too difficult or the project just too closed. Nevertheless, it may be sensible to tie them close, and prevent them from otherwise doing something that is devastating to the project (Eskerod & Jepsen, 2013). As Machiavelli (1961) knew, sometimes keeping your friends close but your enemies closer can be a good strategy.

EXTEND YOUR KNOWLEDGE

All project managers experience tensions and dilemmas. They often relate to stakeholders. Read this article by Boonstra, van Offenbeek, and Vos (2017), 'Tension awareness of stakeholders in large technology projects: A duality perspective', to learn about how you can understand and cope with such tensions through adopting a duality lens. You can also learn about stakeholder roles. You can access the article in the online resources for the book at https://study.sagepub.com/pm.

STAKEHOLDERS AND PROJECT SUCCESS

In general, cooperation with actors outside the project is often necessary. It contributes to knowledge bases, networks, resources and learning (Gulati & Singh, 1998). Costs and uncertainties may also be reduced. In order to make use of such potential resources you will often create networks of relationships, for example in the form of interest alliances, that allow for mutual exploitation and benefit from the different elements that the diverse partners bring to the alliance (Savage et al., 2010).

In the past, stakeholders were mainly managed solely in terms of the probability of project management success increasing. Usually this meant managing the project according to the time, cost and quality framework (Crawford, 2005). Today, the understanding of project success includes the success of the project's product (Miller & Lessard, 2000) for which the quality of stakeholder collaboration can be vital. The question is: How can you work with the stakeholders in a way that enables them to contribute to the relevant delivery of a project outcome?

WATCH THIS!

Watch the YouTube video by Susan Madsen (2015) on 'Dealing with difficult stakeholders', available at: https://study.sagepub.com/pm.

In Chapter 2, we mentioned the politically ambiguous goals that often form the basis for projects. Such goals provide extensive room for interpretation and allow many stakeholders to engage with the project. Keeping various stakeholders engaged can be demanding work. In many cases, it involves an instrumental approach to the stakeholders, one that is necessary because there is little freedom in connection with the design of the project deliverables.

Some stakeholder relations are likely to be conflictual. The project may have certain imperatives associated with it that are injurious for some potential stakeholders. Stakeholders likely to be downsized, made redundant or who have to learn wholly new routines will rarely welcome major change projects, for example. Other times, relations may be much more cooperative: stakeholders' needs can largely be included in the project's execution and delivery so that the project can be regarded as an agent acting on behalf of and protecting stakeholders (Andersen, 2008). We will return to this in the discussion of cooperation strategies.

WATCH THIS!

Sometimes the stakeholders are most unwelcome. Crown Casino's latest construction project was a huge 'high roller' casino on the edge of Sydney Harbour. Crown had a profitable business model flying wealthy Chinese gamblers to Australia to gamble until the Chinese state intervened. ABC's *Four Corners* investigates what went wrong with their business model when the Chinese government decided it was a stakeholder. ABC *Four Corners* (2017), ' Crown Confidential', available at: https://study.sagepub.com/pm.

Picture 10.1   Aswan Dam

Source: Image courtesy of Orlova-tpe, via wikicommons. Shared under the Creative Commons BY-SA 3.0 license.

While identifying and incorporating stakeholders' views early in the project, increasing the potential for benefits realization and value creation, stakeholder management matters not only in the early stages. It must take place throughout the project because the stakeholder landscape is dynamic and changing throughout the project (Mitchell et al., 1997). Stakeholder collaboration is a continuous and recursive process throughout the project process, a process that should be updated in terms of the value being shared at the start of each new phase.

It is impossible to imagine a project without stakeholders (Eskerod & Vaagaasar, 2014). Often, we refer to individuals, groups of individuals or organizations as stakeholders but stakeholders can also include animals as well as nature. Many projects pose extreme risks for ecology and the flora and fauna that inhabit it – think of major dam projects, such as the Aswan Dam in Egypt (Fahim, 2015).

The fact that animals and nature are affected by a project can affect both its execution and the end product it creates. In some projects, the situation related to stakeholders is very demanding, such that stakeholder work becomes a key part of project work. Not all stakeholders must necessarily be handled by the project but it is increasingly common to have both community liasion officers and ecologists involved in major construction projects (Pitsis et al., 2003).

IN PRACTICE

FROGS AND CONSTRUCTION MANAGEMENT

Tryggestad, Justesen, and Mouritsen (2013) tell a story of how frogs were translated from being 'non-existent' into strategic actors in a construction project. They studied a developer who had acquired land and planned to build residential dwellings on it. Since time is of the essence in development projects, the firm was ready to start planning and constructing as soon as the ink on the purchasing agreement dried. However, waterholes were discovered on the site, and soon its residents – 500 protected moor frogs – were identified. The project came to a halt. The frogs, hitherto leading blameless and anonymous semi-aquatic lives in obscurity other than for a few mammalian specialists, became a contested object with several spokespersons claiming to know what was in the frogs' best interests and to speak for them. Such was the articulation of the frogs' interest that the development firm hired their own frog experts as consultants who worked on determining means whereby the frogs could co-exist with the construction workers and trucks and all the noise and destruction of habitat that these would create. That meant learning to adapt to the cyclical time of the frog's life (as opposed to the linear time of project manager's charts) and constructing frog protection devices, such as corridors through which they could move without being bulldozed. The story has a happy ending, when the frogs became themselves strategic protagonists in the marketing campaign to sell the finished buildings in which images of the frogs were used to promote the buildings – who would not want to live in a natural idyll with protected moor frogs? The frog had become a strategic actor shaping the future significantly.

QUESTION

1. Read the article by Tryggestad et al. (2013). In practice, how can we explain the process through which frogs became strategic and powerful? What are the mechanisms that make unconsidered stakeholders strategic?, available in the online resources for the book at https://study.sagepub.com/pm.

Collaborating with stakeholders – an overview

In order to handle stakeholders resourcefully, you need to spend time getting to know them. A stakeholder analysis is often used for this. Based on such an analysis, the project can prioritize which stakeholders it should focus on and how to develop strategies for interaction with these stakeholders (Mitchell et al., 1997). The core of stakeholder collaboration can be seen as a six-step process (see Figure 10.1 below). Although this process may seem relatively sequential in nature, it is clear that the different steps are more or less interwoven. They affect each other.

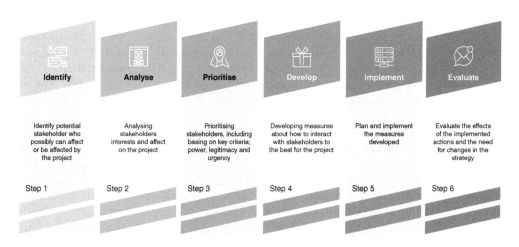

STAKEHOLDER COLLABORATION

A SIX-STEP PROCESS

Identify	Analyse	Prioritise	Develop	Implement	Evaluate
Identify potential stakeholder who possibly can affect or be affected by the project	Analysing stakeholders interests and affect on the project	Prioritising stakeholders, including basing on key criteria; power, legitimacy and urgency	Developing measures about how to interact with stakeholders to the best for the project	Plan and implement the measures developed	Evaluate the effects of the implemented actions and the need for changes in the strategy
Step 1	Step 2	Step 3	Step 4	Step 5	Step 6

Figure 10.1   Stakeholder collaboration – a six-step process

IDENTIFYING STAKEHOLDERS

Efforts to deal with stakeholders usually begin by identifying most of the stakeholders relevant to the project. Here we can use the methods we described in Chapter 8 to identify uncertainty. In order to identify and understand stakeholders, one way is to try and develop a holistic perspective on the project and the environment; not least, this involves taking 'the perspective of others'. A famous headline from *The Times* (22 October 1957) demonstrated a way of not really thinking about the others:

'Heavy Fog in the Channel. Continent Cut Off.'

It may make sense to look at similar projects to assess who the typical stakeholders were on these comparable occasions: Are they likely to be the same in this project? What other factors might be in play, making this project distinctive? Sometimes a distinction is made between internal and external stakeholders (Freeman, 1984). Lettinen & Aaltonen (2020) look at the internal organization of external stakeholders in inter-organizational projects from a value-adding perspective, through governance, values and dynamism. Sometimes, other terms are used, such as direct and indirect stakeholders (Clarkson, 1995) or market and non-market stakeholders (Driessen &

Hillebrand, 2013). These are different ways of referring to stakeholders contractually committed or outside of the project organization.

The internal (direct) stakeholders are actors who are in one way or another directly involved in the project, such as the project owner and management on the client side, and the participants in the project (e.g. suppliers of expertise and other resources). These actors are generally positively tuned in to the project and the project can have a high level of control over how they influence the project. It will be more challenging to identify and control the external stakeholders.

Although project stakeholders vary from project to project, some actors are typical stakeholders in many projects. Regular stakeholders are the owners and sharehold-ers, as well as management at various levels of the organization. Other typical stake-holders are users and customers. The users make demands on the project because the project output, the deliverables, will serve as a useful tool for them, whether it is an office building, an IT system or a work routine. Those who have responsibility for deliveries, those who manage and operate the building, the IT system, etc., are also stakeholders. Whether users are considered as internal or external stakeholders depends on how involved they are in the project. As we will see later, it may be sen-sible for projects to associate external stakeholders as users by making them a part of the project, even if they are not formally contracted to it, for example, by allowing them to be a reference group or a test panel for the project deliveries.

Suppliers, partners and competitors can also have strong interests in the proj-ect. Many projects take an overview of these stakeholders. Often projects may not pay as much attention as they perhaps might to stakeholders such as politicians, public authorities, bureaucrats and other actors who manage regulations, standards and other types of guidelines that the project must relate to. Interest organizations such as trade unions can also provide crucial inputs. Individual stakeholders have different motives (private, commercial and emotional). Financiers, such as credit institutions, as well as media and researchers, are significant stakeholders who must be deal with.

It is crucial that the project team develops an overview of which stakeholders are involved and how best to manage them. It is often the project manager who has the primary responsibility for identifying stakeholders. However, it is common for the rest of the project team to be included in this work in the form of idea work processes (Carlsen et al., 2012; Coldevin et al., 2019). In order to establish a complete picture of the various stakeholders it makes sense to include project owners and participants in the steering group, in order to tap into their knowledge of actors for whom the project may have a relevance that might otherwise be overlooked. It may also be advisable to reflect on who the stakeholders may be, given their organizational attachment to the project (such as those who come from the state, municipality or private sector) or which subjects are considered relevant to the project (e.g. architect, building engineer and technology consultant).

READ THIS!

Read the article to learn about Polish responsible business practices: https://study.sagepub.com/pm

Picture 10.2   A typical silent stakeholder

Source: Anne Live Vaagaasar

ANALYSING STAKEHOLDERS

After the stakeholders have been identified, they can be analysed in order to develop customized interaction strategies. Below are some main areas for such analyses:

1. What are their main interests in the project? Are they attached to:

    a. Special issues?
    b. Phases in the execution?
    c. Final deliverance?

2. Do they most likely have positive or negative attitudes to the project?

    a. Can they be expected to cooperate?
    b. Moreover, will they probably have a significant impact on the project if they want to do so?

3. Do you have the relevant resources for the project to be able to manage these stakeholders (for example, technical, economic, knowledge-based or socio-cultural)?

4. How do these stakeholders tend to work to safeguard their interests? Do they tend to:

    a. Strive for cooperation?
    b. Act positively or negatively?
    c. Use the media to win?
    d. Create coalitions to strengthen their position?

WHAT KIND OF RELATIONSHIP IS POSSIBLE?

By looking at stakeholders' interests, attitudes, resources and orientation, one can assess what kind of relationship it is possible and desirable to have with a given stakeholder. In extending what the project regards as a possible and desirable relationship (given any input from the stakeholder) the project team can begin to develop strategies for furthering their involvement with the project.

WATCH THIS!

Watch a video on stakeholder mapping by Colin Gautrey (2017) and think how to apply it as a project manager at: https://study.sagepub.com/pm.

There are several different frameworks for analysing stakeholders, and often they are based on resource dependence perspectives (e.g. Pfeffer and Salancik's (1978) very familiar perspective) between the project and the stakeholder. Such a framework, which is widely used, is based on two questions (Frooman, 1999):

- Is the project dependent on the stakeholder?
- Is the stakeholder dependent on the project?

If the project is dependent on a given stakeholder, for example if there is a scarcity of expertise within a field of study that is absolutely necessary for the project, it means that the stakeholder has potentially greater power over the project. The degree of power can change over time, across areas and with events.

Similar questions that are common to stakeholder analysis include: (1) What opportunity does the stakeholder have to influence the project? (2) What are the opportunities for cooperation between the two parties? (Savage et al., 1991, inspired by Freeman's [1984] fundamental work related to stakeholder strategies). There are four different combinations of these dimensions (impact and cooperation), which provide four categories of stakeholders (see Figure 10.2).

		Power, potential for threat	
		Low	High
Potential for cooperation	Low	Type: Marginal Strategy: Monitor	Type: Non-supportive Strategy: Defend
	High	Type: Supportive Strategy: Involve	Type: Mixed Blessing Strategy: Collaborate

Figure 10.2 Categorization of type of stakeholder, depending on power, and potential for cooperation

Some call such analyses *harm-and-help analyses*. In short, the project is more dependent on some individual stakeholders than others and some stakeholders have greater potential to contribute positively or harm the project. Based on this type of analysis, the project team can develop strategies to meet the stakeholders' interests (see page 367).

Stakeholders have free will (Barnard, 1938); the project does not control them. Also, what they want will change over time (Kreiner, 1995). Project management cannot dictate to stakeholders but they can try to influence stakeholders to act in the best possible way for the project. When the project team plans the project's execution and deliveries, they often act as if stakeholders can largely be controlled (Eskerod & Vaagaasar, 2014). They tend to believe that they can control their surroundings, including stakeholders (Engwall, 2003).

WHAT IS IMPORTANT TO THE STAKEHOLDER?

The analysis of the stakeholder should contain reflections about what the stakeholders expects to get back for their efforts in the project and what a given stakeholder perceives as fair.

Basically, stakeholders will operate in their own interests. They will evaluate the part of the project they are interested in, considering the consequences it will have for them. They will measure the estimated cost by attempting to influence their field of interest in the project against expected dividends (Eskerod & Jepsen, 2013). Assessments of their efforts in a project, however, will not be isolated. Stakeholders will consider whether they have sufficient inducements for their participation in light of what they perceive other stakeholders enjoy. Often, several stakeholders in a project have contact with each other beyond the boundaries of the project, such that they can compare contributions and rewards and assess the fairness of these. The perception of whether the share is fair depends on three factors: (1) the distribution of benefits, (2) procedures and (3) the interaction.

Initially, stakeholders will typically try to maximize their benefits. However, they will often accept less than the maximum if the deal seems fair compared to what others receive (in light of the effort). If decisions are made on the most objective basis and seem reasonable, stakeholders tend to accept less dividends compared to efforts outlaid. The experience of being treated with respect can also help to reduce their demands. It is often about being asked, being adequately informed and being treated with dignity.

Stakeholders often consider their actions in light of how they see their own identity. They will rarely participate in a project that they see as diminishing their identity. If the project seeks to influence the stakeholder, the choice of strategies requires evaluation in light of the actor's assumed social identity. The project managers must, therefore, motivate relevant stakeholders to participate in the project. They can be proactive and explicitly seek collaboration (Savage et al., 1991). In order to inspire participation, it may be sensible to show that you are willing to compromise on what matters to the stakeholders in question as a sign that you have trust and goodwill to initiate a positive trust spiral (see also Chapter 8).

IN PRACTICE

EUROPEAN CITY OF CULTURE PROGRAMME

One significant European Union institution is the European City of Culture programme. In 2014 the most northerly European city thus far, in the far north of Sweden, Umeå became a Capital of Culture. Stakeholder tensions were present that would not be apparent in most other

(Continued)

Capitals of Culture. The far north is the traditional home of the Sami people, whose reindeer herds roam the tundra. The Sami were featured in the Capitals of Culture project for Umeå in ways that positioned them as examples of exotic semi-nomadic forms of life quite distinct from mainstream urban cultures. Although the project sought to include the Sami as a valuable indigenous culture, subsequent discussion of their role in the Capital of Culture highlighted tensions between being treated only as window-dressing, engaging the Sami people as exotica, with a visualization of Sami culture as a repressed history, a history in danger of never being remembered in its own terms.

Buried deep were issues that many preferred to forget: the ban on the Sami language being spoken in schools; the exclusion of the Sami from the mineral and timber exploitation of the far north; the adverse impact of Swedish eugenics, very prevalent in the inter-war years, which led to the sterilization of Sami women and the treatment of the people as specimens rather than humans possessing the full panoply of human rights (Broberg & Roll-Hansen, 1996; Weingart, 1999). Swedish settlers were encouraged to move to and populate the northern regions through incentives such as rights to access land and water, tax allowances and military exemptions, encroaching on traditional lands, rights and recognition. In the Capital of Culture as a celebration of 'European culture', the Sami were narrated in terms of an exotic and marginal status to that culture, confected as something assumed to be homogeneous.

Picture 10.3   Sami culture

An example of their 'difference' is the eight Sami seasons based on the life of the Sami community that were used when framing the programme. The division of the Sami calendar formed by Sami's nomadic heritage of moving reindeer herds in order to feed them represents the rhythm of nature and the climate conditions in this far northern part of Europe. Each season (translated in the Sami/Swedish/English languages) built a theme for the Capital of Culture year and became a sorting mechanism for the programme activities. However, the contrast between the Sami's regionally embedded seasonality and the overlay of the European 'four seasons' only served to show how the Sami were paradoxical for European memorialization because, in recognition of their marginal status, they were constituted as something *other* to the European project of a common culture serving as a basis for ever-closer integration.

As formalized in the report for the second monitoring and advisory meeting for the European Capitals of Culture 2014, in addition to 'its strong focus on northern Swedish thematic lines, the Panel considers that Umeå 2014 should also better highlight the European features of Umeå being the European Capital of Culture 2014 and the European aspects of its programme'. In no other Capital of Culture would this tension between *European* and *other* be faced so squarely because in few European cities is the legacy of an indigenous people still alive. The temporary event could neither exclude nor wholly incorporate the Sami; its treatment of them as a marginal other neither wholly in nor out of that project had an enduring impact. For Sami leaders, it marked another stage in a struggle for greater recognition of their specificity, one that was in important political respects at odds with the integrative aspects of the European project. Subsidiarity was far closer to their aims than integration. The memory of the Sami past was keying in to a temporary project organization triggering topics that the enduring organization of the municipality and political organization preferred to forget or keep latent. (More information on the project can be found in Wåhlin, Kapsali, Näsholm, and Blomquist, 2016.)

QUESTION

1. When confronted with 'others' with a significant history of 'othering' on the part of authorities yet who will be represented in a major project, what are some of the significant steps that should be followed by the project leaders?

It is not enough to motivate the stakeholder to participate in the project. The interested party must also be able to participate appropriately. Before you dedicate extensive effort to stakeholder participation, it is crucial to assess the stakeholder's knowledge and skills. Are they such that the stakeholder can be involved in a valuable way? If the answer is no but the contribution of the stakeholder is critical to the project, the challenge is to ensure that the stakeholder contributes appropriately through providing information and training. For example, if a subcontractor has signed a contract, it may be profitable to maintain the relationship, even if he or she needs to be taught or taken over some of the tasks the subcontractor should perform. This may be the case if there is scarcity of the supplier's expertise in the market. Another example may be the training of future users to express their needs as the project moves closer to delivery and value creation potential is increased.

In many projects, it is a significant challenge to get stakeholders to participate appropriately. It is an issue that should be taken seriously; assess which stakeholders should be skilled up, how this can be done, what motivates the different stakeholders and what actions the project has to increase the motivation for participation. Many project teams focus too much attention on stakeholders who supposedly could ruin the project's execution, at the expense of efforts to engage those stakeholders who can contribute positively to the project.

WATCH THIS!

Watch the video on how to engage stakeholders from Mike Clayton (2019) who offers five tips for stakeholder engagement at: https://study.sagepub.com/pm.

WHAT WOULD YOU DO?

You are trying to implement a new software solution for handling purchasing and logistics across seven fashion retailers. To make sure that you create a software solution and related procedures that are functional you need to involve multiple stakeholders, including some of the employees working in these shops, to test the different technical solutions and discuss procedures. Many of them are students working part time. Some of them don't see the point of doing this and refrain from participating. You find this to be a problem, as you really need their input. After a while, you manage to get five of the part-time students, across two shops, to participate. The manager in one of the shops encourages them to participate. The managers of the other shops say, I am happy for you to be involved in this as long as you do it in your time, not mine. The students then say they are not willing to participate for the benefit of the store without being paid for it.

QUESTIONS

1. Would you try to influence the opinion of the managers or the students?

2. Would you offer the students compensation? Or would you just keep developing the solution with only the two students that are interested in contributing?

PRIORITIZING STAKEHOLDERS

You will potentially interact with a large number of stakeholders, a situation that may be overwhelming. Often, priority should be given to dealing with some stakeholders, parcelling out how much attention other various stakeholders should receive. Managing stakeholders effectively requires a little Machiavellianism, as not all stakeholders are as critical for the project you are charged with delivering as they think themselves to be.

Three characteristics of the stakeholders can act as key criteria in prioritizing. These are *power, legitimacy* and *urgency* (Mitchell et al., 1997). Do stakeholders hold key positions in the circuits of power? How extensive are their power relations into the project and into external networks? How significant are these networks likely to be for project success? How legitimate are the claims that the stakeholders are making in terms of the project? How can you frame their claims as being more or less legitimate, depending on strategy? What are the institutional bases of their legitimacy? Given the stage of project phases, how urgent is it that the interests they claim to be representing should be attended to? How seamless or fissured are these interests – are the coalitions of interest likely to hold for long? The answers given to these questions say something both about the choice of strategy and what stakeholders should prioritize (Clegg, Carter, et al., 2019). Figure 10.3, derived from Mitchell et al. (1997), describes this situation.

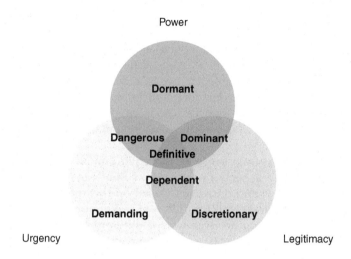

Figure 10.3   Classification of stakeholders

Source: Mitchell et al., 1997

WHO SHOULD BE GIVEN PRIORITY?

Those stakeholders that analysis reveals as having only one of the characteristics can be considered potentially latent stakeholders, depending on the urgency, power and legitimacy of their representations of interest. Such stakeholders should not be prioritized but monitored. Stakeholders who have all three characteristics (the definitive) and also those with two characteristics (those with expectations) are worth prioritizing. Nonetheless, the situation is always in process, dynamic, potentially uncertain. Stakeholder salience can quickly change. Relatively uninterested stakeholders that are powerful and legitimate actors may be enrolled by other stakeholders with less legitimacy and a weaker position in the circuits of power relations, perhaps because of an intersection of interests or networks. It may also be the case that a stakeholder has demands whose legitimacy is acceded to and that are ongoing (urgency) but they have little purchase on the circuits of power; they control no 'obligatory passage points' as far as the project's priorities are concerned, being unable to structure agendas or make decisions (Clegg, 1989). If the project processes change so that these stakeholders become more central to the project's circuits of power – perhaps because they have valuable, rare, inimitable and non-substitutable capabilities essential for the project at this phase, capabilities whose absence leaves a key uncertainty unaddressed – then the stakeholder shifts from being a dependant to becoming a definite stakeholder.

The nature/position of a stakeholder commonly changes due to the alliance formation among stakeholders and the recasting of action nets (Czarniawska, 2004). As the temporality of the project shifts or it moves into new spaces of action then the action nets it needs to construct and stabilize, change. A stakeholder that might previously have been a dependent stakeholder becomes more critical; shifting alliances among stakeholders reposition the actions nets being constructed – both by the project and by those that are or would be stakeholders in the project. Mass or social media might articulate a 'human interest' story that reflects ill on project priorities by highlighting indifference to or harm done to legitimate interests, thus empowering them, however briefly, with a sense of urgency as an issue that has to be fixed. Often the fix consists of taking the news off the front pages or the re-tweets. Throughout the project's life which stakeholders should receive the most attention will be highly variable with a high degree of flexibility and surveillance of the stakeholder scene required, monitoring media, meetings and mobilizations. Some stakeholder urgency will require immediate address; the extent to which they will receive address depends on the project's resources, the temporality of the issues in question as well as the effectiveness of the environmental scanning embedded in the project's capabilities.

The project's overall reconnaissance of the environment needs to include stakeholders, determining those aspects of the project they can influence and how this may affect project processes and outcomes. Based on this intelligence, strategies can be developed to prioritize and minimize different stakeholder concerns. Establishing a stakeholder matrix providing an overview of different types of consequences for different stakeholders, as in Figure 10.4 below, may be a useful tool.

Consequences / Stakeholder	Techno-logical	Legal	Social	Psychological	Economical	Other
Management						
Employees						
Owners						
Customers						
Suppliers						
Competitors						
Public Government						
Employee unions						
Others						

Figure 10.4   Stakeholder matrix

Projects would be wise to document their stakeholder analysis and relations if only because it is a useful resource in case of potential litigation. Such documentation may become useful to later projects that need reference points for their stakeholder management. In long-term projects, how shifting sense was made of the project's stakeholder collaboration over time and how stakeholders had changing impacts on the project along the way, is good archival data. Not only subsequent projects but also interested researchers might find such archives of value.

IN PRACTICE

BUILDING A ROAD

The decision about where to place a road in large construction projects is often quite a controversial matter and involves detailed planning and politics. When the decision is made, it is very seldom that stakeholders manage to change it again. From the newspapers we can learn about an exceptional case where one man in Norway managed to do so after the construction work had started. The drilling and moving of construction loads created dirt, dust and noise and the man found this most disruptive. He approached the project management multiple times over a period of time (urgency), but they did not do anything about it. He then approached the asthma association and convinced them to help him fight for his cause (legitimacy). The man and the asthma association together approached the newspapers to write about this (power). A short time after the newspaper articles, the project started working on how to adapt the alignment of the road to be further away from the man's property and it was moved.

QUESTION

1. The project manager of the road construction was censured by his organization for allowing the story to become front-page news, thus reflecting badly on the organization's legitimacy. What strategy could he have taken to avoid this outcome and what might its implications have been?

Interacting with stakeholders

We have discussed the first three steps in stakeholder collaboration above. In practice, it is impossible to separate these three steps from one another. They are interwoven. Nevertheless, we sought to separate them analytically because all three steps represent significant areas of attention in stakeholder collaboration. There are subsequent steps, however, involving the development of measures for interaction, planning and execution of measures, and evaluation of measures that are more intertwined; thus, it is most appropriate to treat them together.

Based on the analysis of the degree and type of resource dependency (see Figure 10.2), the project manager and team may begin to think of strategies to handle the various stakeholders. Below we present four different interaction strategies. They start with analysis and categorization to identify stakeholders as marginal, supportive, non-supportive and mixed (Freeman, 1984). Projects can have much to learn from such interactions.

-   *Marginal stakeholders* (small impact and little cooperation) require least project attention. They should be monitored for their continuing marginality; where necessary the project might wish to activate or neutralize them as project priorities shift as their interest-representations and know-how shift in utility. Systematic surveillance of stakeholders when major changes are occurring, decisions are being taken, or critical events occupy the project's attention, is advisable. If you think the stakeholders' status may become more significant for the project as time elapses it is advisable to keep them informed about the project's progress. Since such stakeholders are considered marginal, methods that are not too demanding of project resources, such as social media, should be used (Clegg, 2019; Ninan et al., 2019; Ninan & Mahalingam, 2017; Ninan et al., 2019).

- *Supportive stakeholders* (small impact and much cooperation) are those that have only limited impact on the project, but that seek to cooperate. As such, they can be a source of knowledge, networks or other contributions and should be involved, informed and consulted about opportunities for cooperation and value creation. Consultation groups, reference groups or test panels can be stacked with these stakeholders.

- *Non-supportive stakeholders* (high impact and little cooperation) are usually demanding and a source of problems for project execution. Several strategies can be considered. A protective strategy would minimize dependence on such stakeholders. A cooptive strategy would seek to enrol such stakeholders into being supporters through cooptation (Selznick, 1949). Such a strategy can be demanding both in time and in terms of other resources as opponents have to be persuaded, bribed, cajoled or seduced into becoming friends of the project, perhaps through offering them positions of legitimated authority, status or some other honour – the 'ragged trousered philanthropist' strategy (Tressell, 1978). Often, establishing a dialogue in itself can be demanding with such stakeholders. It may require considerable effort, combined with knowledge of what appeals to the other, as well as sensitivity associated with hearing and interpreting the group's expression of its interests and finding a way of binding these to the project. You will have to balance how much time and other resources one can spend on non-supportive stakeholders. If there is little sign that they will change, the protection strategy is more appropriate. Either way, this category of stakeholders should be kept close at hand and well informed, as Machiavelli advises. The project should be careful to adapt its communication to the perceived interests of each and every stakeholder within this category in considering which of the stakeholders should be informed about what key decisions and how.

- *Mixed stakeholders* (significant influence and much cooperation) must be given most attention since they have a high impact while at the same time presenting excellent opportunities for cooperation. Collaboration could, for example, include them in the formal project organization (in the team, reference groups, project councils or steering groups) or in the project network, making them ambassadors for the project. Good formal as well as informal relationships and clear communication are necessary. Creating a community of practice that entails project learning will help the relationship become more supportive (Wenger, 1998). A stakeholder challenging the project before it is even initiated can become a decisive actor when decision-making brings them into a community of practice.

EXTEND YOUR KNOWLEDGE

Read the article by Davis (2018) 'Reconciling the views of project success: A multiple stakeholder model' to understand that what counts as project success and failure is a result of the interpretations used to gauge success by multiple stakeholder groups. You can access the article in the online resources for the book at https://study.sagepub.com/pm.

Picture 10.4   Who do you count as the important stakeholder?

Source: Image courtesy of www.kremlin.ru. Provided under the Creative Commons Attribution 4.0 International license via wikicommons)

WIN–WIN AND WIN–LOSE STRATEGIES?

There are many strategies for dealing with stakeholders. We cannot review all of them but merely note that there are often six main strategies that divide into two broad categories of win–win and win–lose (Savage et al., 2010; see Figure 10.5).

Win–win strategies	Seeking mutual adjustment
	Educating and preparing the stakeholder in contributing to the project
	Following the interests/wishes of the stakeholder
	Leading the stakeholder in supporting the project
Win–lose strategies	Isolating the project from the stakeholder
	Persuading the stakeholder to act in the project's interests

Figure 10.5   Win–win and win–lose strategies

The first four strategies are interaction-oriented in nature and often contribute to win–win situations. With some adjustments you can create the desired outcomes for the client without sacrificing the stakeholder's interests. The other two strategies represent more of a win–lose logic (Savage et al., 2010).

Research has shown that more interaction-oriented strategies are often combined with less friendly strategies (Vaagaasar, 2011). Project teams with many relationships with the same stakeholder can use both metaphorical sticks and carrots to create the most efficient relationship, in a good cop/bad cop strategy. Strategies can also be used sequentially in the same relationship because experience changes over time so that at some time it is appropriate to isolate while at other times more appropriate to lead the stakeholder to the preferred course of action of the project, sometimes through mutual adaptation (Eskerod & Vaagaasar, 2014).

In a large public technology project one of us studied, the project team changed the perception and strategies for handling the subcontractor. Early in the project, there was general optimism that had a spillover effect on how the supplier was considered. In the tender competition, the supplier was considered very competent and reliable. Throughout the process, the supplier showed an inability to produce deliverables, with those provided often being inadequate. Along the way, they received both praise and criticism, threats of fines and demanded structural changes in the organization and the replacement of key personnel. At the same time, the project performed work for the supplier (documentation), taught the supplier (including in project planning and technical fields) and attempted to lead the supplier into the particular context (public administration) in which this project was based. There was joint team development and social activities at the operational level and at the management level contract dimensions and consequences for breach of contract were discussed. A variety of planned strategies and more 'random' situational strategies were observed (Eskerod & Vaagaasar, 2014).

DYNAMIC AND CUSTOMIZED COLLABORATING

The example above shows that stakeholder collaboration is in practice an emergent process, on the basis of analysis, strategies are chosen that have consequences. Based on these consequences, the next strategic will be chosen, more or less consciously (Vaagaasar, 2011). Strategy is a process that is always open because so much depends on the moves that others, that cannot be controlled, might make. General strategies for stakeholder work have to be gradually adapted to the specific stakeholder and development process in relationships between the project and stakeholders. Be aware of these processual aspects, with their inherent political possibilities, rather than assuming a linear and rational relationship that can be mechanically planned and controlled. One mistake in practice is not being willing to see signs of change and act as planned, even though the plan was based on terms that are no longer valid (Kreiner, 1995).

If the project team is willing to be responsive to signals from stakeholders and tries to adapt its interaction pattern, members will be able to develop relational skills that enable them to communicate in a more targeted way with stakeholders and involve them in the most relevant activities at an appropriate time in the schedule. By gradually learning about the interest being represented you can design and target messages. Stories are an instrument used to align stakeholders with many different interests in the same direction because stories play on emotions and create an overall image. Both audiences and stories 'which hit' can promote motivation. At the same time, stories provide room for interpretation so that stakeholders can identify with them (Vaagaasar, 2006).

In other words, stakeholder collaboration is a political process of development and emergence in which strategies are deployed and adjusted as relations pan out and stakeholders respond to what the project team does (Bedwell et al., 2012). For the project team it is a learning process in which they monitor how processes evolve and maintain an ethical concern with proceedings. One must ensure that the processes undertaken can withstand the light of the day. Maintaining cohesive and coherent signalling with the many stakeholders that may well maintain a dialogue with each other means that these collaborations must pass the transparency test.

IN PRACTICE

INTERACTING WITH STAKEHOLDERS

In interacting with stakeholders, you will find that they often come up with a (great) number of suggestions about how to change the delivery or methods of the project, in a way that they find better, which can be quite overwhelming. One can seldom attend to all these suggestions, as it takes time and costs money to do so. Sometimes it can be difficult to know what stakeholders really want for future benefit realization and what they just feel would be nice but not necessary to have.

QUESTION

1.   How would you go about discerning and discriminating among the different requests?

Mo	**MUST HAVE** – THE MOST VITAL THINGS TO INCLUDE
S	**SHOULD HAVE** – THINGS TO BE INCLUDED, IF POSSIBLE
Co	**COULD HAVE** – NICE TO INCLUDE, BUT NOT CRITICAL
W	**WON'T HAVE** – NOT THIS TIME, GET BACK TO THIS LATER

Figure 10.6   Prioritize requirements – MoSCoW analysis

WATCH THIS!

Watch a YouTube video by Susanne Madsen (2017) introducing the MoSCoW technique (Figure 10.6) at: https://study.sagepub.com/pm.

COLLABORATING WITH STAKEHOLDERS: A SHORT AND LONG PERSPECTIVE

In assessing appropriate strategies for interaction with stakeholders, the project involves stakeholders in larger networks of relationships. Stakeholders can form alliances, thereby changing relations of power, urgency and legitimacy (Mitchell et al., 1997). Stakeholders, in turn, also have stakeholders that may be removed and at a distance from the project but whose influence may be felt indirectly as it is translated through those stakeholders of whom the project is aware (Cropanzano, Bowen, & Gilliland, 2007). Stakeholder collaboration is always dynamic and likely to change, sometimes in ways that will not be immediately obvious.

Assessments of how to interact with stakeholders should also be considered in light of whether relationships are recurring. Although an occasion might be the first time a project relates to a given stakeholder there may be others in the project partners that have had a prior relationship with this stakeholder. They can be a source

Picture 10.5 One Central Park, Sydney

Source: Image courtesy of David Stanley, via flickr.com. Shared under the Creative Commons BY 2.0 license.

of valuable intelligence. When an interaction with a specific stakeholder is novel, consider how actions in the here-and-now may influence potential future interaction beyond the life cycle of an individual project. We often think short term and transactionally about what and how we will get something out of a relationship. Longer-term interests may temper transactional tendencies; where the interaction is clearly a one-off transaction it may be worth forcing a result in the short term because in the longer term collaboration with the stakeholder is unlikely to occur on further occasions.

Many of the coordination mechanisms and other interventions discussed in Chapter 6 are in practice also useful in managing stakeholder cooperation, such as plans, roles, routines related to information sharing and other interactions. Deploying milestones and deadlines can promote interaction, knowledge sharing and common problem solving, clarifying those points where actors will mobilize around issues, interests and schedules. For example, research has shown that deadlines can encourage projects to seek collaboration with stakeholders they depend on in order to arrive at decisions needed to drive the project forward.

IN PRACTICE

DECORATING PUBLIC BUILDINGS

The decoration of public buildings is often done with plants and small green trees, providing a pleasant environment for the people working there as well as for visitors. Additionally, it aids sustainability and demonstrates that the building occupants are engaged in an environmentally friendly way. It is good business for the producers of these plants and creates a number of work positions, related not only to producing them but also for interior decorators and exterior landscapers, as well as for the maintenance of the plants in peak condition. On the other hand, production and preservation of these plants often involves using fertilizers, the production of which may not good for the ecology. Likewise, these plants, although beautiful, may not be so good for people that are asthmatic and often have an allergic reaction to their seeds or flowers. In other words, a simple plant can have a number of positive and negative stakeholders attached to them.

QUESTION

1.   Think about the potential stakeholders in these nature projects and draw up a list of them: which would you consider the most critical and why?

Stakeholder involvement in different phases of the project

We have talked about developing specific strategies for interaction with differently strategized stakeholders. Stakeholder collaboration in practice is a process that evolves over time and varies from stage to stage in project execution and as it changes so will strategies. How to work with the various stakeholders in the different phases has a significant impact on the success of the project.

In line with the emphasis on value creation, early planning for benefits realization and making individuals and groups accountable is increasingly emphasized (see Chapter 4). Many of the steps below are typically included in plans for benefits realization.

THE CONCEPT PHASE

At the beginning of the project, it is crucial to use stakeholders to map out requirements, establish overall requirements and encourage idea work (Carlsen et al., 2012; Coldevin et al., 2019). The stakeholders contribute to developing analysis of project requirements. During this phase, stakeholders can also provide input regarding other related (competing) initiatives in progress. These inputs can form the basis for an overall picture of the project's opportunities as well as its risks, especially in projects that involve extensive acquisitions, where the mapping of requirements provides premises for design of acquisitions.

THE PLANNING PHASE

In the next phase of the project, how stakeholders can contribute to the definition and anchoring of the project's goals is a major consideration. A representative selection of stakeholders can be included in the process of identifying and analysing uncertainties likely to arise, with internal stakeholders playing a significant role. It is crucial, for example, that execution plans can be anchored to identification of specific suppliers of expertise and resources, to ensure the most realistic and feasible plan. Then this will be a plan that also reflects competence, capacity and commitment (see Chapter 7) of significant resources. This applies both when the project draws on external resources and when it retrieves resources from its own business (see resource allocation syndrome that we discussed earlier in Chapter 6).

Suppliers may also help investigate and identify possible solutions to issues with project delivery. Internal stakeholders in the form of representatives of the principal play a central role in this phase. They can provide input for planning the project by focusing on the key decision points to ensure that the necessary decisions are covered and that the project is run in the best possible way from the perspective of their product or service provision (decision efficiency and quality discussed in Chapter 3). Commitment is the basis for the interaction between stakeholders at both interpersonal and interorganizational levels (Morgan & Hunt, 1994) and serves to counteract opportunistic behaviour. Suppliers that are critical for project management success and project productiveness may assume specific roles, responsibilities and authority in the project. In more concrete terms, providing information about the project, delivery and future processes and planning is often the basis for communication with stakeholders in this phase. Additionally, discuss with stakeholders how they want to be involved in and affect the execution phase of the project.

THE EXECUTING PHASE

Once the project has moved forward to the execution phase, the task of internal stakeholders, both on the assignment and supplier side, is mainly concerned with acting according to agreements forged in the planning phase. Where what was planned is not possible or desirable to carry out on the part of stakeholders, they must maintain clear communication with the project. During the execution phase, stakeholders (such as users and managers of the delivery, as well as professional experts) can be significant contributors to the quality assurance of the delivery. They can participate in test panels, reference groups and expert panels. Anchoring and involvement with stakeholders increase the potential to mobilize them if necessary.

The various stakeholders should be followed up continuously in the execution phase. The frequency of the interaction depends, as previously mentioned, on the characteristics of the stakeholders and the degree of change in the project (its solutions) and its surroundings. The execution phase is often characterized by requests for changes from stakeholders. They often want other solutions when they see delivery materialized or they want the project to deliver more than the defined and planned scope. As discussed in Chapter 2, this often means an increase in the scope of both the delivery and the project. Assessment depends on the kind of decision, which will sometimes be located in professional staff outside the project, while at other times it will be at the project owner level (if it goes beyond the project's charter). If it is within the charter, it is often handled at the project level. For a more detailed discussion of this, see Chapter 6 on organizing.

EXTEND YOUR KNOWLEDGE

Read the article by Recker, Holten, Hummel, and Rosenkranz (2017), 'How agile practices impact customer responsiveness and development success: A field study', which discusses how agile practices impact on customer responsiveness and development success in projects, available in the online resources for the book at https://study.sagepub.com/pm.

THE FINAL PHASE – ENDING THE PROJECT

When the project is near completion some stakeholders will receive and manage the delivered outcome, a significant interface. A common mistake is that attention to handing over the delivery comes very late in the project. To maximize benefit realization attention should be paid to this from the first day of the project. Those who are to realize the benefits should be involved in the planning of *how* the benefits should be realized, how they should be measured and what responsibilities different roles have for benefits realization. In order to ensure value creation, it is crucial that the project meets or exceeds an unambiguous description of the project's deliverables and how profit is to be realized from the process.

In the final phase it is worth reflecting on the participants in the project team, maintaining the focus of their roles and obligations on what is to be done. It is a well-known phenomenon that project participants tend to focus attention on tasks outside the project in the final phase (for example, those new projects they are about to start) at the expense of completion of the project. The project manager should ensure the participants commit to completing the project and that their line manager enables them to do so.

WHAT WOULD YOU DO?

To move the project forward you must keep the coalition of stakeholders together. They can have divergent interest. One way to do this is through storytelling, something that is much needed in the technological futures being envisaged for us. There are many articles in the popular press generating moral panic about jobs being taken over by robots.

It's crucial to bring a sense of social and environmental responsibility to budding designers and engineers, but how? For one thing, we need a new paradigm for thinking about and designing technology.

One such paradigm is offered by technological stewardship, which refers broadly to 'behaviour that ensures technology is used to make the world a better place for all: more equitable, inclusive, just and sustainable'. It was put forward by the Engineering Change Lab (ECL), a national initiative launched in collaboration with Engineers Canada, Engineers Without Borders and other university, private and public sector partners. ECL has been hosting workshops across the country to encourage deeper conversations about the role engineering should play in guiding the development of technology.

Technological stewardship calls for those who create and influence technology to adopt a more responsible leadership role, arguing for an expansion in how engineers and others see their contributions. Stepping up to that role also involves expanding who participates in decisions about technological design and propagation and which perspectives are considered in design decisions.

The ECL offers Technological Stewardship Principles that describe clear yardsticks for actions, structures, decisions and results. The principles identified by the ECL embody values such as collaboration, inclusivity and responsibility.

Other than the ECL, there has been a proliferation of principle-based declarations about the use of AI and other powerful and potentially disruptive technologies. These include the Canadian Tech for Good Declaration and the Safe Face Pledge sponsored by the Algorithmic Justice League at the Massachusetts Institute of Technology.

CRITICAL CONVERSATIONS

Cynics might see pledges and declarations to be meaningless window dressing, but I see value in those attempts to think more critically about technology. Such conversations are signs of our

(Continued)

collective and sincere willingness to express what we value while also being agile in the face of profound change.

Those conversations are crucial in engineering schools, yet a provocative study suggests that engineering students may actually experience a decrease in social and political concern over the course of their professional education. University of Michigan sociologist Erin Cech refers to this as a culture of disengagement that undergirds many engineering programmes.

But even here there are signs of change: The National Council of Deans of Engineering and Applied Science recently adopted the Calgary Declaration of the Future of Engineering Education. Among other things, this expresses many of the principles associated with technological stewardship.

My home institution of Memorial University is in the midst of incorporating the principles of technological stewardship into our curriculum, from the first-year experience up through to graduation. In partnership with ECL we are aiming to move the needle further in a direction that ensures that technology is made to be as beneficial as possible.

VALUING STEWARDSHIP

If we are serious about technological stewardship in the Fourth Industrial Revolution, design competitions could be an effective way to plant those seeds.

The concept of technological stewardship is still in development, but members of the Engineering Change Lab want to help spark a national conversation not just among engineering professionals and educators, but society at large. At the cusp of the Fourth Industrial Revolution, that conversation matters more than ever before.

Source: Case adapted from Janna Rosales (2019), 'Teaching social and environmental responsibility to engineering students will provide them with valuable skills required for the Fourth Industrial Revolution'. *The Conversation*, 21 August. You can access this at https://study.sagepub.com/pm.

QUESTION

1. What technological stewardship strategies would you use to keep a technology project positive in terms of stakeholder perceptions?

Awareness about the aggregation level and the nuances of interaction with stakeholders

We have already talked about the use of different strategies towards the same stakeholder. Often, stakeholders are treated as if they were a singular actor, even though they may actually be a group (or several groups) collected by a stakeholder label (Vaagaasar, 2006). This applies especially when we refer to entire organizations as one interested party. There are many individuals, departments and other groupings in the same organization. They may have quite different interests or characteristics (such as power, legitimacy and urgency).

For example, the subcontractor is a critical internal stakeholder in many projects. Often, the relationship with an entrepreneurial subcontractor needs to be considered and a strategy developed for managing the interaction. In practice, large projects may involve many (perhaps several hundred) actors interacting in relationships at many levels between the project and the contractor. The relationships can be at many different levels, such as at the senior management level, the project manager level and the operational level, each level having different characteristics.

The project team decides the level of aggregation for managing a certain stakeholder. Early in a relationship, the other party is quite concrete in their identity but as the work progresses, various relationships that are part of this overall relationship are revealed and the identities of the parties representing the relationship become more fluid. Thus, relationships can become more disaggregated (Ackermann & Eden, 2011) and more channels open up to be influenced for both parties. Various and more nuanced strategies tailored to different identities become feasible.

Although obvious, in practice we easily forget how stakeholders, such as organizations that are part of the project's supply chain or environmental protection organizations, are always represented by people with different personalities, motivations and identities. Even though they represent organizations that have strategies and procedures framing their behaviour, other factors will also affect how they act. Sometimes it is expedient that stakeholders are primarily managed by the project manager, while other times it may be more convenient to distribute this work the better to match the interests of the stakeholders or understand their role, context and behaviour. Stakeholder collaboration can sometimes be escalated upwards from the project to a host organization so that the project owner or other members of the top management team can manage individual stakeholders. A lot depends on the extent of the power, legitimacy and urgency of the stakeholders in relation to the project overall.

THE ROLES OF TRUSTING AND CONTRACTING

On occasion, stakeholders should be approached not only structurally and analytically, based on systematic identification and analysis of them, but also more informally and causally, depending on trust relations. Trust is a key dimension in connection with formal–informal interaction (Chapter 7) that also applies to stakeholder relations. Trust implies that a party is willing to make itself vulnerable by trusting that another party actually performs what the party has committed to (Mayer et al., 1995). In these circumstances the exercise of power over the other party can be relaxed. Power over and trust in are mutually opposed variables: where trust is low, the project will strive to maximize power over stakeholders by various means; where trust is high, relations of power over stakeholders by measures such as surveillance, tight contracts and control based on them, can be relaxed. In relationships between project and stakeholders, trust can shift attention from self-interest to 'common interest' and help the parties share more knowledge and other resources (see, among others, Eskerod & Vaagaasar, 2014; Smyth, Gustafsson, & Ganskau, 2010). Trust reduces transaction costs in terms of control and increases the opportunity for positive interaction.

Trust between the project and various stakeholders grows through repeated assessments of whether the other acts in accordance with what it has been said or agreed and appears oriented in their intentions towards a common good (Das & Teng, 1998; Smyth, 2014). In an ongoing stakeholder relationship, the level of trust between the actors can vary, depending on how they assess the behaviour of others at different times. It is time-consuming to gain trust while destroying it can occur rapidly (Elangovan & Shapiro, 1998; Kramer, 2009). Implementation of project activity that is likely to be perceived as dramatic by the stakeholder that might undermine trust needs reflection before action. In any project context, temporality is a key variable, as the temporary project organization that has come into being will fade away when the project is completed. Under these circumstances the shorter the time taken to establish trust between the project and various stakeholders is time won. The positive effects of trust can be exploited to the greatest extent possible. A project seeking to reduce the time it takes to build trust can exploit past positive experiences, a good reputation and expertise. Good instruments in this regard are established norms related to role and task execution and associated interactions, sometimes in the form of a code of conduct that supports integrity and predictability in the action pattern (Tuomela & Tuomela, 2005).

Trust can be produced by the form of contract tying formal stakeholders such as alliance partners and subcontractors in a project. Typically, these contracts, in the form of a competitive tender, do not engender trust so much as exploitative relations in regard to the contract, striving to exploit its potential for indexicality in interpretation by differently interested parties (Clegg, 1975). The result is often zero-sum political games in which a party can only win at another party's expense. Other forms of contract are possible. One such is known as alliancing.

TRUSTING, CONTRACTING AND COLLABORATING: AN EXAMPLE FROM SYDNEY

Stewart Clegg, one of the book's authors, first came to know about alliancing in the context of preparations for the Sydney 2000 Olympics (Pitsis et al., 2003, from which the following account is taken).

A decision to undertake a major project in the run-up to the Sydney 2000 Olympics was taken as part of the State Government Waterways Project in May 1997, designed to clean up rivers, beaches and waterways. Cleaning up the waters of Sydney Harbour was seen as a priority for the Olympics in 2000 given that the 'eyes' of the world

Picture 10.6   Sydney Olympics

Source: Image courtesy of David Shapinsky, via wikicommons.

would be on the city in just over three years. The proposal sought to capture sewerage overflows that occurred during Sydney's sub-tropical storms, when storm water backs up the sewage system and overflows into the harbour, bringing in not only raw sewage but also street detritus such as litter, syringes and dog faeces. The main detail of the project was to build approximately 20km of tunnel in the sandstone under very affluent areas north of Sydney Harbour.

At the time of commencement, relatively little was known about the ground conditions and the tunnel had not been designed. Given the tight time frame, the availability of tunnel boring machines (TBMs) was critical, as these had to be sourced on subcontract from elsewhere in the world. The first stage of the project, of about 18 months, involved a detailed exploration and design phase. Without this, the contractual risks arising from latent conditions would have been unacceptable to any government client. That made completion in an extraordinarily short period of time vital, obviating against a conventional strategic planning process.

The degrees of ambiguity and uncertainty inherent in the project were high because of the deadline, the lack of engineering information, the lack of information about the characteristics of major pieces of technology (the TBMs), and also the characteristics of the communities affected by the project. Because of the higher than usual degree of uncertainty the project was to be managed in a unique way. Instead of a tender process, where the entire project has to be specified in advance and those specifications made public for community comment, Sydney Water invited expressions of interest from companies willing to enter an alliance to deliver the project. The specifications were only 28 pages in length (unheard of in conventional construction where the bill of works and associated contractual documents can run into many thousands of sheets). As the project would involve concurrent engineering much of the design was unspecified. Specified in detail were the agreed principles that the partners were to commit to as the means for resolving issues within the alliance. These differed markedly from traditional detailed construction contracts with the prospect of arbitration when agreement broke down. A typical approach to selecting partners for the alliance was followed, choosing the partners on the basis of their commitment to the envisaged process.

Having thought of the usual way of doing things, with the usual problems that this might entail, with worst- and best-case parameters, they then set about trying to think of unconventional ways of creating the desired outcome. The outcome was easily encapsulated colloquially: 'a lot less shit and rubbish in the harbour' and sparkling blue water for the TV cameras covering Olympic sailing and swimming events, as well as, in the long term, less pollution generally for residents and tourists. Using conventional scenario planning approaches project owners mapped the outcome that would be most likely to occur with the project if they designed and constructed it through traditional planning methods, such as reverse scheduling. But the project partners wanted to achieve breakthrough innovations and outcomes where everyone benefited: the marine life in the harbour (who were a potent symbol in the project iconography); the residents around the foreshore and above the tunnel route; the local communities with whom they would interact in the process; the Olympics organizers; public works contractors throughout the State of New South Wales; and the employees, contractors and client themselves – the members of the alliance. An innovative approach to organizational collaboration framed their thinking and action.

Management consultants experienced in large-scale construction projects helped design a project culture. They recommended that cohesiveness could be fostered through creating a project culture that was explicitly designed and crafted to encourage shared behaviours, decision-making and values. (The design and functioning of this culture is addressed at greater length in Clegg, Pitsis, Rura-Polley, & Marosszeky, 2002.) A list of value statements was produced by the PALT (Project Alliance Leadership Team), which comprised the formal statement of the culture: the two core values were striving to produce solutions that were 'best for project' and having a 'no-blame' culture:

1. Build and maintain a champion team, with champion leadership, which is integrated across all disciplines and organizations
2. Commit corporately and individually to openness, integrity, trust, cooperation, mutual support and respect, flexibility, honesty and loyalty to the project
3. Honour our commitments to one another
4. Commit to a no-blame culture
5. Use breakthroughs and the free flow of ideas to achieve exceptional results in all project objectives
6. Outstanding results provide outstanding rewards
7. Deal with and resolve all issues from within the alliance
8. Act in a way that is 'best for project'
9. Encourage challenging BAU behaviours
10. Spread the alliance culture to all stakeholders.

The basis for the contractors and client benefit was a risk/reward calculation. The project agreement provided for a risk/reward regime based on performance compared to project objectives defined in terms of five key performance indicators (KPIs): cost and schedule – no surprises there – but also safety, community and environment – which are not usually part of construction KPIs. There was one non-negotiable performance criterion – the completion of the project for use by the Olympics. While the alliance had the responsibility of defining BAU objectives in terms of suitable criteria, there was no precedent for a construction project being assessed against such parameters. To ensure independence, external consultants were engaged to review the benchmarks for the non-cost/schedule criteria that had been developed by the alliance. For each area, performance levels, ranging from poor to outstanding, were defined. The specialist consultants also assessed and reported performance against all criteria regularly throughout the project. Success against the non-cost/schedule criteria was critical for project success both in commercial and overall terms and, as such, this area presented the alliance team with significant risks.

There were positive and negative financial outcomes for performance on each of the objectives in the risk/reward process. Financial rewards were payable on a sliding scale for performance above BAU to Outstanding. All objectives, except cost, had a maximum amount. Financial penalties accrued when performance was below BAU with performance in any one area not able to be traded-off against any other area that was represented by the KPIs. Only outstanding performance against all five KPIs would yield the maximum return; less than this in any one area would diminish that return and adverse performance would put the reward at risk as penalty clauses began to bite. Thus, in each area performance processes and outcomes were constructed on which the project would be assessed.

Three specific means of managing using what Pitsis et al. (2003) called a *future perfect strategy* were identified. These means included the creative use of strange conversations, the rehearsal of end games, the practice of workshopping and the projecting of feelings, concerns and issues.

Strange conversations

Karl Weick (1979, p. 200) introduced the notion of strange conversations to the management literature and defined strange conversations as those in which the agenda, process and outcomes were unclear.

A great many community meetings were associated with the project: in each of these, the agenda was unclear, the process highly emergent and the outcomes unknown. In these meetings community members were invited to surface anxieties and make suggestions in relation to the project (almost all of which took place beneath the surface, of which they had little knowledge). What they proposed was often a surprise that, in terms of the rationality of the engineers involved in the project, made little sense: for instance, they were concerned about the visual obtrusiveness of the above-ground works, the noise, mud on the roads, potential loss of access to walk their dogs or for children to play. These were all secondary considerations for the engineers, intent on building the project.

Often, in initial meetings, it was unclear what it was that was being discussed, as talk ranged so widely, in terms of the community members' emotional and aesthetic response to the engineering works. In fact, it was often the case that the eventual outcome informed what it was that the conversations had been about: for instance, once the proposal for the concealment and beautification of one of the sites had emerged, then it crystallized as what had been wanted all along, even though, at the outset, this was not clear at all. Later in the project, community liaison officers found themselves organizing BBQs between community and project members, where more such intriguing conversations occurred.

End games and the practice of workshopping

End games helped concentrate minds on the future perfect strategy in the project. End games occurred frequently, as project completion was enacted in the future perfect. Here is an example that occurred at the January 2000 meeting, when a project leader reminded everybody of the objectives. He said:

> We know where we want to be, where we want to go, and where we want to finish up. We need to plan the end and work out each step to get there so everything is synchronized. We need ownership over the deliverables at the end of the project. The ultimate project is the built product.

The significance of end games was that they worked as aids for visualization of the future perfect and enabled the PALT to focus on the future perfect they were seeking to construct. One of the key techniques used to maintain future perfect focus on the end game was workshopping. When it looked as if the project might run over schedule, the PALT agreed to have a workshop to address the alignment of the five key objectives between headquarters and construction sites (PALT meeting, June 1999). They agreed that by the time of the workshop, one of the project leaders would have met with the programme managers responsible for the key objectives. He would have discussed the alignment of the overall objectives with those of the particular construction sites. Additionally, he would have codified the learning breakthroughs at each construction site, so that they could identify how they had reached their outstanding achievements. Further, he would have discussed the workshop agenda with management consultants and would have arranged a workshop venue.

Projecting feelings, concerns and issues

Although the PALT team were almost all engineers, people with a technical background who were more professionally versed in technical than social construction, there was some explicit recognition of the importance of social construction in one aspect of the PALT meetings. The agenda for each meeting originally contained a section titled 'Projecting Feelings, Concerns and Issues'. Any member could raise anything under this recurring agenda item, with the issue remaining on the agenda until 'it was no longer important or was addressed to the satisfaction of the person who raised the issue in the first place'. The inclusion of this clause was supposed to ensure that future perfect thinking maintained a reality check: if an issue had been constructed in regard to any aspect of the project that was causing concern, then it was reiterated monthly, until it was no longer a matter for concern. While some of these feelings, concerns and issues were quite technical – about scheduling and such like – others concerned more complex community relations.

The technique was significant – it ensured that the future perfect agenda was open and democratic in its projections amongst the top leadership team. A space was created in which emotional aspects of the project could be discussed. Increasingly, the routinized use of the item, which, after a while, became merely a matter for noting rather than action, and was then later abandoned, signalled the limits of future perfect thinking when confronted by community stakeholder matters that were outside of project control.

The project occurred despite the absence of strategic planning decisions made early on, based on minimal information, that lock the process into an inevitable and unquestioned future. Instead, the people who had the greatest opportunity to alter the outcomes were the people who made the strategy up as they went along; normally they would be locked into protecting decisions already made for them through tactics that invariably lead to litigation. Rather than using detailed project scoping and planning to reduce high ambiguity, as is typical of construction (Stinchcombe & Heimer, 1985), the PALT project leaders sought to reduce it through creating a shared culture that enabled future perfect thinking to flourish in an imaginative process oriented to a broad range of imagined outcomes by which they would hold themselves accountable.

Future perfect thinking worked most smoothly where the planners had most control – that is, control of the technological and material context for future action. When external stakeholders critically questioned, achieving the future became more difficult. There were pitfalls in allowing for voice but not providing accompanying responsibility that increased the potential for a project to become hijacked. While project managers may adumbrate a strong culture, they need to avoid being sucked in by its rhetoric and realize that it does not necessarily incorporate all stakeholders.

The project grew from just 28 pages, with no design and no clauses, other than an injunction to think in the future perfect and create a much cleaner Sydney Harbour, to a project that delivered what it set out to do: on time, only slightly over budget, it made Sydney Harbour sufficiently clear that in July 2002, in an ecologically symbolic representation of the success of the project, three 80 ton whales came into the harbour to frolic under the famous Sydney Harbour Bridge, with the equally famous Opera House behind them, although cynics might remark on the clarity of the water due to extensive drought. In living memory whales had never been this far into the Harbour before – the Olympic dream appeared to have been spectacularly realized.

WHAT WOULD YOU DO?

The material in the previous section is drawn from research that Stewart Clegg published with colleagues (Pitsis, 2003 and Clegg, 2002). The case discussed relates to a large technical infrastructure project in Australia.

QUESTION

1. If you were responsible for another type of project, say a potential controversial outdoor music festival in an ecologically sensitive rural area, how could you make use of some of the elements presented in the case above, to:

    - Build trust and manage simple contracts
    - Involve stakeholders
    - Organize for innovative collaboration
    - Meet requirements (KPIs)

Activation and involving stakeholders

Based on the value creation perspective, a key question is to ask how we obtain the highest quality input to make project delivery best for those for whom it is intended? The answer to this may be to address the stakeholders in the lowest priority group according to the above framework (see Figure 10.2), namely those that are just characterized by legitimacy (i.e. discrete stakeholders). In the alliance project just discussed these were represented by the ecology and the community as key stakeholders. Powerful and urgent stakeholders often receive a lot more attention than those with legitimate demands but little access to power relations. By bringing the community and the ecology into the iron triangle, as well as the representatives of organized labour with their interest in health and safety, often overlooked interests from marginally weaker actors were made central. Some projects try to avoid possibly negative stakeholders, such as community members in areas affected by a project, but this is to neglect contributions that such stakeholders can often make to the development of the project.

CREATE GOOD RELATIONSHIPS EARLY

We strongly warn against the project team remaining passive in their interactions with stakeholders, fearing the increased work and problems for the project that engagement might bring. Such an attitude is unfortunate because the project loses constructive input, as discussed above. It's also unfortunate because such stakeholders represent uncertainties about the project that need to be resolved. In general, we can say that when stakeholders are engaged late in the process, the ability to handle them well and to gain from them is reduced and the likelihood of a high level of conflict increased.

ACTIVATE DORMANT STAKEHOLDERS

Many stakeholders have positive interests in the project and possess a lot of knowledge that may be valuable to the project even though not formally engaged. We have already considered how user groups are an example of stakeholders who can provide valuable input for the choice of solutions, in the conceptual, planning and execution phases. Many of these dormant stakeholders can become positive knowledge partners for the project, even though they are not initially active. One challenge for any project is to find out how to stimulate stakeholders so that they want to participate in dialogue and share knowledge with the project, moving the premise of power relations from power over to power with others. As mentioned earlier, there is an opportunity to include these others in the project through participation in reference groups/consultation groups/test panels, or other forums where they can share their knowledge and views, as well as receive information. It can both increase their emotional commitment and form a structural link that can increase their commitment to the project. Networking and other knowledge sharing arenas can be good tools to enable more positive commitment and trust.

READ THIS!

When projects are less successful than hoped then bad news has to be delivered to project stakeholders – Moira Alexander (2019) gives some tips on how to deliver bad news at: https://study.sagepub.com/pm.

NEGOTIATING WITH STAKEHOLDERS

> **Negotiation** entails a bargaining process between two or more parties to discover common ground and reach an agreement.

When two or more parties with partially contradictory interests try to resolve, they negotiate. People negotiate in very many contexts. **Negotiation** can be formal, guided by protocols or be more informal. Often, the project manager must assume the role of a kind of mediator or dealer to find 'the best solution' in the sense of satisfying as many needs as possible (Briner et al., 1993).

The process of negotiating entails:

- Dependency between the parties. Those involved want to achieve something but rely on the other parties involved. Without this dependency, it is not necessary to negotiate.
- Working with the two dimensions of conflict and cooperation in parallel. The parties have both common interests and are opposed to each other. In negotiations, the parties often start from incompatible positions and strive to have the counterparty yield. At the same time, they must identify the interests they have in common if it is to be a constructive and efficient debate. The point will then be to find out how to collaborate for the best possible solution, safeguarding interests while making compromises.

- Finding one or more things in a relationship shared by the parties involved. If there are more things, there are several areas where you can 'give and take'. Discuss which matters are most significant for the different parties and on which they might be prepared to compromise.

For negotiations to be an appropriate tool, the parties must see them as the preferred method to achieve what they want. If one of the parties finds other alternatives, for example finding a solution that does not involve the counterparty, the basis for negotiations will be lacking.

TYPES OF NEGOTIATING

Various types of negotiations can take place between stakeholders and the project, including *distribution negotiations* and *integration negotiations*. In many negotiations, a given amount is distributed so that the gain for one will be a loss to the other in a zero-sum game. However, most negotiations in project contexts are integral negotiations, containing several dimensions and issues. Compromise occurs where all parties' demands are listened to and the outcome is experienced as relatively fair. Cooperation is emphasized to a greater degree in integration negotiations than in distribution negotiations. However, conflict is still potentially present if the parties are not motivated to enter into a possible agreement.

PATHS FOR NEGOTIATING

A project process consists of a large number of situations in which negotiation takes place within the project team (for example, the assignment of tasks between the participants) as well as between internal stakeholder, such as project owners and resources management. Negotiations with future users about solutions to perceived issues are also common. In addition, there are a large number of possible situations where negotiation in the relationships between the project and its external stakeholders occurs. Project managers (and possibly project participants) need to be familiar with basic negotiating principles.

Considering power, legitimacy and urgency can also provide guidance for those stakeholders the project should negotiate with. The impact matrix can reveal the impact of possible solutions. The project must take into consideration the momentum of perceived justice in the negotiation situation. Furthermore, there are four factors in particular that project managers need to note in negotiations with various stakeholders (Larson & Gray, 2011):

- Differentiate between subject matter and person
- Focus on interests, not positions
- Consider which matters to include and assess the effect of the negotiations on related matters
- Use as objective criteria as possible

In order to succeed in projects, strive to identify and understand stakeholders so that you can create the best strategies for interacting with them. We have emphasized that the interaction strategy must be tailored to the individual stakeholder, that it may involve several different relationships with the same stakeholder over time and that it may be both formal and informal in its nature.

Final reflections

Stakeholder management should last throughout the project period and be dynamic as the stakeholder landscape of the individual project changes throughout its entire life cycle. The changes can be applied to stakeholders who over time become critical for the project, whether they stand alone or are part of alliances, and whether they are mixed, positive or negative.

Working with these other parties triggers some questions that should be considered carefully:

- Who are the stakeholders that are involved (in a broad sense)? What characterizes them?
- What do these stakeholders want to achieve overall?
- What part of the project are they particularly interested in?
- How should different stakeholders be engaged or otherwise participate in one or more of the project's processes? What are the prerequisites for this?
- What benefits are required by the project for the stakeholders to be engaged in other processes in the project?
- What relevant measures does the project have to influence the stakeholder to act in a manner appropriate for the project's execution and/or delivery?
- Stakeholder collaboration is a key process in project management, despite limitations. Stakeholders cannot be controlled. They must be worked with interactively, developing trust and shared principles for negotiating with stakeholders: how best to achieve this outcome?

Summary

In this chapter, we have:

- Laid out the differences between internal and external stakeholders and elaborated processes for identifying these different types of stakeholders.
- Described how you can work to understand stakeholders' interests, their characteristics and ways of acting through different forms of analyses. We have also shown how you can prioritize their importance for the project by looking at the stakeholders' power, urgency and legitimacy. We have also highlighted the silent stakeholders and the role of media.
- Provided insights as to how you can develop appropriate interaction strategies with different types of stakeholders and the key aspects on which to base your strategy, and how to think about this in a short and long term perspective.
- Elaborated on the dynamic and continuous processes of managing stakeholders that have to unfold throughout the project, where you monitor how the various stakeholders respond to your strategies, the extent to which their interests and strategies shift and the extent to which changes in their positioning in the stakeholder landscape occurs, for example by stakeholders forming coalitions with other stakeholders.
- Connected the issues of stakeholder management, benefit realization and value creation and explored how you can work with stakeholders from a value creation perspective.

Exercises

1. Can you explicate the difference between internal and external stakeholders? How do you identify them respectively?
2. What are the key steps in stakeholder management?
3. What would be the key characteristics of stakeholders and stakeholders' behaviour that you would look at in order to develop a strategy for handling a set of stakeholders?
4. Why is stakeholder prioritization significant? Can you account for the key issues to consider when prioritizing your attention to stakeholders?
5. Reflect on how stakeholders can change their positioning. What is the role of media in this? What is the role of forming coalitions?
6. Reflect on the relationship between project–stakeholder collaboration and potential benefit realization/value creation.
7. Why should dormant stakeholders be activated?
8. What are three major factors for the project to note in negotiations with various stakeholders?

CASE STUDY

WASTE IN HAMBURG

Gittel is a freshly appointed project manager for a project sponsored by the municipality of Hamburg in Germany. The project is designed to deliver a solution for handling hazardous waste that can be offered throughout Germany. They are building a tunnel under the lake just outside the city of Hamburg as a solution for storing waste. The project has been quite controversial among residents and citizens in surrounding areas. Many are afraid it could affect facilities such as drinking water and also the nature and animals in the area. Others claim it will generate general stress with people just worrying about 'if anything goes wrong…?' On the other hand, there are also stakeholders showing genuine positive interest in the technological development creating this tunnel will entail, as well as the jobs following from this development process. The municipality is struggling to finance all its obligations in terms of health care, caring for the elderly and also the education system. Selling the service of storing hazardous waste for other municipalities and large actors in the industry would be very beneficial to the economy of this municipality. The media has been mostly preoccupied with stressing the potential damage this project could cause to water, nature and people. The political administration favour it for the earnings it will achieve; the opposition parties are much more sceptical on ecological grounds that they have voiced but not yet thoroughly researched.

QUESTIONS

1. What might Gittel's map of stakeholders look like?

(Continued)

2. How can Gittel make an overview of the stakeholders to prioritize her attention and involvement with them?

- Who would be the definitive stakeholders?
- Who else does she really need to deal with?
- Can you think of a typical stakeholder in this case, stealing time from the project as they demand urgent responses, even though they have no real power base behind their claims?
- How should Gittel deal with those?

3. What are your suggestions for Gittel in terms of organizing the stakeholders and involving them in an efficient and appropriate way?

Additional resources

There are many contributions related to stakeholder collaboration. Mitchell et al. (1997) write about how the image of interest is constantly changing and how the project can illuminate this picture so that it makes sensible prioritization of what stakeholders should be most aware of and how they should meet the various stakeholders. Savage et al. (1991) discuss different strategies to interact with stakeholders in a good way. Eskerod and Jepsen (2013) provide a solid and research-based image of stakeholder collaboration in project work that is well worth to look at. The recent work by Ninan et al. (2019) is well worth looking at for some innovative ideas about managing external stakeholders using social media to do so.

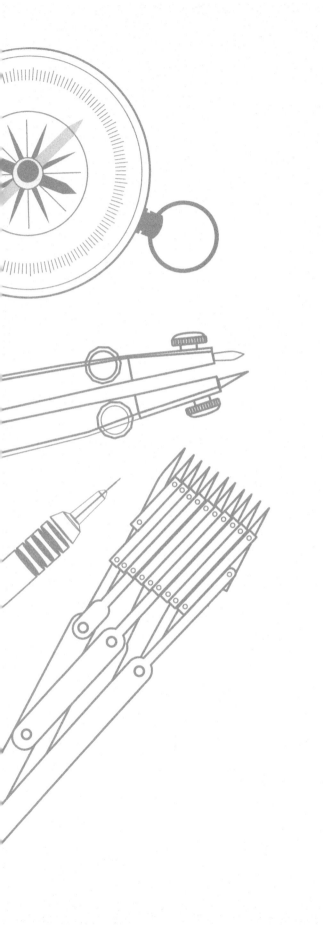
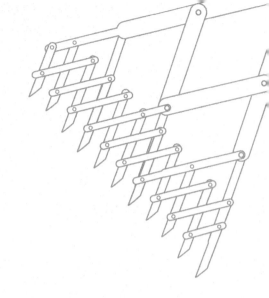

Chapter Roadmap

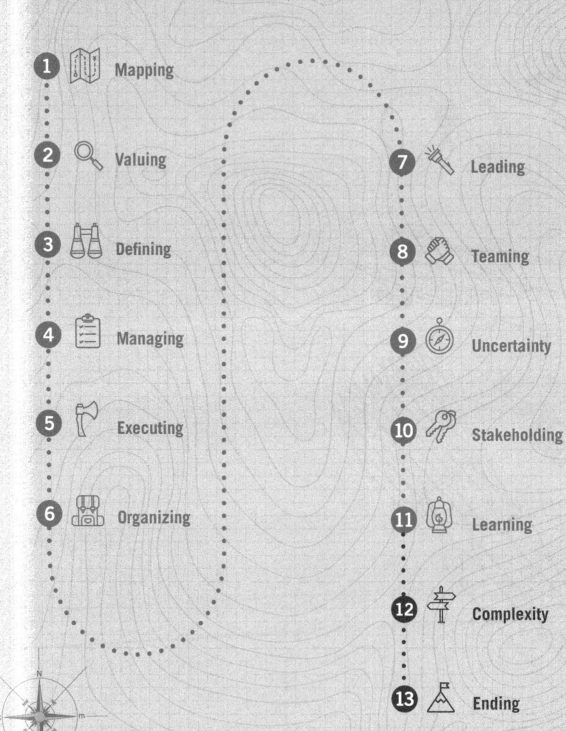

1. Mapping
2. Valuing
3. Defining
4. Managing
5. Executing
6. Organizing
7. Leading
8. Teaming
9. Uncertainty
10. Stakeholding
11. Learning
12. Complexity
13. Ending

11

Learning and Innovating in Projects

Learning objectives

After reading this chapter, you should know:

1 What constitutes project-based learning environments and the difference between different types of knowledge and knowledge processes

2 The key enablers and activities of project-based learning

3 The differences between process and product innovation projects

4 How to use the innovation diamond for projects

5 What the key characteristics of creativity in project teams are and how creativity can be stimulated through idea work

Before you get started

There's no success like failure and failure's no success at all.

– Bob Dylan, 1965

Introduction

Projects are instruments for more than two-thirds of value creation in the Western world. Many complex tasks find their solution through projects. Consequently, there is much to be learnt from projects. Such learning can increase value at both the social and organizational levels. It can provide competitive advantages for organizations and individuals and make individual employees' workdays more productive both personally and organizationally.

There are two problems often related to learning in projects. One is that the project participants do not learn as much as they could have done because there is limited time for reflection, an interaction that is not particularly encouraging for learning or a lack of systems that support learning (Keegan & Turner, 2002). The second problem is that the learning that occurs in projects contributes to organizational learning only to a limited extent (Schindler & Eppler, 2003). Many scholars have pointed out that there is a significant learning loss at the end of projects because the learning that occurred in the project never becomes systematically shared (Davies & Hobday, 2005).

In this chapter, we consider both the learning processes that take place in the project team and learning across the project team. First, we will look at what types of knowledge are relevant in the project context and processes for learning in and between projects. Then we will look at typical pitfalls associated with project-based learning and what can be done to avoid them before moving on to a more general consideration of idea work.

Knowledge, competence and learning

Discussions about learning and learning processes are based on the idea that such processes increase the ability for individuals, projects and organizations to perform better, fulfilling a desire for continuous positive development. In general, the idea is that positive learning beats negative learning – the kind that can be experienced when you learn from events in projects such as accidents at construction sites (Clegg & Kreiner, 2014). Learning can also be negative when dysfunctional habits are acquired, such as project members being late when attending meetings, so that meetings gradually start later with project team members subsequently turning up even later, sowing the seeds for the emergence of a dysfunctional culture.

In this chapter, we will focus on positive learning and innovation that makes organizations better equipped to achieve their work. We concentrate on learning at the project level; that is, how the participants learn while they work on project tasks. Much learning is informal: employees learn from each other through conversations, observation and joint assignment, building collective **communities of practice** (Wenger, 2010) sharing disseminated expertise, shared knowing and common application.

> A **community of practice** is achieved by organizing to promote knowledge flow and skills across individuals, projects and organizations (Wenger, 2010).

When we talk about communities of practice, we mean a group of people who have values, views and perspectives that enable them to converse in common, whether in conflict or collaboration. Conversing, they learn from each other, share know-how and generate enhanced knowing. A common sensemaking emerges as knowledge flows in and among projects. Organizations that want to take project-based learning seriously should encourage employees to seek out and develop communities of practice. Learning in communities of practice can occur when project members try new tasks or encounter new technology or meet with demanding stakeholders from whom they may learn.

> **Workplace learning** that makes a difference occurs where knowledge and skills acquired through experience lead to relatively lasting cognitive, social and organizational changes.

There are many definitions of **workplace learning**.

In general, assembling knowledge is not sufficient to claim that learning has happened. Learning entails something active where the learner alters during the learning process (Huber, 1991). Often learning is seen as synonymous with acquiring new knowledge but is better understood as acquiring new knowing. Knowing is active, embrained, embodied and embedded, whereas knowledge is a device that must be stored and propagated to be of value. Knowing is the enactment of knowledge in processes through which knowledge is applied and recreated when used. Since the beginning of the 2000s the focus on the use of knowledge has shifted from the materialization of knowledge through knowledge management, which sees knowledge recorded in data bases and other storage devices, with the emphasis shifting to how knowing is practised (Gherardi, 2000; Tsoukas, 2009).

Knowledge is of little value if it does not make a difference. Therefore, the importance of competence and competence development is usually emphasized. The main point is that learning must lead to action so that you can solve work tasks better. Competence deals with knowledge, abilities and skills that can be used to perform work. Attitudes are also often included as part of knowing how to do things, underscoring the importance of the ability to act in an empowered way according to situational contingencies. If someone has the knowledge and skills to change practices and make a difference but does not have the will to do so, the learning or knowing is wasted. Competence is a dynamic phenomenon, where the competence developed through learning always builds on skills already held (Kolb, 1984).

READ THIS!

Often learning and development in organizations do not succeed as intended. Read this article by Steve Glaveski (2019) on where organizations often go wrong with learning processes at: https://study.sagepub.com/pm.

While the learning literature has traditionally paid most attention to individuals' learning, contemporary discussions address learning at group and organizational levels. Although learning is often associated with human beings – those who learn – learning in organizations has been recognized as a phenomenon and a relevant discipline. Argyris and Schön (1978) and March (1991) have, for example, made pioneering contributions to the topic of organizational learning, while Senge

> **Organizational learning** represents embedded knowing and explicit knowledge of what is desired to achieve goals or follow strategies.

(2006) has become known for the concept of the learning organization. Organizational learning is embedded in rules, procedures and processes governing and guiding behaviour (Argyris & Schön, 1978), applying even where individuals have forgotten the reason why activities are conducted the way they are ('collective memory loss'). Over time, **organizational learning** grows as the sum of many contributions.

WATCH THIS!

In this YouTube video, Peter Senge (2015) explains how he defines a learning organization and how to develop a learning organization at: https://study.sagepub.com/pm.

Although we emphasize learning in and between projects, such learning must be seen in the light of how an organization develops competence in its ordinary activities. Competitiveness over time depends on continually developing skills by gathering, integrating and disseminating knowledge (Grant, 1996; Kogut & Zander, 1992; Spender & Grant, 1996). The real competitive edge is the ability to combine resources in new ways, something called **dynamic capability** (Clegg et al., 2019; Zollo & Winter, 2002). Dynamic capability refers to the ability to exploit and recombine knowledge and expertise flexibly to respond to situations that require new solutions (Eisenhardt & Martin, 2000; Teece et al., 1997).

> Project **dynamic capabilities** index organizational capacities to integrate, build and reconfigure internal and external resources/competencies to address and shape rapidly changing environments.'

Dynamic capability can develop in projects, as shown by Davies and Brady (2016) in the development of Terminal 5 at Heathrow, where learning, codifying learning experiences and mobilizing them dynamically, as unexpected events occurred, helped resolve unexpected issues. Dynamic capability can be expressed through the establishment of interdisciplinary project teams that integrate their skills so that new types of challenges can be met. Being exposed to learning opportunities increases the ability to learn over time (Cohen & Levinthal, 1990). Projects are therefore useful devices for managing new opportunities and responding to changing needs. Project work thus involves opportunities for learning as well as learning to learn.

WATCH THIS!

In this YouTube video, David Teece and Gary Pissano (2016) explain the concept of dynamic capabilities, at: https://study.sagepub.com/pm.

Project-based learning – an organization perspective: Exploiting and exploring

As mentioned earlier, research shows that much of a company's knowledge is developed in projects (see, for example, Ayas & Zeniuck, 2001; Brady & Davies, 2004; Vaagaasar, 2011). Learning in project-based companies has in recent years received a lot of attention both in practice and in research.

When organizations use projects as a venue for continuous development, they strive both to exploit existing knowledge in their projects and explore opportunities for developing new knowledge (March, 1991). Figure 11.1 shows this dichotomy and the composition of the two dimensions. For a project-based organization, projects become important venues for both utilizing and refining knowledge (exploiting), while being the arenas for exploring new solutions and thus acquiring new knowledge.

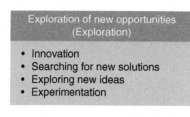
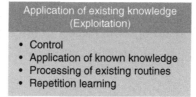

Figure 11.1   Exploration and exploitation

We have pointed out that projects are often created as a response to an issue that is considered novel. To solve the project, one must, to some degree, explore different solutions. The exploration dimension is thus a natural part of all projects. It is extensive in 'Walking in the fog' projects and much less apparent in projects that are mostly the repetition of previous projects, with well-known goals and a known method of getting there, so-called 'Painting by numbers' projects, using the terms introduced in Chapter 3.

Project-based companies use projects to explore new potential solutions and technologies, generating variation in learning experiences (Keegan & Turner, 2002). At the same time, many project-based organizations generally do not exploit this opportunity for learning to any great extent. Industry culture affects the willingness to experiment. For example, the construction industry is more conservative than projects in finance, management, IT and telecom. Rules, procedures and safety requirements inhibit the willingness to experiment. Furthermore, the public sector and large companies seem less willing to experiment and regard projects as opportunities for learning (Keegan & Turner, 2002).

Across industries and sectors, it is the case that organizations assume more commitments than the resources they have at their disposal, often seeking habitual processes and execution of customary types of projects where extant knowledge can be efficiently exploited. Projects characterized by high complexity and uncertainty often try to reduce re-thinking and innovation because it can increase complexity and uncertainty, leading to long-term stagnation (Lenfle & Loch, 2010).

Portfolio projects should be selected to enable both exploitation and exploration over time. In the meantime, 'vanguard projects' should be established (Brady & Davies, 2004), i.e. projects that are established to explore innovative opportunities. This is particularly relevant for organizations operating in markets or with technologies characterized by frequent changes. A 'vanguard project', a path-breaking novel initiative, is a first project in a series of many within what might become a possible new area. Investment in this project may not lead to any return other than learning through exploration if the expected yield does not materialize.

It is important that project-based organizations take care of both knowledge development through exploratory processes and projects and that they are able to utilize their knowledge appropriately. By balancing the exploration and utilization of expertise through the projects they choose to implement and the way they do it, sustainable development is achievable (Brady & Davies, 2004). Figure 11.2 shows that in achieving this balance there are several steps that develop in parallel and affect each other. Within new areas of knowledge, this is a kind of bottom-up learning process in three stages (Brady & Davies, 2004, p. 1607):

Step 1: Implement a vanguard project

Step 2: Learning from project to project (*the economy of repetition*)

Step 3: Learning from Projects to Organization

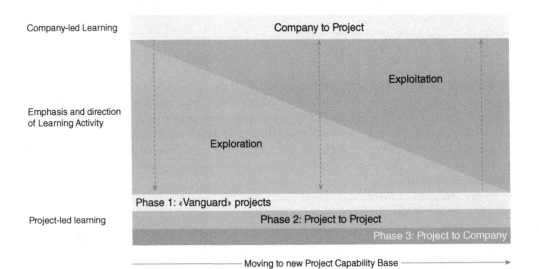

Figure 11.2 Learning process in three phases

Source: Brady & Davies, 2004

Analyses to improve project-to-project learning

We have talked about the importance of using projects as an arena for exploration and exploitation of knowledge, as well as the associated opportunities and challenges.

Organizations aiming to improve their ability in project-based learning might find it appropriate to work with learning landscapes (Prencipe & Tell, 2001). A learning landscape is based on a three-point process where the various points are experiencing accumulation, knowledge articulation and knowledge codification (Zollo & Winter, 2002). *Experience accumulation* is the immediate experience a project acquires in task solving. *Knowledge articulation* is the process of articulating this experience by participants in terms of what happened and why, transforming experience into knowledge that can be shared easily with others, as procedures, rules and messages (Kogut & Zander, 1992; Spender & Grant, 1996). *The knowledge-codification process* stores meaning created by articulation in more general principles, formulating it as knowledge. Literature on project-based learning often emphasizes the codification process but to succeed over time it is important to place emphasis on other processes (Keegan & Turner, 2002), especially on *articulation*.

Knowledge articulation contributes to two things (Zollo & Winter, 2002). First, it contributes to the legitimacy of actions; secondly, to enable participants to increase their understanding of causality in task-solving and expand this repertoire by sharing and discussing views related to the relationships. Based on this, processes in the project-based organization can be analysed:

a. Has the total accumulation of experience been accessed?
b. Have these experiences been articulated?
c. Have these articulations been codified into knowledge?

Furthermore, consider the level of organization at which these processes occur. Is the level:

a. individual?
b. project?
c. organization?

The combination of these provides a nine-field table for analysing learning in project-based companies. Table 11.1 shows an overview of activities/processes that typically belong in the various fields (Prencipe & Tell, 2001).

Table 11.1   Inter-project learning mechanisms

Learning Process	Experience accumulation	Knowledge accumulation	Knowledge codification
Level of Analysis			
Individual	- On-the-job training	- Figurative thinking	- Diary
	- Job rotation	-'Thinking aloud'	- Reporting system
	- Specialization	- Scribbling notes	- Individual system design
	- Re-use of experts		
Project	- Developed groupthink	- Brainstorming sessions	- Project plan/audit
	-Person-to-person communication	- Formal project reviews	- Milestones/deadlines
		- De-briefing meetings	- Meeting minutes
	- Informal encounters	- Ad-hoc meetings	- Case writing
	- Imitation	- Lessons learnt and/or post-mortem meetings	- Project history files
		- Intra-project correspondence	- Intra-project lessons learnt database

(Continued)

Table 11.1 (Continued)

Learning Process	Experience accumulation	Knowledge accumulation	Knowledge codification
Organization	- Informal organizational routines, rule and selection processes - Departmentalization and specialization - Communities of practice	- Project Manager camps - Knowledge retreats - Professional networks - Knowledge facilitators and managers - Inter-project correspondence - Inter-project meetings	- Drawings - Process maps - Project management processes - Lesson learnt database

Source: This figure was published in Prencipe, A., & Tell, F. Inter-project learning: Processes and outcomes of knowledge codification in project-based firms. *Research Policy*, 30(9), 1373–1394. Copyright Elsevier (2001)

Project-based companies can be reflexive about knowledge processes on an individual, project or organizational level. Different processes (accumulation/articulation/codification) can be weighted. These differences can primarily be classified into three different learning landscapes – L, T and stairs landscapes.

THREE DIFFERENT LANDSCAPES

The L-form is based on sharing between individuals where individuals closely link their knowledge. The focus is on individuals sharing knowledge through joint participation in problem-solving through face-to-face communication and interaction in more formal knowledge networks. The organization will be receptive to receiving new knowledge but with few systems for its spread and storage. The organization is person focused in its landscape, typically found in small organizations with a strong culture of learning. See Figure 11.3A.

The T-shape dedicates extensive attention to articulation at all levels, i.e. individual, project and organizational levels. A relatively small set of processes are used to improve project-to-project learning. Experience between projects is systematically shared through routinized meetings between different projects as arenas in which

A

• On-the-job training • Job rotation • Specialisation • Re-use of experts	• Figurative thinking • "Thinking aloud" • Scribbling notes	• Diary • Reporting system • Individual system design
• Developed groupthink • Person-to person communication • Informal encounters • Imitation	•	•
• Informal organizational routines, rules and selection processes • Departmentalisation and specialisation • Oommunities of practice	•	•

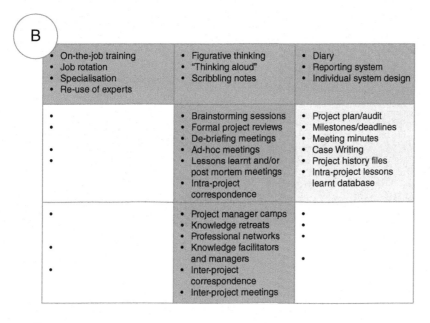

Figure 11.3 Three learning landscapes: L-shaped (A), T-shape (B) and staircase (C)

Source: This figure was published in Prencipe, A., & Tell, F. Inter-project learning: Processes and outcomes of knowledge codification in project-based firms. *Research Policy*, 30(9), 1373–1394. Copyright Elsevier (2001).

to reflect on past experiences and how to benefit from these in other projects. Companies with a T-shaped learning landscape develop mechanisms for more formalized project-to-project learning but do not focus on codification and knowledge processes at the organizational level. (see Figure 11.3B).

The staircase exploits the knowledge that a single individual develops. Project staff actively participate in all three knowledge processes. Organizations document knowledge from projects so that it can be spread to other projects and incorporated into routines, with considerable attention being paid to ICT systems that support the reuse of knowledge. It is primarily larger organizations that make use of ICT tools to support project-to-project learning through systems and templates with which to codify knowledge as an integral part of management systems that work with all three processes. See Figure 11.3C.

Learning levels

There are two approaches to learning at the individual level: **behavioural** and **cognitive learning**. These approaches argue that learning takes place in different ways and they represent different understandings of what knowledge is.

> **Behavioural learning** emphasizes a change in the patterning of action that happens because some actions have positive consequences that lead to the action being repeated.

> **Cognitive learning** involves mental processes through which individuals create meaning in their world.

The classic example of behavioural learning was provided by the physiologist Ivan Pavlov, when he observed that dogs salivated when they were receiving food. If the presentation of food was associated with another stimuli, such as a bell, the dogs learnt to salivate when they heard the bell, in the expectation of food. Skinner, who researched the connection between stimulus of senses and learning in children, is a well-known contributor to behaviourism.

Cognitive learning is the second key approach to individual learning. The starting point for cognitive approaches was a criticism of behaviourism that does not deny the importance of stimuli and response but says learning has more to it than learning as a stimulus-driven response.

Piaget and Vygotsky were prominent contributors to cognitive learning theory. Cognitive learning theory emphasizes that humans are born with cognitive (mental) capacities that are developed through learning. When new knowledge is acquired, it can be incorporated either into existing forms of knowing (assimilation) or it can radically change orientations, creating new ways of new knowing to be established (accommodation). Languages, both verbal and non-verbal, are central to the learning process. Learning is not an automated process whereby knowledge is transmitted directly from one individual to another. There is always a process in which the individual reconstructs knowledge (Vygotsky, 1978); learning to know necessarily involves translation of knowledge from one set of contextual particulars to those of the person learning. Hence, as knowledge travels it is translated (Czarniawska & Sevón, 2005).

Social constructivism could be regarded as a continuation of cognitive learning theory, as it places particular emphasis on the importance of social relationships informing how we construct knowledge.

The social constructivist perspective on workplace learning has received much attention since the mid-1990s (Garrick, 1998). Individuals learn as and when they reflect on the relationship between actions and consequences in their working day, by informal learning through taking part in social relationships (such as practice communities), engaging in practice and interacting with objects (whether they be routines, physical tools or languages). The key point is that learning is always part of a context and that it can only be understood in this context. Being a member of a community of practice means acquiring fluency in its social constructions, central to which are the categorization devices that members use to order their world. Project managers develop a specific set of categorization devices as they learn things such as the Project Management Body of Knowledge (PMBoK). In part, it the learning of this body of prescriptivism that constitutes them as project managers. From this perspective, project management has been less a discipline founded on deep research and more a frame for producing categorization devices through which a global project community of practice has emerged, facilitated by institutionalization of bodies such as the PMI and devices such as the PMBoK. As much of this book makes evident, as research-based knowledge deepens, conventional wisdoms can be questioned and broadened.

> **Social constructivism** states that actors construct the world through those knowledge categories they conventionally use because these categories frame how they relate to the world.

Learning in projects

We learn in projects and from projects. Projects often solve tasks that are relatively special, complex and which require complementary skills for project accomplishment. Doing this makes it necessary for partners that have not collaborated previously to develop new knowledge and to learn from each other (Ayas & Zeniuk, 2001; Söderlund, Vaagaasar, & Andersen, 2008). To address, work on and complete a task, individuals use what they know, what is embrained and embodied in their ways of doing things that have been embedded in their past project experiences. When something unexpected occurs or they do not know how to resolve some aspect of the task, it creates the opportunity for problem-oriented learning.

Problem-oriented learning occurs frequently in projects when you are stuck and don't know what to do. Under these circumstances you might bring in experts, read reports and documentation or test existing procedures and processes in new ways. The reasons why projects are good arenas for learning is that they provide opportunities to:

- Make learning experiences 'hands-on'
- Obtain information and knowledge when something unexpected happens
- Solve tasks with the know-how and tools to hand, perhaps by improvising, generating and experiencing problem-based learning to increase motivation and reflection
- Share knowledge with other professional groups

Through learning, a project team can improve their task definition, implementation and resolution, and increase individual skills. For example, the unique and inherent characteristics of software development requires a collaborative undertaking, involving rapid exchange of information and integration of knowledge, reflection and introspections among team members. Coping with high velocity environments, often found in large and complex projects or innovation projects, demands a collective capacity for dynamic capabilities. When learning outcomes are spread within an organization from one project team to another they can lead to an increase in the capabilities of these other projects as well as of the organization as a whole (Brady & Davies, 2004). However, for this to happen, some way of communicating and learning is required. While storing knowledge in data bases or knowledge management system is one way, it begs a lot of questions. Will people access it; will they read it; will they translate it from the relatively thin context of the data base to the relatively culturally thick example of their situation and project?

Project work is often described by practitioners as a process shaped through the interaction between the individuals, structures and tools that are involved where individual and collective knowing is developed through interaction (Packendorff, 1995). Insights gradually evolve and change over time, as elements of knowledge are related in new contexts and interpreted through collective reflection as novel knowing. Such innovative solutions can be created through organization and project members learning to know and applying this know-how to improvise new solutions and translations of what they have learnt (Söderlund et al., 2008).

Research has repeatedly pointed out that project participants learn a lot of know-how through project work. An international survey shows that 85% of those who primarily work in projects acquire much of their knowledge through experiential learning and project-related exploration (Turner, Huemann, Anbari, & Bredillet, 2010). Project-based learning is a term now widely used (see, for example, Ayas & Zenuik, 2001 and Garrick & Clegg, 2001). Project-based learning embraces both learning in individual projects and the dissemination and translation of this knowledge in the organization. Experience-based informal learning is central to projects so that is what we will discuss next.

IN PRACTICE

PROFESSIONAL SERVICE INDUSTRY

In the professional service industry (advisory, consulting, IT, etc.), a common work practice to create customer value and solve complex problems is cross-disciplinary teams. The concept of 'team learning capability' (TLC) is a recent contribution to the area of team learning, ambidexterity and innovation (Batt-Rawden, Lien, & Slåtten, 2019). A focus is on the favourable 'communities of interaction' that teams can represent. They specifically identify TLC as a 'team-state' that some professional service teams are able to develop. When TLC emerges, the teams are capable of handling both exploitive and explorative knowledge creation. Further, that development of TLC positively affects the team's ability to generate both incremental and more radical service innovation.

In the article, the authors describe TLC as an optimal balance between three cognitive, behavioural and motivational processes. Specifically, (i) 'relationship learning', which is how the team members learn from and *with* each other; (ii) a trusting team climate, which marks perceptions of a 'safe' environment for social risk taking, such as coming with radical ideas or challenge prevailing ideas; (iii) finally, employee commitment which says something about the dedication each member has to the tasks, and their 'stayer' mentality. Importantly, all of these three processes must be present for TLC to emerge.

READ THIS!

The article titled 'Team learning capability – an instrument for innovation?' (Batt-Rawden et al., 2019) is available in online resources at https://study.sagepub.com/pm.

QUESTION

1. Having read the article by Batt-Rawden et al. (2019), do you think TLC could apply to other industries as well? If so, why, and if not, what is special about the context of professional service industries?

EXPERIENCE-BASED INFORMAL LEARNING

Experience-based learning is central to projects. Two principles of experiential learning were introduced by the most famous contributor to learning theory, John Dewey. These are the principle of 'learning by doing' and the principle of 'learning by trial and error' (Dewey, 1938). It is key to both principles that the individual must be active and engaged in the process to promote effective learning. The learning happens as the individuals act, observe the effect of their actions, then reflect on the relationship between actions and consequences. Above all, it entails reflexive learning – learning that is aware of what has been learnt.

Reflection is the core of all experience-based learning (Dewey, 1938; Kolb, 1984) because it allows you to interpret and understand contexts. Interpretation and understanding – sensemaking – entails that meaning is created through and as learning (Weick, 1979). Based on novel sensemaking, you can change your action pattern. Over time, experiential learning can develop an ability continuously to reflect on relationships between phenomena and how knowledge can be combined in new ways to solve different tasks creatively by acting dynamically and better meeting different challenges. Employees with the ability to act dynamically are critical for addressing new challenges, especially if the situation in question is characterized by considerable uncertainty (Keegan & Turner, 2002).

Knowledge acquired through 'learning by doing' contributes to more comprehensive understanding exhibited in knowing. There is a high probability that this knowing will achieve a better fit with the learner than if the same knowledge was transmitted through verbal communication. Knowledge acquired this way can be more easily translated into changed practice (Dewey, 1938). Some of the main criticisms of formal and document-based learning are that it is difficult to put into practice because the abstractness of such knowledge is distanced from the work situation. Through learning in daily project work, through workplace training or by using simulation-oriented methods (as we present below), project staff can learn what they actually need in their work. Therefore, this form of learning has become central in project organizations.

Picture 11.1 Learning by doing

Source: Anne Live Vaagaasar

When we make sense of and share know-how and project-based knowing these processes of translation and sharing enable others to learn also.

Below you will find a description of the connections in experience-based learning (Figure 11.4). The learning process starts with concrete experience, then that the individual observes and reflects on what is happening (action and consequence). Based on the observation and reflection, these are abstracted into more general principles (concepts and generalizations) for action. These implications can then be tested in practice.

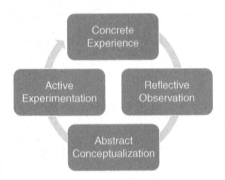

Figure 11.4 Experience-based learning circle

LEARNING TRAPS

Learning cannot be taken for granted; it requires both presences and absences. The most significant absence are **learning traps** (Rich & Gureckis, 2018).

Learning traps are the formation of a stable false belief even with extensive experience.

Learning traps have several sources. In order to learn from experience and develop the ability to act dynamically, there must be time for reflection, often only a small part of the working day (Ayas & Zeniuk, 2001; Raelin, 2002).

The absence of opportunity for reflection is a common learning trap. Reflection tends to be driven out by routine and events in the normal course of doing things. It is well known that the tight concern with temporality in projects can be experienced as stressful and that there often are too many tasks to be solved within a too short time frame, producing stressed-out knowledge workers (Garrick & Clegg, 2001). Lack of time also contributes to short-term thinking (Bakker et al., 2013), further reducing reflection.

WHAT WOULD YOU DO?

You are a project manager at the start of a project that is to develop software for booking hotel rooms for the hotel chain Londurena, as well as the routines needed to implement this system in an efficient way. The development process entails creating some novel solutions. The owner of the project is the marketing director of the hotel chain. The project team consist of members from the client organization, as well as your own organization, which is a consulting company. The team members hold different areas of expertise and their familiarity and experience with project work is also variable. The project time frame appears very limited.

QUESTION

1. What would you do to establish time for reflection in this project? What can you do the enable the team to develop the emergence of novel solutions?

To counter time-poor tendencies, the time frame in projects requires some slack, rather than around the clock urgency to be always doing work. Slack should be combined with a clearly stated expectation that the project team should reflect on contexts they experience during project execution (Söderlund et al., 2008). The project team, along with project owners, at all milestone transitions, can set time aside to reflect on experiences and what they have learnt collectively and individually. Project managers, participants and others involved in establishing the conditions for the project framework and project execution plans find that it is in such reflection that the possibility of improvement and renewal resides.

Localism is a learning trap. There are both challenges and pitfalls associated with experimental learning. A major challenge is that it tends to be local, in the sense that you only make sense of it in the contexts in which it is found. To learn from the learning, to make knowing a source of difference for the future, experience-based learning requires that you are able to see the relationship between action and consequences in a broader context (Levitt and March, 1988). At the same time, individual experiential sensemaking can only be part of a larger context, meaning that informal experience-based learning and knowing is developed based on a small number of events, much less than all relevant contexts in future. Selective sensemaking can occur in terms of seeing what you want to see on an occasion and not recalling it on future occasions. Project participants tend systematically to misinterpret their surroundings, in the sense that they place too much emphasis on certain events in relation to other events in their here-and-now. Events that are experienced as dramatic, as well as events that occurred recently, are often more easily reflected on than other experiences. These are learning traps for project teams (Levinthal & March, 1993).

Experiences are a learning trap. It is also the case that managers and members of projects learn, through experience, to look for specific things (Weick, 1995). Doing this may be good, as it helps discover key issues for project execution, such as critical risk factors. At the same time, looking for specific relationships that are based on past experience is another potential learning trap, as it can make one overlook other relationships (Weick, 1995). To the extent that future situations do not immediately resemble, in terms of sensemaking, the past, knowing generated there-and-then may not easily translate to here-and-now. Project managers and members of the project team need to be aware of these learning issues so that they can utilize their knowledge of challenges and opportunities and look for resemblances with past situations where they have engaged in applying knowing. Doing so enables them scope to reflect on the challenges and opportunities likely to be specific to this project in the light of their broader know-how learnt from many previous projects.

REFLECTION AND EXPERIENCE-BASED LEARNING IN THE PROJECT CONTEXT

Sometimes events occur that disrupt expectations deriving from past routines, work processes and procedures. The distinction between using known processes to problem solve, tinkering with or improving existing systems, compared to radically changing processes that question assumptions, values and beliefs, is the distinction between **single-loop** and **double-loop learning** (Argyris & Schön, 1978; see Figure 11.5).

> **Single-loop learning** is immediate problem resolution applying what is known.
>
> **Double-loop learning** is learning how to do different things, differently.

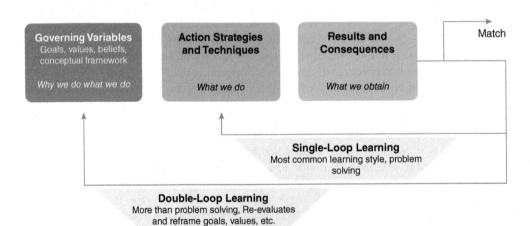

Figure 11.5   Single-loop and double-loop learning

In order to succeed over time, project-based companies must carry out both single- and double-loop learning. The latter can lead to radical changes in terms of changing culture and long-term goals, as well as the organization's basic values and systems. The 'established truths' may be put to the test. Developing new knowledge is often associated with double-loop learning.

A number of processes contribute to significant successful experience-based informal learning. Bob Dylan (1965) once wrote that 'there's no success like failure and failure is no success at all', as we noted at the head of the chapter. Reflection is often triggered by things not going as expected rather than succeeding. Success does not necessarily generate learning so much as complacency in keeping on doing what you are already doing. It is when things fail, when norms are broken, when normal sensemaking is disrupted that learning occurs; as Dylan says, there is no success like failure in order to learn.

Reflection also grows out of the encounter between different perspectives and competencies in the envisioning of how a problem should be solved. In order to share ways of thinking and knowledge in a way that contributes to reflection and learning, individual project members' explorations in double-loop learning entails asking questions and learning from both good and bad experiences (Nonaka & Takeuchi, 1995). One way of doing this is to routinize the expression of concerns and issues by having them addressed as a regular and early item on project management meeting agendas, with items only being removed when those who have brought them up feel satisfied that the issue has been resolved. Not only does doing this enable questioning, it also airs solutions so that more collective learning transpires.

Tacit knowing, which is often almost sub-consciously embrained, is considered critical to the success of projects, especially in the context of open innovation projects. Project managers need to promote a team culture that satisfies members' needs for autonomy, competence and relatedness, allowing them to feel able to share tacit knowing. In the early stage of a project, developing strong informal social relations may be required to facilitate such exchanges – barbeques and beers at the end of the week can unloosen much tacit knowledge sharing!

EXTEND YOUR KNOWLEDEGE

Read the article by Terhorst, Lusher, Bolton, and Wang (2018) on open innovation projects, such as open source software, to learn about how such projects depend on and must enable the use of tacit knowledge of many other people, available at https://study.sagepub.com/pm.

INFRASTRUCTURE FOR EXPERIENCE-BASED INFORMAL LEARNING

In order for project team members to share and learn from each other's experiences, as well as for them to learn from the experiences of previous projects or those running in parallel with the present one, an infrastructure for learning is required (Ayas & Zeniuk, 2001). Many digital tools afford good structures for sharing experiences and knowledge, the status of different activities, discussing solutions and much more. In a typical digital project room, all knowledge about the project can be shared by uploading documentation related to project execution, to professional aspects of the delivery, procedures, images, drawings, video clips and the like, useful things that are relevant for the project team to share. Such digital public spaces are commonly used in projects.

Another form of infrastructure that promotes sharing and integration of knowledge between project members is meeting sequences or other permanent venues to discuss the project. The optimal composition of participants in order to maximize the benefits is a consideration; too many, and the commitment generated by participation diminishes; too few, the onus becomes one of direction by imperative command rather than commitment. The main points in the chapter on work processes and project cooperation (Chapter 8) are usefully considered in this context.

Structures for sharing and integrating knowledge across projects vary. It may be that a project involves experts to assist in demanding processes (e.g. mapping and analysis of uncertainty) or solving specific problems that require detailed disciplinary and technical skills not available in the project team. The start-up meeting can be used to highlight relevant experiences from previous projects by paying attention to reports and analyses or inviting someone to talk about these experiences.

Other forms of organizational learning on projects can come from the conscious design of infrastructures for learning (Figure 11.6). When we think of designs for learning we might think of classrooms, with desks and chairs, a podium, and lecterns – symbols of authority and deference – where disparate people are brought together in one place. Some learning can still be like this, where members gather to listen to an expert or be addressed by senior organizational figures. More informal learning thrives on collocation and the sharing of tacit knowledge whereby project members can easily observe and imitate each other and learn through doing so. Collocation of project participants, whenever possible, is a simple action to promote experience-based learning. Increased interaction provides increased information sharing, better coordination, improved satisfaction and productivity. Being located close to each other makes it easier to arrange for ad hoc meetings, lessons-learned sessions, ideas and debriefings for experience-based learning in projects (Prencipe & Tell, 2001; Schindler & Eppler, 2003). Collocation can also contribute to a common orientation toward what a task entails and how it should be resolved, central to project success (Shenhar & Dvir, 2007).

Picture 11.2   Infrastructure for learning

In Chapter 5, we saw that collocation is a good instrument for effective coordination between project members' activities. Collocation is also a way of facilitating the flow of knowledge and it can be a precursor to the development of communities of practice (Vaagaasar, 2015b). By being collocated (or at least able to communicate with each other digitally), the participants get better acquainted, they know better what experiences others have and can seek out and share experiences (Kokkonen & Vaagaasar, 2018). Knowing each other better also contributes to security so that there is less reticence about being seen to ask questions. Especially when you are in the same place with others, it is easier to set the conditions for common problem solving (Okhuysen & Bechky, 2009). People with prior experience can be brought into a workshop as experienced and knowledgeable people from whom others might learn.

Joint problem solving for sharing and developing knowledge is probably best done face-to-face but can work well with digital communication, especially if there is a problem-solving focus to the digital meeting or it is convened as an exploration of new opportunities to gather opinion. From a problem-solving perspective of single-loop learning project staff might be collocated to address questions such as how can the task be solved as best as possible or what can we learn from each other about the issue to be resolved?

We have previously discussed the importance of routines, procedures and practices for facilitating interaction in the project team (Chapter 8). Routines are also a crucial infrastructure that facilitates the transfer of experience between project participants (Feldman & Pentland, 2003). Where routines are similar or the same across projects the necessity for learning is obviously more economical. Likewise, the risks of not learning are much higher. Project-based organizations balance adapting to changes in their surroundings with preserving and disseminating past experiences and routines effectively (Cacciatori, 2008).

Familiar objects such as templates, drawings and tools are essential devices for learning. In Chapter 5 we examined boundary objects (Carlile, 2002; Star & Griesemer, 1989). These are objects that carry and transfer knowledge, by having a core while being sufficiently open to allow for interpretation and translation in more than one way. Interpretation and translation of meaning allows ideas to move between individuals, projects and departments. Common objects that work in this way in projects are drawings, models, Excel sheets, risk-management strategies and plans.

Infrastructure for experience-based learning	Digital tools
	Meeting sequences
	Structures for sharing and integrating knowledge
	Collocation
	Composition of team members
	Routines
	Objects (models, templates, drawings, tools)

Figure 11.6 Overview for infrastructure for experience-based learning

SOCIAL RELATIONSHIPS FOR EXPERIENCE-BASED LEARNING

Structures for sharing and discussing experiences can be expanded by encouraging participants to develop and utilize social relationships for learning purposes. When we get stuck solving a task, asking a colleague is the most common way to try to move forward (Ajmal & Koskinen, 2001). Close colleagues, the project manager and one's line manager, in practice, will be key sources of knowledge. The larger the network a project employee has to refer to, the less they will seek written sources for reasons of economy of effort as well, perhaps, because of a predilection for oral as opposed to written advice. People enjoy learning socially, through interacting with others that they assume have valuable experiences. It is partly because we are social by nature that it is often more efficient to talk to someone whose know-how you trust rather than searching data bases and documents or seeking advice from experts with whom there is no prior relationship. A conversation is more efficient and faster than hunting out appropriate sources. Google, although useful, means a great deal of sorting of metaphorical wheat from chaff as well as a degree of clarity, that might be lacking, in knowing what questions to ask. Dialogue provides more control for a learner than reading a report: the latter means relating to the content without being able to influence it. We have more control over the direction of a conversation, making it resourceful for the problem at hand. Conversation is dialogical.

Hartmann and Dorée (2015) compared the formal process of recording and using lessons-learned to connecting lessons-learned through social and project activities. Decoupling them, storing them in databases, significantly reduces their value. It is not difficult to capture and store knowledge but to reuse it requires active knowing and that is much more difficult to manage. Connecting knowledge to social and project activities increases the likelihood it will come alive.

Project owners and others with a good overview can enable relationships between individuals who might benefit from interacting with each other. It is crucial that individual's competencies are known so that they may be easily sought for learning purposes. Using the intranet is one way of organizing possibilities for such exchanges. Information about events in projects also helps to highlight experiences that may be interesting (Bragd, 2002; Vaagaasar, 2006). It is beneficial to spend some time developing and maintaining relationships. Discussing events and challenges in the project need not stay in the project; others that are not involved in the project may well be involved. Exclusion of others is often a warning sign for a project, indicating that it is a 'private' space that does not welcome outsiders. Projects characterized by a form of interaction where you are encouraged to share, ask and help each other, develop a helping culture that we discuss in greater depth below (Koskinen, 2008).

In organizations that are distributed, that have projects in many different locations, the most relevant knowledge may not be local to the individual project. Perhaps more relevant experience occurred in a completely different place and project. Thus, it is crucial to distribute experiential stories. Social relations transmit learning but the potential for harvesting and utlizing knowledges increases with the number of relationships to which stories are exposed. Project team members with an overview of what is happening outside their local context can seek relevant experience elsewhere in the organization. Where projects are highly distributed, the development of networks spanning different local contexts increases the ability to create and disseminate expertise and knowing (Nahapiet & Ghoshal, 1998).

ACTIVITIES AND PROCESSES FOR EXPERIENCE-BASED LEARNING IN AND OUT OF PROJECTS

We have presented a number of activities and processes that help share and spread experiences in and between projects. When employees are asked about processes or sources that they know about, they typically point to the following (Davies & Brady, 2000; Prencipe & Tell, 2001):

- *Document management systems* that make it easier to find experiences that have been documented from previous projects, as well as best practice
- *Knowledge data bases* with lessons learned highlighted
- *'Personal' relationships* from whom advice can be sought
- *General knowledge networks*, practice communities and centres of excellence in which experience and other knowledge can be shared
- *Informal interaction and discussion* in common areas (around the coffee machine or water cooler)
- *Travelling experts*, moving between projects and tasks, translating knowledge as they travel
- *Material devices* such as models, sketches and other artefacts that convey knowledge
- *Control activities, evaluations and revisions* (in and after the project process) that help to capture experiences and reflect on them
- *Team development activities, start-up meetings* and the like activities that facilitate sharing and integration of knowledge in the project team
- *Meeting across project teams* where experiences are shared and social networks create common problem solving that helps to share and integrate experiences
- *Learning in the network of suppliers and customers* (by different stakeholders) that provide a wealth of experience that can trigger reflections
- *Standards, design templates, process management tools*, different procedures and routines that carry experience along
- *Master–apprenticeship situations* contributing to direct learning from one project employee to another
- *Job rotation* encouraging individuals to learn by embarking on new tasks
- *Champions for different aspects of the project* – these roles can often be assigned so that the champions are new to the issue or concern, maybe engineers championing ecology – so that learning and affinity are developed as well as issue promotion and translation.

Picture 11.3   Workshop

PROJECT-BASED LEARNING IN ACTION

In this chapter, we have put most emphasis on learning in the project. It is impossible to distinguish clearly between the knowledge processes that take place in and those around the project. Nor is it useful because the main point is that they must support each other and be folded together. When combined, satisfactory learning processes occur in which projects become arenas for project participants' learning and creation of new knowledge, while knowledge developed outside the project can be exploited where relevant. Where valuable learning experiences are safeguarded, stored and spread organizationally, we can talk about work-based learning (Brady & Davies, 2004; Garrick & Clegg, 2001; McIntyre & Symes, 2000).

To make work a learning experience, we need to understand more about what characterizes learning processes and the yield they can give. Here it is crucial to be aware of the different types of knowledge and knowledge processes. Having already introduced the distinction between tacit and explicit knowledge (Figure 11.7), we will take a closer look.

Knowledge: Tacit, explicit and processual

There are many frameworks that deal with different types of knowledge and how knowledge is produced and used in organizations. Some of the most famous are Nonaka and Takuchi (1995), Blackler (1995) and Spender and Grant (1996). They classify knowledge in different ways using different categories. Nonaka and Takuchi (1995) build on Polanyi's (1962) point about some knowledge being difficult to define and codify; the ability to be able to do something without being able to put it into words.

WATCH THIS!

Nonaka and Takuchi have developed a model for knowledge management, labelled SECI. Watch on YouTube a simple presentation of this model (Andre, 2018) at: https://study.sagepub.com/pm.

Nonaka and Takuchi (1995) distinguish between tacit (know-how or knowing) and explicit knowledge. Tacit knowing is characterized by what Nonaka and Takeuchi (1995; 2011) call *Ba*. *Ba* is referred to as the place where knowledge is used and integrated. It may be a physical, mental or virtual place, considered as an interaction between individuals or between individuals and tools but also it could be a framework that enables good work and working with knowledge, involving the sharing of mental models and feelings. *Ba* is a way of thinking that involves the entire individual (including body, senses and feelings) in the production of knowledge.

An image of an iceberg is often used to model the relationship between tacit and explicit knowledge (Figure 11.8); the majority of the berg is underwater, and this part represents that which is tacit. Much of our explicit knowledge is built on tacit knowing – not knowledge so much as knowing that is embrained or embodied in the person or embedded in the organization.

Figure 11.7   Explicit and tacit knowledge

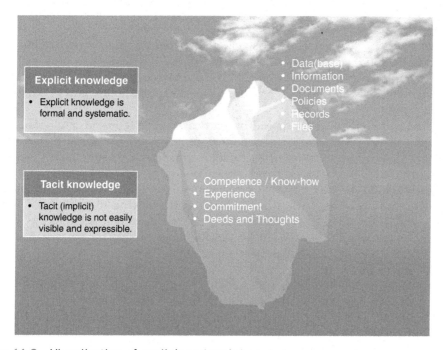

Figure 11.8   Visualization of explicit and tacit knowledge

Explicit knowledge is what we are able to put into words. It is possible to codify and thus easier to transfer as information between actors (e.g. in reports and letters). Tacit knowing is typically embedded in routines, practices and cultures, often rooted in very specific contexts, as situational knowledge. Often such knowing is embodied, as knowing how to ride a bike, or embrained, as in knowing how to speak using correct grammar, or organizationally embedded, as in the project of designing a distinctive collection for each fashion season that is different but retains a certain consistency in style (Lave & Wenger, 1991).

READ THIS!

Creating a fashion collection is a seasonal project. Some designers do it with consistency. Read this article by Anders Christian Madsen (2016) about designers that manage to vary innovation with consistency at: https://study.sagepub.com/pm.

Since tacit knowing cannot be communicated through numbers, formulae and language in documents and other channels of communication that are relatively simple, it is difficult to spread. It often requires rich media of personal knowing being shared in which multiple senses can be used for sensemaking and interpreting what's going on. Rich media, such as being physically in the same room as another person, enables transfer of tacit knowing through multiple sensemaking data. The learner can use all the senses to capture what is difficult to express in words.

Observation and imitation are key processes in the sharing of tacit knowing. You do not have to express in words what you see and imitate. In this process, knowing remains tacit, even though it is transferred from one party to another. This form of model learning can be structured in master–apprenticeship relationships (situational learning) or by project participants staying close to each other and imitating each other. Observation is an effective mechanism for creating a common sensemaking of tasks in complex projects (Koskinen, 2013). Furthermore, it is widely accepted that model learning is an efficient mechanism for transferring and integrating knowledge between project team members.

Tacit knowing can also be shared by parties making repeated attempts to elaborate and explain something to each other; even though the sense made may be quite inadequate at the start, over time tacit knowing, once mastered, may emerge as explicit knowledge. Using stories, metaphors, videos, models and images can enable the transformation of tacit personal knowing into explicit knowledge. Joint problem solving can also enable the transfer from tacit knowing to explicit knowledge (Nonaka and Takeuchi, 1995). For example, visual aids and models in the form of prototypes were widely used in Volvo's development project for the company's XC models. The models and drawings clearly contributed both to sharing and reflecting on multiple tacit knowing.

Knowledge sharing in project contexts tends to focus attention on explicit knowledge, which is easiest to share (Koskinen, 2008). Explicit knowledge, however, can sometimes seem 'a little simple' as well as not immediately purposeful. It is the combination of explicit knowledge with tacit knowing that makes for a comprehensive, meaningful and useful contribution (Newell, Robertson, Scarborough, & Swan, 2009).

Processual knowledge is socially constructed and embedded in practice in specific situations (Orlikowski & Iacono, 2001; Tsoukas, 2009). That it is socially constructed means that it is a local variant of more general knowledge transformed by participants in a social community, such as a project, so that it fits the context in which it will be used. In use, it is knowing in action, constantly evolving as actions are performed and know-how becomes embedded in processes, practices and routines. Elements of knowing are reconstructed in action each time they are used as slight deviations from routine occur that become part of interactions between people. Sometimes radical reconstruction occurs as a result of error or deviance fostering positive learning (Feldman & Orlikowski, 2011).

In complex projects, it is difficult to see how the amount and types of knowledge are woven together (Brady & Davies, 2004). Combinations will include elements, potentially of each of these:

- *Technical knowledge* about the task to be solved (What)
- *Processual knowledge* of how different project activities are to be conducted (How)
- *Strategic knowledge* of the project's relation to the base organization and other projects (Why)

- *Social knowledge* about knowing whom to consult for advice and who the relevant decision-makers are (Who)

Knowledge: Reports, stories and workshops

To succeed in developing and spreading knowledge in project-based organizations widely used tools for transferring and reusing knowledge include reports, stories and workshops.

REPORTS

When talking about the development and reuse of knowledge in a project context, the preparation and use of reports is invariably mentioned. Reports are frequently used to store and transfer experience. However, for several reasons they often do not contribute to the reuse and reconstruction of learning experiences in projects (Keegan and Turner, 2002). Reports include knowledge that can be conveyed (Newell et al., 2009), that is explicit (Polanyi, 1962) in terms of categorized knowledge (Zollo & Winter, 2002).

The content of reports is determined by their author(s). The content selected for inclusion may not match the content that potential users consider useful. Reports are often said to be push-driven while learning is often enabled by the learner selecting and structuring the content to be learned, choosing what is considered useful, increasing the motivation to learn.

A further problem with reports relates to their quality and design (Keegan & Turner, 2002). Experience reports and other project reports are often written late in the project process when time pressure is high, the focus on things other than report writing. Consequently, reports often have low quality.

Organizations might think that they have stored and spread valuable experiences between projects by capturing experience in reports; however, these are rarely written with the key aim of contributing to the learning of others. Thus, they do not become good learning media (Newell et al., 2009). They are often poorly structured and have a wide focus, reducing the motivation of the learner with regard to making use of the reports. Therefore, we must move away from the belief that we learn so much in projects due to multiple reports being produced. In order to increase learning, we should improve the way we prepare reports and choose to report at different points in time other than at the project's end. Reports should be clearly structured and appropriately designed. When documenting a project, it may be sensible to make several reports based on different themes rather than producing one overall final report.

To harvest and disseminate knowledge in contemporary times visualization works well; we live in an increasingly image- rather than text-saturated environment. Use pictures and models, as well as, where possible, links to video clips. Reports that are web-based have many more affordances of technology open to them compared to a printed product. Writing reports could be a continuous process throughout the project life cycle, focusing on, for example, phase transitions and critical events.

For critical events, an excellent tool to capture a project team's or subproject team's experience of what happened systematically (Schindler & Eppler, 2003) is an *after action review*. The review should be a group process focusing on developing a shared interpretation of the event and learning, usually lasting 20 minutes to two hours. Attention will focus on:

- What was supposed to happen?
- What did happen?
- Why did the gap between planned and actual activity occur?
- What can we learn from the processes involved?

The lessons from such sessions can be summarized and stored as mini reports or stored in the form of routines and procedures.

STORIES

Stories aid learning through thematics that memory retains as deep structures that contribute to learning that lasts. Learning becomes more intense. Individuals better remember what they learned from stories because stories are largely able to contextualise the content by placing it in relationships. Stories contribute to a holistic perspective, as the content appears meaningful and so is better remembered. In addition, stories include and elevate emotions. Learning that activates emotions often also contributes to deeper and longer lasting learning.

Organizational storytelling is often the most effective way of transmitting informal experiential knowing (Boje, 2011, 2013; Rosile, Boje, Carlon, Downs, & Saylors, 2013). Project managers can learn from colleagues through stories that are told in the organization. Stories are good formats because they relate the core of an experience (and take the freedom to embellish it a little to make it more interesting). Accounts of how a tricky problem was solved, a deadline met, or a disobedient employee disciplined, communicate the message of how things are done in the organization. Regardless of whether or not these stories are strictly speaking 'true', they form a template for managers' experiences and help make narrative sense of messy situations.

READ THIS!

Storytelling is a powerful way of learning and change. Read what Carmine Gallo (2018) has to say about Jeff Bezos replacing PowerPoints with narratives in meeting, stressing the importance of storytelling at: https://study.sagepub.com/pm.

Stories circulate readily and rapidly because of the temporality of projects as temporary organizations. Occupational mobility from project to project means that many stories travel; project managers have success and disaster stories aplenty from prior projects to inform the present one. Sometimes these stories are formally recounted; other times they circulate as gossip, occasionally becoming part of the informal legends, sagas and mythologies of project life and its characters.

To enable sharing and reuse of experience across simultaneous projects, project managers may be organized to participate systematically in each other's status meetings, meet to update each other or read each other's status reports. More informally, every project is a repository of many stories that circulate from the humblest members' experiences at the hands of previous project managers to the stories of success that circulate in boardrooms and make it into formal corporate mythology.

Stories fascinate when they capture not only past and present but also future expectations, creating comprehensive understanding. Stories have inherent temporality, as events and actions follow in sequence (Czarniawska, 1997), which helps stories to increase understanding of interdependencies in task-solving such as how an action sequence is built up. Good learning stories show that actions have a cause (Clegg & Kreiner, 2014).

It is not just a matter of (neutral) cause–effect correlations. The people involved interpret the situations more or less differently; they have intentions, values and desires. Stories trigger the curiosity of the audience just by presenting the unexpected (Czarniawska, 1997). In a good story, you wonder why an event occurs, and people act as they do. Project-based companies that want to take learning seriously must work with learning media such as stories.

WORKSHOPS

Workshops that seek to simulate some elements of a proposed project can be valuable for learning. An example is the general test workshop that event projects hold prior to an event, such as a theatre set-up, checking that everyone knows how to operate everything, where the controls are, where the cables will go, and so on.

Sharing and integration of knowledge can occur also through workshops designed as roundtable dialogues, where you talk systematically through the events anticipated. You can talk about what's going to happen, in what order, pointing out the interdependencies inherent among the actions. Dialogue is based on issues being presented as a scenario. Each project member explains how the person would have approached and acted in the focal situation. Through this explanation, the role and responsibility of the individual, and who they should collaborate with and how, is clarified and elaborated. Outside expertise can be recruited to address specific issues that might be outside the competencies of the team.

Organized role plays in which project groups train using relevant reality scenarios help members to become aware of what knowledge they lack as well as that which they possess and how what is lacking and what is present can be synthesized. Through the workshop, knowledge will be accumulated, systematized and synthesized personally. Often it is recommended that each participant, immediately after the workshop, describes their own observations and reactions about what happened, focusing on how satisfied they are that:

- Their contribution was useful
- The contributions of others were useful
- The result of the workshop, overall, was useful
- The project team achieved positive results in relation to the issue at hand and work processes
- The desire to improve was fostered

Participants share experiences through such exercises and are encouraged to note interesting or unclear observations/reactions from others for subsequent follow-up. The facilitator manages the review and can ask follow-up questions.

Many organizations possess much valuable knowledge that they have difficulty converting from capabilities into action. The fact that projects do not always perform as planned is often not due to insufficient knowledge but rather inability to make use of the knowledge the project team possesses. The project's knowledge is stored in the employees' awareness and actions, in routines and procedures, in knowing all its guises, as well as collected in various reports.

Visualizing the knowledge elements that the project group holds in order to integrate them in the task solving processes is challenging (Geithner, Menzel, Wolfe, & Kriz, 2016). Visualizing the team members' different knowledge elements helps put them together for situation-based problem solving (Grant, 1996). When practising activities, project team members exercise their skills through training; additionally, these exercises help to visualize, share and integrate knowledge (Carlile, 2002).

EXTEND YOUR KOWLEDGE

Play can be serious. Read the article by Geithner et al. (2016) on the effectiveness of learning through experience and reflection in a project management simulation at: https://study. sagepub.com/pm.

All three tools – reports, stories and workshops – promote learning by serving different but potentially complementary functions. Reports are useful for storing and disseminating forms of codified knowledge but are not suitable for maintaining knowledge related to relationships that are part of practices and the tacit knowing. Stories and exercises are better tools for tacit knowing.

In recent years, there has been a lot of attention to how knowledge integration can take place across individuals, departments, projects and organizations. Project success, it is argued, depends on knowledge integration (Eisenhardt & Tabrizi, 1995). Simulation, roundtable dialogues, stories and communities of practice are useful means for integrating knowledge.

WHAT WOULD YOU DO?

You are still the project manager of the project that is to develop a software for booking hotel rooms for the hotel chain Londurena and the routines that are needed to implement this system in an efficient way. You are now about halfway through the project duration. You have a problem in terms of getting all the team members to contribute what they know, in developing good solutions. There is an expert in the team that seems to be unwilling to share his knowledge. Also, the two members from the client seem negative and rather unmotivated.

QUESTIONS

1. What would you do to motivate the members from the client?

2. What would you do to engage the expert for the sake of the project?

Why is learning from projects limited?

We have pointed out that projects are good learning arenas. Unfortunately, much of the learning happening in projects is lost at the end of the project. The end of the project is often the end of collective project learning and the point at which organizational amnesia begins (Schindler & Eppler, 2003).

Research points out many reasons why there is too little use of project-based learning (Figure 11.9). In line with the research of Keegan and Turner (2002) and Schindler and Eppler (2003), we will look at some of the reasons for limited learning. Project team members are often short of time. Task focus is everything. The project is characterized by short-term thinking. Learning 'costs' in the short term in terms of hours, money and emotions. Learning from the project is a continuous process, not just something that occurs at the end. Often, as the project is coming to a close, there is very limited time and focus on learning as handovers occur, new project teams are assembling, new projects launched. These new projects and related tasks consume most of the attention. Under these circumstances it can be difficult for employees to meet for debriefing; if they do meet it is challenging to achieve focus on the project and remember the valuable learning that occurred.

The complexity of ongoing events in projects with all the judgement and reflection entailed in moving the project forward often overwhelms opportunities for reflection, learning and their consolidation. In retrospect, things tend to look much clearer and simpler and the amount of control that was present can be retrospectively garnished. The sense of emergency and improvisation that actually helped in resolving issues that events threw up is glossed over under the professional rubric of project planning. While being in the situation of decision and actions, what occurs often seems blurrier and more ambiguous than what is selectively remembered and reported. Experiences captured *in situ* from more fuzzy situations would benefit the project in ways that *post hoc* recollection does not. In practice it is difficult to get team members to share knowledge with their colleagues, especially tacit knowing.

Recent studies (Škerlavaj, Connelly, Cerne, & Dysvik, 2018) demonstrate why employees who experience greater time pressure are more likely to engage in forgetting, not recalling or reconstructing accounts of what happened. Such behaviours may be moderated by employees' prosocial motivation (i.e. the intent to benefit others such as helping, sharing and cooperating) and perspective taking. Perspective taking mediates the moderating effect of prosocial motivation, the relationship between time pressure and hiding knowledge.

Learning is also hindered where individual project team members are not made responsible for work related to learning. Learning is often regarded as a centralized responsibility and often not included in the project's management systems. Someone outside the project will be responsible for this, such as the HR department, the competence department or the project management office (Keegan and Turner, 2002). Where learning is not considered a natural and inherent part of the project process, systems and routines for its acquisition and dissemination will be lacking. Sometimes, there is an assumption that the particular project at hand is so special that it is difficult to learn anything generalizable from its processes. Given that one never knows what future projects might be, to judge the utility of the present project on the basis of those done in the past is extremely short-sighted.

Many projects are fully or partially staffed with personnel contracted only for that project; when they disappear so does what they know as they take their lessons with them. Some will not want to share and leave knowledge behind, on the assumption that it will reduce their opportunity to be hired later, by increasing the likelihood of their future redundancy.

Remember there is no success like failure – but who wants to be remembered for failure? People associated with failure are often reluctant to learn from them, as persons and entities such as departments and project teams might be reputationally damaged by their association with these failed aspects of projects.

Obstacles from learning of projects	Do not have the time
	Short-minded thinking
	Short-term costs
	Rather learn at closure of project
	Somebody else responsible
	Not included in project management control system
	Own project so unique
	Hired personel

Figure 11.9   Obstacles to learning of projects

Project learning environments

We have previously discussed the importance of trust for collaboration within in the team and between the team members and various stakeholders. Trust is required for learning (Nerstad et al., 2018) and is a key component of good learning cultures. Trust increases the ability to reflect, ask questions, voice one's opinion and more generally participate in knowledge processes. Trust reduces the need for control (Fox, 1974). Therefore, individuals can gain more independence in their task solution, which also contributes positively to learning.

Self-efficacy relates to trust. We have talked about processes that contribute to high-performance project teams (Chapter 8). A team with high self-efficacy selects more difficult tasks and sets higher goals than teams with lower self-efficacy, start their work faster and put more effort into their task solving over time, contributing very positively to learning. Self-efficacy also contributes positively to learning in many contexts. A recent study of about 1000 employees in five organizations (Nerstad et al., 2018) has demonstrated that when employees perceive an organization as being one in whose culture they are confident, they are also more likely to feel trusted by their leaders and vice versa, facilitating knowledge sharing.

A learning culture is founded on wondering and reflection. Managers that respond positively when team members admit, examine and learn from errors enable learning from mistakes and failure. A feeling of safety and belonging is also critical for project-based learning to occur. It is vital that employees are made accountable for learning processes with regard to reuse, development and dissemination of knowledge. The supportive leader that we discussed in Chapter 6 fits well with this emphasis.

Innovating

Learning leads to knowing; collective knowing how to do things differently or do different things that foster innovation, creating and introducing something new. We will discuss different characteristics of innovation. Organizations increasingly strive for innovation through project-based developments. We will look at different organizational forms by which projects are integrated into an organization (Davies et al., 2011).

When organizations try to facilitate innovation, conflicts can often arise between management's desire to manage the project and the projects' need for autonomy. Organization management must provide a framework that provides the project with the desired direction but at the same time make sure there is sufficient space to be creative and seek novel solutions, as well as elaborating opportunities that arise (Bakker et al., 2013). We will look at how creativity and team processes can contribute to innovations that create value for the companies. First, we address the characteristics of innovation in projects.

Picture 11.4   Creative journeys

INNOVATING IN AND THROUGH PROJECTS

With increased competition and more frequent product and process changes, the interest in, need for and attention paid to **innovation** is constantly increasing (Tidd & Bessant, 2018).

> **Innovation**, simply explained, is a new way of creating value or of using existing ideas to provide *new* forms of *use* value *utilized* in practice.

There are three components of innovation (see Figure 11.10):

1. What is being developed is something other than that which presently exists: it is *new* in context.
2. What is being developed helps to improve a product, process or service: it is *useful*.
3. What is being developed contributes to improved value creation and realization: it is *utilized*.

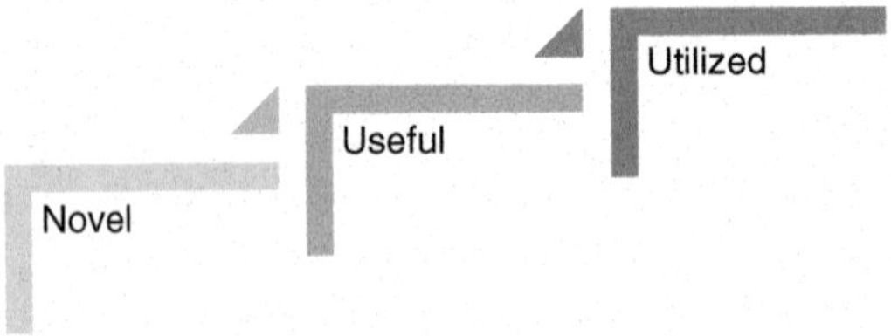

Utilized

Useful

Novel

Figure 11.10   Elements for the term innovation

All projects are always a little innovative in bringing some new product, service or process into being. Even if the project is seemingly as simple as an event associated with an art exhibition it is still an innovation process: the exhibition has to be curated, art chosen, brochures produced, themes devised to market the exhibition. How innovation processes are organized through projects is a central theme for project management.

> **Creativity** entails the production of novel and useful ideas or problem solutions.

Creativity is related to innovation but is not the same. Roughly speaking, creativity is about conceiving and creating an idea or solution, while innovation, somewhat simplified, is to put the idea or solution into practice.

Successful organizations must master three core activities related to creativity (Hill, 2014; see Figure 11.11):

* *Creative resolution*. Ability to make integral, comprehensive decisions that combine different and even contradictory ideas.
* *Creative abrasion*. Skills to generate ideas through discourse and discussion.
* *Creative agility*. Skills to test and experiment through quick pursuit, reflection and adjustments.

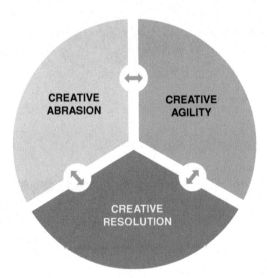

Figure 11.11   Three key activities for successful innovation (after Hill, 2014)

These three key activities provide the basis for managing innovation processes. Note that none of these three basic ideas refer to especially creative individuals. Creativity is not just a matter of individual psychology. Indeed, contemporary creativity research focuses on collective practice (Hargadon & Bechky, 2006; Murphy, 2004; Obstfeld, 2012; Sawyer & DeZutter, 2009; Sonenshein, 2014). Creativity produces new and situationally appropriate ideas or solutions that have *direction and purpose* provided by structuring organization and facilitating innovation. The starting point is to be able to work constructively and creatively but that is not sufficient; the team composition in terms of competencies as well as clarification of goals, expectations and tasks must be present.

THE TEAM AS THE STARTING POINT FOR INNOVATING THROUGH PROJECTS

Team creativity is a key condition for diversity and openness in the team. However, the importance of diversity for the team to work creatively is not sufficient. Research shows that team members also need to be willing to use their resources in the team so that diversity will contribute to better creativity and innovation (Aime et al., 2014). The creative part of a project team working on innovation is not limited to the first phase of the project, where ideas will be clarified to provide direction. Practices of generating, communicating, connecting, evaluating and reshaping ideas contribute to what we call idea work (Coldevin et al., 2019) that sustains innovative projects.

Two aspects of teamwork identified by Coldevin et al. (2019) contribute to creativity underlying innovation. First, the importance of team creativity evolving through the creation of complex compositions that constitute focal ideas through connecting them to the ideas of others, placing them in larger wholes or making analogical inferences that constitute new part–whole relationships. Coldevin et al. (2019) term this *intertextual placing*, where various situational approaches are used to put creative ideas in broader contexts. Intertextual placing might entail prototyping, modelling, linking emergent ideas to proximate comparators experienced or realized in other projects. Second, Coldevin et al. (2019) stress dynamics *legitimating imagining*: this is where ideas of what to do are connected to ideas of what is worth doing and becoming. Legitimating imagining bridges and joins internal aspirations with external expectations of value. Where imaginings are legitimated fragmentary snatches of creative ideas still forming become something that can be believed in.

EXTEND YOUR KNOWLEDGE

Read the article by Coldevin et al. (2019) about how we understand the nature of organizational creativity when dealing with complex, composite ideas rather than singular ones at: https://study.sagepub.com/pm..

IN PRACTICE

MAINSTREAM CREATIVITY THEORY

Coldevin et al. (2019) problematize assumptions that stress the linearity of creative processes and the singularity of ideas in mainstream creativity theory. They draw on the work of Bakhtin

(Continued)

and longitudinal research in two contrasting cases: developing hydrocarbon prospects, and concepts for films and TV series. From these two cases, they highlight two forms of work on ideas: (1) intertextual placing, whereby focal ideas are constituted by being connected to other elements in a larger idea field; and (2) legitimating imaginings, where ideas of what to do are linked to ideas of what is worth doing and becoming. This ongoing constitution and legitimating is not confined to particular stages but takes place in practices of generating, connecting, communicating, evaluating and reshaping ideas, which they call idea work. Their paper contributes to a better understanding of the processual character of creativity and the deeply intertextual nature of ideas, including the multiplicity of idea content and shifting parts–whole relationships. Idea work also serves to explore the neglected role of co-optative power in creativity.

QUESTION

1. Having read Coldevin et al., what inspiration does it offer you for thinking about idea work practices in projects that you have been involved in?

CREATIVITY AND TEAM MANAGEMENT

In creative projects, a project manager will strive to blend mutual trust, understanding of the task and relevant competencies (Tidd & Bessant, 2018). Creative processes require both structure and leadership, with the project manager being the one who takes care of presenting these. Nevertheless, the management function in teams may alternate between several team members as different competencies play a lead role at different stages of the creative process.

Creativity is an ability that can be cultivated, not least through teamwork providing a fruitful interaction between both people, situations and tasks. Some aspects of the persons involved are significant, suggest Amabile, Barsade, Mueller, and Staw (2005). The individual must:

- Possess a certain creative skill for the specific purpose of the task. That is, the ability to approach a problem from different angles, have a strong belief in the idea, and the will to go into the unknown.
- Have sufficient expertise or expertise in the field. It can be difficult to innovate if you do not know about existing knowledge and applications in the area and any of their weaknesses or deficiencies that require improvement.
- Be motivated to contribute and create something and have commitment to the task as meaningful and realizable.

In order to be creative, one must be both knowledgeable and strongly focused on the demands made and the possibilities that exist (Csikszentmihalyi, 2008). Creativity is therefore not something that is reserved for some people who may seem full of original ideas. It is about a driving force towards creating something in an area where one has competence, as well as a certain relevant creative skill, working in teams with others with similar attributes. To innovate in projects, creativity must be developed and challenged in partnership with others in the team and organization.

PRODUCT AND PROCESS INNOVATION

A significant difference exists between product and process forms of innovation. Chapter 2 made it clear that projects can be divided into two types: projects aimed at changing or creating a new product or service, and projects aimed at changing the production and transformation process. The distinction provides the basis for categorizing different project types. For *product innovation projects*, the innovation may be to develop further an existing product or to develop a brand-new product. Delivery of such products might be composed of both product and process innovation: for instance, electrifying an existing range of vehicles.

In projects oriented to *process innovation*, innovation revolves around the way a product is created or acquired and the innovation can apply to both the production process itself and to support functions. The product may change as well as the organization processes involved. An example may be the ways that Thom Yorke and colleagues make and distribute music. By the time of Radiohead's fourth album, *Kid A* (2000), Yorke and the band moved into electronic music, often manipulating his vocals, creating a new product through new processes. Both with Radiohead and in his solo work Yorke has pioneered innovative processes through alternative music release platforms such as pay-what-you-want and BitTorrent, innovating the distribution and marketing of music. Putting on a festival as an event project with Radiohead as headliners could thus entail both product as well as process innovation.

The innovation literature often focuses on **disruptive innovation**, as a form of radical innovation.

> **Disruptive innovation** interferes with and shakes up existing markets.

Disruptive innovation is a product or process that has been improved in a way the market has not expected or foreseen (Christensen, Johnson, & Horn, 2010). An example of disruptive innovation is Amazon's impact on the book industry, where much of the market for books was completely changed with major consequences for distribution of the products. From this initial innovation project Amazon has moved into disrupting many other product markets.

WATCH THIS!

Professor Clayton Christensen (2012) at Harvard Business School explains on this YouTube video the power of disruptive innovation at: https://study.sagepub.com/pm.

Thus far we have distinguished product and process innovation. Product innovation may not be focused on an entirely new product or service but might also offer something that is either new or significantly improved. This may include improvements in components, specifications, materials or functional features. Process innovation may include changes in techniques, equipment or software, or in the way that a product or service is delivered.

When process innovation is organizationally wide-ranging, where it involves new or substantially changed organizational processes, we might refer to organizational innovation, such as changes in business model and organizational structure, networks of relations with suppliers, vendors or other external stakeholders.

Market innovation might include introducing a new marketing and profiling method significantly changed from past practice by the innovation project. For example, there might be significant changes in product design, wrapping, product placement or pricing.

> **Radical innovations** are innovations that lead to major developments, which transform products and/or services in a relatively short period of time.
>
> **Incremental innovations** imply development through small steps, minor changes and adjustments which, over time, can lead to significant innovation.

How fast or comprehensive innovation occurs can be characterized by defining it as either more or less **radical** or **incremental innovation**.

Apple's iTunes and Apple Music and Ford's innovation of the moving production line would be two different examples of radical innovations. Toyota is famous for its incremental innovations; look at the way it introduced the Prius as a hybrid vehicle alongside its regular engine vehicles.

WHAT WOULD YOU DO?

The CEO of a large international company approaches you where you work as a consultant. He is an old-style manager, educated with his MBA years ago and has no lack of self-confidence. Innovation is a term he likes to think he is familiar with. Nevertheless, he wants you to explain the word in more depth by giving you two internal innovation projects he is involved in, as examples.

One is a project where two companies are merging. Company A is a large, old company producing hardware products in a specific branch, while company B is a medium-sized company delivering services to support production related to the product of company A. The company you work at is involved as process facilitators in this merging project.

The other example is a project where the implementation of a new overall IT system in the company is about to start. IT implies exchange of computers and new software. Moreover, it means new routines for handling tasks related to operations to be done via the new IT system.

QUESTION

1. Given the restricted information, how would you categorize those two projects, in terms of innovation? And how would you argue for your choice?

THE INNOVATION DIAMOND

Uncertainty is a central feature of all projects. In Chapter 8 we introduced Shenhar and Dvir's (2007) four dimensions of innovation:

Novelty. How new are key aspects of the project?

Complexity. How complex or compound is the product, the process and the project?

Technology. How technologically dependent are the project and the product?

Pace. How quickly is it necessary to prepare the product?

Based on these four dimensions, Shenhar and Dvir (2007) have developed a diamond model to categorize innovation projects.

NOVELTY

Novelty is the core idea behind innovation and refers to the originality and difference of a product or process. For unique innovations the level of uncertainty in the market in which it may be released will be very high. Uniqueness can be categorized at four levels:

Derivative, where the product is an extension and improvement of the existing product. Example: New version of a mobile phone.

Platform, where one develops a new generation of the product, within a well-established market segment. Example: Development of a new car model.

Market introduction, where a product from a market is adapted and introduced to another market. Example: battery-operated water-flushing domestic devices, modelled on professional dental equipment, with which to floss one's teeth.

Breakthrough, introducing a brand-new concept, a new idea or a completely new way of using a product. Example: when Apple launched the iPad.

The diamond model tends towards discussion of physical and commercial products as innovations. At the same time, it can also be translated and adapted to non-commercial innovation processes. For example, within the public sector one may think of the introduction of patient safety alerts for caregivers as a form of market innovation that changed the way in which care services were offered and performed by municipal services. Subsequently, these security alarms have been extended to include several additional features and services. For more process-related innovations, there will also be degrees of originality. Often, existing 'recipes' for improving different processes, such as total quality management or LEAN production will be used and customized.

COMPLEXITY

How complex is the project and its organization? Complexity depends both on the extent of that which is being developed and the organization required to develop the product. Complexity affects the degree of formalization and coordination needed to manage the project effectively; the more complexity, the higher the levels of these and the larger the effect on system innovation related to the design of workflow processes.

Shenhar and Dvir (2007) differentiate between three levels of complexity:

Assembly projects involving the development of several components that will act as a device and perform a single function. It is thus a single component, whether it is a product or process to be developed. Example: Organizational change within a department.

System projects where development work involves combining a complex set of devices that mutually affect each other, and which will serve more functions at the same time. It may also involve building a new organization that is responsible for a single function. Example: Construction of a residential complex on eco-sustainable principles.

Array projects where a large and scattered register of systems that together have a common purpose require linkage. These may be networks or more complex coordinated devices. Example: Development of transport networks moving container cargo globally.

TECHNOLOGICAL UNCERTAINTY

How much technology is involved in the development process? This point represents the level of technological uncertainty and influences how many cycles are required to design the product and how long it takes before the design is completed. Technological uncertainty can be categorized into four levels:

Low technology, where the development process uses existing technology.

Medium technology, using mainly existing technology, but making some adjustments, and possibly using it in a new way.

High technology, where new systems and practices are used, usually within an industry where rapid changes occur.

Super-high technology, where a new technology is needed to develop the product.

To an even greater degree than novelty, technology is often particularly prominent in the development of physical products. For services and more non-commercial organizations, it may apply to varying degrees.

PACE

Pace determines the critical time aspect of the development process. Pace can be categorized into four levels:

Regular, where the time aspect is not particularly critical.

Fast/competitive, where reaching the market with the product to achieve a competitive advantage is a strategic objective.

Time-critical, where the completion date is absolute and cannot be shifted.

Blitz, where finding a solution or completing a product is essential for success.

Forms of innovation and degrees of uncertainty will vary from project to project and these differences affect how the projects are organized by the client. Based on the four dimensions (novelty, complexity, technology and pace; see Figure 11.12), Shenhar and Dvir (2007) have developed a model that addresses opportunities and potential risks in the various dimensions (Table 11.2).

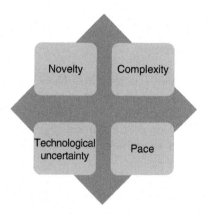

Figure 11.12 Diamond of innovation in projects

Table 11.2 Opportunities and potential risks by dimensions

Dimension	Opportunities	Potential risks
Novelty	Exploring new market opportunities, bypassing competitors, achieving 'first in the market' advantage	Difficult to predict exact market needs, missing customer group, attracting competitors who are copying
Complexity	Improve performance and functionality	Experiencing technological failure, lacking necessary skills
Technology	Larger programmes provide greater profit	Problems with coordination and integration
Pace	Early in the market, can follow up with better products	Crack on deadlines, make arbitrary mistakes

WATCH THIS!

Approaching the innovation diamond must be done in an adaptive way, explains Aaron Shenhar (2013) in a YouTube video on 'The adaptive approach and the diamond model for project success' at: https://study.sagepub.com/pm.

The innovation diamond appears as clear and distinct but somewhat recipe-like. It is based on the assumption that a significant amount of uncertainty can be calculated and is primarily suitable for dealing with major innovation projects for the development of commercial products, although it can be adapted to other innovation projects. Shenhar and Dvir (2007) argue that the innovation diamond can be used to evaluate and measure the potential of the market and products in order to:

- Provide a basis for choosing project design and process
- Be a platform to communicate direction and complexity

- Get a shaky project back on the right track
- Provide a basis for assessing the innovation project's needs for resources and, where appropriate, action rooms

The innovation diamond provides useful insights into how projects and project deliveries differ in terms of complexity, technological uncertainty, pace and novelty and is particularly relevant for 'painting by number' and 'conquest' projects. The diamond model demonstrates that there are a number of different types of innovations that require different types of management in order to succeed in value creation.

WHAT WOULD YOU DO?

You have been handed an assignment as a project manager for a big innovation project. Your project is supposed to develop a new product for an amusement park. The amusement park has a great many existing attractions but needs a new spectacular attraction. You are hired in from an external consulting company as an expert on project management. The principal for the project will be the CEO for the amusement park organization. Moreover, the project includes collaboration with other joint venture partners, such as suppliers of materials and technical solutions, the venue management team as well as other partners. Your project team will consist of team members mainly from the amusement organization but also members from other organizations such as supplier companies.

QUESTION

1. Before you start the project, the principal charges you with identifying what you anticipate will be the major challenges related to this innovation project, in terms of complexity, uncertainty and other elements. How would you apply the innovation diamond to identify this project?

Final reflection

Even though project contexts are characterized by fragmentation and discontinuity that is regarded as antithetical to learning, it does occur and can be improved. To succeed with project-based learning, we must develop an understanding of how learning takes place in the project and how it can be spread across projects. Building the ability to learn and learning in every aspect of project-based companies is the real deal for innovation. Learning can be supported as a natural part of project execution. Project-based learning requires approaching everyday life with a pronounced positive attitude towards development but one that also recalls what Dylan said; that is, there's no success like failure – because when we fail, we should learn from the failings.

Summary

In this chapter, we have:

- Elaborated on the constituents of project-based learning environments. We have looked at how the learning in project-based organizations can be analysed using the framework of learning landscapes.

- Looked at the characteristics of different types of knowledge and knowledge processes. We have seen that experience-based learning is particularly relevant in the context of projects. The key enablers and activities of project-based learning have been outlined, such as social and physical infrastructures and social relationships. We have also looked at learning traps, and some of the reasons why it seems so difficult to learn from projects.
- Discussed how projects and innovation are inseparably linked to organization change and renewal, seeking to create new value. We have discussed the differences between process and product innovation projects.
- How to use the innovation diamond for projects and the importance of management being aware of the opportunities and potential dangers that arise when projects are given autonomy to design innovations through project organization.
- What the key characteristics of creativity in project teams are and how creativity can be stimulated through idea work.

Exercises

1. What are key characteristics of project-based learning? Analysing project-based learning in an organization, what would the three different learning landscapes tell you?
2. Can you describe different activities for sharing knowledge within a project team? What is the difference between explicit and tacit knowledge? What is recommended for working to share tacit knowledge?
3. How would you go about enabling future projects to exploit the learning experiences of an ongoing project that you are involved in – what are the ways you can capture such knowledge?
4. Can you point to three important reasons as to why it is challenging to learn from projects?
5. What are the two forms of innovation processes – and what are the key characteristics of these two forms respectively?
6. What is the key learning to take away from the discussion on the innovation diamond? Do you remember the four key aspects to be considered?
7. What are the key characteristics of creativity in project teams, and what would you do to stimulate creativity in a project team?
8. What can you say about the nature of reflection, why is it so important and how can it be enabled – even in high-paced projects?

CASE STUDY

INNOVATION DECOHERENCE

To explain physical phenomena, there are two sets of laws, one for the large-scale world, and another for the world of particles. Likewise, could we not consider that different 'laws' are required when managing large corporations versus smaller innovative outfits? Large companies

(Continued)

can be defined by their inertia and that of their markets while innovative companies can be defined by indetermination (uncertainty). If this observation is correct, then wouldn't we need to adapt our thinking and perhaps start building new theories that allow us to better analyse the start-up 'state'. In the following paragraphs we build on this logic to show how 'quantum-inspired' factors such as determinism and probability may affect firms differently depending on their size. Building on this analogy we question if we should reconsider how innovative enterprises should be managed and studied.

INEXACT CALCULATIONS

In classical physics, you have determinism. With the proper data, you can anticipate where an object will land when thrown. This is what allows us to have a large degree of certainty that an aircraft will take off and land safely. In the quantum world, though, you can only give an approximation of a particle's position and speed and hence all the subsequent calculations are inexact. Bringing it back to the aeroplane example, this means that there are strong chances the aircraft will land before or by the side of the runway. The same goes with companies. In the world of large enterprises determinism is much more abundant. It is much easier to anticipate a corporation's results than it is for start-ups and predicting the market size for cars or for clothing is much less of a challenge than predicting a non-existing market.

This concept relates to a second important one – probability. In the classical world, the aircraft lands on the runway every time. In quantum physics, the plane can land on and beyond the runway. Here we can make a parallel to investments. Probability is the certainty that an investment will go as expected. While there is high sustainability in the stock of a major corporation, the same doesn't apply to a start-up. Angel investors are more likely to develop a very diverse portfolio of start-up investments because they know that the likelihood of them being successful (that they will land *on* the runway) is limited.

ACCEPTABLE LEVELS OF IMPRECISION

Another angle of understanding of the concept of probability is how it imposes trade-offs. In quantum physics it is impossible to know precisely two types of information from the same particle, at the same time. Worse still, an increase in knowledge (reduction in probability) of one parameter decreases your knowledge of the other. Imagine losing precision in the speed of your aeroplane because you are trying to improve your understanding of your position. This would be a big dilemma for a pilot! Would you prefer knowing where you are going to crash or at what speed!

While large firms do have trade-off challenges, they exist at larger scale and not all trade-offs are mutually exclusive nor create disruptions for another business choice. Coca-Cola does not need to choose between large marketing investments and a new product line. Taking the analogy to a human resource level, these firms have sales teams supported by a marketing teams and also technical teams that rely on precious technical capabilities in the hands of researchers, engineers and technicians. Start-ups, though, with their limited means, need to make trade-offs and find a balance, notably between the technical and the sales activity. They need to accept some level of inaccuracy in building their product and in leading the sales effort. If they insist on utmost precision in one field, it is at the expense of another, like having a great understanding of their whereabouts on the market, but no notion of their speed.

THE EFFECTS OF OBSERVATION

A last specificity is observation. In quantum physics, when particles are observed, they actually change behaviour. When no one is looking, they dance along minding their own business. But as soon as you look at them, they take on a more conventional behaviour and move in a very predictive manner. This would be very odd if applied to an aircraft. Imagine that by simply looking at a plane, it would change the way it flew. However, the phenomenon does exist when observing small entities. Start-ups are very sensitive to observation, whether by the press, investors or potential customers: the final outcome is often influenced by the observer. Is it for the best?

With these parallels in mind, shouldn't we challenge, as it is the case in physics, the way in which we expect large and small firms to produce innovation as well as their fundamental management practices? Accepting a duality in management practices would then entail some form of differentiation among paradigms. New models and ways of studying start-ups could have strong repercussions in the way we manage individuals and projects, by defining for instance, the level of accuracy expected in a project to optimize chances of success. Many individuals underperform because of excessive observation. Many projects are abandoned simply because too much precision was expected from the very onset, or because of the weight of observation and the pressure from investors to follow an overly deterministic plan. By injecting a 'start-up' cursor in our management practices, maybe we could allow a much more adapted approach, thus considerably enhancing the overall efficiency of companies, whether big or small.

Source: adapted from 'Innovation decoherence' by Fernanda Arreola (co-written with Phillipe Carteu), *The Conversation*, 29 November 2018. You can access this at https://study.sagepub.com/pm.

QUESTION

1. Physicists are smart people, by definition. How much smarter would they be if they learnt from the literature of project innovation and what should they learn?

Additional resources

The classic works of Argyris and Schön (1978) provide good insights into learning and competence development in organizations. James March's article (1991) on exploitation and exploration has been widely used and referenced. Prencipe and Tell (2001) contribute insight into the issues of organizational learning in projects and codification of learning. There is a lot of literature to choose from in the areas of innovation and creativity. There are not so many books that deal with both innovation and projects. Shenhar and Dvir's (2007) *Reinventing Project Management* is useful as is Davies and Hobday (2005) *The Business of Projects: Managing Innovation in Complex Products and Systems*. Rosabeth Kanter and Linda Hill have released two valuable contributions in the field, respectively *SuperCorp* (2009) and *Collective Genius* (2014).

Chapter Roadmap

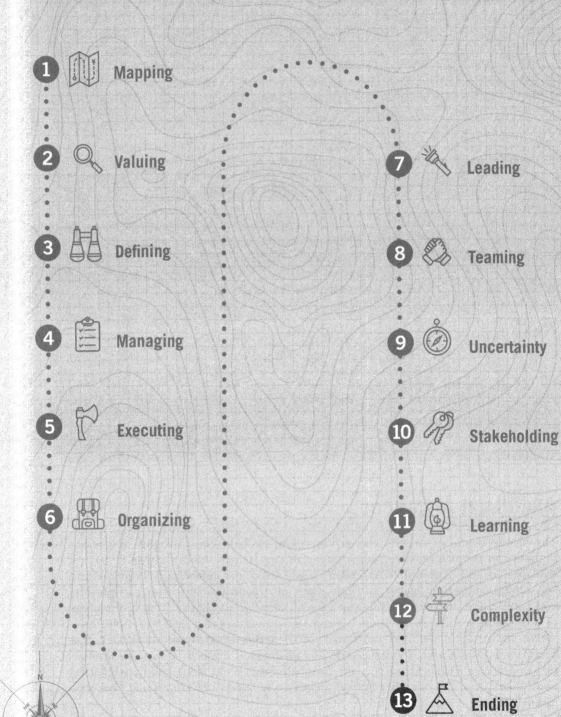

1 Mapping

2 Valuing

3 Defining

4 Managing

5 Executing

6 Organizing

7 Leading

8 Teaming

9 Uncertainty

10 Stakeholding

11 Learning

12 Complexity

13 Ending

12

Complexifying Projects

Learning objectives

After reading this chapter, you should:

1 Recognize projectification as a phenomenon and understand what it means for individuals, processes and structures in business

2 Recognize the characteristics of project programmes and portfolios

3 Understand how complexity increases in interorganizational projects where several actors are involved on the principal and/or executor side

4 Know how to work with project maturity analyses and how project management offices can be useful tools in complex projects

5 Know about key processes to follow and key risks of toxicity to avoid in project management

Before you get started

The greater the potential for reward in the value portfolio, the less risk there is.

– Warren Buffett

Introduction

It is common for companies to have many simultaneous projects, which gives them flexibility, but also a number of challenges. It requires different degrees and forms of coordination between the projects, between the clients and between companies. When these projects occur across fragmented institutional environments in which multiple contradictory institutional logics coexist, such as commercial firms working on public sector projects or Western organizations engaged in development projects in less developed countries (Greenwood, Raynard, Kodeih, Micelotta, & Lounsbury, 2011), then confusion can arise about the appropriate logics. The challenges are many for those involved in several projects and for the organization that must professionalize its project competence by learning from projects. Projects are unique processes and require more resources for management and control than the usual operating tasks. The complexity of an organization therefore drastically increases as the number of projects grows. Successful coordination of several projects in programmes can help to realize strategy. We will look into how projects can be coordinated through programme portfolio management (PPM), contributing to value creation in line with the desired effort.

For organizations that work project-based, a project management office can be a suitable tool for aligning project execution across the project portfolio. The project management office contributes to quality assurance of project implementation according to best practices. For organizations with many parallel projects, competence should be utilized across the projects and the projects enacted in such a way that they do not 'cannibalize' each other. Individuals with special skills are likely to be overloaded if they work on many projects and tasks at the same time. As a result of projectification, a certain amount of maturity is also needed to manage the project form optimally. All of these elements will be highlighted in this chapter.

Multiple projects simultaneously: Projectification

So far, we have in this book mostly focused on the individual project. The reality is that most companies have several projects in parallel. Driven by the necessity and aspirations of innovation and ever faster changes, the project form has had a decisive influence on how organizations adjust their work processes to accommodate **projectification** (Packendorff & Lindgren, 2014) and increases the complexity of managing and leading the projects.

> **Projectification** refers to the cultural and discursive societal processes whereby projects and project-like circumstances are institutionalized in organizing through temporary organizations created to deliver value.

EXTEND YOUR KNOWLEDGE

Projects have become omnipresent in our society and our lives. Drawing on the philosophical cornerstone concepts of activity, time, space, and relations, Jensen, Thuesen, and Geraldi (2016) conceptualize projects as a 'human condition'. Read about this in their article 'The projectification of everything: Projects as a human condition'. The article is available in the online resources at https://study.sagepub.com/pm.

The growth in the use of projects has further led to the development and spread of two related approaches: **programme** and **portfolio** management (Pellegrinelli, Murray-Webster, & Turner, 2015), which together are known as **programme and portfolio management** (PPM). The projects that are part of a programme thus have a common goal that they should work towards. They are also mutually dependent on each other to achieve success. For portfolios, there is often no single common goal that collects the projects together. They must all contribute to reaching the organization's goals.

A **project programme** is a collection of interrelated projects, managed and coordinated to realize value unachievable through the management of the projects individually.

A **project portfolio** is a collection of several projects that are not interrelated but that draw on the same resource base.

Programme and portfolio management (PPM) is the overall organizational ability to select, support and manage the project portfolio strategically and holistically, to create organizational value.

Both project programmes and project portfolios include several projects (Figure 12.1). Programmes have a clearer end, while a portfolio is more continuous, although content can change over time. A project programme is part of the total project portfolio, i.e. its total collection of projects. While a project is clearly a single phenomenon, albeit that it can be broken down into subprojects, a project programme is a collection of interrelated projects. Programme and portfolio management represents a collection of non-correlated projects drawing from the same resource base.

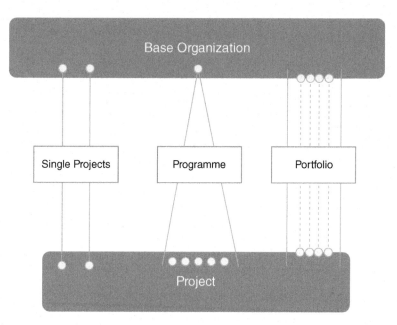

Figure 12.1 Project programmes, portfolio and single projects

Many companies have many project programmes. One can wonder if we are moving from projectification to **programmification** (Maylor, Brady, Cooke-Davies, & Hodgson, 2006).

Programmification means an increasing degree of project programmes being used as an organizational solution to manage complex tasks and changes.

Organizations, in parallel with running operations, increasingly use multiple projects in the form of programmes and portfolios, rather than single projects. Such a programmification has implications for the organization by placing the needs and objectives of the individual projects in a larger context, which may result (Maylor et al., 2006, p. 671) in:

- Less standardized project methods for individual projects
- A greater degree of top management
- Increased need for horizontal communication and coordination
- Increased attention to the value creation of the organization
- Increased potential for learning and reflection

The key issue with programmification is that large organizations, such as municipalities and business groups, increasingly use projects as their (main) mechanism to improve and create value. Project work has become part of their standard way of working and producing, rather than a unique organizational form for special measures. Project implementation has become a permanent form of work.

WATCH THIS!

Watch a Bython Media (2017) YouTube video introducing five steps to effective project portfolio management. Find out how to take those steps from this video at: https://study.sagepub.com/pm.

PORTFOLIO GOVERNANCE

When BP is involved in the extraction of new oil fields, when Vodaphone expands its coverage for 5G, or when Google is expanding customized document management solutions, the work is not organized as isolated single projects. Major strategic initiatives, significant development projects and initiatives where more clients are required are often set up as project programmes or project portfolios.

As mentioned earlier, many organizations have several projects ongoing at all times. This is especially true for companies that are based on selling their products to others in the form of delivery projects. The point of portfolios is to put projects into a broader context in the business, to see the project in the light of other projects in order to coordinate and utilize resources better, as well as add project competence to the projects. Doing this concerns the overall management of the projects in a holistic perspective. Projects can help to realize strategy.

EXTEND YOUR KNOWLEDGE

Read an article by Kock and Gemünden (2019), 'Project lineage management and project portfolio success', available at: https://study.sagepub.com/pm, to learn about the differentiation between *proactive lineage* (planning a roadmap of future projects) and *reactive lineage* (using learning from past projects). Research shows that both practices are positively and independently related to portfolio success.

Portfolio management requires a flexible structure and open communication lines. Portfolio management must not become a major administrative task in addition to the project processes and the base organization's management; it must coordinate in a manner that facilitates realization of value (Martinsuo & Lehtonen, 2009).

Projects and strategy

Increasingly, organizational strategy is delivered through projects. The contemporary focus on strategic oversight and holistic management of project portfolios is even more focused on strategy in practice. It is at the front end of projects that organizational strategy becomes translated into projects and programmes. PPM capabilities are framed by strategic priorities and evolve over the life of many projects as new strategic challenges have to be met. Timely responses to environmental dynamism are executed and real-time decisions have to be made to try and manage project practicalities while acknowledging strategic imperatives.

The importance of practice and context are repeatedly highlighted in PPM research. For example, practice-based studies reveal deviations from expected PPM processes where unauthorised projects consume valuable resources to the detriment of authorised project success (Blichfeldt & Eskerod, 2008) and where decisions are not made following rational assumptions but instead are strongly influenced by context in a process of learning and negotiation (Christiansen & Varnes, 2008).

Attention to the front end of projects brings a strategic focus to bear by exploring the processes that stretch from conception to selection and financial commitment. Williams and Samset (2010, p. 39) identify essential portfolio-level decision-making tasks at the front end of projects, such as identifying the most appropriate concept; aligning the project concept with corporate strategy and goals; making judgements about the future; estimating issues that relate to calculating costs and benefits as well as designing governance in a turbulent environment.

PPM's prevalence in the wider PM research community aligns with the increasing attention to strategy. A participative strategy formulation process, including bottom-up as well as top-down strategy processes, improves the integration of strategic and operative management. These integrative mechanisms can slip out of sight in a focus on either one or the other level. Research into emergent strategy in a telecommunications firm demonstrated how projects initiated to solve local problems and operational issues nonetheless influenced strategic directions (Mirabeau & Maguire, 2014).

Selecting and managing projects in portfolios

Focus on the front end of projects leads to increased scrutiny of the strategic positioning of projects, incorporating both top-down and bottom-up mechanisms. A focus on emergence demonstrates that strategic positioning can be subject to constant re-specification and refocusing, especially in turbulent environments. Ostensive and performative aspects of dynamic capabilities provide a strong theoretical foundation for research on programmes and strategy.

Most organizations have clear objectives and strategies, and portfolios and programmes are established as a direct link in such a strategy. If the strategy is ambiguous and fragmented it becomes more difficult to recognize the links. Similarly, if there is low awareness (in the initiation process) about how the individual project helps to realize the strategy and whether it fits into the project portfolio. While organizations may have many active projects at the same time, doing so may cause some of the projects to be put on hold, with some of them taking too long to complete.

Many simultaneous projects demand portfolio management to achieve desired value creation. Insufficient portfolio management can produce many unwanted results (Cooper, Edgett, & Kleinschmidt, 2001b). They are visualized in Figure 12.2 (Cooper, Edgett, & Kleinschmidt, 2001a).

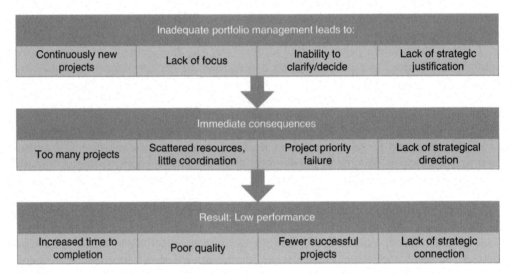

Figure 12.2 Consequences of inadequate strategic portfolio management

Inadequate portfolio management reduces the likelihood of a desired value creation for the organization and helps the project as a whole become less effective.

WATCH THIS!

Watch a YouTube tutorial by Jennifer Witt (2012) on juggling the different components of the project portfolio that also emphasizes the importance of combination and preferences at: https://study.sagepub.com/pm.

Efficient portfolio management requires established processes to enable senior management to select and follow up on the projects that are appropriate to fulfil goals and strategy. Processes that contribute to good portfolio management are characterized by:

- *Senior management's involvement and commitment.* Management must engage in ensuring anchorage and legitimacy, in moving the project portfolio in the desired direction. Also, top management must make decisions about prioritizing among projects. Portfolio management, therefore, requires corporate governance.

- *Compliance with the strategy*. If projects are to contribute to the desired value creation, it is necessary that the project is consistent with the organization's strategy and other initiatives (Patanakul & Shenhar, 2012).
- *Compliance with the organization's other management structures*. The projects should be coordinated and integrated into the financial management and other established management systems to contribute to better resource utilization.
- *Coordinating units*. In order to extract economies of scale and achieve competence development and resource coordination, project management offices or portfolio offices are required.

The projects in a programme thus have a common overall goal that they will realize together. Major focus areas for organizations are often set up as programmes, both in private and public enterprises. Digital renewal provides many examples of large project programmes where a wide range of projects are aimed at developing and establishing good ICT solutions for an organization.

Some consider programmes as scaled-up projects. Sometimes it is advisable to do so but often it's not. It may be more demanding to organize and manage programmes to achieve the desired effects (Lycett et al., 2004). In particular, the work involved in initiating and designing the programmes is significant. Many have pointed out that the management of programmes must think less about technical execution and more about comprehensive implementation and direction (see, for example, Pellegrinelli and Partington, 2007; Thiry, 2004). Nor is it possible that all programmes are equal or can be executed equally or directed alike. Each must be adapted to specific needs and capacity.

Project programmes are organized in several ways (Maylor et al., 2006), where the projects may be:

- sequential, following one another
- parallel
- in a network with a high degree of mutual dependence

Programmes are usually closer to the business strategy than the individual project. The programmes are more visible and are more long-term investments, which means that programme management is often given a lot of attention and that the anchoring is stronger for programmes than for single projects. Since the programmes are running over a long period of time, they are at the same time exposed to significant changes. This may include content items, resource conditions and adjustments of goals. Since programmes are more prolonged than projects, there are further opportunities to think about relationships, culture and trust in a different way. Research has shown that programmes that seek to create value should be more dynamic than projects, more open as systems than individual projects (Pellegrinelli et al., 2006). As discussed in Chapter 11, learning across projects in the programme can be facilitated by working with infrastructures and social relations.

Programme management has many of the same challenges and requirements pertaining to portfolio management. However, programme management is often easier to coordinate because the various projects included in the programme have the same defined strategic objective so that coordination is facilitated. Organizationally, programme management is located in the interface between the permanent organization and the project organization, while portfolio management will be part of line management in an organization that hosts the portfolio (Mikkelsen & Riis, 2017a).

IN PRACTICE

PROJECT PORTFOLIO MANAGEMENT

The following inadequacies have been identified as a source of problems for project portfolio management by Elonen and Artto (2003):

1. Inadequate project level activities

2. Inadequate resources, competencies and methods

3. Inadequate commitment, unclear roles and responsibilities

4. Inadequate portfolio level activities

5. Inadequate information management

6. Inadequate management of project-oriented organization

QUESTIONS

1. Which of these would you address first as a project manager?

2. Why would you choose this inadequacy and what would you do to handle it?

Challenges of project complexity

It is demanding to handle many projects simultaneously. This poses challenges related to resource allocation, competence development, priorities between different initiatives, organizational arrangements, use of personnel and balancing of workload; both structural and human challenges are involved.

In complex environments such as projects, with their multiple organizational actors, organizations may be obliged simultaneously to follow different 'rules of the game' and logics. Organizations rarely integrate practices related to other rationales without tensions and conflicts (Pache & Santos, 2010). They can even less ignore all the requests made to them by their multiple stakeholders, who conform to various logics (Pache & Santos, 2010).

Project complexity		
Macro	Meso	Micro
• Programmification • Interorganizational projects	• Project maturity • Project management office • Project competence	• Overload • Burnout

Figure 12.3   Project complexity – central components at different levels

We will look into this complexity (Figure 12.3). At the macro level, we have looked at programmification. We will also look at interorganizational projects, where several companies jointly carry out projects. We will elucidate the development of competence to handle many simultaneous projects through project maturity and project competence. At the micro level, which deals with the individuals, we will look at project complexity through topics such as overload, burnout, stress and toxicity.

WHAT WOULD YOU DO?

By Michael Maine, Australian National University

The Papua New Guinea liquefied natural gas (LNG) project is the largest resource extraction project in the Asia-Pacific region. Constructed at a stated cost of US$19 billion, it's operated by ExxonMobil in a joint venture with Oil Search and four other partners. The project extracts natural gas from the Papua New Guinea highlands where it is processed before being sent via some 700km of pipeline to a plant near the nation's capital, Port Moresby. The gas is then liquefied and transferred into ships for sale offshore. Construction for the project began in 2010, and the first gas shipment was made in May 2014.

In February 2009, the economic consulting firm Acil Tasman (now Acil Allen) produced a report for ExxonMobil about the project's impact. The purpose of the study, which was posted on ExxonMobil's website but has now been removed, was to provide an analysis of the likely impacts of the project on Papua New Guinea's economy. ExxonMobil did not respond to questions about the removal of the report or the impact of the project on local communities.

The report said the project has the potential to transform the country's economy by boosting GDP and money from exports. These would increase government revenue and provide royalty payments to landowners. It claims the project could potentially improve the quality of life of locals by providing services and enhancing productivity. Workers and suppliers would reap rewards, as would landowners who would also benefit from social and economic infrastructure. But six years on, none of this has come to pass.

A SHAKY AGREEMENT

In the years since construction began, Papua New Guinea's ranking on the United Nations Development Programme's Human Development Index has fallen by two places to 158, having been overtaken by Zimbabwe and Cameroon. Far from enhancing development indicators, the largest development project in PNG's history has coincided with an unprecedented downgrade in the country's development status. In this period, there has been a stream of articles published that highlight the alarming state of Papua New Guinea's economy and criticize the lack of positive economic and development impacts from the LNG project. But very little is known about the actual impact of the project on local landowners. This is largely due to the remote location of the gas field in the mountainous Hela Province. The dire security situation in that part of Papua New Guinea also makes any investigation a highly dangerous undertaking.

Like other such projects in Papua New Guinea, the LNG project was able to begin operations after agreement was reached with landowners on the benefits that were to be

(Continued)

delivered via the extraction and sale of the resource that exists beneath their land. After much negotiation, the PNG LNG Project Umbrella Benefits Sharing Agreement (UBSA) was signed in May 2009.

On its website, ExxonMobil describes the agreement as ensuring a 'fair distribution of the benefits', but neither ExxonMobil, Oil Search nor any of the other joint venture partners are signatories to the UBSA. Rather, the agreement is between the Papua New Guinea state, various levels of government and the landowners themselves. The agreement outlines a variety of income streams to be generated by the project, as well as specific development promises, such as road sealing and township development. Its upshot is that landowners can expect the LNG project to deliver tangible improvements to their lives and to the lives of their children. But the reality – after four years of operation and windfall profits for the project's joint venture partners – is that the project has delivered almost nothing of benefit to landowners. In fact, it has, in important ways, made life worse for the majority of people living in the project area.

DOWNWARD SPIRAL

During my fieldwork with project area landowners, I saw a life of immense frustration, disappointment and palpable anger at the absence of benefits. The township of Komo, which is at the centre of operations, contained a newly built hospital that stood empty with no beds, no staff and no fuel for its generator. It, and its newly constructed staff houses for non-existent staff, are just two of several white elephants built at inflated prices by companies owned by Papua New Guinea's politicians. Promised road sealing and township development, including power supply and schools, have all failed to materialize.

The most terrifying aspect of life in Hela province has been the proliferation of weapons. The Huli-speaking population comprises a complex society of hundreds of individual clans with a history of disputes over land and possessions that can be traced back over many generations. This pre-existing context of intense inter-clan rivalry has been made worse by the frustrations of a population hammered by the broken promises of the nation's largest resource development project.

During the project's construction phase, Komo was a hive of activity. It was home to thousands of international workers as well as PNG nationals attracted to high-paying jobs and the promise of an LNG-driven future. Large amounts of cash were paid to people who had no prior experience of money, and the lack of infrastructure development meant there was little to spend it on other than consumable goods and guns. A black market arms trade has existed between the PNG highlands and the Indonesian military across the border in West Papua for many years. During the course of my fieldwork, I witnessed constant outbreaks of fighting by heavily armed clans, young men gunned down by military assault rifles, and many dozens of houses shot through with holes and razed to the ground.

Much of this fighting is a direct result of payments made to landowners displaced by the project. Compensation money paid to affected clans invariably ends up in the hands of individuals who fail to distribute the funds properly or support their own families, and the money is always paid to men. In 2009, ExxonMobil agreed to pay 700 PNG Kina (approximately US$216) per hectare per year for land occupied by the LNG project, indexed to inflation. The giant Komo airfield that was built to fly in materials for the project's construction occupies an area of approximately 1,500 hectares. Disputes over ownership of that land have resulted in sporadic warfare over the past several years and dozens of deaths.

MILITARY INTERVENTION

In August 2016, several leaders of landowning clans at ExxonMobil's gas conditioning plant at the village of Hides, which is located on a ridge in a remote part of Hela Province, organized to blockade the facility and shut off the gas taps at several wells. Although security guards initially opposed the blockade, the landowners came armed. They forced their way into the plant site before locking its gates and demanding that the government meet their ultimatum to honour the UBSA agreement.

Members of Papua New Guinea's mobile police squad told me they had no intention of acting against the local population, who vastly outnumber and outgun any police and military presence the government is capable of providing. When I interviewed the landowner leaders during the blockade, it became clear that what they were demanding amounted to a better future for their families.

In November 2016, a convoy carrying the Hela Provincial governor, deputy governor and some local level government councillors was blocked on the road by an armed clan. Although the dispute was clan-related, I was informed that the convoy was targeted as a result of frustration over the lack of LNG project benefits and perceived corruption. The resulting shootout left two people dead and one policeman wounded. A few weeks later, the PNG government announced that it would be sending troops with 'logistical support' from ExxonMobil and Oil Search into Hela province, to flush out illegal arms and restore peace to that volatile part of the country. The military intervention in Hela province has thus far been unsuccessful. James Komengi, a Huli who runs a peace NGO based in Hela province, told me that a gun amnesty that's been in place for the past two months has failed to recover anything other than a few home-made shotguns and some non-serviceable factory-made rifles.

Residents of Komo village are reporting that ExxonMobil staff are being transported under heavily armed guard from their arrival at the Komo airfield to the gas conditioning facility at Hides. Recently, a man was gunned down at the Komo market in full view of the police and military contingent that is tasked with ridding the local population of its weapons. According to the blog Papua New Guinea Mine Watch, these forces stood by and watched the killers as they calmly left the scene. They said that they were human beings who are fearful of losing their lives in the face of the enormous task ahead of them. The governor of Hela Province has now declared the gun amnesty to be unsuccessful, with few weapons being surrendered.

The next stage is for the police and army to attempt to forcibly remove thousands of military weapons from hundreds of clans throughout the province. All this is a far cry from the excitement and optimism that characterized the mood of the landowners when the LNG project began construction in 2010. Papua New Guinea now faces a situation where it's compelled to send its army to an area where a major resource extraction project has failed to deliver on its promises to landowners. It may be time for all parties involved – both state and corporate – to consider development as a more effective path to peace.

QUESTION

1. You are the project manager despatched by ExxonMobil to Papua New Guinea to try and sort out the project situation. As things stand, production is at risk, employees are not safe and the situation is escalating. What would be your analysis of the situation and what would you recommend that the project should do in terms of its relations with local stakeholders to try and improve things?

Source: adapted from 'Papua New Guinea gets a dose of the resource curse as ExxonMobil's natural gas project foments unrest' by Michael Main, *The Conversation*, 9 March 2017.

Interorganizational projects

Interorganizational projects occur where two or more organizations work together over time with projects that are widespread. Many of the projects and examples described earlier in the book are examples of such projects. They include multiple actors (supplier level) collaborating to complete the project task. Collaboration between multiple organizations is often chosen when deliveries involve complex products or services and when the environment is characterized by much uncertainty and change, while the requirements for changeability are also high. One way to increase this ability is to collaborate with others. Interorganizational project collaboration has, therefore, become a key factor for the success of many organizations, allowing them to expand their competence bases and accrue other resources (Gransberg, Dillon, Reynolds, & Boyd, 1999).

Interorganizational projects involve at least one client and one supplier. They can also involve hundreds of actors. Such collaborations may be short-lived and organized as a temporary 'umbrella business' (DeFillippi & Arthur, 1998; Eccles, 1981) or be more prolonged and consist of large networks that include several projects. It is because many actors are required that interorganizational projects are particularly common in the construction industry as well as shipbuilding, oil and gas, sporting events, film and marketing.

While interorganizational projects provide opportunities, interaction and coordination across organizational boundaries are demanding. Different management systems, organizational cultures, routines and procedures (Gulati, Wohlgezogen, & Zhelyazkov, 2012) will become entangled, meaning that such projects are also very risky. The yield can be great when the collaboration works, but it can cause big losses and a lot of frustration if it does not work. Much risk is associated with whether the parties will act for the best of the project, not just maximizing self-interest from a short-term perspective.

Many companies enter into such collaborations with a desire to create long-term relationships. This often reduces opportunistic behaviour (Gulati et al., 2012), thus reducing uncertainty. A great uncertainty relates to whether the various companies have capacity in terms of competence and, in other ways, be able to take on the task they have undertaken (the soft uncertainty, Crawford, Morris, Thomas, & Winter, 2006). If a contractor offers tenders on many road projects and wins many of the tenders, they must participate in several parallel projects. This may mean that they do not have enough workforce to fulfil their obligations in all projects at the same time. This is an example of soft uncertainty (see Chapter 9).

It is a challenge in many interorganizational projects that we sometimes know little about what kind of expertise is required to solve a project task. Additionally, it can be difficult for actors to describe what they actually can accomplish; it may turn out that there is a big gap between the skills needed and the competence of a contractual supplier.

We have seen that contracts are a mechanism for distributing and managing uncertainty in interorganizational projects (Chapter 4) and that trust is a key mechanism for promoting cooperation (Smyth, 2014). Trust reduces transaction costs associated with control and increases the possibility of positive interaction where knowledge is shared and integrated so that the implementation process and project delivery produce value (Meyerson et al., 1996). Trust contributes to the parties opening up, sharing more knowledge and other resources and giving more to the common good (Eskerod & Vaagaasar, 2014). There has been a strong positive correlation between actors' trust in each other and how they succeed in the task solution in interorganizational projects.

When organizations work together in projects where they can collaborate to reach common goals or deliver mutual benefits, they are involved in embedded relationships characterized by high levels of necessary trust and mutual commitment (Uzzi, 1997).

Interorganizational projects have two main challenges. One relates to *cooperation* and the other to *coordination*. The core of the former is described above and is about managing expectations, interests and perspectives in the same direction, in common for the project. The latter, coordination challenges, involves integrating resources and activities to design delivery, bringing together the contributions of the parties. Many coordination mechanisms can be used: plans and rules, objects and representations, roles, routines and proximity. As we saw in Chapter 5, the use of these mechanisms creates conditions for coordinated efforts by providing reliability, predictability and a common understanding of the task to be solved (Okhuysen & Bechky, 2009). These mechanisms are highly valid for the coordination of efforts between actors at the employee level, between departments in an organization, and between several organizations. It is usually more demanding to do this across organizations because the differences in culture, routines and procedures will be greater than within one organization. Milestone and deadlines are significant coordination mechanisms for interorganizational projects to strive to ensure that everyone knows when activities are going to take place so that different actors can connect on time.

EXTEND YOUR KNOWLEDGE

Read the article by Eriksson, Leiringer, and Szentes (2017), 'The role of co-creation in enhancing explorative and exploitative learning in project-based settings'. Here you can learn about tracing the ways in which projects provide opportunities for co-learning between collaborators on projects. The article is available in the online resources at https://study.sagepub.com/pm.

Collaboration and coordination support each other in interorganizational projects. That is, better coordination promotes cooperation and vice versa. The experience of integrating knowledge and activities (coordination) will often contribute to less opportunism and more cooperation. The ability and willingness to adapt to each other in an interorganizational project will often emerge over time if the relationship between the parties remains positive. If collaboration is successful, it is easier to repeat the cooperation, thereby developing common practices that are perceived as effective by the parties (Poppo & Zenger, 2002, p. 713).

The reflections above are valid for many projects but are best suited to projects of a certain duration. Project duration may vary from short-term film projects, where filming for a commercial occurs , where filming for a commercial occurs in a few days, to major research projects or infrastructure projects lasting more than ten years. Of course, coordination processes, in particular, are characterized by whether it is a short or long-term project (Jones and Liechtenstein, 2008). Also, it varies if the parties work together for the first time (possibly what they think is the only time) or if they work together repeatedly (Granovetter, 1985). Two or more parties who work together repeatedly learn to know each other, learn from each other, develop practices for interaction, build trust in each other. In such collaboration, macro cultures can be developed; that is, a common understanding of how things should be done, simplifying cooperation. Macro cultures allow trust to occur even in relatively short-term relationships; common understanding serves as a resource that facilitates interaction, including clear role understanding generated by relative agreement across projects. Interorganizational relationships can, therefore, contribute to:

- Managing expectations, interests and perspectives to the common good of the project (cooperation)
- Integrating activities and resources (coordination)
- Gaining trust
- Developing a culture that promotes effective interaction across organizational boundaries

If one organization is in charge of cooperation many of the premises for the cooperation and coordination of activities will be at its behest. Often, it will use its management systems as common practice for the project (Feldman & Orlikowski, 2011). In order for this to work the people involved need to discuss how the contract and management system can be interpreted appropriately in their project, how the goals are to be interpreted, what they should do and who holds the responsibility for what.

In addition to having more parties on the supplier side, projects can also be set up as interorganizational projects with several parties on the client side. When several parties collaborate on the client side, it is often most appropriate that one of the organizations holds the project owner role on behalf of all of them. The other partners are then included in the steering group. Clear agreements on how the various actors will be involved, the individual's mandate in the project, authority, responsibility and obligations, are required. A well-developed information plan and efficient communication between the parties so that each and every one of them can engage in the project in an appropriate manner is desirable. For everyone to succeed with value creation, the organizations must work together to clarify the process of completion of delivery and delivery. The individual organization takes responsibility for clarifying needs and clarifying and managing expectations in their own organization.

IN PRACTICE

HOUSING POLICY IN SOUTH AFRICA

By Richard Ballard, University of the Witwatersrand; Margot Rubin, University of the Witwatersrand

In 2014, the South African government announced a new direction in housing policy. The aim was to phase out smaller low-cost housing projects of a few hundred units and focus primarily on megaprojects – new settlements made of multitudes of housing units combined with a host of social amenities to overcome the inequities resulting from apartheid. The minister favoured megaprojects (also referred to as catalytic projects) as a way of getting delivery back on track. Large human settlement projects weren't entirely new to South Africa. Several were already at an advanced stage of construction in 2014. What was new in this announcement was the idea that all housing would be delivered exclusively through the construction of megaprojects across the country.

RATIONALES FOR MEGAPROJECTS

In a broad sense, megaprojects are glamorous because they are much more visible and impressive than diffuse small-scale projects. As a result, politicians can brand their delivery more effectively. Megaprojects convey a sense of decisive action in which the state can flex its muscle in big hit interventions. More specifically, champions of the megaprojects approach believed that large-scale projects could deliver more houses quicker. When announcing the policy in 2014, the then minister of human settlements, Lindiwe Sisulu, stated that megaprojects would help deliver 1.5 million units by 2019.

Some advocates of the megaprojects approach, notably the Gauteng provincial government, were particularly attracted to the idea of creating whole new 'post-apartheid cities' which could meet the 'live, work and play' needs internally. Starting afresh with new settlements would be a way of designing urban spaces to avoid the inequalities and inefficiencies that beset existing cities. They would also bring major projects to poor areas that had little else to drive any significant economic growth.

Megaprojects were also intended to solve a variety of governance problems. In particular, it was extremely difficult to manage the 11,000 human settlement projects that were at various stages across the country. Consolidating these into just a few dozen projects was a way of focusing government's attention and reducing administrative burdens and costs. The megaprojects approach also seemed to be a way of managing the division of work and some of the tensions between different spheres of government and various departments. With some local authorities having taken on more responsibility for housing projects, national and provincial government considered megaprojects to be a way of bringing housing under more centralized management.

CONCERNS

Big projects take many years to get off the ground, and so delivery can sometimes be suspended for a long time. Some critics are less concerned about the scale of the projects than the fact that they could be poorly located. That's largely because better-located land is more expensive. In addition, there isn't a great deal of well-located land that is large enough to accommodate new settlements of this scale. There is a fear that once the construction jobs run out, residents would have to bear the cost of travelling long distances to jobs outside the settlement. If new projects are located far from sewage, water, electricity and roads then great financial and environmental costs would have to be laid out.

QUESTION

1. The minister of human settlements has established a project to determine whether all housing should be delivered in megaprojects as originally intended by the policy or whether a range of project sizes should be encouraged to facilitate, in particular, urban infill projects within existing urban areas. You are the project director charged with coming up with data and advising a decision on the basis of this data. How would you go about collecting what kind of data to determine the best mode of housing project delivery?

Source: adapted from Richard Ballard and Margot Rubin's 'Why megaprojects to deliver houses in South Africa might not work' (*The Conversation*, 23 May 2018), at: https://theconversation.com/why-megaprojects-to-deliver-houses-in-south-africa-might-not-work-94139.

Project maturity

Maturity in project context concerns the use of the project form in an optimal manner adapted to the nature and needs of the organization. Many events and factors make this difficult to achieve. It can also be difficult to determine what an optimal working form is for a given actor (Andersen & Jessen, 2003). The Project Management Institute (PMI) emphasizes in its definition that it involves the use of knowledge, skills, tools and techniques to meet the project's requirements. We do not disagree with this; nonetheless, we would warn against the misunderstanding that maturity is about utilizing most of the classic tools. In some contexts, it is appropriate to do so but processes and tools must be adapted to the characteristics of the project and the project's surroundings. Thus, as we see it, high project maturity is an expression of both:

- Possessing a large 'toolbox' and project management processes
- Having the ability and willingness to use them in a reflective manner based on what the situation requires

Projectification means that most companies have a portfolio of active projects at all times. How to make the most of these efforts and what measures are to be taken to deliver desired outcomes is a key concern. These assessments should be based on a survey and analysis of current efficiency in delivering projects. In the early nineties different maturity models/frameworks emerged to assess this systematically. Today, there are more than 30 such models/frameworks (Grant & Pennypacker, 2006), the most well-known, OPM3, developed by PMI and based on PMI standards (Crawford et al., 2006).

OPM3 stands for the Organizational Project Management Maturity Model and is intended to be a standardized organizational project management modelling model that many companies can use. There are different maturity models for different industries. Some examples follow:

- SPICE (Structure Process Improvement for Construction Enterprises)
- PM2 (Project Management Process Maturity Model) that integrates critical areas of knowledge
- The European Quality Management Board's 'Business Excellence' model (EFQM)

The various models developed to handle project complexity, alternate with the Capability Maturity Model (CMM), developed for software development by the Software Engineering Institute of Carnegie-Mellon University in the late 1980s (Cooke-Davies & Arzymanow, 2003). The models are addressed to organizations that, over time, have completed many projects, gaining extensive experience in project management. Based on this, one can define five steps in a maturity staircase (Andersen, 2008; see Figure 12.4):

1. *Maturity Level 1 (Initial Processes)*. The work is done without there being descriptions or procedures for how to do it. The work often appears to be random and relatively chaotic. Quality in the work processes depends solely on the employees' expertise and effort because they lack systems that support a performance characterized by quality.
2. *Maturity Level 2 (Structured Processes and Standards)*. Here one has established simple processes that promote good project execution. They focus mostly on

management and follow-up of projects according to a set framework for time, cost and quality.

3. *Maturity Level 3 (Organizational Standards and Institutionalized Processes).* The project work is characterized by professionalism in the sense that definite tools and processes for good project execution are explicated and followed. They include the establishment and completion of projects. They also include a managerial perspective that goes beyond managing under the triple constraint, i.e. the Iron Triangle. Both management and technical aspects are thus included in the project implementation system.

4. *Maturity Level 4 (Controlled Processes).* Procedures for managerial and technical aspects are combined with systematic evaluation of their impact. Attention is focused on the continuous improvement of project competence.

5. *Maturity Level 5 (Optimized Standards and Processes).* Here, attention is focused on optimizing all processes for project execution and value creation, actively seeking qualitative and quantitative feedback to improve. Systems for quality assurance and knowledge sharing are a natural part of the project work. There is great attention to constantly improving the ability of efficient project execution that fits the focal project.

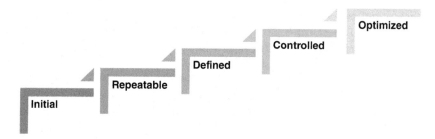

Figure 12.4   Project maturity staircase

The idea is that the further up the levels you are (towards step 5), the more mature you are, which means that you can, in theory, deliver better projects. In principle, maturity increases the likelihood of value creation and competitiveness. In other words, the levels are a scale for measuring maturity in project management to aid continuous improvement. Improvement measures should be prioritized using the scheme in practice. How these measures might be used in conjunction with other measures to develop the organization will obviously require consideration (Backlund, Chronéer, & Sundqvist, 2014).

WATCH THIS!

Watch a YouTube video by Marie-Louise Barry (2014) on self-assessment of project management maturity at: https://study.sagepub.com/pm.

Maturity models/frameworks represent a first step in creating a culture for projects (Crawford et al., 2006). The use of the maturity levels or staircase signals a desire to work with long-term intention to improve the ability of project work.

Models such as OPM also support the organization's development of the ability to manage project programmes and portfolios (Grant & Pennypacker, 2006). It presents a hierarchical structure with a number of best practices presumed. Each of them supports a number of competencies, which in turn can lead to results that can be measured on the three levels: project, programme and portfolio.

It is sensible to look at maturity as something developed over time, in certain steps (i.e. a relatively sequential development process) and that it is part of a learning process as the prerequisite for maturity models. At the same time, it is worth noting that achieving maturity can be a process in which rapid progress may also occur and in which there may also be repeated processes.

The models, rightly, have been criticized for being relatively rigid in nature and that they cannot capture changes in technology, markets, practices and policies. They are mostly aimed at organizations that work with traditional project implementation, with the models being prosaically solution-oriented. They work well for the actual problem description, although they should have more depth. Should they be put into use, they must be combined with clear attention to improvement activities, as well as consider the human aspects of project work. These aspects hardly make an appearance.

MATURITY IS ABOUT CULTURE

It is necessary, but not sufficient, using models, toolboxes and strategic aids, to handle the diversity of projects in organizations. A desired culture cannot be adopted but must be continually pursued to achieve a desired and shared set of values, attitudes and thinking about how specific aspects of the projects will contribute to desired value creation. Without an appropriate project culture, it does not matter how appropriate the tools and project strategies that one has are. Project maturity is also related to organization design, as we shall discuss after the next 'what would you do?' box.

WHAT WOULD YOU DO?

OPERATIONAL RULES ON A PROJECT IN BRAZIL

During the start-up of a project in São Paulo, Brazil, members of the project team were given a policy that stated all employees must arrive at work on time. São Paulo has some of the most congested traffic in the world. It became apparent to the project management office that this was a difficult policy to enforce without creating morale problems: the traffic was so heavy and the congestion so bad that on time was sometimes impossible. Instead of changing the official rule, it was seldom enforced. Later on, an employee was injured crossing an area that was formally marked as unsafe. He, as well as other employees, indicated that they knew the official rules but it took too much time to go around the unsafe area. They assumed that official rules could be ignored if they were difficult to obey. The difference between official and operational rules of the project created a culture that made communication of the priorities difficult.

QUESTION

1. What would you do as the project manager to ensure that operational and official rules coincided?

(Hint: Gouldner (1954), which outlines three patterns of interpretation of the official rules of a plant, might provide some useful insight. The three patterns of bureaucracy were: the mock (the rules are imposed by 'outsiders'); the representative (both union and management initiate the rules) and the punishment-centred (one side initiates and enforces the rules).

Organizational design

Burns and Stalker (1962), in their research in the management of innovation, distinguish between **mechanistic** and **organic structures** based on the contingencies of the environments in which they operated, which effected the processes they adopted.

Henry Mintzberg (1983) also differentiated organizational forms based on functions and the need for differentiated activities. One of the types suited to managing the need for innovation and projects as organizational facilities is **adhocracy**, often referred to in the context of project-based organizations.

The core of adhocracy is a significant degree of decentralized authority, a small degree of formalization of procedures and many cross-links between the organizational units. Given the issue of innovation entailed in any project, their organization is best suited to more organic designs, perhaps even ad hoc designs that respond to the situational specificities faced by projects.

> A **mechanistic structure** may be appropriate when production is fixed, the technology is stable and the environment predictable.
>
> **Organic structures** require a greater degree of adaptation because a highly uncertain environment entails instability in technology and flexibility in processes.

> **Adhocracy** is characterized by adaptive, creative and flexible integration based on non-permanence and spontaneity.

For organizations that have both complex production systems and a complex product portfolio, project-based organization provides more design options. In the chapter on project organization (Chapter 6), we emphasized three types of project organization: within departments, matrix and as an independent organizational unit. They are an expression of differences in autonomy in decision-making but also how strongly project participants are bound to line management in the base organization.

For organizations that have both complex production systems and a complex product portfolio, project-based organization might be arranged as a matrix (Figure 12.5). The figure from Hobday (Davies & Hobday, 2005) illustrates how an organization, or possibly also a large department in an organization, is arranged. In the first option, (A), no project is integrated; in the second alternative (B), there is an example of what we have previously called within-department project organization. These illustrations and types illustrate variations that may be associated with organizing innovation through various forms of project organization, based on both the autonomy given to the project, as well the source and use made of resources.

Projects that are oriented to change and innovation can be divided into three categories (Figure 12.6):

- *Project-driven organizations*: these are organizations that have continuous production within permanent units, where projects are the main vehicle for innovation and knowledge development as a whole. The projects may be either development or change projects.

- *Project-based organizations*: organizations that continuously deliver on projects to external clients, where the majority of the work is organized as projects, previously categorized as mission projects. Examples of such organizations would be corporate architectural practices, large civil and engineering contractors as well as corporate advertising agencies.
- *Project organizations*: the entire organization is geared towards the completion of a project. Typical examples of such type are coalitions established to deliver major events, such as the Olympics.

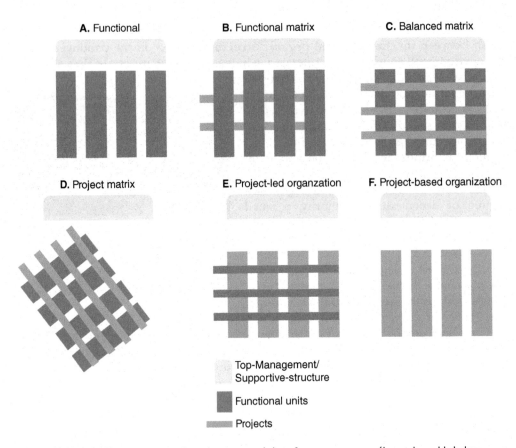

Figure 12.5   Different ways of project organizing for a company (based on Hobday, 2000, p. 877)

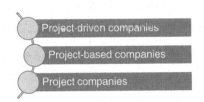

Figure 12.6   Three categories of project organizing

P-FORM ORGANIZATION

Söderlund and Tell (2009, p. 2011) label an organization in which projects are used to create innovation *P-form*. P-form is thus a term for organizations that have project activities as their central core, organized through one of the three ways of project organization mentioned above. The P-form is a continuation of what is called an *M-form* in the strategy literature, a term derived from Chandler's (1962) discussion of American companies, referring to the multi-division form. Since a P-form organization is geared towards promoting innovation through project organization, it has characteristics that differ from those of a more traditional department or division. The P-form and the M-form are not contradictory to each other but represent different approaches, starting points and objectives.

These characteristics indicate that there are some differences between traditional divisional-based companies and those that are more project-oriented. A P-form helps situate customer and external requirements at the centre. It is better suited to integrating different competencies for innovation. In the first place, the P-shape facilitates coordination through close communication because it includes arenas for discussion and development. Decisions relating to the project are taken close to the project and are more autonomous as they are not linked to organizationally permanent units. At the same time, the P-form makes coordinating some issues that do not apply internally to the project more complicated, such as how risk and rewards should be distributed between the players. Söderlund has done notable work on how strategic competence development and project-level knowledge integration are interlinked. He proposes the following areas of competence and knowledge (Table 12.1).

Table 12.1   Some characteristics of organizations applying P-form and M-form

Characteristics	P-Form	M-Form
Production unit	Project	Division/Business unit
Grouping principle	Market and function	Market
Products	Customer adaption	Standardized
User involvement	High degree	Low degree
Time orientation	Deadlines	Continuing
Production system	Unit production and small batches	Large series and mass production
Knowledge approach	Knowledge specialization and integration	Knowledge specialization
Communication	Horizontal	Vertical
Decicion structure	Temporalily decentralized	Partially decentralized

The organizational structure of the permanent organization is significant for the potential of innovation through project organization. Many organizations have their own research and development departments. In a time of frequent changes, new requirements and the need to think across existing competence and conventional thinking organizations that have facilitated innovation and change through having a variant of the P-shape provide a good basic foundation for successful innovation. However, even the best innovation projects have to overcome relations of power and associated cultures in their base organizations. Projects, being temporary, may have less political clout.

PROJECT BARONIES

Project organization, as multiple variations of the P-form, implies significant decentralization of decision-making authority and a break with traditional line organization with clear control and management structures. If one deals with the 'hottest' companies in the digital industry, such as Google and Netflix, those that work with the development of new services and products have a high degree of autonomy. How project units develop their culture and integration with other units is a potential limitation that follows from the project form.

Gann, Salter, Dodgson, and Phillips (2012) have studied a number of organizations that in different ways are project based, including a sample of American, European and Japanese organizations with a variability in size ranging from fewer than 50 to more than 85,000 employees. Selection of the sample was made on the basis of a structurally clear project-oriented profile, a high degree of innovation and sustained success. Gann and his colleagues found that the degree of centralized management varied considerably, which provided the basis for categorizing how project managers were made responsible. To describe the organizational units that carried out projects within organizations for which project organization was central, they introduced the term 'project barons'. It suggests that in various ways these control the organization. They placed the project barons (Figure 12.7) into three categories to describe the different ways project-based organization unfolded:

- *Dominions*. Here an organization pays great attention to its specific skills and performance, aiming at market growth. A significant degree of centralization of decision-making occurs. Projects have low autonomy.
- *Tight federation*. The organization is based on distributed management with an emphasis on collaboration with other entities and clear elements of performance-based approaches. Projects perform freely but are held accountable in fairly strict and routinized terms.
- *Loose federation*. Individual barons or project managers. Characterized by the emphasis on growth, based on opportunism and little emphasis on cooperation with other entities. These are the projects in which polyarchy is likely to flourish.

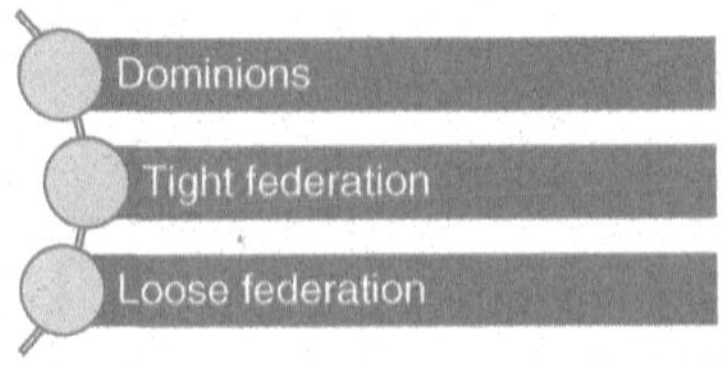

Figure 12.7 Three categories of project baronies

The term *baronies* provide a description of different ways of setting up and managing different project units internally in an organization. Each barony has its potential advantages and weaknesses regarding governance mechanisms, attention areas and success factors. Gann et al. (2012) also draw attention to three areas of governance that will affect the various baronies in different ways:

- *Synthesizing* – The ability the organization has to learn across projects and benefit from this learning
- *Spawning* – Creating new entrepreneurial, risky initiatives in project-based companies
- *Squirrelling* – Collecting funds and profits from the projects to create and reinvest in new projects

A *dominion* has significant centralized management that provides opportunities for fast but also top-level driven decisions. Such a barony often provides the basis for strategic integration of projects, the basis for sharing resources and the capacity to launch major innovative projects. The potential for learning across projects is difficult in this type of project organization. Central management operates tight control and it is potentially more difficult for project barons to influence decisions. There will be fewer entrepreneurial initiatives, while project barons will have less opportunity for squirrelling.

Tight federation has some of the same features as a dominion but has much more autonomy among the individual project barons. They will have less strategic overview but at the same time, there is potential for limited resource sharing. Potential for squirrelling is greater than in dominions and attention will often be directed to more step-by-step innovations.

In a *loose federation*, the project baron is often more protective and able to hide resources rather than sharing them outside the project. A high degree of autonomy means that the project baron performs supportive management and the projects may be characterized by what we called heterarchy in Chapter 8, which makes the relationships more unclear (Aime et al., 2014). Large potential for entrepreneurial activity is also a hallmark while learning from other projects is reduced with a small degree of centralized intervention, creating the opportunities for polyarchy. The project baron in a loose federation has few bureaucratic procedures and considerable flexibility.

The term project baron is somewhat caricatured but illustrates different aspects of the possibilities and limitations of governance and how different power relationships and cultural features in the individual project unit affect the organization as a whole.

Projects that contribute to innovation must be based on *collaborating* internally within the project team but also with the project and base organization. Creating shared understandings and cultures through robust sensemaking around idea work is vital (Carlsen et al., 2012). Where subcultures flourish under project barons with loose federations the organization will less readily cooperate to reach goals. Kanter (2006, p. 80) warns against this: 'Beware of creating two classes of organizational members (employees) – those who have all the fun and those who get all the money.' Learning is highly related to innovation through projects, both at the organizational, team and individual level, and it must be of an exploratory character. Decisions must come both as a result of key initiatives and through bottom-up processes from the individual project teams that help to integrate decisions into the process underway. These three characteristics (collaboration, learning and decisions) contain some paradoxes that need to be balanced and handled consciously but pragmatically. When an organization bases its activities on projects and project teams to contribute to innovation, it must be done by both unleashing and harness (Hill, 2014). See Figure 12.8.

RELEASING		TIGHTENING
The Individual	⟷	The Collective
Bottom-up	⟷	Upside-down
Supportive	⟷	Confrontational
Improvise	⟷	Structuring
Long term	⟷	Short term
Experimenting	⟷	Performing

Figure 12.8   Six paradoxes of managing innovation in organizations (inspired by Hill, 2014)

IN PRACTICE

INTERNATIONAL MEGA-EVENTS

Hosting any mega-event is an opportunity for a country to show its international reputation, management capacity and societal strength, demanding lengthy preparation as well as an enormous amount of investment and massive resource mobilization. Moreover, such megaprojects, with their economic, social, sustainability and legacy costs have far-reaching effects on both the economic and social development of a country. Mega-event projects (MEPs) face remarkable challenges in terms of overrun costs, delayed schedules and political issues. Li, Lu, Ma, and Kwak (2018), in an article on 'Evolutionary governance for mega-event projects (MEPs): A case study of the World Expo 2010 in China', argue that existing studies have ignored the dynamic evolution and adaptation of governance in relation to the success of MEPs. To fill this research gap, they examine the dynamic governance of MEPs on the basis of a new theory – evolutionary governance theory (EGT) – which combines institutional economics, systems theory, and project governance. The study was conducted in three main steps: (1) studying the case of the evolutionary governance of the World Expo 2010 in China during its life-cycle stage, including planning, construction, operation and post-event development; (2) discussing the impact of the hierarchical and cross-functional governance structure of the Expo; and (3) summarizing the theories and best practices of dynamic governance mechanisms for MEPs. The results of the study extend our understanding of the multi-level governance of mega-events during the life-cycle process and demonstrate the evolution of governance transition over the different stages. The article is available in the online resources at https://study.sagepub.com/pm.

QUESTION

1.   MEPs are an extreme case of complexification of projects. What practices for their implementation and governance would you derive from this study?

Creativity

Creativity is required to foster innovation and then there must be room for improvisation and finding things out by breaching accepted limits. While there are frameworks and structures required for the project to proceed in the desired direction and limitations related to time and resources that provide guidance, the paradox to be mastered is comparable to playing jazz. Consider the greatest jazz orchestra ever – that of Duke Ellington. Ellington's collaborations saw the wondrous creativity of his sidemen ending up in compositions through which his genius shone. Key players, such as Bubber Miley's contribution to 'East St. Louis Toodle Oo' and Barney Bigard's contributions to the creation of 'Mood Indigo' as well as Juan Tizol's minor-key theme that introduces 'Caravan', were incorporated by Ellington into his compositions. When Billy Strayhorn joined the band not as a player but as a composer and arranger, Ellington's creativity in absorbing the improvisations of his players became a way of life. Ellington used Strayhorn to complement and sometimes complete his creativity and introduce new musical ideas (Teachout, 2013). Ellington's band and Strayhorn were collaborators that together produced idea work that produced some of the very best music of the twentieth century premised on improvisation. Often the scores would be indicative rather than prescriptive, such as Hodges' solo (referring to Johnny Hodges, the Duke's long-time alto sax player).

A great deal of improvisation, as in Ellington's orchestra, occurs within clear frameworks and structures that emerge from the creative idea work that produces innovation. The innovation research literature suggests in regard to the organization of innovation (Fuglsang and Sundbo, 2005) that most innovations cannot be planned, depending on the situation and context in general but is something that must be developed improvisationally to frame further innovation – much as the Duke Ellington orchestra. Most innovations, as with the Ellington orchestra, are the result of 'grass roots' initiatives (Hill 2014), initiatives that Ellington supported and appropriated. Ellington, as the project owner and manager, had the overview and was responsible for the results.

In many ways, the Ellington orchestra was an ambidextrous organization in that Ellington and Strayhorn's scores and arrangements provided the structure to be exploited; the creative flair of his soloists provided the exploratory improvisation around the structure. We shall explore ambidextrous organizations next.

Ambidexterity

Exploration and exploitation are topics that not only apply to learning processes. Organizations must innovate, through both exploring new opportunities and leveraging existing resources. Projects can help organizations manage innovation while the routines of established operating practices continue undisturbed (Eriksson, 2013). With increasing demands for new products and new ways of implementing processes, it is necessary to keep operations running while refining established processes and at the same time trying to create completely new solutions.

In organizational research, the term *ambidexterity* is used to describe the duality of achieving two incompatible goals at the same time (see Birkinshaw and Gupta, 2013; O'Reilly and Tushman, 2008, for example). Projects also need ambidexterity (Pellegrinelli et al., 2015; Turner, Maylor, & Swart, 2015). Those routines and standards that work well and fit the challenges one is dealing with (the repetition economy) need to be combined with exploring something new, sometimes radically so. Innovation projects are often based on standardized project models developed using fixed procedures and methodologies for management and control; however, while most major projects require some underlying routines and standards, flexibility and autonomy for innovative exploration is required.

One design that bridges with more formal and bureaucratic organization to achieve this flexibility and autonomy is polyarchy, a form that has flourished in broadcasting.

Project polyarchy

Many cultural innovations are organized around projects, for instance in media organizations in fields such as television. A television film – as work by Coldevin, Carlsen, Clegg, Pitsis, and Antonacopoulou (2019) established in the case of Media Tales – is a complex relational composition in which creativity and idea work flourish (Coldevin et al., 2019). In organization studies, discussion of how this flourishing might be organized has been oriented to organization design prescriptions such as **heterarchy** and **responsible autonomy** (Fairtlough, 2005).

Heterarchy (Ogilvy, 2016) describes a situation of multiple rulers, as in partnerships in professional organizations, such as law firms.

Responsible autonomy describes an organizational situation in which control resides in professional experts open to critique and regular audit (Fairtlough, 2005, pp. 31–33).

Polyarchy is a form of organization design in which power is invested in multiple people.

Any unit can govern or be governed by others, depending on circumstances; no one group dominates the rest. Authority is distributed.

Combined, heterarchy and responsible autonomy comprise a form of **polyarchy** as Dahl (1971, p. 8) defined it: a form of organization that is 'highly inclusive and extensively open'.

Clegg, Courpasson, and Phillips (2006), brought Dahl's political science concept of polyarchy into organization studies. When organizational oligarchs take care of the strategic agenda and allow a plurality of relatively autonomous sub-organizational oligarchies to be involved in developing and delivering specific projects within a given organization, polyarchic relations occur. Members have a *de facto* informal right creatively to contest and make decisions within the sub-oligarchy, despite being embedded in a host system of hierarchical authority.

Interrelated changes in technology (digitalization), politics (deregulation and privatization) and culture (shifts to portfolio careers and project organization) create this new type of organization. Temporary in duration, polyarchy's processes are not unique to each occasion. Clegg et al. (2006, p. 338) characterize a polyarchic structure of power as 'soft and decentralized with strict and relatively insuperable social and symbolic boundaries around oligarchic circles', constituting 'strong intermediate bodies often articulated around internal professions and sub elites'. Such structures allow for highly individualized forms of action to generate high levels of internal creative debate.

The development of advanced, cost-effective digital telecommunications services enables central bureaucracies increasingly to become idea and design centres rather than integrated producers. Actual production is outsourced in various ways ranging from insourcing skilled contractors from external organizations for specific contributions to total outsourcing. Production becomes a game of Lego, putting pieces of creative infrastructure together. Agencies contract for a particular period, co-design what they should do and fix the costs and benefits through a contract as a rule of engagement (Barley & Kunda, 2006; Bechky, 2006).

Networks of a polyarchic creative organization have grown substantially in recent years in areas such as television production through project networks (Sydow & Staber, 2002, p. 217) delivering specific programme ideas that nurture longer-term collaborative relationships, beyond the time limitations of particular projects with host organizations. Relatively stable core entrepreneurial teams from outside the host organization, drawn from within a tightly networked institutional field, cross the host organizational boundaries for specific projects (Manning, 2017). In particular, informal contracting for programme production can be for very short periods, sometimes as little as a few days or a week. The form of contracting is based on personal knowledge, informal ties and shared social capital (Adler & Kwon, 2002). Transactions are focused on intermittent projects, delivered by teams of autonomous workers that are composed and recomposed as occasion demands (Bechky, 2006; Jones & Lichtenstein, 2008). Dense networks of independent producers and freelancers in the industry centre on areas such as Soho in London or Ultimo in Sydney.

Independent production firms in the cultural industries are not classical entrepreneurial start-ups (Hesmondhalgh & Baker, 2008, 2010). They are facilitated through 'soft' power relations premised on informality in the project networks. Seemingly, there appears to be little in the way of authoritative restriction imposed on the creativity and 'idea work' (Coldevin et al., 2019) encouraged within these firms, outside of the commissioning organization's framing of deadlines and budgets. Hellgren and Stjernberg (1995) define these networks in terms of a set of relations, in which no single actor may act as the legitimate authority for the network as a whole. These networks have open boundaries and are temporally limited, dynamically changing as well as being reconstructed from one project to the next. In addition, they are strongly task-oriented in accomplishing a project and organizationally coordinated by 'legally autonomous but functionally interdependent firms and individuals' (Sydow & Staber, 2002, p. 216).

Rowlands and Handy (2012, p. 659) state that the 'film industry in most countries utilizes a system of project-based network organization in which diverse teams of highly skilled individuals are assembled for limited periods and disbanded once their part in a production is completed'. Typically, filming occurs only after a complex division of labour assembles the many template elements for production, of cast, crew, location, sets, finance, producers, forming semi-permanent workgroups that are relatively stable (Daskalaki, 2010), sharing collective memories, skills and norms that function as 'latent organizations' (Ebbers & Wijnberg, 2009; Starkey, Barnatt, & Tempest, 2000). Rowlands and Handy (2012) note that fragmentation and casualization inhibit creative innovation. Maintaining creativity and innovation rather than the repetition of trusted programme formulae requires projects that performatively promise an ambiguous mix of adventure and playful passion, which can occur within a disciplined context that polyarchic design provides, suggest Sahlin-Andersson and Söderholm (2002).

Translating polyarchy to organizational terms (Robinson, 2013), the polyarchic design enables creative elites organized in stable sub-oligarchies to compete constructively in doing idea work. They develop scenarios for programme pitches and then collaborate on the script development. This is undertaken in a way that is deeply embedded in the production process that empowers the project team with the 'power to invite, connect, and co-create' (Coldevin et al., 2019, p. 18). While the members of the team are nominally egalitarian, they can coordinate and communicate ideas in an upward direction through the creative sub-oligarchs, who act as promoters for the team. Polyarchic relations are temporally limited and dynamic, revolving around a central creative core, one that is liquid rather than dominated by a central authority, as Hellgren and Stjernberg (1995) suggest and that is also spatially mobile, able to switch from one national institutional field to one in another continent. The critical competencies in being liquid are innovation, commitment, adaptability and achievement (Clegg & Baumeler, 2012). Liquidity requires autonomy, spontaneity, creativity, adaptability, and communicative and relational competence.

In these emergent project organizations significant capacities are invested in social and educational capital and a capacity to develop swift trust in switches from project to project (Meyerson et al., 1996). Distinct relational power configurations characterize the polyarchy. More traditional panoptical power (Lancione & Clegg, 2015) is still evident, vested directly in the overall oligarchic and bureaucratic organization. Two systems of power combine as broadcasting authorities commission creative works from innovative producers. These producers practise polyarchic organizing nesting inside the formal organization of the national broadcaster.

Polyarchy is highly autonomous for projects, leaving them less subject to central control and the pressures these can create, as we will shortly see. Polyarchies and loose federations align well; less well aligned would be dominions or tight federations. These impose far more direct control and reduced autonomy on the project manager; consequently, projects conducted under these auspices might well achieve high levels of project maturity while they are less likely to be highly innovative.

EXTEND YOUR KNOWLEDGE

Read the article by Clegg and Burdon (2019) to learn about how collective innovation can be coordinated in the production of television series. It demonstrates how a new organizational design characterized by a polyarchic structure, which is creatively rich, fluid and decentralized enabled a programme production project that was remarkably successful. The article is available in the online resources at https://study.sagepub.com/pm.

Project management offices for coordination and continuous improvement

Many companies choose to create a device to support project work, to increase project maturity. This will especially be the case of companies that have already climbed some steps in the maturity staircase, clearly valuing such devices. Often this support function forms a project management office. Sometimes it is called project support or 'Centre for Project Excellence' (Hobbs & Aubry, 2007).

The project management office (PMO) is a unit in the permanent organization that aims to enable efficient project execution by developing and managing project management tools and processes, such as manuals, templates, procedures for dealing with uncertainty or stakeholders, planning, estimation, methods, skills and role allocation to ensure the best possible project implementation.

In smaller companies, a project management office's functions can be safeguarded by one or more individuals having the task of safeguarding and developing the project management conditions in the business. For example, an architectural firm might have a resource that assists professionals – primarily architects – with support functions related to the projects they are involved in. Both training and assistance in project management tools, capturing and spreading learning between projects as well as a host of other conditions might be entailed.

Larger companies can formalize support in a different way through their own units and departments. For example, a large oil extraction business will need a unit capable of meeting specific needs related to support and re-implementation of projects. A project management office's tasks are often linked to the following:

- Support for training in and use of project management methods and tools
- Developing and maintaining procedural descriptions, project manuals and routines for use in project work
- Providing and facilitating learning and experience transfer between the projects
- Fronting and developing an understanding of the project form in the organization
- Having an overview of potential project managers in the organization and special categories of project participants
- Assisting with training and competence development within project work

PMOs are a support function outside the other line functions/organizational structures of the organization. They vary across organizations in how decision-making authority is granted to the PMO, over projects such as the design and composition of project teams. Some companies grant the PMO only an advisory function, while others may give them decision-making authority; for example, to put together a project team, including the project manager. It is generally assumed that the application and importance of PMOs increases as the project portfolios increase.

WATCH THIS!

Watch a tutorial video from Mike Clayton (2018) explaining what is the project management office (PMO) at: https://study.sagepub.com/pm.

Stressors, burnout and toxins – and how to avoid them

It is demanding to allocate resources between projects in a portfolio (Gordon & Tulip, 1997). Projects often experience scarcity of resources. Most projects are based on best case implementation. Changes and delays, therefore, cause cascading effects in the portfolio. This can lead to resource crises resolved to redistribute resources between the projects (Engwall & Jerbrant, 2003). We discussed this resource allocation syndrome earlier (Chapter 6). This situation often causes a burden on employees and can lead to negative feelings such as stress and burnout.

Stress is about misalignment between the individual's ability to master certain challenges and the challenges facing the individual. What project team members find stressful varies. Time pressure, expectations from many stakeholders, project assignments combined with tasks employees have in their regular position in the base organization, these are all factors that can affect the perception of stressing work conditions.

Different people involved in the project experience psychosocial aspects of the work differently. One may experience project overload because the workday is perceived as being too busy, or due to constantly switching between tasks and teams when involved in multiple projects simultaneously. Studies have shown that at least every third project team member experiences such an overload. They describe a situation where they have too little opportunity to retrieve, where they do not have proper routines for the work they are going to do and that they get too little time in which it can be completed to their satisfaction.

Too heavy project load often causes the experience of stress, as well as contributing to less competence development and learning and the experience of not mastering tasks within the time available (Zika-Viktorsson, Hovmark, & Nordqvist, 2003; Zika-Viktorsson, Sundström, & Engwall, 2006). If so, there is a risk that project team members experience a burnout (see below). Stress is often due to one or more of the following stressors related to the work situation (Cooper & Marshall, 1978):

- Job factors such as managerial responsibility, undue working hours, physical work environment (e.g. noise and dust).
- Role of the organization; for example, holding the project owner role for many projects or being a user representative under pressure from other stakeholders. Being a project manager can involve high stress in terms of role ambiguity and conflict of interest between different roles.
- Career development (aspirations for a career that has been put on hold or career development has been mandated that does not match the person's wishes, experience or abilities).
- Social relationships in terms of experiencing less support than desired by colleagues in the project team or by one's functional leader, or challenges with cooperation.
- The culture of participation and engagement: few opportunities to help establish goals, participate in decision-making or work with ideas.

WATCH THIS!

Stress. It makes your heart pound, your breathing quicken and your forehead sweat. But while stress has been made into a public health enemy, new research suggests that stress may only be bad for you if you believe that to be the case. Watch this Ted Talk by psychologist Kelly McGonigal (2013) at: https://study.sagepub.com/pm. Maybe you will reconsider stress as a positive?

Freudenberger (1974) established the concept of burnout as the result of multiple stressors such as those that project participants, particularly project managers, can find themselves exposed to. Burnout is often described as having 12 stages:

1. *Manic motivation*. The employee is fired with excitement and enthusiasm for any new project, regardless of the task; the job is self-defining and the person is emotionally dependent on it for recognition and identity.
2. *Job, job, job*. The employee increases the pace – works as fast and as much as possible. Frenetic energy. Shows that the more the context demands hard work, the more indispensable the employee appears to be.
3. *No time for me*. The employee acts as a 'saint' who sacrifices their own needs to solve those of others and the project.
4. *Limbo time*. The employee feels things are not ok, struggling with physical signs such as sleep deprivation, headaches, dyspepsia, etc. These health signals tend to be ignored.
5. *Devaluation of life*. The employee finds only limited pleasure in things. All one relates to are the projects one takes part in.
6. *Cynical and dissatisfied*. The employee criticizes others for their lack of effort and performance. Others do not see things in quite the terms that the employee does.
7. *Withdrawal from the rest of the project team*. The employee attends all meetings but avoids social settings. Feeling indisposed towards others and beginning to register health issues.
8. *Strange behaviour*. Others start talking about this employee; what's wrong with him? The employee avoids everyone as much as possible. When confronted, the person says that everything is all right. That others in the project team work much more than the person in question is not acknowledged.
9. *Nothing else besides the job matters*. The employee experiences a sense of emptiness. Impossible to relax. Recreation is impossible – the employee continuously identifies and engage in new tasks.
10. *Nothing is fun, nothing really matters*. Instead of filling the time with something that will bring joy, the employee fills it with too much food and drink, promiscuous behaviour, games, thus negative over-stimulation.
11. *Depression*. The employee is officially depressed. Does not try to pretend that there is joy in the job and is becoming apathetic.
12. *Full burnout*. The employee is tetchy, mentally erratic, can physically collapse. They are a risk to themselves and should receive professional help.

Counteracting and reducing stress requires social support. The support may be to provide information that makes everyday life more predictable and easier to handle. It may concern offering care if this will help the employee to understand and approach tasks in a more resourceful way, whether this is practical help, such as a meeting or professional assistance. At work, other significant contributions to reducing the negative effects of workload are a supportive leadership style (Chapter 7) and being part of a good project team (Chapter 8) where there is a culture that encourages mastery and development.

The worst thing for stressed out employees, risking burnout, is a toxic culture, where the sources of toxicity go unacknowledged under the imprimatur of a hard-line project manager who drives hard, overloading people beyond their capacities to cope (Frost, 2007). Above we have mentioned the negative effects of overload and how they can be reduced. Although this is presented mostly from the project employee's perspective, it is obviously also applicable to the project manager for it is they who may well be the breeding ground of the toxins at work.

WATCH THIS!

Neil Young (1991) once sang that it is better to burn out than to fade away. Are you the type of person that will burn out? Watch this alarming YouTube video by Dr Geri Puleo (2014) at TEDxSeton Hill University about burnout at: https://study.sagepub.com/pm. Is this the environment you want to be a coproducer of in your future job?

PROJECT MANAGER'S OVERLOADING AS TOXIC

The project is related to the project owner and the permanent organization, and the functional team of the project team, which may affect the project manager's situation. The project manager can become the toxic handler for the pressures that flow down from these sites and that are channelled through their office.

Project work can be exciting, challenging and provide great fulfilment; it can also be miserable, dangerous, unfulfilling and even a lethal place of existence. Frost (2007) prepares the ground for us to think about what happens when projects do bad things to those who work on them. Frost characterizes the emotional pain that undermines hope and self-esteem in people at work as a toxin. To explain how toxicity is created in the workplace, Frost (2007, p. 36) identified sources of toxic emotions which we have adopted to project management:

- **Intentions**: Project managers who are abusive and distrust staff. They manage through control, fear, and constant surveillance. They lead through punishment and fear, lacking the skills and abilities for effective people management. They may be excellent in technical skills but lack the necessary people skills. They are inconsistent in their decisions and lack integrity. Conversely, they may lack faith in their employees' abilities and skills, so they try to control every decision their employees make.
- **Incompetence**: Project managers who lack the skills and abilities for effective people management. They may be excellent in technical skills but lack the necessary people skills. They are inconsistent in their decisions and lack integrity. Conversely, they may lack faith in their employees' abilities and skills, so they try to control every decision their employees make.
- **Infidelity**: Project managers that do not value the trust and confidence of their employees and who betray any discussion made in confidence. Or, such bosses may make promises (e.g. a promotion) and never deliver, and some may take the credit for other people's work.
- **Insensitivity**: Project managers that lack social intelligence. They have no idea, and do not care, how others feel. Such managers may also have no idea how others feel about them. They may be unable to regulate their own emotions and behave in inappropriate ways.

- **Intrusion**: Project managers expect employees to forgo their own social or family lives for their work. They expect people to work long hours, weekends, and so on. They work long hours and expect everyone else to do the same – even if it is to the detriment of the person's family life.

While some toxicity is inevitable and cannot be anticipated or controlled, such as the death of a co-worker on the project, other sources of toxicity, such as those outlined above, can become institutionalized in certain projects, especially when people are expected to act in ways antithetical to their own values and beliefs, their well-being and work–life balance.

Clearly, toxicity at work can take many forms and working in a bad team can be one of the most toxic experiences you can have at work. The sources of the toxicity are often people in formally authoritative and senior roles in the project organization, so there is little that others can actually do to rectify the situation. If projects are run hard and fast, expect toxicity to be pervasive. The best remedy is compassion, but this commodity is often a tender, precious and vulnerable bloom, easily trampled by the foolhardy insensitivity of others, especially those in positions of formal authority.

AVOIDING PROJECT MANAGEMENT TOXICITY

If the project owner and the permanent organization have a good understanding of the project's purpose and are dedicated to the project's content and progress, this provides a good starting point for a project manager. Although the project manager may experience pressure from expectations of the project from the owner and the base organization, while they still share a common opinion about the purpose, direction and objective of the project the pressures can usually be handled if the project is proceeding well. If it is unclear where the project is leading or how well it is faring, it often means that there is less involvement and understanding from key stakeholders, which can lead to a lack of clarification and progress.

Troubles can begin as communication issues between project managers and owners as project progress, for whatever reasons, lags projections of schedules. It is tiresome to be accountable for a lack of results when it is due to circumstances you experience as beyond control. We have repeatedly emphasized the relationship between project owners and project managers. If it does not work, it can cause a lot of stress for both parties. In a good and appropriate relationship, the project manager will more easily clarify significant aspects of project execution – especially progress – and provide support for the project manager's choices and actions, which reduces the number of stressors likely to be experienced.

Team workers who lack time, commitment or competence can also cause stress to the project manager and take up valuable time. Project managers must spend time motivating and tending to such employees, redistributing tasks and possibly taking a greater part in operational work themselves. All of these become potential sources of stress.

Lack of structure, unclear goals and a high level of uncertainty can put a lot of strain on the project manager in a difficult situation with regard to the progress and coordination of tasks for the project team. The project team will experience time pressure for the completion of the delivery but when this occurs in a situation where the project owner, the permanent organization and the project team have clarity on what is actually to be delivered, uncertainty and frustration ensue. The project manager may be exposed to a conflicting pressure from key stakeholders who wish to influence delivery or enforce clarifications and completion.

To avoid, or at least minimize such situations, all parties involved in project execution need to be competent and well informed about their roles and responsibilities. Knowledge of how project management has been designed, clarity about the management tools in use and the accountabilities associated with action being clearly spelled out help the actors around the project manager fulfil their responsibilities. This will facilitate the implementation and therefore help to reduce stress.

WHAT WOULD YOU DO?

Read the article by Alexander on 'How to deal with toxic team members' at https://study.sagepub.com/pm and answer the following question.

QUESTION

1. What would you do to minimize toxicity in a project culture?

Project competence in modern working life

Managing project-based organizations is a matter of managing and enabling the development of expertise and capabilities. Although we have previously discussed competence and learning (Chapter 11), we will discuss this again from an organization perspective and with more specific attention to project competence. In a knowledge economy, modern organizations' competitiveness depends on the fact that they continuously develop their collective competence by collecting, integrating and disseminating knowledge in and between projects (see, for example, Grant, 1996; Kogut and Zander, 1992; Spender & Grant, 1996).

A key field within strategic competence is analysis of the organization's needs and markets, understanding the frameworks, environments, and customer and client groups that are central to the organization. For a municipality, it is an understanding of citizens' needs, knowledge of overall guidelines, suppliers' products and other factors that affect the domain in which the municipality operates. For a PC supplier, it is more obviously about knowledge of the market and understanding customers' needs.

In order to offer products to recipients, be it clients, customers, users or citizens, one must have expertise in how the products are manufactured, i.e. production competence. Knowledge of basic technical elements, as well as of how to acquire new knowledge and create innovations related to the product or process to deliver a product or service, are vital. Organizations have three strategic areas of competence, all of which must be developed and integrated to develop competitive power (Söderlund, 2005, p. 164).

Figure 12.9 illustrates the three strategic areas of competence that must be integrated.

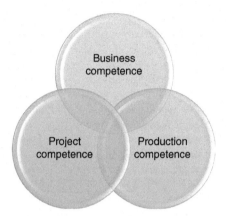

Figure 12.9 A company's three strategical fields of competence/expertise

PROJECT COMPETENCY COMPONENTS

Project competence concerns understanding the mechanisms and elements that apply for projects to be a tool for value creation and how this works together with the other strategic areas of expertise. Competence in organizing and managing projects appropriately is at issue. Project competence consists of an approach to four primary activities concerned with the project (Söderlund, 2005):

- *Project generation* involves understanding the project's basic idea, the resource framework conditions, the uncertainties and the links to the other strategic areas of competence; not least, it implies an understanding of the project's results and effects – the value-creating elements.
- *Project organization* concerns the division of responsibility and authority between key actors, such as project and foundation organization, as well as the relationship between working groups, governing groups and other stakeholders.
- *Project leadership* is linked to competence in the project management role, as well as relations between project owners and project managers in managing project management. It concerns management of the project.
- *Project cooperation* is about competence related to the operational work of the project. It mainly takes place in teams and insights into the components that create good teams, and processes in the project work comprise significant areas of expertise.

In order for projects to generate value, they must integrate the four primary actions (generation, organization, leadership and teamwork) on two levels: in the project and in the organization at the strategic level. Söderlund has done notable work on how strategic competence development and project level knowledge integration are interlinked. He proposes the following areas of competence and knowledge (Table 12.2).

Table 12.2 Strategic competence integration and knowledge integration in projects (after Söderlund, 2005)

Elements	Strategic competence integration Importance of project competence for integration with other strategic competencies	Knowledge integration in project Importance of the elements for the specific project
Project generation	Integrates production and business opportunities, e.g. ideas from specialists and ideas from customers	Early acquisition of knowledge, preparation of premises for the project, creating visions of the future
Project organization	Integrates production and business competencies, e.g. through processes or organizational integration	Knowledge integration between different teams through the design of supportive organizational structures and processes
Project leadership	Collective leadership where responsibility is shared to create superstructure with the other fields of expertise	Gives direction to the knowledge integration, which seems to create memorable events and common language
Project cooperation	Dialogue between team or integrating team where members from other areas participate	Make up the meeting place for operational interaction and knowledge integration in the project

Summary

In this chapter, we have:

- Looked at portfolios and programmes of projects, and how the latter are becoming more widespread due to the phenomenon of projectification and the development of project-based firms.
- Elaborated how programme and portfolio management concerns organizing realization of strategies and goals through projects.
- Discussed how the tendency of increasing portfolios implies increased complexity and fragmentation of organizational structures, which in turn increases the need for coordination and competence development in managing portfolios.
- Described how project management offices (PMOs) can be efficient support offices for projects and also enable increased project maturity.
- Working in projects also includes potential negative side effects for both the organization and the individual. Stress, burnout and toxicity among project staff and project managers can to a large extent be attributed to time pressure, cross-pressures from competing project-oriented interests as well as intense and complex work situations.

Exercises

1. Can you explain the difference between projects, project programmes and project portfolios?
2. What is the implication of programmification for an organization's way of running projects? What can you say about communication, coordination and value creation in light of this? What about the role of top management in this?
3. What characterizes good portfolio management?
4. What are the key characteristics of interorganizational projects and the benefits and key challenges of these projects?

5. Can you explain the concept of project maturity, and what we can do to increase project maturity in an organization?
6. What distinguishes mechanistic and organic organizational structures and what is an adhocracy?
7. What are the key features of organizational hierarchies and polyarchies?
8. Why are stress and overload such important issues of an increasing number of project portfolios and what means do we have available to try to prevent burnouts?

CASE STUDY

WHY GOVERNMENTS ARE SO BAD AT IMPLEMENTING PUBLIC PROJECTS

As Canada's federal government starts looking for a replacement for its failed payroll system (read full article online at https://study.sagepub.com/pm) and the Ontario provincial government launches yet another major shake-up of its health-care system (see www.theglobeandmail.com/canada/article-ontario-government-employee-fired-after-leak-of-fords-health-plan/), it's useful to remind decision-makers of a long history of failures in major public sector implementations.

Research from around the world shows a consistent pattern of failures in public sector policy and project implementation. Yet we continue to embark upon implementation built on bias and faulty logic.

So maybe it's time to better understand the architecture of failure and what can be done to overcome it.

Recent publications from Australia, Canada, the United Kingdom and the United States deliver some consistent messages. *The Blunders of Government,* by Ivor Crewe and Anthony King (2013), delves into the many restarts of the UK National Health Service. The Learning from Failure report (read full article online at https://study.sagepub.com/pm) details major project failures in Australia. In the US, *A Cascade of Failures: Why Government Fails, and How to Stop It* (read full article online at https://study.sagepub.com/pm) reports similar themes. In Canada, the auditor general's latest reports on the Phoenix pay system (read the full article online at https://study.sagepub.com/pm) echo the common basis for implementation failure. It's not often an auditor uses the phrase 'incomprehensible', but there it is.

When distilling all this research and all these investigations, certain themes are common to them all.

First and foremost, in the public sector, announcement was equated with accomplishment. This is the equivalent of thinking that just cutting the ribbon is enough.

A corollary of this is that most projects get lots of attention by both political and bureaucratic leaders at first, but that attention fades as the boring, detail-oriented work begins and the next issue, crisis or bright shiny object comes along.

In many cases, there is a cultural disconnect in the project design that prevents bad news from making it to those at the top of the chain of command, minimizes problems that are often warning signs and deliberately downplays operational issues as minor.

What can be called the 'handover mentality' often takes over between a project's designers and the people who have to actually implement it and get it up and running. It's best characterized by the phrase: 'We design it. You make it work.'

(Continued)

The next element is that when things go wrong, those who speak up about the problems are dismissed, discounted or just plain punished. This leads to groupthink, a failure to challenge assumptions and to just go along, even when danger signs are in full sight.

Policy designers and those who must implement government projects or infrastructure are often guilty of what's known as optimism bias ('What could possibly go wrong?') when, in fact, they should be looking at the end goal. They should be working backwards to identify not only what could go wrong, but how the whole process will roll out.

Instead, they focus on the beginning – the announcement, the first stages.

We hear the word *complexity* a lot when examining government project failures. Indeed, most of the problems examined in the aforementioned research pointed to the increasing complexity in failed implementations that went well beyond IT, and the failure to map those complexities out. But that complexity increases the risks of some moving part of a government project malfunctioning and shutting down the entire system.

GEARS START SLIPPING

People get busy and distracted. If a policy is just the flavour of the week and something else becomes popular next week, the project starts to lose momentum, and needs attention, reaction and adaptation to inevitable challenges. The gears start to slip.

Then there is the churn of officials. At both the political and bureaucratic level, this is a consistent theme in projects failing or in governments responding poorly to crises as they arise.

The champions for a policy simply move on, and their successors are left to decide how much energy to put into someone else's pet project. Similarly, the rapid turnover of senior managers in government often leaves well-intentioned people to respond to emergencies in areas where they have little experience.

An interesting element in all of this research is the confirmation that cognitive biases play a significant role in assessing risks in policy implementation in a number of ways, often in the face of a mountain of contrary evidence.

Cognitive biases tend to confirm beliefs we already have. Biases block new information. While we need biases to short-hand our interpretation of events, they often filter and discount new information. Our experiences are our greatest asset and greatest liability in this process.

The bottom line on the causes of major implementation failure really rests with a culture focused on blame avoidance and getting along. We now know enough to avoid failure, backed by ample evidence that confirms common sense about how to better structure policy, its implementation and our major projects.

Source: adapted from 'Why governments are so bad at implementing public projects', by Andrew Graham, *The Conversation*, 13 February 2019. Read the full article online at https://study.sagepub.com/pm.

QUESTION

1. Thinking about the organization design of innovation projects, bearing in mind the failures referenced in the article, and given what you have learnt about projects and their management and organization design, how would you design a project organization to be more successful than these failures?

Additional resources

In terms of project competence, there are limited books and literature that have a thorough approach to this. However, we are strongly inspired by Jonas Söderlund's book *Project Management & Project Competency* (2005) and recommend it if you want to go deeper. The same book also provides a good insight into the phenomenon of projectification. Peter Frost's (2007) *Toxic Emotions at Work and What You Can do About Them* is a superb book, full of compassion and wisdom.

Chapter Roadmap

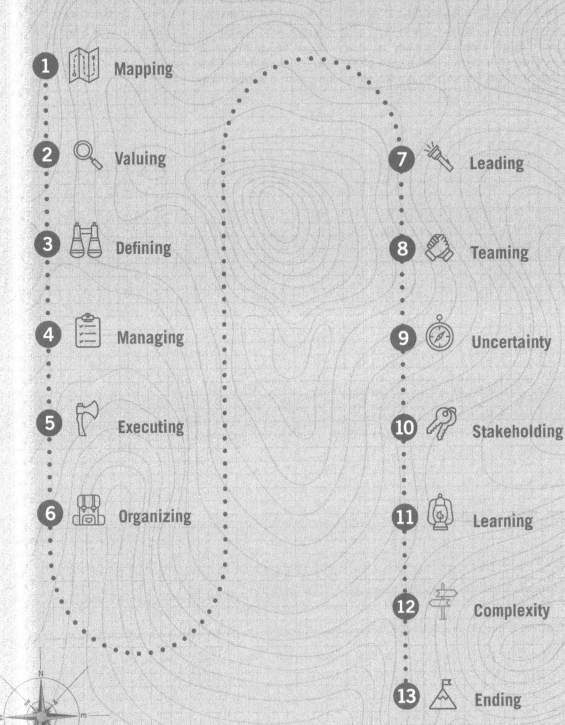

1. Mapping
2. Valuing
3. Defining
4. Managing
5. Executing
6. Organizing
7. Leading
8. Teaming
9. Uncertainty
10. Stakeholding
11. Learning
12. Complexity
13. Ending

13

Ending Projects

Learning objectives

After reading this chapter, you should:

1 Be familiar with current trends in project management as a profession

2 Know why projects sometimes have to be terminated without reaching their goals

3 Know the importance of the activities related to project closure and hand over of project deliveries

4 Understand essential aspects of project delivery, realization, responsibilities and evaluation of the implementation and delivery of projects in terms of success criteria

5 Have a grasp of some new approaches to understanding projects

Before you get started

This is the end, beautiful friend, this is the end, my only friend, the end of our elaborate plans, the end of ev'rything that stands, the end.

– Jim Morrison, 1966, 'The End'

Introduction

We will begin this chapter by considering what being a project manager entails, both ethically and in terms of the profession being joined. One thing that a project manager will have to do, apart from running projects, is closing them. When projects start, you usually have a set date for when to end. We have seen what impact this has on implementing projects, and we will now look at how they should be terminated. At the end of the project, the project manager will hand over the delivery, prepare a final report, complete documentation and reflect on experience from the project. The project should also be phased out and staff reduced and moved on. These moments are the core of this chapter.

Many projects are not completed as planned, and we will look at the different causes of this. The chapter also reflects on the relationship between project completion and assessments of the project's success. It can be difficult to know if the project evolves in the desired manner and will provide project product success and contribute to value creation in the long run or if it has developed in an undesired direction. Project closure must, therefore, be discussed in light of both the quality of the execution and its delivery in terms of possible value creation. The completion will be the penultimate phase of the project before the final phase occurs, namely value creation. We use the concept of value creation as the key here, while also considering the effects of realization and benefits as similar terms that are used that are shades and variants of the same meaningful content. The chapter concludes with an overview of key elements related to project completion and project success assessment.

Being a project manager

Project managers have, as you will gathered from the book, great responsibilities. They are authoritative figures of the contemporary age, heroic in some respects as they guide projects to success. To do so, they must guide ethically. Ethics can be considered at both the macro and a more micro level (Figure 13.1).

At the macro level, ethics in projects focuses on the ethicality of approaches to projects regarding their content and procedures. When the client considers initiating a project, there will be different ethical issues that are reviewed and assessed. If organizations are to create value and be profitable, in the long run they must increasingly be ethically responsible, ensuring that the projects they implement do not harm the environment or otherwise have negative effects. If business performance over time is not sustainable, customers and users will often turn away from their products. Ethics in the project context are closely interlinked and shaped by the attitudes and values of the larger context in which projects are embedded.

Any project is also influenced by the overall *corporate governance* system. Studies have indicated that misleading reports about errors are less common in organizations that clearly state such reports are unacceptable (Smith, Thompson, & Iacovou, 2009). For example, the willingness to report bad news in IT projects is strongly influenced by management's response to such news, in combination with the nature of the communication structures: are they open to producing a flow of information across the project organization and to the management of the organization (Park & Keil, 2009)?

Organizations that strive to appear as ethically conscious and provide a transparent picture of their projects must actively seek to develop learning practices that facilitate ethical reflection and open discussions about difficulties and dilemmas. Control mechanisms alone are insufficient for developing ethical standards; these develop better when project participants trust each other and other stakeholders' intentions. For the project to be ethical as an overall entity the entire value chain must be auditable for ethicality. Indeed, ethics are applicable at different levels in projects.

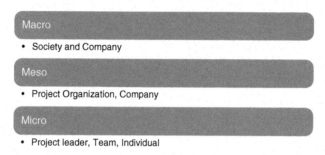

Figure 13.1 Ethics in projects at multiple levels

In projects, it may be more demanding to establish and live up to ethical standards than in project-based organizations (Müller et al., 2013). This is due to several factors. A project is a temporary organization, which makes it difficult to establish shared ethical platforms in the time available. The project also has a clearly defined date for termination – often leaving the issue of liability in the open. Potentially it will be easier for both the principal and other actors involved to be somewhat relaxed about ethical standards. Short deadlines can lead to ethical questions receiving only scant attention. Furthermore, *long-term value chains* involve many actors in projects, some of which are of relatively short duration. Many project actors represent different and partly contradictory interests, especially in interorganizational projects, where different stakeholders often have different embedded ethical cultures and values. Lack of transparency; in both the structure and the collaborative relationships also contributes to making ethics problematic.

At the micro level, it is both the individual project member but especially the project manager for whom ethical issues must be paramount. It is common for project managers to experience ethical dilemmas in situations where there is a lack of transparency; for instance, where reporting of unfortunate events such as accidents or overruns is suppressed. Where there is a close relationship between purchasers and suppliers this can be ethically dubious. In global operations, where projects in the Third World use local rules for health, safety and the environment or for child labour to increase profits, this is unethical by First World standards (Müller et al., 2013; also see Rego, Cunha, and Clegg, 2012).

Managerial and cultural structures that enable 'doing the right thing', for example honesty when unfortunate events or cost overruns occur, are a major ethical asset. Organizations that actively encourage a learning culture and establish structures that promote information flow will tend to be more openly ethical than those that do not. There is a correlation between trust, governance structures and the individual project manager making ethically appropriate choices in different contexts (Müller et al., 2013).

WHAT WOULD YOU DO?

You are a project manager for a medium-sized project supposed to restructure a culture house in your municipality. It involves some rebuilding and some reorganization. The project ambition has grown since the project started. Due to underestimating on some critical issues, the budget is about to run out, way before the project is finished. You have read about cost overruns in other project.

READ THIS!

Read about an example of a project running way over budget and time – Humboldt Forum museum in Berlin, Germany, written by Phillip Otterman (2019) at: https://study.sagepub.com/pm. Think about some of the issues projects like these tend to turn into.

You have become aware of this possible budget breakdown, but the project principal is not yet aware of this. The project principal is a stressed, ambitious person, secretly labelled 'Mini-Trump'. What would you do? Would you inform him, if so how would you do this?

Organizational structures and processes that promote ethical actions will enable purposeful handling of ethical dilemmas with a certain degree of flexibility that makes it possible to capture unforeseen events and reflect on ethical dilemmas. When these help managers 'choose the right solution' in different situations, trust will build and afford confidence in solving the next ethical dilemma. Project managers have a certain 'freedom with responsibility' to act more or less ethically.

Project management as a profession

We have demonstrated significant development in project management from being engineering-based to multidisciplinary as project organizing has become more widespread and knowledge of projects expanded beyond its disciplinary roots. Project management has become a semi-profession aspiring to be a profession characterized by both structural conditions in terms of education and certain criteria and standards for professional qualifications (Hanlon, 1998; Morris, Crawford, Hodgson, Shepherd, & Thomas, 2006). A professional framework includes an attitudinal component that implies that the practitioner has professional ethics related to the attitude towards the work and the way in which the function is exercised. Project management will become more professionalized, among other things, by adopting an active relationship with ethics, often embedded in project management programmes in tertiary education in university and colleges.

The Project Management Institute (PMI) is the largest and most famous of the international member organizations striving to professionalize the area of project management, with over half a million members. PMI offers both courses and education, research programmes and development programmes, along with standardized project tools. The other organizations are the Association for Project Management (APM) and the Project Management Forum (PMF). These bodies build both a common identity and common standards within the field of project management. However, a drawback is that they were established with strong anchoring in the task-oriented approach. Although significant changes are afoot in the field of project management, represented in part by this book, many project managers and others who work with projects in film, competence development programmes or other change and development projects may find the project methodologies that these institutions promote somewhat too prescriptive, restrictive and overly oriented to material projects. For the field to be professionalized, the tendency to over-rationalize the subject must be reduced (Morris et al., 2006). Rather than being standardized, projects vary according to the type and depending on the context they are going to operate within (Shenhar, 2001).

A project manager must have expertise in a wide range of areas. At the same time, the project manager function is determined by both the project type and the context. There is a big difference in being a project manager for a competence development programme in a section in a small municipality, and for the construction of an oil platform. Henry Mintzberg (2009) claims that managing must be learned in practice and that it is an *art* that requires imagination and creative skills to enable the practitioner to understand and solve problems. It is also a *science* in which the manager must apply systematic knowledge and analytical skills in order to handle different situations and make decisions. And not least, management is a *craft* where practical knowledge and experience provide a basis for action and reflection on action. Mintzberg's words also apply to being a project manager (see Figure 13.2).

Figure 13.2 Leading (managing and leadership) as Art, Science and Craft (based on Mintzberg, 2009)

We have identified competencies that are crucial for project managers dealing with projects of different types (Chapter 7), including competence in the areas of administration and management, and relationship and the creation of meaning. Much of the work of a project manager involves communicating and managing information among many teams, not least the project team and the project owner as well as other stakeholders.

Project managers need to be both local and cosmopolitan (Hodgson, Paton & Muzio, 2015), familiar with local project practices regarding methods and methodology, while at the same time being familiar with global methods and practices.

The project manager must handle many stakeholders, time pressures and uncertain and ambiguous situations as well as rapid changes, be able to resolve urgent issues and handle relationships with employees while being a *Project Champion* (Pinto & Slevin, 1989) that manages both projects unfolding in an orderly fashion as well as those unanticipated events that disrupt routines. Modern project management sees the project in relation to other activities, actors and processes as open systems that allow multiple inputs, manage much equivocality and uncertainty and the reality of project processes being dynamic, complex and changeable. Opportunities must be managed and exploited. Boundaries must be drawn around the project (such as defining the project team, managing stakeholders while delivering the project on schedule, on budget, on time, innovatively and creatively). Doing this is demanding. It requires *reflective practitioners* (Schön, 1991; Skyttermoen, 2013) able to be engaged in the processes they are involved in, exploring and interpreting relationships, managing people and teams and being adept at sourcing and using technology, tools and procedures. Finally, projects need to be terminated.

The temporality of projects

Projects are by definition temporary organizations. They must be terminated after completion of their assignment. Nevertheless, project scholars have paid only limited attention to the impact of temporality on organizing processes, like the collaboration, the development of trust among the involved actors, the leadership, etc. Some projects, such as short film projects, may last only a few days while others last for many years. A few projects, such as large infrastructure projects, can last for more than a decade. How does the actual certainty about the short and long duration shape the project processes differently? We observe that temporality is a hot topic. Together with the increasing awareness of the importance of time for the design and development of the project processes, there has been an interest in understanding time in itself in project contexts.

In Chapter 1 we looked at the change from considering time in projects as exclusively linear, to consider cyclical times, such as occurs in an enterprise annually, for example budgeting. This can also be the case in projects, but it is often the case that you move through the project in a spiral-like process. The project implementation will then be repeated in cycles, i.e. iterations, where you move through the project in two-step-forward-and-back thinking. One never returns to the exact same process, while the work takes place in many repeating loops (processes) where each loop is relatively similar to the other. This is expressed in the implementation models; for example, when we have discussed classic waterfall models, milestone models and agile implementation models.

Often time is experienced as a given phenomenon, one that everyone in and around a project perceives the same. It is considered as one-dimensional, while it may be multi-dimensional. Recent research argues that time is a complex, social construction that includes elements such as: *time frame* (i.e. focusing primarily on what is happening here and now, far ahead of time or in the past), *pace* (how fast will things happen), *timing, synchronization* (integration) of activities, *duration and sequence* (order of activities) (Halbesleben et al., 2003).

Project members and others can all have different perceptions of each of these dimensions. These are intertwined and contribute to complexity in the coordination of resources, tasks and deliveries in projects because each individual can have his own and local construction of time. Managers and other employees in projects need to be aware of the different perceptions of pace, sequence, duration and the elements mentioned above, both within the group and among the project's other stakeholders. In order to identify differences and to establish the most united understanding of time, this should be discussed as part of the planning process. Working with time as a multi-dimensional phenomenon implies that time can be understood in different ways. It also means that we can organize and spend time across projects and permanent organizations (Orlikowski & Yates, 2002).

Above we took into account different conditions in regard to the assessment of project success and failure. To minimize projects failing, be aware of the potentially adverse factors. If project results are to be successful over time, the base organization, as the principal, needs to be aligned with the project organization. The base organization has a responsibility to allocate resources, contribute to attitudinal changes and otherwise support the project outcome. If the project takes longer than originally planned the importance of project success in terms of desired effects and value creation should still remain uppermost.

A broad overview of key elements for how project success can be ensured, assessed and measured is provided in Table 13.1. It is not meant to be an exhaustive overview but as a contribution to focusing on project completion and various dimensions of project success.

Table 13.1 Termination of projects – assessing and evaluating

Element	Area	Areas of attention
Project termination	End activities	End the tasks in the product, update and disseminate an overview of activities that have not been completed. Terminate contracts and project accounts.
	Hand over of product/delivery	The delivery is handed over to the client and taken into use by the customer/base organization. Have taken care of any necessary training/introduction.
	Evaluation	Documentation and control of the delivery and any suggestions for use and further development. Assessment of process and learning. Usually included as part of the final report. Depending on, among other things, size and type, the evaluation will be external or internally performed by the project organization itself.
	The final report	Submit final report by agreed forms and moments. Often consists of a summary of the project delivery's core results, assessment of the achievement of project and effect goals.
	Dissolution of the project organization	Prepare team members and project manager for termination and transition to other tasks. For internal projects, prepare the basic organization for return in position. Be prepared for various emotional and motivational reactions.
Project success – central dimensions		
Project effiency	Central stakeholder – main perspective	Project owner/principal
	What to measure	Implementation of the project's time and cost frameworks. Project management tools and expediency.
	Challenges	Any changes during the project? How to assess this?
	Aspect of time	Assessment of the extent to which the project was completed within the project's time frames. Reasons for the time dimension.
	Costs/resources	Assessment of budget, accounting and investment. Identification and explanations for deviations from plans.
	Project management methodology	Assessment of the use of project plans, routines and tools, and appropriateness. Assessment of how tools such as milestone plans, activity plans and follow-up at this level were appropriate.
	Methodological elements	The time aspect is assessed on the basis of the timetables of any reasons for deviations. The cost aspect is assessed on the basis of the resource limits and any reasons for deviations.
	Time of assessment	Immediately after the completion of the project. Included in project final report.
	Core points	Time and cost limits, use of project management tools. Assessment of what could have done differently
Performance goals (Delivery)	Central stakeholder – main perspective	Principal, clients
	What to measure	The defined performance goals for the project.
	Challenges	Adjusted and changed objectives/goals along the way. Target conflicts between goals.

Element	Area	Areas of attention
	Quality criteria	Measure and evaluate the quality criteria set for the delivery.
	The defined performance goals	Assess the individual defining the performance goals. Separately and collectively, must be measured and evaluated.
	Methodological elements	Measure each of the project goals, consider these in context. Can imply goal conflicts. For technical parts, measuring tools can be applied, can be more difficult for 'soft' targets.
	Time of assessment	Immediately after the completion of the project. Included in project final report.
	Core points	Assessment of operationalized performance goals.
Learning and team development	Central stakeholder – main perspective	Principal, base organization, project leader, project team
	What to measure	Learning elements for the principal. Project implementation elements, content aspects, teamwork and development.
	Challenges	Establish moments and criteria for measuring and assessing success. Set aside time and attention for assessment of learning and team development.
	Learning aspect	Learning along the way must be reflected over, embedded and shared. Include both learning related to the project's content but also the project form and teamwork.
	Methodological elements	Establish learning arenas. Use of reports, simple appropriate routines for sharing reflection and experience.
	Time of assessment	After the completion of the project. May be included in project final report. Possibly an own evaluation report.
	Core points	Awareness of learning during the project. Arenas and culture for learning, attention to team development and project professional learning, as well as transfer of experience to educators and customers of content experience and learning in the project.
Purpose and value creation	Central stakeholder – main perspective	Principal, base organization, clients/users, suppliers, competitors, etc.
	What to measure	Effects of the delivery and how the delivery has contributed to value creation.
	Challenges	Isolate the effect of the project delivery from other factors that may affect. Be aware that potential effects may change over time. Attention that some project goals may be mutually contradictory.
	Delivery	The project's delivery must be assessed against value creation. The most important part of the project.
	Methodological elements	Benefits realization plan to assess effects. Clarify how effects should be measured and assessed. Attention to both 'hard' and 'soft' goals.
	Time of assessment	When the project result has worked for a period. Big differences between projects. Should be part of the company's strategic assessments.
	Core points	Attention on the desired effects the delivery should provide for value creation. Also, note other effects.
Innovation and preparing for the future	Central stakeholder – main perspective	Principal, base organization, clients/users, suppliers, competitors, etc.
	What to measure	Degree of innovation and contribution to improved business situation.
	Challenges	Time for measurement will often be long before it can be assessed. Changed framework conditions entail great uncertainty about effect.

(Continued)

Table 13.1 (Continued)

Element	Area	Areas of attention
	Focus	Attention to changed product and process. New business models will often come in this category, but also innovations in the product itself, or the work process.
	Methodological elements	Can be difficult to measure, but set criteria in advance, which is assessed after a period. Can be both 'hard' and 'soft' measurement indicators.
	Time of assessment	When the project result has worked for a period. Big differences between projects. Should be part of the company's strategic assessments.
	Core points	Forward setting for change.

Project management is a complex and challenging area. We have dealt with the most relevant topics within the project management area, based on both classical and recent research, as we believe it provides the basis for a relevant understanding of this subject. Our goal has been to align updated research and relevant practices throughout the book, as research provides new insights that enable us to execute projects so that value creation can be enhanced.

There are many reasons why projects are terminated. We will look at some of them as rendered in Figure 13.3.

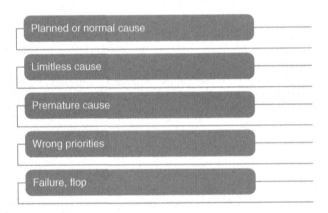

Figure 13.3 Reasons for project termination

Ending projects

PLANNED OR NORMAL CAUSE

Most often, projects are completed as planned, classified as a *normal reason for project completion*. There are more elements than just the 'Iron Triangle of the project' that are in play when the project is to be considered terminate but time, cost and delivery (quality) are key criteria.

Some projects, such as event projects, are controlled by some absolute time frames. An Olympic championship cannot be shifted in time, even if the criteria or objectives of the project delivering it are not fully met. Nevertheless, if it is held, it is considered a normal conclusion. When a building or plant is completed it can also be termed a normal termination, even when it is not completed within the planned framework.

Picture 13.1   A simple project completed

Source: Torgeir Skyttermoen

LIMITLESS CAUSE

Projects have the potential to start *living their own lives*, especially when there are no clearly defined requirements and frameworks or where project plans and follow-up do not have the necessary clarity (Vaagaasar, 2006). Project implementation can be characterized by delays because requirements and specifications change with elements constantly being added, as the scope of the project increases. At the same time, project implementation is often linked to the expectations and prestige of the project as well as the considerable resources invested, such that it may be difficult to stop or substantially change the project. The project is considered necessary and desirable.

Development projects in which new IT systems are being introduced may fall into the category of being limitless. An IT project that starts with clear ambitions but that does not have a clear framework is often able to sustain constant additions, new specifications and changes (Skyttermoen & Vaagaasar, 2015). Tress-90 was a large and comprehensive Norwegian IT project the intention behind which was to develop and implement a common system for the then National Welfare Administration (now NAV). It was intended to be the replacement for INFOTRYGD, a case-worker support system, used by the Norwegian National Insurance Administration. There were many reasons why the project grew in scope, complexity and, not least, cost. In the end, the project was eventually abandoned with a total cost of NOK 1.2bn ($200m), constituting the largest IT failure in Norwegian history. The project assumed new forms, developed its own dynamics and understanding, and the connection to the original purpose became somewhat unclear as it developed. The government, as the project owner, stopped the project, creating Norway's largest project *breakdown*.

The client has different options for action when projects start to develop in the wrong direction. As we saw in the example above with Tress-90, a decision may be made to stop the project completely. Other alternatives may be to redefine the project radically, making it a more or less new project. This can be done by redefining the project itself, with many of the same elements, such as individual objectives and management frameworks, as well as personnel, remaining part of a revised project. Another option is to redefine the project and replace many of the management frameworks and staff that were included in the original project. Often, a change of project manager will be relevant for this type of change, as a project manager may appear as the symbol of the completed project.

Increasing engagement (escalation of commitment) is a phenomenon that can be applied when projects are exposed to high risk, and where the attempt to correct problems with new solutions creates new or worsened problems. This causes the project's challenges to increase while reducing the likelihood of success, not an unusual phenomenon. Various explanations can be given (Staw & Ross, 1987):

Psychological factors among decision-makers where project managers and others convince themselves and others that they are doing the right thing

Social factors that need the justification of the project against competition with other actors in the market

Organizational factors where the institutional environment has expectations for the project and that the project is aligned with organization values and objectives

There is no easy way to prevent escalating involvement in a project but the use of management frameworks, especially in the form of milestone plans and uncertainty assessments, reduces the likelihood of such escalation.

PREMATURE CAUSE

Many projects start from a thin knowledge basis and with great uncertainty. Sometimes this is due to lack of preparation and investigation before start-up. For example, small projects such as the introduction of a new system or a management development project might be initiated on the basis of a leader's inspiration, perhaps as a result of a course or seminar attended. Other times, the project is premature simply because the uncertainty associated with the project is so great that it is not possible to clarify project parameters and develop the concept to a particular extent. The project may also be premature because those who work on clarifying the concept and preparing the case for it do not have sufficient competence. Projects designed with deliverables that seem to be a good idea before they are tested on potential future users sometimes, after testing with future users takes place, then the project learns that the delivery is not pertinent to these users. Bearing this in mind, that rather reinforces some of the insights of design thinking – try and have the users involved in the project and its scope from the outset; use prototypes and models to demonstrate current thinking; engage with the future users in terms that they can understand.

INAPPROPRIATE PRIORITIES

Organizations have many tasks and functions that need to be taken care of. Modern organizations are characterized by an excess of constraints. Expectations and demands from many different teams relate to when and how a project will solve or accomplish different tasks. While many projects are initiated by carefully considered priorities among the tasks and expectations, sometimes projects are set up to meet expectations without being so carefully considered. Sometimes, meeting one set of priorities makes meeting overall priorities very difficult, something that happened in a Norwegian government plan analysed by Dille, Söderlund and Clegg (2018) to develop a new national emergency communication system across the three main emergency services (Fire, Police, Health). The plan for building a new, digital emergency network was launched in the early 1990s. A project administrative office was established in the late 1990s in the Ministry of Justice and Police as a coordinating unit to develop the initiative. The project administrative group focused mainly on identifying and communicating the needs and requirements of the three emergency services. It soon became apparent, however, that the three main stakeholders were putting pressure on the project coordinators to comply with their specific demands.

The three emergency services are embedded in quite different structures, ranging from municipalities to national government. For instance, the Police service is run by the state, the Fire services are run by the municipalities, whereas Healthcare services are organized by five regional healthcare authorities with municipalities responsible for primary healthcare service and local emergency wards. Cooperation and coordination between these public-sector organizations and private contractors was critical. Synchronized implementation across a challenging topography and regionalized delivery systems implied high order technical and organizational complexity that was not achieved wholly in practice.

The project management team faced conflicting temporal requirements among the three subprojects. There was a central administration for the Police service, the National Police Directorate located in Oslo, which was capable of rapid time reckoning and decision. The Fire and Health services were much less centralized than the Police, with Fire and Rescue services being run by local municipalities. The national public fire protection authority, the Norwegian Directorate for Civil Protection, defined and regulated public requirements for fire prevention in the municipalities. Health had even greater complexity. The Norwegian Ministry of Health and Care Services administers four regional health authorities in Norway with many specialist agencies. The responsibility for specialist care lies with the state as the owner of the regional health authorities, which in turn own the hospital trusts. Municipalities are responsible for primary care and enjoy a great deal of freedom in organizing health services. Finding a common system with common features that suited all project stakeholders proved impossible; the project ended up delivering a system that suited the least demanding stakeholder, the police, but did not satisfy the features demanded by the other services (see Dille et al., 2018; and Dille, Hernes, & Vaagaasar, 2020, for the full story).

Often projects are created under conditions linked to available resources or markets that change during the course of the project: they have *drifting environments* (Kreiner, 1995). When this occurs it can make it very costly or risky to continue the project and the value of the project deliverables will be significantly reduced, such that it may be wise to discontinue the project in favour of other tasks. A responsible project owner might stop the project and relocate resources and attention to other projects. Nonetheless, many projects continue to run and consume resources long after they should have been closed. Once a project is established it often continues through an escalation of commitment as happened with many well-known megaprojects, such as the Channel Tunnel, Sydney Opera House and Tress-90 – although the latter was discontinued, eventually. Flyvbjerg (2003; 2007, 2014b) points out that many major projects, megaprojects, end up as failures.

From the portfolio management discussion in Chapter 12, remember that resource allocation is often made difficult to handle because the sum of many small and medium-sized projects is difficult to account for globally. Responsible owners must dare to quit projects when necessary. Another situation where this may be a wise decision is where a project is dependent on specific types of expertise or key personnel, having limited resources with which to acquire and maintain their commitment. In these cases, projects with such resources may be outflanked by the demands of other tasks or resources and the projects may end up being given a lower priority and terminated. Smaller projects, such as organizational change management projects, often fail also. Intentions to achieve more efficient processes and more appropriate organization will not always be fulfilled by a change project. Projects often concern innovation and innovation threatens embedded interests: hence, it is not unusual that one does not always succeed with innovation projects. Innovation and projects are associated with a significant degree of uncertainty and we will discuss a little further what makes a project fail or not.

READ THIS!

Why do projects fail? Two papers that are available in the online resources at https://study.sagepub.com/pm answer this question in relation to Volswagen's diesel-gate scandal, by Rhodes (2016) and Ghaim, Clegg, & Cunha, (2019).

Assessing project completion criteria

Milestones, plans, decision gates and clarity of responsibilities are tools to try and control project direction (and project teams) in terms of project intention. They provide the basis for evaluating early completion of the project before the scheduled end date. Milestones are aids for assessing whether the project is on the right course in terms of project intent. If failure to achieve the milestones cannot be corrected with minor changes, the project basis might need to be reviewed again. The results of these assessments can give rise to different conclusions such as adding resources, changing delivery times, adjusting quality criteria for delivery or some combination of these, perhaps even renegotiating or exiting the project (Figure 13.4).

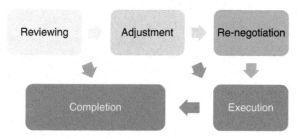

Figure 13.4   Assessments of project completion criteria

When early completion of a project is considered, two main factors should be emphasized: these are the extent to which expected results were achieved and success criteria fulfilled. Invested costs and resources used are key factors for assessing whether projects should be terminated earlier than planned. If the assessment is that the project has succeeded in reaching the goals that were set, it would be appropriate to quit. If the goals have not been realized sufficiently, there will have to be consideration of the balance between the amount invested in resources, effort and attention, given what has been achieved or will soon be achieved.

IN PRACTICE

HS2

Major rail projects are often characterized by concerns about cost, the exact route of the line and their effect on those living close by the rail works. One project that has been the subject of much criticism and contestation is the HS2 railway proposed as a high-speed line to connect London to Birmingham and then further north with one branch to Leeds and another to Manchester (originally due to open in 2032–33 but now pushed back to 2035–2040) where, eventually, it is proposed it will connect with a cross-Pennines East–West fast route that will be built at some unspecified time in the future. The initial plan is for 400m-long trains with as many as 1100 seats per train that would be capable of reaching speeds of up to 250mph and run as often as 14 times per hour in each direction.

The project began originally under the Labour government in 2009 and is the second high-speed rail project. The first was HS1 (High Speed 1), linking St Pancras International in London with the Channel Tunnel, opened in 2003. Since HS2 was planned it has run into considerable criticism in part because of delays and the billions of pounds that have already

(Continued)

been spent with little to show for the expenditure. The first phase of the railway between London and Birmingham was due to open at the end of 2026 but it is now projected that it will be 2028–2031 before the first trains run on the route, if they ever do. Opposition has been vociferous, especially in the wealthy home counties north of London, where ecological concerns about habitat have been predominant.

The constituency MPs representing the areas that the line traverses as it comes out of London are predominantly Conservative, the ruling political party at the time of writing, who have considerable political clout in objecting to the railway for its claimed loss of amenity and the compulsory purchase orders being issued to clear a path for the proposed route. Backing up this position is the pressure group Stop HS2 that argues that the line will cause increasing carbon emissions as well as damage areas of natural beauty and their ecosystems. Other opposition has been mounted targeting the increasing cost of the project, which on the current estimates has risen from £62bn to between £81bn and £88bn, up from £56bn in 2015 prices, the initial estimate for the cost. Further sources of opposition have framed around the benefits of the project: the time to travel from London to Birmingham would be reduced by 29 minutes. Here the objection is that, given the costs, is it worth it so that a relatively few people will be able to travel a small distance a little bit faster? Against the objections there is an argument that HS2 will generate thousands of jobs and revitalize the balance of economic growth between London and its southeast hinterland and the rest of the country.

Many people thus believe that the development should never have been adopted, given the real costs. The present government at the time of writing has announced that HS2 will go ahead. The decision was made prior to the COVID-19 crisis during which time travel was curtailed and many people learnt to Zoom rather than travel for meetings.

QUESTION

1. Using Google search and concentrating on the British media, track what has happened to the HS2 project recently, looking at the arguments for going ahead and for not doing so.

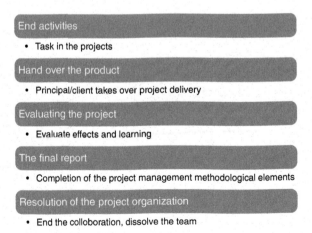

Figure 13.5 Elements related to project termination

End activities

Several issues must be clarified in the final phase. These are related to the project content, delivery of the product, project management elements including a final report, and an evaluation of the project (Figure 13.5).

A project is usually completed at the time of delivery, unless the project organization is contracted to be responsible for the project for a contracted period of time, as often happens with BOOT (Build Own Operate Transfer) contracts. In the latter case, tasks and activities will continue to be carried out in the project after it is realized. In other cases, if the project is oriented to producing a new product this product should be ready for use. If it is an event, then the event should have been staged. Depending on the type and size of the project, there will be many activities that are included in the actual completion work of the project, for example:

- *Contract termination*. The purpose is to ensure that formal contracts are terminated in an orderly manner.
- *Update and disseminate activities that have not been completed*. It is not uncommon that the project does not 'rush' to perform all planned activities or prepare all products before the project ends, when it will be taken over by the base organization. For the base organization to be able to handle this, these deficiencies need to be rectified by the project.
- *Completion of project accounts*. The economic elements of the project will be updated and completed through a project account under the agreement.
- *Exit and save project documentation*. This involves completing and storing management tools and other documentation from the project. There may also be the completion of test documentation related to systems and technical deliveries.

EXTEND YOUR KNOWLEDGE

Read the article by Wen and Qiang (2019) on the competencies project managers need for managing project closing, available at https://study.sagepub.com/pm.

HANDING OVER THE PRODUCT

The client is the recipient of the project's delivery. Some project types are concrete, such that it is obvious what will be handed over to the recipient as a final product. If it is a building, it is clear what surrender of the product entails: it is that the owner takes over the building, usually symbolized with a key being transferred from the project manager to the principal.

In an event project, the project's delivery is the completion of the event itself, with the project usually being closed with a final report. Something similar will apply to a change project, such as a reorganization of a departmental unit. The change itself is completed and delivery is marked by the project manager handing over a final report.

EVALUATING THE PROJECT

Evaluation in project context involves looking at the implementation of the project and the results achieved to gain an overall understanding of the project. Such evaluation is a source of continuous development of project competence. Evaluation is a systematic and analytical study conducted to obtain data on relationships related to a process and/or the outcome of the process, which can be evaluated either as the project unfolds or afterwards. The extent of evaluation obviously depends on the purpose of the evaluation. Roughly, evaluations can be divided into two main types, each with a different purpose, target group and basis:

- *Documentation and control*, where the purpose is to develop reliable information on what has been done, thereby contributing to accountability and openness. It is primarily those stakeholders that have contributed resources that are strongly affected by the impact of the project that require such evaluation. Evaluation is usually done in the form of data collection and analysis made in accordance with the mandate of the client.
- *The potential for performance improvement*, where the purpose is evaluation aimed at improving current and future projects through project-based learning. The principal, the base organization and the project organizers are the key target group but other stakeholders may also be relevant. The basis for the evaluation will be an open process, whose theme and facilities will be decided by those who sponsor the evaluation.

Evaluation by project owners is often initiated. Often, evaluation is conducted routinely according to the organization's project management systems. Different skills will obviously be required to evaluate project processes and to evaluate technical deliveries from a project. The independence of the review process is necessary to conduct a proper evaluation.

Different practices relate to who conducts the evaluation of projects. In smaller projects and projects where there have been no special events or consequences, *internal evaluation* is common. Usually, the project manager is central in terms of the elements to be evaluated and the actual implementation of the evaluation. In larger or more controversial projects, they may be subject to external evaluation of project implementation and results. Often these reviews will be done by one of the big four consultancy companies. Typically, the consultants that come in and carry out the evaluation will be specialists on the implementation of the type of projects to be considered. The result is usually a report with suggestions for improvements.

Many organizations routinely perform post-project evaluations of their projects. Often this will occur two to three years after the end of the project, primarily oriented to knowing if the stakeholder-users are satisfied with the delivery. Many builders, for example, make such a follow-up with the users to see how the buildings work in operation and whether they meet the needs of the users.

EXTEND YOUR KNOWLEDGE

Read the article by Gong, Zhang, and Xia (2019). It has interesting reflections on what experiences firms learn from. Do they learn from small or big successes and failures? The article is available in the online resources at https://study.sagepub.com/pm.

WATCH THIS!

Watch this SkillPath (2014) YouTube video that shows one way of explaining project evaluation at: https://study.sagepub.com/pm.

THE FINAL REPORT

The final report is included as a core part of most project closures. For the project organization, it marks termination and signifies to recipients that delivery is now their responsibility. A final report matters for project owners because it helps the project's results be evaluated properly and affords an opportunity for learning experiences from the project to be recorded and registered. While experiential learning is central to the continuous development of project-oriented companies, ending projects often involves a significant loss of learning that leaks away as the project team disperses. Final reports assume different formats and scopes. For smaller and more limited projects, the reports will usually be concise; for bigger projects, more detailed. A good final report is one that is referred and used so its design should enable easy and broad communication. A final report is usually a documentation of both the process and the results of the project, often containing a learning component. The learning component should give rise to future improvements in performance, especially for the principal and the base organization, as well as for other relevant stakeholders, including users. The documentation communicates relevant and reliable information about the delivery and project process, its coordination and control.

The content of and the format of the final report depends on the type of project and the delivery, size and complexity, as well as a number of other factors. The final report should be designed in such a way that it is relevant for the recipient. Usually it will contain most of the following information: a summary of project delivery core results and the project objectives that were achieved, in terms of performance goals. A brief description of the achievement of the individual performance targets, possibly with reference to previous project management documentation, will probably be included. An evaluation of the extent of value creation is also usually included along with an assessment of the potential effects of the project's delivery, depending on the degree of clarity that is possible, given the projected time horizon for use. Recommendations will be made to the client as to how the client should handle the delivery further.

In the overall evaluation of the project there will be a description of those success factors that have been central to goal achievement as well as of those factors that did not contribute positively. Key uncertainties that arose and how they were handled will also usually be included as one of the significant learning points concerning project implementation. User documentation and description of the product delivered will be included in the final report, including a description of project products, possibly with requirement specifications and quality requirements.

End of project reports will also address accounting and financial conditions; contractual conditions along with project management documentation on the background and motivation of the project; its milestones and how they were managed as well as how anomalies and events that arose unexpectedly were dealt with; the performance of various contractors, subcontractors and the members of the project management team will also be valuated, in the case of the latter the quality of their performance will have significant implications for their future career as a project manager or even as an aspirant to the upper echelons of the host organization (Clegg & Courpasson, 2004).

Finally, ideas and suggestions made throughout the process, which for various reasons were not included in the project itself but which may have value for the client in other contexts, will also be included in the final report. Much of the documentation and more detailed descriptions can be included as an attachment to the report.

READ THIS!

Stephanie Ray (2019) offers advice on how to write a project management report at: https://study.sagepub.com/pm.

DISSOLUTION OF THE PROJECT ORGANIZATION

The project organization has a different connection with and commitment to the principal and the base organization. For projects that deliver a material outcome, such as a building or a railway, as well as some other projects with looser formal binding between the actors in the project organization and the base organization, completion of the project and dissolution of the project organization and team can be relatively uncomplicated. If several of the project team members belong to the base organization, how people respond to project dissolution will probably differ depending on their future situation. Where the personnel in question are looking forward to taking on new tasks and have new projects slated that they will be attached to at the project end is usually not a problem; otherwise it clearly will be as project precariousness becomes evident.

The dissolution phase, when the team disbands, can mean that the participants both feel emptiness and loss. If the project work has been demanding and strained, the conclusion may be a relief but where the project has been particularly well organized, in which there has been considerable room for participation and autonomous action, the project termination can feel to be window closing with no assurances that the next project will generate similar levels of commitment or be organized on similar participative lines. In many projects, the project leader role is central and dominant, involving the investment of considerable time, commitment and attention to the job. Where the project was large, long term and for an 'external' client project, closure will usually be more extensive and stressful, especially if future tasks are uncertain.

Project members react differently to the dissolution of a project. Some feel a sense of loss and need some time; some need time to turn to new tasks while others look forward to launching new tasks, whether they are of a project or operational nature. A chosen few may achieve elevation in the organization, where evaluations rate them as having kept below budget, exceeded in innovation, completed ahead of schedule and contributed surplus value.

WHAT WOULD YOU DO?

You have been the project manager for an internal project in the organization for which you work. The project team consists of internal employees inside your medium-sized organization. Three out of four have been engaged full time. All of the members have loved working on this project during its two-year period. The project is about to end.

QUESTION

1. How will you procede in this shutdown/closure process as the project team is about to dissolute?

Delivering value

BENEFITS REALIZATION

Many projects involve major investments, and often it will be uncertain as to whether the investments will yield a proper return. Because projects are primarily a means to achieve goals, the effects and value creation will be visible only after the project has been completed. The client and others involved will have had this made clear from the project assessment, even if in many cases this will be long after the project itself has been completed. Benefits realization is about realizing the desired gains and effects that formed the basis for initiating the project. Benefits realization is a process that starts with project assessment, which lasts a long time after the project has been completed because the variables are many and the causality associated with effects often unclear. Seemingly small things, such as insurance claim settlements, can take some time to be settled and their results can alter the value profile noticeably. Karlsen (2013) argues that the impact of projects' effects requires attention through three steps (see Figure 13.6).

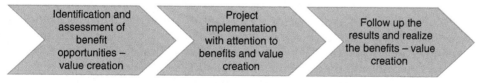

Figure 13.6   Process for benefit realization

It is not automatic that the results achieved in project delivery also realize the effects anticipated. Whether it is a reorganization or the introduction of a new IT system, the recipients must use the results to achieve the effects desired. Value matters in terms of use value to the end users of the project's outcomes as well in the surplus value, constituting profit after all overhead charges are subtracted, that project completion should yield for the project management organization. In order for value benefits to be realized it is necessary to audit the various stakeholders and see if the plans for when, how and who will contribute to the delivery being utilized appropriately were met: did meeting them yield the desired value creation? (Cooke-Davies, 2002).

The potential effects of a project will change over time and rarely be the same as at the start of the project. This is due to both new knowledge acquired through the project, changes in the context and other related conditions (Kreiner, 1995). The base organization involved in the project processes will focus attention on the value-added elements, not just the actual delivery. Both the client and the base organization need to be proactive in finding potential for discovering and benefiting from unplanned effects. Whatever the project results are, they will be realized at different times and at different levels, making success criteria multi-faceted.

EXTEND YOUR KNOWLEDGE

Read the article by Laursen (2018) linking value constellations and project networks, and outlining four key value creating activities, available at: https://study.sagepub.com/pm.

Project success – what does it really mean?

Nearly everyone that establishes a project wants it to be successful and most people who participate in projects want to achieve project success. Often it is implied that the project should be carried out within the framework of the Iron Triangle; however, there is also increasing attention to the fact that the delivery being created is implemented successfully. We have looked at multi-dimensional success criteria (Chapter 2). When project success is to be considered, it is good to emphasize this again.

Since many projects do not meet their time or cost estimates it is often assumed that these projects are unsuccessful. Questions of the success of projects must be considered in terms broader than these criteria alone. Research shows that most companies do not survive for more than a few years (Söderlund, 2005, p. 26) with very few companies having longevity. The Titans of yesteryear, such as PanAm and TWA, are but distant memories today. Project failures such as Concorde, the high-speed supersonic aeroplane that began life as a French–British joint venture, become famous for the costs and extent of their lack of success. Projects often fail to achieve the goals set but organizations that seem in their time, to be permanent, also fail in achieving goals.

The Sydney Opera House is a case in point. At the time of its completion few recognized quite what a success it actually was; today, it is one of the few modern buildings that is instantly recognizable. It would be correct to say that the Opera House is one of the most iconic designs of the modern era, quite unlike anything that preceded it and absolutely central to Sydney's identity as a city and global destination.

Many of the elements associated with megaprojects may also apply to smaller projects. In many ways, implementing projects always involves varying degrees of uncertainty, as well as stakeholder influence on the design of the project, its interpretation and implementation. Optimism and assessment bias in the decision-making process is a pervasive possibility that does not always end with the engineers and the architects unable to communicate with each other, being at loggerheads over design issues, as occurred in the Opera House. However, the implementation of any project that requires coordination and communication between different disciplines striving to interpret highly 'indexical' plans – plans that different disciplines read by indexing different possibilities for interpretation – often produces tensions, contradictions and conflicts that may herald creativity and success, as in the Opera House, but may also be a harbinger of project fail-ure. In the case of the Opera House short-term failure gave way in interpretation to long-term perceived success.

Projects largely deal with *innovation*. Not all innovations can be expected to be successful. On the contrary, most innovations are not particularly successful but that does not mean that even if you do not succeed with all attempts at innovation that it should be forsaken as an activity. It is necessary to continue striving to succeed in innovation combined with learning from experience in utilizing project knowledge when designing and implementing projects.

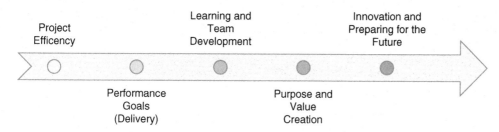

Figure 13.7   Dimensions of project success in an arrow of time

There are many *stakeholders* who will be involved in the process of evaluating whether the project has been successful or not. It also means that there will be differ-ent assessments of what is perceived as success factors. For example, in a project to build a new motorway, the success rate will be different depending on the emphasis given to factors such as faster transport, environmental emissions, land use, changing traffic patterns, etc. The perspective of the principal and the base organization will be the most central; however, in a context where other stakeholders' attention is central, consider bringing in more perspectives when project success is the issue. It may not be immediately apparent to project engineers that the success of the motorways may well be judged by community members by the effect it has on their social networks rather than the movement of traffic.

The time for assessing success is also significant, as illustrated in Figure 13.7. Some of the dimensions of project success can be considered immediately after project completion, while others cannot be considered before a certain amount of time has elapsed. For example, the effects of investing in environmentally friendly solutions in a new product cannot be considered before sufficient representative data on use and end of life disposal of the product have been completed; some effects, however, such as a more positive image that, in turn, may drive higher revenue, will soon be evident.

There will also be different challenges associated with the possibilities for *measuring* the effects and possible project success in the various dimensions. Some can be relatively easily considered in terms of, for example, increased earnings and sales in both the short and the long term, or lower production costs, while other goals and criteria are more difficult to measure (see Chapter 3). Some success criteria are 'hard' in the sense that there are concrete, quantifiable goals, while others are 'soft' in that they may contain altered behaviours or attitudes that cannot as easily be measured. Projects may also contain several objectives that give rise to conflicting effects, making extra complications for assessment of project success.

READ THIS!

Read the article by Amoako-Gyampah, Meredith, and Loyd (2018), which is available at https://study.sagepub.com/pm. It has interesting reflections on understanding how top management's actions impact project success and show how project success is strengthened by the enhancement of social capital through top management commitment.

PROJECT EFFICIENCY

For the project organization in isolation, especially for the project manager and team, the project framework is key. Projects are time limited. When considering a project, the time dimension is the easiest to assess. The assessment should then be conducted according to established criteria, whether deadlines have been met and the extent to which these have been appropriate.

Cost estimates concern resources in the project. There will be significant differences between different projects as to where the central value of accounting, investment and economic aspects will reside. Huge differences in financial cost frames will be associated with different types of project. Especially where public funds are in use, the use of resources must be documented and evaluated, so that the use to which funds have been put can be defended and understood. As explained, it will usually not be possible accurately to calculate expected return on investments until some time after project delivery.

Organizations apply different project management-related methods and tools to project management. As part of the assessment of project management success, it is useful to include an assessment of which project tools and methods were used and what they contributed to success. Did milestone plans prove helpful, were plans and follow-ups appropriately designed? How successful was the 'learning and teamwork' that occurred?

PERFORMANCE GOALS (DELIVERY)

The project's delivery arrives at that moment when the final product is handed over to the client. When assessing the degree of success, project results are assessed in relation to the project's objectives. The project's objectives, in terms of performance goals, would have been formulated before the project's commencement but it is not unusual to change these as projects unfold and priorities change. Changes and adjustments may be a consequence of innovations, changing assumptions or other factors that have influenced the project's frameworks and objectives. The latest updated goals for the project should be assessed in relation to the degree of project success. Performance goals and how they are met are the most common means used for evaluating project success (Cooke-Davies, 2002). Normally, an assessment of performance goals is done immediately after completion of the project. If the project is an event, the objectives can be considered after the main activity is concluded; whether it is a development of a new product or the introduction of a new IT system, the performance targets can be assessed shortly after the end of the project.

In assessing the extent to which project success has been achieved based on project performance goals, several indicators need to be emphasized. They must be assessed against the specified quality goals set for delivery. There may be purely technical specifications for the delivery, such as software functionality for an IT system. Or, there may be other, softer criteria, such as the competence goals to be achieved among users for a competence development project.

It might appear to be relatively uncomplicated to assess project success based on the performance targets set for the project delivery but there are often challenges related to the measurability of the goals and often a project will achieve several goals simultaneously, confounding measurement as they may be difficult to untangle them. There are also challenges related to situations in which goals conflict with each other.

LEARNING AND TEAM DEVELOPMENT

Learning for the client and organization links to systematic assessments of the project's planning, implementation and completion. Organization members need to develop expertise in using projects, with learning being a central element in their capability to do so. Training designed to address continuous development of core competencies improves by capturing relevant experiences from the project.

There are many *stakeholders* who are in some way involved and are affected by the project. Assessments of success related to learning will also include how subcontractors, customers, competitors and others learn from some of the projects they use in their own work.

We have included *teams* as a separate element in this dimension. It is not because teamwork is unique and especially related to the project's success but because such a large part of organization development work takes place in teams. Teamwork as a phenomenon is therefore particularly significant (Edmondson & Nembhard, 2009).

Team members will at some point join other teams, and quality teamwork is a key factor in success in projects that succeed in innovation (Hoegl & Gemuenden, 2001).

PURPOSE AND VALUE CREATION

If project delivery does not generate surplus value over and above project costs, the project has failed. It is often difficult to assess the impact of project deliveries, especially when several project owners and clients and many powerful stakeholders are involved. Then some effects may be perceived as positive by some stakeholders, while others may be negative. Time may be of the essence for some types of projects. After some projects are delivered, time will have to elapse before value can be assessed. A new toll road or tunnel, for instance, needs to be used for a period to be able to measure average use of the tunnel (Shenhar & Dvir, 2007). Often projected expectations are not met. This was the case with the Lane Cove Tunnel that was opened on 25 March 2007, two months ahead of schedule. Connector Motorways was supposed to operate the tunnel concession until 2037 but the projected number of vehicles did not use it and cash flow suffered. Consequently, the project was a disaster for the company, which went into receivership in January 2010 after a string of losses. When the tunnel opened in 2007 with about a third of the predicted traffic volumes, it was suggested in Supreme Court hearings held in litigation in the aftermath that forecasters came up with traffic figures based on commercial objectives (Saulwick, 2014). There was a considerable shortfall between these projections and what transpired in practice.

INNOVATION AND PREPARATION FOR THE FUTURE

While all projects may be innovative to some extent there are great variations in the degree of innovation geared towards a changing future for the business. Projects that pay particular attention to long-term gains in innovation and infrastructure for the future extend value creation beyond the immediate project. The project becomes an enabler of future value, a situation often applicable in industries operating in competitive markets with constant changes. Projects of this type are largely of an exploratory character, in which there will be a considerable uncertainty as to whether the projects envisaged will, in fact, contribute the desired effects and achieve anticipated value creation. These may be projects through which organizations try entering new markets or developing new technology but they may also be based on changes in infrastructure. The time in which project success is to be measured should vary in the same way as the value creation dimension. Often it will take a long time before success can be measured in terms of future innovation.

READ THIS!

In an article in the *Guardian* by Kathryn Dobson (2013), 'Lessons from London 2012 Olympics: a cribsheet for major projects', which in turn is a digest of Emma Norris, Jill Rutter, and Jonny Medland's (2013) report for the Institute of Government, titled *Making the Games: What government can learn from London 2012*, seven crucial elements are argued to have been crucial for the success of the London 2012 Olympics. While the article is rather old the lessons learned from this successful project are still applicable. After reading the articles, consider where these elements should be categorized in terms of dimensions of project success. From a superficial consideration, are there other success elements you would like to add, and in which categories of the dimensions of project success would you place those? The article can be found at: https://study.sagepub.com/pm.

Contemporary perspectives on projects

A 'THIRD WAVE' FOCUS

In recent years, scholars have abandoned the idea that all projects are similar. Projects take many forms; they are complex and interchangeable. This means that we cannot approach them as if they were uniform. In other words, projects have different characteristics and relationships (Svejvig & Andersen, 2015). The way we work on their overall management framework, plan processes and follow them up, should be aligned with their nature and development process. It should also be reflected in the way we organize, manage and work with uncertainty, stakeholders, innovation and learning.

The discipline has recently become 'softer' and the classic industrial approach is no longer unique. A simplified way of saying this is that the minds that dominated the first 40 years of the development of the discipline (1950–1990) have gained competition from topics within the organization and management field in the last 25 years. These changes are manifested in clear attention now being paid to the project leader's role, the project team and its development and organizational processes in order to achieve good coordination and coordination of activities. It is evident that learning, trust, motivation and teamwork are key subjects of the contemporary project management discipline. Since these themes are relatively new within our discipline, we have devoted attention to them.

The emphasis has shifted from the implementation of the individual project to seeing projects in a larger context from the perspective of project-based organizations. The book reflects this through the discussion of projects as tools for realizing strategy (often organized as project programmes), projects as a tool for process and product innovations, as well as a learning arena to strengthen competitiveness. Researchers based in the project discipline describe the emergent paradigm for the areas as a 'third wave' (Morris et al., 2011). A paradigm is a pattern or a common, shared approach and understanding of a phenomenon – in this case, the project subject. The first wave generally refers to what we have described as the task perspective, the second wave the project as a temporary organization (what we can simplify as the organizational perspective). The third wave is characterized by seven features (Morris et al., 2011):

- Interest for the theoretical foundation and the history of the project discipline.
- An awareness of the importance of the contextual factors for the projects.
- An acknowledgement of the link between project and organization – in the form of the client and the base organization.
- An interest in the link between strategy and project and thus the project's role for innovation in companies.

- A valuation of the corporate governance function as a basis for the efficient use of resources.
- Increased recognition of leadership role and challenges associated with building trust and developing relevant competencies.
- An acknowledgement that projects are complex organizations that often include interorganizational relationships that will deal with innovation and uncertainty and meet these challenges through learning and knowledge integration.

This book is in line with the third wave and is based on research that discuses relevant processes and practices for project management in a nuanced and future-oriented manner. Throughout the book we have emphasized that projects ideally create value while working with both risks and opportunities throughout the project. Moreover, actors, both in project and client organizations are responsible for delivering value. Benefits realization needs dedicated responsibility to be delivered. Active ownership management is necessary if value creation is to be achieved (project product success). Value creation takes place through effective project implementation and deliberate work on risk, opportunities and stakeholders. Attention to value creation often results in a more flexible implementation of the project than has traditionally been the case when using stage gate models. Increased flexibility produces more choice and decisions throughout the duration of the project. Project execution requires engaged decision-makers at all levels. Employees need to know their mandate and have an ability to communicate so that optimal decisions are made on time in line with the decision-making authority of the different actors.

Practice and process orientations

In recent years there has been a keen interest in taking a more process-oriented and practice-oriented approach to projects. This means seeing projects as a continues development process, shaped as actors act to solve tasks and assign meaning to their doing so (Tsoukas & Chia, 2002). Projects and all aspects of how they are implemented can best be understood by following how the people involved interact, what kind of technology, tools and devices affect this interaction and how interaction patterns are shaped by procedures, governance structures, routines and culture. Do not just look at a project's organizational structure as it is designed, but how it is expressed over time through the practices of the parties involved. Practice, how individuals act in a specific setting, is the key (Hällgren & Söderholm, 2011).

Projects are typically designed, organized and delivered as mainly engineering-based (Giezen, 2012); typically the rational, linear, quantitative and value-neutral (Cicmil, Williams, Thomas, & Hodgson, 2006) aspects of project management are favoured. The dominant scientific, normative and dualist assumptions of traditional project management define these projects mainly in terms of project structure and prescriptive processes. Such assumptions ignore underlying power dynamics both in the start-up phase and in subsequent actions characterizing project practice (Cicmil & Hodgson, 2006; Clarke, 1999).

From a practice perspective one would not prescribe or predicate linear processes so much as expect processes where diverse practices are entangled, intertwined, affecting each other. Complexity, ambiguity and indexical interpretation require attention. Practice is placed in the centre, whether the practice is accomplished by actors or actants – that is material artefacts or devices such as software, building information modelling, three-dimensional models or plans. In this perspective not only humans act and have consequences but so do material and other artefacts.

While some successful project managers become adept at the 'dark arts' of managing organizational politics they often do so less through formal instruction and more through embedded custom and practice learnt on the job of serial projects. Making the education of project managers more explicitly concerned with the politics of organizations would be a significant innovation, given the polyphonic, plural and constrained contexts in which they will be likely to operate. There is some progress in this direction. Recent research, instead of aiming towards the development of universal models for abstracted conceptualization of project management, emphasizes instead a social science-based, process-oriented tradition of research (Blomquist, Hällgren, Nilsson, & Soderholm, 2010; Blomquist & Packendorff, 1998; Engwall, 2003; Söderlund, 2002). Practice-oriented studies emphasize that projects and their underlying processes are relational, evolving over time.

People make sense as they act upon their world and, typically, accept new practices insofar as they do not contradict their taken-for-granted knowing of what constitutes appropriate practice. The forming of a practice coming-into-being is always constituting and reconstituting itself: it is becoming per se (Bjørkeng, Clegg, & Pitsis, 2009, p. 156).

Practice-oriented project management studies view projects as a 'social and organized setting in which numerous conceptual organizational theories and organizational behaviour frameworks can be applied and developed' (Blomquist et al., 2010, p. 6). The major contribution of the practice perspective is that projects must also be understood as social processes incorporating the complexities of social life (Cicmil & Hodgson, 2006). Traditional assumptions about projects as objective realities are challenged. The project manager is seen as a reflective practitioner who resolves issues in a context-dependent, pragmatic and political fashion (Cicmil & Hodgson, 2006), since 'there is considerable agreement that conventional, universal statements of what management is about and what managers do – planning, organizing, coordinating and controlling – do not tell us much about organizational reality, which is often messy, ambiguous, fragmented and political in character' (Alvesson & Deetz, 2000, p. 60).

The usual form of project process is one of messy muddling through, in which various bounded rationalities clash over project specifications, process and outcomes, using various practices of pooled, sequential and reciprocal interdependencies (Thompson, 1967b) to secure interests, outflank those whose interests do not align over whatever is at issue at the time, while gaining small wins in specific episodes of power.

Project management must increasingly deal with many forms of professional and occupational practice, bringing many different forms of power/knowledge into play. To the extent that each profession and occupation has its own ways of coding knowledge these do not always translate effortlessly. The classic examples have to do with the different trades and professions' capacity and propensity to read the same set of 3D plans or models differently, with different relevancies. Small matters of interpretation can blow out into big matters of cost, time, design and function. As megaprojects entail a degree of complexity that is greatly in excess of more standard projects, the opportunities for these different forms of sensemaking to spark confrontational power relations related to matters of responsibility is high (Lukes, 2005). Where the usual trades and professions are joined by esoteric knowledge embodied in social science, ecological, community, political and economic expertise, the opportunities for conflictual power relations between people secure in their own knowledge areas but unfamiliar with that of those with whom they are obliged to collaborate escalates the potential for conflictual relations in which negative power comes into play.

IN PRACTICE

MODELS AT WORK

Projects are replete with digital devices, models, plans and other artefacts such as machines that act, do things, have consequences. For instance, in a paper by Naar and Clegg (2018) that investigates the use made of three-dimensional material models by the starchitect Frank Gehry, a novel approach to the role of models in innovation processes is outlined. The article demonstrates how innovative architectural outcomes result from the strategic management of multiple physical models in a design process. Drawing on actor-network theory, they explore architect Frank Gehry's designing in action to trace the work done in translating design ideas with architectural models. They observe how certain practices constituted around material models are Gehry's means for unsettling and resetting the clients' receptiveness and willingness to embark upon a particular architectural path. They find that the physical models, as actants in these activity flows, are rendered strategic in ways currently overlooked. When approval for an innovative design is secured, through the unfolding of models, their strategic role is realized. Their approach goes beyond current accounts of the role and nature of architectural models to reveal how architectural models as strategic actants are mobilized in an innovation process. The article in question is available at the website for the book at https://study.sagepub.com/pm.

QUESTION

1. What work do models do in your understanding of this paper on a Gehry project?

Sensemaking practices

It is in and through practices that roles are defined, competencies related to process and product developed, as well as skill in handling social and organizational relations. Classical understanding of and research on 'projects' fails to take on board the practice perspective, favouring instead a degree of prescriptivism that is theoretically unrealistic when contrasted with actual practice (Blomquist et al., 2010). All practice is socially constructed and, as with all social constructions, it is phenomenology that determines reality.

The underlying perspective is perhaps best articulated by Schutz (1967, p. 230), when he states that it 'is the meaning of our experiences and not the ontological structure of the objects which constitutes reality'. From this perspective projects can be seen as 'a space whose boundaries and possibilities for action are marked by subjectivity, meanings, perceptions, and emotions, as opposed to the external imperatives coming from the "objective" system' (Passy & Giugni, 2000, p. 122). Sensemaking is in play everywhere. For instance, any large-scale project entails a substantial amount of documentation. Project managers have to be highly skilled and competent in managing to make sense of what they do, the key competency of sensemaking, defined by Weick (1993, p. 635) as 'the ongoing retrospective development of plausible images that rationalize what people are doing'.

Much of what happens in organizations entails a constant process of sensemaking. The characteristic activities that constitute sensemaking are captured well in Weick's definition. First, sensemaking is ongoing: we are always making sense, and our sense of what we are experiencing is always of the moment – fleeting, experiential, changing, and contextual. Second, sensemaking is retrospective: we make sense of something as it is elapsing and we are constantly reviewing the sense we make in terms of additional sense data. Third, the sense we make is plausible, as we never make perfect sense but only make provisional sense, sense that is good enough for the matter and people at hand. It allows us to go on with what we are trying to do. While accuracy may be desirable, reasonable constructions that are continuously updated provide directional guides, especially when things are changing fast. Plausible sense is always provisional in another way as well: it depends on the interest that we have there and then in making *that* sense and not another. We shall return to this aspect in more detail. Fourth, sensemaking is a material practice: it is made using representations of things such as models, plans and mental maps that are used to try and navigate meanings and actions, steering them in certain directions – directions that others may well resist. Our stock of knowledge is political, emergent and likely to be contested by others with different interests in sensemaking. Fifth, with sensemaking we rationalize the meaning of things in terms of the interest we vest in them. Sixth, although organizations contain many actants that are not people – such as computers and keypads – it is people who do the sensemaking, doing so using material things and devices that perform as actants. Seventh, it is through performing practices that actors construct and negotiate the sense of what they are doing that may be different between actors engaged in the same projects even when they think they are dealing with the same cues and seek to collaborate, which is not always the case in negotiations around projects.

Project organizations have a considerable interest in members making common sense, particularly of documentary materials. A vital part of the project management task is to try and produce cues for common sensemaking. The project manager's job includes creating, adapting and using common frames of meaning that characterize the organization and its members. Making sensemaking common is no easy matter.

In practice, as projects unfold, uncommon sensemaking becomes normalized. Variation orders will be submitted exploiting elements of indexicality in interpreting project plans and contractual documents – and there always will be such indexicality where there are different interests being brought to bear on documentary and other materials (Clegg, 1975). For one thing, the contractual materials are invariably very complex. Not only that, there will be a great deal of detail of a great deal of complexity. Megaprojects are extremely complex accomplishments constituted by many documents produced by many hands in many different places, all of which are saturated with meaning. Hence, when these documents are used in context, their meaning is always subject to indexical interpretation (Garfinkel, 1967).

It is not just that documents will be interpreted differently. Differentially interested actors in the project processes will have differential interests in different aspects of the sensemaking associated with the project. Contract complexity created by skilled lawyers for contractors can be a trap for unwary clients, especially from the public sector, lacking the deep knowledge, experience and learning that enables them to interpret the material effectively. Moreover, a common sensemaking pattern in project management is for different actors to try and exploit different indexical meanings of documents that constitute the project (Clegg, 1975). Different stakeholders interpret ellipses, ambiguities and contradictions in the documents in terms of the specific interests that, organizationally, they strive to achieve; hence, they index meaning in different ways that are politically and organizationally interested. The contractual particulars thus become an arena for politicking, politicking that is embedded in projects from the outset.

Managers use tools to try and accomplish things that are understood in common: accounting systems, resource planning models, PERT, and so on. These tools are designed to be rational instruments to aid managing. Tools do nothing on their own – they have to be used; they have to be made sense of in terms of the specific context of their application, the time available to do something, the information that is at hand, the skills and capabilities that are available. Thus, managing is actively constructed – made sense of – by actors going about their everyday organizational life, using such resources as come to hand including rational tools, instruments, and designs. It is the *use to which they are put* – not that they *merely exist* – that matters and that there is a distinct individual who is the user and who is making sense of the context and situations of use. A number of factors thus enter into sensemaking.

Sensemaking is a complex phenomenon. It involves *social context*: sensemaking is influenced by the actual, implied or imagined presence of others. If other people think that a particular interpretation makes sense, then you are more likely to do so as well. *Personal identity* effects sensemaking. Certain situations may subvert or reinforce this sense of identity. What people notice in elapsed events, how far back they look and how well they remember the past – in other words, *retrospective meaning* – all influence sensemaking. Organizationally, the most significant decisions are often the least apparent: decisions made by minutes secretaries – what to keep and what to discard – can provide the basis for any later sense that can possibly be made by project members. While these are not strategic or conspicuous decisions, they construct the organizational past. Project managers derive *salient cues* from their past experiences; thus, they project their pasts onto their futures. Given the temporality and fluidity of project experience most actors will have a great many distinct experiences to draw on when making sense. Project planning tools provide *structure* to divide the unfolding of events into different patterns. Sensemaking creates meaning that is sufficiently *plausible* to carry on with current projects; such meaning is always enacted here-and-now and thus is always subject to revision as new data emerges or new interpretations of old data. Sensemaking involves redrafting an emerging story so that it becomes more comprehensive as events unfold and are interpreted, framing details as relevant, to isolate particular themes in an emerging story and provide an answer to the question, 'What's going on?' (adapted from Weick, 1995, 2008).

Sensemaking is endemic in project life. Project organizations are full of plausible stories – rumour, gossip, official statements, business plans and websites – each sensible in its own way but none necessarily coherent with the others. People talk all the time at work. Much of what they say is formal; yet, *even more is not formal*, which is to say that it is neither constitutive of, nor mandated by, the occupational and organizational roles that organization members fill.

How project organization relations actually pan out will always depend on the specific sensemaking that we find in local situations, discourses and practices. Different types of sensemaking occur especially where things are uncertain or not as we would have expected them to be, when sense just breaks down, or cannot be made, and normal expectations just do not work. When we make sense of breaches in everyday understanding, suggests Weick (2008), we look first for reasons that will enable us to keep on doing whatever it was that we were doing – we are averse to change. We make sense using devices such as what everybody knows, or apply rational analysis, or we ask others what they think is going on. Much of the project management literature and the many models it produces should best be thought of as metaphorical frames designed to try and facilitate common sensemaking.

IN PRACTICE

NORMAL CLAY

Practice in complex projects entails negotiation processes between different disciplines and stakeholders interpreting different senses of what are frequently highly indexical elements of documentation. Clegg (1975) explored these practices in a contribution that looked at the ways in which different interests involved in a project made different sense of the contractual documents, exploiting the interpretative sensemaking they were able to make of materials that did not, that could not, prescribe the sense that was to be made. A key example was that of 'normal clay'. A dispute on a construction site arose because the contractor had removed extra fill on site in preparation for foundations. The documentation was unclear; some referred to excavating three metres, while others, in an engineering consultants' report, suggested excavation to sandy stony clay. On a day on which the site was not being supervised by the client's representative, a substantial amount of excavation occurred and a variation order (VO) for a significant amount of excavation works tendered in consequence. The VO became the object of acrimony and the technical discussion that ensued was about the quality of 'normal clay': was it the sandy, stony clay that it was claimed was a variable depth strata across the site or was it the 'puddle clay' that could be found at three metres depth? The VO represented a significant source of value to the project's management on behalf of the contractors on a project that was on a very tight margin. In this instance the materiality of clay was being socially constructed in diverse ways by different interests whose practice relied on differing indexical interpretations of the contractual artefacts.

QUESTION

1. What is 'normal clay' and how does it become defined as such? (Hint: the discussion of normal clay in Clegg (1975), may be useful.)

Consideration of sensemaking necessarily entails consideration of temporality: different parties make different sense at different times and with different interests in any specific project in different ways. Hence, a sophisticated grasp of temporality is necessary for social science understanding of the temporary organizations created to deliver projects.

We can consider this temporal sensemaking in terms of several different elements of phenomenology: the financialization of project practices and the resistance and the memorialization required to secure a temporal legacy, best addressed as attempts to freeze time. Each of these phenomenologies is temporally saturated and deeply embedded in complex power relations in different ways. A basic approach to political phenomenology would start by seeing projects as political arenas, a theme with which we will end our account of project management.

Political phenomenology of projects

Projects should be considered as arenas in which players from various fields, such as government, private sector contractors, subcontractors, architects, unions, community groups, regulatory authorities, etc., are engaged. Each of these players has their own interests as stakeholders in the project, interests that shift in terms and alignments as projects unfold. At the project outset, as Flyvbjerg (2014b) suggests, there may well be good organizational reasons for bad organizational projections of costs, benefits and completion: costs prove to be probabilistically underestimated while the latter two tend to be overestimated in terms of what they deliver and how quickly they will deliver. These projections, of course, are a kind of power: they are productive in gaining commitments, harnessing resources, persuading key actors and constituencies that projects are viable. An essential element of positive power – which the cynical might call 'spin' – is often necessary to make projects happen.

Once upon a time many large-scale projects would have been public sector initiatives. As a result of the mega-costs associated with megaprojects and cuts in government spending, an increasing number of megaprojects rely on private investments from banks, private investors or capital funds. Investors have their own objectives, which may not be entirely aligned with the overall objectives of the project per se, making the megaproject arena an even more fertile ground for power dynamics to affect project progress. External involvement of private sector capital means that continuation of vital project funding becomes partially contingent on third-party considerations of medium-term return on investment, which can affect key decisions throughout the project life cycle. These questions of financial calculation and related considerations dramatically change the nature of negotiations and the decision-making processes in megaprojects. In other words, megaprojects face major social, political and cultural challenges, especially in the context of multiple stakeholders whose objectives, goals and strategies will, in all probability, not be aligned, other than through various expressions of financial motivation.

In recent years governments have increasingly used public private partnerships (PPPs) as a way of structuring public infrastructure investments. Governments frequently partner with private companies to develop and provide what were once typically thought of as distinctly public works and services. They have done so to such an extent that the public sector bodies that used to build and run things no longer have the resources financially or in terms of human capital to do so. As more aspects of the organization of the public sector have been despatched to the private sector the former has been declining in human and capital resources and the trajectory becomes self-fulfilling. As capabilities, capital and competencies diminish, the public sector simply cannot do what it might once have done such that the phenomenology of financial partnering becomes ever more compelling.

The upshot of financialization tendencies is that the temporality of projects is far greater than their apparent duration; the PPP may well construct finance streams to the private sector from public usage or from taxpayers up to 25 years into the future. One may think of this as the financialization of project infrastructure investments. It has been argued that the benefits of PPPs are largely undemonstrated and their costs well documented, according to Van Waeyenberge (2016). The financialization of infrastructure investments as an asset class, involving hedge funds and institutional investors, makes the relationship between the state, other stakeholders, and PPP investor(s) and the ability of the state to participate in and/or effectively regulate infrastructure investments deeply problematic. One major attraction of PPPs is to enable governments to shift costs and liabilities off their balance sheets in the near term. However, as Guven and Johnson (2018) suggest, PPPs may impose longer-term risks and contingent liabilities that are not adequately measured, tracked or accounted for, and which can have significant implications for governments and their constituents. Additionally, while there are diverse stakeholders whose basic needs and fundamental rights can be directly and severely impacted by the performance, cost, availability and governance of infrastructure and related services, private ownership and operation of such services can impact, often negatively, those stakeholders' abilities to hold infrastructure owners and operators accountable for providing quality, accessible and affordable services. Whereas the first questions that decision-makers should focus on are whether and under what circumstances a PPP should be considered, it is too commonly assumed that public infrastructure will be more efficiently provided by the private sector, with the key question instead becoming how to structure the deal.

Financialization predisposes decision-makers to the presupposition that private financing is always more efficient and appropriate than using governmental accounts. Instead of the government building and paying for major projects directly, they get private firms to borrow to finance their construction, under a deal that the government will pay them back over, say, 25 years, through a BOOT scheme, with monopoly rights to sources of finance, such as tolls.

The metaphors of mainstream project management imply a unitary and objectivist view of the world, suggesting that commitment to early definition is both valid and desirable for megaprojects. The results of this can be seen in pressure for early progress and commitment to poor estimates. Jennings (2012) has noted that political acceleration of the Sydney Opera House project led to scope creep and uncertainty. Pressure from the New South Wales government in 1959 resulted in the project starting ahead of schedule while engineering design was still incomplete.

Government parties to infrastructure PPPs often have to respond to investors' attempts to change the terms of the deal after that deal had been agreed. The recent impasse that surrounds the extension of Light Rail in the Sydney CBD is a case in point; whether or not the claims or counter-claims that are presently keeping some of Sydney's more expensive barristers busy are decided one way or the other, there will always be a suspicion that the strategy of seeking variation in the contract is a normal strategy of companies engaged in PPPs to maximize returns on contracts bid low.

Phenomenologically, it is often recognized that private partners in PPPs do not necessarily have the same priorities or interests as their government partners or infrastructure users and that, indeed, the private and public objectives might conflict. These conflicts can result from many differences, with what Flyvbjerg (2008) calls optimism bias in forecasts of usage of infrastructure such as tunnels and roads, being particularly important. Without the optimism bias being in place, phenomenologically, project sponsorship might have difficulty in achieving project launch. Flyvbjerg (2014a) notes that one of the major reasons why megaprojects rarely come in on time and on budget, and with design integrity, is because they can often only be launched with an implicit optimism bias inherent and with political support of the project from powerful stakeholders, usually in government.

Large-scale temporary organizations that are time-limited and project-focused mélanges of actors and organizations are increasingly used for developing infrastructure, achieving economic growth, targeting welfare, and managing health and safety concerns. For such *inter-institutional temporary organizations*, operating under conditions of institutional complexity and pluralism is a normal condition and an essential raison d'être. These organizations are characterized by designed temporal limitations and explicitly formulated deadlines (Lindkvist, Soderlund, & Tell, 1998) that require actors to align nested and interdependent activities (Thompson, 1967). Intense collective agency is essential for realizing evermore challenging system-wide goals with regards to limited budgets, time pressure and stakeholder benefits (Merrow, 2011).

While all projects are alike in their temporary duration each project-focused organization is unique in its tightly integrated orientation and demands for intense collaboration and synchronization among the actors involved. Such project-focused organizations constitute 'temporal zones' designed to facilitate collective action among sovereign actors and organizations. Because different rituals and norms shape organizational practices and structures such organizations are institutionally pluralistic (Friedland & Alford, 1991; Meyer & Rowan, 1977; Whittington, 2003). Differences can range across professional codes (Anderson-Gough, Grey, & Robson, 2001), time horizons (Judge & Speitzfaden, 1995), time orientations (Lawrence & Lorsch, 1967; Mosakowski & Earley, 2000), language communities and spatial separation (van Marrewijk et al., 2016). Of particular significance, in the context of financialization and the pressures for evaluation of value by diverse stakeholders, is the alignment of different time reckoning systems.

Summary

- -

After reading this chapter, you should:

- Be familiar with current trends in project management as a profession, and have gained some reflections on the ethical aspects of project, and also reflections on how the notions of time and temporality in projects is far from straightforward.
- Know why projects sometimes have to be terminated without reaching their goals, the different reasons for this, and also know what the important aspects to consider are when projects face the possibility of being terminated.
- Know the end activities and their importance, such as creating a good final report and evaluating the project, and also what to think about when dissolving the project organization.
- Understand essential aspects of project delivery and benefit realization, the distribution of responsibilities for implementing the deliveries, and effecting the aimed-for benefits. We have elaborated on how project success includes multiple dimensions at individual, team, project and organizational level.

- Be able to outline new approaches to understanding projects and underline that contemporary understanding of projects do not seem them as rational, linear instruments that can be easily managed and controlled. Rather, they are processes of ongoing sensemaking.

Exercises

1. What can you say about the temporality of projects – how has this understanding evolved? How is the temporality of project different from the understanding of time in more permanent organizations?
2. What are the key reasons for terminating a project before planned ending? What could be the reason for not terminating projects that in hindsight should have been terminated?
3. When considering an early completion of projects, what are the two key aspects to think through?
4. What are the main activities at the end of the project? Who is the main recipient of the project deliveries?
5. What is the key content of the final report? How can you develop a useful final report?
6. Benefit realization is key in projects. Who holds the main responsibility for benefit realization? When can benefits be realized?
7. What can you say about the role of various stakeholders in realizing benefits?
8. What are the contemporary trends of project management – the understanding of the discipline?

CASE STUDY

PROJECTS FOR A SUSTAINABLE FUTURE
SUSTAINABLE DEVELOPMENT GOALS

Projects for a sustainable future concern many people and organizations. Young people, in particular, engage in this all-embracing issue. Swedish teenager Greta Thunberg has in many ways become a reluctant figurehead for a movement raising consciousness around the world.

READ THIS!

An article in *The Conversation* on why Thunberg's success is due in part to the fact that she's had a substantial impact in alerting many people, especially the young, to the unfolding climate catastrophe of the Anthropocene. (Read the full article online at https://study.sagepub.com/pm)

WATCH THIS!

Greta Thunberg's infamous speech at the Climate Action Summit 2019, available at: https://study.sagepub.com/pm.

At an overall global level, the United Nations (UN) has formed Sustainable Development Goals (SDGs) (see https://sustainabledevelopment.un.org/). SDGs were established in 2015 as a project supposed to end in 2030. Having our 'project-lenses' on, achieving these goals could be regarded as a project programme encompassing 17 goals (see Figure 13.8), involving numerous projects around the world. Having looked at these important goals early in the book we return to them here; projects need increasingly to address them.

Figure 13.8 UN Sustainable Development Goals

Source: www.un.org/sustainabledevelopment/news/communications-material/

VALUE CREATION AT STAKE

Most people agree on the importance of a sustainable future. However, there is significant disagreement as to how these goals may be achieved. Value is at stake. On the one hand there is a strong focus on the topic of what should be considered the essential values and how these are to be achieved. On the other hand, there is some agreement on the importance of achieving and maintaining global economic prosperity in the context of a sustainable future. However, on this issue, there is substantial disagreement as to what constitutes economic value and how and where this value is created. Can economic value be maintained while the value of planetary boundaries are preserved or are these irreconcilable goals?

READ THIS!

The Anthropocene, a fundamental concept, is explained in Heikkurinen, Clegg, Pinnington, Nicolopoulou, & Alcaraz.(2019), available at: https://study.sagepub.com/pm. A shorter version of the paper by Clegg (2020) titled 'Management of Climate Crisis and Planetary Boundaries through Eco Taxation' can be downloaded from *Manage Magazine*.

WATCH THIS!

One of the leading academic figures contributing to the topic of what is value is Professor Marianna Mazzucato (2018a). She argues that economic value creation is more than some businesses doing trade on the market. Public organizations are a salient part of value creation and must be taken into account when considering what value creation is and who contributes to its achievement. In this YouTube video available at https://study.sagepub.com/pm, Mazzucato talks about how we understand value creation, how this perspective has shifted over the years, and to see value creation as something that is collectively produced.

READ THIS!

To gain a better understanding of the complexity of what value is and who the 'takers and makers' are, read the article 'Takers and Makers: Who Are the Real Value Creators?' by Professor Mariana Mazzucato (2018c).

A PROJECT PERSPECTIVE

All these elements related to what is value, what are values, and what is valued are huge issues and involve most people and organizations on the planet. Life on Earth is a stakeholder if we remember the example of the frogs in Chapter 10. Putting on our 'project lenses' again, trying to sort out the map and the terrain, there are a lot of subjects and elements here, to name a few:

- The importance of what kind of value creation for whom in projects
- The complexity and ambiguity of value as a concept
- Projects and programmes organizing value and their values
- Stakeholders and collaborations organizing value and their values
- Uncertainty about fundamentals: what does this project do to harm or enhance life on Earth?

These questions underlay the variety of projects in general, as well as the importance projects have for our life on Earth. Moreover, in terms of this significant issue, we certainly have to operate with various types of maps as guides to a terrain that is exceptionally complicated to traverse and is always in process.

Nevertheless, having gained value from the book, we challenge you to answer some questions related to project management from a value creation approach.

QUESTIONS

1. There are a significant number of stakeholders and categories of them in SDGs. Take a look at the categorization of them and consider if this an adequate mapping of

(Continued)

stakeholders.[1] How would you categorize Greta Thunberg as a stakeholder? Provide a reasoned argument.

2. Value creation is a critical issue both for project management and for SDGs. Go online and choose one of the topics for Goal number 11 'Sustainable cities and communities'.[2] Consider what types of values the project/topic is supposed to achieve. If you were to start a project in your region, how would you link your project to these values?

3. Furthermore, follow the start-up of a major infrastructure project in your country, city or region and consider how the competence gained through reading this book might contribute to such a project. What would you argue are the most critical subjects and tools to bring to the project that you have chosen?

_____

[1]https://sustainabledevelopment.un.org/mgos

[2]https://sustainabledevelopment.un.org/

Additional resources

If you want further insight into what is happening on the research front in project management, key journals include the *International Journal of Project Management*, the *Project Management Journal* and the *International Journal of Managing Projects in Business*. *The Oxford Handbook of Project Management* edited by Morris et al. (2011) elaborates some key topics in project management as does the more recent Sankaran, Müller, & Drouin (2017) *Cambridge Handbook of Organizational Project Management*.

REFERENCES

Chapter 1

Aaker, D.A. (1996). *Building Strong Brands*. New York: Free Press.

Andersen, E.S. (2008). *Rethinking Project Management: An Organisational Perspective*. Harlow: Prentice Hall/Financial Times.

Andersen, E.S., Soderlund, J., & Vaagaasar, A.L. (2010). Projects and politics: Exploring the duality between action and politics in complex projects. *International Journal of Management and Decision Making*, *11*(2), 121–139.

Barnett, C., Clarke, N., Cloke, P., & Malpass, A. (2014). The elusive subjects of neo-liberalism: Beyond the analytics of governmentality. In S. Binkley & J. Littler (eds), *Cultural Studies and Anti-consumerism* (pp. 116–145). London: Routledge.

Bateson, G. (1972). *Steps to an Ecology of Mind*. New York: Ballantine Books.

Batista, M.d.G., Clegg, S., Pina e Cunha, M., Giustiniano, L., & Rego, A. (2016). Improvising prescription: Evidence from the emergency room. *British Journal of Management*, *27*(2), 406–425.

Brodie, R.J., Ilic, A., Juric, B., & Hollebeek, L. (2013). Consumer engagement in a virtual brand community: An exploratory analysis. *Journal of Business Research*, *66*(1), 105–114.

Buchanan, D., & Badham, R. (2020). *Power, Politics, and Organizational Change: Winning the Turf Game* (3rd edn). London: Sage.

Bulman, M., & Shukla, A. (2019). Grenfell Tower report: Fire service's 'stay put' advice cost lives, long awaited public inquiry conclude. *The Independent*, 30 October. Available at: www.independent.co.uk/news/uk/home-news/grenfell-tower-london-cladding-public-inquiry-report-martin-moore-bick-a9175291.html (accessed 15 January 2020).

Burnstein, W. (2016). The map is not the territory. Medium.com. Available at: https://medium.com/parachuting/the-map-is-not-the-territory-4772ec3125d3 (accessed 15 January 2020).

Burnton, S. (2018). World Cup stunning moments: Germany humiliate Brazil 7–1. *Guardian*, 23 May.

Bygballe, L.E., Swärd, A.R., & Vaagaasar, A.L. (2016). Coordinating in construction projects and the emergence of synchronized readiness. *International Journal of Project Management*, *34*(8), 1479–1492. Available at: https://doi.org/10.1016/j.ijproman.2016.08.006 (accessed 15 January 2020).

Carlsson, I., Ramphal, S., Alatas, A., & Dahlgren, H. (1995). *Our Global Neighbourhood: The Report of the Commission on Global Governance*. Oxford: Oxford University Press.

Clegg, S. (1975/2013). *Power, Rule and Domination: A Critical and Empirical Understanding of Power in Sociological Theory and Organizational Life*. London: Routledge & Kegan Paul.

Clegg, S.R., & Pitsis, T.S. (2012). Phronesis, projects and power research. In B. Flyvbjerg, T. Landman, & S. Schram (eds), *Real Social Science* (pp. 66–91). Oxford: Oxford University Press.

Clegg, S., Pitsis, T.S., Rura-Polley, T., & Marosszeky, M. (2002). Governmentality matters: Designing an alliance culture of inter-organizational collaboration for managing projects. *Organization Studies*, *23*(3), 317–337.

Clegg, S.R., Sankaran, S., Biesenthal, C., & Pollack, J. (2017). Power and sensemaking in megaprojects. In B. Flybjerg (ed.), *The Oxford Handbook of Megaproject Management*. Oxford: Oxford University Press.

Clegg, S., Killen, C.P., Biesenthal, C., & Sankaran, S. (2018). Practices, projects and portfolios: Current research trends and new directions. *International Journal of Project Management*, *36*(5), 762–772. Available at: https://doi.org/10.1016/j.ijproman.2018.03.008 (accessed 15 January 2020).

Coldevin, G.H., Carlsen, A., Clegg, S., Pitsis, T.S., & Antonacopoulou, E.P. (2019). Organizational creativity as idea work: Intertextual placing and legitimating imaginings in media development and oil exploration. *Human Relations*, *72*(8), 1369–1397. Available at: https://doi.org/10.1177%2F0018726718806349 (accessed 15 January 2020).

Colville, I.D., Waterman, R.H., & Weick, K.E. (1999). Organizing and the search for excellence: Making sense of the times in theory and practice. *Organization*, *6*(1), 129–148.

Cooper, C. (2015). Entrepreneurs of the self: The development of management control since 1976. *Accounting, Organizations and Society*, *47*, 14–24.

Davies, A. (2017). *Projects: A Very Short Introduction*. Oxford: Oxford University Press.

Dean, M. (2010). *Governmentality: Power and Rule in Modern Society*. London: Sage.

DeBarro, T., MacAulay, S., Davies, A., Wolstenholme, A., Gann, D., & Pelton, J. (2015). Mantra to Method: Lessons from Managing Innovation on Crossrail, UK. Paper presented at the Proceedings of the Institution of Civil Engineers-Civil Engineering.

du Gay, P. (2000). Enterprise and its futures: A response to Fournier and Grey. *Organization*, *7*(1), 165–183.

Engwall, M. (2003). No project is an island: Linking projects to history and context. *Research Policy*, *32*(5), 19.

Fayol, H. (1917). *Administration industrielle et générale: Prévoyance, organisation, commandement, coordination*. Paris: H. Dunod et E. Pinat.

Fleming, P., & Spicer, A. (2014). Power in management and organization science. *The Academy of Management Annals*, *8*(1), 237–298.

Flyvbjerg, B. (2001). *Making Social Science Matter: Why Social Inquiry Fails and how it can Succeed Again*. Cambridge: Cambridge University Press.

Flyvbjerg, B. (2005). Design by deception: The politics of megaproject approval. *Harvard Design Magazine*, *22*, 50–59. Available at: https://ssrn.com/abstract=2238047 (accessed 15 January 2020).

Flyvbjerg, B. (2006). Making organization research matter: Power, values, and phronesis. In S.R. Clegg, C. Hardy, T.B. Lawrence, & W.R. Nord (eds), *Handbook of Organization Studies* (2nd edn., pp. 370–387). Thousand Oaks, CA: Sage.

Flyvbjerg, B., Bruzelius, N., & Rothengatter, W. (2003). *Megaprojects and Risk: An Anatomy of Ambition*. Cambridge: Cambridge University Press.

Foucault, M. (1982). The subject and power. In H. Dreyfus & P. Rabinow (eds), *Michel Foucault: Beyond Structuralism and Hermeneutics* (pp. 208–226). Chicago: University of Chicago Press.

Foucault, M. (1997). *Ethics: Subjectivity and Truth. The Essential Works of Michel Foucault, 1954–1984 (Vol. 1)*. New York: The New Press.

Foucault, M. (2007). *Security, Territory, Population: Lectures at the Collège de France, 1977–78*. Berlin: Springer.

Garel, G. (2013). A history of project management models: From pre-models to the standard models. *International Journal of Project Management*, *31*(5), 663–669.

Geertz, C. (1973). *Thick Descriptions: Towards an Interpretive Theory of Cultures. Selected Essays*. New York: Basic Books.

Gil, N. (2017). A collective-action perspective on the planning of megaprojects. In B. Flyvbjerg (ed.), *The Oxford Handbook of Megaproject Management*. Oxford: Oxford University Press.

Golsorkhi, D., Rouleau, L., Seidl, D., & Vaara, E. (2016). *Cambridge Handbook of Strategy as Practice*. Cambridge: Cambridge University Press.

Henisz, W.J. (2016). The dynamic capability of corporate diplomacy. *Global Strategy Journal*, *6*(3), 183–196.

Korzybski, A. (1933). Science and Sanity: A Non-Aristotelian System and its Necessity for Rigour in Mathematics and Physics. New York: *Institute of General Semantics*.

Kreiner, K. (1995). In search of relevance: Project management in drifting environments. *Scandinavian Journal of Management, 11*(4), 335–346. Available at: https://doi.org/10.1016/0956–5221(95)00029-U (accessed 15 January 2020).

Lect, C.I. (2012). Basic notions of branding: Definition, history, architecture. *Journal of Media Research, 5*(3), 110.

Lefebvre, H. (1991). *The Production of Space*. Cambridge, MA: Blackwell.

Lemke, T. (2002). Foucault, governmentality, and critique. *Rethinking Marxism, 14*(3), 49–64.

Lenfle, S., & Loch, C. (2010). Lost roots: How project management came to emphasize control over flexibility and novelty. *California Management Review, 53*(1), 32–55. Available at: https://doi.org/10.1525%2Fcmr.2010.53.1.32 (accessed 15 January 2020).

Loch, C.H., DeMeyer, A., & Pich, M. (2011). *Managing the Unknown: A New Approach to Managing High Uncertainty and Risk in Projects*. Hoboken, NJ: John Wiley & Sons.

Lukes, S. (2005). *Power: A Radical View* (2nd edn). Basingstoke: Palgrave Macmillan.

MacIntyre, A. (1971). *Against the Self-images of the Age: Essays on Ideology and Philosophy*. London: Duckworth.

Marcuse, H. (1964). *One Dimensional Man*. London: Routledge & Kegan Paul.

Marks, J. (2000). Foucault, Franks, Gauls: Il faut defendre la société: The 1976 lectures at the Collège de France. *Theory, Culture & Society, 17*(5), 127–147.

Milani, T.M. (2009). At the intersection between power and knowledge: An analysis of a Swedish policy document on language testing for citizenship. *Journal of Language and Politics, 8*(2), 287–304.

Miller, R., & Lessard, D.R. (2000). *The Strategic Management of Large Engineering Projects: Shaping Institutions, Risks, and Governance*. Cambridge, MA: MIT Press.

Morris, P.W.G. (2013). *Reconstructing Project Management*. Chicester: John Wiley & Sons.

Morris, P.W.G., Pinto, J.K., & Söderlund, J. (eds) (2011). *The Oxford Handbook of Project Management*. Oxford: Oxford University Press.

Müller, R., Pemsel, S., & Shao, J. (2014). Organizational enablers for governance and governmentality of projects: A literature review. *International Journal of Project Management, 32*(8), 1309–1320.

Müller, R., Zhai, L., & Wang, A. (2017). Governance and governmentality in projects: Profiles and relationships with success. *International Journal of Project Management, 35*(3), 378–392.

Müller, R., Sankaran, S., Drouin, N., Vaagaasar, A.-L., Bekker, M.C., & Jain, K. (2018). A theory framework for balancing vertical and horizontal leadership in projects. *International Journal of Project Management, 36*(1), 83–94. Available at: https://doi.org/10.1016/j.ijproman.2017.07.003 (accessed 15 January 2020).

Ninan, J., Clegg, S.R., & Mahalingam, A. (2019). Branding and governmentality for infrastructure megaprojects: The role of social media. *International Journal of Project Management, 37*(1), 59–72.

Pinto, J.K. (2000). Understanding the role of politics in successful project management. *International Journal of Project Management, 18*(2), 85–91. Available at: doi:10.1016/S0263-7863(98)00073–8 (accessed 15 January 2020).

Pitsis, T.S., Sankaran, S., Gudergan, S., & Clegg, S.R. (2014). Governing projects under complexity: Theory and practice in project management. *International Journal of Project Management, 32*(8), 1285–1290.

Project Management Institute (2017). *A Guide to the Project Management Body of Knowledge* (6th edn). Newtown Square, PA: Project Management Institute, Inc.

Pugh, D.S., Hickson, D.J., Hinings, C.R., Macdonald, K.M., Turner, C., & Lupton, T. (1963). A conceptual scheme for organizational analysis. *Administrative Science Quarterly, 8*, 289–315.

Sanchez, H., Robert, B., Bourgault, M., & Pellerin, R. (2009). Risk management applied to projects, programs, and portfolios. *International Journal of Managing Projects in Business, 2*(1), 14–35.

Schön, D.A. (1991). *The Reflective Practitioner: How Professionals Think in Action*. Aldershot: Avebury.

Scott, D.M. (2010). *The New Rules of Marketing and PR: How to Use Social Media, Blogs, News Releases, Online Video, and Viral Marketing to Reach Buyers Directly*. Hoboken, NJ: John Wiley & Sons.

Sewell, G. (1998). The discipline of teams: The control of team-based industrial work through electronic and peer surveillance. *Administrative Science Quarterly, 43*(2), 397–428.

Turnbull, D. (1998). Mapping encounters and (en)countering maps: a critical examination of cartographic resistance. *In Research in Science and Technology Studies: Knowledge Systems. Knowledge and Society.* Ed. Shirey Gorenstein. Vol. *11*. Greenwich, CT: JAI Press, 15–44.

Turnbull, D. (2008). Maps and mapmaking of the Australian Aboriginal people. In H. Selin (ed.) *Encyclopaedia of the History of Science, Technology, and Medicine in Non-Western Cultures.* Dordrecht: Springer, pp. 1277–1278.

Vaagaasar, A.L. (2011). Development of relationships and relationship competencies in complex projects. *International Journal of Managing Projects in Business, 4*(2), 294–307.

Van Marrewijk, A., Clegg, S.R., Pitsis, T.S., & Veenswijk, M. (2008). Managing public–private megaprojects: Paradoxes, complexity, and project design. *International Journal of Project Management, 26*(6), 591–600.

Weick, K.E. (1995). *Sensemaking in Organizations.* Thousand Oaks, CA: Sage.

Yu, M., Vaagaasar, A.L., Müller, R., Wang, L., & Zhu, F. (2018). Empowerment: The key to horizontal leadership in projects. *International Journal of Project Management.* Available at: https://doi.org/10.1016/j.ijproman.2018.04.003 (accessed 15 January 2020).

Chapter 2

Allal-Chérif, O. (2019). Airbus A380: from high-tech marvel to commercial flop, available at: https://theconversation.com/airbus-a380-from-high-tech-marvel-to-commercial-flop-112086, 20 February (accessed 23 February 2020).

Andersen, E., Birchall, D., A. Jessen, S., & Money, A. (2006). Exploring project success. *Baltic Journal of Management, 1*(2) 127–147.

Andersen, E.S. (2008). *Rethinking Project Management: An Organisational Perspective.* Harlow: Prentice Hall/Financial Times.

Baccarini, D. (1996). The concept of project complexity - A review. *International Journal of Project Management, 14*(4), 201–204. doi:10.1016/0263–7863(95)00093–3.

Barraket, J., & Loosemore, M. (2018). Co-creating social value through cross-sector collaboration between social enterprises and the construction industry. *Construction Management and Economics, 36*(7), 394–408.

Berggren, C., Järvik, J., & Söderlund, J. (2008). Lagomizing, organic integration, and systems emergency wards: Innovative practices in managing complex systems development projects. *Project Management Journal, 39*(1), S111–S122.

Bozeman, B. (2007). *Public Values and Public Interest – Counterbalancing Economic Individualism.* Washington, DC: Georgetown University Press.

Brady, T., & Davies, A. (2004). Building project capabilities: From exploratory to exploitative learning. *Organization Studies, 25*(9), 1601–1621.

Cantarelli, C.C., Flybjerg, B., Molin, E.J.E., & van Wee, B. (2013). Cost overruns in large-scale transportation infrastructure projects: Explanations and their theoretical embeddedness. *European Journal of Transport and Infrastructure Research, 10*(1): 5–18.

Capka, J.R. (2004). Megaprojects: They are a different breed. *Public Roads, 68*(1), 2–9.

Carlton, D. (2018). Lack of technical knowledge in leadership is a key reason why IT projects fail, *The Conversation*, 11 September. Available at: https://theconversation.com/lack-of-technical-knowledge-in-leadership-is-a-key-reason-why-so-many-it-projects-fail-101889 (accessed 23 February 2020).

Cooke-Davies, T. (2002). The 'real' success factors on projects. *International Journal of Project Management, 20*(3), 185–190. Available at: http://dx.doi.org/10.1016/S0263-7863(01)00067–9 (accessed 21 January 2020).

Crawford, L., Morris, P., Thomas, J., & Winter, M. (2006). Practitioner development: From trained technicians to reflective practitioners. *International Journal of Project Management, 24*(8), 722–733.

Daniel, E.I., & Pasquire, C. (2019). Creating social value within the delivery of construction projects: The role of lean approach. *Engineering, Construction and Architectural Management, 26*, 1105–1128.

Davies, A., & Frederiksen, L. (2010). Project-based innovation: The world after Woodward. In N. Phillips, G. Sewell, & D. Griffiths (eds), *Technology and Organization: Essays in Honour of Joan Woodward* (Research in the Sociology of Organizations, Vol. *29*) (pp. 177–215). Bingley: Emerald Group Publishing.

Davis, K. (2014). Different stakeholder groups and their perceptions of project success. *International Journal of Project Management, 32*(2), 189–201.

Eisenhardt, K.M., & Tabrizi, B.N. (1995). Accelerating adaptive processes: Product innovation in the global computer industry. *Administrative Science Quarterly, 40*(1), 84–110.

Engwall, M. (2003). No project is an island: Linking projects to history and context. *Research Policy, 32*(5), 19.

Flyvbjerg, B. (2008). Curbing optimism bias and strategic misrepresentation in planning: Reference class forecasting in practice. *European Planning Studies, 16*(1), 3–21.

Flyvbjerg, B. (2014). What you should know about megaprojects and why: An overview. *Project Management Journal, 45*(2), 6–19.

Flyvbjerg, B., Bruzelius, N., & Rothengatter, W. (2003). *Megaprojects and Risk: An Anatomy of Ambition.* Cambridge: Cambridge University Press.

Frick, K.T. (2008). The cost of the technological sublime: Daring ingenuity and the new San Francisco–Oakland Bay Bridge. In H. Priemus, B. Flyvbjerg, & B. van Wee (eds), *Decision-Making On Mega-Projects: Cost–benefit Analysis, Planning, and Innovation.* Cheltenham: Edward Elgar.

Gil, N.A. (2015). Sustaining Highly-Fragile Collaborations: A Study of Planning Mega Infrastructure Projects in the UK. Available at: https://papers.ssrn.com/sol3/papers.cfm?abstract_id=2557370 (accessed 21 January 2020)..

Green, S.D. & Sergeeva, N. (2019). Value creation in projects: Towards a narrative perspective. *International Journal of Project Management, 37*(5), 636–651.

Greer, N., & Ksaibati, K. (2019). Development of benefit cost analysis tools for evaluating transportation research projects. *Transportation Research Record, 2673*(1), 123–135.

Hall, P. (1980). Great planning disasters: What lessons do they hold?. *Futures, 12*(1), 45–50.

Hernes, T., Simpson, B., & Söderlund, J. (2013). Managing and temporality. *Scandinavian Journal of Management, 29*(1), 1–6. Available at: http://dx.doi.org/10.1016/j.scaman.2012.11.008 (accessed 21 January 2020).

Jennings, W. (2012). Executive politics, risk and the mega-project paradox. In M. Lodge & K. Wegrich (eds), *Executive Politics in Times of Crisis.* Basingstoke: Palgrave Macmillan.

Jørgensen, S., & Pedersen, L.J.T. (2018). *RESTART Sustainable Business Model Innovation.* Basingstoke: Palgrave Macmillan.

Jugdev, K., & Müller, R. (2005). A retrospective look at our evolving understanding of project success. *Project Management Journal, 36*(4), 19–31.

Kaplan, R.S., & Norton, D.P. (1996). *The balanced Scorecard: Translating Strategy into Action.* Boston, MA: Harvard Business School Press.

Kloppenborg, T.J., Manolis, C., & Tesch, D. (2009). Successful project sponsor behaviors during project initiation: An empirical investigation. *Journal of Managerial Issues, 21*(1), 140–159.

Lee, C. L., Liang, J., & Koo, K. (2019). Rail works lift property prices, pointing to value capture's potential to fund city infrastructure, *The Conversation.* Available at: https://theconversation.com/rail-works-lift-property-prices-pointing-to-value-captures-potential-to-fund-city-infrastructure-123757 (accessed 23 February 2020).

Levitt, T. (1960). Marketing myopia. *Harvard Business Review, 38*(4), 45–56. Available at: https://hbr.org/2004/07/marketing-myopia (accessed 21 January 2020).

Li, Y., Lu, Y., Ma, L., & Kwak, Y. H. (2018). Evolutionary governance for mega-event projects (MEPs): A case study of the World Expo 2010 in China. *Project Management Journal, 49*(1), 57–78.

Loosemore, M. (2016). Social procurement in UK construction projects. *International Journal of Project Management, 34*(2), 133–144.

Loosemore, M., & Higgon, D. (2015). *Social Enterprise in the Construction Industry Building Better Communities*. London: Routledge.

Lusch, R.F., & Vargo, S.L. (2014). *Service-dominant Logic: Premises, Perspectives, Possibilities*. Cambridge: Cambridge University Press.

March, J.G. (1991). Exploration and exploitation in organizational learning. *Organization Science*, *2*(1), 71–87. Available at: www.jstor.org/stable/2634940?origin=JSTOR-pdf (accessed 21 January 2020).

Miller, R., & Lessard, D.R. (2000). *The Strategic Management of Large Engineering Projects: Shaping Institutions, Risks, and Governance*. Cambridge, MA: MIT Press.

Miller, R., Lessard, D., & Sakhrani, V. (2017). Megaprojects as games of innovation. In B. Flybjerg (ed.), *The Oxford Handbook of Megaproject Management* (pp. 249–259). Oxford: Oxford University Press.

Morris, P.W.G. (1994). *The Management of Projects*. London: Thomas Telford.

Morris, P.W.G. (2011). A brief history of project management. In P.W.G. Morris, J.K. Pinto, & J. Söderlund (eds), *The Oxford Handbook of Project Management*. Oxford: Oxford University Press.

Morris, P.W.G., & Hough, G.H. (1987). *The Anatomy of Major Projects: A Study of the Reality of Project Management*. Chichester: Wiley.

Morris, P.W.G., Pinto, J.K., & Söderlund, J. (eds) (2011). *The Oxford Handbook of Project Management*. Oxford: Oxford University Press.

Müller, R., & Turner, R. (2007). The influence of project managers on project success criteria and project success by type of project. *European Management Journal*, *25*(4), 298–309. Available at: http://dx.doi.org/10.1016/j.emj.2007.06.003 (accessed 21 January 2020).

Ng, A., & Loosemore, M. (2007). Risk allocation in the private provision of public infrastructure. *International Journal of Project Management*, *25*(1), 66–76.

Nielsen, C., Lund, M., & Thomsen, P. (2017). Killing the balanced scorecard to improve internal disclosure. *Journal of Intellectual Capital*, *18*(1), 45–62.

Osterwalder, A., & Pigneur, Y. (2010). *Business Model Generation: A Handbook for Visionaries, Game Changers, and Challengers*. Hoboken, NJ: John Wiley & Sons.

Payne, J.H., & Turner, J.R. (1999). Company-wide project management: The planning and control of programmes of projects of different type. *International Journal of Project Management*, *17*(1), 55–59.

Phillips, G. (2007). Analysis of Sydney Public-Private Partnership road tunnels. In 19th National Conference of the Australian Society for Operations Research.

Pinto, J.K., & Prescott, J.E. (1988). Variations in critical success factors over the stages in the project life cycle. *Journal of Management*, *14*(1), 5–18.

Pinto, J.K., & Slevin, D. (1988). Critical success factors in effective project implementation. In D.I. Cleland, & W.R. King (eds), *Project Management Handbook*. New York: Van Nostrand Reinhold.

Pitsis, A., Clegg, S., Freeder, D., Sankaran, S., & Burdon, S. (2018). Megaprojects redefined: Complexity vs cost and social imperatives. *International Journal of Managing Projects in Business*, *11*(1), 7–34.

Priemus, H., Flyvbjerg, B., & van Wee, B. (2008). *Decision-making on Mega-Projects: Cost-Benefit Analysis, Planning and Innovation*. Cheltenham: Edward Elgar Publishing.

Raidén, A., Loosemore, M., King, A., & Gorse, C. (2018). *Social Value in Construction*. London: Routledge.

Sayyadi, M. (2019). How effective leadership of knowledge management impacts organizational performance. *Business Information Review*, *36*(1), 30–38.

Schindler, M., & Eppler, M.J. (2003). Harvesting project knowledge: A review of project learning methods and success factors. *International Journal of Project Management*, *21*(3), 219–228.

Serrador, P., & Turner, J. (2013). The impact of the planning phase on project success. *IRNOP*, Oslo, Norway.

Shenhar, A.J., & Dvir, D. (1996). Toward a typological theory of project management. *Research Policy*, *25*(4), 607–632.

Shenhar, A.J., & Dvir, D. (2007). *Reinventing Project Management: The Diamond Approach to Successful Growth and Innovation*. Boston, MA: Harvard Business School Press.

Social Enterprise UK, (2012). *The Shadow State: A Report About Outsourcing of Public Services*. Social Enterprise UK: London

Söderlund, J. (2005). *Projektledning & projektkompetens: Perspektiv på konkurrenskraft*. Malmö: Liber.

Stinchcombe, A.L., & Heimer, C.A. (1985). *Organization Theory and Project Management: Administering Uncertainty in Norwegian Offshore Oil*. Oslo: Norwegian University Press.

Sturup, S. (2009). Mega projects and governmentality. *World Academy of Science, Engineering and Technology, International Journal of Humanities and Social Sciences, 3*(6), 862–871.

Sun, J., & Zhang, P. (2011). Owner organization design for mega industrial construction projects. *International Journal of Project Management, 29*(7), 828–833.

Takeuchi, H., & Nonaka, I. (1986). The new new product development game. *Harvard Business Review, 64*, 137.

Tatikonda, M.V., & Rosenthal, S.R. (2000). Successful execution of product development projects: Balancing firmness and flexibility in the innovation process. *Journal of Operations Management, 18*(4), 401–425.

Tereso, A., Ribeiro, P., Fernandes, G., Loureiro, I., & Ferreira, M. (2019). Project management practices in private organizations. *Project Management Journal, 50*(1), 6–22.

Turner, J.R., Anbari, F., & Bredillet, C. (2013). Perspectives on research in project management: The nine schools. *Global Business Perspectives, 1*(1), 3–28.

Turner, J.R., & Müller, R. (2005). The project manager's leadership style as a success factor on projects: A literature review. *Project Management Journal, 36*(2), 49–61.

Verweij, S., & Gerrits, L.M. (2019). *Evaluating infrastructure project planning and implementation: A study using qualitative comparative analysis*. Sage Research Methods Cases in Business and Management. https://dx.doi.org/10.4135/9781526467997

Wachs, M. (1989). When planners lie with numbers. *Journal of the American Planning Association, 55*(4), 476.

Wateridge, J. (1995). IT projects: A basis for success. *International Journal of Project Management, 13*(3), 169–172.

Weick, K.E. (1995). *Sensemaking in Organizations*. Thousand Oaks, CA: Sage.

Chapter 3

Andersen, E.S., Soderlund, J., & Vaagaasar, A.L. (2010). Projects and politics: Exploring the duality between action and politics in complex projects. *International Journal of Management and Decision Making, 11*(2), 121–139.

Batselier, J., & Vanhoucke, M. (2016). Practical application and empirical evaluation of reference class forecasting for project management. *Project Management Journal, 47*(5), 36–51.

Brady, T., & Davies, A. (2004). Building project capabilities: From exploratory to exploitative learning. *Organization Studies, 25*(9), 1601–1621.

Brunsson, K., & Brunsson, N. (2017). *Decisions: The complexities of individual and organizational decision-making*: Cheltenham: Edward Elgar.

Brunsson, N. (2000). *The irrational Organization: Irrationality as a Basis for Organizational Action and Change*. Bergen: Fagbokforlaget.

Brunsson, N. (2006). *Mechanisms of Hope: Maintaining the Dream of the Rational Organization*. Copenhagen Business School Press

Brunsson, N. (2007). *The Consequences of Decision-making*. Oxford: Oxford University Press.

Brunsson, N., & Adler, N. (1989). *The Organization of Hypocrisy: Talk, Decisions and Actions in Organizations* (2nd edn). Oslo: Universitetsforlaget.

Carlsen, A., Clegg, S.R., & Gjersvik, R. (2012). *Idea Work: Lessons of the Extraordinary in Everyday Creativity*. Oslo: Cappelen Damm akademisk.

Carlton, D. (2018) Lack of technical knowledge in leadership is a key reason why IT projects fail, *The Conversation*, 11 September. Available at: https://theconversation.com/lack-of-technical-knowledge-in-leadership-is-a-key-reason-why-so-many-it-projects-fail-101889 (accessed 23 February 2020).

Clegg, S.R. (1989). *Frameworks of Power*. London: Sage Publications.

Clegg, S.R. and Burdon, S. (2019) Exploring polyarchic creativity and innovation in broadcasting, *Human Relations*, https://doi.org/10.1177/0018726719888004

Clegg, S.R., Pitsis, T.S., Rura-Polley, T., & Marosszeky, M. (2002). Governmentality matters: Designing an alliance culture of inter-organizational collaboration for managing projects. *Organization Studies*, *23*(3), 317–337.

Clegg, S., Kornberger, M., Pitsis, T.S., & Mount, M. (2019). *Managing & Organizations: An Introduction to Theory and Practice* (5th edn). London: Sage.

Cohen, M.D., March, J.G., & Olsen, J.P. (1972). A garbage can model of organizational choice. *Administrative Science Quarterly*, *17*(1), 1–25.

Coldevin, G.H., Carlsen, A., Clegg, S.R., Pitsis, T.S., & Antonacopoulou, E.P. (2018). Organizational creativity as idea work: Intertextual placing and legitimating imaginings in media development and oil exploration. *Human Relations*, *72*(8), 1369–1397.

Cunha, M.P., Viera, D.V., Rego, A. & Clegg, S.R. (2018) Why does performance management not perform?, *International Journal of Productivity and Performance Management*, *67*(4), 673–692.

Danso-Wiredu, E.Y., & Midheme, E. (2017). Slum upgrading in developing countries: Lessons from Ghana and Kenya. *Ghana Journal of Geography*, *9*(1), 88–108.

Davies, A., & Brady, T. (2000). Organisational capabilities and learning in complex product systems: Towards repeatable solutions. *Research Policy*, *29*(7), 931–953. Available at: https://doi.org/10.1016/S0048-7333(00)00113-X (accessed 22 January 2020).

Davies, A., Brady, T., Prencipe, A., & Hobday, M. (2011). Innovation in complex products and systems: Implications for project-based organizing. *Advances in Strategic Management*, *28*, 3–26.

Garvin, D.A., & Roberto, M.A. (2001). What you don't know about making decisions. *Harvard Business Review*, *79*(8), 108.

Giezen, M., Salet, W., & Bertolini, L. (2015). Adding value to the decision-making process of mega projects: Fostering strategic ambiguity, redundancy, and resilience. *Transport Policy*, *44*, 169.

Giones, F. (2019). Horizon Europe: the EU plans to spend €100 billion on research – here's how to get the most from it, *The Conversation*, 6 September. Available at: https://theconversation.com/horizon-europe-the-eu-plans-to-spend-100-billion-on-research-heres-how-to-get-the-most-from-it-122276 (accessed 23 February 2020).

Hamylton, S., & Balez, R. (2018). How a trip to Antarctica became a real-life experiment in decision-making, *The Conversation*, 23 May. Available at: https://theconversation.com/how-a-trip-to-antarctica-became-a-real-life-experiment-in-decision-making-96726 (accessed 23 February 2020).

Hill, P. (2015). More is less? Health in the Sustainable Development Goals, *The Conversation*, 23 September. Available at: https://theconversation.com/more-is-less-health-in-the-sustainable-development-goals-47627 (accessed 23 February 2020).

Jones, J., & Barry, M.M. (2018). Factors influencing trust and mistrust in health promotion partnerships. *Global Health Promotion*, *25*(2), 16–24.

Jørgensen, S., & Pedersen, L J.T. (2018). *RESTART Sustainable Business Model Innovation*. Basingstoke: Palgrave Macmillan.

Kahneman, D. (2012). *Thinking, Fast and Slow*. London: Penguin Books.

Kahneman, D., & Tversky, A. (2000). *Choices, Values, and Frames*. Cambridge: Cambridge University Press.

Loch, C., & Sommer, S. (2019). The tension between flexible goals and managerial control in exploratory projects. *Project Management Journal*, *50*(5), 524–537.

Lovallo, D., & Kahneman, D. (2003). Delusions of success. *Harvard Business Review*, *81*(7), 56–63. Available at: https://hbr.org/2003/07/delusions-of-success-how-optimism-undermines-executives-decisions (accessed 22 January 2020).

March, J.G., & Olsen, J.P. (1976). *Ambiguity and Choice in Organizations.* Bergen: Universitetsforlaget.

Obeng, E. (1996). *The Project Leader's Secret Handbook: All Change!* London: Financial Times/ Prentice Hall.

Okyere, S.A., Tasnatab, J.C., & Abunyewah, M. (2018). Accra's informal settlements are easing the city's urban housing crisis, *The Conversation*, 7 October. Available at: https://theconversation.com/accras-informal-settlements-are-easing-the-citys-urban-housing-crisis-104266 (accessed 23 February 2020).

Patanakul, P., & Shenhar, A.J. (2012). What project strategy really is: The fundamental building block in strategic project management. *Project Management Journal, 43*(1), 4–20.

Plato (1973). *Laches; Charmides* (2nd edn). New York: Bobbs-Merril.

Simon, H.A. (1965). *Administrative Behavior: A Study of Decision-making Processes in Administrative Organization.* New York: Free Press.

Simon, H.A. (1991). Bounded rationality and organizational learning. *Organization Science, 2*(1), 125–134.

Teece, D.J., Pisano, G., & Shuen, A. (1997). Dynamic capabilities and strategic management. *Strategic Management Journal, 18*(7), 509–533.

Tidd, J., & Bessant, J. (2018). *Managing Innovation: Integrating Technological, Market and Organizational Change* (6th edn). Hoboken, NJ: Wiley.

Vaagaasar, A.L. (2006). *From Tool to Actor: How a Project Came to Orchestrate its Own Life and That of Others* (Vol. *10*). Oslo: Handelshøyskolen BI.

Vaagaasar, A. L. (2011). Development of relationships and relationship competencies in complex projects. *International Journal of Managing Projects in Business,4*(2), 294–307.

Vanhoucke, M. (2018). Data-driven project management is good for your business: A business novel tells you why. Available at: https://projectdesignmanagement.com.br/wp-content/uploads/2018/08/Vanhoucke_Book_Content_Summary.pdf (accessed 22 January 2020).

Weick, K.E. (1995). *Sensemaking in Organizations.* Thousand Oaks, CA: Sage.

Yamaura, J., Muench, S.T., & Willoughby, K. (2019). Factors influencing adoption of information technologies for public transportation project inspection: A WSDOT case study. *Transportation Research Record: Journal of the Transportation Research Board.* Available at: https://doi.org/10.1177/0361198118823198 (accessed 22 January 2020).

Chapter 4

Andersen, E.S. (2008). *Rethinking Project Management: An Organisational Perspective.* Harlow: Prentice Hall/Financial Times.

Andersen, E.S. (2014). Value creation using the mission breakdown structure. *International Journal of Project Management, 32*(5), 885–892. Available at: http://dx.doi.org/10.1016/j.ijproman.2013.11.003 (accessed 24 January 2020).

Andersen, E.S., Grude, K.V., & Haug, T. (2009). *Goal Directed Project Management: Effective Techniques and Strategies* (3rd edn). London: Kogan Page Publishers.

Ballard, D.I., & Seibold, D.R. (2003). Communicating and organizing in time: A meso-level model of organizational temporality. *Management Communication Quarterly, 16*(3), 380–415.

Beauregard, R. (2018). The entanglements of uncertainty. *Journal of Planning Education and Research.* Available at: https://doi.org/10.1177%2F0739456X18783038 (accessed 24 January 2020).

Bechky, B.A., & Okhuysen, G.A. (2011). Expecting the unexpected? How SWAT officers and film crews handle surprises.*The Academy of Management Journal, 54*(2), 239–261.

Bos-de Vos, M., Volker, L., & Wamelink, H. (2019). Enhancing value capture by managing risks of value slippage in and across projects. *International Journal of Project Management, 37*(5), 767–783.

Brodie, R.J., Ilic, A., Juric, B., & Hollebeek, L. (2013). Consumer engagement in a virtual brand community: An exploratory analysis. *Journal of Business Research, 66*(1), 105–114.

Browning, T.R. (2019). Planning, tracking, and reducing a complex project's value at risk. *Project Management Journal, 50*(1), 71–85.

Carlsen, A., Clegg, S.R., & Gjersvik, R. (2012). *Idea Work: Lessons of the Extraordinary in Every-day Creativity*. Oslo: Cappelen Damm akademisk.

Chamberlin, J. (2011). Who put the 'ART' in SMART goals. *Management Services, 55*(3), 22–27.

Christensen, T., & Lægreid, P. (2007). The whole-of-government approach to public sector reform. *Public Administration Review, 67*(6), 1059–1066. Available at: https://doi.org/10.1111/j.1540–6210.2007.00797.x (accessed 24 January 2020).

Clayton, M. (2017) What is Milestone Planning? Project Management in Under 5. Available at: https://www.youtube.com/watch?v=aJcd1rQ0Z9w (accessed 24 February 2020).

Clegg, S.R., Pitsis, T.S., Rura-Polley, T., & Marosszeky, M. (2002). Governmentality matters: Designing an alliance culture of inter-organizational collaboration for managing projects. *Organization Studies, 23*(3), 317–337.

Clegg, S., Carter, C., Kornberger, M., & Schweitzer, J. (2019). *Strategy: Theory and Practice* (3rd edn). London: Sage Publications.

Collins, J.C., & Porras, J.I. (1994). *Built to last: Successful Habits of Visionary Companies*. New York: HarperBusiness.

Cormack, Z. (2019) How Kenya's mega wind power project is hurting communities, *The Conversation*, 3 September. Available at: https://theconversation.com/how-kenyas-mega-wind-power-project-is-hurting-communities-122061 (accessed 23 February 2020).

Crawford, L., Cooke-Davies, T., Hobbs, B., Labuschagne, L., Remington, K., & Chen, P. (2008). Governance and support in the sponsoring of projects and programs. *Project Management Journal, 39*(S1), S43–S55. Available at: https://doi.org/10.1002/pmj.20059 (accessed 24 January 2020).

Das, T.K., & Teng, B.-S. (1998). Between trust and control: Developing confidence in partner cooperation in alliances. *The Academy of Management Review, 23*(3), 491–512. Available at: https://doi.org/10.2307/259291 (accessed 24 January 2020).

Deming, W.E. (2000). *Out of the Crisis*. Cambridge, MA: MIT Press.

DFØ (2014). *Guidance in Profit Liberalization by Digitizing the Procurement Process*. Oslo: DFØ.

Doerr, J. (2018a). *Measure What Matters: How Google, Bono, and the Gates Foundation Rock the World with OKRs*. London: Penguin.

Doerr, J. (2018b) Why the secret to success is setting the right goals, *Ted Talks*, 8 July 8. Available at: www.youtube.com/watch?v=L4N1q4RNi9I (accessed 23 February 2020).

Doran, G.T. (1981). There's a S.M.A.R.T. way to write managements's goals and objectives. *Management Review, 70*(11), 35.

Drucker, P.F. (1976). *People and Performance: The Best of Peter Drucker on Management: Management Editions (Europe)*.

Duhigg, C. (2016). *Smarter Faster Better: The Secrets of Being Productive in Life and Business*. New York: Random House.

Eisenhardt, K.M., & Tabrizi, B.N. (1995). Accelerating adaptive processes: Product innovation in the global computer industry. *Administrative Science Quarterly, 40*(1), 84–110.

Engineer4Free (2014). Use forward and backward pass to determine project duration and critical path. Available at: www.youtube.com/watch?v=4oDLMs11Exs (accessed 24 February 2020).

Engwall, M. (2003). No project is an island: Linking projects to history and context. *Research Policy, 32*(5), 19.

Fitzgerald, B. (1996). Formalized systems development methodologies: A critical perspective. *Information Systems Journal, 6*(1), 3–23.

Flyvbjerg, B. (2006). From Nobel Prize to project management: Getting risks right. *Project Management Journal, 37*(3), 5.

Fox, A. (1974). *Beyond Contract: Work, Power and Trust Relations*. London: Faber.

Goggin, C.L., Barrett, T., Leys, J., Summerell, G., Gorrod, E., Waters, S., Littleboy, M., Auld, T.D., Drielsma, M., & Jenkins, B.R. (2019). Incorporating social dimensions in planning, managing and evaluating environmental projects. *Environmental Management, 63*(2), 215–232.

Hackman, J.R., & Wageman, R. (2005). A theory of team coaching. *Academy of Management Review, 30*(2), 269–287. Available at: https://doi.org/10.5465/AMR.2005.16387885 (accessed 24 January 2020).

Hughes, D.J. (1995). *Moltke on the Art of War: Selected Writings.* New York: Random House.

Jenner, S. (2010). *Transforming Government and Public Services: Realising Benefits Through Project Portfolio Management.* Farnham: Gower.

Kahneman, D. (2012). *Thinking, Fast and Slow.* London: Penguin Books.

Kamski, B. (2019). Why Ethiopia's showcase sugar projects face huge challenges, *The Conversation*, 15 September. Available at: https://theconversation.com/why-ethiopias-showcase-sugar-projects-face-huge-challenges-122871 (accessed 24 February 2020).

Kauser, Mrs. (2016) PERT – Project Evaluation Review and Technique in Project Management. Available at: www.youtube.com/watch?v=WrAf6zdteXI (accessed 24 February 2020).

Kerr, S., & Landauer, S. (2004). Using stretch goals to promote organizational effectiveness and personal growth: General Electric and Goldman Sachs. *Academy of Management Perspectives, 18*(4), 134–138.

Larson, E.W., & Gray, C.F. (2011). *Project Management: The Managerial Process.* Boston: McGraw-Hill.

McGivern, G., Dopson, S., Ferlie, E., Fischer, M., Fitzgerald, L., Ledger, J., & Bennett, C. (2018). The silent politics of temporal work: A case study of a management consultancy project to redesign public health care. *Organization Studies, 39*(8), 1007–1030.

Matthews, T., Ambry, C., Baker, D., & Byrne, J. (2016). Here's how green infrastructure can easily be added to the urban planning toolkit, *The Conversation*, 25 April. Available at: https://theconversation.com/heres-how-green-infrastructure-can-easily-be-added-to-the-urban-planning-toolkit-57277 (accessed 25 February 2020).

Maylor, H. (2010). *Project Management* (4th edn). Harlow: Financial Times Prentice Hall.

Mikkelsen, H., & Riis, J.O. (2017). *Project Management: A Multi-Perspective Leadership Framework.* Bingley, UK: Emerald Publishing.

Mitchell, R.K., Agle, B.R., & Wood, D.J. (1997). Toward a theory of stakeholder identification and salience: Defining the principle of who and what really counts. *The Academy of Management Review, 22*(4), 853–886. Available at: https://doi.org/10.2307/259247 (accessed 24 January 2020).

Müller, R. (2016). *Governance and Governmentality for Projects: Enablers, Practices, and Consequences.* London: Routledge.

Müller, R., Drouin, N., & Sankaran, S. (2019). Modeling organizational project management. *Project Management Journal, 50*(4), 499–513.

Müller, R., & Lecoeuvre, L. (2014). Operationalizing governance categories of projects. *International Journal of Project Management, 32*(8), 1346–1357. Availablw at: http://dx.doi.org/10.1016/j.ijproman.2014.04.005 (accessed 24 January 2020).

Müller, R., Turner, J.R., Andersen, E.S., Shao, J., & Kvalnes, Ø. (2016). Governance and ethics in temporary organizations: The mediating role of corporate governance. *Project Management Journal, 47*(6), 7–23.

Ninan, J., Clegg, S., & Mahalingam, A. (2019). Branding and governmentality for infrastructure megaprojects: The role of social media. *International Journal of Project Management, 37*(1), 59–72.

Patanakul, P., & Shenhar, A.J. (2012). What project strategy really is: The fundamental building block in strategic project management. *Project Management Journal, 43*(1), 4–20. Available at: https://doi.org/10.1002/pmj.20282 (accessed 24 January 2020).

Paul, S. (2019). *Managing Development Programs: The Lessons of Success.* London: Routledge.

Pina E. Cunha, M., Giustiniano, L., Rego, A., & Clegg, S.R. (2017). Mission impossible? The paradoxes of stretch goal setting. *Management Learning, 48*(2), 140–157. Available at: https://doi.org/10.1177/1350507616664289 (accessed 23 January 2020).

Pinto, J.K. (2014). Project management, governance, and the normalization of deviance. *International Journal of Project Management, 32*(3), 376–387.

Pinto, J.K., & Slevin, D. (1988). Critical success factors in effective project implementation. In D.I. Cleland & W.R. King (eds), *Project Management Handbook*. New York: Van Nostrand Reinhold.

Pitsis, T.S., Clegg, S.R., Marosszeky, M., & Rura-Polley, T. (2003). Constructing the Olympic dream: A future perfect strategy of project management. *Organization Science, 14*(5), 574–590.

Pitsis, T.S., Clegg, S.R., Marosszeky, M., & Rura-Polley, T. (2003). Constructing the Olympic dream: A future perfect strategy of project management. *Organization Science, 14*(5), 574–590.

Serra, C.E.M., & Kunc, M. (2015). Benefits Realisation Management and its influence on project success and on the execution of business strategies. *International Journal of Project Management, 33*(1), 53–66. Available at: https://doi.org/10.1016/j.ijproman.2014.03.011 (accessed 24 January 2020).

Serrador, P., & Turner, J. (2013). *The Impact of the Planning Phase on Project Success*. Oslo: IRNOP.

Sitkin, S.B., See, K.E., Miller, C.C., Lawless, M.W., & Carton, A.M. (2011). The paradox of stretch goals: Organizations in pursuit of the seemingly impossible. *Academy of Management Review, 36*(3), 544–566.

Söderlund, J., & Tell, F. (2009). The P-form organization and the dynamics of project competence: Project epochs in Asea/ABB, 1950–2000. *International Journal of Project Management, 27*(2), 101–112. Available at: https://doi.org/10.1016/j.ijproman.2008.10.010 (accessed 24 January 2020).

Söderlund, J., & Tell, F. (2012). *Styrning: med projekt och kunskap i fokus*. Lund: Studentlitteratur.

Stemmie, C. (2019). What is the planning fallacy (and how can it derail your time management efforts)? Available at: www.developgoodhabits.com/planning-fallacy/ (accessed 24 February 2020).

Thwaites, J. & Ferraro, J. (2016). 2050 climate targets: nations are playing the long game in fighting global warming. Available at: https://theconversation.com/2050-climate-targets-nations-are-playing-the-long-game-in-fighting-global-warming-69334 (accessed 24 February 2020).

Torfing, J., Sørensen, E., & Røiseland, A. (2019). Transforming the public sector into an arena for co-creation: Barriers, drivers, benefits, and ways forward. *Administration & Society, 51*(5), 795–825. Available at: https://doi.org/10.117/0095399716680057 (accessed 24 January 2020).

Valverde, M., & Moore, A. (2019). The performance of transparency in public–private infrastructure project governance: The politics of documentary practices. *Urban Studies, 56*(4), 689–704. Available at: https://doi.org/10.1177/0042098017741404 (accessed 24 January 2020).

Chapter 5

Adler, P. (1995). 'Democratic Taylorism': The Toyota production system at NUMMI. In S. Babson (ed.), *Lean Work: Empowerment and Exploitation in the Global Auto Industry* (pp. 207–219). Detroit: Wayne State University Press.

Adler, P.S., Goldoftas, B., & Levine, D.I. (1999). Flexibility versus efficiency? A case study of model changeovers in the Toyota production system. *Organization Science, 10*(1), 43–68. Available at: https://doi.org/10.1287/orsc.10.1.43 (accessed 27 January 2020).

Albalate, D., & Bel, G. (2009). Regulating concessions of toll motorways: An empirical study on fixed vs. variable term contracts. *Transportation Research Part A: Policy and Practice, 43*(2), 219–229.

Andersen, E.S., Grude, K.V., & Haug, T. (2009). *Goal Directed Project Management: Effective Techniques and Strategies* (3rd edn). London: Kogan Page Publishers.

Andi (2006). The importance and allocation of risks in Indonesian construction projects. *Construction Management and Economics, 24*(1), 69–80.

Arndt, R.H. (1998). Risk allocation in the Melbourne city link project. *Journal of Structured Finance, 4*(3), 11.

Atkins, G., Wajzer, C., Hogarth, R., Davies, N., & Norris, E. (2017). What's wrong with infrastructure decision making?. London: Institute for Government.

Bing, L., Akintoye, A., Edwards, P.J., & Hardcastle, C. (2005). The allocation of risk in PPP/PFI construction projects in the UK. *International Journal of Project Management, 23*(1), 25–35.

Boehm, B., & Turner, R. (2005). Management challenges to implementing agile processes in traditional development organizations. *IEEE Software, 22*(5), 30–39.

Bresnen, M., & Marshall, N. (2002). The engineering or evolution of co-operation? A tale of two partnering projects. *International Journal of Project Management, 20*(7), 497–505.

Brown, T. (2009). Designers – think big! Ted Talk. Available at: www.ted.com/talks/tim_brown_designers_think_big?language=en (accessed 24 February 2020).

Brown, T.L., Potoski, M., & Van Slyke, D.M. (2018). Complex contracting: Management challenges and solutions. *Public Administration Review, 78*(5), 739–747.

Buchanan, R. (1992). Wicked problems in Design Thinking. *Design Issues, 8*(2), 5–21. Available at: https://doi.org/10.2307/1511637 (accessed 27 January 2020).

Bygballe, L.E., Dewulf, G., & Levitt, R.E. (2015). The interplay between formal and informal contracting in integrated project delivery. *Engineering Project Organization Journal, 5*(1), 22–35.

Carlsen, A., Clegg, S.R., & Gjersvik, R. (2012). *Idea Work: Lessons of the Extraordinary in Everyday Creativity*. Oslo: Cappelen Damm akademisk.

Chang, A., Hatcher, C., & Kim, J. (2013). Temporal boundary objects in megaprojects: Mapping the system with the integrated master schedule. *International Journal of Project Management, 31*(3), 323–332.

Clark, K., & Fujimoto, T. (1989). Overlapping problem-solving in product development. In K. Ferdows (ed.), *Managing International Manufacturing*. Amsterdam: Elsevier.

Clayton. M. (2017) What is a milestone planning? Available at: www.youtube.com/watch?v=a-Jcd1rQ0Z9w (accessed 24 February 2020).

Clegg, S.R., & Kornberger, M. (2015). Analytical frames for studying power in strategy as practice and beyond. In D. Golsorkhi (ed.), *Cambridge Handbook of Strategy as Practice* (2nd edn). Cambridge: Cambridge University Press.

Clegg, S.R., Pitsis, T.S., Rura-Polley, T., & Marosszeky, M. (2002). Governmentality matters: Designing an alliance culture of inter-organizational collaboration for managing projects. *Organization Studies, 23*(3), 317–337.

Clegg, S.R., Kornberger, M., Pitsis, T., & Mount, M. (2019). *Managing & Organizations: An Introduction to Theory & Practice* (5th edn). London: SAGE.

Coldevin, G.H., Carlsen, A., Clegg, S.R., Pitsis, T.S., & Antonacopoulou, E.P. (2018). Organizational creativity as idea work: Intertextual placing and legitimating imaginings in media development and oil exploration. *Human Relations, 72*(8). Available at: https://doi.org/10.1177/0018726718806349 (accessed 27 January 2020).

Cooper, R.G. (1990). Stage-gate systems: A new tool for managing new products. *Business Horizons, 33*(3), 44–54. Available at: https://doi.org/10.1016/0007–6813(90)90040-I (accessed 27 January 2020).

Coughlan, P., Suri, J.F., & Canales, K. (2007). Prototypes as (design) tools for behavioral and organizational change: A design-based approach to help organizations change work behaviors. *Journal of Applied Behavioral Science, 43*(1), 122–134. Available at: https://doi.org/10.1177/0021886306297722 (accessed 27 January 2020).

Cova, B., Ghauri, P.N., & Salle, R. (2002). *Project Marketing: Beyond Competitive Bidding*. Chichester: John Wiley.

Deming, W.E. (2000). *Out of the Crisis*. Cambridge, MA: MIT Press.

Drummond, C. (2020). Scrum: Learn how to scrum with the best of 'em. Available at: https://www.atlassian.com/agile/scrum (accessed 24 February 2020).

Eisenhardt, K.M., & Tabrizi, B.N. (1995). Accelerating adaptive processes: Product innovation in the global computer industry. *Administrative Science Quarterly, 40*(1), 84–110.

Elsbach, K.D., & Stigliani, I. (2018). Design Thinking and organizational culture: A review and framework for future research. *Journal of Management, 44*(6), 2274–2306.

European Commission (2003). *Guidelines for Successful Public–Private Partnerships.* Available at: https://ec.europa.eu/regional_policy/sources/docgener/guides/ppp_en.pdf (accessed 27 January 2020).

Fisk, E. (1997). *Construction Project Administration.* New Jersey: Prentice Hall.

Fitzgerald, B. (1996). Formalized systems development methodologies: A critical perspective. *Information Systems Journal, 6*(1), 3–23.

Fleming, P. (2019). Robots and organization studies: Why robots might not want to steal your job. *Organization Studies, 40*(1), 23–38. Available at: https://doi.org/10.1177/0170840618765568 (accessed 27 January 2020).

Forsberg, K., Mooz, H., & Cotterman, H. (1996). *Visualizing Project Management.* New York: Wiley.

Garland, R. (2009). *Project Governance: A Practical Guide to Effective Project Decision Making.* London: Kogan Page.

Grimsey, D., & Lewis, M.K. (2002). Evaluating the risks of public private partnerships for infrastructure projects. *International Journal of Project Management, 20*(2), 107–118.

Heslin, P. A. (2019) Three ways to achieve your New Year's resolutions by building 'goal infrastructure', *The Conversation.* Available at: https://theconversation.com/three-ways-to-achieve-your-new-years-resolutions-by-building-goal-infrastructure-105292 (accessed 24 February 2020).

Hobbs, B., & Petit, Y. (2017). Agile methods on large projects in large organizations. *Project Management Journal, 48*(3), 3–19. Available at: https://doi.org/10.1177/875697281704800301 (accessed 27 January 2020).

Irwin, T., Klein, M., Perry, G.E., & Thobani, M. (1998). *Dealing with Public Risk in Private Infrastructure.* Washington DC: The World Bank.

Jin, X.-H. (2009). Determinants of efficient risk allocation in privately financed public infrastructure projects in Australia. *Journal of Construction Engineering and Management, 136*(2), 138–150.

Jones, C., & Lichtenstein, B.B. (2008). Temporary inter-organizational projects. In S. Cropper, M. Ebers, C. Huxham, & P.S. Ring (eds), *The Oxford Handbook of Inter-organizational Relations.* Oxford: Oxford University Press.

Khoury, J. (2018). Waterfall model definition and example. Available at: https://www.youtube.com/watch?v=Y_A0E1ToC_I (accessed 24 February 2020).

Kwak, Y.H., & Anbari, F.T. (2009). Analyzing project management research: Perspectives from top management journals. *International Journal of Project Management, 27*(5), 435–446.

Kwon, H., & Kang, C. W. (2019). Improving project budget estimation accuracy and precision by analyzing reserves for both identified and unidentified risks. *Project Management Journal, 50*(1), 86–100.

Larson, E., & Gray, C. (2017). *Project Management: The Managerial Process with MS Project.* New York: McGraw-Hill Education.

Liker, J.K., & Morgan, J.M. (2006). The Toyota way in services: The case of lean product development. *The Academy of Management Perspectives, 20*(2), 5. Available at: https://doi.org/10.5465/AMP.2006.20591002 (accessed 27 January 2020).

Lindkvist, L., Soderlund, J., & Tell, F. (1998). Managing product development projects: On the significance of fountains and deadlines. *Organization Studies, 19*(6), 931–951.

Mahmoud-Jouini, S. B., Midler, C. & Silberzahn, P. (2016). Contributions of design thinking to project management in an innovation context. *Project Management Journal, 47*(2), 144–156.

Meso, P., & Jain, R. (2006). Agile software development: Adaptive systems principles and rest practices. *Information Systems Management, 23*(3), 19–30. Available at: https://doi.org/10.1201/1078.10580530/46108.23.3.20060601/93704.3 (accesssed 27 January 2020).

Michlewski, K. (2008). Uncovering design attitude: Inside the culture of designers. *Organization Studies, 29*(3), 373–392. doi:10.1177/0170840607088019 (accessed 27 January 2020).

Miller, R., & Lessard, D.R. (2000). *The Strategic Management of Large Engineering Projects: Shaping Institutions, Risks, and Governance*. Cambridge, MA: MIT Press.

Mok, K.Y., Shen, G.Q., & Yang, J. (2015). Stakeholder management studies in mega construction projects: A review and future directions. *International Journal of Project Management*, *33*(2), 446–457.

Müller, R., & Turner, J.R. (2005). The impact of principal–agent relationship and contract type on communication between project owner and manager. *International Journal of Project Management, 23*(5), 398–403. Available at: https://doi.org/10.1016/j.ijproman.2005.03.001 (accessed 27 January 2020).

Naar, L., & Clegg, S.R. (2015). *Gehry in Sydney: The Dr Chau Chak Wing Building, UTS*. Mulgrave, Victoria, Australia: The Images Publishing Group Pty Ltd.

Naar, L., and Clegg, S.R. (2018). Models as strategic actants in innovative architecture, *Journal of Management Inquiry, 27*(1), 26–39

Nerur, S., & Balijepally, V. (2007). Theoretical reflections on agile development methodologies – The traditional goal of optimization and control is making way for learning and innovation. *Communications of the ACM, 50*(3), 79–83. Available at: https://doi.org/10.1145/1226736.1226739 (accessed 27 January 2020).

Nerur, S., Mahapatra, R., & Mangalaraj, G. (2005). Challenges of migrating to agile methodologies. *Communications of the ACM, 48*(5), 72–78. Available at: https://doi.org/10.1145/1060710.1060712 (accessed 27 January 2020).

Peckiene, A., Komarovska, A., & Ustinovicius, L. (2013). Overview of risk allocation between construction parties. *Procedia Engineering, 57*, 889–894.

Pitsis, T.S., Clegg, S.R., Marosszeky, M., & Rura-Polley, T. (2003). Constructing the Olympic Dream: A Future perfect strategy of project management. *Organization Science, 14*(5), 574–590.

Pries, K.H., & Quigley, J.M. (2010). *Scrum Project Management*. Boca Raton, FL: CRC Press.

Project Management Institute (2017). *Agile Practice Guide*. Philadelphia, PN: PMI.

Rotter, T., Plishka, C., Lawal, A., Harrison, L., Sari, N., Goodridge, D., ... & Willoughby, K. (2019). What is lean Management in Health Care? Development of an operational definition for a Cochrane systematic review. *Evaluation & the health professions, 42*(3), 366–390.

Sastoque, L.M., Arboleda, C.A., & Ponz, J.L. (2016). A proposal for risk allocation in social infrastructure projects applying PPP in Colombia. *Procedia Engineering, 145*, 1354–1361.

Schön, D.A. (1992). The theory of inquiry: Dewey's legacy to education. *Curriculum Inquiry, 22*(2), 119. Available at: https://doi.org/10.1080/03626784.1992.11076093 (accessed 27 January 2020).

Serrador, P., & Pinto, J.K. (2015). Does Agile work? A quantitative analysis of agile project success. *International Journal of Project Management, 33*(5), 1040–1051. Available at: http://dx.doi.org/10.1016/j.ijproman.2015.01.006 (accessed 27 January 2020).

Smyth, H.J. (2014). *Relationship Management and the Management of Projects*. New York: Routledge.

Takeuchi, H., & Nonaka, I. (1986). The new new product development game. *Harvard Business Review, 64*, 137.

Trullen, J., & Bartunek, J.M. (2007). What a design approach offers to organization development. *The Journal of Applied Behavioral Science, 43*(1), 23–40. Available at: https://doi.org/10.1177/0021886306297549 (accessed 27 January 2020).

Turner, J.R. (2017). *Contracting for Project Management*. London: Routledge.

University of Technology Sydney (2015). Introducing the Frank Gehry designed Dr Chau Chak Wing Building, now home to UTS Business School. Available at: www.youtube.com/watch?v=G5Z-QjSo8Nc (accessed 24 February 2020).

van Oorschot, K.E., Sengupta, K., & Van Wassenhove, L.N. (2018). Under pressure: The effects of iteration lengths on agile software development performance. *Project Management Journal, 49*(6), 78–102. Available at: https://doi.org/10.1177/8756972818802714 (accessed 27 January 2020).

van Veen, A. R. (2017) Atkins Norway – Lean and Agile approach to Bergen Art and Design School. Available at: www.youtube.com/watch?v=GyL11KJDB2k (accessed 24 February 2020).

Wang, W., Chen, Y., Zhang, S., & Wang, Y. (2018). Contractual complexity in construction projects: Conceptualization, operationalization, and validation. *Project Management Journal*, *49*(3), 46–61. Available at: https://doi.org/10.1177/8756972818770589 (accessed 27 January 2020).

Wheelwright, S.C., & Clark, K.B. (1992). *Revolutionizing Product Development: Quantum Leaps in Speed, Efficiency, and Quality*. New York: Simon and Schuster.

Williams, T. (2017). The nature of risk in complex projects. *Project Management Journal*, *48*(4), 55–66. Available at: https://doi.org/10.1177/875697281704800405 (accessed 27 January 2020).

Zaghloul, R., & Hartman, F.T. (2002). Reducing contract cost: The trust issue. *AACE International Transactions*, CD161.

Chapter 6

Allen, T.J. (1977). *Managing the Flow of Technology: Technology Transfer and the Dissemination of Technological Information within the R&D Organization*. Cambridge, MA: MIT Press.

Andersen, E.S. (2008). *Rethinking Project Management: An Organisational Perspective*. Harlow: Prentice Hall/Financial Times.

Andersen, E.S., Grude, K.V., & Haug, T. (2009). *Goal Directed Project Management: Effective Techniques and Strategies* (3rd edn). London: Kogan Page Publishers.

Argote, L. (1982). Input uncertainty and organizational coordination in hospital emergency units. *Administrative Science Quarterly*, *27*, 420–434.

Argyris, C., & Schön, D.A. (1996). *Organizational Learning II: Theory, Method, and Practice*. Reading, MA: Addison-Wesley.

Bechky, B.A. (2006). Gaffers, gofers, and grips: Role-based coordination in temporary organizations. *Organization Science*, *17*(1), 3–21.

Bechky, B.A., & Okhuysen, G.A. (2011). Expecting the unexpected? How SWAT officers and film crews handle surprises. *Academy of Management Journal*, *54*(2), 239–261. Available at: https://doi.org/10.5465/amj.2011.60263060 (accessed 30 January 2020).

Berggren, C., Järkvik, J., & Söderlund, J. (2008). Lagomizing, organic integration, and systems emergency wards: Innovative practices in managing complex systems development projects. *Project Management Journal*, *39*(1), S111–S122.

Bourne, L., & Walker, D.H.T. (2005). Visualising and mapping stakeholder influence. *Management Decision*, *43*(5), 649–660. Available at: https://doi.org/10.1108/00251740510597680 (accessed 30 January 2020).

Bresnen, M., & Marshall, N. (2002). The engineering or evolution of co-operation? A tale of two partnering projects. *International Journal of Project Management*, *20*(7), 497–505.

Buchanan, D.A., & Badham, R.J. (2020). *Power, Politics and Organizational Change: Winning the Turf Game*. (3rd ed.) London: SAGE.

Bygballe, L.E., Swärd, A.R., & Vaagaasar, A.L. (2016). Coordinating in construction projects and the emergence of synchronized readiness. *International Journal of Project Management*, *34*(8), 1479–1492. Available at: http://dx.doi.org/10.1016/j.ijproman.2016.08.006 (accessed 30 January 2020).

Cicmil, S., & Marshall, D. (2005). Insights into collaboration at the project level: Complexity, social interaction and procurement mechanisms. *Building Research & Information*, *33*(6), 523–535.

Clegg, S.R. (1975/2013). *Power, Rule and Domination: A Critical and Empirical Understanding of Power in Sociological Theory and Organizational Life*. London: Routledge & Kegan Paul.

Clegg, S.R. (1989). *Frameworks of Power*. London: Sage Publications.

Clegg, S.R. (2019). Governmentality. *Project Management Journal*, *50*(3), 266–270.

Clegg, S.R., & Haugaard, M. (2009). *The SAGE Handbook of Power*. London: SAGE Publications.

Clegg, S.R., & Kreiner, K. (2013). Power and politics in construction projects. In N. Drouin, R. Müller, & S. Sankaran (eds), *Novel Approaches to Organizational Project Management*

Research: Translational and Transformational. Copenhagen: Copenhagen Business School Press DK.

Clegg, S.R., Pitsis, T.S., Rura-Polley, T., & Marosszeky, M. (2002). Governmentality matters: Designing an alliance culture of inter-organizational collaboration for managing projects. *Organization Studies, 23*(3), 317–337.

Clegg, S.R., Hardy, C., Lawrence, T.B., & Nord, W.R. (2006). *The SAGE Handbook of Organization Studies*. London: SAGE Publications.

Clegg, S.R., Kornberger, M., Pitsis, T., & Mount, M. (2019). *Managing and Organizations: An Introduction to Theory and Practice* (5th edn). London: SAGE.

Clegg, S.R., Pitelis, C., Schweitzer, J., & Whittle, A. (2020). *Strategy: Theory & Practice*. London: Sage.

Deal, T.E., & Kennedy, A.A. (1982). *Corporate Cultures: The Rites and Rituals of Corporate Life*. Reading, MA: Addison-Wesley.

Elstad, B. and De Paoli, D. (2014). *Organisering og ledelse av kunst og kultur*. Cappelen Damm akademisk.

Engwall, M., & Jerbrant, A. (2003). The resource allocation syndrome: The prime challenge of multi-project management? *International Journal of Project Management, 21*(6), 403–409. Available at: https://doi.org/10.1016/S0263-7863(02)00113-8 (accessed 30 January 2020).

Eskerod, P. (1998). The human resource allocation process when organising by projects. In R.A. Lundin & C. Midler (eds), *Projects as Arenas for Renewal and Learning Processes* (pp. 125–131). Boston, MA: Springer US.

Feldman, M.S., & Pentland, B.T. (2003). Reconceptualizing organizational routines as a source of flexibility and change. *Administrative Science Quarterly, 48*(1), 94–118.

Feldman, M.S., & Rafaeli, A. (2002). Organizational routines as sources of connections and understandings. *Journal of Management Studies, 39*(3), 309–331.

Flyvbjerg, B. (2002). Bringing power to planning research: One researcher's praxis story. *Journal of Planning Education and Research, 21*(4), 353–366. Available at: https://doi.org/10.1177/0739456X0202100401 (accessed 30 January 2020).

Flyvbjerg, B., Bruzelius, N., & Rothengatter, W. (2003). *Megaprojects and Risk: An Anatomy of Ambition*. Cambridge: Cambridge University Press.

Gersick, C.J., & Hackman, J.R. (1990). Habitual routines in task-performing groups. *Organizational Behavior and Human Decision Processes, 47*(1), 65–97.

Hackman, J.R. (2002). *Leading Teams: Setting the Stage for Great Performances*. Boston: Harvard Business School Press.

Halman, J.I., & Burger, G. (2002). Evaluating effectiveness of project start-ups: An exploratory study. *International Journal of Project Management, 20*(1), 81–89.

Hargadon, A.B. (2002). Brokering knowledge: Linking learning and innovation. *Research in Organizational Behavior, 24*, 41–85.

Helm, J., & Remington, K. (2005). Effective project sponsorship: An evaluation of the role of the executive sponsor in complex infrastructure projects by senior project managers. *Project Management Journal, 36*(3), 51–61.

Hickson, D.J., Hinings, C.R., Lee, C., Schneck, R., & Pennings, J. (1971). A strategic contingencies theory of intra-organizational power. *Administrative Science Quarterly, 16*, 216–229.

Hickson, D.J., Pugh, D.S., & Pheysey, D.C. (1969). Operations technology and organization structure: An empirical reappraisal. *Administrative Science Quarterly, 14*(3), 378–397. Available at: https://doi.org/10.2307/2391134 (accessed 30 January 2020).

Hodgson, D., & Cicmil, S. (2007). The politics of standards in modern management: Making 'the project' a reality. *Journal of Management Studies, 44*(3), 431–450. Available at: https://doi.org/10.1111/j.1467–6486.2007.00680.x (accessed 30 January 2020).

Hofstede, G. (2001). *Culture's Consequences: Comparing Values, Behaviors, Institutions, and Organizations Across Nations*. Thousand Oaks, CA: Sage.

Hydle, K.M., Kvålshaugen, R., & Breunig, K.J. (2014). Transnational practices in communities of task and communities of learning. *Management Learning, 45*(5), 609–629.

Janis, I.L. (1972). *Victims of Groupthink: A Psychological Study of Foreign Policy Decisions and Fiascoes*. Atlanta, GA: Houghton Mifflin.

Jugdev, K., & Müller, R. (2005). A retrospective look at our evolving understanding of project success. *Project Management Journal, 36*(4), 19–31.

Kamoche, K., & Cunha, M.P.E. (2001). Minimal structures: From jazz improvisation to product innovation. *Organization Studies, 22*(5), 733–764.

King, W.R., & Cleland, D.I. (1975). The design of management information systems: An information analysis approach. *Management Science, 22*(3), 286–297.

Kniberg, H. (2012). Agile product ownership in a nutshell. Available at: www.youtube.com/watch?v=502ILHjX9EE (accessed 24 February 2020).

Koskinen, K.U. (2008). Boundary brokering as a promoting factor in competence sharing in a project work context. *International Journal of Project Organisation and Management, 1*(1), 119–132.

Kreiner, K. (1995). In search of relevance: Project management in drifting environments. *Scandinavian Journal of Management, 11*(4), 335–346. Available at: https://doi.org/10.1016/0956–5221(95)00029-U (accessed 30 January 2020).

Lappi, T., Karvonen, T., Lwakatare, L. E., Aaltonen, K., & Kuvaja, P. (2018). Toward an improved understanding of agile project governance: a systematic literature review. *Project Management Journal, 49*(6), 39–63.

Larson, E.W., & Gobeli, D.H. (1987). Matrix management: Contradictions and insights. *California Management Review, 29*(4), 126. Available at: https://doi.org/10.2307/41162135 (accessed 30 January 2020).

Latour, B. (1988). *The Pasteurization of France*. Cambridge, MA: Harvard University Press.

Latour, B. (1996). *Aramis, or The Love of Technology*. Cambridge, MA: Harvard University Press.

Lechler, T.G., & Cohen, M. (2009). Exploring the role of steering committees in realizing value from project management. *Project Management Journal, 40*(1), 42–54.

Lukes, S. (2005). *Power: A Radical View* (2nd edn). Basingstoke: Palgrave Macmillan.

Maher, L. (2018). Parliament House construction milestones and their symbols to help form new display, ABC Radio Canberra. Available at: https://mobile.abc.net.au/news/2018–01–24/treasure-trove-parliament-house-construction-objects/9314620?pfmredir=sm&source=rss (accessed 25 February 2020).

Martin, J. (1992). *Cultures in Organizations: Three Perspectives*. New York: Oxford University Press.

Martin, J., Feldman, M.S., Hatch, M.J., & Sitkin, S.B. (1983). The uniqueness paradox in organizational stories. *Administrative Science Quarterly, 28*(3), 438–453. Available at: https://doi.org/10.2307/2392251 (accessed 30 January 2020).

Meso, P., & Jain, R. (2006). Agile software development: Adaptive systems principles and rest practices. *Information Systems Management, 23*(3), 19–30. Available at: https://doi.org/10.1201/1078.10580530/46108.23.3.20060601/93704.3 (accessed 30 January 2020).

Miller, R., & Lessard, D.R. (2000). *The Strategic Management of Large Engineering Projects: Shaping Institutions, Risks, and Governance*. Cambridge, MA: MIT Press.

Morris, P.W., Pinto, J.K., & Söderlund, J. (2011). *The Oxford Handbook of Project Management*. Oxford: Oxford University Press.

Muller, R. (2009). *Project Governance: Fundamentals of Project Management*. Farnham: Gower.

Müller, R., & Lecoeuvre, L. (2014). Operationalizing governance categories of projects. *International Journal of Project Management, 32*(8), 1346–1357. Available at: http://dx.doi.org/10.1016/j.ijproman.2014.04.005 (accessed 30 January 2020).

Müller, R., & Turner, J.R. (2005). The impact of principal–agent relationship and contract type on communication between project owner and manager. *International Journal of Project Management, 23*(5), 398–403. Available at: http://dx.doi.org/10.1016/j.ijproman.2005.03.001 (accessed 30 January 2020).

Nelson, R. R., & Winter, S. G. (1982). *An Evolutionary Theory of Economic Change*. Harvard, MA: Harvard University Press.

Nerur, S., & Balijepally, V. (2007). Theoretical reflections on agile development methodologies: The traditional goal of optimization and control is making way for learning and innovation. *Commun. ACM, 50*(3), 79–83. Available at: http://doi.org/10.1145/1226736.1226739 (accessed 30 January 2020).

Ninan, J., Mahalingam, A., & Clegg, S.R. (2019). External stakeholder management strategies and resources in megaprojects: An organizational power perspective. *Project Management Journal, 50*(6). Available at: https://doi.org/10.1177%2F8756972819847045 (accessed 30 January 2020).

Okhuysen, G.A., & Bechky, B.A. (2009). Coordination in organizations: An integrative perspective. *The Academy of Management Annals, 3*(1), 463–502.

Partogi, J. (2020). What are the differences between project manager and scrum master. Available at: www.youtube.com/watch?v=7TyOlxmoOYo (accessed 24 February 2020).

Perrow, C. (1967). A framework for the comparative analysis of organizations. *American Sociological Review, 32*(2), 194. Available at: https://doi.org/10.2307/2091811 (accessed 30 January 2020).

Pfeffer, J., & Salancik, G.R. (2003). *The External Control of Organizations: A Resource Dependence Perspective.* Stanford, CA: Stanford Business Books.

Pinto, M.B., Pinto, J.K., & Prescott, J.E. (1993). Antecedents and consequences of project team cross-functional cooperation. *Management Science, 39*(10), 1281–1297.

Pitsis, T.S., Clegg, S.R., Marosszeky, M., and Rura-Polley, T. (2003). Constructing the Olympic Dream: Managing innovation through the future Perfect. *Organization Science,* (14)5, 574–590.

Schein, E.H. (2010). *Organizational Culture and Leadership* (4th edn). San Fransisco, CA: Jossey-Bass.

Schön, D.A. (1983). *The Reflective Practitioner: How Professionals Think in Action.* London: Routledge.

Serrador, P., & Pinto, J.K. (2015). Does Agile work? A quantitative analysis of agile project success. *International Journal of Project Management, 33*(5), 1040–1051. Available at: http://dx.doi.org/10.1016/j.ijproman.2015.01.006 (accessed 30 January 2020).

Shenhar, A.J. (2001). One size does not fit all projects: Exploring classical contingency domains. *Management Science, 47*(3), 394–414.

Shenhar, A.J., & Dvir, D. (2007). *Reinventing Project Management: The Diamond Approach to Successful Growth and Innovation.* Boston, MA: Harvard Business School Press.

Star, S.L., & Griesemer, J.R. (1989). Institutional ecology, translations and boundary objects: Amateurs and professionals in Berkeley's Museum of Vertebrate Zoology, 1907–39. *Social Studies of Science, 19*(3), 387–420.

Suchman, M.C. (1995). Managing legitimacy: Strategic and institutional approaches. *Academy of Management Review, 20*(3), 571–610.

Swan, J., Scarbrough, H., & Newell, S. (2010). Why don't (or do) organizations learn from projects? *Management Learning, 41*(3), 325–344.

Swärd, A. (2013). *Trust Processes in Fixed-duration Alliances: A Multi-level, Multi-dimensional, and Temporal View on Trust.* Oslo: BI Norwegian Business School.

Tabassi, A. A., Abdullah, A., & Bryde, D. J. (2019). Conflict management, team coordination, and performance within multicultural temporary projects: Evidence from the construction industry. *Project Management Journal, 50*(1), 101–114.

Takeuchi, H., & Nonaka, I. (1986). The new new product development game. *Harvard Business Review, 64*, 137.

Thompson, J.D. (1967). *Organizations in Action: Social Science Bases of Administrative Theory.* New York: McGraw-Hill.

Trice, H.M., & Beyer, J.M. (1993). *The Cultures of Work Organizations.* Englewood Cliffs, NJ: Prentice Hall.

Trottier, J. & Forrest, M.-A. (2018). Collaborative creativity: beyond traditional methods https://www.youtube.com/watch?v=rvPnWtHIaVs (accessed 24 February 2020).

Turner, J.R., & Keegan, A. (2001). Mechanisms of governance in the project-based organization: Roles of the broker and steward. *European Management Journal, 19*(3), 254–267.

Turner, J.R., & Müller, R. (2005). The project manager's leadership style as a success factor on projects: A literature review. *Project Management Journal, 36*(2), 49–61.

Unterhitzenberger, C., & Bryde, D. J. (2019). Organizational justice, project performance, and the mediating effects of key success factors. *Project Management Journal, 50*(1), 57–70.

Vaagaasar, A.L. (2006). *From Tool to Actor: How a Project Came to Orchestrate its own Life and that of Others*. Oslo: Handelshøyskolen BI.

Vaagaasar, A.L. (2015). A spatial perspective to leadership in knowledge-intensive projects. In A. Ropo, S. Perttu, E. Sauer, & D. De Paoli (eds), *Leadership, Spaces and Organizing*. Cheltenham: Edward Elgar.

van Marrewijk, A.H., Ybema, S.B., Smits, K.C.M., Clegg, S.R., & Pitsis, T. (2016). Clash of the Titans: Temporal organizing and collaborative dynamics in the Panama Canal Megaproject. *Organization Studies, 37*(12), 1745–1769. Available at: http://doi.org/10.1177/0170840616655489 (accessed 30 January 2020)

Ven, A.H.V.D., Delbecq, A.L., & Koenig, R. (1976). Determinants of coordination modes within organizations. *American Sociological Review, 41*(2), 322. Available at: http://doi.org/10.2307/2094477 (accessed 30 January 2020).

Weber, M. (1978). *Economy and Society: An Outline of Interpretive Sociology* (Vol. *2*). Berkeley, CA: University of California Press.

Wheelwright, S.C., & Clark, K.B. (1992). *Revolutionizing Product Development: Quantum Leaps in Speed, Efficiency, and Quality*. New York: Simon & Schuster.

Wiley, V.D., Deckro, R.F., & Jackson Jr, J.A. (1998). Optimization analysis for design and planning of multi-project programs. *European Journal of Operational Research, 107*(2), 492–506.

Woodward, J. (1958). *Management and Technology* (Vol. *5*). London: HMSO.

Zaker, R., & Coloma, E. (2018). Virtual reality-integrated workflow in BIM-enabled projects collaboration and design review: A case study. *Visualization in Engineering, 6*(1), 4. Available at: http://doi.org/10.1186/s40327-018–0065–6 (accessed 30 January 2020).

Chapter 7

Alvehus, J. (2019). Emergent, distributed, and orchestrated: Understanding leadership through frame analysis. Leadership, *15*(5), 535–554. Available at: http://doi.org/10.1177/1742715018773832 (accessed 31 January 2020).

Amundsen, S., & Martinsen, Ø.L. (2014). Empowering leadership: Construct clarification, conceptualization, and validation of a new scale. *The Leadership Quarterly, 25*(3), 487–511. Available at: http://dx.doi.org/10.1016/j.leaqua.2013.11.009 (accessed 31 January 2020).

Andersen, E.S. (2008). *Rethinking Project Management: An Organisational Perspective*. Harlow: Prentice Hall/Financial Times.

Amabile, T. (2011). The Progress principle, Ted Talk, 12 October. Available at: www.youtube.com/watch?v=XD6N8bsjOEEA (accessed 25 February 2020).

Arnulf, J.K. (2014). *A Brief Introduction to Leadership*. Oslo: Universitetsforlaget.

Barrick, M.R., & Mount, M.K. (1991). The big five personality dimensions and job performance: A meta-analysis. *Personnel Psychology, 44*(1), 1–26.

Bass, B.M., & Bass, R.R. (2008). *The Bass Handbook of Leadership: Theory, Research, and Managerial Applications*. New York: Free Press.

Bass, B.M., & Riggio, R.E. (2006). *Transformational Leadership*. Mahwah, NJ: L. Erlbaum Associates.

Birkinshaw, J. (2013). *Becoming a Better Boss: Why Good Management is so Difficult*. San Francisco, CA: Jossey-Bass.

Bredillet, C., Tywoniak, S., & Dwivedula, R. (2015). What is a good project manager? An Aristotelian perspective. *International Journal of Project Management, 33*(2), 254–266. Available at: http://dx.doi.org/10.1016/j.ijproman.2014.04.001 (accessed 31 January 2020).

Briner, W., Geddes, M., & Hastings, C. (1993). *Project Leadership*. Farnham: Gower.

Burns, J.M. (1978). *Leadership*. New York: Harper & Row.

Cain, S. (2013). *Quiet: The Power of Introverts in a World that Can't Stop Talking*. New York: Broadway Books.

Clegg, S.R., & Courpasson, D. (2004). Political hybrids: Tocquevillean views on project organizations. *Journal of Management Studies, 41*(4), 525–547.

Clegg, S.R., Courpasson, D., & Phillips, N. (2006). *Power and Organizations*. London: Sage.

Clegg, S.R., Kornberger, M., Pitsis, T., & Mount, M. (2019). *Managing and Organizations: An Introduction to Theory and Practice* (5th edn). London: SAGE.

Clegg, S.R., Pitelis, C., Schweitzer, J., & Whittle, A. (2020). *Strategy; Theory and Practice* (3rd edn). London: Sage.

Crawford, L., Morris, P., Thomas, J., & Winter, M. (2006). Practitioner development: From trained technicians to reflective practitioners. *International Journal of Project Management, 24*(8), 722–733.

Crevani, L., Lindgren, M., & Packendorff, J. (2010). Leadership, not leaders: On the study of leadership as practices and interactions. *Scandinavian Journal of Management, 26*(1), 77–86.

Cuddy, A. (2012). Your body language may shape who you are. Available at: www.youtube.com/watch?v=Ks-_Mh1QhMc (accessed 25 February 2020).

Czarniawska, B., & Sevón, G. (2003). *The Northern Lights: Organization Theory in Scandinavia*. Malmö: Abstrakt.

Daney, L. (2013) The introverts guide to surviving teamwork, *Psychology Today*, 14 August. Available at: www.psychologytoday.com/au/blog/making-your-team-work/201308/the-introverts-guide-surviving-teamwork (accessed 25 February 2020).

Davies, A. (2017). *Projects: A Very Short Introduction*. Oxford: Oxford University Press.

Davies, A., & Hobday, M. (2005). *The Business of Projects: Managing Innovation in Complex Products and Systems*. Cambridge: Cambridge University Press.

De Meyer, A., Loch, C., & Pich, M. (2002). Managing project uncertainty: From variation to chaos. *MIT Sloan Management Review, 43*(2), 60–67.

Drouin, Nathalie & Müller, Ralf, & Sankaran, Shankar. (2018). Balancing vertical and horizontal leadership in projects: Empirical studies from Australia, Canada, Norway and Sweden. *International Journal of Managing Projects in Business. 11*(4), 986–1006.

Dwivedula, R., & Bredillet, C.N. (2010). Profiling work motivation of project workers. *International Journal of Project Management, 28*(2), 158–165.

Dysvik, A., & Kuvaas, B. (2013). Intrinsic and extrinsic motivation as predictors of work effort: The moderating role of achievement goals. *British Journal of Social Psychology, 52*(3), 42–430. Available at: http://doi.org/10.1111/j.2044–8309.2011.02090.x (accessed 31 January 2020).

Dysvik, A., Buch, R., & Kuvaas, B. (2015). Knowledge donating and knowledge collecting: The moderating roles of social and economic LMX. *Leadership and Organization Development Journal, 36*(1), 35–53. Available at: http://doi.org/10.1108/LODJ-11–2012-0145 (accessed 31 January 2020).

Flyvbjerg, B., Bruzelius, N., & Rothengatter, W. (2003). *Megaprojects and Risk: An Anatomy of Ambition*. Cambridge: Cambridge University Press.

Frame, J.D. (2003). *Managing Projects in Organizations: How to Make the Best Use of Time, Techniques, and People* (3rd edn). San Francisco, CA: Jossey-Bass.

George, B. (2003). *Authentic Leadership: Rediscovering the Secrets to Creating Lasting Value*: Chicester: John Wiley & Sons.

Grant, A. (2018). Your hidden personality, *Ted Talks*. Available at: www.ted.com/talks/worklife_with_adam_grant_is_your_personality_more_flexible_than_you_think (accessed 25 February 2020).

Gruden, N., & Stare, A. (2018). The influence of behavioral competencies on project performance. *Project Management Journal, 49*(3), 98–109. Available at: http://doi.org/10.1177/8756972818770841 (accessed 31 January 2020).

Hackman, J.R. (2002). *Leading Teams: Setting the Stage for Great Performances*. Boston, MA: Harvard Business School Press.

Hackman, J.R. (2011). *Collaborative Intelligence: Using Teams to Solve Hard Problems*. San Francisco: Berrett-Koehler.

Hobsbawn, E.J. (1975). *The Age of Capital*. London: Weidenfield & Nicholson.

Hoegl, M., & Gemuenden, H.G. (2001). Teamwork quality and the success of innovative projects: A theoretical concept and empirical evidence. *Organization Science, 12*(4), 435–449.

Hoskin, K., Macve, R., & Stone, J. (1997). The Historical Genesis of Modern Business and Military Strategy: 1850–1950. Paper presented at the Proceedings of the Interdisciplinary Perspectives on Accounting Conference, Manchester.

Judge, T.A., Heller, D., & Mount, M.K. (2002). Five-factor model of personality and job satisfaction: A meta-analysis. *Journal of Applied Psychology, 87*(3), 530.

Keegan, A.E., & Den Hartog, D.N. (2004). Transformational leadership in a project-based environment: A comparative study of the leadership styles of project managers and line managers. *International Journal of Project Management, 22*(8), 609–617.

Keller, R.T. (2006). Transformational leadership, initiating structure, and substitutes for leadership: A longitudinal study of research and development project team performance. *Journal of Applied Psychology, 91*(1), 202.

Koeslag, M., van den Bossche, P., Hoven, M., van der Klink, M.R., & Gijselaers, W. (2018). When leadership powers team learning: A meta-analysis. *Small Group Research, 49*(4), 475–513. Available at: http://doi.org/10.1177/1046496418764824 (accessed 31 January 2020).

Kreiner, K. (1995). In search of relevance: Project management in drifting environments. *Scandinavian Journal of Management, 11*(4), 335–346. Available at: http://doi.org/10.1016/0956–5221(95)00029-U (accessed 31 January 2020).

Laub, J.A. (1999). *Assessing the Servant Organization. Development of the Organizational Leadership Assessment (OLA) Instrument.* Dissertation, Florida Atlantic University.

Lindgren, M., & Packendorff, J. (2009). Project leadership revisited: Towards distributed leadership perspectives in project research. *International Journal of Project Organisation and Management, 1*(3), 285–308.

Lindgren, M., Packendorff, J., & Sergi, V. (2014). Thrilled by the discourse, suffering through the experience: Emotions in project-based work. *Human Relations, 67*(11), 1383–1412.

Lloyd-Walker, B., & Walker, D. (2011). Authentic leadership for 21st century project delivery. *International Journal of Project Management, 29*(4), 383–395.

Machiavelli, N. (1961). *The Prince.* London: Penguin Books.

Meyer, M.W., & Zucker, L.G. (1989). *Permanently Failing Organizations.* Thousand Oaks, CA: Sage Publications.

Meyerson, D., Weick, K.E., & Kramer, R.M. (1996). Swift Trust and Temporary Groups. In R.K.T. Tyler (ed.), *Trust in Organizations: Frontiers of Theory and Research* (pp. 166–196). Thousand Oaks, CA: SAGE Publications, Inc.

Mintzberg, H. (2004). *Managers not MBAs: A Hard Look at the Soft Practice of Managing and Management Development.* San Francisco, CA: Berrett-Koehler.

Mintzberg, H. (2009). *Managing.* San Francisco, CA: Berrett-Koehler.

Müller, R, Drouin, N. and Shankar, S. (2019). *Organizational Project Management: Theory and Implementation.* Cheltenham: Elgar.

Müller, R., & Turner, J.R. (2010). *Project-oriented Leadership.* Farnham: Gower.

Müller, R., & Turner, R. (2007). The influence of project managers on project success criteria and project success by type of project. *European Management Journal, 25*(4), 298–309. Available at: http://dx.doi.org/10.1016/j.emj.2007.06.003 (accessed 31 January 2020).

Northouse, P.G. (2017). *Introduction to Leadership: Concepts and Practice.* London: Sage Publications.

Obenauer, W. (2015). The Big Five Personality Model. Available at: www.youtube.com/watch?v=gtiRNxd_qL4 (accessed 25 February 2020).

Petridis, A. (2019). Stormzy at Glastonbury 2019 review – a glorious victory lap for black British culture. *Guardian*, 29 June. Available at: www.theguardian.com/music/2019/jun/29/stormzy-glastonbury-review-pyramid-stage (accessed 31 January 2020).

Pfeffer, J., & Sutton, R.I. (2006). *Hard facts, Dangerous Half-truths, and Total Nonsense: Profiting from Evidence-based Management.* Boston, MA: Harvard Business School Press.

Pinto, J.K., & Slevin, D.P. (1989). The project champion: Key to implementation success. *Project Management Journal, 20*(4), 15–20.

Prencipe, A., & Tell, F. (2001). Inter-project learning: Processes and outcomes of knowledge codification in project-based firms. *Research Policy, 30*(9), 1373–1394. Available at: http://doi.org/10.1016/S0048-7333(01)00157-3 (accessed 31 January 2020).

Ritzer, G. (2008). *The McDonaldization of Society*. Los Angeles, CA: Pine Forge Press.

Schön, D.A. (1991). *The Reflective Practitioner: How Professionals Think in Action*. Aldershot: Avebury.

Selznick, P. (1949). *TVA and the Grass Roots: A Study in the Sociology of Formal Organization*. Berkeley, CA: University of California Press.

Shenhav, Y. (1999). *Manufacturing Rationality: The Engineering Foundations of the Managerial Revolution*. Oxford: Oxford University Press.

Shenhav, Y. (2003). The historical and epistemological foundations of organization theory: Fusing sociological theory with engineering discourse. In H. Tsoukas & C. Knudsen (eds), *The Oxford Handbook of Organization Theory* (pp. 183–209). Oxford: Oxford University Press.

Tabassi, A.A., Roufechaei, K.M., Bakar, A.H.A., & Yusof, N.A. (2017). Linking Team condition and team performance: A transformational leadership approach. *Project Management Journal*, *48*(2), 22–38. Available at: https://doi.org/10.1177/875697281704800203 (accessed 31 January 2020).

Taylor, F.W. (1911). *The Principles of Scientific Management*. New York: Harper & Brothers.

Thompson, K.N. (2010). *Servant-leadership: An Effective Model for Project Management*. Doctoral dissertation, Capella University, Minnesota.

Thucydides (1963) *History of the Peloponnesian War* (revised edition) London: Penguin.

Turner, J.R. (1999). *The Handbook of Project-based Management: Improving the Processes for Achieving Strategic Objectives* (2nd edn). London: McGraw-Hill.

Tuffley, D. (2017). How to manage self-motivated, intelligent workers, *The Conversation*, 26 February. Available at: https://theconversation.com/how-to-manage-self-motivated-intelligent-workers-72668 (accessed 17 June 2020).

Turner, J.R., & Müller, R. (2005). The project manager's leadership style as a success factor on projects: A literature review. *Project Management Journal*, *36*(2), 49–61.

Tyssen, A.K., Wald, A., & Heidenreich, S. (2014a). Leadership in the context of temporary organizations: A study on the effects of transactional and transformational leadership on followers' commitment in projects. *Journal of Leadership & Organizational Studies*, *21*(4), 376–393. Available at: http://doi.org/10.1177/1548051813502086 (accessed 31 January 2020).

Tyssen, A.K., Wald, A., & Spieth, P. (2014b). The challenge of transactional and transformational leadership in projects. *International Journal of Project Management*, *32*(3), 365–375. Available at: http://dx.doi.org/10.1016/j.ijproman.2013.05.010 (accessed 31 January 2020).

van Marrewijk, A., Ybema, S., Smits, K., Clegg, S.R., & Pitsis, T. (2016). Clash of the Titans: Temporal organizing and collaborative dynamics in the Panama Canal Megaproject. *Organization Studies*, *37*(12), 1745–1769. Available at: http://doi.org/10.1177/0170840616655489 (accessed 31 January 2020).

Vaughan, D. (1996). *The Challenger Launch Decision: Risky Technology, Culture, and Deviance at NASA*. Chicago: University of Chicago Press.

Von Bertalanffy, L. (1968). *General System Theory*. New York: George Braziller.

Watts, S.L. (1991). *Order Against Chaos: Business Culture and Labor Ideology in America, 1880–1915*. New York: Greenwood Press.

William-Grut, O. (2016). Deutsche Bank, Airbnb, and McKinsey use this personality test to find 'millennial talent'. *The Independent*, 6 October. Available at: www.independent.co.uk/news/business/deutsche-bank-airbnb-and-mckinsey-use-this-personality-test-to-find-a7348636.html (accessed 25 February 2020).

Wright, K. (2013). Leadership – engage your team – create a culture of engagement. Available at: www.youtube.com/watch?v=IZA94smSkQg (accessed 25 February 2020).

Yu, L., & Zellmer-Bruhn, M. (2018). Introducing team mindfulness and considering its safeguard role against conflict transformation and social undermining. *Academy of Management Journal*, *61*(1), 324–347.

Yukl, G.A. (2013). *Leadership in Organizations*. Boston, MA: Pearson Education.

Zika-Wiktorsson, A., Sundström, P., & Engwall, M. (2006). Project Overload: An exploratory study of work and management in multi-project settings. *International Journal of Project Management*, *24*(5), 385–394. Available at: http://doi.org/10.1016/j.ijproman.2006.02.010 (accessed 31 January 2020).

Chapter 8

Aime, F., Humphrey, S., Derue, D.S., & Paul, J.B. (2014). The riddle of heterarchy: Power transitions in cross-functional teams. *Academy of Management Journal, 57*(2), 327–352. Available at: https://doi.org/10.5465/amj.2011.0756 (accessed 3 February 2020).

Allen, T., Katz, R., Grady, J., & Slavin, N. (1988). Project team aging and performance: The roles of project and functional managers. *R&D Management, 18*(4), 295–308.

Amabile, T.M., Barsade, S.G., Mueller, J.S., & Staw, B.M. (2005). Affect and creativity at work. *Administrative Science Quarterly, 50*(3), 367–403. Available at: https:/doi.org/10.2189/asqu.2005.50.3.367 (accessed 10 February 2020).

Amabile, T., & Kramer, S. (2011). *The Progress Principle: Using Small Wins to Ignite Joy, Engagement, and Creativity at Work.* Boston, MA: Harvard Business Press.

Ancona, D.G., & Caldwell, D.F. (1992). Bridging the boundary: External activity and performance in organizational teams. *Administrative Science Quarterly, 37*(4).

Argyris, C. (1957). The individual and organization: Some problems of mutual adjustment. *Administrative Science Quarterly, 2*(1), 1–24.

Asch, S.E. (1956). Studies of independence and conformity: I. A minority of one against a unanimous majority. *Psychological Monographs: General and Applied, 70*(9), 1.

Bakker, R.M., Boroș, S., Kenis, P., & Oerlemans, L.A. (2013). It's only temporary: Time frame and the dynamics of creative project teams. *British Journal of Management, 24*(3), 383–397.

Bandura, A. (1986). *Social Foundations of Thought and Action: A Social Cognitive Theory.* Englewood Cliffs, NJ: Prentice-Hall.

Bandura, A. (1997). Self-efficacy and health behaviour. *Cambridge Handbook of Psychology, Health and Medicine* (pp. 160–162).

Baum, A., Newman, S., Weinman, J., McManus, C., & West, R. (Eds.). (1997). *Cambridge Handbook of Psychology, Health and Medicine.* Cambridge: Cambridge University Press.

Bechky, B.A. (2006). Gaffers, gofers, and grips: Role-based coordination in temporary organizations. *Organization Science, 17*(1), 3–21.

Bechky, B.A., & Okhuysen, G.A. (2011). Expecting the unexpected? How SWAT officers and film crews handle surprises. *Academy of Management Journal, 54*(2), 239–261. Available at: https://doi.org/10.5465/amj.2011.60263060 (accessed 3 February 2020).

Belbin, R. M. (1993). *Team Roles at Work.* Oxford: Butterworth-Heinemann.

Belbin, R. M. (2000). *Beyond the Team.* Oxford: Butterworth-Heinemann.

Belbin, R.M. (2011). *Team Roles at Work.* Oxford: Butterworth-Heinemann.

Carte, T.A., Chidambaram, L., & Becker, A. (2006). Emergent leadership in self-managed virtual teams. *Group Decision and Negotiation, 15*(4), 323–343.

Chen, X. (2016). Groupthink Challenger Disaster. Available at: www.youtube.com/watch?v=XD6N8bsjOEEA (accessed 25 February 2020).

Cialdini, R.B. (2016). *Pre-suasion: A Revolutionary Way to Influence and Persuade.* London: Random House.

Coldevin, G.H., Carlsen, A., Clegg, S.R., Pitsis, T.S., & Antonacopoulou, E.P. (2019). Organizational creativity as idea work: Intertextual placing and legitimating imaginings in media development and oil exploration. *Human Relations, 72*(8), 1369–1397. Available at: https://doi.org/10.1177/0018726718806349 (accessed 3 February 2020).

Courpasson, D., Dany, F., & Clegg, S.R. (2012). Resisters at work: Generating productive resistance in the workplace. *Organization Science, 23*(3), 801–819.

Courtright, S.H., McCormick, B.W., Mistry, S., Wang, J., & Chen, G. (2017). Quality charters or quality members? A control theory perspective on team charters and team performance. *Journal of Applied Psychology, 102*(10), 1462–1470. Available at: https://doi.org/10.1037/apl0000229 (accessed 3 February 2020).

Coyle, D. (2018). *The Culture Code: The Secrets of Highly Successful Groups.* New York: Bantam.

Cunha, M.P.e., Clegg, S.R., Rego, A., & Neves, P. (2014). Organizational improvisation: From the constraint of strict tempo to the power of the avant-garde. *Creativity and Innovation Management, 23*(4), 359–373.

Cunha, M.P.e., Neves, P., Clegg, S.R., & Rego, A. (2015). Tales of the unexpected: Discussing improvisational learning. *Management Learning, 46*(5), 511–529. Available at: https://doi.org/10.1177/1350507614549121 (accessed 3 February 2020).

De Paoli, D. (2014). Disappearing bodies in virtual leadership? In A. Ropo (ed.), *The Physicality of Leadership: Gesture, Entanglement, Taboo, Possibilities* (Vol. *6*, pp. 59–79). Bingley: Emerald Group Publishing Limited.

DeChurch, L.A., & Mathieu, J.E. (2009). *Thinking in Terms of Multiteam Systems.* London: Routledge.

Druskat, V.U., & Kayes, D.C. (2000). Learning versus performance in short-term project teams. *Small Group Research, 31*(3), 328–353.

Duhigg, C. (2016). *Smarter Faster Better: The Secrets of Being Productive in Life and Business.* New York: Random House.

Durham, C.C., Knight, D., & Locke, E.A. (1997). Effects of leader role, team-set goal difficulty, efficacy, and tactics on team effectiveness. *Organizational Behavior and Human Decision Processes, 72*(2), 203–231. Available at: http://dx.doi.org/10.1006/obhd. 1997.2739 (accessed 3 February 2020).

Edmondson, A. (1999). Psychological safety and learning behavior in work teams. *Administrative Science Quarterly, 44*(2), 350–383.

Edmondson, A. (2002) Managing the risk of learning. In M. West (ed.), *International Handbook of Organizational Teamwork.* London: Blackwell.

Edmondson, A.C. (2012). *Teaming: How Organizations Learn, Innovate, and Compete in the Knowledge Economy.* San Francisco, CA: Jossey-Bass.

Edmondson, A. (2014). Building a psychologically safe workplace, Ted Talk, 4 May. Available at: www.youtube.com/watch?v=LhoLuui9gX8 (accessed 25 February 2020).

Edmondson, A. (2017). How to turn a group of strangers into a team, Ted Talk, October. Available at: www.ted.com/talks/amy_edmondson_how_to_turn_a_group_of_strangers_into_a_team/transcript?language=en (accessed 25 February 2020).

Edmondson, A.C. (2018). *The Fearless Organization: Creating Psychological Safety in the Workplace for Learning, Innovation, and Growth*: Hoboken, NJ: John Wiley & Sons.

Engwall, M., & Westling, G. (2004). Peripety in an R&D drama: Capturing a turnaround in project dynamics. *Organization Studies, 25*(9), 1557–1578.

Eskerod, P., & Jepsen, A.L. (2013). *Project Stakeholder Management.* Farnham: Gower.

Frame, J.D. (2003). *Managing Projects in Organizations: How to Make the Best Use of Time, Techniques, and People* (3rd edn). San Francisco, CA: Jossey-Bass.

Furst, S.A., Reeves, M., Rosen, B., & Blackburn, R. S. (2004). Managing the life cycle of virtual teams. *Academy of Management Perspectives, 18*(2), 6–20.

Gersick, C.J. (1988). Time and transition in work teams: Toward a new model of group development. *Academy of Management Journal, 31*(1), 9–41.

Giddens, A. (1991). *Modernity and Self-identity: Self and Society in the Late Modern Age.* Cambridge: Polity Press.

Gully, S.M., Incalcaterra, K.A., Joshi, A., & Beaubien, J.M. (2002). A meta-analysis of team-efficacy, potency, and performance: Interdependence and level of analysis as moderators of observed relationships. *Journal of Applied Psychology, 87*(5), 819.

Hackman, J.R. (1987). The design of work teams. In J.W. Lorsch (ed.), *Handbook of Organizational Behavior.* Englewood Cliffs, NJ: Prentice-Hall.

Hackman, J.R. (2011). *Collaborative Intelligence: Using Teams to Solve Hard Problems.* San Francisco, CA: Berrett-Koehler

Hackman, J.R., & Oldham, G.R. (1980). *Work Redesign.* Reading, MA: Addison-Wesley.

Hackman, J.R. & Wageman, R. (2004). When and How Team Leaders Matter. *Research in Organizational Behavior, 26*, 37–74.

Hackman, J.R., & Wageman, R. (2005). A theory of team coaching. *Academy of Management Review, 30*(2), 269–287. Available at: https://doi.org/10.5465/AMR.2005.16387885 (accessed 3 February 2020).

Hansen, M.T. (2018). Great at work: How to fight and unite. *Leader to Leader, 89*, 7–13. Available at: https://doi.org/10.1002/ltl.20369 (accessed 3 February 2020).

Heath, C. (1999). On the social psychology of agency relationships: Lay theories of motivation overemphasize extrinsic incentives. *Organizational Behavior and Human Decision Processes, 78*(1), 25–62.

Herzberg, F., Mausner, B., & Snyderman, B.B. (1959). *The Motivation to Work* (2nd edn). New York: Wiley.

Hobfoll, S.E. (2011). Conservation of resource caravans and engaged settings. *Journal of Occupational and Organizational Psychology, 84*(1), 116–122.

Hoegl, M., & Gemuenden, H.G. (2001). Teamwork quality and the success of innovative projects: A theoretical concept and empirical evidence. *Organization Science, 12*(4), 435–449.

Hoegl, M., & Muethel, M. (2016). Enabling shared leadership in virtual project teams: A practitioners' guide. *Project Management Journal, 47*(1), 7–12. Available at: https://doi.org/10.1002/pmj.21564 (accessed 3 February 2020).

Hoegl, M., & Proserpio, L. (2004). Team member proximity and teamwork in innovative projects. *Research Policy, 33*(8), 1153–1165.

Holland, S., Gaston, K., & Gomes, J. (2000). Critical success factors for cross-functional teamwork in new product development. *International Journal of Management Reviews, 2*(3), 231. Available at: https://doi.org/10.1111/1468-2370.00040 (accessed 3 February 2020).

Janis, I.L. (1972). *Victims of Groupthink: A Psychological Study of Foreign-policy Decisions and Fiascoes.* Atlanta, GA: Houghton Mifflin.

Katzenbach, J.R. (1998). *Teams at the Top: Unleashing the Potential of Both Teams and Individual Leaders.* Boston, MA: Harvard Business School Press.

Knoll, K., & Jarvenpaa, S.L. (1998). Working together in global virtual teams. In M. Igbaria and M. Tan (eds), *The Virtual Workplace* (pp. 2–23). Idea Group Publishing.

Larson, E.W., & Gray, C.F. (2011). *Project Management: The Managerial Process.* Boston: McGraw-Hill.

Levi, D. (2015). *Group Dynamics for Teams.* London: Sage Publications.

Locke, E.A., & Latham, G.P. (1990). *A Theory of Goal Setting & Task Performance.* Englewood Cliffs, NJ: Prentice-Hall.

Luhmann, N. (1979). *Trust and Power.* Chichester: John Wiley.

Mathieu, J.E., & Rapp, T.L. (2009). Laying the foundation for successful team performance trajectories: The roles of team charters and performance strategies. *Journal of Applied Psychology, 94*(1), 90–103. Available at: https://doi.org/10.1037/a0013257 (accessed 3 February 2020).

Mathieu, J.E., Gallagher, P.T., Domingo, M.A., & Klock, E.A. (2019). Embracing complexity: Reviewing the past decade of team effectiveness research. *Annual Review of Organizational Psychology and Organizational Behavior, 6*(1), 17–46. Available at: https://doi.org/10.1146/annurev-orgpsych-012218-015106 (accessed 3 February 2020).

McLeod, S. (2016). What is conformity? Available at: www.simplypsychology.org/conformity.html (accessed 25 February 2020).

Meyerson, D., Weick, K.E., & Kramer, R.M. (1996). Swift trust and temporary groups. In R.M. Kramer & T. Tyler (eds), *Trust in Organizations: Frontiers of Theory and Research* (pp. 166–196). Thousand Oaks, CA: SAGE Publications, Inc.

Morgan, J. (2015). Why Smaller Teams Are Better Than Larger Ones, *Forbes*, 15 April. Available at: www.forbes.com/sites/jacobmorgan/2015/04/15/why-smaller-teams-are-better-than-larger-ones/#4468a1861e68 (accessed 25 February 2020).

Mullen, B., & Copper, C. (1994). The relation between group cohesiveness and performance: An integration. *Psychological Bulletin, 115*(2), 210.

Nicolini, D. (2002). In search of 'project chemistry'. *Construction Management & Economics, 20*(2), 167–177.

Nordqvist, S., Hovmark, S., & Zika-Viktorsson, A. (2004). Perceived time pressure and social processes in project teams. *International Journal of Project Management, 22*(6), 463–468.

Pinto, M.B., & Pinto, J.K. (1990). Project team communication and cross-functional cooperation in new program development. *Journal of Product Innovation Management, 7*(3), 200–212.

Ring, P.S., & Van De Ven, A.H. (1994). Developmental processes of cooperative interorganizational relationships. *The Academy of Management Review, 19*(1), 90–118.

Roberts, L.M., Dutton, J.E., Spreitzer, G.M., Heaphy, E.D., & Quinn, R.E. (2005). Composing the reflected best-self portrait: Building pathways for becoming extraordinary in work organizations. *Academy of Management Review, 30*(4), 712–736.

Roethlisberger, F., & Dickson, W. (1939). *Management and the Worker*. Cambridge, MA: Harvard University Press.

Saunders, C.S., & Ahuja, M.K. (2006). Are all distributed teams the same? Differentiating between temporary and ongoing distributed teams. *Small Group Research, 37*(6), 662–700.

Schlesinger, A.M. (1965). *A Thousand Days: JF Kennedy in the White House*. Boston, MA: Houghton Mifflin.

Seligman, A.B. (1997). *The Problem of Trust*. Princeton, NJ: Princeton University Press.

Simmel, G. (1990). *The Philosophy of Money*. London: Routledge.

Smyth, H., Gustafsson, M., & Ganskau, E. (2010). The value of trust in project business. *International Journal of Project Management, 28*(2), 117–129. Available at: https://doi.org/10.1016/j.ijproman.2009.11.007 (accessed 3 February 2020).

Sunstein, C.R., & Hastie, R. (2015). *Wiser: Getting Beyond Groupthink to Make Groups Smarter*. Boston, MA: Harvard Business Press.

Susstein, C. (2015). Getting beyond groupthink. Available at: www.youtube.com/watch?v=7jFfx-suoZQU (accessed 25 February 2020).

Sydow, J., Lindkvist, L., & DeFillippi, R. (2004). Project-based organizations, embeddedness and repositories of knowledge. *Organization Studies, 25*(9). Available at: https://doi.org/10.1177%2F0170840604048162 (accessed 3 February 2020).

Terhorst, A., Lusher, D., Bolton, D., Elsum, I., & Wang, P. (2018). Tacit knowledge sharing in open innovation projects. *Project Management Journal, 49*(4), 5–19.

Tuckman, B.W., & Jensen, M.A.C. (1977). Stages of small-group development revisited. *Group & Organization Studies, 2*(4), 419–427.

Tuomela, R., & Tuomela, M. (2005). Cooperation and trust in group context. *Mind & Society, 4*(1), 49–84.

Turner, J.R., Anbari, F., & Bredillet, C. (2013). Perspectives on research in project management: The nine schools. *Global Business Perspectives, 1*(1), 3–28. Available at: https://doi.org/10.1007/s40196-012-0001-4 (accessed 3 February 2020).

van Marrewijk, A., Ybema, S., Smits, K., Clegg, S.R., & Pitsis, T. (2016). Clash of the Titans: Temporal organizing and collaborative dynamics in the Panama Canal megaproject. *Organization Studies, 37*(12), 1745–1769. Available at: https://doi.org/10.1177/0170840616655489 (accessed 3 February 2020).

Weick, K.E. (1984). Small wins: Redefining the scale of social problems. *American Psychologist, 39*(1), 40.

Weick, K.E. (1993). The collapse of sensemaking in organizations: The Mann Gulch disaster. *Administrative Science Quarterly, 38*(4), 628–652. Available at: https://doi.org/10.2307/2393339 (accessed 3 February 2020).

Weick, K.E. (1995). *Sensemaking in Organizations*. Thousand Oaks, CA: Sage.

West, M.A., Smith, K.G. & Tjosvold, D. (2003). *International Handbook of Organizational Teamwork and Cooperative Working* (1st ed.). GB: Wiley.

Wood, R., & Bandura, A. (1989). Social cognitive theory of organizational management. *Academy of Management Review, 14*(3), 361–384.

Wu, W.-Y., Rivas, A.A.A., & Liao, Y.-K. (2017). Influential factors for team reflexivity and new product development. *Project Management Journal, 48*(3), 20–40.

Zander, L., Mockaitis, A.I., & Butler, C.L. (2012). Leading global teams. *Journal of World Business, 47*(4), 592–603.

Zhu, Y.-Q., Gardner, D.G., & Chen, H.-G. (2018). Relationships between work team climate, individual motivation, and creativity. *Journal of Management, 44*(5), 2094–2115.

Zimbardo, P. (2012) Asch Conformity Experiment. Available at: www.youtube.com/watch?v=NyDDyT1lDhA (accessed 25 February 2020).

Chapter 9

Adner, R., & Levinthal, D.A. (2004). What is not a real option: Considering boundaries for the application of real options to business strategy. *The Academy of Management Review, 29*(1), 74–85. Available at: https:/doi.org/10.2307/20159010 (accessed 5 February 2020).

Alvarez, S.A., & Barney, J.B. (2007). Discovery and creation: Alternative theories of entrepreneurial action. *Strategic Entrepreneurship Journal, 1*(1–2), 11–26.

Argote, L. (1982). Input uncertainty and organizational coordination in hospital emergency units. *Administrative Science Quarterly, 27*(3), 420–434. Available at: https:/doi.org/10.2307/2392320 (accessed 5 February 2020).

Arrow, K.J., & Hahn, F. (1999). Notes on sequence economies, transaction costs, and uncertainty. *Journal of Economic Theory, 86*(2), 203.

Atkinson, R., Crawford, L., & Ward, S. (2006). Fundamental uncertainties in projects and the scope of project management. *International Journal of Project Management, 24*(8), 687.

Austin, R.D., Devin, L., & Sullivan, E.E. (2012). Accidental innovation: Supporting valuable unpredictability in the creative process. *Organization Science, 23*(5), 1505–1522.

Bennett, N., & Lemoine, G.J. (2014). What a difference a word makes: Understanding threats to performance in a VUCA world. *Business Horizons, 57*(3), 311–317. Available at: https://doi.org/10.1016/j.bushor.2014.01.001 (accessed 5 February 2020).

Bennis, W., & Nanus, B. (1985). *Leaders: The Strategies for Taking Charge*. New York: Harper Row.

Berggren, C., Järkvik, J., & Söderlund, J. (2008). Lagomizing, organic integration, and systems emergency wards: Innovative practices in managing complex systems development projects. *Project Management Journal, 39*(1_suppl), S111–S122.

Bewley, T.F. (1986). Knightian decision theory: Part 1. Cowles Foundation for Research in Economics Discussion Paper No. 807, Yale University.

Bewley, T.F. (2002). Knightian decision theory: Part I. *Decisions in Economics and Finance, 25*(2), 79–110.

Bradley, R., & Drechsler, M. (2014). Types of uncertainty. *An International Journal of Scientific Philosophy, 79*(6), 1225–1248. Available at: https://doi.org/10.1007/s10670-013-9518-4 (accessed 5 February 2020).

Brown, T. (2009). *Change by Design: How Design Thinking Transforms Organizations and Inspires Innovation*. New York: Collins Business.

Browning, T.R. (2019). Planning, tracking, and reducing a complex project's value at risk. *Project Management Journal, 50*(1), 71–85. Available at: https://doi.org/10.1177/8756972818810967 (accessed 5 February 2020).

Camerer, C.F., & Weber, M. (1992). Recent developments in modeling preferences uncertainty and ambiguity. *Journal of Risk and Uncertainty, 5*(4), 325–370. Available at: http:/doi.org/10.1007/BF00122575 (accessed 5 February 2020).

Chapman, C., & Ward, S. (1996). *Project Risk Management: Processes, Techniques and Insights*. John Wiley.

Chapman, C., & Ward, S. (2008). Developing and implementing a balanced incentive and risk sharing contract. *Construction Management and Economics, 26*(6), 659–669. Available at: http:/doi.org/10.1080/01446190802014760 (accessed 5 February 2020).

Chapman, C.B., & Ward, S. (2012). *How to Manage Project Opportunity and Risk: Why Uncertainty Management can be a Much Better Approach than Risk Management*. Hoboken, NJ: Wiley.

Clare, R. (2011). Top 10 mistakes made in managing project risks. Available at: www.pmi.org/learning/library/mistakes-made-managing-project-risks-6239 (accessed 25 February 2020).

Clayton, M. (2017). What is project risk management? Available at: www.youtube.com/watch?v=QgALrPHrsk4 (accessed 25 February 2020).

Clegg, S. (1975/2013). *Power, Rule and Domination: A Critical and Empirical Understanding of Power in Sociological Theory and Organizational Life*. London: Routledge & Kegan Paul.

Clegg, S.R. (1992) Contracts cause conflicts. In P. Fenn and R. Gameson (eds), *Construction Conflict Management and Resolution* (pp. 128–144). London: E and FN Spon.

Clegg, S.R., Pitsis, T., Rura-Polley, T., and Marosszeky, M. (2002) Governmentality matters: Designing an alliance culture of inter-organizational collaboration for managing projects. *Organization Studies, 23*(3), 317–337.

Clegg, S.R., Pitelis, C., Schweitzer, J., & Whittle, A. (2019). *Strategy; Theory and Practice* (3rd edn). London: Sage.

Connor-Linton, J. & Petit, M. (2010). Indexicality. Available at: www.youtube.com/watch?v=7FVE HKYz6qg (accessed 25 February 2020).

Crossan, M.M., & Apaydin, M. (2010). A multi-dimensional framework of organizational innovation: A systematic review of the literature. *Journal of management studies, 47*(6), 1154–1191.

Cyert, R.M., & March, J. G. (1963). *A Behavioral Theory of the Firm*. Englewood Cliffs, NJ: Prentice Hall.

De Meyer, A.C.L., Loch, C.H., & Pich, M.T. (2002). Managing project uncertainty: From variation to chaos. *MIT Sloan Management Review, 43*(2), 60.

Dequech, D. (2000). Fundamental uncertainty and ambiguity. *Eastern Economic Journal, 26*(1), 41–60.

Dequech, D. (2011). Uncertainty: A typology and refinements of existing concepts. *Journal of Economic Issues, 45*(3), 621–640. Available at: https:/doi.org/10.2753/JEI0021-3624450306 (accessed 5 February 2020).

Deroy, X., & Clegg, S. (2011). When events interact with business ethics. *Organization, 18*(5), 637–653. Available at: https:/doi.org/10.1177/1350508410393773 (accessed 5 February 2020).

Dosi, G., & Egidi, M. (1991). Substantive and procedural uncertainty: An exploration of economic behaviours in changing environments. *Journal of Evolutionary Economics, 1*(2), 145–168. Available at: https:/doi.org/10.1007/BF01224917 (accessed 5 February 2020).

Drummond, H. (2018). Megaproject escalation of commitment. In B. Flybjerg (ed.), *The Oxford Handbook of Megaproject Management*. Oxford: Oxford University Press.

Einhorn, H.J., & Hogarth, R.M. (1986). Decision making under ambiguity. *The Journal of Business, 59*(4), S225. Available at: https:/doi.org/10.1086/296364 (accessed 5 February 2020).

Ellsberg, D. (1961). Risk, ambiguity, and the savage axioms. *Quarterly Journal of Economics, 75*(4), 643–669. Available at: https:/doi.org/10.2307/1884324 (accessed 5 February 2020).

Feduzi, A. (2007). On the relationship between Keynes's conception of evidential weight and the Ellsberg paradox. *Journal of Economic Psychology, 28*(5), 545–565.

Flyvbjerg, B. (2014a). *Megaproject Planning and Management: Essential Readings*. Cheltenham: Edward Elgar Publishing.

Flyvbjerg, B. (2014b). What you should know about megaprojects and why: An overview. *Project Management Journal, 45*(2), 6–19.

Flyvbjerg, B., & Budzier, A. (2011). Why your IT project may be riskier than you think. *Harvard Business Review, 89*(9), 23–25.

Flyvbjerg, B., Bruzelius, N., & Rothengatter, W. (2003). *Megaprojects and Risk: An Anatomy of Ambition*. Cambridge: Cambridge University Press.

Geraldi, J.G., Lee-Kelley, L., & Kutsch, E. (2010). The Titanic sunk, so what? Project manager response to unexpected events. *International Journal of Project Management, 28*(6), 547–558.

Guttag, J. (2017a). Confidence Intervals. Available at: www.youtube.com/watch?v=rUxP7TM8-wo (accessed 25 February 2020).

Guttag, J. (2017b). Monte Carlo simulation. Available at: www.youtube.com/watch?v=OgO1gpXSUzU (accessed 25 February 2020).

Hackman, J.R. & Wageman, R. (2004). When and How Team Leaders Matter. *Research in Organizational Behavior*, 26, 37–74.

Hällgren, M., & Wilson, T.L. (2008). The nature and management of crises in construction projects: Projects-as-practice observations. *International Journal of Project Management, 26*(8), 830–838.

Herring, G.C. (1986). *America's Longest War: The United States and Vietnam, 1950–1975* (2nd edn). New York: Knopf.

Hidalgo, E.S. (2019). Adapting the scrum framework for agile project management in science: Case study of a distributed research initiative. *Heliyon, 5*(3), e01447.

Hillson, D.A. (1997). Towards a risk maturity model. *The International Journal of Project & Business Risk Management, 1*(1), 35–45.

Hillson, D., & Murray-Webster, R. (2007). *Understanding and Managing Risk Attitude* (2nd edn). Aldershot: Gower.

Keynes, J.M. (1921). *A Treatise on Probability. The Collected Writings of John Maynard Keynes* (Vol. *8*). London: Macmillan.

Keynes, M. (1936). *The General Theory of Employment Interest and Money*. London: Macmillan.

Knight, F.H. (1921). *Risk, Uncertainty and Profit*. New York: Hart, Schaffner, & Marx.

Levinthal, D. (2011). A behavioral approach to strategy – what's the alternative? *Strategic Management Journal, 32*(13), 1517–1523.

Loch, C.H., Solt, M.E., & Bailey, E.M. (2008). Diagnosing unforeseeable uncertainty in a new venture. *Journal of Product Innovation Management, 25*(1), 28.

March, J.G., & Simon, H. A. (1958). *Organizations*. Oxford: Wiley.

Mengis, J., Nicolini, D., & Swan, J. (2018). Integrating knowledge in the face of epistemic uncertainty: Dialogically drawing distinctions. *Management Learning, 49*(5), 595–612. Available at: https://doi.org/10.1177/1350507618797216 (accessed 6 February 2020).

Millar, C.C.J.M., Groth, O., & Mahon, J.F. (2018). Management innovation in a VUCA world: Challenges and recommendations. *California Management Review, 61*(1), 5–14. Available at: https:/doi.org/10.1177/0008125618805111 (accessed 6 February 2020).

Mintzberg, H., & Waters, J. (1985). Of strategies, deliberate and emergent. *Strategic Management Journal, 6*(3), 257.

Norsk Oil & Gas (2005). Black Swans – an enhanced understanding of risk. Available at: https://www.youtube.com/watch?v=w3mxDP0C6Nk (accessed 25 February 2020).

Obeng, E. (1996). *The Project Leader's Secret Handbook: All Change!* London: Financial Times/ Prentice Hall.

Packard, M., Clark, B., & Klein, P. (2017). Uncertainty types and transitions in the entrepreneurial process. *Organization Science, 28*(5), 840–856. Available at: https://doi.org/10.1287/orsc.2017.1143 (accessed 6 February 2020).

Perrow, C. (1994). The limits of safety: The enhancement of a theory of accidents. *Journal of Contingencies and Crisis Management, 2*(4), 212–220. Available at: https:/doi.org/10.1111/j.1468-5973.1994.tb00046.x (accessed 6 February 2020).

Pitsis, T., Clegg, S.R., Marosszeky, M., and Rura-Polley, T. (2003) Constructing the Olympic Dream: Managing innovation through the future perfect. *Organization Science, 14*(5), 574–590.

Raz, T., Shenhar, A.J., & Dvir, D. (2002). Risk management, project success, and technological uncertainty. *R & D Management, 32*(2), 101.

Rumsfeld, D. (2009). Unknown unknowns! Available at: www.youtube.com/watch?v=-GiPe1OiKQuk (accessed 25 February 2020).

Sanchez, H., Robert, B., Bourgault, M., & Pellerin, R. (2009). Risk management applied to projects, programs, and portfolios. *International Journal of Managing Projects in Business, 2*(1), 14–35.

Shenhar, A J., & Dvir, D. (2007). *Reinventing Project Management: The Diamond Approach to Successful Growth and Innovation*. Boston, MA: Harvard Business School Press.

Söderholm, A. (2008). Project management of unexpected events. *International Journal of Project Management, 26*(1), 80–86.

Sommer, S.C., & Loch, C. (2004). Selectionism and learning in projects with complexity and unforeseeable uncertainty. *Management Science, 50*(10), 1334–1347.

Sommer, S.C., Loch, C.H., & Dong, J. (2009). Managing complexity and unforeseeable uncertainty in startup companies: An empirical study. *Organization Science, 20*(1), 118–133. Available at: https://doi.org/10.1287/orsc.1080.0369 (accessed 6 February 2020).

Taleb, N.N. (2007). *The Black Swan: The Impact of the Highly Improbable*. London: Allen Lane.

Taleb, N.N. (2008) What is a black swan? Available at: www.youtube.com/watch?v=BD buJtAiABA (accessed 25 February 2020).

Thiry, M. (2002). Combining value and project management into an effective programme management model. *International Journal of Project Management, 20*(3), 221–227.

Tidd, J. (2001). Innovation management in context: environment, organization and performance. *International Journal of Management Reviews, 3*(3), 169–183.

Townsend, D.M., Hunt, R.A., McMullen, J.S., & Sarasvathy, S.D. (2018). Uncertainty, knowledge problems, and entrepreneurial action. *Academy of Management Annals, 12*(2), 659–687.

Turner, J.R., & Cochrane, R.A. (1993). Goals-and-methods matrix: Coping with projects with ill defined goals and/or methods of achieving them. *International Journal of Project Management, 11*(2), 93–102.

Vesper, J. (2014). Risk assessment methods. Available at: www.youtube.com/watch?v=olMKw MzEcyU (accessed 19 June 2020).

Ward. S. & Chapman, C. (2003). Transforming project risk management into project uncertainty management. *International Journal of Project Management, 21*(2), 97–105.

Ward, S., & Chapman, C. (2008). Stakeholders and uncertainty management in projects. *Construction Management and Economics, 26*(6), 563–577.

Williams, T. (2017). The nature of risk in complex projects. *Project Management Journal, 48*(4), 55–66. Available at: https://doi.org/10.1177/875697281704800405 (accessed 6 February 2020).

Chapter 10

ABC Four Corners (2017). *Crown Confidential*. Available at: www.abc.net.au/4corners/crown-promo/8319302 (accessed 25 February 2020).

Ackermann, F., & Eden, C. (2011). Strategic management of stakeholders: Theory and practice. *Long Range Planning, 44*(3), 179–196.

Alexander, M. (2019). How to deliver bad news to project stakeholders. Available at: https://www.techrepublic.com/article/how-to-deliver-bad-news-to-project-stakeholders/ (accessed 25 February 2020).

Andersen, E.S. (2008). *Rethinking Project Management: An Organisational Perspective*. Harlow: Prentice Hall/Financial Times.

Barnard, C.I. (1938). *The Functions of the Executive*. Cambridge, MA: Harvard University Press.

Bedwell, W.L., Wildman, J.L., DiazGranados, D., Salazar, M., Kramer, W.S., & Salas, E. (2012). Collaboration at work: An integrative multilevel conceptualization. *Human Resource Management Review, 22*(2), 128–145.

Boonstra, A., van Offenbeek, M.A., & Vos, J.F. (2017). Tension awareness of stakeholders in large technology projects: A duality perspective. *Project Management Journal, 48*(1), 19–36.

Briner, W., Geddes, M., & Hastings, C. (1993). *Project Leadership*. Farnham: Gower Publishing Company.

Broberg, G., & Roll-Hansen, N. (1996). *Eugenics and the Welfare State : Sterilization Policy in Denmark, Sweden, Norway and Finland*. East Lansing, MI: Michigan State University Press.

Carlsen, A., Clegg, S., & Gjersvik, R. (2012). *Idea Work: Lessons of the Extraordinary in Everyday Creativity*. Oslo: Cappelen Damm akademisk.

Clarkson, M.E. (1995). A stakeholder framework for analyzing and evaluating corporate social performance. *Academy of Management Review, 20*(1), 92–117.

Clayton, M. (2019). Stakeholder Engagement Tips: 5 Tips For Project Managers. Available at: www.youtube.com/watch?v=APc9S_8v7YY (accessed 25 February 2020).

Clegg, S. (1975/2013). *Power, Rule and Domination: A Critical and Empirical Understanding of Power in Sociological Theory and Organizational Life*. London: Routledge & Kegan Paul.

Clegg, S. (1989). *Frameworks of Power*. London: Sage Publications.

Clegg, S. (2019). Governmentality. *Project Management Journal, 50*(3), 266–270.

Clegg, S., Pitsis, T.S., Rura-Polley, T., & Marosszeky, M. (2002). Governmentality matters: Designing an alliance culture of inter-organizational collaboration for managing projects. *Organization Studies, 23*(3), 317–337.

Clegg, S.R., Carter, C., Kornberger, M., & Schweitzer, J. (2019). *Strategy: Theory and Practice* (3rd edn). London: Sage Publications.

Coldevin, G.H., Carlsen, A., Clegg, S., Pitsis, T.S., & Antonacopoulou, E.P. (2019). Organizational creativity as idea work: Intertextual placing and legitimating imaginings in media development and oil exploration. *Human Relations, 72*(8), 1369–1397. Available at: https:/doi.org/10.1177/0018726718806349 (accessed 7 February 2020).

Courpasson, D., Dany, F., & Clegg, S. (2012). Resisters at work: Generating productive resistance in the workplace. *Organization Science, 23*(3), 801–819.

Crawford, L. (2005). Senior management perceptions of project management competence. *International Journal of Project Management, 23*(1), 7–16.

Cropanzano, R., Bowen, D.E., & Gilliland, S.W. (2007). The management of organizational justice. *Academy of Management Perspectives, 21*(4), 34–48.

Czarniawska, B. (2004). On time, space, and action nets. *Organization, 11*(6), 773–791.

Das, T.K., & Teng, B.-S. (1998). Between trust and control: Developing confidence in partner cooperation in alliances. *The Academy of Management Review, 23*(3), 491–512. Available at: http:/doi.org/10.2307/259291 (accessed 7 February 2020).

Davis, K. (2018). Reconciling the views of project success: A multiple stakeholder model. *Project Management Journal, 49*(5), 38–47. Available at: http:/doi.org/10.1177/8756972818786663 (accessed 7 February 2020).

Driessen, P.H., & Hillebrand, B. (2013). Integrating multiple stakeholder issues in new product development: An exploration. *Journal of Product Innovation Management, 30*(2), 364–379.

Elangovan, A.R., & Shapiro, D. (1998). Betrayal of trust in organizations. *Academy of Management Review, 23*(3), 547–566.

Engwall, M. (2003). No project is an island: Linking projects to history and context. *Research Policy, 32*(5), 789–808.

Eskerod, P., & Jepsen, A.L. (2013). *Project Stakeholder Management*. Farnham: Gower.

Eskerod, P., & Vaagaasar, A.L. (2014). Stakeholder management strategies and practices during a project course. *Project Management Journal, 45*(5), 71–85. Available at: http:/doi.org/10.1002/pmj.21447 (accessed 7 February 2020).

Ewa, J. (2016). Natural environment as a silent stakeholder of a socially responsible company. Good business practices in Poland, Logistyka Odzysku, *4*(21s), 80–82.

Fahim, H.M. (2015). *Dams, People and Development: The Aswan High Dam Case*. London: Elsevier.

Freeman, R.E. (1984). *Strategic Management: A Stakeholder Approach*. Boston, MA: Pitman/Ballinger.

Frooman, J. (1999). Stakeholder influence strategies. *Academy of Management Review, 24*(2), 191–205.

Gautrey, C. (2017). Stakeholder Mapping Process. Available at: www.youtube.com/watch?v=Ifqm_yYsXt0 (accessed 25 February 2020).

Gulati, R., & Singh, H. (1998). The architecture of cooperation: Managing coordination costs and appropriation concerns in strategic alliances. *Administrative Science Quarterly, 43*(4), 781–814. Available at: https://doi.org/10.2307/2393616 (accessed 7 February 2020).

Kramer, R.M. (2009). Rethinking trust. *Harvard Business Review, 87*(6), 68–77, 113.

Kreiner, K. (1995). In search of relevance: Project management in drifting environments. *Scandinavian Journal of Management, 11*(4), 335–346.

Larson, E.W., & Gray, C.F. (2011). *Project Management: The Managerial Process*. Boston, MA: McGraw-Hill.

Machiavelli, N. (1961). *The Prince*. London: Penguin Books..

Madsen., S. (2015). Dealing with difficult stakeholders. Available at: www.youtube.com/watch?v=iV4BAQCBpF4 (accessed 25 February 2020).

Madsen, S. (2017). How to prioritize with the MoSCoW technique. Available at: www.youtube.com/watch?v=v__x5O_E5Ho (accessed 26 February 2020).

Mayer, R. C., Davis, J. H., & Schoorman, F. D. (1995). An integrative model of organizational trust. *Academy of Management Review, 20*(3), 709–734.

Miles, S. (2012). Stakeholder: Essentially contested or just confused? *Journal of Business Ethics, 108*(3), 285–298.

Miller, R., & Lessard, D.R. (2000). *The Strategic Management of Large Engineering Projects: Shaping Institutions, Risks, and Governance.* Cambridge, MA: MIT Press.

Mitchell, R.K., Agle, B.R., & Wood, D.J. (1997). Toward a theory of stakeholder identification and salience: Defining the principle of who and what really counts. *The Academy of Management Review, 22*(4), 853–886. Available at: https://doi.org/10.2307/259247 (accessed 7 February 2020).

Morgan, R.M., & Hunt, S.D. (1994). The commitment-trust theory of relationship marketing. *Journal of Marketing, 58*(3), 20–38.

Ninan, J., & Mahalingam, A. (2017). Stakeholder Management Strategies in Infrastructure Megaprojects – A Dimension of Power Perspective. Paper presented at the Proceedings of the Engineering Project Organization Conference.

Ninan, J., Clegg, S., & Mahalingam, A. (2019). Branding and governmentality for infrastructure megaprojects: The role of social media. *International Journal of Project Management, 37*(1), 59–72.

Ninan, J., Mahalingam, A., & Clegg, S. (2019). External stakeholder management strategies and resources in megaprojects: An organizational power perspective. *Project Management Journal, 50*(6). Available at: https://doi.org/10.1177%2F8756972819847045 (accessed 7 February 2020).

Pfeffer, J., & Salancik, G.R. (1978). The design and management of externally controlled organizations. In J. Pfeffer and G.R. Salancik, *The External Control of Organizations: A Resource Dependence Perspective* (pp. 257–287). New York: Harper & Row.

Pitsis, T.S., Clegg, S.R., Marosszeky, M., & Rura-Polley, T. (2003). Constructing the Olympic dream: a future perfect strategy of project management. *Organization Science, 14*(5), 574–590.

Recker, J., Holten, R., Hummel, M., & Rosenkranz, C. (2017). How agile practices impact customer responsiveness and development success: A field study. *Project Management Journal, 48*(2), 99–121.

Roe, M. (2019) Why America's CEOs are talking about stakeholder capitalism. *Project Syndicate*, 4 November. Available at: www.project-syndicate.org/commentary/america-business-roundtable-ceos-corporate-purpose-by-mark-roe-2019–11?barrier=accesspaylog (accessed 25 February 2020).

Savage, G., Bunn, M., Gray, B., Xiao, Q., Wang, S., Wilson, E., & Williams, E. (2010). Stakeholder collaboration: Implications for stakeholder theory and practice. *Journal of Business Ethics, 96*, 21–26. Available at: https://doi.org/10.1007/s10551-011-0939-1 (accessed 7 February 2020).

Selznick, P. (1949). *TVA and the Grass Roots: A Study in the Sociology of Formal Organization* (Vol. 3). Berkeley, CA: University of California Press.

Shenhar, A.J. (2001). One size does not fit all projects: Exploring classical contingency domains. *Management Science, 47*(3), 394–414.

Smyth, H. (2014). *Relationship Management and the Management of Projects.* New York: Routledge.

Smyth, H., Gustafsson, M., & Ganskau, E. (2010). The value of trust in project business. *International Journal of Project Management, 28*(2), 117–129.

Stinchcombe, A.L., & Heimer, C.A. (1985). *Organization Theory and Project Management: Administering Uncertainty in Norwegian Offshore Oil.* Oxford: Oxford University Press.

Tressell, R. (1978). *The Ragged Trousered Philanthropists.* London: Lawrence & Wishart.

Tryggestad, K., Justesen, L., & Mouritsen, J. (2013). Project temporalities: How frogs can become stakeholders. *International Journal of Managing Projects in Business, 6*(1), 69–87.

Tuomela, R., & Tuomela, M. (2005). Cooperation and trust in group context. *Mind & Society, 4*(1), 49–84.

Vaagaasar, A.L. (2006). *From Tool to Actor: How a Project Came to Orchestrate its own Life and that of Others* (Vol. 10). Oslo: Handelshøyskolen BI.

Vaagaasar, A.L. (2011). Development of relationships and relationship competencies in complex projects. *International Journal of Managing Projects in Business*, 4(2), 294–307.

Wåhlin, N., Kapsali, M., Näsholm, M.H., & Blomquist, T. (2016). *Urban Strategies for Culture-driven Growth: Co-creating a European Capital of Culture*. Cheltenham: Edward Elgar Publishing.

Weick, K.E. (1979). *The Social Psychology of Organizing* (2nd edn). Reading, MA: Addison-Wesley.

Weingart, P. (1999). Science and political culture: Eugenics in comparative perspective. *Scandinavian Journal of History*, 24(2), 163–177. Available at: https://doi.org/10.1080/03468759950115782 (accessed 7 February 2020).

Wenger, E. (1998). Communities of practice: Learning as a social system. *Systems Thinker*, 9(5), 2–3.

Chapter 11

Aime, F., Humphrey, S., Derue, D.S., & Paul, J.B. (2014). The riddle of heterarchy: Power transitions in cross-functional teams. *Academy of Management Journal*, 57(2), 327–352. Available at: https:/doi.org/10.5465/amj.2011.0756 (accessed 10 February 2020).

Ajmal, M.M., & Koskinen, K. U. (2008). Knowledge transfer in project-based organizations: an organizational culture perspective. *Project Management Journal*, 39(1), 7–15.

Andre, D. (2018). Knowledge Management – The SECI model (Nonaka & Takeuchi 1996). Available at: www.youtube.com/watch?v=Rr02SdqmY2A (accessed 26 February 2020).

Anonymous (2018). The dynamic capacilities of firms: David Teece & Gary Pissano. Available at: www.youtube.com/watch?v=KsJ4yTh9sMc (accessed 25 February 2020).

Argyris, C., & Schön, D.A. (1978). *Organizational Learning: A Theory of Action Perspective*. Reading, MA: Addison-Wesley.

Ayas, K., & Zeniuk, N. (2001). Project-based learning: Building communities of reflective practitioners. *Management Learning*, 32(1), 61–76. Available at: https:/doi.org/10.1177/1350507601321005 (accessed 10 February 2020).

Bakker, R.M., Boroø, S., Kenis, P., & Oerlemans, L.A. (2013). It's only temporary: Time frame and the dynamics of creative project teams. *British Journal of Management*, 24(3), 383–397.

Batt-Rawden, V., Lien, G., & Slåtten, T. (2019). Team learning capability – an instrument for innovation ambidexterity? *International Journal of Quality and Service Sciences*, 11(4): 473–486.

Blackler, F. (1995). Knowledge, knowledge work and organizations: An overview and interpretation. *Organization Studies*, 16(6), 1021–1046.

Boje, D.M. (2011). *Storytelling and the Future of Organizations: An Antenarrative Handbook*. New York: Routledge.

Boje, D.M. (2013). *Storytelling Organizational Practices: Managing in the Quantum Age*. London: Routledge.

Brady, T., & Davies, A. (2004). Building project capabilities: From exploratory to exploitative learning. *Organization Studies*, 25(9), 1601–1621.

Bragd, A. (2002). *Knowing Management. An Ethnographic Study of Tinkering with a New Car*. Gothenburg: BAS Publisher.

Cacciatori, E. (2008). Memory objects in project environments: Storing, retrieving and adapting learning in project-based firms. *Research Policy*, 37(9), 1591–1601.

Carlile, P.R. (2002). A pragmatic view of knowledge and boundaries: Boundary objects in new product development. *Organization Science*, 13(4), 442–455.

Christensen, C. (2012). Disruptive Innovation Explained. Available at: www.youtube.com/watch?v=qDrMAzCHFUU (accessed 26 February 2020).

Christensen, C.M., Johnson, C.W., & Horn, M.B. (2010). *Disrupting Class*. New York: McGraw-Hill.

Clegg, S.R., & Kreiner, K. (2014). Fixing concrete: Inquiries, responsibility, power and innovation. *Construction Management & Economics*, 32(3), 262–278. Available at: https://doi.org/10.1080/01446193.2013.848996 (accessed 10 February 2020).

Clegg, S.R., Pitelis, C., Schweitzer, J., & Whittle, A. (2019). *Strategy: Theory and Practice* (3rd edn). London: Sage.

Cohen, W.M., & Levinthal, D.A. (1990). Absorptive capacity: A new perspective on learning and innovation. *Administrative Science Quarterly, 35*(1), 128–152.

Coldevin, G.H., Carlsen, A., Clegg, S., Pitsis, T.S., & Antonacopoulou, E.P. (2019). Organizational creativity as idea work: Intertextual placing and legitimating imaginings in media development and oil exploration. *Human Relations, 72*(8), 1369–1397. Available at: https:/doi.org/10.1177/0018726718806349 (accessed 10 February 2020).

Csikszentmihalyi, M. (2008). *Flow*. New York: HarperPerennial.

Czarniawska, B. (1997). *Narrating the Organization: Dramas of Institutional Identity*. Chicago: University of Chicago Press.

Czarniawska, B., & Sevón, G. (2005). *Global Ideas: How Ideas, Objects and Practices Travel in the Global Economy*. Copenhagen: Samfundslitteratur.

Davies, A., & Brady, T. (2000). Organisational capabilities and learning in complex product systems: Towards repeatable solutions. *Research Policy, 29*(7), 931–953. Available at: https://doi.org/10.1016/S0048-7333(00)00113-X (accessed 10 February 2020).

Davies, A., & Brady, T. (2016). Explicating the dynamics of project capabilities. *International Journal of Project Management, 34*(2), 314–327. Avalable at: doi:https://doi.org/10.1016/j.ijproman.2015.04.006 (accessed 10 February 2020).

Davies, A., & Hobday, M. (2005). *The Business of Projects: Managing Innovation in Complex Products and Systems*. Cambridge: Cambridge University Press.

Davies, A., Dodgson, M., & Gann, D. (2016). Dynamic capabilities in complex projects: The case of London Heathrow Terminal 5. *Project Management Journal, 47*(2), 26–46.

Davies, A., Brady, T., Prencipe, A., & Hobday, M. (2011). Innovation in complex products and systems: Implications for project-based organizing. *Advances in Strategic Management, 28*, 3–26. Available at: https://doi.org/10.1108/S0742-3322(2011)0000028005 (accessed 10 February 2020).

Dewey, J. (1938). *Logic: The Theory of Enquiry*. New York: Holt, Rinehart & Winston.

Dylan, B. (1965). Love minus zero/no limit. On *Bringing It All Back Home*. New York: Colombia.

Eisenhardt, K.M., & Martin, J.A. (2000). Dynamic capabilities: What are they? *Strategic Management Journal, 21*(10–11), 1105–1121.

Eisenhardt, K.M., & Tabrizi, B.N. (1995). Accelerating adaptive processes: Product innovation in the global computer industry. *Administrative Science Quarterly, 40*(1), 84–110.

Feldman, M.S., & Orlikowski, W.J. (2011). Theorizing practice and practicing theory. *Organization Science, 22*(5), 1240.

Feldman, M.S., & Pentland, B.T. (2003). Reconceptualizing organizational routines as a source of flexibility and change. *Administrative Science Quarterly, 48*(1), 94–118.

Fox, A. (1974). *Beyond Contract: Trust and Power Relations*. London: Faber.

Gallo, C. (2018). Jeff Bezos banned PowerPoint in meetings. Available at: www.inc.com/carmine-gallo/jeff-bezos-bans-powerpoint-in-meetings-his-replacement-is-brilliant.html (accessed 25 February 2020).

Garrick, J. (1998). *Informal Learning in the Workplace: Unmasking Human Resource Development*. London: Routledge.

Garrick, J., & Clegg, S. (2001). Stressed-out knowledge workers in performative times: A postmodern take on project-based learning. *Management Learning, 32*(1), 119–134. Available at: https:/doi.org/10.1177/1350507601321008 (accessed 10 February 2020).

Geithner, S., Menzel, D., Wolfe, J., & Kriz, W. (2016). Effectiveness of learning through experience and reflection in a project management simulation. *Simulation & Gaming, 47*(2), 228–256. Available at: https://doi.org/10.1177/1046878115624312 (accessed 10 February 2020).

Gherardi, S. (2000). Practice-based theorizing on learning and knowing in organizations. *Organization, 7*(2), 211–223. Available at: https:/doi.org/10.1177/135050840072001 (accessed 10 February 2020).

Glaveski, S. (2019) Where companies go wrong with learning and development. *Harvard Business Review*. Available at: https://hbr.org/2019/10/where-companies-go-wrong-with-learning-and-development (accessed 25 February 2020).

Grant, R.M. (1996). Toward a knowledge-based theory of the firm. *Strategic Management Journal, 17*, 109–122.

Hargadon, A., & Bechky, B.A. (2006). When collections of creatives become creative collectives: A field study of problem solving at work. *Organization Science, 17*(4), 484–500.

Hartmann, A., & Dorée, A. (2015). Learning between projects: More than sending messages in bottles. *International Journal of Project Management, 33*(2), 341–351.

Hill, L.A. (2014). *Collective Genius: The Art and Practice of Leading Innovation*. Boston, MA: Harvard Business School Press.

Huber, G.P. (1991). Organizational learning: The contributing processes and the literatures. *Organization Science, 2*(1), 88–115. Available at: htps://doi.org/10.1287/orsc.2.1.88 (accessed 10 February 2020).

Kanter, R.M. (2009). *Supercorp: How Vanguard Companies Create Innovation, Profits, Growth, and Social Good*. New York: Crown Business.

Keegan, A., & Turner, J.R. (2002). The management of innovation in project-based firms. *Long Range Planning, 35*(4), 367–388. doi:http://dx.doi.org/10.1016/S0024-6301(02)00069–9 (accessed 10 February 2020).

Kogut, B., & Zander, U. (1992). Knowledge of the firm, combinative capabilities, and the replication of technology. *Organization Science, 3*(3), 383–397.

Kokkonen, A., & Vaagaasar, A.L. (2018). Managing collaborative space in multi-partner projects. *Construction Management and Economics, 36*(2), 83–95. Available at: https:/doi.org/10.108 0/01446193.2017.1347268 (accessed 10 February 2020).

Kolb, D.A. (1984). *Experiential Learning: Experience as the Source of Learning and Development*. Englewood Cliffs, NJ: Prentice-Hall.

Koskinen, K.U. (2008). Boundary brokering as a promoting factor in competence sharing in a project work context. *International Journal of Project Organisation and Management, 1*(1), 119–132.

Koskinen, K. U. (2012). Organizational learning in project-based companies: A process thinking approach, *Project Management Journal, 43*(3), 40–49.

Lave, J., & Wenger, E. (1991). *Situated Learning: Legitimate Peripheral Participation*. Cambridge: Cambridge University Press.

Lenfle, S., & Loch, C. (2010). Lost roots: How project management came to emphasize control over flexibility and novelty. *California Management Review, 53*(1), 32–55.

Levinthal, D.A., & March, J.G. (1993). The myopia of learning. *Strategic Management Journal, 14*, 95–112.

Levitt, B., & March, J.G. (1988). 'Organizational learning.' *Annual Review of Sociology, 14*(1), 319–338.

Madsen, A. C. (2016). Clothes, consistency and constant change, 1-D. Available at: https://i-d.vice.com/en_au/article/mbew54/clothes-consistency-and-constant-change (accessed 25 February 2020).

March, J.G. (1991). Exploration and exploitation in organizational learning. *Organization Science, 2*(1), 71–87.

McIntyre, J., & Symes, C. (2000). *Working Knowledge: The New Vocationalism and Higher Education*. Buckingham: Society for Research into Higher Education & Open University Press.

Murphy, K.M. (2004). Imagination as joint activity: The case of architectural interaction. *Mind, Culture, and Activity, 11*(4), 267–278.

Nahapiet, J., & Ghoshal, S. (1998). Social capital, intellectual capital, and the organizational advantage. *The Academy of Management Review, 23*(2), 242–266.

Nerstad, C., Searle, R., černe, M., Dysvik, A., Škerlavaj, M., & Scherer, R. (2018). Perceived mastery climate, felt trust, and knowledge sharing. *Journal of Organizational Behavior, 39*(4), 429–447.

Newell, S., Robertson, H., Scarborough, H., & Swan, J. (2009). *Managing Knowledge Work and Innovation* (2nd edn). Basingstoke: Palgrave Macmillan.

Nonaka, I., & Takeuchi, H. (1995). *The Knowledge-creating Company: How Japanese Companies Create the Dynamics of Innovation*. New York: Oxford University Press.

Nonaka, I., & Takeuchi, H. (2011). The wise leader. *Harvard Business Review, 89*(5).

Obstfeld, D. (2012). Creative projects: A less routine approach toward getting new things done. *Organization Science, 23*(6), 1571–1592.

Okhuysen, G.A., & Bechky, B.A. (2009). Coordination in organizations: An integrative perspective. *The Academy of Management Annals, 3*(1), 463–502.

Orlikowski, W.J., & Iacono, C.S. (2001). Research commentary: Desperately seeking the 'IT' in IT research – A call to theorizing the IT artifact. *Information Systems Research, 12*(2), 121–134.

Packendorff, J. (1995). Inquiring into the temporary organization: New directions for project management research. *Scandinavian Journal of Management, 11*(4), 319–333.

Polanyi, M. (1962). *Personal Knowledge: Towards a Post-critical Philosophy*. Chicago, London: University of Chicago Press, Routledge & Kegan Paul.

Prencipe, A., & Tell, F. (2001). Inter-project learning: Processes and outcomes of knowledge codification in project-based firms. *Research Policy, 30*(9), 1373–1394.

Radiohead (2000). *Kid A*. London: Parlophone.

Raelin, J.A. (2002). 'I don't have time to think!' versus the art of reflective practice. *Reflections: The SoL Journal, 4*(1), 66–79.

Rich, A.S., & Gureckis, T.M. (2018). The limits of learning: Exploration, generalization, and the development of learning traps. *Journal of Experimental Psychology: General, 147*(11), 1553.

Rosile, G.A., Boje, D.M., Carlon, D.M., Downs, A., & Saylors, R. (2013). Storytelling diamond: An antenarrative integration of the six facets of storytelling in organization research design. *Organizational Research Methods, 16*(4), 557–580.

Sawyer, R.K., & DeZutter, S. (2009). Distributed creativity: How collective creations emerge from collaboration. *Psychology of Aesthetics, Creativity, and the Arts, 3*(2), 81–92. Available at: https:/doi.org/10.1037/a0013282 (accessed 10 February 2020).

Schindler, M., & Eppler, M.J. (2003). Harvesting project knowledge: A review of project learning methods and success factors. *International Journal of Project Management, 21*(3), 219–228.

Senge, P.M. (2006). *The Fifth Discipline: The Art and Practice of the Learning Organization* (rev. and updated edn). New York: Currency/Doubleday.

Senge, P. (2015). How do you define a learning organization? Available at: www.youtube.com/watch?v=vc2ruCErTok (accessed 25 February 2020).

Shenhar, A. (2013). The adaptive approach and the diamond model for project success. Available at: https://yt.ax/watch/the-adaptive-approach-and-the-diamond-model-for-project-success-19623111/ (accessed 26 February 2020).

Shenhar, A.J., & Dvir, D. (2007). *Reinventing Project Management: The Diamond Approach to Successful Growth and Innovation*. Boston, MA: Harvard Business School Press.

Škerlavaj, M., Connelly, C.E., Cerne, M., & Dysvik, A. (2018). Tell me if you can: Time pressure, prosocial motivation, perspective taking, and knowledge hiding. *Journal of Knowledge Management, 22*(7), 1489–1509.

Söderlund, J., Vaagaasar, A.L., & Andersen, E.S. (2008). Relating, reflecting and routinizing: Developing project competence in cooperation with others. *International Journal of Project Management, 26*(5), 517–526. Available at: http://dx.doi.org/10.1016/j.ijproman.2008.06.002 (accessed 10 February 2020).

Sonenshein, S. (2014). How organizations foster the creative use of resources. *Academy of Management Journal, 57*, 814–848.

Spender, J.C., & Grant, R.M. (1996). Knowledge and the firm: An overview. *Strategic Management Journal, 17*(S2), 5–9. Available at: https://doi.org/10.1002/smj.4250171103 (accessed 10 February 2020).

Star, S.L., & Griesemer, J.R. (1989). Institutional ecology, translations and boundary objects: Amateurs and professionals in Berkeley's Museum of Vertebrate Zoology, 1907–39. *Social Studies of Science, 19*(3), 387–420.

Teece, D. (2016). Dynamic capabilities and strategic management. Available at: www.youtube. com/watch?v=F6t5t9dnUF8 (accessed 25 February 2020).

Teece, D.J., Pisano, G., & Shuen, A. (1997). Dynamic capabilities and strategic management. *Strategic Management Journal, 18*(7), 509–533.

Terhorst, A., Lusher, D., Bolton, D., Elsum, I., & Wang, P. (2018). Tacit knowledge sharing in open innovation projects. *Project Management Journal, 49*(4), 5–19.

Tidd, J., & Bessant, J. (2018). *Managing Innovation: Integrating Technological, Market and Organizational Change* (6th edn). Hoboken, NJ: Wiley.

Tsoukas, H. (2009). A dialogical approach to the creation of new knowledge in organizations. *Organization Science, 20*(6), 941–957. Available at: https://doi.org/10.1287/orsc.1090.0435 (accessed 10 February 2020).

Turner, R., Huemann, M., Anbari, F.T., & Bredillet, C.N. (2010). *Perspectives on Projects*. London: Routledge.

Vaagaasar, A.L. (2006). *From Tool to Actor: How a Project Came to Orchestrate its own Life and that of Others* (Vol. *10*). Oslo: Handelshøyskolen BI.

Vaagaasar, A.L. (2011). Development of relationships and relationship competencies in complex projects. *International Journal of Managing Projects in Business, 4*(2), 294–307.

Vaagaasar, A.L. (2015). A spatial perspective to leadership in knowledge-intensive projects. In A. Ropo, P. Salovaara, D. De Paoli, & E. Sauer (eds), *Leadership, Spaces and Organizing* (pp. 71–86). Cheltenham: Edward Elgar.

Vygotsky, L. S. (1978). *Mind in Society: The Development of Higher Psychological Processes* (ed. M. Cole, V. John-Steiner, S. Scribner, & E. Souberman). Cambridge, MA: Harvard University Press.

Weick, K.E. (1979). *The Social Psychology of Organizing* (2nd edn). Reading, MA: Addison-Wesley.

Weick, K.E. (1995). *Sensemaking in Organizations* (1st edn). Thousand Oaks, CA: Sage.

Wenger, E. (2010). Communities of practice and social learning systems: The career of a concept. In C. Blackmore (ed.), *Social Learning Systems and Communities of Practice* (pp. 179–198) London: Springer.

Zollo, M., & Winter, S.G. (2002). Deliberate learning and the evolution of dynamic capabilities. *Organization Science, 13*(3), 339–351.

Chapter 12

Adler, P.S., & Kwon, S.-W. (2002). Social capital: Prospects for a new concept. *Academy of Management Review, 27*(1), 17–40.

Aime, F., Humphrey, S., Derue, D.S., & Paul, J.B. (2014). The riddle of heterarchy: Power transitions in cross-functional teams. *Academy of Management Journal, 57*(2), 327–352. Available at: https://doi.org/10.5465/amj.2011.0756 (accessed 12 February 2020).

Andersen, E.S. (2008). *Rethinking Project Management: An Organisational Perspective*. Harlow: Prentice Hall/Financial Times.

Andersen, E.S., & Jessen, S.A. (2003). Project maturity in organisations. *International Journal of Project Management, 21*(6), 457–461. Available at: http://dx.doi.org/10.1016/S0263-7863(02)00088–1 (accessed 12 February 2020).

Backlund, F., Chronéer, D., & Sundqvist, E. (2014). Project management maturity models – a critical review: A case study within Swedish engineering and construction organizations. *Procedia – Social and Behavioral Sciences, 119*, 837–846. Available at: https://doi.org/10.1016/j.sbspro.2014.03.094 (accessed 12 February 2020).

Barley, S.R., & Kunda, G. (2006). Contracting: A new form of professional practice. *Academy of Management Perspectives, 20*(1), 45–66.

Barry, M-L. (2014). Project management maturity. Available at: www.youtube.com/watch?v=VAC JEbYwnEc (accessed 26 February 2020).

Bechky, B.A. (2006). Gaffers, gofers, and grips: Role-based coordination in temporary organizations. *Organization Science, 17*(1), 3–21.

Birkinshaw, J., & Gupta, K. (2013). Clarifying the distinctive contribution of ambidexterity to the field of organization studies. *Academy of Management Perspectives, 27*(4), 287–298. Available at: https://doi.org/10.5465/amp.2012.0167 (accessed 12 February 2020).

Blichfeldt, B.S., & Eskerod, P. (2008). Project portfolio management: There's more to it than what management enacts. *International Journal of Project Management, 26*(4), 357–365.

Burns, T., & Stalker, G.M. (1962). *The Management of Innovation.* Oxford: Oxford University Press.

Bython Media (2017). 5 Steps of Project Portfolio Management. Available at: www.youtube. com/watch?v=dgaSCe-ZuNs (accessed 26 February 2020).

Carlsen, A., Clegg, S., & Gjersvik, R. (2012). *Idea Work: Lessons of the Extraordinary in Everyday Creativity.* Oslo: Cappelen Damm akademisk.

Chandler, A.D. (1962). *Strategy and Structure: Chapters in the History of the Industrial Enterprise.* Cambridge, MA: MIT Press.

Christiansen, J.K., & Varnes, C. (2008). From models to practice: Decision making at portfolio meetings. *International Journal of Quality & Reliability Management, 25*(1), 87–101. Available at: https://doi.org/10.1108/02656710810843603 (accessed 12 February 2020).

Clayton, M. (2018). What is the PMO? Available at: www.youtube.com/watch?v=cdAfZijI_Hc (accessed 26 February 2018).

Clegg, S.R., & Baumeler, C. (2012). From life in cages to life in projects: Metaphors for moderns. In A. Davila, M.M. Elvira, J. Ramirez, & L. Zapata-Cantu (eds), *Understanding Organizations in Complex, Emergent and Uncertain Environments* (pp. 185–206). London: Springer.

Clegg, S.R., & Burdon, S. (2019). Exploring polyarchic creativity and innovation in broadcastin. *Human Relations.* Available at: https://doi.org/10.1177/0018726719888004 (accessed 12 February 2020).

Clegg, S.R., Courpasson, D., & Phillips, N. (2006). *Power and Organizations.* London: Sage.

Coldevin, G.H., Carlsen, A., Clegg, S., Pitsis, T.S., & Antonacopoulou, E.P. (2019). Organizational creativity as idea work: Intertextual placing and legitimating imaginings in media development and oil exploration. *Human Relations, 72*(8), 1369–1397. Available at: https:/doi.org/10.1177/0018726718806349 (accessed 12 February 2020).

Cooke-Davies, T.J., & Arzymanow, A. (2003). The maturity of project management in different industries. *International Journal of Project Management, 21*(6), 471–478. Available at: https://doi.org/10.1016/S0263-7863(02)00084-4 (accessed 12 February 2020).

Cooper, C.L., & Marshall, J. (1978). *Understanding Executive Stress.* London: Springer.

Cooper, R., Edgett, S., & Kleinschmidt, E. (2001a). *Portfolio Management for New Product Development* (Vol. *31*). Cambridge, MA: Perseus Publication.

Cooper, R., Edgett, S., & Kleinschmidt, E. (2001b). Portfolio management for new product development: Results of an industry practices study. *R & D Management, 31*(4), 361–380.

Crawford, L., Morris, P., Thomas, J., & Winter, M. (2006). Practitioner development: From trained technicians to reflective practitioners. *International Journal of Project Management, 24*(8), 722–733.

Dahl, R.A. (1971). *Polyarchy: Participation and Opposition.* New Haven, CT: Yale University Press.

Daskalaki, M. (2010). Building 'bonds' and 'bridges': Linking tie evolution and network identity in the creative industries. *Organization Studies, 31*(12), 1649–1666.

Davies, A., & Hobday, M. (2005). *The Business of Projects: Managing Innovation in Complex Products and Systems.* Cambridge: Cambridge University Press.

DeFillippi, R.J., & Arthur, M.B. (1998). Paradox in project-based enterprise: The case of film. *California Management Review, 40*(2), 125–139.

Ebbers, J.J., & Wijnberg, N.M. (2009). Latent organizations in the film industry: Contracts, rewards and resources. *Human Relations, 62*(7), 987–1009.

Eccles, R.G. (1981). The quasifirm in the construction industry. *Journal of Economic Behavior & Organization, 2*(4), 335–357. Available at: https://doi.org/10.1016/0167-2681(81)90013-5 (accessed 12 February 2020).

Elonen, S., & Artto, K.A. (2003). Problems in managing internal development projects in multi-project environments. *International Journal of Project Management, 21*(6), 395–402. Available at: https://doi.org/10.1016/S0263-7863(02)00097-2 (accessed 12 February 2020).

Engwall, M., & Jerbrant, A. (2003). The resource allocation syndrome: The prime challenge of multi-project management? *International Journal of Project Management, 21*(6), 403–409. Available at: https:/doi.org/10.1016/S0263-7863(02)00113–8 (accessed 12 February 2020).

Eriksson, P.E. (2013). Exploration and exploitation in project-based organizations: Development and diffusion of knowledge at different organizational levels in construction companies. *International Journal of Project Management, 31*(3), 333–341. doi:http://dx.doi.org/10.1016/j.ijproman.2012.07.005 (accessed 12 February 2020).

Eriksson, P.E., Leiringer, R., & Szentes, H. (2017). The role of co-creation in enhancing explorative and exploitative learning in project-based settings. *Project Management Journal, 48*(4), 22–38.

Eskerod, P., & Vaagaasar, A.L. (2014). Stakeholder management strategies and practices during a project course. *Project Management Journal, 45*(5), 71–85. Available at: https://doi.org/10.1002/pmj.21447 (accessed 12 February 2020).

Fairtlough, G. (2005). *The Three Ways of Getting Things Done: Hierarchy, Heterarchy & Responsible Autonomy in Organizations* (international edn). Bridport: Triarchy Press.

Feldman, M.S., & Orlikowski, W.J. (2011). Theorizing practice and practicing theory. *Organization Science, 22*(5), 1121–1367.

Freudenberger, H.J. (1974). Staff burn-out. *Journal of Social Issues, 30*(1), 159–165.

Frost, P.J. (2007). *Toxic Emotions at Work and What You Can Do About Them*. Boston, MA: Harvard Business Press.

Fuglsang, L., & Sundbo, J. (2005). The organizational innovation system: Three modes. *Journal of Change Management, 5*(3), 329–344.

Gann, D., Salter, A., Dodgson, M., & Phillips, N. (2012). Inside the world of the project baron. *MIT Sloan Management Review, 53*(3), 63–71.

Gordon, J., & Tulip, A. (1997). Resource scheduling. *International Journal of Project Management, 15*(6), 359–370. doi:https://doi.org/10.1016/S0263-7863(96)00090–7 (accessed 12 February 2020).

Gouldner, A.W. (1954). *Patterns of Industrial Bureaucracy*. New York: Free Press.

Granovetter, M. (1985). Economic action and social structure: The problem of embeddedness. *American Journal of Sociology, 91*(3), 481–510.

Gransberg, D.D., Dillon, W.D., Reynolds, L., & Boyd, J. (1999). Quantitative analysis of partnered project performance. *Journal of Construction Engineering and Management, 125*(3), 161.

Grant, K.P., & Pennypacker, J.S. (2006). Project management maturity. An assessment of project management capabilities among and between selected industries. *IEEE Transactions on Engineering Management, 53*(1), 10.

Grant, R.M. (1996). Toward a knowledge-based theory of the firm. *Strategic Management Journal, 17*, 109–122.

Greenwood, R., Raynard, M., Kodeih, F., Micelotta, E.R. & Lounsbury, M. (2011). Institutional complexity and organizational responses. *Academy of Management Annals, 5*(1), 317–371.

Gulati, R., Wohlgezogen, F., & Zhelyazkov, P.I. (2012). 'The two facets of collaboration: Cooperation and coordination in strategic alliances. *Academy of Management Annals, 6*, 531–583.

Hellgren, B., & Stjernberg, T. (1995). Design and implementation in major investments – a project network approach. *Scandinavian Journal of Management, 11*(4), 377–394.

Hesmondhalgh, D., & Baker, S. (2008). Creative work and emotional labour in the television industry. *Theory, Culture & Society, 25*(7–8), 97–118.

Hesmondhalgh, D., & Baker, S. (2010). 'A very complicated version of freedom': Conditions and experiences of creative labour in three cultural industries. *Poetics, 38*(1), 4–20.

Hill, L.A. (2014). *Collective Genius: The Art and Practice of Leading Innovation*. Boston, MA: Harvard Business School Press.

Hobday, M. (2000). The project-based organisation: an ideal form for managing complex products and systems?. *Research policy, 29*(7–8), 871–893.

Hobbs, B., & Aubry, M. (2007). A multi-phase research program investigating project management offices (PMOs): The results of phase 1. *Project Management Journal, 38*(1), 74–86.

Jensen, A., Thuesen, C., & Geraldi, J. (2016). The projectification of everything: Projects as a human condition. *Project Management Journal, 47*(3). Available at: https://doi.org/10.1177%2F875697281604700303 (accessed 10 February 2020).

Jones, C., & Lichtenstein, B. (2008). Temporary inter-organizational projects: How temporal and social embeddedness enhance coordination and manage uncertainty. In S. Cropper, M. Ebers, C. Huxham, & P.S. Ring (eds), *The Oxford Handbook of Inter-organizational Relations*. Oxford: Oxford University Press.

Kanter, R.M. (2006). Innovation: The classic traps. *Harvard Business Review, 84*(11), 72–83.

King, A., & Crewe, I. (2014). *The Blunders of Our Governments*. London: Oneworld Publications.

Kock, A., & Gemünden, H.G. (2019). Project lineage management and project portfolio success. *Project Management Journal, 50*(5). Available at: https://doi.org/10.1177%2F8756972819870357 (accessed 10 February 2020).

Kogut, B., & Zander, U. (1992). Knowledge of the firm, combinative capabilities, and the replication of technology. *Organization Science, 3*(3), 383–397.

Lancione, M., & Clegg, S.R. (2015). The lightness of management learning. *Management Learning, 46*(3), 280–298. Available at: https://doi.org/10.1177/1350507614526533 (accessed 12 February 2020).

Li, Y., Lu, Y., Ma, L., & Kwak, Y.H. (2018). Evolutionary governance for mega-event projects (MEPs): A case study of the World Expo 2010 in China. *Project Management Journal, 49*(1), 57–78.

Lycett, M., Rassau, A., & Danson, J. (2004). Programme management: a critical review. *International Journal of Project Management, 22*(4), 289–299.

Manning, S. (2017). The rise of project network organizations: Building core teams and flexible partner pools for interorganizational projects. *Research Policy, 46*(8), 1399–1415.

Martinsuo, M., & Lehtonen, P. (2009). Project autonomy in complex service development networks. *International Journal of Managing Projects in Business, 2*(2), 261–281.

Maylor, H., Brady, T., Cooke-Davies, T., & Hodgson, D. (2006). From projectification to programmification. *International Journal of Project Management, 24*(8), 663–674.

McGonigal, K. (2013). How to make stress your friend, *Ted Talk*. Available at: www.youtube.com/watch?v=RcGyVTAoXEU (accessed 26 February 2020).

Meyerson, D., Weick, K.E., & Kramer, R.M. (1996). Swift trust and temporary groups. In R.M. Kramer & T. Tyler (eds), *Trust in Organizations: Frontiers of Theory and Research* (pp. 166–196). Thousand Oaks, CA: SAGE Publications, Inc.

Midler, C., Maniak, R., & de Campigneulles, T. (2019). Ambidextrous program management: The case of autonomous mobility. *Project Management Journal, 50*(5), 571–586. Available at: https://doi.org/10.1177/8756972819869091 (accessed 12 February 2020).

Mikkelsen, H., & Riis, J.O. (2017). *Project Management: A Multi-perspective Leadership Framework*. Bingley: Emerald Group Publishing Limited.

Mintzberg, H. (1983). *Structure in Fives: Designing Effective Organizations*. Englewood Cliffs, NJ: Prentice-Hall.

Mirabeau, L., & Maguire, S. (2014). From autonomous strategic behavior to emergent strategy. *Strategic Management Journal, 35*(8), 1202–1229. Available at: https://doi.org/10.1002/smj.2149 (accessed 12 February 2020).

O'Reilly III, C.A., & Tushman, M.L. (2008). Ambidexterity as a dynamic capability: Resolving the innovator's dilemma. *Research in Organizational Behavior, 28*, 185–206. Available at: http://dx.doi.org/10.1016/j.riob.2008.06.002 (accessed 12 February 2020).

Ogilvy, J. (2016). Heterarchy – an idea finally ripe for its time. *Forbes*, 4 February. Available at: www.forbes.com/sites/stratfor/2016/02/04/heterarchy-an-idea-finally-ripe-for-its-time/#3158c52747a7 (accessed 12 February 2020).

Okhuysen, G.A., & Bechky, B.A. (2009). Coordination in organizations: An integrative perspective. *The Academy of Management Annals, 3*(1), 463–502. Available at: https://doi.org/10.1080/19416520903047533 (accessed 12 February 2020).

Pache, A.-C., & Santos, F. (2010). When worlds collide: The internal dynamics of organizational responses to conflicting institutional demands. *Academy of Management Review, 35*(3), 455–476.

Packendorff, J., & Lindgren, M. (2014). Projectification and its consequences: Narrow and broad conceptualisations. *South African Journal of Economic and Management Sciences*, *17*(1), 7–21.

Patanakul, P., & Shenhar, A.J. (2012). What project strategy really is: The fundamental building block in strategic project management. *Project Management Journal*, *43*(1), 4–20. Available at: https://doi.org/10.1002/pmj.20282 (accessed 12 February 2020).

Pellegrinelli, S., Murray-Webster, R., & Turner, N. (2015). Facilitating organizational ambidexterity through the complementary use of projects and programs. *International Journal of Project Management*, *33*(1), 153–164. Available at: https://doi.org/10.1016/j.ijproman.2014.04.008 (accessed 12 February 2020).

Poppo, L., & Zenger, T. (2002). Do formal contracts and relational governance function as substitutes or complements? *Strategic Management Journal*, *23*(8), 707–725.

Puleo, G. (2014). Burnout and post-traumatic stress disorder, Ted Talk. Available at: www.youtube.com/watch?v=hFkI69zJzLI (accessed 26 February 2020).

Robinson, W.I. (2013). Promoting polyarchy: 20 years later. *International Relations*, *27*(2), 228–234.

Rowlands, L., & Handy, J. (2012). An addictive environment: New Zealand film production workers' subjective experiences of project-based labour. *Human Relations*, *65*(5), 657–680.

Sahlin-Andersson, K., & Söderholm, A. (2002). The Scandinavian school of project studies. In K. Sahlin-Andersson & A. Söderholm (eds), *Beyond Project Management. New Perspectives on the Temporary–Permanent Dilemma* (pp. 11–24). Stockholm: Liber.

Smyth, H.J. (2014). *Relationship Management and the Management of Projects*. New York: Routledge.

Söderlund, J. (2005). *Projektledning & Projektkompetens: Perspektiv på Konkurrenskraft*. Malmö: Liber.

Söderlund, J., & Tell, F. (2009). The P-form organization and the dynamics of project competence: Project epochs in Asea/ABB, 1950–2000. *International Journal of Project Management*, *27*(2), 101–112. Available at: https://doi.org/10.1016/j.ijproman.2008.10.010 (accessed 12 February 2020).

Spender, J.C., & Grant, R.M. (1996). Knowledge and the firm: An overview. *Strategic Management Journal*, *17*(S2), 5–9. Available at: https://doi.org/10.1002/smj.4250171103 (accessed 12 February 2020).

Starkey, K., Barnatt, C., & Tempest, S. (2000). Beyond networks and hierarchies: Latent organizations in the UK television industry. *Organization Science*, *11*(3), 299–305.

Sydow, J., & Staber, U. (2002). The institutional embeddedness of project networks: The case of content production in German television. *Regional Studies*, *36*(3), 215–227.

Teachout, T. (2013). *Duke – A Life of Duke Ellington*. New York: Gotham Books.

Thiry, M. (2004). "For DAD": a programme management life-cycle process. *International Journal of Project Management*, *22*(3), 245–252.

Turner, N., Maylor, H., & Swart, J. (2015). Ambidexterity in projects: An intellectual capital perspective. *International Journal of Project Management*, *33*(1), 177–188. Available at: http://dx.doi.org/10.1016/j.ijproman.2014.05.002 (accessed 12 February 2020).

Uzzi, B. (1997). Social structure and competition in interfirm networks: The paradox of embeddedness. *Administrative Science Quarterly*, *42*(1), 35–67.

Williams, T., & Samset, K. (2010). Issues in front-end decision making on projects. *Project Management Journal*, *41*(2), 38–49. Available at: http://doi.org/10.1002/pmj.20160 (accessed 12 February 2020).

Witt, J. (2012). Project Portfolio Management Defined. Available at: www.youtube.com/watch?v=bbVPqUl3jfM (accessed 26 February 2020).

Young, N. (1991). My my, hey hey (out of the blue). *Weld*. Hollywood: Reprise.

Zika-Viktorsson, A., Hovmark, S., & Nordqvist, S. (2003). Psychosocial aspects of project work: A comparison between product development and construction projects. *International Journal of Project Management*, *21*(8), 563–569.

Zika-Viktorsson, A., Sundström, P., & Engwall, M. (2006). Project overload: An exploratory study of work and management in multi-project settings. *International Journal of Project Management, 24*(5), 385–394.

Chapter 13

Aaker, D.A. (1996). *Building Strong Brands*. New York: Free Press.

Ackermann, F., & Eden, C. (2011). Strategic management of stakeholders: Theory and practice. *Long Range Planning, 44*(3), 179–196.

Adler, P. (1995). 'Democratic Taylorism': The Toyota production system at NUMMI. In S. Babson (ed.), *Lean Work: Empowerment and Exploitation in the Global Auto Industry* (pp. 207–219). Detroit: Wayne State University Press.

Adler, P.S., Goldoftas, B., & Levine, D.I. (1999). Flexibility versus efficiency? A case study of model changeovers in the Toyota production system. *Organization Science, 10*(1), 43–68. doi:10.1287/orsc.10.1.43

Adler, P.S., & Kwon, S.-W. (2002). Social capital: Prospects for a new concept. *Academy of Management Review, 27*(1), 17–40.

Adner, R., & Levinthal, D.A. (2004). What is not a real option: Considering boundaries for the application of real options to business strategy. *The Academy of Management Review, 29*(1), 74–85. doi:10.2307/20159010

Agile Practice Guide. (2017). Project management Institute.

Aime, F., Humphrey, S., Derue, D.S., & Paul, J.B. (2014). The riddle of heterarchy: Power transitions in cross-functional teams. *Academy of Management Journal, 57*(2), 327–352. doi:10.5465/amj.2011.0756

Albalate, D., & Bel, G. (2009). Regulating concessions of toll motorways: An empirical study on fixed vs. variable term contracts. *Transportation Research Part A: Policy and Practice, 43*(2), 219–229.

Allen, T., Katz, R., Grady, J., & Slavin, N. (1988). Project team aging and performance: The roles of project and functional managers. *R&D Management, 18*(4), 295–308.

Allen, T.J. (1977). *Managing the Flow of Technology: Technology Transfer and the Dissemination of Technological Information within the R&D Organization.* Cambridge, MA: MIT Press.

Alvehus, J. (2018). Emergent, distributed, and orchestrated: Understanding leadership through frame analysis. *Leadership, 15*(5). doi:10.1177/1742715018773832

Alvesson, M., & Deetz, S. (2000). *Doing Critical Management Research.* London: SAGE Publications.

Amabile, T., & Kramer, S. (2011). *The Progress Principle: Using Small Wins to Ignite Joy, Engagement, and Creativity at Work*: Harvard Business Press.

Amabile, T.M., Barsade, S.G., Mueller, J.S., & Staw, B.M. (2005). Affect and creativity at work. *Administrative Science Quarterly, 50*(3), 367–403. doi:10.2189/asqu.2005.50.3.367

American Management Association (2019). Do You Have What It Takes to be a Project Manager? Available at: https://www.amanet.org/articles/do-you-have-what-it-takes-to-be-a-project-manager/ (accessed 26 February 2020).

Amoako-Gyampah, K., Meredith, J., & Loyd, K. W. (2018). Using a social capital lens to identify the mechanisms of top management commitment: a case study of a technology project. *Project Management Journal, 49*(1), 79–95.

Amundsen, S., & Martinsen, Ø.L. (2014). Empowering leadership: Construct clarification, conceptualization, and validation of a new scale. *The Leadership Quarterly, 25*(3), 487–511. doi:http://dx.doi.org/10.1016/j.leaqua.2013.11.009

Ancona, D.G., & Caldwell, D.F. (1992). Bridging the boundary: External activity and performance in organizational teams. *Administrative Science Quarterly, 37*(4).

Andersen, E.S. (2008). *Rethinking project management: an organisational perspective.* Harlow: Prentice Hall/Financial Times.

Andersen, E.S. (2014). Value creation using the mission breakdown structure. *International journal of project management, 32*(5), 885–892. doi:http://dx.doi.org/10.1016/j.ijproman.2013.11.003

Andersen, E.S., Grude, K.V., & Haug, T. (2009). *Goal Directed Project Management: Effective Techniques and Strategies* (3rd edn). London: Kogan Page Publishers.

Andersen, E.S., & Jessen, S. A. (2003). Project maturity in organisations. *International journal of project management, 21*(6), 457–461. doi:http://dx.doi.org/10.1016/S0263-7863(02)00088–1

Andersen, E.S., Soderlund, J., & Vaagaasar, A. L. (2010). Projects and politics: Exploring the duality between action and politics in complex projects. *International Journal of Management and Decision Making, 11*(2), 121–139.

Anderson-Gough, F., Grey, C., & Robson, K. (2001). Tests of time: Organizational time-reckoning and the making of accountants in two multi-national accounting firms. *Accounting, Organizations and Society, 26*(2), 99–122. doi:10.1016/S0361-3682(00)00019–2

Andi. (2006). The importance and allocation of risks in Indonesian construction projects. *Construction Management and Economics, 24*(1), 69–80.

Argote, L. (1982). Input uncertainty and organizational coordination in hospital emergency units. *Administrative Science Quarterly: dedicated to advancing the understanding of administration through empirical investigation and theoretical analysis, 27*(3), 420–434. doi:10.2307/2392320.

Argyris, C. (1957). The individual and organization: Some problems of mutual adjustment. *Administrative Science Quarterly*, 1–24.

Argyris, C., & Schön, D. A. (1978). *Organizational Learning: A Theory of Action Perspective.* Reading, MA: Addison-Wesley.

Argyris, C., & Schön, D. A. (1996). *Organizational Learning II: Theory, Method, and Practice.* Reading, MA: Addison-Wesley.

Arndt, R. H. (1998). Risk allocation in the Melbourne city link project. *Journal of Structured Finance, 4*(3), 11.

Arnulf, J. K. (2014). *A Brief Introduction to Leadership.* Oslo: Universitetsforlaget.

Arrow, K. J., & Hahn, F. (1999). Notes on sequence economies, transaction costs, and uncertainty. *Journal of Economic Theory, 86*(2), 203.

Asch, S. E. (1956). Studies of independence and conformity: I. A minority of one against a unanimous majority. *Psychological Monographs: General and Applied, 70*(9), 1.

Atkinson, R., Crawford, L., & Ward, S. (2006). Fundamental uncertainties in projects and the scope of project management. *International Journal of Project Management, 24*(8), 687.

Ayas, K., & Zeniuk, N. (2001). Project-based learning: Building communities of reflective practitioners. *Management Learning, 32*(1), 61–76. doi:10.1177/1350507601321005

Baccarini, D. (1996). The concept of project complexity – A review. *International Journal of Project Management, 14*(4), 201–204. doi:10.1016/0263–7863(95)00093–3

Backlund, F., Chronéer, D., & Sundqvist, E. (2014). Project management maturity models – A critical review: A case study within Swedish engineering and construction organizations. *Procedia - Social and Behavioral Sciences, 119*, 837–846. doi:https://doi.org/10.1016/j.sbspro.2014.03.094

Bakker, R.M., Boroş, S., Kenis, P., & Oerlemans, L. A. (2013). It's only temporary: time frame and the dynamics of creative project teams. *British Journal of Management, 24*(3), 383–397.

Ballard, D.I., & Seibold, D. R. (2003). Communicating and organizing in time: A meso-level model of organizational temporality. *Management Communication Quarterly, 16*(3), 380–415.

Bandura, A. (1986). *Social Foundations of Thought and Action: A Social Cognitive Theory.* Englewood Cliffs, N.J: Prentice-Hall.

Barley, S. R., & Kunda, G. (2006). Contracting: A new form of professional practice. *Academy of Management Perspectives, 20*(1), 45–66.

Barnard, C.I. (1938). *The functions of the Executive.* Cambridge, MA: Harvard University Press.

Barnett, C., Clarke, N., Cloke, P., & Malpass, A. (2014). The elusive subjects of neo-liberalism: Beyond the analytics of governmentality. In *Cultural Studies and Anti-Consumerism* (pp. 116–145). Routledge.

Barraket, J., & Loosemore, M. (2018). Co-creating social value through cross-sector collaboration between social enterprises and the construction industry. *Construction Management and Economics, 36*(7), 394–408.

Barrick, M.R., & Mount, M. K. (1991). The big five personality dimensions and job performance: a meta-analysis. *Personnel Psychology, 44*(1), 1–26.

Bass, B.M., & Bass, R.R. (2008). *The Bass Handbook of Leadership: Theory, Research, and Managerial Applications.* New York: Free Press.

Bass, B.M., & Riggio, R.E. (2006). *Transformational Leadership.* Mahwah, NJ: L. Erlbaum Associates.

Bateson, G. (1972). *Steps to an Ecology of Mind.* New York: Ballantine Books.

Batista, M.d.G., Clegg, S., Pina e Cunha, M., Giustiniano, L., & Rego, A. (2016). Improvising prescription: evidence from the emergency room. *British Journal of Management, 27*(2), 406–425.

Batselier, J., & Vanhoucke, M. (2016). Practical application and empirical evaluation of reference class forecasting for project management. *Project Management Journal, 47*(5), 36–51. doi:10.1177/875697281604700504

Batt-Rawden, V., Lien, G., & Slåtten, T. (2019). Team Learning Capability - an Instrument for Innovation Ambidexterity? . *To be updated.*

Beauregard, R. (2018). The entanglements of uncertainty. *Journal of Planning Education and Research,* 0739456X18783038.

Bechky, B.A. (2006). Gaffers, gofers, and grips: Role-based coordination in temporary organizations. *Organization Science, 17*(1), 3–21. doi:10.2307/25146010

Bechky, B.A., & Okhuysen, G.A. (2011). Expecting the unexpected? How SWAT officers and film crews handle surprises. In (pp. 239–261).

Bedwell, W.L., Wildman, J.L., DiazGranados, D., Salazar, M., Kramer, W. S., & Salas, E. (2012). Collaboration at work: An integrative multilevel conceptualization. *Human Resource Management Review, 22*(2), 128–145.

Belbin, R. M. (2011). *Team Roles at Work.* Oxford: Butterworth-Heinemann.

Bell, A. (2014). Project closure. Available at: www.youtube.com/watch?v=Ln9eNowUYgY (accessed 26 February 2020).

Bennett, N., & Lemoine, G. J. (2014). What a difference a word makes: Understanding threats to performance in a VUCA world. *Business Horizons, 57*(3), 311–317. doi:https://doi.org/10.1016/j.bushor.2014.01.001

Bennis, W., & Nanus, B. (1985). *Leaders: The Strategies for Taking Charge.* New York: Harper. Row.

Berggren, C., Järkvik, J., & Söderlund, J. (2008). Lagomizing, organic integration, and systems emergency wards: Innovative practices in managing complex systems development projects. *Project Management Journal, 39*(1_suppl), S111–S122.

Bewley, T. F. (2002). Knightian decision theory. Part I. *Decisions in economics and finance, 25*(2), 79–110.

Bing, L., Akintoye, A., Edwards, P. J., & Hardcastle, C. (2005). The allocation of risk in PPP/PFI construction projects in the UK. *International Journal of Project Management, 23*(1), 25–35.

Birkinshaw, J. (2013). *Becoming a Better Boss: Why Good Management Is So Difficult.* San Francisco, CA: Jossey-Bass.

Birkinshaw, J., & Gupta, K. (2013). Clarifying the distinctive contribution of ambidexterity to the field of organization studies. *Academy of Management Perspectives, 27*(4), 287–298. doi:10.5465/amp.2012.0167

Bjørkeng, K., Clegg, S.R., & Pitsis, T. (2009). Becoming (a) practice. *Management Learning, 40*(2), 145–159.

Blackler, F. (1995). Knowledge, knowledge work and organizations: An overview and interpretation. *Organization Studies, 16*(6), 1021–1046.

Blichfeldt, B.S., & Eskerod, P. (2008). Project portfolio management – There's more to it than what management enacts. *International Journal of Project Management, 26*(4), 357–365.

Blomquist, T., Hällgren, M., Nilsson, A., & Soderholm, A. (2010). Project-as-practice: In search of project management research that matters. *Project Management Journal*, *41*(1), 5–16. doi:10.1002/pmj.20141

Blomquist, T., & Packendorff, J. (1998). Learning from renewal projects: Content, context and embeddedness. In R.A. Lundin & C. Midler (eds.), *Projects as Arenas for Renewal and Learning Processes* (pp. 37–46). Dordrecht: Kluwer Academic Publishers.

Boehm, B., & Turner, R. (2005). Management challenges to implementing agile processes in traditional development organizations. *IEEE Software*, *22*(5), 30–39.

Boje, D.M. (2011). *Storytelling and the Future of Organizations: An Antenarrative Handbook*. New York: Routledge.

Boje, D.M. (2013). *Storytelling Organizational Practices : Managing in the Quantum Age.* London: Routledge.

Boonstra, A., van Offenbeek, M.A., & Vos, J.F. (2017). Tension awareness of stakeholders in large technology projects: A duality perspective. *Project Management Journal*, *48*(1), 19–36.

Bos-de Vos, M., Volker, L., & Wamelink, H. (2019). Enhancing value capture by managing risks of value slippage in and across projects. *International Journal of Project Management*, *37*(5), 767–783.

Bourne, L., & Walker, D.H.T. (2005). Visualising and mapping stakeholder influence. *Management Decision*, *43*(5), 649–660. doi:10.1108/00251740510597680

Boutinet, J. P. (1999). *Anthropologie du projet* (5th edn). Paris: Presses universitaires de France.

Bozeman, B. (2007). *Public Values and Public Interest – Counterbalancing Economic Individualism*. Washington, DC: Georgetown University Press.

Bradley, R., & Drechsler, M. (2014). Types of uncertainty. *An International Journal of Scientific Philosophy*, *79*(6), 1225–1248. doi:10.1007/s10670-013–9518–4

Brady, T., & Davies, A. (2004). Building project capabilities: From exploratory to exploitative learning. *Organization Studies*, *25*(9), 1601–1621.

Bragd, A. (2002). *Knowing Management: An Ethnographic Study of Tinkering with a New Car*. Gothenburg: BAS Publisher.

Bredillet, C., Tywoniak, S., & Dwivedula, R. (2015). What is a good project manager? An Aristotelian perspective. *International Journal of Project Management*, *33*(2), 254–266. doi:http://dx.doi.org/10.1016/j.ijproman.2014.04.001

Bresnen, M., & Marshall, N. (2002). The engineering or evolution of co-operation? A tale of two partnering projects. *International Journal of Project Management*, *20*(7), 497–505.

Briner, W., Geddes, M., & Hastings, C. (1993). *Project Leadership*: Gower Publishing Company, Limited.

Broberg, G., & Roll-Hansen, N. (1996). *Eugenics and the Welfare State: Sterilization Policy in Denmark, Sweden, Norway and Finland* East Lansing, MI: Michigan State University Press.

Brodie, R. J., Ilic, A., Juric, B., & Hollebeek, L. (2013). Consumer engagement in a virtual brand community: An exploratory analysis. *Journal of Business Research*, *66*(1), 105–114.

Brown, T. (2009). *Change by Design: How Design Thinking Transforms Organizations and Inspires Innovation*. New York: Collins Business.

Brown, T.L., Potoski, M., & Van Slyke, D.M. (2018). Complex contracting: Management challenges and solutions. *Public Administration Review*, *78*(5), 739–747.

Browning, T.R. (2019). Planning, tracking, and reducing a complex project's value at risk. *Project Management Journal*, *50*(1), 71–85. doi:10.1177/8756972818810967

Brunsson, K., & Brunsson, N. (2017). *Decisions: The Complexities of Individual and Organizational Decision-Making*. Cheltenham: Edward Elgar.

Brunsson, N. (2000). *The Irrational Organization: Irrationality as a Basis for Organizational Action and Change*. Bergen: Fagbokforlaget.

Brunsson, N. (2006). *Mechanisms of Hope: Maintaining the Dream of the Rational Organization*. Copenhagen Business School Press.

Brunsson, N. (2007). *The Consequences of Decision-Making*. Oxford: Oxford University Press.

Brunsson, N., & Adler, N. (1989). *The Organization of Hypocrisy: Talk, Decisions and Actions in Organizations* (2nd edn). Oslo: Universitetsforlaget.

Buchanan, D., & Badham, R. (2020). *Power, Politics, and Organizational Change: Winning the Turf Game* (3rd edn). London: Sage.

Buchanan, R. (1992). Wicked problems in design thinking. *Design Issues*, *8*(2), 5–21. doi:10.2307/1511637

Bulman, M., & Shulman, A. (2019). Grenfell Tower report: Fire service's 'stay put' advice cost lives, long awaited public inquiry conclude. *The Independent*, 30 October. Retrieved from https://www.independent.co.uk/news/uk/home-news/grenfell-tower-london-cladding-public-inquiry-report-martin-moore-bick-a9175291.htm

Burns, J.M. (1978). *Leadership*. New York: Harper & Row.

Burns, T., & Stalker, G. M. (1962). *The Management of Innovation*. Oxford: Oxford University Press.

Burnstein, W. (2016). The map is not the territory. Medium.com. Retrieved from https://medium.com/parachuting/the-map-is-not-the-territory-4772ec3125d3

Burnton, S. (2018). World Cup stunning moments: Germany humiliate Brazil 7–1 *The Guardian*, 23 May.

Bygballe, L.E., Dewulf, G., & Levitt, R. E. (2015). The interplay between formal and informal contracting in integrated project delivery. *Engineering Project Organization Journal*, *5*(1), 22–35.

Bygballe, L.E., Swärd, A.R., & Vaagaasar, A.L. (2016). Coordinating in construction projects and the emergence of synchronized readiness. *International journal of project management*, *34*(8), 1479–1492. doi:http://dx.doi.org/10.1016/j.ijproman.2016.08.006

Cacciatori, E. (2008). Memory objects in project environments: Storing, retrieving and adapting learning in project-based firms. *Research Policy*, *37*(9), 1591–1601.

Cain, S. (2013). *Quiet: The Power of Introverts in a World that Can't Stop Talking*: New York: Broadway Books.

Camerer, C.F., & Weber, M. (1992). Recent developments in modeling preferences uncertainty and ambiguity. *Journal of Risk and Uncertainty : JRU*, *5*(4), 325–370. doi:10.1007/BF00122575

Cantarelli, C.C., Flybjerg, B., Molin, E. J. E., & van Wee, B. (2013). Cost overruns in large-scale transportation infrastructure projects: Explanations and their theoretical embeddedness, arXiv preprint arXiv:1307.2176.

Capka, J.R. (2004). Megaprojects - They are a different breed. *Public Roads*, *68*(1), 2–9.

Carlile, P.R. (2002). A pragmatic view of knowledge and boundaries: Boundary objects in new product development. *Organization Science*, *13*(4), 442–455.

Carlsen, A., Clegg, S.R., & Gjersvik, R. (2012). *Idea Work: Lessons of the Extraordinary in Everyday Creativity*. Oslo: Cappelen Damm akademisk.

Carlsson, I., Ramphal, S., Alatas, A., & Dahlgren, H. (1995). *Our Global Neighbourhood: The Report of the Commission on Global Governance*. Oxford: Oxford University Press.

Carreyrou, J. (2015a, 27 December 2015). At Theranos, many strategies and snags; Elizabeth Holme's blood-testing ambition has long collided with technological problems. *The Wall Street Journal Online*.

Carreyrou, J. (2015b, 16 October 2015). Hot startup Theranos has struggled with its blood-test Technology. *The Wall Street Journal Online*.

Carreyrou, J. (2015c, 15 October 2015). A prized startup's struggles --- Silicon Valley lab Theranos is valued at $9 billion but isn't using its technology for all the tests it offers. *The Wall Street Journal*.

Carreyrou, J. (2015d, 21 December 2015). U.S. probes Theranos complaints --- Blood-testing startup's practices investigated over concerns about accuracy, protocol. *The Wall Street Journal*.

Carreyrou, J. (2016). Theranos results could throw off medical decisions, study finds; Researchers find that lab-testing company's results on cholesterol tests were lower by an average of 9.3% than Quest and LabCorp. *The Wall Street Journal Online*, 28 March.

Carte, T.A., Chidambaram, L., & Becker, A. (2006). Emergent leadership in self-managed virtual teams. *Group Decision and Negotiation*, *15*(4), 323–343.

Chamberlin, J. (2011). Who put the 'ART'in SMART goals. *Management Services, 55*(3), 22–27.

Chandler, A.D. (1962). *Strategy and Structure: Chapters in the History of the Industrial Enterprise*. Cambridge, MA: MIT Press.

Chang, A., Hatcher, C., & Kim, J. (2013). Temporal boundary objects in megaprojects: Mapping the system with the integrated master schedule. *International Journal of Project Management, 31*(3), 323–332.

Chapman, C., & Ward, S. (2008). Developing and implementing a balanced incentive and risk sharing contract. *Construction Management and Economics, 26*(6), 659–669. doi:10.1080/01446190802014760

Chapman, C.B., & Ward, S. (2012). *How to Manage Project Opportunity and Risk: Why Uncertainty Management Can Be a Much Better Approach than Risk Management*. Hoboken, NJ: Wiley.

Christensen, C.M., Johnson, C.W., & Horn, M.B. (2010). *Disrupting Class*. New York: McGraw-Hill.

Christensen, T., & Lægreid, P. (2007). The whole-of-government approach to public sector reform. *Public Administration Review, 67*(6), 1059–1066. doi:10.1111/j.1540–6210.2007.00797.x

Christiansen, J.K., & Varnes, C. (2008). From models to practice: decision making at portfolio meetings. *International Journal of Quality & Reliability Management, 25*(1), 87–101. doi:10.1108/02656710810843603

Cialdini, R. B. (2016). *Pre-suasion: A Revolutionary Way to Influence and Persuade*. London: Random House.

Cicmil, S., & Hodgson, D. (2006). New possiblities for project management theory: A critical engagement. *Project Management Journal, 37*(3), 111–122. Retrieved from http://sims-rad.net.ocs.mq.edu.au/login?url=http://search.ebscohost.com/login.aspx?direct=true&db=buh&AN=22149380&site=ehost-live

Cicmil, S., & Marshall, D. (2005). Insights into collaboration at the project level: Complexity, social interaction and procurement mechanisms. *Building Research & Information, 33*(6), 523–535.

Cicmil, S., Williams, T., Thomas, J., & Hodgson, D. (2006). Rethinking project management: Researching the actuality of projects. *International Journal of Project Management, 24*(8), 675–686.

Clark, K., & Fujimoto, T. (1989). Overlapping problem-solving in product development. In K. Ferdows (ed.), *Managing International Manufacturing*. North-Holland: Elsevier Science Publications.

Clarke, A. (1999). A practical use of key success factors to improve the effectiveness of project management. *International Journal of Project Management, 17*(3), 139–145.

Clarkson, M.E. (1995). A stakeholder framework for analyzing and evaluating corporate social performance. *Academy of Management Review, 20*(1), 92–117.

Clegg, S.R. (1975/2013). *Power, Rule and Domination: A Critical and Empirical Understanding of Power in Sociological Theory and Organizational Life*. London: Routledge & Kegan Paul.

Clegg, S.R. (1989). *Frameworks of Power*. London: Sage Publications.

Clegg, S.R. (2019). Governmentality. *Project Management Journal, 50*(3), 266–270.

Clegg, S.R. (2020). Management of climate crisis and planetary boundaries through eco taxation. *ManageMagazine*. Available at: https://managemagazine.com/article-bank/strategic-management-article-bank/management-of-climate-crisis-and-planetary-boundaries-eco-taxation/ (accessed 26 February 2020).

Clegg, S.R., Carter, C., Kornberger, M., & Schweitzer, J. (2019). *Strategy: Theory and Practice* (3rd edn). London: Sage Publications.

Clegg, S.R., & Courpasson, D. (2004). Political hybrids: Tocquevillean views on project organizations. *Journal of Management Studies, 41*(4), 525–547.

Clegg, S.R., Hardy, C., Lawrence, T. B., & Nord, W. R. (2006). *The SAGE Handbook of Organization Studies*. London: SAGE Publications.

Clegg, S.R., & Haugaard, M. (2009). *The SAGE Handbook of Power*. London: SAGE.

Clegg, S.R., Killen, C.P., Biesenthal, C., & Sankaran, S. (2018). Practices, projects and portfolios: Current research trends and new directions. *International Journal of Project Management, 36*(5), 762–772. doi:10.1016/j.ijproman.2018.03.008

Clegg, S.R., & Kornberger, M. (2015). Analytical frames for studying power in strategy as practice and beyond. In D. Golsorkhi (ed.), *Cambridge Handbook of Strategy as Practice* (2nd edn). Cambridge: Cambridge University Press.

Clegg, S.R., Kornberger, M., Pitsis, T. S., & Mount, M. (2019). *Managing & Organizations: An Introduction to Theory and Practice* (5th edn). London: SAGE.

Clegg, S.R., & Kreiner, K. (2013). Power and politics in construction projects. In N. Drouin, R. Müller, & S. Sankaran (eds.), *Novel Approaches to Organizational Project Management Research: Translational and Transformational*. Copenhagen: Copenhagen Business School Press DK.

Clegg, S.R., & Kreiner, K. (2014). Fixing concrete: Inquiries, responsibility, power and innovation. *Construction Management & Economics, 32*(3), 262–278. doi:10.1080/01446193.2013.848996

Clegg, S.R., Pitsis, T. S., Rura-Polley, T., & Marosszeky, M. (2002). Governmentality matters: Designing an alliance culture of inter-organizational collaboration for managing projects. *Organization Studies, 23*(3), 317–337.

Clegg, S.R., & Baumeler, C. (2012). From life in cages to life in projects: Metaphors for moderns. In *Understanding Organizations in Complex, Emergent and Uncertain Environments* (pp. 185–206). Springer.

Clegg, S.R., & Burdon, S. (2019). Exploring polyarchic creativity and innovation in broadcastin. *Human Relations*. Retrieved from https://doi.org/10.1177/0018726719888004

Clegg, S.R., Courpasson, D., & Phillips, N. (2006). *Power and Organizations*. London: Sage.

Clegg, S. R., Pitelis, C., Schweitzer, J., & Whittle, A. (2019). *Strategy; Theory and Practice* (3rd edn.). London: Sage.

Clegg, S.R., & Pitsis, T. S. (2012). Phronesis, projects and power research. In B. Flyvbjerg, T. Landman, & S. Schram (eds.), *Real Social Science* (pp. 66–91). Oxford: Oxford University Press.

Clegg, S.R., Sankaran, S., Biesenthal, C., & Pollack, J. (2017). Power and sensemaking in megaprojects. In B. Flybjerg (ed.), *The Oxford Handbook of Megaproject Management*. Oxford: Oxford University Press.

Cohen, M. D., March, J. G., & Olsen, J. P. (1972). A garbage can model of organizational choice. *Administrative Science Quarterly, 17*(1), 1–25. doi:10.2307/2392088

Cohen, W. M., & Levinthal, D. A. (1990). Absorptive capacity: A new perspective on learning and innovation. *Administrative Science Quarterly, 35*(1), 128–152.

Coldevin, G.H., Carlsen, A., Clegg, S.R., Pitsis, T. S., & Antonacopoulou, E. P. (2019). Organizational creativity as idea work: Intertextual placing and legitimating imaginings in media development and oil exploration. *Human Relations, 72*(8), 1369–1397. doi:10.1177/00187 26718806349

Collins, J. C., & Porras, J. I. (1994). *Built to Last: Successful Habits of Visionary Companies*. New York: HarperBusiness.

Colville, I.D., Waterman, R. H., & Weick, K. E. (1999). Organizing and the search for excellence: Making sense of the times in theory and practice. *Organization, 6*(1), 129–148.

Cooke-Davies, T. (2002). The "real" success factors on projects. *International Journal of Project Management, 20*(3), 185–190. doi:http://dx.doi.org/10.1016/S0263-7863(01)00067–9

Cooke-Davies, T. J., & Arzymanow, A. (2003). The maturity of project management in different industries. *International Journal of Project Management, 21*(6), 471–478. doi:10.1016/S0263-7863(02)00084–4

Cooper, C. (2015). Entrepreneurs of the self: The development of management control since 1976. *Accounting, Organizations and Society, 47*, 14–24.

Cooper, C. L., & Marshall, J. (1978). *Understanding Executive Stress*. Springer.

Cooper, R., Edgett, S., & Kleinschmidt, E. (2001a). *Portfolio Management for New Product Development* (Vol. *31*). Cambridge, MA: Perseus Publication.

Cooper, R., Edgett, S., & Kleinschmidt, E. (2001b). Portfolio management for new product development: Results of an industry practices study. *R & D Management, 31*(4), 361.

Cooper, R.G. (1990). Stage-gate systems: A new tool for managing new products. *Business Horizons, 33*(3), 44–54. doi:10.1016/0007–6813(90)90040-I

Coughlan, P., Suri, J.F., & Canales, K. (2007). Prototypes as (design) tools for behavioral and organizational change: A design-based approach to help organizations change work behaviors. *Journal of Applied Behavioral Science, 43*(1), 122–134. doi:10.1177/0021886306297722

Courpasson, D., Dany, F., & Clegg, S.R. (2012). Resisters at work: Generating productive resistance in the workplace. *Organization Science, 23*(3), 801–819.

Courtright, S.H., McCormick, B. W., Mistry, S., Wang, J., & Chen, G. (2017). Quality charters or quality members? A control theory perspective on team charters and team performance. *Journal of Applied Psychology, 102*(10), 1462–1470. doi:10.1037/apl0000229

Cova, B., Ghauri, P. N., & Salle, R. (2002). *Project Marketing: Beyond Competitive Bidding* Chichester: John Wiley.

Crawford, L. (2005). Senior management perceptions of project management competence. *International Journal of Project Management, 23*(1), 7–16.

Crawford, L., Cooke-Davies, T., Hobbs, B., Labuschagne, L., Remington, K., & Chen, P. (2008). Governance and support in the sponsoring of projects and programs. *Project Management Journal, 39*(S1), S43–S55. doi:10.1002/pmj.20059

Crawford, L., Morris, P., Thomas, J., & Winter, M. (2006). Practitioner development: From trained technicians to reflective practitioners. *International Journal of Project Management, 24*(8), 722–733.

Crevani, L., Lindgren, M., & Packendorff, J. (2010). Leadership, not leaders: On the study of leadership as practices and interactions. *Scandinavian Journal of Management, 26*(1), 77–86.

Cropanzano, R., Bowen, D. E., & Gilliland, S. W. (2007). The management of organizational justice. *Academy of Management Perspectives, 21*(4), 34–48.

Crow, D. (2015). Theranos exemplifies clash of new versus old in-vitro test models. *Financial Times*, 15 December.

Crow, D., & Samson, A. (2015). Theranos blood labs under fresh scrutiny on staffing and quality. *Financial Times*, 23 October.

Csikszentmihalyi, M. (2008). *Flow*. New York: HarperPerennial <on.

Cunha, M.P.e., Clegg, S.R., Rego, A., & Neves, P. (2014). Organizational Improvisation: From the Constraint of Strict Tempo to the Power of the Avant-Garde. *Creativity and Innovation Management, 23*(4), 359–373.

Cunha, M. P. e., Neves, P., Clegg, S. R., & Rego, A. (2015). Tales of the unexpected: Discussing improvisational learning. *Management Learning, 46*(5), 511–529. doi:10.1177/1350507614549121

Cunha, M.P.e., Giustiniano, L., Rego, A., & Clegg, S. (2017). Mission impossible? The paradoxes of stretch goal setting. *Management Learning, 48*(2), 140–157. doi:10.1177/13505076 16664289

Czarniawska, B. (1997). *Narrating the Organization: Dramas of Institutional Identity*. Chicago: University of Chicago Press.

Czarniawska, B. (2004). On time, space, and action nets. *Organization, 11*(6), 773–791.

Czarniawska, B., & Sevón, G. (2003). *The Northern Lights: Organization Theory in Scandinavia*. Malmö: Abstrakt.

Czarniawska, B., & Sevón, G. (2005). *Global Ideas: How Ideas, Objects and Practices Travel in the Global Economy*. Copenhagen: Samfundslitteratur.

Dahl, R.A. (1971). *Polyarchy: Participation and Opposition*. New Haven, CT: Yale University Press.

Daisey, M. (2015). We should be suspicious of Silicon Valley unicorns and their exorbitant valuations. *TheGuardian*, 25 October.

Daniel, E.I., & Pasquire, C. (2019). Creating social value within the delivery of construction projects: the role of lean approach. *Engineering, Construction and Architectural Management*.

Danso-Wiredu, E. Y., & Midheme, E. (2017). Slum upgrading in developing countries: Lessons from Ghana and Kenya. *Ghana Journal of Geography, 9*(1), 88–108.

Das, T.K., & Teng, B.-S. (1998). Between trust and control: Developing confidence in partner cooperation in alliances. *The Academy of Management Review, 23*(3), 491–512. doi:10.2307/259291

Daskalaki, M. (2010). Building 'bonds' and 'bridges': Linking tie evolution and network identity in the creative industries. *Organization Studies, 31*(12), 1649–1666.

Davies, A. (2017). *Projects: A Very Short Introduction*. Oxford: Oxford University Press.

Davies, A., & Brady, T. (2000). Organisational capabilities and learning in complex product systems: Towards repeatable solutions. *Research Policy, 29*(7), 931–953. doi:https://doi.org/10.1016/S0048-7333(00)00113-X

Davies, A., & Brady, T. (2016). Explicating the dynamics of project capabilities. *International Journal of Project Management, 34*(2), 314–327. doi:https://doi.org/10.1016/j.ijproman.2015.04.006

Davies, A., Brady, T., Prencipe, A., & Hobday, M. (2011). Innovation in complex products and systems: Implications for project-based organizing. *Advances in Strategic Management, 28*, 3–26. doi:10.1108/S0742-3322(2011)0000028005

Davies, A., & Frederiksen, L. (2010). Project-based innovation: The world after Woodward. In *Technology and Organization: Essays in Honour of Joan Woodward* (pp. 177–215). Bingley: Emerald Group Publishing Limited.

Davies, A., & Hobday, M. (2005). *The Business of Projects: Managing Innovation in Complex Products and Systems.* Cambridge: Cambridge University Press.

Davis, K. (2018). Reconciling the views of project success: A Multiple Stakeholder model. *Project Management Journal, 49*(5), 38–47. doi:10.1177/8756972818786663

De Meyer, A., Loch, C., & Pich, M. (2002). Managing project uncertainty: From variation to chaos. MIT Sloan Management Review. Rev., 43(2), 60–7.

De Meyer, A. C. L., Loch, C. H., & Pich, M. T. (2002). Managing project uncertainty: From variation to chaos. *MIT Sloan Management Review, 43*(2), 60.

De Paoli, D. (2014). Disappearing bodies in virtual leadership? In A. Ropo (ed.), *The Physicality of Leadership: Gesture, Entanglement, Taboo, Possibilities* (pp. 59–79) *Bingley*: Emerald Group Publishing Limited.

Deal, T.E., & Kennedy, A. A. (1982). *Corporate Cultures: The Rites and Rituals of Corporate Life.* Reading, MA: Addison-Wesley.

Dean, M. (2010). *Governmentality: Power and Rule in Modern Society.* London: Sage.

DeBarro, T., MacAulay, S., Davies, A., Wolstenholme, A., Gann, D., & Pelton, J. (2015). Mantra to method: lessons from managing innovation on Crossrail, UK. Paper presented at the Proceedings of the Institution of Civil Engineers-Civil Engineering.

DeChurch, L.A., & Mathieu, J. E. (2009). *Thinking in Terms of Multiteam Systems.* London: Routledge.

DeFillippi, R.J., & Arthur, M. B. (1998). Paradox in project-based enterprise: The case of film. *California Management Review, 40*(2), 125–139. Retrieved from https://login.ezproxy.hil.no/login?url=http://search.ebscohost.com/login.aspx?direct=true&db=buh&AN=348756&site=ehost-live&scope=site

Deming, W.E. (2000). *Out of the Crisis.* Cambridge, MA: MIT Press.

Dequech, D. (2000). Fundamental uncertainty and ambiguity. *Eastern Economic Journal, 26*(1), 41–60.

Dequech, D. (2011). Uncertainty: A typology and refinements of existing concepts. *Journal of Economic Issues, 45*(3), 621–640. doi:10.2753/JEI0021-3624450306

Deroy, X., & Clegg, S.R. (2011). When events interact with business ethics. *Organization, 18*(5), 637–653. doi:10.1177/1350508410393773

Dewey, J. (1938). *Logic: The Theory of Enquiry.* New York: Holt Rinehart & Winston.

Dille, T., Hernes, T. & Vaagaasar, A.L. (2019). Coordinating multiple organizational actors: The temporal challenge of temporary organizations. *Paper presented at the European Group for Organization Studies*, 2-4 July, 2019, Edinburgh, Scotland.

Dille, T., Söderlund, J., & Clegg, S.R. (2018). Temporal conditioning and the dynamics of inter-institutional projects. *International Journal of Project Management, 36*(5), 673–686. doi:10.1016/j.ijproman.2018.03.007

Dobson, K. (2013). Lessons from London 2012 Olympics: A cribsheet for major projects, *Guardian*, 22 January. Available at: www.theguardian.com/public-leaders-network/2013/jan/22/lessons-london-2012-government-projects (accessed 26 February 2020).

Doerr, J. (2018). *Measure What Matters: How Google, Bono, and the Gates Foundation Rock the world with OKRs.* London: Penguin.

Doran, G.T. (1981). There's a S.M.A.R.T. way to write managements's goals and objectives. *Management Review, 70*(11), 35. Retrieved from https://login.ezproxy.hil.no/login?url=

Dosi, G., & Egidi, M. (1991). Substantive and procedural uncertainty: An exploration of economic behaviours in changing environments. *Journal of Evolutionary Economics, 1*(2), 145–168. doi:10.1007/BF01224917

Driessen, P.H., & Hillebrand, B. (2013). Integrating multiple stakeholder issues in new product development: An exploration. *Journal of Product Innovation Management, 30*(2), 364–379. doi:10.1111/j.1540–5885.2012.01004.x

Drucker, P. F. (1976). *People and Performance: The Best of Peter Drucker on Management* London: Routledge.

Drummond, H. (2018). Megaproject escalation of commitment. In B. Flybjerg (ed.), *The Oxford Handbook of Megaproject Management.* Oxford: Oxford University Press.

Druskat, V.U., & Kayes, D. C. (2000). Learning versus performance in short-term project teams. *Small Group Research, 31*(3), 328–353.

du Gay, P. (2000). Enterprise and its futures: A response to Fournier and Grey. *Organization, 7*(1), 165–183.

Duhigg, C. (2016). *Smarter Faster Better: The Secrets of Being Productive in Life and Business.* New York: Random House.

Durham, C. C., Knight, D., & Locke, E. A. (1997). Effects of leader role, team-set goal difficulty, efficacy, and tactics on team effectiveness. *Organizational Behavior and Human Decision Processes, 72*(2), 203–231. doi:http://dx.doi.org/10.1006/obhd.1997.2739

Dwivedula, R., & Bredillet, C. N. (2010). Profiling work motivation of project workers. *International Journal of Project Management, 28*(2), 158–165.

Dylan, B. (1965). Love minus zero/no limit. On *Bringing It All Back Home* (LP). New York: Colombia.

Dysvik, A., Buch, R., & Kuvaas, B. (2015). Knowledge donating and knowledge collecting The moderating roles of social and economic LMX. *Leadership and Organization Development Journal, 36*(1), 35–53. doi:10.1108/LODJ-11–2012–0145

Dysvik, A., & Kuvaas, B. (2013). Intrinsic and extrinsic motivation as predictors of work effort: The moderating role of achievement goals. British Journal of Social Psychology, 52(3), 412–430.

Ebbers, J. J., & Wijnberg, N. M. (2009). Latent organizations in the film industry: Contracts, rewards and resources. *Human Relations, 62*(7), 987–1009.

Eccles, R. G. (1981). The quasifirm in the construction industry. *Journal of Economic Behavior & Organization, 2*(4), 335–357. doi:https://doi.org/10.1016/0167–2681(81)90013–5

Edmondson, A. (1999). Psychological safety and learning behavior in work teams. *Administrative Science Quarterly, 44*(2), 350–383.

Edmondson, A.C. (2012). *Teaming: How Organizations Learn, Innovate, and Compete in the Knowledge Economy.* San Francisco, CA: Jossey-Bass.

Edmondson, A.C. (2018). *The Fearless Organization: Creating Psychological Safety in the Workplace for Learning, Innovation, and growth.* Chichester: John Wiley & Sons.

Edmondson, A.C., & Nembhard, I. M. (2009). Product development and learning in project teams: The challenges are the benefits. *Journal of Product Innovation Management, 26*(2), 123–138.

Einhorn, H. J., & Hogarth, R. M. (1986). Decision making under ambiguity. *The Journal of Business, 59*(4), S225. doi:10.1086/296364

Eisenhardt, K.M., & Martin, J. A. (2000). Dynamic capabilities: What are they? *Strategic Management Journal, 21*(10–11), 1105–1121.

Eisenhardt, K.M., & Tabrizi, B. N. (1995). Accelerating adaptive processes: Product innovation in the global computer industry. *Administrative Science Quarterly, 40*(1), 84–110.

Elangovan, A.R., & Shapiro, D. (1998). Betrayal of trust in organizations. *Academy of Management Review, 23*(3), 547–566.

Ellsberg, D. (1961). Risk, ambiguity, and the savage axioms. *Quarterly Journal of Economics, 75*(4), 643–669. doi:10.2307/1884324

Elonen, S., & Artto, K.A. (2003). Problems in managing internal development projects in multi-project environments. *International Journal of Project Management, 21*(6), 395–402. doi:10.1016/S0263-7863(02)00097–2

Elsbach, K. D., & Stigliani, I. (2018). Design Thinking and Organizational Culture: A Review and Framework for Future Research. *Journal of Management, 44*(6), 2274–2306.

Engwall, M. (2003). No project is an island: Linking projects to history and context. *Research Policy, 32*(5), 789–808.

Engwall, M., & Jerbrant, A. (2003). The resource allocation syndrome: The prime challenge of multi-project management? *International Journal of Project Management, 21*(6), 403–409. doi:10.1016/S0263-7863(02)00113–8

Engwall, M., & Westling, G. (2004). Peripety in an R&D drama: Capturing a turnaround in project dynamics. *Organization Studies, 25*(9), 1557–1578.

Eriksson, P.E. (2013). Exploration and exploitation in project-based organizations: Development and diffusion of knowledge at different organizational levels in construction companies. *International Journal of Project Management, 31*(3), 333–341. doi:http://dx.doi.org/10.1016/j.ijproman.2012.07.005

Eriksson, P. E., Leiringer, R., & Szentes, H. (2017). The role of co-creation in enhancing explorative and exploitative learning in project-based settings. *Project Management Journal, 48*(4), 22.

Eskerod, P. (1998). The human resource a process when organising by projects. In R. A. Lundin & C. Midler (eds.), *Projects as Arenas for Renewal and Learning Processes* (pp. 125–131). Boston, MA: Springer US.

Eskerod, P., & Jepsen, A. L. (2013). *Project Stakeholder Management*. Farnham: Gower.

Eskerod, P., & Vaagaasar, A. L. (2014). Stakeholder management strategies and practices during a project course. *Project Management Journal, 45*(5), 71–85. doi:10.1002/pmj.21447

European_Commission. (2003). *Guidelines for Successful Public – Private Partnerships*. Retrieved from Brussel: https://ec.europa.eu/regional_policy/sources/docgener/guides/ppp_en.pdf

Fahim, H.M. (2015). *Dams, People and Development: The Aswan High Dam Case*. Elsevier.

Fairtlough, G. (2005). *Three Ways of Getting Things Done: Hierarchy, Heterarchy and Responsible Autonomy in Organizations*.

Fayol, H. (1917). *Administration industrielle et générale; prévoyance,* Axminster: Triarchy press. *Organisation, commandement, coordination*. Paris: H. Dunod et E. Pinat.

Feduzi, A. (2007). On the relationship between Keynes's conception of evidential weight and the Ellsberg paradox. *Journal of Economic Psychology, 28*(5), 545–565.

Feldman, M. S., & Orlikowski, W. J. (2011). Theorizing practice and practicing theory. *Organization Science, 22*(5), 1240.

Feldman, M. S., & Pentland, B. T. (2003). Reconceptualizing organizational routines as a source of flexibility and change. *Administrative Science Quarterly, 48*(1), 94–118.

Feldman, M. S., & Rafaeli, A. (2002). Organizational routines as sources of connections and understandings. *Journal of Management Studies, 39*(3), 309–331.

Fisk, E. (1997). *Construction Project Administration*. Upper Saddle River, NJ: Prentice Hall.

Fitzgerald, B. (1996). Formalized systems development methodologies: A critical perspective. *Information Systems Journal, 6*(1), 3–23.

Fleming, P. (2019). Robots and organization studies: Why robots might not want to steal your job. *Organization Studies, 40*(1), 23–38. doi:10.1177/0170840618765568

Fleming, P., & Spicer, A. (2014). Power in management and organization science. *The Academy of Management Annals, 8*(1), 237–298.

Flyvbjerg, B. (2001). *Making Social Science Matter: Why Social Inquiry Fails and How It Can Succeed Again*. Cambridge: Cambridge University Press.

Flyvbjerg, B. (2002). Bringing power to planning research one researcher's praxis story. *Journal of Planning Education and Research, 21*(4), 353–366. doi:10.1177/0739456X0202100401

Flyvbjerg, B. (2005). Design by deception: The politics of megaproject approval. *Harvard Design Magazine* (22), 50–59. Retrieved from https://ssrn.com/abstract=2238047"\t

Flyvbjerg, B. (2006a). From Nobel Prize to project management: getting risks right. *Project Management Journal, 37*(3), 5.

Flyvbjerg, B. (2006b). Making organization research matter: Power, values, and phronesis. In S. R. Clegg, C. Hardy, T. B. Lawrence, & W. R. Nord (eds.), *Handbook of Organization Studies* (2nd edn, pp. 370–387). Thousand Oaks, CA: Sage.

Flyvbjerg, B. (2007). *Megaproject Policy and Planning: Problems, Causes, Cures*. Aalborg: Institut for Samfundsudvikling og Planlægning, Aalborg Universitet.

Flyvbjerg, B. (2008). Curbing optimism bias and strategic misrepresentation in planning: Reference class forecasting in practice. *European Planning Studies, 16*(1), 3–21.

Flyvbjerg, B. (2014a). *Megaproject Planning and Management: Essential Readings* Cheltenham: Edward Elgar Publishing.

Flyvbjerg, B. (2014b). What you should know about megaprojects and why: An overview. *Project Management Journal, 45*(2), 6–19.

Flyvbjerg, B., Bruzelius, N., & Rothengatter, W. (2003). *Megaprojects and Risk: An Anatomy of Ambition*. Cambridge: Cambridge University Press.

Flyvbjerg, B., & Budzier, A. (2011). Why your IT project may be riskier than you think. *Harvard Business Review, 89*(9), 23–25.

Forsberg, K., Mooz, H., & Cotterman, H. (1996). *Visualizing Project Management*. New York: Wiley.

Foucault, M. (1982). The subject and power. In H. Dreyfus & R. P. (eds.), *Michel Foucault: Beyond Structuralism and Hermeneutics* (pp. 208–226). Chicago: University of Chicago Press.

Foucault, M. (1997). *Ethics: Subjectivity and Truth: The Essential Works of Michel Foucault, 1954–1984* (Vol. *1*). New York: The New Press.

Foucault, M. (2007). *Security, Territory, Population: Lectures at the Collège de France, 1977–78*. Berlin: Springer.

Frame, J.D. (2003). *Managing Projects in Organizations: How to Make the Best Use of Time, Techniques, and People* (3rd edn). San Francisco, CA: Jossey-Bass.

Freeman, R. E. (1984). *Strategic Management: A Stakeholder Approach*. Boston, MA: Pitman/Ballinger.

Freudenberger, H.J. (1974). Staff burn-out. *Journal of Social Issues, 30*(1), 159–165.

Frick, K. T. (2008). The cost of the technological Sublime: Daring ingenuity and the new San Francisco-Oakland Bay Bridge. In H. Priemus, B. Flyvbjerg, & B. van Wee (eds.), *Decision-Making On Mega-Projects: Cost–Benefit Analysis, Planning, and Innovation*. Cheltenham: Edward Elgar.

Friedland, R., & Alford, R.R. (1991). Bringing society back: Symbols, practices, and institutional contradictions. In W. W. Powell & P. DiMaggio (eds.), *The New Institutionalism in Organizational Analysis*. Chicago: University of Chicago Press.

Frooman, J. (1999). Stakeholder influence strategies. *Academy of Management Review, 24*(2), 191–205.

Frost, P. J. (2007). *Toxic Emotions at Work and What You Can Do About Them*. Boston, MA: Harvard Business Press.

Gann, D., Salter, A., Dodgson, M., & Phillips, N. (2012). Inside the world of the project baron. *MIT Sloan Management Review, 53*(3), 63–71.

Garel, G. (2013). A history of project management models: From pre-models to the standard models. *International Journal of Project Management, 31*(5), 663–669.

Garfinkel, H. (1967). *Studies in Ethnomethodolgy*. Evanston, IL: Prentice Hall.

Garland, R. (2009). *Project Governance: A Practical Guide to Effective Project Decision Making*. London: Kogan Page.

Garrick, J. (1998). *Informal Learning in the Workplace: Unmasking Human Resource Development*. London: Routledge.

Garrick, J., & Clegg, S.R. (2001). Stressed-out knowledge workers in performative times: A postmodern take on project-based learning. *Management Learning, 32*(1), 119–134. doi:10.1177/1350507601321008

Garvin, D. A., & Roberto, M. A. (2001). What you don't know about making decisions. *Harvard Business Review, 79*(8), 108.

Geertz, C. (1973). *Thick Descriptions: Towards an Interpretive Theory of Cultures. Selected Essays*. New York: Basic Books.

Geithner, S., Menzel, D., Wolfe, J., & Kriz, W. (2016). Effectiveness of learning through experience and reflection in a project management simulation. *Simulation & Gaming, 47*(2), 228–256. doi:10.1177/1046878115624312

George, B. (2003). *Authentic Leadership: Rediscovering the Secrets to Creating Lasting Value.* Chichester: John Wiley & Sons.

Geraldi, J.G., Lee-Kelley, L., & Kutsch, E. (2010). The Titanic sunk, so what? Project manager response to unexpected events. *International Journal of Project Management, 28*(6), 547–558. doi:10.1016/j.ijproman.2009.10.008

Gersick, C.J. (1988). Time and transition in work teams: Toward a new model of group development. *Academy of Management Journal, 31*(1), 9–41.

Gersick, C.J., & Hackman, J. R. (1990). Habitual routines in task-performing groups. *Organizational Behavior and Human Decision Processes, 47*(1), 65–97.

Ghaim, M., Clegg, S. R. and Cunha, M. P. e (2019). Managing impressions rather than emissions: Volkswagen and the false mastery of paradox, *Organization Studies,* 0170840619891199.

Gherardi, S. (2000). Practice-based Theorizing on learning and knowing in organizations. *Organization, 7*(2), 211–223. doi:10.1177/135050840072001

Giddens, A. (1991). *Modernity and Self-identity: Self and Society in the Late Modern Age.* Cambridge: Polity Press.

Giezen, M. (2012). Keeping it simple? A case study into the advantages and disadvantages of reducing complexity in mega project planning. *International Journal of Project Management, 30*(7), 781–790. doi:10.1016/j.ijproman.2012.01.010

Giezen, M., Salet, W., & Bertolini, L. (2015). Adding value to the decision-making process of mega projects: Fostering strategic ambiguity, redundancy, and resilience. *Transport Policy, 44,* 169–178.

Gil, N. (2017). A collective-action perspective on the planning of megaprojects. In B. Flybjerg (ed.), *The Oxford Handbook of Megaproject Management.* Oxford: Oxford University Press.

Gil, N.A. (2015). Sustaining highly-fragile collaborations: A study of planning mega infrastructure projects in the UK. *Available at SSRN 2557370.*

Goggin, C.L., Barrett, T., Leys, J., Summerell, G., Gorrod, E., Waters, S., . . . Jenkins, B. R. (2019). Incorporating social dimensions in planning, managing and evaluating environmental projects. *Environmental Management, 63*(2), 215–232.

Goldman, D. (2015). Mega-hot biotech startup Theranos calls WSJ take-down 'baseless'. *CNN,* 15 October.

Golsorkhi, D., Rouleau, L., Seidl, D. & Vaara, E. (2016). *Cambridge Handbook of Strategy as Practice.* Cambridge: Cambridge University Press.

Gong, Y., Zhang, Y. & Xia, J. (2019). Do firms learn more from small or big successes and failures? A test of the outcome-based feedback learning perspective. *Journal of Management, 45*(3), 1034–1056.

Gordon, J. & Tulip, A. (1997). Resource scheduling. *International Journal of Project Management, 15*(6), 359–370. doi:https://doi.org/10.1016/S0263-7863(96)00090-7

Gouldner, A. W. (1954). *Patterns of Industrial Bureaucracy.* New York: Free Press.

Granovetter, M. (1985). Economic action and social structure: The problem of embeddedness. *American Journal of Sociology, 91*(3), 481–510.

Gransberg, D.D., Dillon, W.D., Reynolds, L., & Boyd, J. (1999). Quantitative analysis of partnered project performance. *Journal of Construction Engineering and Management, 125*(3), 161.

Grant, K.P. & Pennypacker, J. S. (2006). Project management maturity. An assessment of project management capabilities among and between selected industries. *IEEE Transactions on Engineering Management, 53*(1), 10.

Grant, R.M. (1996). Toward a knowledge-based theory of the firm. *Strategic Management Journal, 17,* 109–122.

Green, S.D. & Sergeeva, N. (2019). Value creation in projects: towards a narrative perspective. *International journal of project management, 37*(5), 636–651.

Greenwood, R. Raynard, M., Kodeih, F., Micelotta, E. R. & Lounsbury, M. (2011). Institutional complexity and organizational responses. *Academy of Management annals, 5*(1), 317–371.

Greer, N. & Ksaibati, K. (2019). Development of benefit cost analysis tools for evaluating transportation research projects. *Transportation Research Record, 2673*(1), 123–135.

Grimsey, D. & Lewis, M. K. (2002). Evaluating the risks of public private partnerships for infrastructure projects. *International Journal of Project Management, 20*(2), 107–118.

Gruden, N. & Stare, A. (2018). The influence of behavioral competencies on project performance. *Project Management Journal, 49*(3), 98–109. doi:10.1177/8756972818770841

Guide, P. (2017). *A Guide to the Project Management Body of Knowledge* (6th edn). Project Management Institute, Inc.

Gulati, R. & Singh, H. (1998). The architecture of cooperation: managing coordination costs and appropriation concerns in strategic alliances. *Administrative Science Quarterly, 43*(4), 781–814. doi:10.2307/2393616

Gulati, R. Wohlgezogen, F. & Zhelyazkov, P. I. (2012). The Two Facets of Collaboration: Cooperation and Coordination in Strategic Alliances.

Gully, S. M., Incalcaterra, K. A., Joshi, A. & Beaubien, J. M. (2002). A meta-analysis of team-efficacy, potency, and performance: Interdependence and level of analysis as moderators of observed relationships. *Journal of Applied Psychology, 87*(5), 819.

Guven, B. & Johnson, L. (2018). PPPs and ISDS: A risky combination. Retrieved from http://investmentpolicyhub.unctad.org/Blog/Index/65

Hackman, J.R. (1987). The design of work teams. In J. W. Lorsch (ed.), *Handbook of Organizational Behavior*. Englewood Cliffs, NJ: Prentice-Hall.

Hackman, J.R. (2002). *Leading Teams: Setting the Stage for Great Performances*. Boston, MA: Harvard Business School Press.

Hackman, J.R. (2011). *Collaborative Intelligence: Using Teams to Solve Hard Problems*.

Hackman, J.R. & Coutu, D. (2009). Why teams don't work. *Harvard Business Review, 87*(5).

Hackman, J.R. & Oldham, G. R. (1980). *Work Redesign*. Reading, MA: Addison-Wesley.

Hackman, J.R. & Wageman, R. (2004). When and How Team Leaders Matter. *Research in Organizational Behavior, 26*, 37–74.

Hackman, J. R. & Wageman, R. (2005). A Theory of Team Coaching. *Academy of management review, 30*(2), 269–287. doi:10.5465/AMR.2005.16387885

Halbesleben, J. R. B., Novicevic, M. M., Harvey, M. G. & Buckley, M. R. (2003). Awareness of temporal complexity in leadership of creativity and innovation: A competency-based model. *Leadership Quarterly, 14*(4/5), 433. doi:10.1016/S1048-9843(03)00046-8

Halman, J. I. & Burger, G. (2002). Evaluating effectiveness of project start-ups: an exploratory study. *International Journal of Project Management, 20*(1), 81–89.

Hanlon, G. (1998). Professionalism as enterprise: Service class politics and the redefinition of professionalism. *Sociology, 32*(1), 43–63.

Hansen, M.T. (2018). Great at work: how to fight and unite. *Leader to Leader, 2018*(89), 7–13. doi:10.1002/ltl.20369

Hargadon, A. & Bechky, B. A. (2006). When collections of creatives become creative collectives: A field study of problem solving at work. *Organization Science, 17*(4), 484–500.

Hargadon, A. B. (2002). Brokering knowledge: Linking learning and innovation. *Research in Organizational Behavior, 24*, 41–85.

Harrison, V. (2015). Young and super rich: Top 10 billionaires under 40. *CNN*, 4 March.

Hartmann, A. & Dorée, A. (2015). Learning between projects: More than sending messages in bottles. *International Journal of Project Management, 33*(2), 341–351.

Heath, C. (1999). On the social psychology of agency relationships: Lay theories of motivation overemphasize extrinsic incentives. *Organizational Behavior and Human Decision Processes, 78*(1), 25–62.

Heikkurinen, P., Clegg, S., Pinnington, A. H., Nicolopoulou, K. & Alcaraz, J. M. (2019). Managing the Anthropocene: Relational agency and power to respect planetary boundaries. *Organization & Environment*, 1086026619881145.

Hellgren, B. & Stjernberg, T. (1995). Design and implementation in major investments—a project network approach. *Scandinavian Journal of Management, 11*(4), 377–394.

Helm, J. & Remington, K. (2005). Effective project sponsorship an evaluation of the role of the executive sponsor in complex infrastructure projects by senior project managers. *Project Management Journal, 36*(3), 51–61.

Henisz, W.J. (2016). The dynamic capability of corporate diplomacy. *Global Strategy Journal, 6*(3), 183–196.

Hernes, T., Simpson, B. & Söderlund, J. (2013). Managing and temporality. *Scandinavian Journal of Management, 29*(1), 1–6. doi:http://dx.doi.org/10.1016/j.scaman.2012.11.008

Herring, G.C. (1986). *America's Longest War: The United States and Vietnam, 1950–1975* (2nd edn). New York: Knopf.

Herzberg, F., Mausner, B. & Snyderman, B. B. (1959). *The Motivation to Work* (2nd edn). New York: Wiley.

Hesmondhalgh, D. & Baker, S. (2008). Creative work and emotional labour in the television industry. *Theory, Culture & Society, 25*(7–8), 97–118.

Hesmondhalgh, D. & Baker, S. (2010). 'A very complicated version of freedom': Conditions and experiences of creative labour in three cultural industries. *Poetics, 38*(1), 4–20.

Hickson, D., Hinings, C., Lee, C., Schneck, R. & Pennings, J. (1971). A strategic contingencies theory of intra-organizational power. *Administrative Science Quarterly, 16*.

Hickson, D.J., Pugh, D. S. & Pheysey, D. C. (1969). Operations technology and organization structure: an empirical reappraisal. *Administrative Science Quarterly, 14*(3), 378–397. doi:10.2307/2391134

Hidalgo, E. S. (2019). Adapting the scrum framework for agile project management in science: Case study of a distributed research initiative. *Heliyon, 5*(3), e01447.

Hill, L.A. (2014). *Collective Genius: The Art and Practice of Leading Innovation*. Boston, MA: Harvard Business School Press.

Hillson, D. & Murray-Webster, R. (2007). *Understanding and Managing Risk Attitude* (2nd edn). Aldershot: Gower.

Hillson, D. A. (1997). Towards a risk maturity model. *The International Journal of Project & Business Risk Management, 1*(1), 35–45.

Hobbs, B. & Aubry, M. (2007). A multi-phase research program investigating project management offices (PMOs): the results of phase 1. *Project Management Journal, 38*(1), 74–86.

Hobbs, B. & Petit, Y. (2017). Agile methods on large projects in large organizations. *Project Management Journal, 48*(3), 3–19. doi:10.1177/875697281704800301

Hobday, M. (2000). The project-based organisation: an ideal form for managing complex products and systems?. *Research policy, 29*(7–8), 871–893.

Hobfoll, S. E. (2011). Conservation of resource caravans and engaged settings. *Journal of Occupational and Organizational Psychology, 84*(1), 116–122.

Hobsbawn, E. J. (1975). *The Age of capital*. London: Weidenfield & Nicholson.

Hodgson, D. & Cicmil, S. (2007). The politics of standards in modern management: Making 'the project' a reality. *Journal of Management Studies, 44*(3), 431–450. doi:10.1111/j.1467-6486.2007.00680.x

Hoegl, M. & Gemuenden, H. G. (2001). Teamwork quality and the success of innovative projects: a theoretical concept and empirical evidence. *Organization Science, 12*(4), 435–449.

Hoegl, M. & Muethel, M. (2016). Enabling shared leadership in virtual project teams: A practitioners' guide. *Project Management Journal, 47*(1), 7–12. doi:10.1002/pmj.21564

Hoegl, M. & Proserpio, L. (2004). Team member proximity and teamwork in innovative projects. *Research Policy, 33*(8), 1153–1165.

Hofstede, G. (2001). *Culture's Consequences: Comparing Values, Behaviors, Institutions, and Organizations across Nations*. Thousand Oaks, CA: Sage.

Holland, S., Gaston, K. & Gomes, J. (2000). Critical success factors for cross-functional teamwork in new product development. *International Journal of Management Reviews, 2*(3), 231. doi:10.1111/1468-2370.00040

Hoskin, K., Macve, R. & Stone, J. (1997). The historical genesis of modern business and military strategy: 1850–1950. Paper presented at the Proceedings of the Interdisciplinary Perspectives on Accounting Conference, Manchester.

Huber, G.P. (1991). Organizational learning: The contributing processes and the literatures. *Organization Science, 2*(1), 88–115. doi:10.1287/orsc.2.1.88

Hughes, D.J. (1995). *Moltke on the Art of War: Selected Writings*: Random House Digital, Inc.

Hydle, K.M., Kvålshaugen, R., & Breunig, K. J. (2014). Transnational practices in communities of task and communities of learning. *Management Learning, 45*(5), 609–629.

Hällgren, M & Söderholm, A. (2011). Project as practice. New Approach. new insight. In P. W.G. Morris, J. K. Pinto, & J. Söderlund (eds.), *The Oxford Handbook of Project Management*. Oxford: Oxford University Press.

Hällgren, M., & Wilson, T. L. (2008). The nature and management of crises in construction projects: Projects-as-practice observations. *International Journal of Project Management, 26*(8), 830–838. doi:10.1016/j.ijproman.2007.10.005

Hodgson, D., Paton, S., & Muzio, D. (2015). Something old, something new: Competing logics and the hybrid nature of new corporate professions. *British Journal of Management, 26*(4), 745–759.

Irwin, T., Klein, M., Perry, G. E. & Thobani, M. (1998). *Dealing with Public Risk in Private Infrastructure*. Washington, DC: The World Bank.

Janis, I.L. (1972). *Victims of groupthink: A Psychological Study of Foreign-policy Decisions and Fiascoes*. Atlanta, GA: Houghton Mifflin.

Jenner, S. (2010). *Transforming Government and Public Services: Realising Benefits through Project Portfolio Management*.

Jennings, W. (2012). Executive politics, risk and the mega-project paradox. In M. Lodge & K. Wegrich (eds), *Executive Politics in Times of Crisis*. Basingstoke: Palgrave Macmillan.

Jin, X.-H. (2009). Determinants of efficient risk allocation in privately financed public infrastructure projects in Australia. *Journal of Construction Engineering and Management, 136*(2), 138–150.

Johnson, C. (2015). FDA approves Theranos' $9 finger stick blood test for herpes; Theranos announced that the FDA had approved the test for herpes simplex 1 virus. *The Washington Post*, 2 July.

Johnson, C. (2015). The wildly hyped $9 billion blood test company that no one really understands. *Washington Post*, 16 October.

Johnson, C., & Eunjung, C. A. (2015). A comprehensive guide to Theranos's troubles and what it means for you: A Wall Street Journal investigation has raised questions about the company's technology. *The Washington Post*, 17 October.

Jones, C., & Lichtenstein, B. (2008). Temporary inter-organizational projects: How temporal and social embeddedness enhance coordination and manage uncertainty. In S. Cropper, M. Ebers, C. Huxham, & P. S. Ring (eds), *The Oxford Handbook of Inter-organizational Relations*. Oxford: Oxford University Press.

Jones, C., & Lichtenstein, B. B. (2008). Temporary inter-organizational projects. In S. Cropper, M. Ebers, C. Huxham, & P. S. Ring (eds), *The Oxford Handbook of Inter-organizational Relations*. Oxford: Oxford University Press.

Jones, J., & Barry, M. M. (2018). Factors influencing trust and mistrust in health promotion partnerships. *Global Health Promotion, 25*(2), 16–24. doi:10.1177/1757975916656364

Judge, T. A., Heller, D., & Mount, M. K. (2002). Five-factor model of personality and job satisfaction: A meta-analysis. *Journal of Applied Psychology, 87*(3), 530.

Judge, W.Q., & Speitzfaden, M. (1995). The management of strategic time horizons within biotechnology firms: The impact of cognitive complexity on time horizon diversity. *Journal of Management Inquiry, 4*(2), 179–196.

Jugdev, K., & Müller, R. (2005). A retrospective look at our evolving understanding of project success. In (pp. 19–31).

Jørgensen, S., & Pedersen, L. J. T. (2018). *RESTART Sustainable Business Model Innovation*. Basingstoke: Palgrave Macmillan.

Kahneman, D. (2012). *Thinking, Fast and Slow*. London: Penguin Books.

Kahneman, D. & Tversky, A. (2000). *Choices, Values, and Frames*. Cambrigde: Cambridge University Press.

Kamoche, K., & Cunha, M. P. E. (2001). Minimal structures: From jazz improvisation to product innovation. *Organization Studies, 22*(5), 733–764.

Kanter, R.M. (2006). Innovation: The classic traps. *Harvard Business Review, 84*(11), 72–83.

Kanter, R.M. (2009). *Supercorp: How Vanguard Companies Create Innovation, Profits, Growth, and Social Good*. New York: Crown Business.

Kaplan, R.S., & Norton, D. P. (1996). *The Balanced Scorecard: Translating Strategy into Action*. Boston, MA: Harvard Business School Press.

Karlsen, J.T. (2013). *Prosjektledelse: fra initiering til gevinstrealisering*. Oslo: Universitetsforl.

Katzenbach, J. R. (1998). *Teams at the Top: Unleashing the Potential of Both Teams and Individual Leaders*. Boston, MA: Harvard Business School Press.

Keegan, A., & Turner, J. R. (2002). The management of innovation in project-based firms. *Long Range Planning, 35*(4), 367–388. doi:http://dx.doi.org/10.1016/S0024-6301(02)00069-9

Keegan, A.E., & Den Hartog, D. N. (2004). Transformational leadership in a project-based environment: A comparative study of the leadership styles of project managers and line managers. *International Journal of Project Management, 22*(8), 609–617.

Keller, R. T. (2006). Transformational leadership, initiating structure, and substitutes for leadership: A longitudinal study of research and development project team performance. *Journal of Applied Psychology, 91*(1), 202.

Kerr, S. & Landauer, S. (2004). Using stretch goals to promote organizational effectiveness and personal growth: General Electric and Goldman Sachs. Academy of Management Perspectives, 18(4), 134–138.

Keynes, J.M. (1921). *A Treatise on Probability: The Collected Writings of John Maynard Keynes*. London: Macmillan

Keynes, M. (1936). *The General Theory of Employment Interest and Money*. London: Macmillan.

King, W.R., & Cleland, D. I. (1975). The design of management information systems an information analysis approach. *Management Science, 22*(3), 286–297.

Kloppenborg, T. J., Manolis, C. & Tesch, D. (2009). Successful project sponsor behaviors during project initiation: An empirical investigation. *Journal of Managerial Issues, 21*(1), 140–159.

Knight, F.H. (1921). *Risk, Uncertainty and Profit*. New York: Hart, Schaffner, and Marx.

Knoll, K. & Jarvenpaa, S. L. (1998). Working together in global virtual teams. In *The Virtual Workplace* (pp. 2–23).

Koeslag, M., van den Bossche, P., Hoven, M., van der Klink, M. R., & Gijselaers, W. (2018). When leadership powers team learning: A meta-analysis. *Small Group Research, 49*(4), 475–513. doi:10.1177/1046496418764824

Kogut, B., & Zander, U. (1992). Knowledge of the firm, combinative capabilities, and the replication of technology. *Organization Science, 3*(3), 383–397.

Kokkonen, A., & Vaagaasar, A. L. (2018). Managing collaborative space in multi-partner projects. *Construction Management and Economics, 36*(2), 83–95. doi:10.1080/01446193.2017.1347268

Kolb, D.A. (1984). *Experiential Learning: Experience as the Source of Learning and Development*. Englewood Cliffs, NJ: Prentice-Hall.

Koskinen, K.U. (2008). Boundary brokering as a promoting factor in competence sharing in a project work context. *International Journal of Project Organisation and Management, 1*(1), 119–132.

Kramer, R.M. (2009). Rethinking trust. *Harvard Business Review, 87*(6), 68–77, 113.

Kreiner, K. (1995). In search of relevance: Project management in drifting environments. *Scandinavian Journal of Management, 11*(4), 335–346. doi:10.1016/0956-5221(95)00029-U

Kwak, Y.H. & Anbari, F.T. (2009). Analyzing project management research: Perspectives from top management journals. *International Journal of Project Management, 27*(5), 435–446.

Lancione, M., & Clegg, S.R. (2015). The lightness of management learning. *Management Learning, 46*(3), 280–298. doi:10.1177/1350507614526533

Larson, E., & Gray, C. (2017). *Project Management: The Managerial Process with MS Project*. New York: McGraw-Hill Education.

Larson, E.W., & Gobeli, D.H. (1987). Matrix management: contradictions and insights. *California Management Review, 29*(4), 126. doi:10.2307/41162135

Larson, E.W., & Gray, C.F. (2011). *Project Management: The Managerial Process*. Boston: McGraw-Hill.

Latour, B. (1988). *The Pasteurization of France*. Cambridge, MA: Harvard University Press.

Latour, B. (1996). *Aramis, or The love of technology*. Cambridge, MA: Harvard University Press.

Laub, J.A. (1999). *Assessing the servant organization. Development of the organizational leadership assessment (OLA) instrument*.

Laursen, M. (2018). Project networks as constellations for value creation. *Project Management Journal, 49*(2), 56–70.

Lave, J., & Wenger, E. (1991). *Situated Learning: Legitimate Peripheral Participation*. Cambridge: Cambridge University Press.

Lawrence, P. R. & Lorsch, J. W. (1967). Differentiation and integration in complex organizations. *Administrative Science Quarterly*, 1–47.

Lechler, T. G., & Cohen, M. (2009). Exploring the role of steering committees in realizing value from project management. *Project Management Journal, 40*(1), 42–54.

Lect, C.I. (2012). Basic notions of branding: Definition, history, architecture. *Journal of Media Research, 5*(3), 110.

Lee, C.L., Liang, J., & Koo, K. (2019) Rail works lift property prices, pointing to value capture's potential to fund city infrastructure. Available at: https://theconversation.com/rail-works-lift-property-prices-pointing-to-value-captures-potential-to-fund-city-infrastructure-123757 (accessed 23 February 2020).

Lefebvre, H. (1991). *The Production of Space*. Cambridge, MA: Blackwell.

Lemke, T. (2002). Foucault, governmentality, and critique. *Rethinking Marxism, 14*(3), 49–64.

Lenfle, S., & Loch, C. (2010). Lost roots: how project management came to emphasize control over flexibility and novelty. *California Management Review, 53*(1), 32–55. Retrieved from https://login.ezproxy.hil.no/login?url=http://search.ebscohost.com/login.aspx?direct=true&db=buh&AN=55117757&site=ehost-live&scope=site

Levi, D. (2015). *Group Dynamics for Teams*. London: Sage Publications.

Levinthal, D. (2011). A behavioral approach to strategy – what's the alternative? *Strategic Management Journal, 32*(13), 1517.

Levinthal, D. A., & March, J. G. (1993). The myopia of learning. *Strategic Management Journal, 14*, 95–112. doi:10.2307/2486499

Levitt, T. (1960). Marketing myopia. *Harvard Business Review, 38*(4), 45–56. Retrieved from https://login.ezproxy.hil.no/login?url=http://search.ebscohost.com/login.aspx?direct=true&db=buh&AN=6774995&site=ehost-live&scope=site

Li, Y., Lu, Y., Ma, L., & Kwak, Y. H. (2018). Evolutionary governance for mega-event projects (MEPs): A case study of the World Expo 2010 in China. *Project Management Journal, 49*(1), 57.

Liker, J. K., & Morgan, J. M. (2006). The Toyota way in services: The case of lean product development. *The Academy of Management Perspectives, 20*(2), 5. doi:10.5465/AMP.2006.20591002

Lindgren, M., & Packendorff, J. (2009). Project leadership revisited: Towards distributed leadership perspectives in project research. *International Journal of Project Organisation and Management, 1*(3), 285–308.

Lloyd-Walker, B., & Walker, D. (2011). Authentic leadership for 21st century project delivery. *International Journal of Project Management, 29*(4), 383–395.

Loch, C., & Sommer, S. (2019). The tension between flexible goals and managerial control in exploratory projects. *Project Management Journal, 50*(5), 524–537.

Loch, C.H., DeMeyer, A. & Pich, M. (2011). *Managing the Unknown: A New Approach to Managing High Uncertainty and Risk in Projects*. Chichester: John Wiley & Sons.

Loch, C.H., Solt, M.E., & Bailey, E.M. (2008). Diagnosing unforeseeable uncertainty in a new venture. *Journal of Product Innovation Management, 25*(1), 28.

Locke, E.A., & Latham, G.P. (1990). *A Theory of Goal Setting & Task Performance*. Prentice-Hall, Inc.

Loosemore, M. (2016). Social procurement in UK construction projects. *International Journal of Project Management, 34*(2), 133–144.

Loosemore, M., & Higgon, D. (2015). *Social Enterprise in the Construction Industry: Building Better Communities*. London: Routledge.

Lovallo, D., & Kahneman, D. (2003). Delusions of success. *Harvard Business Review, 81*(7), 56–63. Retrieved from https://login.ezproxy.hil.no/login?url=http://search.ebscohost.com/login.aspx?direct=true&db=buh&AN=10147066&site=ehost-live&scope=site

Luhmann, N. (1979). *Trust and Power.* Chichester: John Wiley.

Lukes, S. (2005). *Power: A Radical View* (2nd edn). Basingstoke: Palgrave Macmillan.

Lusch, R. F., & Vargo, S. L. (2014). *Service-dominant Logic: Premises, Perspectives, Possibilities.* Cambridge: Cambridge University Press.

Machiavelli, N. (1961). *The Prince.* London: Penguin Books.

MacIntyre, A. (1971). *Against the Self-images of the Age: Essays on Ideology and Philosophy.* London: Duckworth.

Manning, S. (2017). The rise of project network organizations: Building core teams and flexible partner pools for interorganizational projects. *Research Policy, 46*(8), 1399–1415.

March, J.G. (1991). Exploration and exploitation in organizational learning. *Organization Science, 2*(1), 71–87. Retrieved from https://login.ezproxy.hil.no/login?url=http://search.ebscohost.com/login.aspx?direct=true&db=buh&AN=4433770&site=ehost-live&scope=site

March, J. G., & Olsen, J. P. (1976). *Ambiguity and Choice in Organizations.* Bergen: Universitetsforlaget.

Marcuse, H. (1964). *One Dimensional Man.* London: Routledge & Kegan Paul.

Marks, J. (2000). Foucault, Franks, Gauls: Il faut defendre la société: The 1976 lectures at the Collège de France. *Theory, Culture & Society, 17*(5), 127–147.

Martin, J. (1992). *Cultures in Organizations: Three Perspectives.* New York: Oxford University Press.

Martin, J., Feldman, M.S., Hatch, M. J. & Sitkin, S. B. (1983). The uniqueness paradox in organizational stories. *Administrative Science Quarterly, 28*(3), 438–453. doi:10.2307/2392251

Martinsuo, M., & Lehtonen, P. (2009). Project autonomy in complex service development networks. *International Journal of Managing Projects in Business, 2*(2), 261–281.

Mathieu, J.E., Gallagher, P. T., Domingo, M. A., & Klock, E. A. (2019). Embracing complexity: Reviewing the past decade of team effectiveness research. *Annual Review of Organizational Psychology and Organizational Behavior, 6*(1), 17–46. doi:10.1146/annurev-orgpsych-012218–015106

Mathieu, J.E., & Rapp, T. L. (2009). Laying the foundation for successful team performance trajectories: The roles of team charters and performance strategies. *Journal of Applied Psychology, 94*(1), 90–103. doi:10.1037/a0013257

Maylor, H. (2010). *Project Management* (4th edn). Harlow: Financial Times Prentice Hall.

Maylor, H., Brady, T., Cooke-Davies, T., & Hodgson, D. (2006). From projectification to programmification. *International Journal of Project Management, 24*(8), 663–674.

Mazzucato, M. (2018a). *The Value of Everything: Making and Taking in the Global Economy.* London: Allen Lane.

Mazzucato, M. (2018b). Redefining economic value. Royal Society of Arts Lecture. Available at: www.youtube.com/watch?v=xJgjLfx-Bcs (accessed 26 February 2020).

Mazzacuto, M. (2018c). Takers and makers: Who are the real value creators? Available at: https://evonomics.com/value-of-everything-mariana-mazzucato/ (accessed 26 February 2020).

McIntyre, J., & Symes, C. (2000). *Working Knowledge: The New Vocationalism and Higher Education: Society for Research into Higher Education & Open University Press.*

Mengis, J., Nicolini, D., & Swan, J. (2018). Integrating knowledge in the face of epistemic uncertainty: Dialogically drawing distinctions. *Management Learning, 49*(5), 595–612. doi:10.1177/1350507618797216

Merrow, E. W. (2011). *Industrial Megaprojects : Concepts, Strategies, and Practices for Success.* Hoboken, NJ: John Wiley & Sons.

Meso, P., & Jain, R. (2006). Agile software development: Adaptive systems principles and rest practices. *Information Systems Management, 23*(3), 19–30. doi:10.1201/1078.10580530/46108.23.3.20060601/93704.3

Meyer, J. W., & Rowan, B. (1977). Institutionalized organizations: Formal structure as myth and ceremony. *American Journal of Sociology, 83*(2), 340–363. doi:10.1086/226550

Meyer, M.W., & Zucker, L.G. (1989). *Permanently Failing Organizations*. London Sage Publications, Inc.

Meyerson, D., Weick, K.E., & Kramer, R.M. (1996). Swift trust and temporary groups. In R. M. Kramer & T. Tyler (eds), *Trust in Organizations: Frontiers of Theory and Research* (pp. 166–196). Thousand Oaks, CA: SAGE Publications, Inc.

Michlewski, K. (2008). Uncovering design attitude: Inside the culture of designers. *Organization Studies, 29*(3), 373–392. doi:10.1177/0170840607088019

Midler, C., Maniak, R., & de Campigneulles, T. (2019). Ambidextrous program management: The case of autonomous mobility. *Project Management Journal, 50*(5), 571–586. doi:10.1177/8756972819869091

Mikkelsen, H., & Riis, J. O. (2017b). *Project Management: A Multi-perspective Leadership Framework*. Bingley: Emerald Publishing.

Milani, T. M. (2009). At the intersection between power and knowledge: An analysis of a Swedish policy document on language testing for citizenship. *Journal of Language and Politics, 8*(2), 287–304.

Miles, S. (2012). Stakeholder: Essentially contested or just confused? *Journal of Business Ethics, 108*(3), 285–298.

Millar, C.C.J. M., Groth, O., & Mahon, J.F. (2018). Management innovation in a VUCA world: Challenges and recommendations. *California Management Review, 61*(1), 5–14. doi:10.1177/0008125618805111

Miller, R., Lessard, D., & Sakhrani, V. (2017). Megaprojects as games of innovation. In B. Flybjerg (Ed.), *The Oxford Handbook of Megaproject Management* (pp. 249–259). Oxford: Oxford University Press.

Miller, R., & Lessard, D. R. (2000). *The Strategic Management of Large Engineering Projects: Shaping Institutions, Risks, and Governance*. Cambridge, MA: MIT Press.

Mintzberg, H. (1973). *The Nature of Managerial Work*. New York: Harper & Row.

Mintzberg, H. (1983). *Structure in Fives: Designing Effective Organizations*. Englewood Cliffs, N.J: Prentice-Hall.

Mintzberg, H. (2004). *Managers Not MBAs: A Hard Look at the Soft Practice of Managing and Management Development*. San Francisco, CA: Berrett-Koehler.

Mintzberg, H. (2009). *Managing*. San Francisco, CA: Berrett-Koehler.

Mintzberg, H., & Waters, J. A. (1985). Of strategies, deliberate and emergent. *Strategic Management Journal, 6*(3), 257–272. doi:10.1002/smj.4250060306

Mirabeau, L., & Maguire, S. (2014). From autonomous strategic behavior to emergent strategy. *Strategic Management Journal, 35*(8), 1202. doi:10.1002/smj.2149

Mitchell, R.K., Agle, B.R., & Wood, D.J. (1997). Toward a theory of stakeholder identification and salience: Defining the principle of who and what really counts. *The Academy of Management Review, 22*(4), 853–886. doi:10.2307/259247

Mok, K.Y., Shen, G. Q., & Yang, J. (2015). Stakeholder management studies in mega construction projects: A review and future directions. *International Journal of Project Management, 33*(2), 446–457.

Morgan, R.M., & Hunt, S.D. (1994). The commitment-trust theory of relationship marketing. *Journal of Marketing, 58*(3), 20–38.

Moritz, M. (2015). The subprime 'unicorns' that do not look a billion dollars. *Financial Times,* 16 October.

Morris, P. W. (1994). *The Management of Projects*. Thomas Telford.

Morris, P. W., Crawford, L., Hodgson, D., Shepherd, M. M., & Thomas, J. (2006). Exploring the role of formal bodies of knowledge in defining a profession – The case of project management. *International Journal of Project Management, 24*(8), 710–721.

Morris, P. W., Pinto, J. K., & Söderlund, J. (2011). *The Oxford Handbook of Project Management*. Oxford: Oxford University Press.

Morris, P.W.G. (2011). A brief history of project management. In P. W. G. Morris, J. K. Pinto, & J. Söderlund (eds), *The Oxford Handbook of Project Management*. Oxford: Oxford University Press.

Morris, P.W.G. (2013). *Reconstructing Project Management*. Chicester: John Wiley & Sons.

Morris, P.W.G., & Hough, G. H. (1987). *The Anatomy of Major Projects: A Study of the Reality of Project Management*. Chichester: Wiley.

Morris, P. W. G., Pinto, J. K., & Söderlund, J. (eds). (2011). *The Oxford Handbook of Project Management*. Oxford: Oxford University Press.

Mosakowski, E., & Earley, P. C. (2000). A selective review of time assumptions in strategy research. *Academy of Management Review, 25*(4), 796–812.

Mullen, B., & Copper, C. (1994). The relation between group cohesiveness and performance: An integration. *Psychological Bulletin, 115*(2), 210.

Muller, R. (2009). *Project Governance: Fundamentals of Project Management. Farnham: Gower*.

Murphy, K. M. (2004). Imagination as joint activity: The case of architectural interaction. *Mind, Culture, and Activity, 11*(4), 267–278.

Müller, R. (2016). *Governance and Governmentality for Projects: Enablers, Practices, and Consequences* (Vol. 9).

Müller, R., Andersen, E. S., Kvalnes, Ø., Shao, J., Sankaran, S., Turner, J. R., . . . Gudergan, S. (2013). The Interrelationship of governance, trust, and ethics in temporary organizations. *Project Management Journal, 44*(4), 26–44. doi:10.1002/pmj.21350

Müller, R., Drouin, N., & Sankaran, S. (2019). Modeling organizational project management. *Project Management Journal, 50*(4), 499–513.

Müller, R., & Lecoeuvre, L. (2014). Operationalizing governance categories of projects. *International Journal of Project Management, 32*(8), 1346–1357. doi:http://dx.doi.org/10.1016/j.ijproman.2014.04.005

Müller, R., Pemsel, S., & Shao, J. (2014). Organizational enablers for governance and governmentality of projects: A literature review. *International Journal of Project Management, 32*(8), 1309–1320.

Müller, R., Sankaran, S., Drouin, N., Vaagaasar, A.-L., Bekker, M. C., & Jain, K. (2018). A theory framework for balancing vertical and horizontal leadership in projects. *International journal of Project Management, 36*(1), 83–94. doi:https://doi.org/10.1016/j.ijproman.2017.07.003

Müller, R., & Turner, J. R. (2005). The impact of principal–agent relationship and contract type on communication between project owner and manager. *International Journal of Project Management, 23*(5), 398–403. doi:http://dx.doi.org/10.1016/j.ijproman.2005.03.001

Müller, R., & Turner, J. R. (2010). *Project-oriented Leadership*. Farnham: Gower.

Müller, R., Turner, J. R., Andersen, E. S., Shao, J., & Kvalnes, Ø. (2016). Governance and ethics in temporary organizations: The mediating role of corporate governance. In (pp. 7–23).

Müller, R. & Turner, R. (2007). The influence of project managers on project success criteria and project success by type of project. *European Management Journal, 25*(4), 298–309. doi:http://dx.doi.org/10.1016/j.emj.2007.06.003

Müller, R., Zhai, L., & Wang, A. (2017). Governance and governmentality in projects: Profiles and relationships with success. *International Journal of Project Management, 35*(3), 378–392.

Naar, L., & Clegg, S.R. (2015). *Gehry in Sydney: The Dr Chau Chak Wing Building, UTS*. Mulgrave, Victoria: The Images Publishing Group Pty Ltd.

Nahapiet, J., & Ghoshal, S. (1998). Social capital, intellectual capital, and the organizational advantage. *The Academy of Management Review, 23*(2), 242–266.

Nerstad, C., Searle, R., Černe, M., Dysvik, A., Škerlavaj, M., & Scherer, R. (2018). Perceived mastery climate, felt trust, and knowledge sharing. *Journal of Organizational Behavior, 39*(4), 429–447.

Nerur, S., & Balijepally, V. (2007). Theoretical reflections on agile development methodologies – The traditional goal of optimization and control is making way for learning and innovation. *Commun. ACM, 50*(3), 79–83. doi:10.1145/1226736.1226739

Nerur, S., Mahapatra, R., & Mangalaraj, G. (2005). Challenges of migrating to agile methodologies. *Communications of the ACM, 48*(5), 72–78. doi:10.1145/1060710.1060712

Newell, S., Robertson, H., Scarborough, H. & Swan, J. (2009). *Managing Knowledge Work and Innovation* (2nd edn). Basingstoke: Palgrave Macmillan.

Nicolini, D. (2002). In search of project chemistry. *Construction Management & Economics*, *20*(2), 167–177.

Nielsen, C., Lund, M., & Thomsen, P. (2017). Killing the balanced scorecard to improve internal disclosure. *Journal of Intellectual Capital, 18*(1), 45–62.

Ninan, J., Clegg, S., & Mahalingam, A. (2019). Branding and governmentality for infrastructure megaprojects: The role of social media. *International Journal of Project Management, 37*(1), 59–72.

Ninan, J. & Mahalingam, A. (2017). Stakeholder Management Strategies in Infrastructure Megaprojects – A Dimensions of Power Perspective. Paper presented at the Proceedings of the Engineering Project Organization Conference.

Ninan, J., Mahalingam, A., & Clegg, S.R. (2019). External stakeholder management strategies and resources in megaprojects: An organizational power perspective. *Project Management Journal*, 8756972819847045.

Nonaka, I., & Takeuchi, H. (1995). *The Knowledge-creating Company: How Japanese Companies Create the Dynamics of Innovation*. New York: Oxford University Press.

Nonaka, I., & Takeuchi, H. (2011). The wise leader. *Harvard Business Review, 89*(5), n/a.

Nordqvist, S., Hovmark, S., & Zika-Viktorsson, A. (2004). Perceived time pressure and social processes in project teams. *International Journal of Project Management, 22*(6), 463–468.

Norris, E., Rutter, J. & Medland, J. (2013). *Making the Games: What Government Can Learn from London 2012*. Available at: www.instituteforgovernment.org.uk/sites/default/files/publications/Making%20the%20Games%20final_0.pdf (accessed 26 February 2020).

Northouse, P.G. (2017). *Introduction to Leadership: Concepts and Practice*. London: Sage Publications.

O'Reilly Iii, C. A., & Tushman, M. L. (2008). Ambidexterity as a dynamic capability: Resolving the innovator's dilemma. *Research in Organizational Behavior, 28*, 185–206. doi:http://dx.doi.org/10.1016/j.riob.2008.06.002

Obeng, E. (1996). *The Project Leader's Secret Handbook: All Change!* London: Financial Times/Prentice Hall.

Obstfeld, D. (2012). Creative projects: A less routine approach toward getting new things done. *Organization Science, 23*(6), 1571–1592.

Ogilvy, J. (2016). Heterarchy—An idea finally ripe for its time. Retrieved from www.stratfor.com/

Okhuysen, G.A., & Bechky, B.A. (2009). Coordination in organizations: An integrative perspective. *The Academy of Management Annals, 3*(1), 463–502. doi:10.1080/19416520903047533

Orlikowski, W.J. & Iacono, C.S. (2001). Research commentary: Desperately seeking the "IT" in IT research—A call to theorizing the IT artifact. *Information Systems Research, 12*(2), 121–134.

Orlikowski, W. J. & Yates, J. (2002). It's about time: Temporal structuring in organizations. *Organization Science, 13*(6), 684–700. Retrieved from https://login.ezproxy.hil.no/login?url=http://search.ebscohost.com/login.aspx?direct=true&db=buh&AN=8681205&site=ehost-live&scope=site

Osterwalder, A., & Pigneur, Y. (2010). *Business Model Generation: A Handbook for Visionaries, Game Changers, and Challengers*. Chichester: John Wiley & Sons.

Otterman, P. (2019). Berliners wary as €600m super-museum is latest project to overrun. *Guardian*, 16 June. Available at: www.theguardian.com/world/2019/jun/16/berliners-wary-600m-super-museum-latest-project-overrun-humboldt-forum (accessed 26 February 2020).

Pache, A.-C., & Santos, F. (2010). When worlds collide: The internal dynamics of organizational responses to conflicting institutional demands. *Academy of Management Review, 35*(3), 455–476.

Packard, M., Clark, B., & Klein, P. (2017). Uncertainty types and transitions in the entrepreneurial process. *Organization Science, 28*(5), 840–856. doi:10.1287/orsc.2017.1143

Packendorff, J. (1995). Inquiring into the temporary organization: New directions for project management research. *Scandinavian Journal of Management, 11*(4), 319–333.

Packendorff, J. & Lindgren, M. (2014). Projectification and its consequences: Narrow and broad conceptualisations. *South African Journal of Economic and Management Sciences, 17*(1), 7–21.

Park, C., & Keil, M. (2009). Organizational silence and whistle-blowing on IT projects: An integrated model. *Decision Sciences, 40*(4), 901–918.

Passy, F., & Giugni, M. (2000). Life-spheres, networks, and sustained participation in social movements: A phenomenological approach to political commitment. Paper presented at the Sociological Forum.

Patanakul, P., & Shenhar, A. J. (2012). What project strategy really is: The fundamental building block in strategic project management. *Project Management Journal, 43*(1), 4–20. doi:10.1002/pmj.20282

Paul, S. (2019). *Managing Development Programs: The Lessons of Success*. London: Routledge.

Payne, J. H., & Turner, J. R. (1999). Company-wide project management: The planning and control of programmes of projects of different type. *International Journal of Project Management, 17*(1), 55–59.

Peckiene, A., Komarovska, A. & Ustinovicius, L. (2013). Overview of risk allocation between construction parties. *Procedia Engineering, 57*, 889–894.

Pellegrinelli, S., Murray-Webster, R., & Turner, N. (2015). Facilitating organizational ambidexterity through the complementary use of projects and programs. *International Journal of Project Management, 33*(1), 153–164. doi:10.1016/j.ijproman.2014.04.008

Perrow, C. (1967). A framework for the comparative analysis of organizations. *American Sociological Review, 32*(2), 194. doi:10.2307/2091811

Perrow, C. (1994). The limits of safety: The enhancement of a theory of accidents. *Journal of Contingencies and Crisis Management, 2*(4), 212–220. doi:10.1111/j.1468–5973.1994.tb00046.x

Petridis, A. (2019). Stormzy at Glastonbury 2019 review – a glorious victory lap for black British culture. *Guardian*. Retrieved from www.theguardian.com/music/2019/jun/29/stormzy-glastonbury-review-pyramid-stage

Pfeffer, J., & Salancik, G. R. (1978). The design and management of externally controlled organizations. In *The External Control of Organizations: A Resource Dependence Perspective* (pp. 257–287). Stanford, CA: Stanford Business Books.

Pfeffer, J., & Salancik, G. R. (2003). *The External Control of Organizations: A Resource Dependence Perspective*. Stanford, CA: Stanford Business Books.

Pfeffer, J., & Sutton, R. I. (2006). *Hard Facts, Dangerous Half-truths, and Total Nonsense: Profiting from Evidence-based Management*. Boston, MA: Harvard Business School Press.

Pinto, J.K. (2000). Understanding the role of politics in successful project management. *International Journal of Project Management, 18*(2), 85–91. doi:10.1016/S0263-7863(98)00073–8

Pinto, J.K. (2014). Project management, governance, and the normalization of deviance. *International Journal of Project Management, 32*(3), 376–387. doi:10.1016/j.ijproman.2013.06.004

Pinto, J.K., & Prescott, J. E. (1988). Variations in critical success factors over the stages in the project life cycle. *Journal of Management, 14*(1), 5–18.

Pinto, J.K., & Slevin, D. (1988). Critical success factors in effective project implementation. In D. I. Cleland & W. R. King (eds), *Project Management Handbook*. New York: Van Nostrand Reinhold.

Pinto, J.K., & Slevin, D. P. (1989). *The Project Champion: Key to Implementation Success*.

Pinto, M.B., & Pinto, J. K. (1990). Project team communication and cross-functional cooperation in new program development. *Journal of Product Innovation Management: An International Publication of the Product Development & Management Association, 7*(3), 200–212.

Pinto, M.B., Pinto, J.K., & Prescott, J.E. (1993). Antecedents and consequences of project team cross-functional cooperation. *Management Science, 39*(10), 1281–1297.

Pitsis, A., Clegg, S., Freeder, D., Sankaran, S., & Burdon, S. (2018). Megaprojects redefined–complexity vs cost and social imperatives. *International Journal of Managing Projects in Business, 11*(1), 7–34.

Pitsis, T.S., Clegg, S. R., Marton, M., & Rura-Polley, T. (2003). Constructing the Olympic dream: A future perfect strategy of project management. *Organization Science, 14*(5), 574–590. Retrieved from www.jstor.org.ezproxy.inn.no/stable/4135150

Pitsis, T.S., Sankaran, S., Gudergan, S. & Clegg, S.R. (2014). Governing projects under complexity: Theory and practice in project management. *International Journal of Project Management, 32*(8), 1285–1290.

Plato. (1973). *Laches; Charmides* (2nd edn). New York.

Polanyi, M. (1962). *Personal Knowledge: Towards a Post-critical Philosophy* (corr. edn). Chicago, London: University of Chicago Press, Routledge & Kegan Paul.

Pollack, A., & Abelson, R. (2015). Theranos, a blood test start-up, faces F.D.A. scrutiny. *The New York Times*, 17 October.

Poppo, L., & Zenger, T. (2002). Do formal contracts and relational governance function as substitutes or complements? *Strategic Management Journal, 23*(8), 707–725.

Prencipe, A., & Tell, F. (2001). Inter-project learning: Processes and outcomes of knowledge codification in project-based firms. *Research Policy, 30*(9), 1373–1394. doi:10.1016/S0048-7333(01)00157-3

Priemus, H., Flyvbjerg, B., & van Wee, B. (2008). *Decision-making on Mega-projects: Cost – Benefit Analysis, Planning and Innovation*. Cheltenham: Edward Elgar Publishing.

Pries, K.H., & Quigley, J. M. (2010). *Scrum Project Management*. CRC Press.

Pugh, D.S., Hickson, D. J., Hinings, C. R., Macdonald, K. M., Turner, C., & Lupton, T. (1963). A conceptual scheme for organizational analysis. *Administrative Science Quarterly*, 289–315.

Radiohead. (2000). *Kid A*. London: Parlophone.

Raelin, J.A. (2002). 'I don't have time to think!' versus the art of reflective practice. *Reflections: The SoL Journal, 4*(1), 66–79. doi:10.1162/152417302320467571

Raidén, A., Loosemore, M., King, A., & Gorse, C. (2018). *Social Value in Construction*. London: Routledge.

Ray, S. (2019). 5 steps to project closure (checklist included). Available at: www.projectmanager.com/blog/project-closure (accessed 26 February 2020).

Raz, T., Shenhar, A. J., & Dvir, D. (2002). Risk management, project success, and technological uncertainty. *R & D Management, 32*(2), 101.

Recker, J., Holten, R., Hummel, M., & Rosenkranz, C. (2017). How agile practices impact customer responsiveness and development success: A field study. *Project Management Journal, 48*(2), 99–121.

Rego, A., Cunha, M. P., & Clegg, S. R. (2012). *The Virtues of Leadership: Contemporary Challenges for Global Managers*. Oxford: Oxford University Press.

Rhodes, C. (2016). Democratic business ethics: Volkswagen's emissions scandal and the disruption of corporate sovereignty. *Organization Studies, 37*(10), 1501–1518.

Rich, A.S., & Gureckis, T. M. (2018). The limits of learning: Exploration, generalization, and the development of learning traps. *Journal of Experimental Psychology: General, 147*(11), 1553.

Ring, P.S., & Van De Ven, A. H. (1994). Developmental processes of cooperative interorganizational relationships. *The Academy of Management Review, 19*(1), 90–118.

Ritzer, G. (2008). *The McDonaldization of Society 5*. Los Angeles, CA: Pine Forge Press.

Roberts, L.M., Dutton, J. E., Spreitzer, G. M., Heaphy, E. D., & Quinn, R. E. (2005). Composing the reflected best-self portrait: Building pathways for becoming extraordinary in work organizations. *Academy of Management Review, 30*(4), 712–736.

Robinson, W.I. (2013). Promoting polyarchy: 20 years later. *International Relations, 27*(2), 228–234.

Roethlisberger, F., & Dickson, W. (1939). *Management and the Worker*. Cambridge, MA: Harvard University Press.

Rosile, G.A., Boje, D.M., Carlon, D.M., Downs, A. & Saylors, R. (2013). Storytelling diamond: An antenarrative integration of the six facets of storytelling in organization research design. *Organizational Research Methods, 16*(4), 557–580.

Rowlands, L., & Handy, J. (2012). An addictive environment: New Zealand film production workers' subjective experiences of project-based labour. *Human Relations, 65*(5), 657–680.

Sahlin-Andersson, K. & Söderholm, A. (2002). The Scandinavian school of project studies. *Beyond Project Management: New Perspectives on the Temporary-Permanent dilemma* (pp. 11–24). Stockholm: Liber.

Sanchez, H., Robert, B., Bourgault, M. & Pellerin, R. (2009). Risk management applied to projects, programs, and portfolios. *International Journal of Managing Projects in Business, 2*(1), 14–35.

Sankaran, S., Müller, R., & Drouin, N. (2017). *Cambridge Handbook of Organizational Project Management*. Cambridge: Cambridge University Press.

Sastoque, L.M., Arboleda, C.A., & Ponz, J.L. (2016). A proposal for risk allocation in social infrastructure projects applying PPP in Colombia. *Procedia Engineering, 145*, 1354–1361.

Saulwick, J. (2014). WestConnex adviser "engineered" traffic numbers on Lane Cove Tunnel disaster. *Sydney Morning Herald*. Retrieved from www.smh.com.au/national/westconnex-adviser-engineered-traffic-numbers-on-lane-cove-tunnel-disaster-20140811-102vqf.html (accessed 4 October 2019).

Saunders, C.S., & Ahuja, M.K. (2006). Are all distributed teams the same? Differentiating between temporary and ongoing distributed teams. *Small Group Research, 37*(6), 662–700.

Savage, G., Bunn, M., Gray, B., Xiao, Q., Wang, S., Wilson, E., & Williams, E. (2010). Stakeholder collaboration: Implications for stakeholder theory and practice. *Journal of Business Ethics, 96*, 21–26. doi:10.1007/s10551-011-0939-1

Sawyer, R.K., & DeZutter, S. (2009). Distributed creativity: How collective creations emerge from collaboration. *Psychology of Aesthetics, Creativity, and the Arts, 3*(2), 81–92. doi:10.1037/a0013282

Sawyer, K. & Thoroughgood, C. (2017). Fixing a toxic culture like ubers requires more than just a new CEO. *The Conversation*, 20 June, *10*, https://theconversation.com/fixing-a-toxic-culture-like-ubers-requires-more-than-just-a-new-ceo-79102

Sayyadi, M. (2019). How effective leadership of knowledge management impacts organizational performance. *Business Information Review, 36*(1), 30–38.

Schein, E.H. (2010). *Organizational Culture and Leadership* (4th edn). San Fransisco, CA: Jossey-Bass.

Schindler, M., & Eppler, M. J. (2003). Harvesting project knowledge: A review of project learning methods and success factors. *International Journal of Project Management, 21*(3), 219–228.

Schlesinger, A.M. (1965). *A Thousand Days: JF Kennedy in the White House*. Boston, MA: Houghton Mifflin.

Schutz, A. (1967). *The Phenomenology of the Social World*. Evanston, IL: Northwestern University Press.

Schön, D.A. (1991). *The Reflective Practitioner: How Professionals Think in Action*. Aldershot: Avebury.

Schön, D.A. (1992). The theory of inquiry: Dewey's legacy to education. *Curriculum Inquiry, 22*(2), 119. doi:10.1080/03626784.1992.11076093

Schön, D.A. (1983). *The Reflective Practitioner: How Professionals Think in Action*. London: Routledge.

Scott, D.M. (2010). *The New Rules of Marketing and PR: How to Use Social Media, Blogs, News Releases, Online Video, and Viral Marketing to Reach Buyers Directly*. Hoboken, NJ: John Wiley & Sons.

Seligman, A. B. (1997). *The Problem of Trust*. Princeton, NJ: Princeton University Press.

Selznick, P. (1949). *TVA and the Grass Roots: A Study in the Sociology of Formal Organization* (Vol. *3*). Berkeley, CA: University of California Press.

Senge, P.M. (2006). *The Fifth Discipline: The Art and Practice of the Learning Organization* (rev. and updated edn). New York: Currency/Doubleday.

Serra, C.E.M., & Kunc, M. (2015). Benefits Realisation Management and its influence on project success and on the execution of business strategies. *International Journal of Project Management, 33*(1), 53–66. doi:10.1016/j.ijproman.2014.03.011

Serrador, P., & Pinto, J. K. (2015). Does Agile work? — A quantitative analysis of agile project success. *International Journal of Project Management, 33*(5), 1040–1051. doi:http://dx.doi.org/10.1016/j.ijproman.2015.01.006

Serrador, P., & Turner, J. (2013). The impact of the planning phase on project success. *IRNOP (Oslo, Norway)*.

Sewell, G. (1998). The discipline of teams: The control of team-based industrial work through electronic and peer surveillance. *Administrative Science Quarterly*, 397–428.

Shenhar, A.J. (2001). One size does not fit all projects: Exploring classical contingency domains. *Management Science, 47*(3), 394–414.

Shenhar, A.J. & Dvir, D. (1996). Toward a typological theory of project management. *Research Policy, 25*(4), 607–632.

Shenhar, A.J. & Dvir, D. (2007). *Reinventing Project Management: The Diamond Approach to Successful Growth and Innovation*. Boston, MA: Harvard Business School Press.

Shenhav, Y. (1999). *Manufacturing Rationality: The Engineering Foundations of the Managerial Revolution*. Oxford: Oxford University Press.

Shenhav, Y. (2003). The historical and epistemological foundations of organization theory: Fusing sociological theory with engineering discourse. In H. Tsoukas & C. Knudsen (eds), *The Oxford Handbook of Organization Theory* (pp. 183–209). Oxford: Oxford University Press.

Simmel, G. (1990). *The Philosophy of Money*. London: Routledge.

Simon, H. A. (1965). *Administrative Behavior: A Study of Decision-making Processes in Administrative Organization*. New York: Free Press.

Simon, H.A. (1991). Bounded rationality and organizational learning. *Organization Science*, 2(1), 125–134. doi:10.1287/orsc.2.1.125

Sitkin, S. B., See, K. E., Miller, C. C., Lawless, M. W. & Carton, A. M. (2011). The paradox of stretch goals: Organizations in pursuit of the seemingly impossible. *Academy of Management Review*, 36(3), 544–566.

Škerlavaj, M., Connelly, C. E., Cerne, M., & Dysvik, A. (2018). Tell me if you can: Time pressure, prosocial motivation, perspective taking, and knowledge hiding. *Journal of Knowledge Management*, 22(7), 1489–1509.

SkillPath (2014). Project management essentials: Closing. Available at: www.youtube.com/watch?v=MWu8B8rcS2g (accessed 26 February 2020).

Skyttermoen, T. (2013). *En narrativ beretning om et prakademisk utviklingsarbeid: profileringsdokument* (Vol. *nr 158/2013*). Lillehammer: Høgskolen i Lillehammer.

Skyttermoen, T., & Vaagaasar, A. L. (2015). *Value Creating Project Management [In Norwegian: Verdiskapende prosjektledelse]*. Oslo: Cappelen Damm akademisk.

Smith, H.J., Thompson, R., & Iacovou, C. (2009). The impact of ethical climate on project status misreporting. *Journal of Business Ethics*, 90(4), 577.

Smyth, H., Gustafsson, M., & Ganskau, E. (2010). The value of trust in project business. *International Journal of Project Management*, 28(2), 117–129. doi:10.1016/j.ijproman.2009.11.007

Smyth, H.J. (2014). *Relationship Management and the Management of Projects*. New York: Routledge.

Söderlund, J., Vaagaasar, A. L., & Andersen, E. S. (2008). Relating, reflecting and routinizing: Developing project competence in cooperation with others. *International Journal of Project Management*, 26(5), 517–526.

Söderholm, A. (2008). Project management of unexpected events. *International Journal of Project Management*, 26(1), 80–86. doi:10.1016/j.ijproman.2007.08.016

Söderlund, J. (2002). Managing complex development projects: Arenas, knowledge processes and time. *R and D Management*, 32(5), 419–430.

Söderlund, J. (2005). *Projektledning & projektkompetens: perspektiv på konkurrenskraft*. Malmö: Liber.

Söderlund, J., & Tell, F. (2009). The P-form organization and the dynamics of project competence: Project epochs in Asea/ABB, 1950–2000. *International Journal of Project Management*, 27(2), 101–112. doi:https://doi.org/10.1016/j.ijproman.2008.10.010

Söderlund, J., & Tell, F. (2012). *Styrning: med projekt och kunskap i fokus*. Studentlitteratur.

Söderlund, J., Vaagaasar, A. L., & Andersen, E. S. (2008). Relating, reflecting and routinizing: Developing project competence in cooperation with others. *International Journal of Project Management*, 26(5), 517–526. doi:http://dx.doi.org/10.1016/j.ijproman.2008.06.002

Solomon, S.D. (2016). David Boies's dual roles at Theranos set up conflict. *The New York Times*, 3 February.

Sommer, S.C., & Loch, C. (2004). Selectionism and learning in projects with complexity and unforeseeable uncertainty. *Management Science*, 50(10), 1334–1347.

Sommer, S.C., Loch, C. H., & Dong, J. (2009). Managing complexity and unforeseeable uncertainty in startup companies: An empirical study. *Organization Science*, 20(1), 118–133. doi:10.1287/orsc.1080.0369

Sonenshein, S. (2014). How organizations foster the creative use of resources. *Academy of Management Journal*, 57, 814–848.

Spender, J.C., & Grant, R. M. (1996). Knowledge and the firm: An overview. *Strategic Management Journal, 17*(S2), 5–9. doi:10.1002/smj.4250171103

Star, S.L., & Griesemer, J. R. (1989). Institutional ecology,translations' and boundary objects: Amateurs and professionals in Berkeley's Museum of Vertebrate Zoology, 1907–39. *Social Studies of Science, 19*(3), 387–420.

Starkey, K., Barnatt, C., & Tempest, S. (2000). Beyond networks and hierarchies: Latent organizations in the UK television industry. *Organization Science, 11*(3), 299–305.

Staw, B.M. & Ross, J. (1987). Knowing when to pull the plug. *Harvard Business Review, 65*(2), 68–74.

Stewart, J. (2015). The narrative frays for Theranos and Elizabeth Holmes. *The New York Times*, 30 October.

Stinchcombe, A.L., & Heimer, C.A. (1985). Organization theory and project management: Administering uncertainty in Norwegian offshore oil.

Sturup, S. (2009). Mega projects and governmentality. *World Academy of Science, Engineering and Technology, International Journal of Social, Behavioral, Educational, Economic, Business and Industrial Engineering, 3*(6), 862–871.

Suchman, M.C. (1995). Managing legitimacy: Strategic and institutional approaches. *Academy of Management Review, 20*(3), 571–610.

Sun, J. & Zhang, P. (2011). Owner organization design for mega industrial construction projects. In (pp. 828–833).

Sunstein, C.R., & Hastie, R. (2015). *Wiser: Getting beyond Groupthink to Make Groups Smarter*. Boston, MA Harvard Business Press.

Svejvig, P., & Andersen, P. (2015). Rethinking project management: A structured literature review with a critical look at the brave new world. *International Journal of Project Management, 33*(2), 278–290. doi:http://dx.doi.org/10.1016/j.ijproman.2014.06.004

Swan, J., Scarbrough, H., & Newell, S. (2010). Why don't (or do) organizations learn from projects? *Management Learning, 41*(3), 325–344.

Swärd, A. (2013). *Trust Processes in Fixed-duration Alliances: A Multi-level, Multi-dimensional, and Temporal View on Trust*. (2/2013). BI Norwegian Business School, Oslo.

Sydow, J., Lindkvist, L., & DeFillippi, R. (2004). Project-based organizations, embeddedness and repositories of knowledge. In Thousand Oaks, CA: Sage.

Sydow, J. & Staber, U. (2002). The institutional embeddedness of project networks: The case of content production in German television. *Regional Studies, 36*(3), 215–227.

Tabassi, A.A., Roufechaei, K.M., Bakar, A.H.A. & Yusof, N.A. (2017). Linking team condition and team performance: A transformational leadership approach. *Project Management Journal, 48*(2), 22–38. doi:10.1177/875697281704800203

Takeuchi, H. & Nonaka, I. (1986). The new new product development game. *Harvard Business Review, 64*, 137.

Taleb, N.N. (2007). *The Black Swan: The Impact of the Highly Improbable*. London: Allen Lane.

Tatikonda, M.V., & Rosenthal, S. R. (2000). Successful execution of product development projects: Balancing firmness and flexibility in the innovation process. *Journal of Operations Management, 18*(4), 401–425.

Taylor, F.W. (1911). *The Principles of Scientific Management*. New York: Harper & Brothers.

Teachout, T. (2013). *Duke – A Life of Duke Ellington*. New York: Gotham Books.

Tech Republic (2018). TechRepublic 10 signs you may not be cut out for project management. Available at: www.techrepublic.com/blog/10-things/10-signs-that-you-arent-cut-out-to-be-a-project-manager/ (accessed 26 February 2020).

Teece, D.J., Pisano, G., & Shuen, A. (1997). Dynamic capabilities and strategic management. *Strategic Management Journal, 18*(7), 509–533. doi:10.1002/(SICI)1097–0266(199708)18:7<509::AID-SMJ882>3.0.CO2–Z

Tereso, A., Ribeiro, P., Fernandes, G., Loureiro, I., & Ferreira, M. (2019). Project management practices in private organizations. *Project Management Journal, 50*(1), 6–22.

Terhorst, A., Lusher, D., Bolton, D., Elsum, I., & Wang, P. (2018). Tacit knowledge sharing in open innovation projects. *Project Management Journal, 49*(4), 5–19.

Thiry, M. (2002). Combining value and project management into an effective programme management model. *International Journal of Project Management, 20*(3), 221–227. doi:10.1016/S0263-7863(01)00072-2

Thompson, J.D. (1967a). *Organizations in Action: Social Sience Bases of Administrative Theory.* New York: McGraw-Hill.

Thompson, J.D. (1967b). *Organizations in Action: Social Science Bases of Administrative Theory.* London: Routledge.

Thompson, K.N. (2010). Servant-leadership: An effective model for project management. Doctoral dissertation. Retrieved from Minneapolis, MN: Capella University:

Thucydides. (1963). *History of the Peloponnesian War.* London: Penguin.

Tidd, J. & Bessant, J. (2018). *Managing Innovation: Integrating Technological, Market and Organizational Change* (6th edn). Hoboken, NJ: Wiley.

Torfing, J., Sørensen, E., & Røiseland, A. (2019). Transforming the public sector into an arena for co-creation: Barriers, drivers, benefits, and ways forward. *Administration & Society, 51*(5), 795–825. doi:10.1177/0095399716680057

Townsend, D. M., Hunt, R. A., McMullen, J. S., & Sarasvathy, S. D. (2018). Uncertainty, knowledge problems, and entrepreneurial action. *Academy of Management Annals, 12*(2), 659–687.

Tressell, R. (1978). *The Ragged Trousered Philanthropists.* London: Lawrence & Wishart.

Trice, H.M., & Beyer, J. M. (1993). *The Cultures of Work Organizations.* Englewood Cliffs, NJ: Prentice Hall.

Trullen, J., & Bartunek, J. M. (2007). What a design approach offers to organization development. *The Journal of Applied Behavioral Science, 43*(1), 23–40. doi:10.1177/0021886306297549

Tryggestad, K., Justesen, L., & Mouritsen, J. (2013). Project temporalities: How frogs can become stakeholders. *International Journal of Managing Projects in Business, 6*(1), 69–87.

Tsoukas, H. (2009). A dialogical approach to the creation of new knowledge in organizations. *Organization Science, 20*(6), 941–957. doi:10.1287/orsc.1090.0435

Tsoukas, H., & Chia, R. (2002). On organizational becoming: Rethinking organizational change. *Organization Science, 13*(5), 567–582.

Tuckman, B.W., & Jensen, M.A.C. (1977). Stages of small-group development revisited. *Group & Organization Studies, 2*(4), 419–427. Retrieved from https://login.ezproxy.hil.no/login?url=http://search.ebscohost.com/login.aspx?direct=true&db=buh&AN=6547692&site=ehost-live&scope=site

Tuomela, R. & Tuomela, M. (2005). Cooperation and trust in group context. *Mind & Society, 4*(1), 49–84.

Turner, J.R. (1999). *The Handbook of Project-based Management: Improving the Processes for Achieving Strategic Objectives* (2nd edn). London: McGraw-Hill.

Turner, J. R. (2017). *Contracting for Project Management.* London: Routledge.

Turner, J.R., Anbari, F., & Bredillet, C. (2013). Perspectives on research in project management: The nine schools. *Global Business Perspectives, 1*(1), 3–28. doi:10.1007/s40196-012-0001-4

Turner, J.R., & Cochrane, R. A. (1993). Goals-and-methods matrix: Coping with projects with ill defined goals and/or methods of achieving them. *International Journal of Project Management, 11*(2), 93–102.

Turner, J.R., & Keegan, A. (2001). Mechanisms of governance in the project-based organization:: Roles of the broker and steward. *European Management Journal, 19*(3), 254–267.

Turner, J.R., & Müller, R. (2005). The project manager's leadership style as a success factor on projects: A literature review. *Project Management Journal, 36*(2), 49–61. Retrieved from https://login.ezproxy.hil.no/login?url=http://search.ebscohost.com/login.aspx?direct=true&db=buh&AN=17533881&site=ehost-live&scope=site

Turner, N., Maylor, H., & Swart, J. (2015). Ambidexterity in projects: An intellectual capital perspective. *International Journal of Project Management, 33*(1), 177–188. doi:http://dx.doi.org/10.1016/j.ijproman.2014.05.002

Turner, R., Huemann, M., Anbari, F. T., & Bredillet, C. N. (2010). *Perspectives on Projects.* London: Routledge.

Tyssen, A.K., Wald, A., & Heidenreich, S. (2014). Leadership in the context of temporary organizations: A study on the effects of transactional and transformational leadership on followers' commitment in projects. *Journal of Leadership & Organizational Studies, 21*(4), 376–393. doi:10.1177/1548051813502086

Tyssen, A.K., Wald, A., & Spieth, P. (2014). The challenge of transactional and transformational leadership in projects. *International Journal of Project Management, 32*(3), 365–375. doi:http://dx.doi.org/10.1016/j.ijproman.2013.05.010

Uzzi, B. (1997). Social structure and competition in interfirm networks: The paradox of embeddedness. *Administrative Science Quarterly, 42*(1), 35.

Vaagaasar, A.L. (2006). *From Tool to Actor: How a Project Came to Orchestrate Its Own Life and That of Others* (Vol. *10*). Oslo: Handelshøyskolen BI.

Vaagaasar, A.L. (2015a). A spatial perspective to leadership in knowledge-intensive projects. In A. Ropo, S. Perttu, E. Sauer, & D. De Paoli (eds), *Leadership, Spaces and Organizing.* London: Edward Elgar.

Vaagaasar, A.L. (2015b). A spatial perspective to leadership in knowledge-intensive projects. In A. Ropo, P. Salovaara, D. De Paoli, & E. Sauer (eds), *Leadership, Spaces and Organizing* (pp. 71–86). Cheltenham: Edward Elgar.

Van Marrewijk, A., Clegg, S. R., Pitsis, T. S., & Veenswijk, M. (2008). Managing public–private megaprojects: Paradoxes, complexity, and project design. *International Journal of Project Management, 26*(6), 591–600.

van Marrewijk, A., Ybema, S., Smits, K., Clegg, S. R., and Pitsis, T. S. (2016) Clash of the Titans: Temporal organizing and collaborative dynamics in the Panama Canal megaproject, *Organization Studies*, (Special Issue on Temporary Organizations), 37 (12), 1745–1769.

van Oorschot, K.E., Sengupta, K., & Van Wassenhove, L. N. (2018). Under pressure: The effects of iteration lengths on agile software development performance. *Project Management Journal, 49*(6), 78–102. doi:10.1177/8756972818802714

Van Waeyenberge, E. (2016). *The Private Turn in Development Finance.* Retrieved from

Vanhoucke, M. (2018). Data-driven project management is good for your business: A business novel tells you why.

Vaughan, D. (1996). *The Challenger Launch Decision: Risky Technology, Culture, and Deviance at NASA.* Chicago: University of Chicago Press.

Ven, A.H.V. D., Delbecq, A. L., & Koenig, R. (1976). Determinants of coordination modes within organizations. *American Sociological Review, 41*(2), 322. doi:10.2307/2094477

Verweij, S. & Gerrits, L. M. (2019). Evaluating infrastructure project planning and implementation: A study using qualitative comparative analysis. *Sage Research Methods Cases in Business and Management.* https://dx.doi.org/10.4135/9781526467997

Von Bertalanffy, L. (1968). *General System Theory.* New York: George Braziller.

Vygotsky, L.S. (1978). *Mind in Society: The Development of Higher Psychological Processes* (ed. M. Cole, V. John-Steiner, S. Scribner, & E. Souberman). Cambridge, MA: Harvard University Press.

Wachs, M. (1989). When planners lie with numbers. *Journal of the American Planning Association, 55*(4), 476.

Wang, W., Chen, Y., Zhang, S., & Wang, Y. (2018). Contractual complexity in construction projects: Conceptualization, operationalization, and validation. *Project Management Journal, 49*(3), 46–61. doi:10.1177/8756972818770589

Ward, S. & Chapman, C. (2008). Stakeholders and uncertainty management in projects. *Construction Management and Economics, 26*(6), 563–577.

Wateridge, J. (1995). IT projects: A basis for success. *International Journal of Project Management, 13*(3), 169–172. doi:10.1016/0263–7863(95)00020-Q

Watts, S.L. (1991). *Order Against Chaos: Business Culture and Labor Ideology in America, 1880–1915.* Praeger.

Weber, M. (1978). *Economy and Society: An Outline of Interpretive Sociology* (Vol. *2*). Berkeley, CA: University of California Press.

Weick, K.E. (1979). *The Social Psychology of Organizing* (2nd edn). Reading, MA: Addison-Wesley.

Weick, K.E. (1984). Small wins: Redefining the scale of social problems. *American Psychologist, 39*(1), 40.

Weick, K.E. (1993). The collapse of sensemaking in organizations: The Mann Gulch disaster. *Administrative Science Quarterly, 38*(4), 628–652. doi:10.2307/2393339

Weick, K.E. (1995). *Sensemaking in Organizations*. Thousand Oaks, CA: Sage.

Weick, K.E. (2008). Sensemaking. In S. Clegg & J. R. Bailey (eds), *The Sage International Encyclopedia of Organization Studies* (pp. 1403–1406). Thousand Oaks, CA: SAGE.

Weingart, P. (1999). Science and political culture: Eugenics in comparative perspective. *Scandinavian Journal of History*, *24*(2), 163–177. doi:10.1080/03468759950115782

Wen, Q. & Qiang, M. (2019). Project managers' competences in managing project Closing. *Project Management Journal*, *50*(3), 361–375.

Wenger, E. (1998). Communities of practice: Learning as a social system. *Systems Thinker*, *9*(5), 2–3.

Wenger, E. (2010). Communities of practice and social learning systems: The career of a concept. In *Social Learning Systems and Communities of Practice* (pp. 179–198). Springer.

West, Michael A., Smith, K.G. & Tjosvold, D. (2003). *International Handbook of Organizational Teamwork and Cooperative Working*, 1st edition. GB: Wiley.

Wheelwright, S.C. & Clark, K.B. (1992). *Revolutionizing Product Development: Quantum Leaps in Speed, Efficiency, and Quality*. Simon & Schuster.

Whittington, R. (2003). The work of strategizing and organizing: For a practice perspective. *Strategic Organization*, *1*(1), 117–125.

Whyte, J. (2019). How digital information transforms project delivery models. *Project Management Journal*, *5*(2), 177–194.

Wiley, V.D., Deckro, R.F., & Jackson Jr, J.A. (1998). Optimization analysis for design and planning of multi-project programs. *European Journal of Operational Research*, *107*(2), 492–506.

Williams, T. (2017). The nature of risk in complex projects. *Project Management Journal*, *48*(4), 55–66. doi:10.1177/875697281704800405

Williams, T. & Samset, K. (2010). Issues in front-end decision making on projects. *Project Management Journal*, *41*(2), 38–49. doi:10.1002/pmj.20160

Witt, J. (2013). How to capture lessons learned at the end of a project. Available at: www.youtube.com/watch?v=DBUqW_ek4hI (accessed 26 February 2020).

Wood, R. & Bandura, A. (1989). Social cognitive theory of organizational management. *Academy of Management Review*, *14*(3), 361–384.

Woodward, J. (1958). *Management and Technology* (Vol. 5). London: HMSO.

Wu, W.-Y., Rivas, A. A. A., & Liao, Y.-K. (2017). Influential factors for team reflexivity and new product development. *Project Management Journal*, *48*(3), 20–40.

Wåhlin, N., Kapsali, M., Näsholm, M. H., & Blomquist, T. (2016). *Urban Strategies for Culture-driven Growth: Co-creating a European Capital of Culture*. Cheltenham: Edward Elgar Publishing.

Yamaura, J., Muench, S. T., & Willoughby, K. (2019). Factors influencing adoption of information technologies for public transportation project inspection: A WSDOT case study. *Transportation Research Record*, <xocs:firstpage xmlns:xocs=""/>. doi:10.1177/0361198118823198

Young, N. (1991). My my, hey hey (out of the blue). *Weld*. Hollywood: Reprise.

Yu, M., Vaagaasar, A. L., Müller, R., Wang, L., & Zhu, F. (2018). Empowerment: The key to horizontal leadership in projects. *International Journal of Project Management*. doi:https://doi.org/10.1016/j.ijproman.2018.04.003

Yukl, G.A. (2013). *Leadership in Organizations*. Boston, MA: Pearson Education.

Zaghloul, R. & Hartman, F. T. (2002). Reducing contract cost: The trust issue. *AACE International Transactions*, CD161.

Zander, L., Mockaitis, A.I., & Butler, C.L. (2012). Leading global teams. *Journal of World Business*, *47*(4), 592–603.

Zhu, Y.-Q., Gardner, D.G., & Chen, H.-G. (2018). Relationships between work team climate, individual motivation, and creativity. *Journal of Management*, *44*(5), 2094–2115.

Zika-Viktorsson, A., Hovmark, S., & Nordqvist, S. (2003). Psychosocial aspects of project work: A comparison between product development and construction projects. *International Journal of Project Management*, *21*(8), 563–569.

Zika-Wiktorsson, A., Sundström, P., & Engwall, M. (2006). Project overload: An exploratory study of work and management in multi-project settings. *International Journal of Project Management*, *24*(5), 385–394. doi:10.1016/j.ijproman.2006.02.010

Zollo, M. & Winter, S.G. (2002). Deliberate learning and the evolution of dynamic capabilities. *Organization Science*, *13*(3), 339–351.

INDEX

NOTE: Page numbers in *italic* type refer to figures and pictures.